Lecture Notes in Computer Science 2651
Edited by G. Goos, J. Hartmanis, and J. van Leeuwen

Springer
*Berlin
Heidelberg
New York
Hong Kong
London
Milan
Paris
Tokyo*

Didier Bert   Jonathan P. Bowen
Steve King   Marina Waldén (Eds.)

ZB 2003:
Formal Specification and Development in Z and B

Third International Conference of B and Z Users
Turku, Finland, June 4-6, 2003
Proceedings

Springer

Series Editors

Gerhard Goos, Karlsruhe University, Germany
Juris Hartmanis, Cornell University, NY, USA
Jan van Leeuwen, Utrecht University, The Netherlands

Volume Editors

Didier Bert
CNRS, Laboratoire LSR-IMAG
681, rue de la Passerelle, BP 72, 38402 Saint-Martin-d'Heres Cedex, France
E-mail: Didier.Bert@imag.fr

Jonathan P. Bowen
London South Bank University
CISM, Borough Road, London SE1 0AA, UK
E-mail: jonathan.bowen@sbu.ac.uk

Steve King
University of York
Department of Computer Science, Heslington, York YO10 5DD, UK
E-mail: king@cs.york.ac.uk

Marina Waldén
Åbo Akademi University
Department of Computer Science, Lemminkäineng. 14 A, 20520 Turku, Finland
E-mail: marina.walden@abo.fi

Cataloging-in-Publication Data applied for

A catalog record for this book is available from the Library of Congress.

Bibliographic information published by Die Deutsche Bibliothek
Die Deutsche Bibliothek lists this publication in the Deutsche Nationalbibliografie;
detailed bibliographic data is available in the Internet at <http://dnb.ddb.de>.

CR Subject Classification (1998): D.2.1, D.2.2, D.2.4, F.3.1, F.4.2, F.4.3

ISSN 0302-9743
ISBN 3-540-40253-5 Springer-Verlag Berlin Heidelberg New York

This work is subject to copyright. All rights are reserved, whether the whole or part of the material is
concerned, specifically the rights of translation, reprinting, re-use of illustrations, recitation, broadcasting,
reproduction on microfilms or in any other way, and storage in data banks. Duplication of this publication
or parts thereof is permitted only under the provisions of the German Copyright Law of September 9, 1965,
in its current version, and permission for use must always be obtained from Springer-Verlag. Violations are
liable for prosecution under the German Copyright Law.

Springer-Verlag Berlin Heidelberg New York
a member of BertelsmannSpringer Science+Business Media GmbH

http://www.springer.de

© Springer-Verlag Berlin Heidelberg 2003
Printed in Germany

Typesetting: Camera-ready by author, data conversion by PTP-Berlin GmbH
Printed on acid-free paper   SPIN: 10934463   06/3142   5 4 3 2 1 0

Preface

These proceedings record the papers presented at the third International Conference of B and Z Users (ZB 2003), held in the city of Turku in the south of Finland. This conference builds on the success of the first and second conferences in this series, ZB 2000, held at the University of York in the UK and ZB 2002, held at the *Laboratoire Logiciels Systèmes Réseaux* within the *Institut d'Informatique et Mathématiques Appliquées de Grenoble* (LSR-IMAG) in Grenoble, France. The location of ZB 2003 in Turku reflects the important work in the area of formal methods carried out at Åbo Akademi University and the Turku Centre for Computer Science (TUCS), especially involving the B method. In particular, Ralph-Johan Back, Professor of Computer Science at Åbo Akademi University and an Academy Professor at the Academy of Finland, has made an important contribution to the development of refinement calculus, influential and relevant to many formal methods, including B and Z. He was an invited speaker at the previous ZB 2002 conference.

B and Z are two important formal methods that share a common conceptual origin; they are leading approaches in industry and academia for the specification and development (using formal refinement) of computer-based systems. At ZB 2003 the B and Z communities met once again to hold a third joint conference that simultaneously incorporated the 14th International Z User Meeting and the 5th International Conference on the B method. Although organized logistically as an integral event, editorial control of the joint conference remained vested in two separate but cooperating program committees that respectively determined its B and Z content, but in a coordinated manner.

All the papers in these proceedings have been peer reviewed by at least three reviewers drawn from the B or Z committee depending on the subject matter of the paper. Reviewing and initial selection were undertaken electronically. The Z committee met at South Bank University in London on 4th February 2003 to determine the final selection of Z papers. The B committee met on 5th February 2003 at the *Conservatoire National des Arts et Métiers* (CNAM) in Paris to select B papers. A joint committee meeting was held at South Bank University on 6th February 2003 to resolve the final paper selection and a draft program for the conference.

The conference featured a range of contributions by distinguished invited speakers drawn from both industry and academia. The invited speakers addressed significant recent industrial applications of formal methods, as well as important academic advances serving to enhance their potency and widen their applicability. Our invited speakers for ZB 2003 were drawn from France, Switzerland, and the USA.

Jean-Raymond Abrial, a consultant based in Marseille, France, was the progenitor of both Z and B. It was a great delight to have him as an invited speaker at ZB 2003 where he delivered a lecture sponsored by Formal Methods Europe (FME). Prof. Dr. Bertrand Meyer is Chair of Software Engineering in the Department of Computer Science at the world renowned ETH, the Swiss Federal Institute of Technology in Zürich, Switzerland. He has undertaken important work in the area of object-oriented software technology and continues in the footsteps of the great computing pioneer, Niklaus Wirth, who was based at the same institution, and designed Pascal, Modula-2, and other programming languages. Daniel Jackson is the Ross Career Development Professor of Software Technology in the Department of Electrical Engineering and Computer Science at MIT, USA. He leads the Software Design Group in the Laboratory for Computer Science and is the son of Michael Jackson, the originator of JSP and JSD, making him one of a handful of second generation computer scientists. He has developed Alloy, a lightweight modeling language based on a subset of the Z notation, and the Alloy Analyzer, a tool for automatically analyzing models.

Besides its formal sessions the conference included tool demonstrations, exhibitions, and tutorials. In particular, a workshop on *Refinement of Critical Systems: Methods, Tools, and Experience* (RCS 2003) was organized on 3rd June 2003 with the support of members of the EU IST-RTD Project *MATISSE: Methodologies and Associated Technologies for Industrial Strength Systems Engineering*, in association with the ZB 2003 meeting. In addition, the International B Conference Steering Committee (APCB) and the Z User Group (ZUG) used the conference as a convenient venue for open meetings intended for those interested in the B and Z communities respectively.

The topics of interest to the conference included: industrial applications and case studies using Z or B; integration of model-based specification methods in the software development lifecycle; derivation of hardware-software architecture from model-based specifications; expressing and validating requirements through formal models; theoretical issues in formal development (e.g., issues in refinement, proof process, or proof validation, etc.); software testing versus proof-oriented development; tools supporting tools for the Z notation and the B method; development by composition of specifications; validation of assembly of COTS by model-based specification methods; Z and B extensions and/or standardization.

The ZB 2003 conference was jointly initiated by the Z User Group (ZUG) and the International B Conference Steering Committee (APCB). Åbo Akademi and the Turku Centre for Computer Science (TUCS) provided all the local organization and financial backing for the conference. Without the great support from local staff at Åbo Akademi and TUCS, ZB 2003 would not have been possible. Particular mention should be made of the Local Committee Chair, Marina Waldén. ZB 2003 was sponsored by ClearSy System Engineering, Nokia, BCS-FACS (the British Computer Society Formal Aspects of Computing Science specialist group), FME (Formal Methods Europe), and ZUG (Z User Group). BCS-FACS specifically sponsored prizes for the best papers at the conference. We are grateful to all those who contributed to the success of the conference. ZUG sponsored students to attend the conference.

Online information concerning the conference is available under the following Uniform Resource Locator (URL):

http://www.tucs.fi/zb2003/

This also provides links to further online resources concerning the B method and Z notation.

We hope that all participants and other interested readers benefit scientifically from these proceedings and also find them stimulating in the process.

March 2003

Didier Bert
Jonathan Bowen
Steve King
Marina Waldén

Program and Organizing Committees

The following people were members of the ZB 2003 Z program committee and reviewed papers for the conference:

    Conference Chair: Jonathan Bowen, South Bank University, London, UK
    Program Chair: Steve King, University of York, UK

    Rob Arthan, Lemma 1, Reading, UK
    Neville Dean, Anglia Polytechnic University, UK
    John Derrick, The University of Kent at Canterbury, UK
    Mark d'Inverno, University of Westminster, UK
    Wolfgang Grieskamp, Microsoft Research, USA
    Henri Habrias, University of Nantes, France
    Ian Hayes, University of Queensland, Australia
    Martin Henson, University of Essex, UK
    Jonathan Jacky, University of Washington, USA
    Kevin Lano, Kings College London, UK
    Yves Ledru, LSR-IMAG, Grenoble, France
    Fiona Polack, University of York, UK
    Norah Power, University of Limerick, Ireland
    Steve Reeves, University of Waikato, New Zealand
    Mark Saaltink, ORA, Ottawa, Canada
    Thomas Santen, Technical University of Berlin, Germany
    Graeme Smith, University of Queensland, Australia
    Susan Stepney, University of York, UK
    Ian Toyn, University of York, UK
    Mark Utting, University of Waikato, New Zealand
    Sam Valentine, LiveDevices, UK
    John Wordsworth, University of Exeter, UK

The following served on the ZB 2003 B program committee and reviewed papers for the conference:

Program Chair: Didier Bert, CNRS, LSR-IMAG, Grenoble, France
Co-chair: Marina Waldén, Åbo Akademi University, Finland

Christian Attiogbé, University of Nantes, France
Richard Banach, University of Manchester, UK
Juan Bicarregui, CLRC, Oxfordshire, UK
Egon Börger, University of Pisa, Italy
Michael Butler, University of Southampton, UK
Lilian Burdy, GemPlus Research Laboratory, France
Dominique Cansell, LORIA, University of Metz, France
Pierre Chartier, RATP, Paris, France
Steve Dunne, University of Teesside, UK
Mamoun Filali, CNRS, IRIT, Toulouse, France
Marc Frappier, University of Sherbrooke, Canada
Andy Galloway, University of York, UK
Jacques Julliand, University of Franche-Comté, Besançon, France
Brian Matthews, CLRC, Oxfordshire, UK
Luis-Fernando Mejia, Alstom Transport Signalisation, France
Jean-Marc Meynadier, Siemens Transportation Systems, France
Louis Mussat, DCSSI, France
Marie-Laure Potet, LSR-IMAG, Grenoble, France
Ken Robinson, The University of New South Wales, Australia
Emil Sekerinski, McMaster University, Canada
Bill Stoddart, University of Teesside, UK
Helen Treharne, Royal Holloway, UK
Véronique Viguié Donzeau-Gouge, CNAM, Paris, France

The following people helped particularly with the organization of the conference in various capacities:

Conference Chair:	Jonathan Bowen, South Bank University
Local Committee Chair:	Marina Waldén, Åbo Akademi University
B submissions:	Didier Bert, LSR-IMAG, Grenoble
Z submissions:	Steve King, University of York
Tools demonstrations & exhibitions:	{ Kevin Lano, King's College London Ulf Tigerstedt, Åbo Akademi University
Tutorials:	Henri Habrias, University of Nantes
Proceedings:	Didier Bert, LSR-IMAG, Grenoble
Grants:	Steve King, University of York
Local arrangements:	Orieta Celiku, Åbo Akademi University
Finances:	Anna Karlsson, Åbo Akademi University
Website:	Nina Kivinen, Åbo Akademi University

We are especially grateful to the above for their efforts in ensuring the success of the conference.

External Referees

We are grateful to the following people who aided the program committees in the reviewing of papers, providing additional specialist expertise:

>Pascal André, University of Yamoussoukro, Ivory Coast
>Diyaa-Addein Atiya, University of York, UK
>Jean-Paul Boidevex, IRIT, Toulouse, France
>Alain Giogetti, University of Franche-Comté, Besançon, France
>Linas Laibinis, Åbo Akademi University, Finland
>Régine Laleau, CNAM, France
>Bruno Legeard, University of Franche-Comté, Besançon, France
>Richard Paige, University of York, UK
>Pascal Poizat, University of Evry, France
>Mike Poppleton, University of Southampton, UK
>Gwen Salaun, University of Nantes, France
>Marianne Simonot, CNAM, Paris, France
>Colin Snook, University of Southampton, UK
>David Streader, University of Waikato, New Zealand
>Carsten Sühl, FhG FIRST, Germany
>Bruno Tatibouet, University of Franche-Comté, Besançon, France
>Thai Son Hoang, University of New South Wales, Australia
>Nikolai Tillmann, Microsoft Research, USA

Support

ZB 2003 greatly benefited from the support of the following organizations:

>Åbo Akademi University
>TUCS

and sponsorship from:

>ClearSy System Engineering
>Nokia
>BCS-FACS
>FME
>Z User Group

Table of Contents

Alloy: A Logical Modelling Language 1
  Daniel Jackson

An Outline Pattern Language for Z: Five Illustrations and Two Tables ... 2
  Susan Stepney, Fiona Polack, Ian Toyn

Patterns to Guide Practical Refactoring: Examples Targetting
Promotion in Z 20
  Susan Stepney, Fiona Polack, Ian Toyn

Reuse of Specification Patterns with the B Method 40
  Sandrine Blazy, Frédéric Gervais, Régine Laleau

Composing Specifications Using Communication 58
  Helen Treharne, Steve Schneider, Marchia Bramble

When Concurrent Control Meets Functional Requirements, or Z +
Petri-Nets 79
  Frédéric Peschanski, David Julien

How to Diagnose a Modern Car with a Formal B Model? 98
  Guilhem Pouzancre

Parallel Hardware Design in B 101
  Stefan Hallerstede

Operation Refinement and Monotonicity in the Schema Calculus 103
  Moshe Deutsch, Martin C. Henson, Steve Reeves

Using Coupled Simulations in Non-atomic Refinement 127
  John Derrick, Heike Wehrheim

An Analysis of Forward Simulation Data Refinement 148
  Moshe Deutsch, Martin C. Henson

$B^{\#}$: Toward a Synthesis between Z and B 168
  Jean-Raymond Abrial

Introducing Backward Refinement into B 178
  Steve Dunne

Expression Transformers in B-GSL 197
  Bill Stoddart, Frank Zeyda

Probabilistic Termination in B 216
  Annabelle McIver, Carroll Morgan, Thai Son Hoang

Probabilistic Invariants for Probabilistic Machines 240
  Thai Son Hoang, Zhendong Jin, Ken Robinson, Annabelle McIver, Carroll Morgan

Proving Temporal Properties of Z Specifications Using Abstraction 260
  Graeme Smith, Kirsten Winter

Compositional Verification for Object-Z 280
  Kirsten Winter, Graeme Smith

Timed CSP and Object-Z 300
  John Derrick

Object Orientation without Extending Z 319
  Mark Utting, Shaochun Wang

Comparison of Formalisation Approaches of UML Class Constructs
in Z and Object-Z 339
  Nuno Amálio, Fiona Polack

Towards Practical Proofs of Class Correctness 359
  Bertrand Meyer

Automatically Generating Information from a Z Specification
to Support the Classification Tree Method 388
  Robert M. Hierons, Mark Harman, Harbhajan Singh

Refinement Preserves *PLTL* Properties 408
  Christophe Darlot, Jacques Julliand, Olga Kouchnarenko

Proving Event Ordering Properties for Information Systems 421
  Marc Frappier, Régine Laleau

ZML: XML Support for Standard Z 437
  Mark Utting, Ian Toyn, Jing Sun, Andrew Martin, Jin Song Dong, Nicholas Daley, David Currie

Formal Derivation of Spanning Trees Algorithms 457
  Jean-Raymond Abrial, Dominique Cansell, Dominique Méry

Using B Refinement to Analyse Compensating Business Processes 477
  Carla Ferreira, Michael Butler

A Formal Specification in B of a Medical Decision Support System 497
  Christine Poerschke, David E. Lightfoot, John L. Nealon

Extending B with Control Flow Breaks 513
  Lilian Burdy, Antoine Requet

Towards Dynamic Population Management of Abstract Machines
in the B Method 528
    Nazareno Aguirre, Juan Bicarregui, Theo Dimitrakos, Tom Maibaum

Author Index 547

Alloy: A Logical Modelling Language

Daniel Jackson

MIT Lab for Computer Science
dnj@mit.edu

Abstract. Alloy, like Z, is a language for modelling software systems. Indeed, it draws many of its good ideas from Z: in particular, representing all data structures with sets and relations, and representing behaviour and properties with simple formulas. Unlike Z, however, Alloy was designed with automatic analysis in mind. A constraint solver based on reduction to SAT can check properties of Alloy models, and simulate execution (even of implicit operations). The key idea is to consider all possible bindings of a formula that assign no more than some small number of atoms to each given type. The result is a flexible mechanism that provides rapid and concrete feedback during evolution of a model. It cannot prove properties, but by exhausting all small test cases, it usually succeeds in finding bugs rapidly.

In my talk, I'll explain the fundamental ideas underlying Alloy and its analysis: its basis in relation rather than sets, and the compromises (notably a restriction to first order structures and formulas) that make analysis possible. I'll compare Alloy's specification-structuring mechanism, the signature, to Z's schema. I'll illustrate some modelling idioms that we have developed in using Alloy, focusing on how mutation is represented. I'll also show some examples of typical analyses, including a trace-based analysis that employs the idea of 'machine diameter' from bounded model checking to ensure that all reachable states are considered.

More information about Alloy can be found at
http://sdg.lcs.mit.edu/alloy.

An Outline Pattern Language for Z: Five Illustrations and Two Tables

Susan Stepney, Fiona Polack, and Ian Toyn

Department of Computer Science, University of York,
Heslington, York, YO10 5DD, UK.
{susan, fiona, ian}@cs.york.ac.uk

Abstract. We introduce a pattern language for using formal methods in computer system engineering. We focus on the Z notation, but many of the patterns are adaptable to other formal notations, or can be used to help choose a notation, or to decide on a style of formality. As in other pattern languages, we are providing a new presentation of existing practice, to make it accessible to computer systems engineering. We propose an initial classification of Z patterns, present selected examples, and outline issues of tool support.

Keywords: Z, patterns, development methods

1 Introduction

Formal methods have been used in computer systems development for decades. The most mature forms, particularly those used for hardware design, are compact, well-defined, and well integrated in the development process: they are specialised methods (or tools) for specialist developers. However, most software-oriented formalisms are under-exploited in commercial-scale development, because they are not properly integrated in existing development processes, and are poorly supported by development tools.

In mature development approaches, the stages and steps of development are clear and generally-accepted, whereas in these immature areas there is more art than science; development success depends more on the character and skills of personnel than on the power of the methods. Notations, methods and tools for formal software specification and development currently require specialist knowledge, in an area that is not generally recognised as meriting any development specialism.

2 Motivation

This paper is a contribution to the commercial acceptance of formality, specifically of Z. Z is a powerful *notation*, with few inbuilt assumptions about any design philosophy or development *method* of its own. This power and freedom can make it hard for the newcomer to decide how to structure and develop a Z specification, and hard for a reviewer or implementor to comprehend a specification written in an unfamiliar style.

Our motivation is a desire to make Z more usable by commercial non-specialist developers. Our reason for investigating patterns comes from experience in the industrial use of Z. One of the authors was a member of Logica UK's Formal Methods Team, where she worked extensively on large-scale commercial specification and proof, including a compiler [Stepney & Nabney 2003]; an electronic Purse [Stepney et al. 2000]; and a Smart Card Operating System [Stepney & Cooper 2003]. [Stepney 1998] reports on issues to do with performing proofs on these industrial-scale Z specifications, and sketches requirements for proof tool support to help in this task.

Z textbooks introduce the mathematical bases of Z, the notation, and essential elements of the use of Z. However, few books provide advice on how to "do" Z in practice. Illustrations clearly show how a feature was used by the author, but context and intent are implicit, and there is rarely any advice on how to reuse or adapt the Z text. The work in this paper is a new presentation of well-known material, with the concept of *pattern* applied to enhance the "semantic structure" of Z, thereby helping the writing, reading and presentation of Z. Formalisms such as Z have a role to play in general software development. So the patterns should enable

- writing of formal texts by generalists, because the patterns present formal solutions to common problems
- development of tools to support the use of formal methods by generalists, by recognising and assisting in the application of patterns, and by breaking down the formal concepts into mechanisable or tool-supportable components

3 Patterns

Patterns, originally introduced by [Alexander et al. 1977] in the context of architecture, have been introduced into software engineering, to document and promote best practice, and to share expertise. A pattern provides a *solution to a problem in a context*. Existing patterns cover a wide range of issues, from coding standards [Beck 1997], through program design [Gamma et al. 1995], to domain analysis [Fowler 1997], and meta-concerns such as team structures and project management [Coplien 1995].

Patterns do not stand in isolation. As [Alexander et al. 1977] explain, a *Pattern Language* is a collection of patterns, expressed at different levels, that can be used together to give a structure at *all* levels to the system under development. The names of the patterns provide a *vocabulary* for describing problems and design solutions.

Typically, a pattern comprises a template or algorithm and a statement of its range of applicability. A catalogue records pattern descriptions, organised to facilitate pattern selection. In providing for the selection of appropriate patterns, the description of the *intent* of the pattern is crucial. This describes the situation for which the pattern is appropriate.

The pattern catalogue uses meaningful pattern names to guide users to appropriate patterns. It is also common to use a visual representation. For instance, [Gamma et al. 1995] and [Larman 2001] use UML diagrams to visualise object-oriented program and design patterns. A good pattern catalogue can be applied to assist all elements of construction of a description (program, design, etc).

Some patterns are general purpose, occurring in similar forms across many media (for example, across languages, development phases, contexts). For example, all notations require commentary which is clear, consistent, and adds meaning to the text, and all notations have common usage conventions that can be expressed as patterns.

Some patterns are specific to the language for which they are written. For example, [Gamma et al. 1995] note that some patterns provided for Smalltalk programming are built-in features of other object oriented programming languages. In the formal language context, some Z patterns for identifying proof obligations would be irrelevant in the tool-supported B Method, in which the corresponding proof obligations are automatically generated. Equally, if a Z practitioner is using an architectural pattern other than Delta/Xi, then most of the patterns written for use with the Delta/Xi pattern (promotion, change part of the state etc) are irrelevant.

4 Antipatterns

The concept of patterns in software engineering has been extended to *antipatterns* [Brown et al. 1998]. An antipattern presents an example of poor practice, a pit into which developers (etc) often fall, and a way of avoiding or mitigating the results.

In [Brown et al. 1998], most of the antipatterns describe universally poor practice. However, in other contexts, and particularly in notations such as Z, one developer's antipattern may be another's pattern. This is because a formal text can have many purposes: a pattern that is used to simplify the proof of formal conjectures may reduce the readability of the Z text. In writing antipatterns (and indeed patterns), and in selecting patterns for application, it is therefore important to consider the purpose of the description. The patterns presented here are most appropriate when the primary purpose of the Z specification is communication; we are also working on patterns for other purposes including refinement, implementation and proof.

5 Patterns in Z

5.1 Motivation

Z provides a core language. (We refer to the two main variants of Z as ZRM [Spivey 1992b] and as ISO-Z [ISO-Z 2002]. By *Mathematical Toolkit*, we mean those well-known definitions in [Spivey 1992b, chapter 4] and [ISO-Z 2002, annex B].) Additionally, it is usual to use the Z Mathematical Toolkit, which adds many practical constructs to the core notation. This toolkit is generally assumed to be part of the core, and its scope mistakenly considered to impose fundamental restrictions (such as its definition of only *finite* sequences).

There are currently only a small number of well-known conventions for using Z, and many users are unaware that other approaches are possible. For example, the Delta/Xi style ("state and operations") is often taken to be a characteristic of Z itself, ignoring alternatives such as functional and algebraic styles.

It is common for Z specifications to be coerced into these conventions, no matter how inappropriate. By separating out and describing toolkit patterns, and by naming the Delta/Xi pattern and its associated subpatterns, we hope to make it clear that these are just one choice of many.

We are only beginning to understand the power of patterns in Z; our catalogue headings and pattern formats are still developing.

5.2 Structure of Z Pattern Descriptions

Each reference work has its own structure for describing patterns. We use the following structure.

- Name: conveys the essence, and expands the community "vocabulary"
- *Intent*: a summary of what the pattern provides
- *Problem*: a detailed description of the problem in context
- *Example*: a specific instance of the problem
- *Solution*: a description of the structure that can solve the problem
- *Illustration*: an illustration of the effect of applying the solution
- *Constraint*: something that affects the use of the pattern
- *Variants*: modifications of the pattern for certain circumstances, particularly where ZRM and ISO-Z solutions differ
- *Related patterns*: other patterns to be used with, or in place of, this one
- *Specimens*: references to the literature where the pattern is used (often only implicitly)
- □ : indicates the end of the pattern description

Because of Z's generality and power, there are often several ways to solve a problem, with some solutions being better in some contexts. We include *choice patterns*, describing these various solutions and when they are most appropriate.

Some patterns can be *elaborated* in more significant ways than are covered by the *Variants* heading, the elaborations being almost further patterns in their own right. We describe such elaborations in abbreviated pattern form after the main pattern (see [Stepney *et al.* 2003b] for elaborations of the promotion pattern).

5.3 Diagram Patterns

There are many diagram styles appropriate for summarising different Z structures. For example, Venn diagrams can be used to represent set-theoretic statements; state machines summarise event-based structures; data-flow diagrams can represent functional styles.

We have distilled diagrammatic sub-patterns for specifications using the Delta/Xi and morph architecture patterns. The full details of these can be found in [Stepney et al. 2003c] [Stepney et al. 2003a]; the Delta/Xi sub-pattern is outlined below.

6 Catalogue of Z Patterns

6.1 Introduction

In writing about patterns, we use the following categories (further work is needed on the developing and refining these categories):

- Presentation patterns: ways of presenting, formatting and laying out Z specifications and documents.
- Idiom patterns: styles of writing individual Z phrases
- Structure patterns: ways of structuring small pieces of Z specifications
- Architecture patterns: ways of structuring an entire specification
- Domain patterns: support for specific application domains.
- Development patterns: assistance in parts of an engineering process, ranging from assistance in selecting appropriate formal methods and for applying formality at appropriate levels of rigour, to notation-specific development patterns for a particular system.

Under each category we also list certain *antipatterns*.

Themes re-occur in the different categories, and to some extent the divisions among categories are arbitrary. For example, patterns relating to naming and formatting exist at most levels. Patterns are context-dependent. So, for example, the particular details of a presentation pattern may be affected by the architecture, style, and purpose of the Z description, and by the application domain.

Table 1 categorises the Z patterns that we have identified so far.

6.2 Presentation Patterns

Presentation patterns are analogous to low-level coding standards: how to comment, how to cross reference, how to format. These patterns seem self-evident to people used to structured programming or trained to follow company styles for presentation. However, much published Z is not presented in a consistent manner. These patterns are based on experience of constructing and proving large formal texts, and the needs of the checkers and reviewers of these documents (eg [Stepney et al. 2000]).

6.3 Idiom Patterns

Z is a powerful notation, and there can be several ways of achieving a particular end. It is often useful to choose a particular idiomatic way of doing something, and sticking to it. The idiom itself then becomes part of the vocabulary.

Table 1. Z Pattern Catalogue. In this table we use particular fonts to indicate the patterns, the *antipatterns*, and those with associated `generative` patterns and elaborations.

Category	Sub-category		
	Documentation	Style	Usage
Presentation	Comment the intention Provide navigation Name consistently *Overlong name* *Overmeaningful name*	Format to expose structure	
Idiom		Assemble from chunks Representing many-many mappings Use free types for unions Making a schema binding Making a local declaration *Belated constraint* *Abused mu* *Bemused lambda* *Overloaded numbers*	
Structure	Name meaningful chunks Name predicates	Use generics to control detail *Fortran* *Sørensen shorty*	Modelling optional elements Modelling product types Modelling membership or flags *Boolean flag* *Partial precondition*
Architecture		Morph Event traces Object Orientation Algebraic style Goldilocks chunks *Unsuitable Delta/Xi pattern*	Promotion Delta/Xi
Domain		Application oriented theory	Domain specific toolkits Schema operator toolkit
Development		Focus the formality Use integrated methods	Do a `refinement` Animate Do sanity checks Express implicit properties Apply syntax and type checking Prove rigorously Prove formally

6.4 Structure Patterns

At the intermediate structural level, structure patterns guide the selection and construction of components of the formal description. Whilst some of these patterns represent presentational issues, several capture solutions to potentially hard practical problems.

6.5 Architecture Patterns

Architecture patterns capture conventional ways of using the formal language to produce an overall architecture that achieves the goals of the developer. Some architecture patterns draw on conventional wisdom in the construction of large or complex computer programs: such patterns are generalisable to other formal notations. Other patterns relate specifically to Z.

Architecture patterns help to express a description in Z. They also help the reader of the text. For example, the recognition that a particular form of expression is an architecture pattern allows the reader to concentrate on the system-specific detail rather than the structure of the Z – this would apply to, for example, Delta/Xi: change part of the state, Delta/Xi: project away clutter, and promotion, among others.

Even experienced formalists find it difficult to take on a new style of specification. This can result in inappropriate use of common architecture patterns, and inelegant specifications that do not map cleanly on to the solution architecture. We have identified some alternatives to the widely-used Delta/Xi pattern.

6.6 Domain Patterns

Almost all high-level programming languages use class libraries and packages to provide incidental utilities and domain-specific concepts. In Z, toolkits play a similar role. The Mathematical Toolkit provides generic definitions, laws and constructs for use with sets, relations and predicates. However, its aim is to provide a sufficient set of laws, rather than a complete language.

We envisage that further toolkit libraries will be developed with their associated patterns in future engineering support for Z-based formal methods.

Toolkits could range in level and sophistication, from straightforward extensions to the Mathematical Toolkit, to complete application-specific support with template structures, special operators, and a full set of laws.

6.7 Development Patterns

Development patterns give an engineering context for formal methods. Patterns can be written to assist the choice of whether to use a formal method, in the choice of a specific formal method, and in guiding the (top level) style of formality.

It is easy to write gibberish in a formal notation. There are various ways during the development process of helping to validate a specification: to ensure that it is well-formed, meaningful, and says what is intended. These are captured as usage patterns.

Do a refinement, a generative pattern with elaborations, is outlined briefly and illustrated using the diagram the structure pattern.

7 Five illustrative Patterns

Table 1 shows the Z patterns that we have identified so far. We illustrate these with the examples below; they have been selected to illustrate the pattern structure, antipatterns, good Z style, and some of the new patterns available with ISO-Z. The promotion pattern, which is itself an elaboration of Delta/Xi, is covered in detail in [Stepney et al. 2003b]. The remaining patterns are described in the full Z pattern catalogue [Stepney et al. 2003c].

Comment the Intention

Intent: Communicate the intent of every part of the specification, with a uniform commenting style.

Problem: A Z specification that comprises only mathematics is not readable or maintainable. The mathematics provides a reasonably unambiguous specification, but the variable names are an insufficient link to the real world.

Example: an unambiguous but obscure Z schema:

$$
\begin{array}{|l}
\text{\_\_ Memory _____} \\
ram, rom : ADDR \nrightarrow BYTE \\
inmap, outmap : \mathbb{P}\, ADDR \\
\hline
\text{disjoint}\langle \text{dom } ram, \text{dom } rom \rangle \\
inmap \cup outmap \subseteq \text{dom } ram \\
\text{disjoint}\langle inmap, outmap \rangle \\
\end{array}
$$

Solution: Provide a commentary in a particular style at a number of levels. The text needs to be written and maintained with as much care as the Z, and must add to the value of the mathematical statements: the text is not just a "translation" of the maths.

- If necessary, include an introductory overview of the domain, as context for the specification; use diagrams to capture the architecture.
- In the body of the specification, write a short sentence that conveys the intent of every Z paragraph, linking to the real world; if the Z is long, provide further commentary describing the intent of the internals.
- Where a Z paragraph has internal structure let the comment structure clearly follow that of the Z paragraph. For a schema, for example, precede the Z paragraph with commentary on declarations (global names), follow the paragraph with commentary on internals.

Illustration:

The schema *Memory* defines the memory state of the device.
- *ram* describes the dynamic memory, as a mapping from memory addresses to the byte values they contain
- *rom* describes the read-only memory, as for *ram*
- *inmap*, *outmap* are the memory-mapped input/output memory locations

$$
\begin{array}{|l}
\text{\_\_ Memory _____} \\
ram, rom : ADDR \nrightarrow BYTE \\
inmap, outmap : \mathbb{P}\, ADDR \\
\hline
\text{disjoint}\langle \text{dom } ram, \text{dom } rom \rangle \\
inmap \cup outmap \subseteq \text{dom } ram \\
\text{disjoint}\langle inmap, outmap \rangle \\
\end{array}
$$

- *ram* and *rom* have distinct address spaces
- the memory mapped i/o lies within *ram*
- no address is both input and output

□

Overloaded Numbers

Intent: Exploit the Z type system and typechecking tools to catch as many errors as possible.

Problem: Subsets of ℕ or ℤ are often used as convenient models of labels and identifiers in specifications, but a typechecker cannot catch cases where the wrong kind of label is being used.

Solution: Use given sets and free types, rather than subsets of ℕ or ℤ, where possible.

Specimen: [Brown 1979] quotes his eighth deadly sin as "to use numbers for objects that are not numbers".

□

Modelling Product Types (Choice)

Intent: Choose the more appropriate product constructor for a context.

Problem: Z has two nearly-isomorphic product type constructors. Which one should be used in a given context?

Solution choice:

1. Modelling product types: schema
   Component names are meaningful (for example, *memory.register* would refer to the *register* component of the schema binding *memory*). This fits the intention of name meaningful chunks. However, constructing particular schema bindings is relatively verbose. Use a schema product where the names convey some helpful meaning, and where component selection is common.
2. Modelling product types: Cartesian product
   Components are located by position (for example, *memory*.3), which communicates little meaning. However, the tuple construction syntax is terse. Use a Cartesian product when terseness is valuable, for example, the main use of the product is writing explicit values, as in **algebraic style** operator definitions. Use a Cartesian product when there are no meaningful names to be had, for example, if the components are bundled into a tuple simply in order to return multiple results from a function.

Specimens: of schemas: [Polack *et al.* 1993], [Mander & Polack 1995]; of tuples: many Mathematical Toolkit definitions.

Variants: In ZRM, schema components can be directly selected, as in $S.foo$, but schema bindings cannot be directly written (a mu-expression is often used, as in $\mu S \bullet foo = x \land bar = y$); tuples can be directly written, as in (x, y, z), but their components cannot be directly selected (a lambda-expression with a characteristic tuple is often used, as in $\lambda x : X; y : Y; z : Z \bullet z$). ISO-Z allows

schema bindings to be directly written, as in ⦇ $foo == x, bar == y$ ⦈, and tuple components to be directly selected, as in $t.3$, but there is still a difference in the terseness of construction.
□

Delta/Xi: Diagram the Structure

Intent: Summarise the structure of a Delta/Xi specification using a diagram.

Problem: Since a Z specification is presented 'bottom-up' (declaration before use) and can be factored into many pieces, it may become difficult to 'see the wood for the trees'.

Solution: Construct a diagram to record the structure of the state and operation schemas, highlighting any Delta/Xi-related patterns used.

Do not worry over-much about being consistent and complete, and about distinguishing every small difference: the purpose of the diagram is to give a graphical overview of structure, not to be an alternative formal notation.

The following components are recommended.

– distinguish schemas by purpose
  • draw state schemas as named rectangles
  • draw operation schemas as named hexagons
  • draw other data types as named parallelograms
  • schemas not defined in the specification may be used in the diagram, for clarity. Indicate these by a dashed box. (Use of the Delta/Xi: strict convention sub-pattern means that ΔS and ΞS boxes are always dashed.)
– for schema inclusion, use solid arrows pointing from the including schema to the included schema
  • for state inclusion, use a single line
  • for an operation including a state schema, S, via ΔS (and thus introducing a before- and an after-state), use a double line and a delta arrowhead, pointing to the rectangle, S.
  • for an (initialisation) operation that includes only an after-state (S'), use a single line and an after-state ' by the arrowhead
  • an arrow directly to a box may be elided if there is an alternative path to that box
– indicate other uses of schemas by dashed lines from the referring data type to the referenced schema
– use highlighting (line thickness, box shading) to distinguish important parts of the diagram
  • if a description uses a pattern described with a diagrammatic form, the diagram of the description can be constructed by instantiating the structure of the pattern. Use highlighting to distinguish the pattern from other structural elements
  • highlight the full operations, as contrasted to intermediate definitions

As much as possible, without distorting the diagram, inclusion arrows are drawn upwards, so that the simplest schemas are at the top of the diagram, and constructs that are more complex are further down the page.

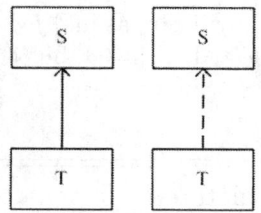

Fig. 1. (a) schema T includes schema S. (b) schema T references schema S.

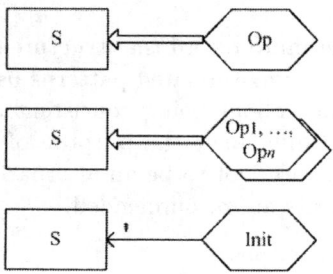

Fig. 2. (a) operation Op includes ΔS. (b) several operations Op_i include ΔS. (c) initialisation operation $Init$ includes $S\,'$.

- If schema T includes schema S, either as declaration as $T == [\,S;\,\ldots\,|\,\ldots\,]$, or as a predicate as $T == [\,\ldots\,|\,S \wedge \ldots\,]$, it can be drawn as figure 1a.
- If schema T refers to schema S other than by inclusion, for example as $T == [\,f : x \nrightarrow S \ldots\,|\,\ldots\,]$, it can be drawn as figure 1(b)
- If operation schema Op includes schema S as $Op == [\,\Delta S \ldots\,|\,\ldots\,]$, it can be drawn as figure 2(a)
- If multiple schemas S_i have precisely the same relationships with other schemas, their names can be listed in the same box, thereby drawing attention to their similar structures, as with Op_i in figure 2(b)
- If initialisation schema $Init$ includes schema S as $Init == [\,S\,' \ldots\,|\,\ldots\,]$, it can be drawn as figure 2(c)

Illustration: [Stepney et al. 2003c] shows the diagrams of a large Delta/Xi specification.

Variants:

- The notation can be extended to show conjectures (as in the do a refinement pattern, below).
  - conjectures are drawn in an oval, labelled with a suitable name, pointing to referenced schemas
- For large specifications, a diagram may be split into sub-diagrams for clarity. It may be appropriate to draw a separate diagram for each operation, or family of operations, reproducing (relevant parts of) the diagram.

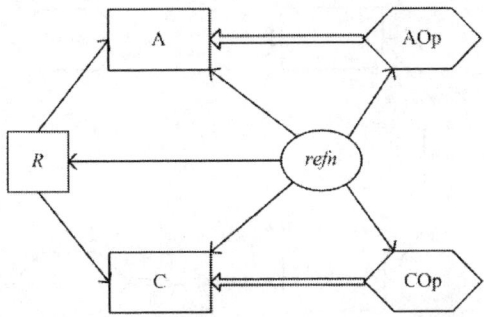

Fig. 3. Structure of the do a refinement pattern using diagram the structure.

- schemas or other data type boxes occurring in more than one subdiagram are represented as rounded boxes on subsequent occurrences (see the example in [Stepney et al. 2003c]).
- If your application uses schemas in some particular way, extend the notation to capture your structure.

Specimen: this pattern is adapted from [d'Inverno & Luck 2001].
□

Do a Refinement

Intent: connect, by formal proof of a refinement conjecture, specifications of the same system at different levels of abstraction.

Solution: Use the generative refinement patterns:

- Do a refinement: abstract model – provide an abstract specification
- Do a refinement: concrete model – provide an equivalent specification at a lower level of detail
- Do a refinement: retrieve relation – formally express the mapping between each abstract component and its concrete equivalent
- Do a refinement: conjecture – prove that the concrete operations and invariant maintain the invariant of the abstract specification

The underlying structure of a refinement is summarised in figure 3. The retrieve relation is the schema R. The refinement conjecture is represented as the ellipse, *refn*.

The conjecture statement refers to all states and operations. To clarify the structure, we choose to replace it by a dotted line linking the corresponding concrete and global operations referenced in the conjecture, and labelled with the relevant retrieve relation, figure 4.

The do a refinement pattern has a large number of elaborations, some of which are listed in table 2, below.
□

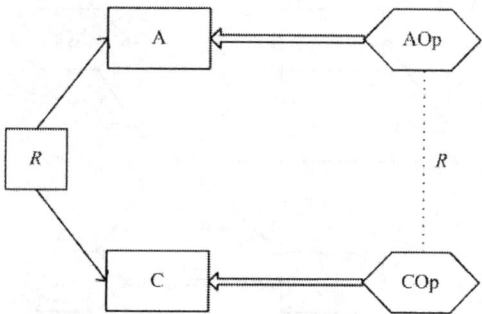

Fig. 4. Structure of the do a refinement pattern, abbreviated form.

8 Z Generative Patterns

In object-oriented programming, generative patterns are an element of adaptive programming. Patterns written in a meta-language are used to automatically derive programs in the object-oriented language. This is analogous to conventional compilation of a high-level program into a lower-level program [Lopes & Lieberherr 1994].

A looser meaning of generative pattern in object-oriented patterns work is the application of a series of patterns to create a program. Note that this is quite different from the creational patterns of [Gamma *et al.* 1995]: the latter are patterns that can be used to create specific elements of a program (classes, structures, generic operations etc).

It is impossible to automatically generate a specification from a meta-language template alone. The process of (commercial) specification establishes the requirements and progressively assembles an abstract description of a suitable system to meet the requirements. There can be no safe meta-level for a description that is continually and actively evolving. However, the looser definition of generative patterns is clearly applicable.

Generative patterns are appropriate for any Z concept that is expressed in a series of steps or components. Simple generative patterns could be used to initiate beginners into the writing of specifications in any format. They form the beginnings of a method for Z. At the hard end of formal notations, generative patterns are proposed to assist in refinement, retrenchment and proof.

Elaborations exist for all the proposed generative patterns. For example, the refinement pattern has elaborations to deal with particularly problematic elements of practical refinements. Patterns can be used to determine the kind(s) of refinement to use: forward or backward rules, blocking or non-blocking semantics, etc. In addition, there are elaborations that help the specifier to arrive at refinements. These could be used to guide the weakening of preconditions, and the making deterministic of the abstract specification (or their inverses for abstraction).

Table 2. Generative Z Patterns and their Elaborations. Note that `promotion` is both an elaboration of `Delta/Xi`, and a generative parttern in its own right.

Generative Pattern	Elaboration	Intention
Delta/Xi: state operations disjoin errors		Specify a system as a state, and operations based on that state.
	Promotion	(see below)
diagram the structure strict convention change part of the state project away clutter hide a state component partial precondition		
Promotion: local state and operations global state framing schemas global operations		Specify a system characterised as a collection of local states, and of operations based on those defined on the local state.
	global constraints	Add global state components to the collection of local instances.
diagram the structure	internal identifiers	Use a native element of the local instances as the identifier.
	combine promotions	Specify a system that conforms to the local-global format for the Promotion architecture pattern, but has different sorts of local instance.
	multi-promotion	Specify a system that comprises multiple instances, but has global operations that may affect more than one local instance.
Do a refinement: abstract model concrete model retrieve relation refinement conjecture		Reduce the level of abstraction by provable refinements
	weakest concrete form	Use the retrieve relation to calculate the weakest concrete form.
	widen precondition	(Various patterns)
	reduced non-determinism	(Various patterns)
	backwards refinement	Apply reverse refinement rules
	blocking semantics	Allow a blocking semantics in concrete specification

Table 2 identifies some generative patterns. The table is not exhaustive, either in terms of the list of generative patterns, or in the detail of elaborations and component patterns. See [Stepney *et al.* 2003b] for more details of the promotion generative patterns.

9 Tool Support

9.1 Introduction

The use of (generative sets of) patterns to produce Z specifications goes some way towards a Z method – particularly in conjunction with existing Z tools. However, commercial specification developers need more, and better-targeted, tools. The required tools should both exploit and support patterns:

- Where a pattern or some part of it is fixed-form, a tool should support it directly (perhaps as a built-in generic pattern instantiated by the user).

- Where a pattern provides a template, or where various forms apply in different contexts, the tool should guide the user.
- New Z tools should aim to support documentation formats, presentation patterns and alternation between well-defined choice patterns.
- Existing Z tools might be refactored to exploit patterns.

9.2 Existing Tool Support

Manual application of patterns during development is difficult – even simple things like name consistently can be overlooked, especially if the naming convention is evolving with the specification. Conforming to patterns during maintenance is even more difficult, especially if the particular patterns used have not been documented.

In the object-oriented community, there is work on integrating patterns into the development process. Some schemes have been invented for encoding patterns in classes, but the match is not good. Patterns are at a different level from the language constructs. Mostly, naming conventions and comments are used to indicate the use of patterns in the code. But some tool support is possible, both in software development and in formal notations. Before trying to invent a new general purpose meta-language to support the identified patterns, tool developers should concentrate on supporting the individual patterns explicitly.

Current Z tools are mostly syntax- and type-checkers, and proof tools. Compared to programming language IDEs, they provide relatively unsophisticated development environments.

The presentation patterns are supported to a greater or lesser extent by current Z tools, but even there little is automatic. Existing tools format to expose structure: most LaTeX-based tools, for example, [Spivey 1992a], give the user complete control over line breaks, indentation and white space within phrases; other tools such as CADiZ [Toyn 2002] and Formaliser [Stepney 2001] have automatic 'pretty-printing' layouts, but they do not always give optimal readability, and are not configurable to different layout standards. Similarly, provide navigation is supported in LaTeX-based tools via the LaTeX \index command and in HTML-based tools via hyperlinks. Z-Eves [Saaltink 1997] has a good navigation interface. Name consistently is partially supported by search and replace; such operations are even more useful when scope-sensitive. Graphical tools for GUI design show how a tool can automatically generate underlying code such that user changes to that code are reflected back in the GUI design. A similar approach could be used to support many of the Z patterns.

Z development process patterns are, perhaps surprisingly, the best supported, because many of the identified patterns are validation patterns requiring proof, for which proof tools exist. But even proof tools provide little *explicit* support for validation proof patterns – they are general purpose, rather than sensitive to the particular proofs required. There is some support for animation, ranging from conventions for semi-automatic translation of Z to an executable form [West & Eaglestone 1992], [Hewitt et al. 1997], to executable subsets of Z itself

[Valentine 1992]. Making such conventions and tools sensitive to particular patterns would greatly smooth the process.

9.3 A Better Way of Supporting Patterns

Template support for presentation patterns such as comment the intention could be provided: addition of a declaration or predicate would cause a new comment line to be provided, with a prompt to the developer to explain the addition (either on the new comment line or in an existing comment line). The tool should manage the linking of comment lines to the Z lines; reordering of declaration or predicates should cause corresponding reordering of their associated comments.

Tool support for choice patterns would allow users to change their minds. As a trivial example, Formaliser can convert between a horizontal and vertical schema display. Support for modelling product types, to assist in changing the representation between schemas and Cartesian products, could be implemented by adaptation from existing tool support for *schema expansion*.

Architecture patterns are not yet well supported by tools. Delta/Xi is supported, simply because its naming conventions are partly encoded in the Z core language, yet tools need to 'understand' whether a particular schema is a state, an operation, or a piece of scaffolding.

Interactive support in the form of state and operation templates, framing schema templates for promotion, and function definitions broken down over free types for morph, could all be automated. The Delta/Xi diagrams presented above show the schema components and their interrelationships; these could form a framework for "intelligent" structural support, extending the existing tool facilities for tracking named component usage in a specification.

One day tools may be configurable to support different specification aims (readability, provability, etc). They may be able to detect antipatterns in each style of specification, and able to guide the developer to a better representation, based on the patterns appropriate to that form of specification.

10 Conclusion

Z patterns have something in common with many of the software engineering pattern languages. [Beck 1997]'s Smalltalk coding standards provide inspiration for commenting and presentation. [Gamma *et al.* 1995]'s design patterns are similar in intent to many of the Z presentation, architecture and structure patterns. [Larman 2001]'s UML patterns can be compared to the higher-level architecture patterns, and the generative use of patterns.

A Pattern Language for Z, which is essentially a packaging of existing language elements and usage according to their context of use, helps to make explicit the wider range of conventions and styles available. In addition, it helps to provide good solutions to well-known recurrent problems.

References

[Alexander et al. 1977] Christopher Alexander, Sara Ishikawa, Murray Silverstein, Max Jacobson, Ingrid Fiksdahl-King, and Shlomo Angel. *A Pattern Language: Towns, Buildings, Construction.* Oxford University Press, 1977.

[Beck 1997] Kent Beck. *Smalltalk Best Practice Patterns.* Prentice Hall, 1997.

[Bowen et al. 1997] J. P. Bowen, M. G. Hinchey, and D. Till, editors. *ZUM'97: The Z Formal Specification Notation, 10th International Conference of Z Users, Reading, UK*, volume 1212 of *LNCS*. Springer, 1997.

[Brown et al. 1998] William J. Brown, Raphael C. Malveau, Hays W. McCormick III, and Thomas J. Mowbray. *AntiPatterns.* Wiley, 1998.

[Brown 1979] Peter J. Brown. *Writing Interactive Compilers and Interpreters.* Wiley, 1979.

[Coplien 1995] James O. Coplien. A generative development-process pattern language. In James O. Coplien and Douglas C. Schmidt, editors, *Pattern Languages of Program Design.* Addison-Wesley, 1995.

[d'Inverno & Luck 2001] Mark d'Inverno and Michael Luck. *Understanding Agent Systems.* Springer Verlag, 2001.

[Fowler 1997] Martin Fowler. *Analysis Patterns.* Addison-Wesley, 1997.

[Gamma et al. 1995] Erich Gamma, Richard Helm, Ralph Johnson, and John Vlissides. *Design Patterns.* Addison-Wesley, 1995.

[Hewitt et al. 1997] M. A. Hewitt, C. M. O'Halloran, and C. T. Sennett. Experiences with PiZA, an animator for Z. In [Bowen et al. 1997], pages 37–51.

[ISO-Z 2002] ISO/IEC 13568. *Information Technology—Z Formal Specification Notation—Syntax, Type System and Semantics: International Standard*, 2002.

[Larman 2001] Craig Larman. *Applying UML and Patterns, 2nd edition.* Prentice Hall, 2001.

[Lopes & Lieberherr 1994] Cristina Videira Lopes and Karl Lieberherr. Generative patterns. In *ECOOP'94 Workshop on Patterns, Bologna, Italy*, 1994.

[Mander & Polack 1995] Keith C. Mander and Fiona Polack. Rigorous specification using structured systems analysis and Z. *Information and Software Technology*, 37(5):285–291, 1995.

[Polack et al. 1993] Fiona Polack, Mark Whiston, and Keith C. Mander. The SAZ project : Integrating SSADM and Z. In *FME'93 : Industrial Strength Formal Methods, Odense, Denmark*, volume 670 of *LNCS*, pages 541–557. Springer, 1993.

[Saaltink 1997] Mark Saaltink. The Z/EVES system. In [Bowen et al. 1997], pages 72–85.

[Spivey 1992a] J. Michael Spivey. *The fuzz Manual.* The Spivey Partnership, 2nd edition, 1992. ftp://ftp.comlab.ox.ac.uk/pub/Zforum/fuzz.

[Spivey 1992b] J. Michael Spivey. *The Z Notation: a Reference Manual.* Prentice Hall, 2nd edition, 1992.

[Stepney & Cooper 2003] Susan Stepney and David Cooper. Smart card operating system: Specification, refinement, and proof. Technical Report YCS-2003, York, 2003. (in press).

[Stepney & Nabney 2003] Susan Stepney and Ian Nabney. The DeCCo papers. Technical Report YCS-2003, York, 2003. (in press).

[Stepney et al. 2000] Susan Stepney, David Cooper, and Jim Woodcock. An electronic purse: Specification, refinement, and proof. Technical Monograph PRG-126, Programming Research Group, Oxford University Computing Laboratory, 2000.

[Stepney et al. 2003a] Susan Stepney, Fiona Polack, and Ian Toyn. A meta-pattern for diagram patterns. 2003. (in preparation).
[Stepney et al. 2003b] Susan Stepney, Fiona Polack, and Ian Toyn. Patterns to guide practical refactoring. 2003. (these proceedings).
[Stepney et al. 2003c] Susan Stepney, Fiona Polack, and Ian Toyn. A Z patterns catalogue I: specification and refactoring, v0.1. Technical Report YCS-2003-349, York, 2003.
[Stepney 1998] Susan Stepney. A tale of two proofs. In *Third Northern Formal Methods Workshop*. BCS-FACS, 1998.
[Stepney 2001] Susan Stepney. Formaliser Home Page. http://public.logica.com/~formaliser/, 2001.
[Toyn 2002] Ian Toyn. CADiZ web pages. http://www-users.cs.york.ac.uk/~ian/cadiz/, 2002.
[Valentine 1992] Samuel H. Valentine. Z^{--}, an executable subset of Z. In J. E. Nicholls, editor, *Z User Workshop, York 1991*, Workshops in Computing, pages 157–187. Springer, 1992.
[West & Eaglestone 1992] M. M. West and B. M. Eaglestone. Software development: Two approaches to animation of Z specifications using Prolog. *IEE/BCS Software Engineering Journal*, 7(4):264–276, July 1992.

Patterns to Guide Practical Refactoring: Examples Targetting Promotion in Z

Susan Stepney, Fiona Polack, and Ian Toyn

Department of Computer Science, University of York,
Heslington, York, YO10 5DD, UK.
{susan, fiona, ian}@cs.york.ac.uk

Abstract. Formal methods such as Z are generally criticised for their lack of practical applicability. As in other areas of software engineering, *patterns* help to construct, analyse and describe formal texts. Once a method has a catalogue of patterns, development can proceed by applying patterns, and by moving from one sort of pattern to another. This paper illustrates a developmental use of patterns. First, we describe the set of patterns that collectively represent the well-known Z structure, *promotion*. We then show how *refactoring* can be used to take an unstructured Z specification in to a promotion structure.

Keywords: Z, patterns, refactoring, development methods

1 Introduction

Pattern languages [Alexander *et al.* 1977] [Gamma *et al.* 1995] and refactoring [Fowler 1999] are programming techniques that can also be fruitfully applied to specification [Stepney *et al.* 2003a] [Stepney *et al.* 2002].

In this paper, we illustrate how patterns and refactoring can be applied, using the example of Z promotion as an *elaboration* of the Delta/Xi pattern [Stepney *et al.* 2003a]. We describe the simplest case of the promotion pattern in terms of a set of sub-patterns that can be used as steps in *generating* a promoted specification. We then provide various *elaboration* patterns, showing how the simple case can be adapted to different circumstances. Finally we use the promotion generative sub-patterns as a basis for *refactoring*, to take an unstructured Z specification into a promotion structure.

2 The Promotion Pattern, and Its Generative Sub-patterns

Promotion

Intent: Specify a global system in terms of multiple instances of a local state, and of operations that manipulate a local state.

Problem: A system that is essentially a hierarchy of components has operations and state at different levels in the hierarchy. This is difficult to specify directly, requiring Z structures such as μ and θ schema bindings.
Solution: Build a specification for local state and operations. Build the global state as a composite of local states. Define framing schemas to promote the local operations. Use schema calculus to construct appropriate global operations. (These steps are expanded further in the four sub-patterns below.)
Specimens: Unix File System [Morgan & Sufrin 1984] (first published example); [Woodcock & Davies 1996] (useful refinement laws); [Stepney & Cooper 2000] (an operating system for managing processes on a smart card).
□

We structure the promotion pattern into four sub-patterns, used to guide the generation of a promoted specification. For reasons of space, we merely summarise these sub-patterns here, giving the *intent* and the *solution* only. See [Barden et al. 1994, chapter 19] for a fuller description of the underlying structure. [Stepney et al. 2003b] gives an example of using these sub-patterns to generate a promoted specification, starting from a local state specification.

The sub-pattern illustrations are documented according to the presentation pattern comment the intent, and illustrated by diagramming the structure [Stepney et al. 2003a].

Promotion: Local State and Operations

Intent: describe the state, operations, initialisation and (precondition for) finalisation, for a single instance of the multi-instance system.
Solution:

> $Local == $ [state components | constraints]
> $LocalOp == $ [$\Delta Local$; $a?: IN$; $b!: OUT$ | constraints]
> $LocalInit == $ [$Local\,'$ | constraints]
> $LocalFinalise == $ [$Local$ | constraints]

□

Promotion: Global State

Intent: describe the global context of a multi-instance system.
Solution:

- the global state requires a set, $[ID]$ of identities
- gbl maps identities to instances of the local state

> $Global == $ [$gbl: ID \nrightarrow Local$]

□

Promotion: Framing Schemas

Intent: provide a context that describes how the global state is updated by the results of local operations.

Solution: the context, or "frame" is written as a "framing schema". This establishes the relationship of the state of a local instance to the global state, then shows how the after-state of an operation on that local instance is used to update the global state (the after-state of any suitable global operation) – no details of the global operation or the local operation are required; the frame merely deals with states established by operations defined elsewhere.

The following frame is for any operation that updates the state(s).

- $\Delta Global$, $\Delta Local$ introduce before and after global and local states
- $x?$ is the global identity of an (existing) local instance

$$
\begin{array}{|l}
\Phi Update \\
\Delta Global \\
\Delta Local \\
x? : ID \\
\hline
x? \in \mathrm{dom}\ gbl \\
\theta Local = gbl\ x? \\
gbl' = gbl \oplus \{x? \mapsto \theta Local\,'\}
\end{array}
$$

- $x?$ is in the global set of local instances
- the before state of *Local* is the current local state associated with $x?$
- the global state is updated by overriding the *gbl* function with the maplet from $x?$ to the after-state of *Local*

The frame for introducing a new local instance to the global state is similar to an initialisation.

- declarations are as above, except that there is no *Local* before state

$$
\begin{array}{|l}
\Phi New \\
\Delta Global \\
Local\,' \\
x? : ID \\
\hline
x? \notin \mathrm{dom}\ gbl \\
gbl' = gbl \cup \{x? \mapsto \theta Local\,'\}
\end{array}
$$

- $x?$ does not have a mapping in the global state (it is an unused identity)
- The *gbl* function is updated by set union, adding the mapping from $x?$ to the after-state of *Local*

The frame for an operation to remove a local instance from the global state, $\Phi Remove$, is similar, but removes the local instance from the global mapping. The frame is needed only where the removal of a local instance must be verified using operations at the local level.

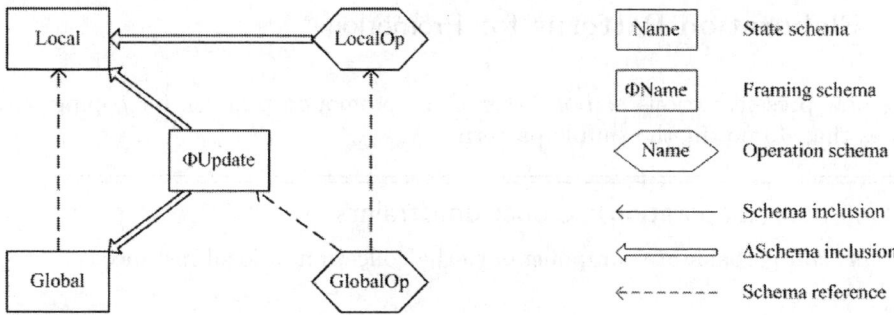

Fig. 1. Structure of the promotion pattern.

- declarations are as above, except that there is no *Local* after state

$$
\begin{array}{|l}
\varPhi Delete \\
\Delta Global \\
Local \\
x? : ID \\
\hline
x? \in \mathrm{dom}\, gbl \\
\theta Local = gbl\ x? \\
gbl' = \{x?\} \vartriangleleft gbl
\end{array}
$$

- $x?$ is in the global set of local instances
- the before-state of *Local* is the current local state associated with $x?$
- the global state is updated by removing the relevant maplet from gbl

□

Promotion: Global Operations

Intent: write a global operation in terms of the defined local operations.
Solution: Use schema calculus to extract the relevant local operation (or after-state of a local operation) and conjoin the appropriate framing schema.

$GlobalOp == \exists\, \Delta Local \bullet \varPhi Update \wedge LocalOp$

$GlobalNew == \exists\, Local\,' \bullet \varPhi New \wedge LocalInit$

$GlobalRemove == \exists\, Local \bullet \varPhi Remove \wedge LocalFinalise$

Define an appropriate global initialisation:

$GlobalInit == [\ Global\,' \mid constraints\ ]$

Note that the type of $GlobalOp$ is $[\ \Delta Global;\ x? : ID;\ a? : IN;\ b! : OUT\ ]$.

A diagrammatic representation of the promoted update operations is shown in figure 1. (For a fuller description of the diagrammatic notation, based on an extension of that in [d'Inverno & Luck 2001], see [Stepney *et al.* 2003a].)

□

3   Elaboration Patterns for Promotion

We now present various *elaborations* of the promotion pattern, for coping with cases that do not fit the simple pattern.

Promotion (Elaboration): Global Constraints

Intent: add global state components to the collection of local instances
Solution:

```
┌─ GlobalWithState ────────────────────────────────┐
│ Global                                           │
│ purely global state components                   │
│ ───────────────────────────────                  │
│ constraints on global state                      │
│ constraints relating local states                │
└──────────────────────────────────────────────────┘
```

The addition of global state components may require addition of constraints (a) on the global state, and (b) relating the local instance states; the promoted local operations may affect the global state through such constraints. There may also be operations that act on the global state components alone.

Illustration: [Stepney et al. 2000] defines a collection of concrete (that is, refined from the abstract) electronic purses. The global state has additional mechanisms to control interoperability of the purses. The extended global state is:

- *conPurse* is the global state for the local purses, *ConPurse*, using identities from the set, *NAME*
- *ether* and *archive* are global-only state elements

```
┌─ ConWorld ───────────────────────────────────────┐
│ conPurse : NAME ⇸ ConPurse                       │
│ ether : ℙ Message                                │
│ archive : NAME ↔ Message                         │
│ ───────────────────────────────                  │
│ ...                                              │
│ dom archive ⊆ dom conPurse                       │
└──────────────────────────────────────────────────┘
```

- the global state element, *archive*, is constrained to only known local purses

All the single purse operations are promoted to the global level. The inputs and outputs from the local operation, $m?$ and $m!$, are not simply mapped into global inputs and outputs; they are also linked to the *ether* (the message transport mechanism) by the framing schema, which extends the framing schemas pattern:

$$
\begin{array}{|l}
\_\Phi\mathit{UpdateCon}_____\\
\Delta\mathit{ConWorld}\\
\Delta\mathit{ConPurse}\\
m?, m! : \mathit{MESSAGE}\\
\mathit{name}? : \mathit{NAME}\\
\hline
\mathit{name}? \in \mathrm{dom}\ \mathit{conPurse}\\
m? \in \mathit{ether}\\
\theta\mathit{ConPurse} = \mathit{conPurse}\ \mathit{name}?\\
\mathit{conPurse}' = \mathit{conPurse} \oplus \{\mathit{name}? \mapsto \theta\mathit{ConPurse}\ '\}\\
\mathit{ether}' = \mathit{ether} \cup \{m!\}\\
\mathit{archive}' = \mathit{archive}
\end{array}
$$

In addition to the promoted operations, there are some global-only operations, for example to add messages in the *ether* to the *archive*
□

Promotion (Elaboration): Internal Identifiers

Intent: use a native element of the local state as the identifier. (The global identifiers used in promotion are arbitrary. Where the local state has its own identity, this may be a suitable global identifier.)
Solutions:
There are two solutions, depending on whether the promotion uses only internal identity, or uses both internal and global identity redundantly.
Solution 1: Internal identity only
Adapt Promotion: local state and operations thus:
  Include the identity as a native attribute of the local state

  $\mathit{Local} == [\ \mathit{self} : \mathit{ID};\ \ldots\ ]$

Include a constraint in local operations that the identity is not changed by the operation

  $\mathit{LocalOp} == [\ \Delta\mathit{Local};\ \ldots\ |\ \mathit{self}' = \mathit{self} \wedge \ldots\ ]$

Adapt Promotion: global state thus:
  Make the global state the set of local instances, with different local states having different identities.

  $\mathit{Global} == [\ \mathit{gbl} : \mathbb{P}\ \mathit{Local}\ |\ \forall\, x, y : \mathit{glb}\ |\ x \neq y \bullet x.\mathit{self} \neq y.\mathit{self}\ ]$

Global operations must include constraints to check the identity of local instances. For exapmle, the frame for the update operations modifies the predicates of the framing schemas pattern as follows.

$$
\begin{array}{|l}
\hline
\varPhi\mathit{Update} \\
\Delta\mathit{Global} \\
\Delta\mathit{Local} \\
x?: \mathit{ID} \\
\hline
\mathit{self} = x? \\
\theta\mathit{Local} \in \mathit{gbl} \\
\mathit{gbl}' = (\mathit{gbl} \setminus \{\theta\mathit{Local}\}) \cup \{\theta\mathit{Local}\,'\} \\
\hline
\end{array}
$$

- the local state's *self* component matches the given identifier, x?
- the local instance occurs in the global state *gbl*
- the update replaces the local instance in the global set of instances with the result of the local operation

The frame for the operation to add a new piece of local state is as follows.

$$
\begin{array}{|l}
\hline
\varPhi\mathit{New} \\
\Delta\mathit{Global} \\
\mathit{Local}\,' \\
x?: \mathit{ID} \\
\hline
\forall x : \mathit{gbl} \bullet x.\mathit{self} \neq x? \\
\mathit{self}' = x? \\
\mathit{gbl}' = \mathit{gbl} \cup \{\theta\mathit{Local}\,'\} \\
\hline
\end{array}
$$

- no pre-existing local state has the given identifier, x?
- the new local state has identifier x?
- the update adds the new local state to the global set

Solution 2: External and internal identities

The local state and operation definitions are the same as for solution 1.

Adapt Promotion: global state thus:

Make the global function an injection, capturing the one-to-one correspondence between 'external' and 'internal' names, and ensure that, for any instance, external and internal identities are the same.

$$\mathit{Global} == [\; \mathit{gbl} : \mathit{ID} \rightarrowtail \mathit{Local} \mid \forall x : \mathrm{dom}\, \mathit{gbl} \bullet (\mathit{gbl}\, x).\mathit{self} = x \;]$$

Example: In the concrete specification of the electronic purse, the purse has a name; this is the name that the purse is known by at the external level. The local state is *ConPurse*:

$$\mathit{ConPurse} == [\; \mathit{name} : \mathit{NAME};\; \ldots \mid \ldots \;]$$

Adapt Promotion: global state thus:

- *ConWorld* uses the same type as the local identifier for the domain of the global *conPurse*.

```
┌─ ConWorld ─────────────────────────────────────────────┐
│ conPurse : NAME ↦→ ConPurse                            │
│ ...                                                     │
├─────────────────────────────────────────────────────────┤
│ ∀ n : dom conPurse • (conPurse n).name = n             │
│ ...                                                     │
└─────────────────────────────────────────────────────────┘
```

– every purse's internal name must be the same as the name by which it is known in the global system.

The framing schemas pattern is applicable, as the additional constraint is carried forward in the $\Delta ConWorld$ inclusion.

Specimen: Hall's style [Stepney et al. 1992, chapter 3] combines both these variants. It has a set of local states, and it has a *derived* mapping from (external) identities to local states:

```
┌─ HallStyle ────────────────────────────────────────────┐
│ gbl : 𝔽 Local                                          │
│ idGbl : ID ↦→ Local                                    │
├─────────────────────────────────────────────────────────┤
│ idGbl = { l : gbl • l.self ↦ l }                       │
└─────────────────────────────────────────────────────────┘
```

□

Promotion (Elaboration): Combine Promotions

Intent: specify a system that conforms to the local-global format for the promotion pattern, but has different kinds of local instance.

Solution:

- Each kind of local instance is associated with a separate component of the global state.

$$Global == [\ gbl1 : ID1 \twoheadrightarrow Local1;\ \ldots;\ gbln : IDN \twoheadrightarrow LocalN\ ]$$

- Constraints could be added as appropriate.

Example: [Stepney & Cooper 2000]'s specification of a Smart Card Operating System specifies three types of application instance that the operating system has to control: fixed ISO applications, user programmable applications, and (for modelling reasons) 'absent' applications. It is possible to promote these three types of local instances individually:

- **fixed** and **user** follow the **global state** pattern.
- **absent** has no local state other than an identifier, so the **internal identifier** pattern of promotion is applied.

$$\begin{array}{|l}
\hline
\textit{CardGlobal} \\
\hline
\textit{fixed} : ID \nrightarrow \textit{Fixed} \\
\textit{user} : ID \nrightarrow \textit{Appl} \\
\textit{absent} : \mathbb{P}\, ID \\
\hline
\text{disjoint}\langle \text{dom}\, \textit{fixed}, \text{dom}\, \textit{user}, \textit{absent} \rangle \\
\hline
\end{array}$$

- In this case, the global identifiers for each promotion are drawn from the same set, ID, and so are constrained to be disjoint.

Alternatively, combine the various local types with a free type disjoint union, and use this in the simple promotion pattern. (This results in much extracting of state from the free type machinery, however.)
□

Promotion (Elaboration): Multi-promotion

Intent: specify a system that comprises multiple instances, but has global operations that may affect more than one local instance.

Solutions: the local state and operations and global state patterns are applied. The framing schemas include multiple local instances. There are two possible patterns. The first applies when the global operations affect a fixed number of local instances. The second is more general, and applies when the number of local operations affected by the global operation is variable or unknown.

Solution 1: A fixed number of local instances, illustrated for two instances, but extensible to as many as are practical or desired.

Adapt Promotion: framing schemas thus:

- The (otherwise identical) local states are declared twice, distinguished by decorations. (Note that in $\Delta \textit{Local}_1$, the decoration applies to the whole $\Delta \textit{Local}$ phrase, and thus yields $\textit{Local}_1$ and $\textit{Local}'_1$.)

$$\begin{array}{|l}
\hline
\Phi\textit{Update2} \\
\hline
\Delta \textit{Global} \\
\Delta \textit{Local}_1 \\
\Delta \textit{Local}_2 \\
x?, y? : ID \\
\hline
\{x?, y?\} \subseteq \text{dom}\, \textit{gbl} \\
x? \neq y? \\
\theta \textit{Local}_1 = \textit{gbl}\, x? \\
\theta \textit{Local}_2 = \textit{gbl}\, y? \\
\textit{gbl}' = \textit{gbl} \oplus \{x? \mapsto \theta \textit{Local}'_1, y? \mapsto \theta \textit{Local}'_2\} \\
\hline
\end{array}$$

- the provided identifiers are different instances from the set of identifiers used in the global system
- each local state instance is bound to one of the input identifiers

— the result of the global operation overrides the global state with the mappings from each identifier to the after-state of the local operation on its local state

Then the global operation becomes

$$GlobalOp == \exists \Delta Local_1;\ \Delta Local_2 \bullet$$
$$\Phi Update2 \wedge ALocalOp_1 \wedge AnotherLocalOp_2$$

The type of $GlobalOp$ is [$\Delta Global;\ x?: ID;\ a?_1, a?_2 : IN;\ b!_1, b!_2 : OUT$]. If the inputs or output need to be the same for both operations, renaming is required.

Illustration: This pattern is illustrated in the specification of the electronic purse transfer operations, section 4.5.

Solution 2: An arbitrary number of local instances

If there is an arbitrary number of local states all affected by the same operation, they can be bundled into a sequence ls, with a corresponding sequence of inputs, $xs?$, which identifies which local instances are being promoted. The framing schema becomes

$$\begin{array}{l} \Phi UpdateAll \\ \hline \Delta Global \\ ls : \text{seq } \Delta Local \\ xs? : \text{iseq } ID \\ \hline \#xs? = \#ls \\ \text{ran } xs? \subseteq \text{dom } gbl \\ \forall i : \text{dom } ls \bullet \exists \Delta Local \mid \theta \Delta Local = ls\ i \bullet \theta Local = gbl(xs?\ i) \\ gbl' = gbl \oplus \{\ i : \text{dom } ls;\ \Delta Local \mid \theta \Delta Local = ls\ i \bullet xs?\ i \mapsto \theta Local\ '\ \} \end{array}$$

The local operation is cast into a form for use with the framing schema:

$$\begin{array}{l} LocalOpS \\ \hline ls : \text{seq } \Delta Local \\ as? : \text{seq } IN \\ bs! : \text{seq } OUT \\ \hline \#ls = \#as? = \#bs! \\ \forall i : \text{dom } ls \bullet \\ \quad \exists \Delta Local;\ a? : IN, b! : OUT \mid \\ \quad\quad \theta \Delta Local = ls\ i \wedge a? = as?\ i \wedge b! = bs!\ i \\ \quad \bullet LocalOp \end{array}$$

Then the global operation becomes

$$GlobalOp == \exists ls : \text{seq } \Delta Local \bullet \Phi UpdateAll \wedge LocalOpS$$

The type of $GlobalOp$ is [$\Delta Global;\ xs? : \text{iseq } ID;\ as? : \text{seq } IN;\ bs! : \text{seq } OUT$].

Illustration: Consider a local state, *Counter* that holds an incrementable natural number. An operation on the local state resets the number to zero. Following the local state and operations pattern, these are defined:

$$Counter == [\ c : \mathbb{N}\ ]$$
$$Reset == [\ \Delta Counter\ |\ c' = 0\ ]$$

A global system of counters can be defined using the global state pattern:

$$CounterSystem == [\ sys : NAME \nrightarrow Counter\ ]$$

To simultaneously reset all the identified counters to zero (assuming a $\Phi UpdateAll$ defined following the pattern above, but using the names of this example):

$$\begin{array}{|l}
\_ResetS _____ \\
ls : \text{seq}\,\Delta Counter \\
\hline
\forall\, i : \text{dom}\,ls \bullet \exists\,\Delta Counter\ |\ \theta\Delta Counter = ls\ i \bullet Reset
\end{array}$$

$$ResetAll == \exists\, ls : \text{seq}\,\Delta Counter \bullet \Phi UpdateAll \wedge ResetS$$

This is equivalent to

$$\begin{array}{|l}
\_ResetAll _____ \\
\Delta CounterSystem \\
xs? : \text{iseq}\,NAME \\
\hline
\text{ran}\,xs? \subseteq \text{dom}\,sys \\
\{xs?\} \triangleleft sys' = \{xs?\} \triangleleft sys \\
\forall\, x : \text{ran}\,xs? \bullet \\
\quad \exists\,\Delta Counter \bullet \\
\quad\quad \theta Counter = sys\ x \wedge Reset \wedge sys'\ x = \theta Counter\,'
\end{array}$$

□

4 Using the Promotion Patterns

The promotion pattern and its sub-patterns can be used to generate a specification with a promotion structure. For example, [Stepney et al. 2003b] show how to use the patterns to generate a promoted bank account specification from a single account specification.

Here we focus on using the promotion patterns to generate a refactoring of an existing unstructured specification. We start with an initial specification closely based on the 'Abstract World' specification from the electronic purse development [Stepney et al. 2000].

The structural promotion pattern is the target pattern for the refactoring, and the generative patterns guide the refactoring steps. Some of the refactor transformations do not seem obvious and might be missed without the generative patterns as a reference. Indeed, some of the transformations temporarily make the specification structure more baroque.

4.1 Starting Point: The Existing Specification

– purses are identified by a name

$[NAME]$

The abstract world comprises two mappings

- *balance* maps purse names to their balances
- *lost* maps purse names to the total amount they have lost because of failed transfer operations
- modelling notes: We wish to distinguish empty purses from non-existent purses, so we use a partial function rather than a bag. We use a finite function to ensure that the total balance in the system is well-defined.

$World == [\ balance, lost : NAME \nrightarrow \mathbb{N}\ |\ \mathrm{dom}\ balance = \mathrm{dom}\ lost\ ]$

- the *balance* and *lost* domains are the same, and define the purse names known to the system

There is a standard precondition for operations involving transfer between two purses. This is specified separately and included in each operation to aid readability (following the name predicates pattern [Stepney et al. 2003b]).

- transfer operations always have two input purse names and an input representing the value to be transferred between the purses

$$
\begin{array}{|l}
\hline
\ TransferPre \\
\ World \\
\ from?, to? : NAME \\
\ value? : \mathbb{N} \\
\hline
\ \{from?, to?\} \subseteq \mathrm{dom}\ balance \\
\ to? \neq from? \\
\ value? \leq balance\ from? \\
\hline
\end{array}
$$

- the two identified purses are known and distinct (it does not make sense to transfer money from one purse to itself)

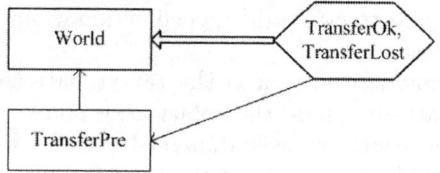

Fig. 2. Structure of the abstract world of electronic purses, before refactoring

– there is sufficient funds for the transfer

There are two transfer operations; one that succeeds, and one that fails. Both have the same declarations.

─── *TransferOkay* ─────────────────────────────
$\Delta World$
$from?, to? : NAME$
$value? : \mathbb{N}$
─────────────────────────
$TransferPre$
$balance' = balance \oplus \{from? \mapsto balance\ from? - value?,$
$\qquad\qquad\qquad to? \mapsto balance\ to? + value?\}$
$lost' = lost$
──

– a successful transfer decrements *value?* from the *from?* purse's balance, and adds it to the *to?* purse's balance, leaving all other balances unchanged
– success means the *lost* components are unchanged

─── *TransferLost* ─────────────────────────────
$\Delta World$
$from?, to? : NAME$
$value? : \mathbb{N}$
─────────────────────────
$TransferPre$
$balance' = balance \oplus \{from? \mapsto balance\ from? - value?\}$
$lost' = lost \oplus \{from? \mapsto lost\ from? + value?\}$
──

– a lost transfer decrements *value?* from the *from?* purse's balance, and loses it, modelled by adding it to the *from?* purse's *lost* component
– no other purse is affected

Figure 2 represents the structure of the specification before refactoring. It is a simple Delta/Xi pattern; there is also a schema included (as a precondition) in the operations.

The purse system is a Delta/Xi specification that matches the multi-promotion intent: it describes a system made up of instances of a local state and global operations based on operations on multiple (two) local states.

The refactoring steps are based on the four elements of the generative pattern for promotion. The first generative pattern, local state and operations, requires substantial refactoring over several steps. The second generative pattern, global state, emerges as a side effect.

4.2 Step 1: Introduce Local State

The first goal for refactoring is to define the local state. The system described above has a collection of purses, so the purse becomes the local instance.

The individual purses each have a *balance* and a *lost* component. The schema is formed by removing the identifying functions and predicates from the original state specification. The result matches the state of local state and operations:

$Purse == [\ balance, lost : \mathbb{N}\ ]$

Global elements of the original state are refactored to match global state:

$[NAME]$
$World == [\ purse : NAME \twoheadrightarrow Purse\ ]$

The preservation of meaning for *purse* can be established by a *schema expansion* refactoring [Stepney et al. 2002] to a single function from $NAME$ to the schema binding of *balance* and *lost*. This is isomorphic to the original state schema, *World*.

To complete these refactorings, and to preserve the full sense of the original specification, the original precondition and operation specifications have to be refactored to use the local and global states.

– The precondition schema declarations are not affected: purses are still identified by name, even though the name has been relocated to the global context.

$$\begin{array}{|l}
\_TransferPre _____ \\
World \\
from?, to? : NAME \\
value? : \mathbb{N} \\
\hline
\{from?, to?\} \subseteq \mathrm{dom}\ purse \\
to? \neq from? \\
value? \leq (purse\ from?).balance \\
\end{array}$$

– Each reference to the *balance* function in the original precondition is replaced by a suitable reference to the *purse* function. Otherwise, the precondition predicates are unchanged.

The operations introduce global and local state schemas. To allow global operations to use the local state, explicit after-state purses are constructed.

– A successful transfer involves explicitly two purses. The refactoring is influenced by the form of the elaboration pattern, multi-promotion, in its version for a fixed number of local instances. The declarations are made accordingly. Making a schema binding: ZRM [Stepney *et al.* 2003b] is used to construct purse instances.

$$
\begin{array}{|l}
\_\_ TransferOkay _____ \\
\Delta World \\
\Delta Purse_1 \\
\Delta Purse_2 \\
from?, to? : NAME \\
value? : \mathbb{N} \\
\hline
TransferPre \\
Purse'_1 = (\ \mu\, \Delta Purse \mid \theta Purse = purse\ from? \\
\qquad\qquad\quad \wedge\ balance' = balance - value? \\
\qquad\qquad\quad \wedge\ lost' = lost \\
\qquad\quad \bullet\ Purse'\ ) \\
Purse'_2 = (\ \mu\, \Delta Purse \mid \theta Purse = purse\ to? \\
\qquad\qquad\quad \wedge\ balance' = balance + value? \\
\qquad\qquad\quad \wedge\ lost' = lost \\
\qquad\quad \bullet\ Purse'\ ) \\
purse' = purse \oplus \{from? \mapsto \theta Purse'_1, to? \mapsto \theta Purse'_2\}
\end{array}
$$

– $Purse_1$ has *value?* subtracted from its *balance*; no other elements is changed.
– $Purse_2$ has *value?* added to its *balance*; no other elements is changed.
– The global world mappings to the instances of the two purses are overwritten with the after-states of each purse.

The lost case is refactored similarly.

– an unsuccessful transfer involves exactly one purse (we call this $Purse_1$ to use it with the general framing schema)

$$
\begin{array}{|l}
\_\_ TransferLost _____ \\
\Delta World \\
\Delta Purse_1 \\
from?, to? : NAME \\
value? : \mathbb{N} \\
\hline
TransferPre \\
Purse'_1 = (\ \mu\, \Delta Purse \mid \theta Purse = purse\ from? \\
\qquad\qquad\quad \wedge\ balance' = balance - value? \\
\qquad\qquad\quad \wedge\ lost' = lost + value? \\
\qquad\quad \bullet\ Purse'\ ) \\
purse' = purse \oplus \{from? \mapsto \theta Purse'_1\}
\end{array}
$$

- *Purse* has *value?* subtracted from its *balance*, and added to *lost*
- the global world mapping to the purse is overwritten with the purse's after-state

This intermediate refactoring preserves the meaning of the original specification, but is otherwise considerably more obscure than the original. Further refactoring is required[1].

4.3 Step 2: Introduce Local Operations

Having extracted the local and global states, attention now turns to the extraction of local operations. These are specified to include the local part of the precondition schema.

- the declaration of *World* has been replaced by the local *Purse*
- The *from?* and *to?* purse declarations are not relevant at the local level.
- The other declaration is as for the original precondition schema.

```
┌─ TransferPre ─────────────────────────────┐
│ Purse                                     │
│ value? : N                                │
├───────────────────────────────────────────┤
│ value? ≤ balance                          │
└───────────────────────────────────────────┘
```

- The predicate is the remaining local one from the original precondition schema.

The local operations separately specify transfer from a purse, transfer to a purse and the lost transfer. The schemas are taken to be self-explanatory.

```
┌─ TransferFrom ────────────────────────────┐
│ ΔPurse                                    │
│ value? : N                                │
├───────────────────────────────────────────┤
│ TransferPre                               │
│ balance' = balance − value?               │
│ lost' = lost                              │
└───────────────────────────────────────────┘
```

---

[1] This first refactoring is, in fact, closer to the form of the actual Purse specification [Stepney *et al.* 2000]. It was written in this form because the multi-promotion pattern was unknown to the authors at the time. See [Stepney *et al.* 2003b] for diagrams of the full specification.

┌─ *TransferTo* ─────────────────────────────┐
│ $\Delta Purse$
│ $value? : \mathbb{N}$
│ ─────────────────────
│ *TransferPre*
│ $balance' = balance + value?$
│ $lost' = lost$
└──┘

┌─ *TransferLost* ───────────────────────────┐
│ $\Delta Purse$
│ $value? : \mathbb{N}$
│ ─────────────────────
│ *TransferPre*
│ $balance' = balance - value?$
│ $lost' = lost + value?$
└──┘

4.4 Step 3: Introduce Framing Schemas

The next generative pattern is framing schemas. Each kind of operation requires a frame. All the local operations are simple changes to the local state. However, at the global level, a successful transfer updates the state of two purses whilst the unsuccessful transfer updates only one purse.

The validity of the purses involved in a transfer must be checked at the global level, since the name identifiers have been assigned only to the global state. This check needs to appear as part of the frame(s).

┌─ $\Phi Transfer$ ──────────────────────────┐
│ $\Delta World$
│ $\Delta Purse_1$
│ $\Delta Purse_2$
│ $from?, to? : NAME$
│ $value? : \mathbb{N}$
│ ─────────────────────
│ $\{from?, to?\} \subseteq \text{dom } balance$
│ $from? \neq to?$
│ $\theta Purse_1 = purse\ from?$
│ $\theta Purse_2 = purse\ to?$
│ $purse' = purse \oplus \{from? \mapsto \theta Purse'_1, to? \mapsto \theta Purse'_2\}$
└──┘

- the identities of the two purses are checked against the known identities, and are distinct

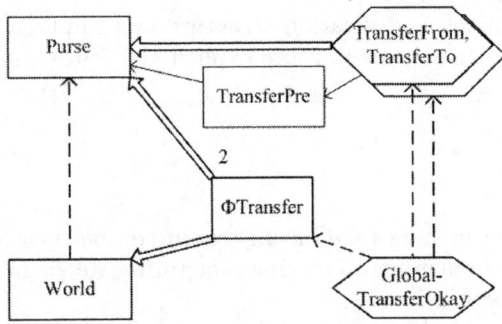

Fig. 3. Structure of the abstract world of electronic purses, after refactoring to a two-state promotion, for the *GlobalTransferOkay* operation

- the *purse* after-state is formed by overriding the mappings for the two instances with the results of the local operations

The single purse *TransferLost* could be provided with a framing schema by an application of the framing schemas pattern. However, it is equally valid, and requires fewer definitions, to think of the unsuccessful global operation as affecting two purses, one of which is unchanged.

4.5 Step 4: Define the Global Operations

The final step applies the global operations pattern.

$GlobalTransferOkay == \exists \Delta Purse_1; \Delta Purse_2 \bullet$
$\qquad \Phi Transfer \wedge TransferFrom_1$
$\qquad \wedge TransferTo_2[value?_1/value?_2]$

$GlobalTransferLost == \exists \Delta Purse_1; \Delta Purse_2 \bullet$
$\qquad \Phi Transfer \wedge TransferLost_1 \wedge \Xi Purse_2$

4.6 Resulting Specification, Summary

Gathering together all the pieces produced above, the complete specification of the abstract purse world comprises (a) local specifications, (b) framing schema(s) and (c) global transfer operations that promote the local transfer elements. This could be demonstrated to be isomorphic to the original by a *schema expansion* refactoring [Stepney et al. 2002] of both versions, and simplifying. Alternatively, conjectures on the operations could be formulated and proved. Neither is demonstrated here.

The specification using promotion is slightly longer, but more readable. Writing further operations that change purses is straightforward: the local component operations are added, and the global operation pattern applied.

Figure 3 represents the structure of the specification after refactoring. This diagram looks more complicated than the pre-refactoring diagram (figure 2); this demonstrates how much specification structure was implicit before (hidden in the state and operation schemas). More explicit structure makes a specification easier to comprehend.

5 Conclusion

The refactorings shown here take an unstructured specification into a specific pattern by a series of meaning preserving refactoring steps, guided by the target patterns and sub-patterns.

Refactoring can also be used to take a specification in one pattern in to a different pattern: Z patterns include a number of choice patterns that are equivalent (in some sense) formulations of the same concept; some are better for communication, and some are better for proof or refinement.

Meaning preservation is a crucial component in refactoring. Whilst it may be desirable to evolve the meaning of a specification by a series of small, controlled steps, this is not what is normally meant by refactoring. (In [Stepney et al. 2002] we refer to this as *benefactoring*.) In code refactoring, the meaning preservation is demonstrated if all the original functionality is preserved by the refactoring (same inputs lead to same outputs). In specification, meaning preservation may be defined in terms of isomorphic semantic models; it may be defined in terms of mutual refinement; it may be defined in terms of what (refactored) conjectures can be proved true (and, if relevant, proved false). France (private communication) uses a much looser definition of meaning preservation, relating to the intent of the specifiers, a preservation that could not be mechanically checked. The definition can be chosen to suit the application.

Some refactoring is clearly supportable by tools: some tools can already refactor, as part of a proof-assistant role. Thus, schemas can be expanded, preconditions calculated, and other equivalent structures substituted. These refactorings follow a strict mathematical meaning preservation. However, practical refactoring is more likely to need to preserve the properties of a specification, and to demonstrate preservation by reproving the conjectures. This occurred during the commercial specifications that are the motivation for this paper [Cooper & Stepney 2000], [Stepney & Cooper 2000].

More work on refactoring proofs is under way. Such refactorings, especially where guided by patterns, have the potential to guide proof, refinement, and other aspects of formal software engineering.

Acknowledgements: We thank the anonymous referee whose careful reading of an earlier version of this paper resulted in many improvements.

References

[Alexander et al. 1977] Christopher Alexander, Sara Ishikawa, Murray Silverstein, Max Jacobson, Ingrid Fiksdahl-King, and Shlomo Angel. *A Pattern Language: Towns, Buildings, Construction.* Oxford University Press, 1977.

[Barden et al. 1994] Rosalind Barden, Susan Stepney, and David Cooper. *Z in Practice*. BCS Practitioner Series. Prentice Hall, 1994.

[Bowen et al. 2000] Jonathan P. Bowen, Steve Dunne, Andy Galloway, and Steve King, editors. *ZB2000: First International Conference of B and Z Users*, volume 1878 of *LNCS*. Springer, 2000.

[Cooper & Stepney 2000] David Cooper and Susan Stepney. Segregation with communication. In [Bowen et al. 2000], pages 451–470.

[d'Inverno & Luck 2001] Mark d'Inverno and Michael Luck. *Understanding Agent Systems*. Springer, 2001.

[Fowler 1999] Martin Fowler. *Refactoring: improving the design of existing code*. Addison-Wesley, 1999.

[Gamma et al. 1995] Erich Gamma, Richard Helm, Ralph Johnson, and John Vlissides. *Design Patterns*. Addison-Wesley, 1995.

[Morgan & Sufrin 1984] Carroll Morgan and Bernard Sufrin. Specification of the UNIX filing system. *IEEE Trans. Softw. Eng*, 10(2):128–142, 1984.

[Stepney & Cooper 2000] Susan Stepney and David Cooper. Formal methods for industrial products. In [Bowen et al. 2000], pages 374–393.

[Stepney et al. 1992] Susan Stepney, Rosalind Barden, and David Cooper, editors. *Object Orientation in Z*. Springer, 1992.

[Stepney et al. 2000] Susan Stepney, David Cooper, and Jim Woodcock. An electronic purse: Specification, refinement, and proof. Technical Monograph PRG-126, Programming Research Group, Oxford University Computing Laboratory, 2000.

[Stepney et al. 2002] Susan Stepney, Fiona Polack, and Ian Toyn. Refactoring in maintenance and development of Z specifications and proofs. In *REFINE 2002, Copenhagen*, volume 70(3) of *ENTCS*. Elsevier, 2002.

[Stepney et al. 2003a] Susan Stepney, Fiona Polack, and Ian Toyn. An outline pattern language for Z. 2003. (these proceedings).

[Stepney et al. 2003b] Susan Stepney, Fiona Polack, and Ian Toyn. A Z patterns catalogue I: specification and refactoring, v0.1. Technical Report YCS-2003-349, York, 2003.

[Woodcock & Davies 1996] J. C. P. Woodcock and J. Davies. *Using Z: Specification, Refinement, and Proof*. Prentice–Hall, 1996.

Reuse of Specification Patterns
with the B Method

Sandrine Blazy, Frédéric Gervais, and Régine Laleau

Institut d'Informatique d'Entreprise, Laboratoire CEDRIC
18, Allée Jean Rostand, F-91025 ÉVRY Cedex, France
{blazy, gervais, laleau}@iie.cnam.fr

Abstract. This paper describes an approach for reusing specification patterns. Specification patterns are design patterns that are expressed in a formal specification language. Reusing a specification pattern means instantiating it or composing it with other specification patterns. Three levels of composition are defined: juxtaposition, composition with inter-patterns links and unification. This paper shows through examples how to define specification patterns in B, how to reuse them directly in B, and also how to reuse the proofs associated with specification patterns.

Keywords: Design pattern, specification pattern, reuse, B.

1 Introduction

Component-based development is a technology that has been widely used for many years during the implementation phase of the software life cycle. This technology has also been adapted to the design phase. Design patterns expressed in UML are frequently reused in order to simplify the design of new applications. The most famous design patterns are called the Gang of Four (or GoF) patterns [7]. During the development of a new application, most designers refer to the GoF patterns, even if there is no precise definition of these patterns. This lack of a formal definition allows designers to adapt freely the GoF patterns to their needs and has contributed to the success of the GoF patterns.

As formal specifications are now well-known in industry, the reuse of formal specifications based on design patterns becomes a challenging issue. Reusing a formal specification means firstly to formally define components of formal specifications (or specification patterns). Secondly, it means to define how to combine components together in order to build a new application. Other problems such as the definition of a library for storing the components must also be solved. A few works address the problem of defining specification patterns. Each of these works define also a specific way to combine specification patterns together but there is no consensus on the definition of a specification pattern or on the combination of patterns.

We use the B language to formally specify the notion of specification pattern, and several ways to combine specification patterns together. Our approach aims at helping the designer to firstly formally specify a new application that reuses design patterns and secondly to assist him with a tool. We have chosen the B language for the following reasons:

- Where B is already being used, then there is no need to learn a new formalism to define and reuse specification patterns.
- B is supported by tools that validate the specification. We will use them to validate the definition of specification patterns and the different reuse mechanisms. A designer will thus reuse not only pieces of formal specifications but also proofs concerning these pieces of formal specifications.

This paper describes our approach through examples and is organised as follows. The next section is an introduction to patterns. Section 3 deals with a state of the art about the reuse of specification patterns with formal methods. Section 4 is a discussion of the notion of reuse in B: our approach is presented and illustrated by an example. Finally, we conclude this work in Sect. 5 with the perspectives and the limits of this approach.

2 About Patterns

The aim of this section is to present in an informal way how to specify an application with UML patterns. This section identifies also several ways to reuse the patterns.

2.1 Examples of Patterns

Two examples of design patterns are presented in this section. They will be used in the remainder of the paper.

Figure 1 presents with the UML notation the class diagram of the **Composite** design pattern [7]. This pattern is a solution to describe the tree structure of a composite, which is an object composed of several other objects. Two classes are defined to represent composite objects (`Composite` class) and basic objects (`Leaf` class). An abstract class called `Component` represents both composite and basic objects. An association is defined between `Composite` and `Component` classes with the `father` and `children` roles. A `Composite` can have several `Component` children which can be `Leaf` or `Composite` objects.

Operations (methods) are defined in the different classes. The set of components of a composite object is given by the `GetChild` method. `Operation` is a generic operation and deals with both leaf and composite objects. This operation is redefined in the `Composite` and `Leaf` classes by `Operation_Composite` and `Operation_Leaf`.

Figure 2 presents the class diagram of the **Resource Allocation** pattern described in [5]. Four classes are defined. The `Resource` class represents a resource to allocate. A resource provides facilities, represented in this pattern by the `ResourceFacility` class. A resource is allocated to job occurrences represented by the `JobOccurrence` class. Finally, `JobCategory`, which stands for the

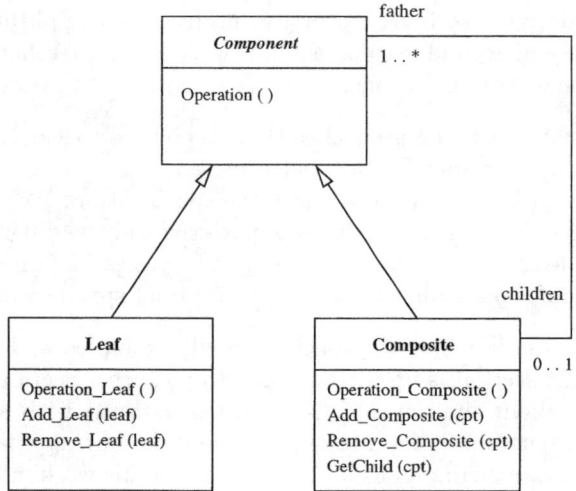

Fig. 1. Class diagram of the **Composite** design pattern

job categories, is linked to the last two classes. The requirements of the resource facilities are supported only by specific job categories. A job is represented by an association between JobOccurrence and JobCategory.

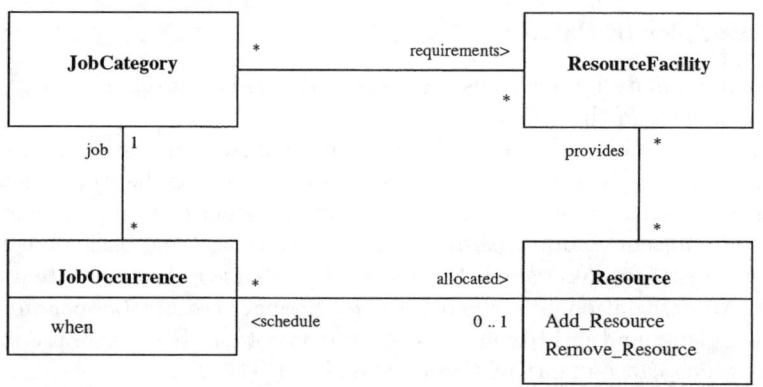

Fig. 2. Class diagram of the **Resource Allocation** pattern

2.2 Design by Reuse

To motivate the need for reuse of specification patterns, we use the simple example of designing in UML the allocation of directories to secretaries. A directory is composed of files and other directories. Figure 3 gives a solution obtained by "instantiating" both patterns **Composite** and **Resource Allocation**. In the first pattern, a directory is considered as a Composite object and a file as a Leaf object. The Component class is renamed as Element (note that we could have kept the name Component). In the pattern **Resource Allocation**, an element is considered as a Resource object and a secretary as a JobCategory object.

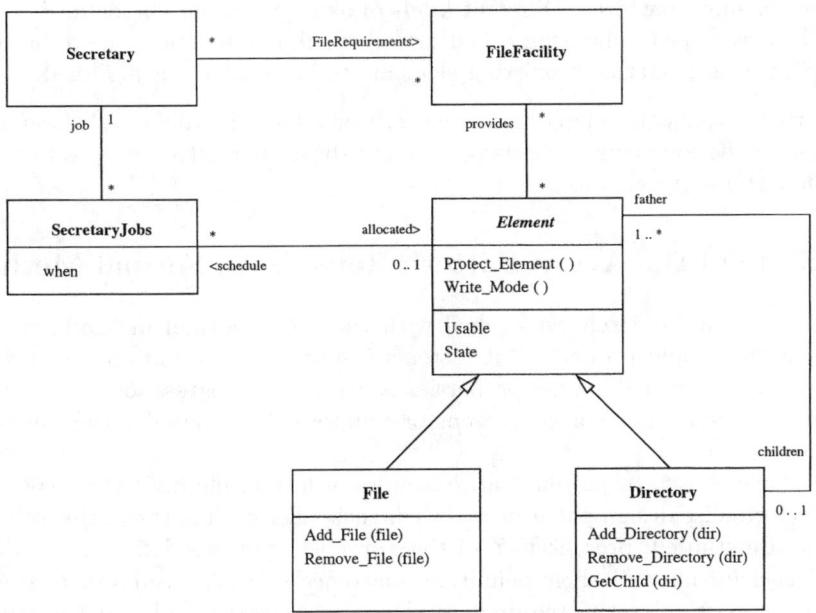

Fig. 3. An example of design by pattern reuse

Compared to both original patterns, some operations are renamed. For instance, Add_Composite becomes Add_Directory in Fig. 3. Other operations such as Protect_Element and Write_Mode are created once the patterns have been instantiated. New variables called State and Usable are introduced to describe the protection mode of a file or a directory which is declared as usable.

2.3 Main Operations on Patterns

Two kinds of operations can be distinguished: pattern definition and mechanisms for reusing patterns.

Pattern Definition. Two ways exist to define a new pattern. The pattern can either be defined "ex nihilo" or it can be deduced from existing patterns: this kind of reuse is aiming to create new patterns. In this case, mechanisms are defined at the pattern level in order to link and compare several patterns.

Reuse Mechanisms. Three basic mechanisms exist for reusing patterns in order to design an application: instantiation, composition and extension [16]. They allow patterns to be adapted to the design in progress.

- The *instantiation*, also called imitation, is a mechanism which allows different elements of a pattern to be renamed.
- The *composition* mechanism, also called integration mechanism, associates two or more patterns. Different kinds of association may be defined.
- The last reuse mechanism, called *extension*, allows new elements to be added to existing patterns or existing elements to be removed or modified.

Formal specification languages are very well adapted to define all these mechanisms. In the following sections, we present different existing propositions, before describing our solution.

3 State of the Art of Pattern Reuse with Formal Methods

Up to now, our research works deal with the use of formal methods in order to verify functional properties of systems (especially information systems [9]). Taking into account dynamic properties is a work in progress [6]. Therefore, in this paper, we do not consider event or temporal logic based formal methods such as [10,14].

We have chosen to present four examples of formal methods that have been used to formalise design patterns and their reuse. For each of them, the following criteria are studied: presentation of the approach, pattern definition, available reuse mechanisms and their definition, existence of tools, usability of the approach, in particular the required mathematical background and the level of abstraction patterns that are defined and reused. More details can be found in [8].

3.1 UML-B Patterns Reuse

In [12,13], design patterns are specified in both UML and B.

Pattern Definition. Patterns are defined in two ways. In [12], patterns are defined "ex nihilo". The UML diagram of a GoF pattern is translated from UML to B using a set of rules. Thus the B specification can be proved, using a B tool. In [13], a pattern can be defined as a refinement (also called specialisation) of a more generic pattern, thanks to the refinement mechanism of the B method.

Reuse Mechanisms. The instantiation of a pattern is defined on the UML description of a pattern. The resulting diagram is again translated to B with the set of rules. This process has not been formalised, so the resulting B specification must be proved again.

Tools. A tool based on the B and UML environments has been developed. No specific tools are defined to implement the reuse.

Usability. This approach requires knowledge of UML and B. Pattern reuse is defined on the UML representation. Consequently, reuse mechanisms cannot be formally defined. Proofs associated with a pattern cannot be directly reused to achieve the proofs of its instantiation. However the definition of patterns by refinement of other patterns is quite interesting and original.

3.2 Frameworks in Catalysis

Catalysis [11] is a component-based specification method. Framework is the name used for pattern in Catalysis. The idea is to formally specify the frameworks by adapting the existing Catalysis features.

Pattern Definition. A specification framework is defined with algebraic specifications using many-sorted first order logic. Axioms concerning the framework are specified in Catalysis with first order logic predicates. Rather than considering the initial model traditionally used in algebraic specifications as the referring model for the framework semantics, the theory is here represented by an isoinitial model which is very interesting, especially for proving formulas using negation, because it preserves the negation property contrary to the initial model[1]. Nevertheless, the existence of the isoinitial model cannot be always guaranteed and axioms must be added to ensure its existence.

Reuse Mechanisms. The instantiation is implemented by parameterisation. A parameter is a sort or a relation between sorts. Additional axioms involving parameters are defined. The axioms must be satisfied by the instantiation of parameters.

The frameworks composition is likewise. A parameterised framework F_1 may be composed with a parameterised framework F_2 if the involved axioms are satisfied. Firstly, a renaming map is defined from F_1 to F_2. The aim is to link each element of the F_2 signature to one element of the F_1 signature. Then the framework resulting from the composition of F_1 and F_2 is characterised as follows : its signature is the renamed signature of F_1 and its axioms are the union of the axioms of F_1 and F_2. Note that this composition is associative but not commutative.

Tools. No other tools than those existing in the Catalysis approach are used.

Usability. This approach formally defines the notions of framework specification, instantiation and composition. The choice of adapting an existing approach (Catalysis) is interesting because it avoids the introduction of new languages or tools. The isoinitial theory chosen for the framework semantics simplifies the soundness proof. However, additional axioms must be defined in order to ensure that an isoinitial model exists. Furthermore, it requires knowledge about algebraic specification and about isoinitial theories.

---

[1] In an initial theory, the falsity of a ground atom A corresponds to the non-provability of A, while in an isoinitial theory, it corresponds to the provability of $\neg A$.

3.3 Pattern Specification with RSL

The idea of this approach is to formalise with RSL (RAISE Specification Language) [4] design patterns described by UML diagrams. RSL is based on VDM and an algebraic specification language.

Pattern Definition. A formal model of pattern is defined. It represents a pattern as a head, a structure and a list of collaborations. The head section describes the name, purpose and scope of the pattern. The pattern structure specifies the classes and associations in RSL. In the last section, the list of collaborations specifies constraints on the order of operation calls.

Reuse Mechanisms. The instantiation mechanism is implemented by a renaming map. However, a pattern can be instantiated only once. The resulting RSL specification can then be extended by new elements. The composition mechanism is only illustrated through examples.

Tools. To our knowledge, no tool has been implemented.

Usability. Patterns for oriented-object programming have been studied extensively in this approach. That is why a lot of oriented-object programming features have been specified, thus giving specifications described at a low level of abstraction.

3.4 LePUS, a Language for Patterns Specification

The idea in this approach is the definition of a new formal language, LePUS (LanguagE for Patterns Uniform Specification) [3], dedicated to the specification of patterns. This language is based on higher order monadic logic (HOML).

Pattern Definition. The aim is to formalise the GoF patterns. The main properties of these patterns are expressed by higher order predicates built on higher order sets of classes and methods. A pattern is then represented by a conjunction of predicates. New patterns can be defined from existing ones by projection of the higher order sets. Roughly speaking, a projection consists in reducing the order of a set. Thus, these patterns are more concrete than the original ones.

Reuse Mechanisms. The instantiation of a pattern consists in instantiating the sets involved in the pattern predicate.

Tools. To our knowledge, no tool has been implemented.

Usability. This approach needs a strong background in mathematics. Moreover, this very formal method is difficult to apply, because the user must exhibit classes, methods and higher order sets in order to define an instance of a pattern. Defining a higher order set means defining all the sets with a lower order level and so on up to classes and methods.

3.5 State of the Art: Conclusion

Table 1 is a comparison between the four above-mentioned approaches and our approach, presented in the next section.

Table 1. Formal approaches for pattern reuse

Approach	UML-B	Framework	RSL	LePUS	Ours
Section	3.1	3.2	3.3	3.4	4
Specification models:	UML and B machines	algebraic specification	VDM	HOML	B
Direct Definition of Pattern:	UML to B translation	isoinitial theory	RSL formal model	conjunction of predicates	B machine
Pattern Definition by Reuse:	refinement	no	no	projection	no
Instantiation:	UML	parameters	map	parameters	inclusion and renaming
Composition:	UML	not commutative	no	no	inclusion and new invariant
Extension:	UML	no	yes	no	inclusion and refinement
Tools:	UML and B tools	Catalysis	no	no	B tools
Usability	+	+	−	−−	+

The LePUS approach is the most advanced specification method for defining and instantiating design patterns, but it is also the most difficult to apply. The instantiation notion is defined in all the approaches: by the UML instantiation mechanism for UML-B, by parameterised frameworks for Catalysis, by a renaming map for RSL and by an instantiation of parameters for LePUS. The composition mechanism seems to be more difficult to define, since only a non commutative operation is defined for frameworks. The extension is only treated by RSL and UML-B. Even if the UML-B approach seems to be close to our work, it differs significantly since the reuse mechanisms are not formally defined.

4 An Approach for Reusing Patterns in B

The aim of this section is to investigate the ability of B to specify patterns and the different reuse mechanisms. We have chosen to consider the B language as it is. This means that we want to define the reuse mechanisms only with the different B mechanisms such as refinement, inclusion, and so on. Thus, the proofs generated during the reuse process are only those generated by the corresponding B mechanisms.

For each mechanism, we present an implementation in B and its limits. We refer to the example presented in Sect. 2.2. The B specification is introduced step by step, the complete specification is given in [1].

The last subsection presents a summary of the proof activity generated by the approach.

4.1 Definition of Patterns

The way a pattern is defined is strongly dependent on how the reuse mechanisms are defined. Ideally, a pattern should be specified by several machines (for instance, one machine for each class of the UML diagram), all included in a machine which stands for an interface of the pattern (see UML-B approach in Sect. 3.1 and [15]).

For technical reasons, some B mechanisms such as refinement require the use of a single abstract machine. Consequently, a pattern is specified by a single abstract machine. This is a first limit of our approach, and perhaps the more annoying one.

In order to implement the composition mechanism (see Sect. 4.3), the given sets of the pattern must be specified as parameters of the machine. For instance, the **Composite** pattern is specified with the following Composite_Pattern machine:

MACHINE Composite_Pattern(COMPONENT)
VARIABLES Component, Composite, Leaf, Father
INVARIANT
  Component $\subseteq$ COMPONENT $\wedge$
  Composite $\subseteq$ Component $\wedge$
  Leaf $\subseteq$ Component $\wedge$
  Father $\in$ Component $\twoheadrightarrow$ Composite $\wedge$
  Leaf $\cup$ Composite = Component $\wedge$
  Leaf $\cap$ Composite = $\emptyset$
  ...

OPERATIONS
  children $\longleftarrow$ GetChild(father) = ...
  cpt $\longleftarrow$ New_Composite(comp) = ...
  Add_Composite(cpt,comp) = ...
  leaf $\longleftarrow$ New_Leaf = ...
  Add_Leaf(leaf) = ...

Remove_Composite(cpt) = ...
Remove_Leaf(leaf) =
pre
   leaf ∈ Leaf ∧
   leaf ∈ dom(Father)
then
   ...
end
Operation(cpt) = ...

The variables **Component**, **Composite** and **Leaf** represent three classes, while the variable **Father** stands for the association link between the UML classes **Component** and **Composite** (see Sect. 2.1). The types of the classes and associations are formally specified in the B invariants. In the same way, the **Resource Allocation** pattern is specified in B.

MACHINE Resource_Allocation(JOBS, CATEGORY,
   FACILITY, RESOURCE)
SETS DATE
VARIABLES
   JobOccurrence, When, JobCategory, Resource, ResourceFacility,
   Job, Requirements, Provides, Allocated
INVARIANT
   JobOccurrence ⊆ JOBS ∧
   When ∈ JobOccurence → DATE ∧
   ...
OPERATIONS
Add_Resource(res) = ...
Remove_Resource(res) =
pre
   res ∈ RESOURCE
then
   Resource := Resource − {res} ∥
   Provides := {res} ⩤ Provides ∥
   Allocated := Allocated ⩥ {res}
end
   ...

4.2 Instantiation Mechanism

The instantiation mechanism is implemented in B by the inclusion of machines. The machine corresponding to the pattern is included in the machine corresponding to the instantiation of the pattern.

In the example, the machine `Directory_Renaming` includes the machine of the **Composite** pattern. The given sets, defined as parameters of the machine, can be renamed by instantiation of the parameters. In our example, COMPONENT is renamed by ELEMENT:

MACHINE Directory_Renaming
SETS ELEMENT
INCLUDES Composite_Pattern(ELEMENT)
...

The **DEFINITIONS** clause allows us to rename variables from the included machine. Composite and Leaf are respectively renamed by Directory and File.

DEFINITIONS
　　Directory == Composite
　　File == Leaf

Renaming operations is not so straightforward. There are two cases. Firstly, if an operation is directly reused without renaming we use the **PROMOTES** clause. Secondly, a renamed operation is specified in the **OPERATIONS** clause. It consists of a call statement to the corresponding pattern operation. In our example, the Remove_Leaf operation is renamed by Remove_File:

OPERATIONS
　Remove_File(file) =
　pre
　　file ∈ File ∧
　　file ∈ dom(Father)
　then
　　Remove_Leaf(file) /* operation defined in Composition_Pattern */
　end

The preconditions must be the same as those of the called operation, except that the variables and sets are the renamed ones.

4.3 Composition Mechanism

A first step is to precisely define the composition mechanism. We distinguish three levels of composition according to whether or not there exist links between the composed patterns. In the three cases, composition is achieved by the inclusion mechanism of B: all the machines representing the composed patterns are included in the machine representing the composition, called the composition machine.

Juxtaposition. Patterns are composed without defining any link between them. This composition is only a juxtaposition of each pattern. We use the **EXTENDS** mechanism which allows all the operations of the two composed patterns to be considered as genuine operations of the composition machine:

MACHINE Composition_By_Juxtaposition
SETS COMPONENT; JOBS; CATEGORY; FACILITY; RESOURCE
EXTENDS
　　Composite_Pattern(COMPONENT),
　　Resource_Allocation(JOBS, CATEGORY, FACILITY, RESOURCE)
...

Composition with Inter-patterns Links. New relations between variables of the composed patterns can be added. For instance, a bijection called `CompRes` may be defined between `Component` (from `Composite_Pattern`) and `Resource` (from `Resource_Allocation`).

MACHINE Composition_By_InterPatterns_Links
SETS COMPONENT; JOBS; CATEGORY; FACILITY; RESOURCE
INCLUDES
    Composite_Pattern(COMPONENT),
    Resource_Allocation(JOBS, CATEGORY, FACILITY, RESOURCE)
VARIABLES CompRes
INVARIANT CompRes $\in$ Component $\rightarrowtail\!\!\!\rightarrow$ Resource

According to the type of the new variables, the operations of the composed patterns involving the linked variables must be modified. For instance, the operation `Remove_Leaf` from `Composite_Pattern` removes a `leaf` from `Component`. This operation cannot be only renamed in the machine `Composition_By_Inter-Patterns_Links`. It must be composed with the operation `Remove_Resource` from `Resource_Allocation` and with a substitution on the variable `CompRes` in order to preserve the new invariant. The resulting operation is `Remove_Thing_1`:

Remove_Thing_1(thing) =
pre
    thing $\in$ Leaf $\wedge$
    thing $\in$ dom(Father)
then
    Remove_Leaf(thing) $\|$
    Remove_Resource(CompRes(thing)) $\|$
    CompRes := {thing} $\vartriangleleft\!\!\!-$ CompRes
end

A composition mechanism between operations must be defined. It could be automated provided that each composed pattern specifies the elementary operations to be composed on each variable.

Other operations of the composed patterns can be promoted to become genuine operations of the composition machine.

Unification. This composition allows some variables of the composed patterns to be merged. Up to now, only variables corresponding to classes or associations in the patterns may be unified. This property is specified in the **INVARIANT** clause of the composition machine. Two variables may be unified only if they have the same type, that is why we need to define the given sets as parameters of a pattern machine (see Sect. 4.1). For example, we can compose the two patterns `Composite_Pattern` and `Resource_Allocation` by unifying the variables `Component` and `Resource`. This yields the following machine:

MACHINE Composition_By_Unification
SETS ELEMENT; JOBS; CATEGORY; FACILITY

INCLUDES
    Composite_Pattern(ELEMENT),
    Resource_Allocation(JOBS, CATEGORY, FACILITY, ELEMENT)
INVARIANT Component = Resource

Let us note that the parameters COMPONENT and RESOURCE are now replaced by the same set called ELEMENT.

As in the composition by inter-patterns links, operations of the composed patterns involving the unified variables must be redefined. The operation Remove_Leaf involves the variable Component which is now unified with Resource. Then the operation resulting from the composition is:

Remove_Thing_2(thing) =
pre
    thing ∈ Leaf ∧
    thing ∈ dom(Father)
then
    Remove_Leaf(thing) ∥
    Remove_Resource(thing)
end

From a methodological point of view, an instantiation and a composition can be achieved in one step, before applying the extension mechanism. For the next subsection, we assume that firstly we have composed the two patterns Composite_Pattern and Resource_Allocation by unifying the variables Component and Resource and secondly instantiated them by renaming elements with the names used in the class diagram of Fig. 3. The resulting B machine is called Comp_By_Unif_Inst:

MACHINE Comp_By_Unif_Inst
SETS ELEMENT; JOBS; CATEGORY; FACILITY
INCLUDES
    Composite_Pattern(ELEMENT),
    Resource_Allocation(JOBS, CATEGORY, FACILITY, ELEMENT)
DEFINITIONS
    Directory == Composite;
    File == Leaf;
    SecretaryJobs == JobOccurrence;
    Secretary == JobCategory;
    FileFacility == ResourceFacility;
    FileRequirements == Requirements;
    Element == Resource
INVARIANT Component = Resource
    ...
PROMOTES GetChild
OPERATIONS
    dir ⟵ Add_Directory(files) = ...

file ⟵ Add_File = ...
Remove_Directory(dir) = ...
Remove_File(file) = ...
...

In this machine, the above-mentioned operation Remove_Thing_2 is renamed by Remove_File.

4.4 Extension

Most often an extension consists in defining new variables, modifying existing operations to take into account these new variables and adding new operations, in the result of a composition and/or an instantiation, specified in a B machine called the before-extension machine. Two solutions exist to implement this mechanism in B, with arguments on both sides. The first solution consists in including the before-extension machine into a new machine. The main drawback is that we cannot modify an included operation. Then, if we want to modify an operation of the before-extension machine, we need to rename it. We prefer using the refinement mechanism with the idea of adding more details to a specification. We will see later the limits of the refinement mechanism.

Let us take our example: the machine Comp_By_Unif_Inst which is the before-extension machine is refined by the machine Extension.

REFINEMENT Extension
REFINES Comp_By_Unif_Inst
SETS ELEMENT; JOBS; SECRETARY; FILEFACILITY;
    STATE = {write,protected}
INCLUDES
    Composite_Pattern(ELEMENT),
    Resource_Allocation(JOBS, SECRETARY, FILEFACILITY,
        ELEMENT)
VARIABLES State, Usable
INVARIANT
    Usable ⊆ Element ∧
    State ∈ Usable ⇸ STATE
INITIALISATION Usable, State := ∅,∅
    ...

Existing operations may be extended in only one way: new substitutions using the new variables can be specified. For instance, Remove_File is refined by:

Remove_File(file) =
pre
    file ∈ File ∧
    file ∈ dom(Father)

then
   Remove_Leaf(file) ∥ Remove_Resource(file) ∥
   Usable := Usable − {file} ∥ State := {file} ⊲ State
end

New operations cannot be added during the refinement process. Thus, in order to define a new operation, two solutions are possible. Either the before-extension machine is extended with the **EXTENDS** clause, to add new operations, specified as "skip". Or the before-extension machine is modified by adding these new operations also specified as "skip". For the sake of concision, we present the second option. Then, in both cases, each new operation is refined with new substitutions involving only new variables that are not related to variables in the gluing invariant and with calls to operations of the included machines. The refinement is then correct.

In our example, the new operation Protect_Element sets the state of an element to protected. This operation is defined in the Comp_By_Unif_Inst machine by:

Protect_Element(el) =
pre
   el ∈ Element
then
   skip
end

The operation is then refined in the machine Extension by:

Protect_Element(el) =
pre
   el ∈ Element
then
   State(el) := protected ∥ Usable := Usable ∪ {el}
end

4.5 Summary and Analysis of the Proof Activity

The machines corresponding to the different patterns (Composite_Pattern and Resource_Allocation) have been proved with the Atelier B [2] (see Tab. 2). We will now present a summary of the proofs generated by the reuse mechanisms.

The instantiation mechanism does not generate new proof obligations since nothing new has been specified. By construction, operations are automatically proved. Thus the proofs of the machine corresponding to an instantiation are obvious: they have already been proved in the included machine.

The composition by juxtaposition of different machines gives a machine which is automatically proved, since nothing new has been specified. The compositions with inter-patterns links and by unification generate proof obligations which are to be automatically discharged if the composition of operations has been correctly elaborated.

For the extension mechanism, the new proof obligations concern, on one hand, the invariants and operations which have been added and, on the other hand, the refinement of the modified operations.

Table 2 summarises the proofs of the example described in Sect. 4.4. **nObv** is the number of obvious proofs generated and trivially discharged by the Atelier B. **nPO** represents the number of proof obligations (PO) to discharge. **nAut** represents the number of POs automatically discharged and **nInt** the number of POs interactively discharged. All the interactive proofs have been discharged.

Table 2. Proofs result

Machines	nObv	nPO	nAut	nInt
Composite_Pattern	32	59	47	12
Resource_Allocation	42	16	15	1
Comp_By_Unif_Inst	43	10	10	0
Extension_Machine	284	33	23	10

For Extension_Machine, only ten proofs have been interactively proved. Six proof obligations are linked to the preservation of the following invariant:

State $\in$ Usable $\nrightarrow$ STATE

These proof obligations depend on the new specifications introduced in the refinement: they are linked to the extension mechanism.

Four proof obligations concern the refinement of operations. These four proof obligations have been proved in the same way: their goal is false because one of their hypotheses is false. Whatever the extension is, this kind of proof obligations is always generated: the proof obligations do not depend on the new specifications, but on the refinement mechanism. Once they have been proved, we can use the same strategy in order to prove them again in another extension.

In comparison with our approach, we have specified the same example (see Fig. 3) directly in B without using patterns. The resulting machine, called Direct_Example, has been proved with the Atelier B (see Tab. 3 for the proofs result). The complete specification can be found in [1].

Table 3. Proofs result of Direct_Example

Machines	nObv	nPO	nAut	nInt
Direct_Example	167	87	67	20

For the same example, the Direct_Example machine obviously requires less proof activity than with our pattern reuse method, since only one abstract specification is used compared to the two specification patterns, the before-extension machine and the refinement used in our approach. However, if we assume that the two specification patterns are previously specified and proved, our approach requires only forty-three POs (10+33) which have to be compared to the eighty-seven for the direct specification. Moreover, once POs have been automatically discharged, only ten POs (0 + 10) must be interactively proved in our approach by pattern reuse, compared to the twenty POs that must be interactively discharged for the Direct_Example machine.

In conclusion, since four POs are "reusable" in our approach, the reuse of specification patterns to specify the example described in Sect. 2.2 allows us to save fourteen POs to interactively discharge, provided that the two specification patterns Composite_Pattern and Resource_Allocation are previously specified and proved. Let us note that the Direct_Example machine is inspired by the result of the specification by pattern reuse described in Fig. 3. One would have undoubtedly specified the same example differently and consequently the generated proofs could be different.

5 Conclusion, Limits and Perspectives

In this paper, we have presented an approach for reusing patterns with the B method. We have implemented the different mechanisms linked to the reuse of patterns by using only the B mechanisms. It is interesting because the mechanisms are formally defined and we can benefit from the advantages of the B method, especially the "reuse" of proofs and the tool. There are two major drawbacks. The first one is that a pattern is defined in one machine, which can produce a big machine, difficult to read and maintain. The second one is the obligation of defining the new operations of an extension before actually applying the extension mechanism.

Concerning the pattern reuse mechanisms, the composition of several instances of the same pattern has not been studied. We also have to precisely define the mechanism of operations composition. The following necessary step will be the development of a tool to assist the designer during the specification of an application by pattern reuse. The example presented in this paper is rather simple. However, the used patterns are those described in [7], which are patterns largely tested in real designs. A more complex example just involves more patterns but the method presented in the paper is still applicable, provided that a tool is available.

In this paper, we have introduced the notion of reuse of proofs. The aim is to define the notion of proof linked to a machine and to specify the reuse of proofs with the B method. This perspective is new, since the reuse of proofs is not possible with a formal method like B. However, such a possibility requires several works on new examples in order to analyse the consequences on the proof obligations.

References

1. Blazy, S., Gervais, F., Laleau, R.: Un exemple de réutilisation de patterns de spécification avec la méthode B. Techn. rep. **395**, CEDRIC Laboratory, Évry, France, 2002. Available at http://cedric.cnam.fr/PUBLIS/RC395.ps.gz
2. Clearsy: http://www.atelierb-societe.com
3. Eden, A., Hirshfeld, Y., Yehudai, A.: LePUS - a declarative pattern specification language. Techn. rep. **326/98**, Department of Computer Science, Tel Aviv University, 1998.
4. Flores, A., Reynoso, L., Moore, R.: A formal model of object-oriented design and GoF design patterns. Techn. rep. **200**, UNU/IIST, Macau, 2000. Available at http://www.iist.unu.edu/
5. Fowler, M.: Analysis patterns: reusable object models. Addison-Wesley, 1997.
6. Frappier, M., Laleau, R.: Proving Event Ordering Properties for Information Systems. Proc. ZB2003, LNCS, Springer-Verlag, Turku, Finland, June 4-6, 2003.
7. Gamma, E., Helm, R., Johnson, R., Vlissides, J.: Design patterns: elements of reusable object-oriented software. Addison-Wesley, 1995.
8. Gervais, F.: Réutilisation de composants de spécification en B. Master's thesis, DEA IIE(CNAM)-University of Évry-INT, Évry, France, July 2002. Available at http://cedric.cnam.fr/PUBLIS/RC394.ps.gz
9. Laleau, R., Mammar, A.: An overview of a method and its support tool for generating B specifications from UML notations. Proc. ASE: 15th IEEE Conference on Automated Software Engineering, IEEE Computer Society Press, Grenoble, France, September 2000.
10. Lano, K., Bicarregui, J., Goldsack, S.: Formalising Design Patterns. Proc. BCS-FACS Northern Formal Methods Workshop, Springer-Verlag, 1997, Ilkley, United Kingdom, September 3-4, 1996.
11. Lau, K., Ornaghi, M.: OOD frameworks in component-based software development in computational logic. Proc. LOPSTR'98, LNCS **1559**, pages 101–123, Springer-Verlag, 1999, Manchester, United Kingdom, June 15-19, 1998.
12. Marcano, R., Meyer, E., Levy, N., Souquieres, J.: Utilisation de patterns dans la construction de spécifications en UML et B. Proc. AFADL'2000: Approches formelles dans l'assistance au développement de logiciels, Tech. rep. **A00-R-009**, LSR Laboratory, Grenoble, France, January 26-28, 2000.
13. Marcano-Kamenoff, R., Levy, N., Losavio, F.: Spécification et spécialisation de patterns en UML et B. Proc. LMO'2000: Langages et modèles à objets, Hermès Science Publications, Mont Saint-Hilaire, Québec, Canada, January 25-27, 2000.
14. Mikkonen, T.: Formalizing design patterns. Proc. of the 20th International Conference on Software Engineering, IEEE Computer Society, pages 115–124, Kyoto, Japan, April 19-25, 1998.
15. Nguyen, H.P.: Dérivation de spécifications formelles B à partir de spécifications semi-formelles. Ph.D. Thesis, CEDRIC Laboratory, CNAM, Évry, France, 1998. Available at http://www.iie.cnam.fr/~laleau/
16. Prieto-Diaz, R., Freeman, P.: Classifying software for reusability. IEEE Software, 4(1), pages 6–16, January 1987.

Composing Specifications Using Communication

Helen Treharne, Steve Schneider, and Marchia Bramble

Department of Computer Science, Royal Holloway,
University of London, Egham, Surrey, TW20 0EX, UK
{helen, steve, marchia}@cs.rhul.ac.uk

Abstract. This paper develops a case study using the process algebra CSP to enable controlled interaction between B machines. This illustrates how B machines are essential components within a combined communicating system. The development steps used to build the case study are new: they are applications of theoretical results which allow us to focus on the external interface of a combined communicating system, compositionally verify it, and show that it is a refinement of a more abstract specification described in CSP. This allows safety and liveness properties to be established for combinations of communicating B machines.

Keywords: B-Method, CSP, Composing Specifications, Combining Formalisms, Concurrency.

1 Introduction

This paper focuses on a case study which illustrates how the B-Method [1] and the process algebra of Communicating Sequential Processes (CSP) [3] can be used together to specify a combined communicating system. The overall specification of a combined communicating system is comprised of two separate specifications; a number of CSP process descriptions and a collection of B machines. Our aim when using B and CSP is to factor out as much of the "data-rich" aspects of a system as possible into B machines.

Previously, we focused on proving that a collection of *controllers* (*Ps*) are consistent with their underlying *machines* (*Ms*) [10,12,13,14]. A single controller P_i is a CSP process which can encapsulate a single flow of control for a B machine M_i and some of its events correspond directly to B operations. Each P_i is from the collection *Ps* and each M_i is from the collection *Ms*. We view a particular CSP/B component pair as $P_i \parallel M_i$. Then *Ps* $\parallel$ *Ms* is the parallel combination of all the controllers and all the underlying machines. Such a parallel composition is meaningful because a B machine is itself interpretable as a communicating process whose event-traces are the possible execution sequences of its operations. The invoking of an operation outside its precondition within such a trace is defined as divergence [4,14]. Therefore, our notion of consistency is that a combined communicating system *Ps* $\parallel$ *Ms* is *divergence-free* and also *deadlock-free*.

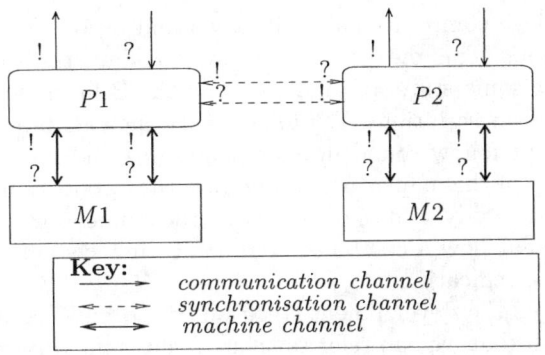

Fig. 1. An architecture for concurrent B machines

Recent results [11] also enable us to verify that a specification of a combined communicating system is a refinement of a more abstract specification described using CSP processes. This allows safety and liveness properties to be established for the combined system. All our theoretical results allow us to perform the desired verifications in a compositional way, by focusing on either on the collection of controllers, Ps, or on each component pair, $P_i \parallel M_i$. We never need to attempt to verify a combined communicating system $Ps \parallel Ms$ as one large verification step. This compositional verification is made possible due to an architecture we use to co-ordinate interaction between controllers and their underlying B machines. This architecture, shown in Figure 1, was first identified in [10] and is again adopted in this paper so that any communication is between a component pair $(P_i \parallel M_i)$, between two or more controllers, or between a controller and its external environment.

The architecture adopted in this paper was not used in our early work [12, 14] because external events interacting with the system were only used to set up appropriate values for B variables modelling the environment of an embedded system, and thus we permitted their flow of control to permeate into the underlying B machines. In our current work we view a B machine as a component which interacts only with its immediate environment which is a CSP controller. In this paper we view the combined communicating system entirely from the perspective of the controlling CSP processes with the overall interface of the system defined as interactions with the external environment in the CSP process descriptions. However, we emphasise the important role B machines play when complex state information needs to be specified and their impact on the CSP process descriptions. Note that in general our (CSP $\parallel$ B) approach does not preclude B operations of a machine from contributing to the overall interface but we do not discuss this in this paper.

In practice, when verifying the consistency of a particular combined communicating system and showing that safety and liveness properties are being preserved, we find that it is not always possible to segregate all the state aspects of the system solely within B machines. This is due to the fact that some state is critical to achieve compositional verification and needs to be included in the process descriptions. This means that we have to adapt the specification of the system and move some state information from the B machines into the appropriate CSP process descriptions. We do not make such adaptations in an ad-hoc fashion; instead we follow sound development steps underpinned by theorems. The contributions of this paper are to illustrate the application of these steps in developing the case study, and to demonstrate the applicability of our theoretical results, in particular how a combined communicating system is a refinement of a more abstract specification.

We now outline the development steps we use to build combined communicating systems, so that we can refer to them throughout the paper.

Step 1 Define the individual B machines,
Step 2 Give CSP controllers for them that describe the flow of control for their use,
Step 3 Prove consistency between each of the B machines and their controllers to establish divergence freedom,
Step 4 Prove deadlock freedom for the combination of the controllers,
Step 5 Establish that hiding internal events does not introduce any further divergences (livelock freedom),
Step 6 Verify safety and liveness properties of the system.

Observe that Steps 3 and 4 may only be possible if we introduce appropriate guards and assumptions, and extra events, into the CSP process descriptions. Steps 5 and 6 can be performed independently but both need to be achieved by the end of the development of a particular system. Furthermore, Steps 5 and 6 may only be possible if we introduce state as necessary into the CSP. Such state can be dropped following verification to end up with the system we originally had in Step 5 and 6 (but which has now been verified). Any introduction of guards, assumptions, or the introduction of more state has an iterative effect on the development and the steps will need to be revisited. When more state is added to the CSP it is likely to be more difficult to achieve Step 3 due to the complex interaction of B machines and their controllers.

This paper is organised as follows: Section 2 introduces the CSP controller language and semantics; Section 3 introduces the theoretical results which underpin our CSP∥ B approach; Section 4 describes the case study development in detail; and Section 5 ends with a discussion. The paper assumes familiarity with AMN; further details can be found in [1].

2 CSP Controllers and B Machines

2.1 Notation for Controllers

CSP is a language for describing processes of concurrent systems and their patterns of interactions. The unit of interaction is the atomic *event* which processes perform and on which they may synchronise. Events can be unstructured (such as *start*), or they can have some structure, generally of the form of a channel name c and some values v that are passed along a channel. Thus the occurrence of $c?3!5$ may be understood as the passing of the input value 3 and output value 5 along the channel c. The *occurrence* of events is atomic. The set of all events is denoted Σ.

We will use a subset of CSP to describe the controllers for B machines. The language we use is based on the language in [10,13,14] and is given by the following pseudo-BNF rule;

$$P ::= a \to P \mid c?x\langle E(x)\rangle \to P \mid d!v\{E(v)\} \to P \mid$$
$$e!v?x\{E(x)\} \to P \mid e!v?x\langle E(x)\rangle \to P \mid$$
$$P_1 \square P_2 \mid P_1 \sqcap P_2 \mid \sqcap_{x \mid E(x)} P \mid \text{if } b \text{ then } P_1 \text{ else } P_2 \text{ end} \mid S(p)$$

where a, c and d can be both *communication* and *synchronisation channels*, and e is a *machine channel*, x represents all data variables on a channel, v represents all data values being passed along a channel, $E(x)$ is a predicate on x (it may be elided, in which case it is considered to be *true*), b is a boolean expression, and p is a process expression. Note that the notation for machine channels has reverted to standard CSP notation, where '?' denotes input to the process, and '!' denotes output from the process. Previously in [10,14] we considered CSP processes as wrappers for the B machines rather than controllers, and so the notation described communications on machine channels from the point of view of the B machine (i.e. ! for output from the machine, and ? for input to it). Although the semantics remains the same, the change in notation reflects the shift in our view of the CSP process.

The process $a \to P$ can perform an event a and then behave as P. The input process $c?x\langle E(x)\rangle \to P(x)$ denotes a process that can accept any input x along channel c, provided x satisfies the guard E. It will block other inputs. Having accepted x, it will behave as $P(x)$. Conversely, the output process $d!v\{E(v)\} \to P$ will initially output v along channel d. If v meets the assumption E then it will behave as P, otherwise it will diverge.

Communication on machine channels involves both input and output, though special cases might drop one or even both of these. A machine channel e will correspond to an operation $x \longleftarrow e(v)$ of the underlying B machine, matching the input v of the operation to the output from the CSP, and the output x of the operation to the CSP input. This communication can include either an assumption or a guard. The communication $e!v?x\{E(x)\} \to P(x)$ can accept any x as input, but will diverge if $E(x)$ is not satisfied. Conversely, the communication $e!v?x\langle E(x)\rangle \to P(x)$ can only accept inputs x which satisfy the guard $E(x)$. Inputs which fail the guard are blocked.

The external choice, $P_1 \square P_2$, is initially prepared to behave either as P_1 or as P_2, with the choice being made on occurrence of the first event. The choice of the first event is made by the environment of the choice. Conversely, the choice $P_1 \sqcap P_2$ chooses internally whether to behave as P_1 or as P_2, and its environment has no control over the way the choice is resolved. Indexed internal choice ($\sqcap$) chooses a value x such that is meets the predicate $E(x)$ and then behaves as the process P which may depend on the value of x. Another form of choice is controlled by the value of a boolean expression in an **if** expression.

$S(p)$ is a process name where p is an expression. Each process expression contains a recursive call, $S(p)$. For example, a process which manages a set of values can be described by two recursive families Set and $Flush$ indexed by sets:

$$Set(S) = in?x\langle x \notin S\rangle \to Set(S \cup \{x\})$$
$$\square\ (\sqcap_{v \in S}\ out!v \to Set(S - \{v\}))$$
$$\square\ flush \to Flush(S)$$

$$Flush(S) = \textbf{if}\ S = \{\}\ \textbf{then}\ Set(S)\ \textbf{else}\ (\sqcap_{v \in S}\ out!v \to Flush(S - \{v\}))$$

Observe the use of the guard on the input channel in to block the input of any value which is already in the set S; and that some arbitrary member of S is selected for output. If the event $flush$ is chosen then the behaviour is described by $Flush$, which only allows outputs until the set is empty.

2.2 Composing Controllers

In addition to the language for controllers, CSP provides a number of composition operators. These can be used to combine controller processes, and can also be applied to B machines considered as CSP processes, since they can be given a CSP semantics. The operators we are concerned about in this paper are the following:

$$P_1 \parallel P_2 \mid \parallel_i P_i \mid P_1 \parallel_A P_2 \mid P_1 \mid\mid\mid P_2 \mid \mid\mid\mid_i P_i \mid P \setminus A$$

The *parallel composition* operator, $P_1 \parallel P_2$, executes P_1 and P_2 concurrently, requiring that they synchronise on events in both their alphabets, and allowing independent performance of events outside their alphabets. In this paper the alphabet of a process will be all the events that it can perform. This allows messages to pass along channels. There is also an indexed form $\parallel_i P_i$, and $P_1 \parallel_A P_2$ which requires synchronisation only on those events appearing in a common interface set A.

For example, if the processes $Copy$ and $Copy2$ are defined as follows

$$Copy = in?x \to mid!x \to Copy$$
$$Copy2 = mid?y \to out!y \to Copy2$$

then $Copy \parallel Copy2$ can input values v on in, have both components synchronise on $mid.v$ which passes the value to $Copy2$, and then have $Copy2$ independently output v on out.

A special form of parallel composition is *interleaving*, which allows concurrent processes to execute completely independently. The combination $P_1 \mid\mid\mid P_2$

executes both P_1 and P_2 in parallel, but without any synchronisation, even on common events. For example, $Copy ||| Copy$ behaves as a bag of capacity 2: it can accept up to two messages on channel in, and can output them independently on channel mid. There is also an indexed interleaving operator $|||_i P_i$.

Finally (for this paper), the *hiding* operator $P \setminus A$ executes P with the set of events A as internal events. This is often used on parallel combinations of processes to make their communication channels internal once they have been connected together. For example, the process $(Copy \parallel Copy2) \setminus \{| mid |\}$ behaves as a two place buffer with input channel in and output channel out.

2.3 CSP Semantics

CSP processes are identified with the observations that can be made of them: thus the semantics of a CSP process will be a set of observations. The precise form of the observations will describe the CSP model. The *traces model* uses traces as observations. The *stable failures model* uses traces along with subsequent refusals. The *failures/divergences model* uses traces, divergences, and failures. We briefly describe them here. A fuller explanation can be found in [8].

A *trace tr* of a process P is a finite sequence of events that it may be observed to engage in. The *traces model* identifies a process with its set of traces.

A *divergence* of a process P is a sequence of events tr such that P reaches a divergent state (which may be thought of as entering a non-terminating loop, or in specification terms as a specification which allows any behaviour) during the performance of the sequence of events tr. A process is *divergence-free* if it has no divergences. Divergence denotes undesirable behaviour, and it is generally useful to establish that a process is divergence-free.

A *refusal* of a process P is a set X of events that P might be initially prepared to refuse. A *stable failure* of a process P is a trace/refusal pair (tr, X) such that P can initially perform the sequence of events tr, and reach a non-divergent state in which every event in X is refused. The stable failures of P is denoted $\mathcal{F}_{SF}[\![P]\!]$.

If for some tr $(tr, \Sigma) \in \mathcal{F}_{SF}[\![P]\!]$ then P can reach a state in which no event at all is possible, and we say that P has a *deadlock*. If there is no such stable failure, then P is *deadlock-free*.

The semantic models allow *refinement*: $P \sqsubseteq Q$ means that the semantics of Q is a subset of the semantics of P. This allows a process P to be treated as a specification of allowed behaviours, and Q meets the specification if $P \sqsubseteq Q$. In this paper we use trace refinement $\sqsubseteq_T$ and stable failures refinement $\sqsubseteq_F$.

The CSP model-checker FDR [5] allows checks for refinement between processes. It also allows checks for deadlock and divergence freedom to be made automatically for CSP processes.

3 Results on Combining Communicating Systems

The development steps 3-6 (outlined in Section 1) are justified in terms of our theoretical results which allow us to use CSP and B together to specify combined communicating systems. In this section we present these results and note that Steps 3 and 4 are applications of Results 1 and 2 respectively. Step 5 is related to Results 3 and 4. Step 6 is related to Result 5. Our observations regarding dropping some state from the CSP descriptions following verification is justified due to Result 6.

Result 1. If each component pair $P_i \parallel M_i$ is divergence-free, then so is the entire parallel combination, $Ps \parallel Ms$. This is a useful result, since we already know how to establish that an individual $P_i \parallel M_i$ is divergence-free using the control loop invariant (CLI) technique from [12,13,14]. The CLI technique examines sequences of operations and ensures that all the precondition of an operation holds when it is invoked.

Result 2. If a combined communicating system $Ps \parallel Ms$, is divergence-free, and the collection of controllers *without their controlled B machines*, Ps, is deadlock-free, then the entire parallel combination is deadlock-free. This is a valuable result, since the parallel combination of CSP controllers, $Ps = \parallel_i P_i$, can be automatically checked using FDR. This enables the outcome of such a check to be lifted to include the B components.

Result 2 above shows that results about the CSP part of a combined system can be lifted to the entire combination. Recent results [11] have identified further ways in which checks on the CSP part of the combined system can provide results about the overall combination. In particular, the following results are useful. Results 3 and 4 are in the context of a divergence-free combination $Ps \parallel Ms$, so these results are applicable only after divergence-freedom has been established. (Here the M_i machines are completely independent and do not communicate directly, so they are combined using interleaving, $Ms = \parallel\parallel_i M_i,$).

Result 3. If $Ps \setminus Int$ is divergence-free, then so too is $(Ps \parallel Ms) \setminus Int$. If we want to declare some channels as internal (Int), this might introduce some divergent behaviour, so it is necessary to check in any particular case that this has not occurred. This result enables this check to be carried out purely on the CSP part of the combination.

Result 4. If Ps and Ps' differ only on the divergences of Ps (i.e., any failure (tr, X) of one but not the other must have that tr is a divergence of Ps) then $Ps \parallel Ms = Ps' \parallel Ms$. In other words, the behaviour of Ps and Ps' *in the context of Ms* is the same. Informally, this is because Ms prevents Ps from reaching any of its divergent behaviour. In practice, as will be illustrated in the case-study, this result enables assumptions on CSP channels to be dropped or transformed into guards. This is because assumptions are simply predicates on values which lead to divergent behaviour if the predicate is false. If $P_i \parallel M_i$ is divergence-free then all the assumptions must be true. Replacing assumptions in P_i with the same predicate as a guard, or removing the assumption entirely, yields a process P'_i which is the same as P_i on the non-divergent behaviour of P_i. This means that the combination Ps can be transformed to a combination Ps' which is the same on the non-divergent behaviour of Ps, and which might be more suitable for checking in FDR.

Result 5. If αM is the set of all channels of the B machines, and $\alpha M \subseteq \mathit{Int}$, and Ps does not have any guards on any of its channels, then $Ps \setminus \mathit{Int} \sqsubseteq_F (Ps \parallel Ms) \setminus \mathit{Int}$. In other words, once all the communications with the underlying state machines are hidden (and possibly others), then to show some failures property of the system $SPEC \sqsubseteq_F (Ps \parallel Ms) \setminus \mathit{Int}$, it is sufficient to show that the same property holds purely for the CSP controllers Ps when those channels are hidden: $SPEC \sqsubseteq_F Ps \setminus \mathit{Int}$. This result relies on the fact that the B machines that we are concerned with do not block on any channel, and that the CSP processes do not partially block on any internal channel in Int: in other words, they must be open to any input on a channel if they are open to some. A similar argument holds for trace refinement so that if we can show that a trace property holds for a restricted controller interface it can also be lifted up to the combination.

We will also make use of a folk theorem (which is also given in [11]) concerning mutual recursion:

Result 6. If the behaviour of a CSP process is completely independent of an index in its recursive definition, then that index can be dropped.

4 Example

The example in this section is of a bank control system which processes the flow of customers through a bank. The bank contains only one counter and a number of queues in which customers line up. They can proceed from these queues to the counter in order to process their business. Customers can enter the bank provided the bank has not reached its limit of customers. Customers can also leave the bank once they have finished their business. This example was originally inspired by the distributed buffer example described in Circus [2] where the cache and various flags were described separately from the ring.

The development is highly iterative because placing the state appropriately within the architecture to facilitate verification is not straightforward. Thus, we go through several incremental versions as follows;

Version 1 identifies all the important state and models it solely within B machines (**Step 1**). When required this state information is then passed via parameters into and retrieved from the CSP as appropriate. Having developed the controllers (**Step 2**) the consistency of the combined system (**Step 3 and 4**) is established. Then an attempt to verify the desired system properties (**Steps 5 and 6**) is made and mostly fails.

Version 2 re-structures the architecture so that more state is added to the CSP in order to restrict its behaviour sufficiently so that a better attempt can be made at verifying the desired properties. This re-structuring eliminates the need for one of the B machines, but the state in the other machine is so complicated that expressing it solely in CSP is not appropriate, and so it is an essential part of the system. As we stated in Section 1 this re-structuring means that we have to re-do **Steps 1-6**. The advantage of the resulting architecture is that it minimises the synchronous communication

MACHINE *Counter*
SEES *Types*
VARIABLES *currentCustomer* , *queueNo*
INVARIANT *currentCustomer* $\in$ *CUSTOMER* $\wedge$ *queueNo* $\in$ *QUEUENUM*
INITIALISATION
   currentCustomer := *defaultCustomer* $\parallel$ *queueNo* := *1*
OPERATIONS
   setCustomer ($cc \in CUSTOMER$) $\widehat{=}$ *currentCustomer* := cc ;
   $cc \longleftarrow$ **getCustomer** $\widehat{=}$ $cc := currentCustomer$;
   setnextQueue ($qNo \in QUEUENUM$) $\widehat{=}$ *queueNo* := qNo ;
   $qq \longleftarrow$ **getQueueNo** $\widehat{=}$ $qq := queueNo$
END

Fig. 2. *Counter* Machine

needed between controllers before appropriate underlying state changes can occur (since less retrieval of state occurs from the underlying B).

Version 3 differs only slightly from Version 2. Nonetheless, this version is needed so that we can confidently check (using FDR) that the bank system is free from any additional divergences which could have been introduced by the hiding of internal events.

The B-Toolkit [6] and FDR source files for the example can be downloaded[1].

4.1 Version 1 of the Bank System

In the overview of this version above we stated that all the main state of the system is captured in B machines. We separate the state into two machines so that one machine tracks all the information related to the counter and the other deals with queues and the waiting customers. These two machines are called *Counter* and *Queues*, which are defined in Figures 2 and 3 respectively.

The single bank counter is captured in the *Counter* machine. It introduces the variable *currentCustomer* to track the person currently being serviced. The set of all possible customers, *CUSTOMER* is declared in a separate context machine, *Types*, as shown in Figure 4. Similarly, the set of queue numbers, *QUEUENUM*, is declared in the same context machine. This global visibility of types is typical in B developments.

Four very simple operations are offered by *Counter*: *setCustomer* simply assigns a customer to the counter; *getCustomer* queries the current counter; *setNextQueue* updates the queue number to the next one to be serviced; and *getQueueNo* outputs the queue value.

The *Queues* machine tracks customers in the different queues within a bank by updating the *customerQueues* variable appropriately. The invariant of the

---
[1] http://www.cs.rhul.ac.uk/home/helen/papers/zb2003/sources.tar.gz

MACHINE $Queues$
SEES $Types$
VARIABLES $customerQueues$
INVARIANT $customerQueues \in QUEUENUM \rightarrow$ iseq ($CUSTOMER$) $\wedge$
card (union (ran ($customerQueues$))) $\leq maxQueueingCustomers \wedge$
$\forall$ ($c1$, $c2$) . ($c1 \in$ dom ($customerQueues$) $\wedge$
$c2 \in$ dom ($customerQueues$) $\wedge$
$c1 \neq c2 \Rightarrow$ ran ($customerQueues$ ($c1$)) $\cap$ ran ($customerQueues$ ($c2$)) = $\varnothing$)
INITIALISATION $customerQueues := QUEUENUM \times \{\,[\,]\,\}$

OPERATIONS
  joinQueue ($cc \in CUSTOMER$) $\,\widehat{=}\,$
    PRE $cc \notin$ ran (union (ran ($customerQueues$))) $\wedge$
     card (union (ran ($customerQueues$))) $< maxQueueingCustomers$
    THEN
     ANY $number$ **WHERE** $number \in$ dom ($customerQueues$) $\wedge$
      size ($customerQueues$ ($number$)) =
      min (ran ($\lambda\ xx$. ($xx \in$ dom ($customerQueues$) |
         size ($customerQueues$ (xx)))))
     THEN
      $customerQueues$ ($number$) := $customerQueues$ ($number$) $\leftarrow cc$
     END
    END ;
  $cc \longleftarrow$ **leaveQueue** ($queueNo \in QUEUENUM$) $\,\widehat{=}\,$
    PRE $customerQueues$ ($queueNo$) $\neq [\,]$ **THEN**
     $cc :=$ first ($customerQueues$ ($queueNo$)) $\|$
     $customerQueues$ ($queueNo$) := tail ($customerQueues$ ($queueNo$))
    END ;
  $bb \longleftarrow$ **queryQueueEmpty** ($queueNo \in QUEUENUM$) $\,\widehat{=}\,$
    IF $customerQueues$ ($queueNo$) = $[\,]$ **THEN**
     $bb := yes$
    ELSE
     $bb := no$
    END ;
  $bb \longleftarrow$ **queryIsInQueue** ($cc \in CUSTOMER$) $\,\widehat{=}\,$
    IF $cc \in$ ran (union (ran ($customerQueues$))) **THEN**
     $bb := yes$
    ELSE
     $bb := no$
    END
END

Fig. 3. $Queues$ Machine

MACHINE *Types*
SETS $CUSTOMER$; $QUEUENUM$; $QSTATUS = \{\ yes\ ,\ no\ \}$
CONSTANTS *defaultCustomer* , *maxQueueingCustomers* , *numQueues*
PROPERTIES *defaultCustomer* $\in CUSTOMER \land$ *maxQueueingCustomers* $\in \mathbb{N} \land$ *numQueues* $\in \mathbb{N}_1 \land QUEUENUM = 1\ ..\ numQueues$
END

Fig. 4. *Types* Machine

machine provides constraints on the queues of customers, stating that customers should only ever appear in at most one queue, and in at most one position. It also captures the fact that there is a safety limit of *maxQueueingCustomers* representing the total number of queueing customers allowed in the bank.

Four operations are offered by the machine. The operation *joinQueue* non-deterministically adds a customer to the end of one of the shortest queues. The precondition needs to state that the customer is not already in some other queue and that the *maxQueueingCustomers* constraint has not been reached. The operation *leaveQueue* removes the customer from the head of a particular queue and then all the other customers can move along. Neither updating operation is robust (i.e. it is not always safe to call these operations). Therefore, the CSP controllers will have to protect the flow of control appropriately. In order to assist with this we provide two query operations. The operation *queryQueueEmpty* reports whether a particular queue of customers is empty or not. Note that if the output is *no* we know that it is safe to call the *leaveQueue* operation. We also provide the operation *queryIsInQueue* to determine whether a customer is already in a queue. This will be useful when it comes to ensuring that the precondition of the *joinQueue* operation is met. We need not provide a query operation for the cardinality constraint because there will be enough information in the CSP controllers to discharge this.

Now let us consider the controllers which drive the *Counter* and *Queues* machines so that the operations of these B machines are called appropriately within the overall system. We define one controller for each machine, *CounterCtrl* and *QueuesCtrl*, and so our combined system is *BankSystem* = ((*CounterCtrl* ∥ *Counter*) ∥ (*QueuesCtrl* ∥ *Queues*)). Figure 5 illustrates the overall architecture of the whole system and highlights all the channels involved. The main external interface of the system is given by the *enterBank*, *report*, and *leaveBank* communication channels.

CounterCtrl is a controller which deals with customer requests, and is given in Figure 6. This is the process which takes overall control of communicating with the environment. It is defined in terms of a parameterised recursion. The parameter *num* represents the number of people in the bank (i.e. the customer at the counter and all the ones in queues). Initially, there are no such customers and so *num* is set to zero. There are two main execution paths, described using sub-

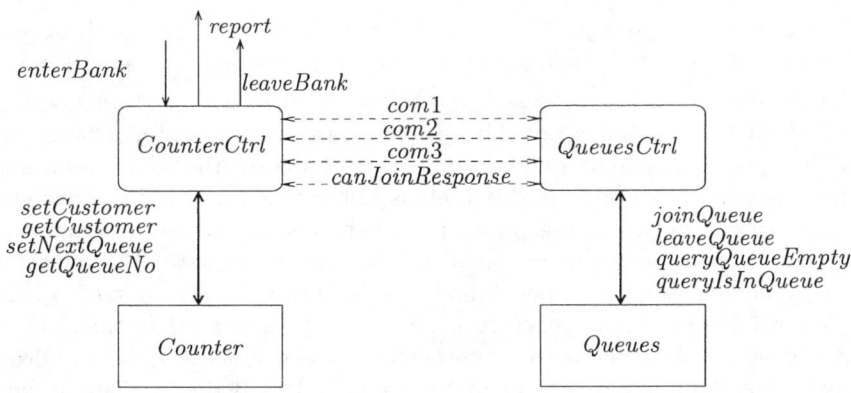

Fig. 5. Communication Architecture of *BankSystem* - Version 1

$CounterCtrl \quad\quad = CurrentCtrl(0)$
$CurrentCtrl(num) = JoinCtrl(num) \;\Box\; LeaveCtrl(num)$
$JoinCtrl(num) =$
    $num < maxLimit \;\&\; enterBank?cc \rightarrow$
    $((num = 0 \;\&\; report!success \rightarrow setCustomer!cc \rightarrow CurrentCtrl(num+1))$
    $\Box$
    $(num > 0 \;\&\; getCustomer?currentCust \rightarrow$
        if $(cc = currentCust)$
        then
            $report!fail \rightarrow CurrentCtrl(num)$
        else
            $com1!cc \rightarrow canJoinResponse?bb \rightarrow report!bb \rightarrow$
            (**if** $(bb = success)$
            then
                $CurrentCtrl(num+1)$
            else
                $CurrentCtrl(num)) \quad))$

$LeaveCtrl(num) =$
    $(num = 1 \;\&\; getCustomer?cc \rightarrow leaveBank!cc \rightarrow$
    $setCustomer!defaultCustomer \rightarrow CurrentCtrl(0))$
    $\Box$
    $(num > 1 \;\&\; getCustomer?cc \rightarrow leaveBank!cc \rightarrow$
    $getQueueNo?qNo \rightarrow com2!qNo \rightarrow com3?newCust?newQNo \rightarrow$
    $setCustomer!newCust \rightarrow setNextQueue!newQNo \rightarrow CurrentCtrl(num-1))$

Fig. 6. *Counter* Controller

processes, which are controlled by an external choice. The first path processes customers entering the bank and the second allows customers to leave the bank.

Let us first look at the process, *JoinCtrl*, which deals with customers entering the bank. It is not always possible to allow customers to enter a bank, since there is a maximum limit on the number of people in the bank, represented by the constant *maxLimit*. If this limit is not reached and a customer enters the bank there are two further branches. First, if there are no customers at all (i.e. when *num* is zero) the customer can proceed straight to the counter and so the event *setCustomer* is performed, and in turn this corresponds to setting the B variable *currentCustomer* to *cc*. Second, if there are customers present in the bank we must check that the new *cc* passed along the communication channel *enterBank* is not the one at the counter. If it is then we simply ignore the request to allow *cc* to enter for a second time, and we report that the request was unsuccessful with a *fail* communication along the channel *report*. However, if *cc* is a different customer to the one at the counter we can send a synchronisation communication (to the *QueuesCtrl* described below) to indicate that *cc* should join an appropriate queue.

Now let us consider the process, *LeaveCtrl*, which deals with leaving customers and there are two main possible behaviours. First, if there is only one customer then the customer to leave the bank is the one associated with *cc* (i.e. the one at the counter). This information is retrieved using the *getCustomer* event. Then a communication along *leaveBank* indicates *cc*'s departure, after which we update the current customer to a default value and reset the number of people in the bank to zero. Second, if there is more than one customer in the bank, then the person to leave is again the one at the counter but in this case we must also move a person from a queue to the counter to be serviced next. We do this by querying which queue is to be serviced using *getQueueNo* and send this information along *com2* so that the *QueueCtrl* can extract the appropriate customer. We then wait for this information to be received along *com3* along with the new queue number (which is the next queue to be serviced next time round). Following this synchronised communication we can perform the setting events to update the counter and queue information. The process ends with a recursive call in which the total number of people in the bank is decremented by one.

The other main controller is *QueuesCtrl* which drives the *Queues* machine to process the queueing customers in the bank. *QueuesCtrl* is defined in Figure 7, in terms of a parameterised mutual recursion. The parameter *s* holds the maximum number of queueing customers (one less that the bank limit). Initially, there are no such customers.

There are two main possible execution paths in *QueuesCtrl*; the first deals with joining a queue, and the second processes leaving a queue. The first branch receives a communication requesting that *cc* joins a queue. As we stated earlier the operation *joinQueue* is not robust and so this is reflected in the CSP by a query event and then wrapping an if statement around the main *joinQueue* event (which effectively changes the underlying B state). If the customer *cc* is already

$QueuesCtrl = QCtrl(0)$
$QCtrl(s) =$
$\quad\quad (s < maxQueueingCustomers\ \&\ com1?cc \rightarrow queryIsInQueue!cc?bb \rightarrow$
$\quad\quad\quad\quad \textbf{if } (bb = yes)$
$\quad\quad\quad\quad \textbf{then}$
$\quad\quad\quad\quad\quad\quad canJoinResponse!fail \rightarrow QCtrl(s)$
$\quad\quad\quad\quad \textbf{else}$
$\quad\quad\quad\quad\quad\quad canJoinResponse!success \rightarrow joinQueue!cc \rightarrow QCtrl(s+1))$
$\quad\quad \square$
$\quad\quad (s > 0\ \&\ com2?qNo \rightarrow NextQCtrl(s, qNo))$
$NextQCtrl(s, queueNo) =$
$\quad\quad queryQueueEmpty!queueNo?bb \rightarrow$
$\quad\quad \textbf{if } (bb = no)$
$\quad\quad \textbf{then}$
$\quad\quad\quad\quad leaveQueue!queueNo?cc \rightarrow com3!cc!inc(queueNo) \rightarrow QCtrl(s-1)$
$\quad\quad \textbf{else}$
$\quad\quad\quad\quad NextQCtrl(s, inc(queueNo))$
$inc(queueNo) = (queueNo\ \%\ numQueues) + 1$
$A = \{\!|\ com1, com2, com3, canJoinResponse\ |\!\}$
$B = \{\!|\ joinQueue, leaveQueue, queryQueueEmpty, queryIsInQueue, getCustomer,$
$\quad\quad setCustomer, getQueueNo, setNextQueue\ |\!\}$
$BankSystemControllers = CounterCtrl\ \underset{A}{\|}\ QueuesCtrl \setminus (A \cup B)$

Fig. 7. *Queues* Controller and *BankSystemControllers*

in another queue the request to join fails and the appropriate communication is sent back to the *CounterCtrl*, otherwise it can proceed and the number of people s can be incremented. The second path synchronises on the receipt of a queue number. Subsequently, a call to the *NextQCtrl* sub-process occurs. The main event in this process is the one which effectively removes a customer from the queue, *leaveQueue*, but again the corresponding B precondition needs to hold. Therefore, we use a query operation and an if statement in a similar way to the previous branch. From this we can clearly see that the underlying B machine has a direct impact on the style of specification of a controller when we have complete information hiding and fragile operations.

If there is a queue of customers associated with the queue number qNo we can then extract a customer and communicate this to the *CounterCtrl* along *com3*. We also pass the new queue information back to the other controller. Finally, we make a recursive call to *QCtrl* so that we are prepared to deal with further queueing related requests.

The *NextQCtrl* controller is itself an iterative process because if qNo is associated with an empty queue the controller needs to cycle through the queues in the bank until a non-empty queue is found.

The above completes our discussion of **Steps 1** and **2** for this first version of the bank system. Now we turn to the verification steps; **Step 3** requires that we verify *CounterCtrl* $\|$ *Counter* and *QueuesCtrl* $\|$ *Queues* to be divergence-free.

$SPEC = |||_{i \in \{1..maxLimit\}} CUST$
$CUST = enterBank?i \rightarrow (report!fail \rightarrow CUST$
$\Box$
$report!success \rightarrow leaveBank!i \rightarrow CUST)$

$SPEC2 = NEWSPEC(0)$
$NEWSPEC(num) =$
  $num < maxLimit \& enterBank?cc \rightarrow$
  $(report!success \rightarrow NEWSPEC(num+1) \sqcap report!fail \rightarrow NEWSPEC(num))$
  $\Box$
  $(num > 0 \& \sqcap_{cc \in CUSTOMER} leaveBank!cc \rightarrow NEWSPEC(num-1))$

Fig. 8. Desired Properties of $BankSystem \setminus (A \cup B)$

The *CLI* for *CounterCtrl* ∥ *Counter* is simply *true* because we do not have to ensure any preconditions are met other than typing ones. An appropriate *CLI* for *QueuesCtrl* ∥ *Queues* is

$$s = \Sigma_{i \in dom(customerQueues)} size(customerQueues(i))$$

and again we can show that this holds true. Informally, this is because each time we add a customer to a queue we increment s by one and the cardinality of one of the queues will also increase by one. Similarly, when we remove a person from the queue we decrement s and this is reflected by the removal of a customer from a queue. Establishing deadlock-freedom of the *BankSystem* (**Step 4**) simply involves checking that $CounterCtrl \parallel_A QueuesCtrl$ is deadlock-free (which is the case).

The remaining checks to be performed are livelock freedom (**Step 5**) of the *BankSystemControllers*, defined in Figure 7, and the verification of safety and liveness properties (**Step 6**). We cannot prove livelock freedom because a *yes* result can always be passed along the *queryQueueEmpty* channel and thus we loop round the *NextQCtrl* process infinitely.

A desired safety property of our system is one where a customer entering the bank can also leave at some point later and customers are allowed to use the bank independently. An appropriate liveness property will guarantee that the system should always offer the possibility of letting a customer enter or leave the bank whenever possible (given that there is a limit on the number of people allowed in the bank at any one time). Figure 8 captures these properties as CSP processes. We need to show that the *BankSystemControllers* meet these specification using FDR and thus we can show that they apply to the whole of the $BankSystem \setminus (A \cup B)$ (**Result 5**). The results of these checks are shown in Figure 9. We see that this first version succeeds on only one check.

The checks mostly fail because all the important state is hidden within B but some state is required in the CSP to ensure that the properties hold for the controller processes (using FDR). This need for some state information in the CSP controllers is clearly exhibited when we fail to show that $SPEC \sqsubseteq_T$

Version (V)	LivelockFreedom	$SPEC \sqsubseteq_T V$	$SPEC2 \sqsubseteq_T V$	$SPEC2 \sqsubseteq_F V$
1	No	No	Yes	No
2	No	Yes	Yes	Yes
3	Yes	Yes	Yes	Yes

Fig. 9. Verification of *BankSystemControllers* in FDR

BankSystemControllers (*version1*) because the controllers allow more behaviours than the specification permits. Consider the following trace

$\langle enterBank?c1, report!success, setCustomer!c1, getCustomer?c2, leaveBank!c2 \rangle$

which illustrates the customer $c2$ attempting to leave the bank without having first entered it. This trace is not allowed by the process *SPEC* but it is permitted by *BankSystemControllers*. This is because the channel *getCustomer* accepts any cc as input (since no guards are enforced) and so *leaveBank!c2* is a visible event when it should not be.

A similar counter example can be identified when we attempt to verify $SPEC2 \sqsubseteq_F BankSystemControllers(version1)$. The root cause of the verification failure is again the complete hiding of state purely within B.

Note, in the table, we do not check for the stable failures refinement of *SPEC* against the *BankSystemControllers* in any of the development versions because it would require the bank system to allow users to use the bank completely independently. For example, after *enterBank?c1*, the event *enterBank?c2* is still possible in *SPEC* (due to the interleaving). However, the *BankSystemControllers* definition refuses it, because it will not allow anything else until a report is provided. This is perfectly reasonable, the bank system is not expected to process customers completely independently. Hence, *SPEC* as a liveness specification ($SPEC \sqsubseteq_F BankSystemControllers$) is unreasonable.

4.2 Version 2 of the Bank System

In the previous version we noted that retrieving any customer, cc, along the channel *getCustomer* does not restrict the CSP behaviour appropriately, but there was no state in the CSP which could be used to express such a restriction on that communication allowed. Therefore, in this second version we re-design *BankSystemControllers* to include some useful state. We begin by representing the *currentCustomer* as state within the CSP description. One option is to duplicate the state in both the B and the CSP (as we had shown in our example in [10]). In this paper we minimise duplication, and so we do not capture *currentCustomer* in the *Counter* machine. Given this change to the *Counter* machine we note that the only other variable in this machine is *queueNo*. This number is not used within *CounterCtrl* to restrict the flow of control and begs the question, why capture it in that part of the system? Would it not be more appropriate in the queues partition of the system? We had initially considered moving it to the *Queues* machine but since it is only a natural number it can

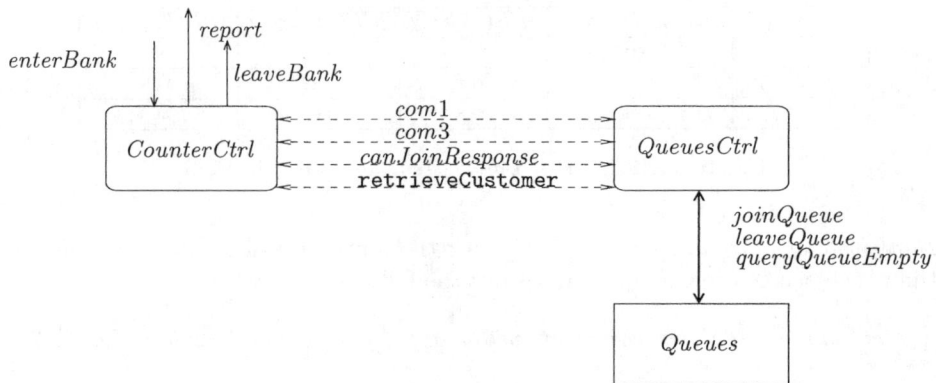

Fig. 10. Communication Architecture of *BankSystem* - Version 2

be easily captured solely in the *QueuesCtrl*. This means that we no longer need the *com2* channel to communicate the queue number across the distributed system. Furthermore, *com3* is simplified to only passing the next customer to be serviced along its channel. Thus, the overall simpler architecture of the second version is shown in Figure 10. The *Counter* machine is no longer needed but the *Queues* machine contains complex state and remains almost unchanged (as we shall discuss below).

The second version of the *BankSystemControllers* is defined fully in Figure 11. The processes have similar execution paths but utilise fewer B query and setting operations. This version achieves all the verification aims of **Steps 3**, **4**, and **6** for the system, but was achieved after some iteration. Our first attempt at **Step 4** showed the controllers reaching a deadlock situation. It was possible for the *CounterCtrl* to have processed two customers and then be attempting to allow another person to join the queues by sending a communication along *com1*. The *QueuesCtrl* on the other hand had already resolved its choice internally and was attempting to allow a customer to leave but was forced to wait for a communication along *com2*. Thus, both synchronisation channels were waiting for each others' co-operation to continue execution. This was caused because we had limited the external interface of the bank system and so the CSP controllers were allowed to make internal progress when they should not be doing so. Therefore, we introduced a new synchronisation channel retrieveCustomer on one of the problematic branches to prevent this undesirable progress. Hence, *BankSystemControllers(version2)* can now be shown to be deadlock-free.

Our first attempt at **Step 5** highlighted the fact that we could not again prove $SPEC \sqsubseteq_T BankSystemControllers(version2)$. As with the first version this was due to the fact that we could allow customers to leave the bank who had not entered. This problem was solved by introducing *custSet* as extra state in the CSP, which is an abstraction of the customers held in queues. Then only customers who had entered the bank could proceed from queues to the counter, and subsequently leave. Hence, we can show that the safety property is preserved.

$CounterCtrl = CurrentCtrl(0, defaultCustomer)$
$CurrentCtrl(num, currentCust) =$
$\qquad JoinCtrl(num, currentCust) \;\Box\; LeaveCtrl(num, currentCust)$

$JoinCtrl(num, currentCust) =$
$\quad num < maxLimit \,\&\, enterBank?cc \rightarrow$
$\quad ((num = 0 \,\&\, report!success \rightarrow CurrentCtrl(num + 1, cc))$
$\qquad \Box$
$\quad ((num > 0 \,\&\, \neg(cc = currentCust)) \,\&\, com1!cc \rightarrow$
$\qquad\qquad canJoinResponse?bb \rightarrow report!bb \rightarrow$
$\qquad\qquad \textbf{if } (bb = success)$
$\qquad\qquad \textbf{then}$
$\qquad\qquad\qquad CurrentCtrl(num + 1, currentCust)$
$\qquad\qquad \textbf{else}$
$\qquad\qquad\qquad CurrentCtrl(num, currentCust))$
$\quad \Box$
$\quad ((num > 0 \,\&\, (cc = currentCust)) \,\&\, report!fail \rightarrow CurrentCtrl(num, currentCust)))$

$LeaveCtrl(num, currentCust) =$
$\qquad (num = 1 \,\&\, leaveBank!currentCust \rightarrow CurrentCtrl(0, defaultCustomer))$
$\qquad \Box$
$\qquad (num > 1 \,\&\, leaveBank!currentCust \rightarrow$
$\qquad\qquad \textbf{retrieveCustomer} \rightarrow com3?cc-> CurrentCtrl(num - 1, cc))$

$QueuesCtrl = QCtrl(0, 1, \varnothing)$
$QCtrl(s, queueNo, custSet) =$
$\quad (s < maxQueueingCustomers \,\&\, com1?cc \rightarrow$
$\qquad \textbf{if } (cc \in custSet)$
$\qquad \textbf{then}$
$\qquad\quad canJoinResponse!fail \rightarrow QCtrl(s, queueNo, custSet)$
$\qquad \textbf{else}$
$\qquad\quad canJoinResponse!success \rightarrow joinQueue!cc \rightarrow$
$\qquad\quad QCtrl(s + 1, queueNo, custSet \cup \{cc\}))$
$\quad \Box$
$\quad (s > 0 \,\&\, \textbf{retrieveCustomer} \rightarrow NextQCtrl(s, queueNo, custSet))$

$NextQCtrl(s, queueNo, custSet) =$
$\quad queryQueueEmpty!queueNo?bb \rightarrow$
$\quad \textbf{if } (bb = no)$
$\quad \textbf{then}$
$\qquad leaveQueue!queueNo?\{cc : custSet\} \rightarrow com3!cc \rightarrow$
$\qquad QCtrl(s - 1, inc(queueNo), custSet - \{cc\}))$
$\quad \textbf{else}$
$\qquad NextQCtrl(s, inc(queueNo), custSet)$
$inc(queueNo) = (queueNo \,\%\, numQueues) + 1$
$A = \{|\; com1, com3, canJoinResponse, \textbf{retrieveCustomer}\;|\}$
$B = \{|\; joinQueue, leaveQueue, queryQueueEmpty\;|\}$
$BankSystemControllers = CounterCtrl \parallel_{A} QueuesCtrl \setminus (A \cup B)$

Fig. 11. *BankSystemControllers* - Version 2

$NextQCtrl(s, queueNo, lastQueueNo, custSet) =$
  $(queryQueueEmpty!queueNo?bb\langle queueNo = lastQueueNo \Rightarrow bb = no\rangle \rightarrow$
      if $(bb = no)$
      then
          $leaveQueue!queueNo?\langle cc \in custSet\rangle \rightarrow com3!cc \rightarrow$
          $QCtrl(s - 1, inc(queueNo), custSet - \{cc\})$
      else
          $NextQCtrl(s, inc(queueNo), lastQueueNo, custSet))$

Fig. 12. Extra state in *NextQCtrl* to prevent livelock - Version 3

Carrying around this extra information in the CSP had an impact on the first branch of the *QueuesCtrl*. The precondition of *joinQueue* states that the joining customer *cc* cannot already be in any queue. In Version 1, we guaranteed this by first calling a query operation. In this version we can make use of *custSet* and use this as an alternative way of checking that *cc* is not already a member of this set. Consequently, we do not need to use the *queryIsInQueue* operation from the *Queues* machine in this version (which is why it is missing from Figure 10). Adding the extra state meant iterating through the development steps again. Ensuring divergence-freedom (**Step 3**) of *QueuesCtrl* ∥ *Queues* is more involved because the relationship between the CSP and B (captured in the *CLI*) is as follows;

$$s = \Sigma_{i \in dom(customerQueues)} size(customerQueues(i)) \wedge$$
$$custSet = ran(\bigcup(ran(customerQueues)))$$

4.3 Version 3 of the Bank System

Version 2 above does not ensure livelock freedom of the *BankSystem* (and hence *BankSystem* \ $(A \cup B)$) when examining the CSP in isolation (**Step 5**). It is not possible as it stands because the assumption ($\{cc \in custSet\}$) in the CSP description introduces a possible divergence. An application of **Result 4** enables us to transform the assumption into a guard to obtain an equivalent controller for the B machines. Having removed this assumption the only remaining way divergence can arise is from an internal loop.

In fact, as in Version 1, the CSP description does allow an internal loop in *NextQCtrl*, forever obtaining *queryQueueEmpty!queueNo?yes* on every *queueNo* input in turn. However, *NextQCtrl* will always terminate because we only call it when $s > 0$, and so there is at least one non-empty queue which will give a result *queryQueueEmpty!queueNo?no* and exit the internal loop. We need to include this information into the CSP controller if we wish to establish results purely from checking the CSP part of the system.

One way to achieve this is by introducing an additional item of state in order to express a guard on the values provided by the *Queues* machine: the last queue that will have to be checked in order to obtain a *no* result. When entering the loop, this value is set to be the queue preceding the first queue to be checked — this will be reached only if all other queues are empty. This change is given in the new *NextQCtrl* process, defined in Figure 12. The process is called within *QCtrl* with the parameters (s, *queueNo*, $dec(queueNo)$, *custSet*). The guard enforces that if the last queue is being queried the answer must be *no*.

This extra state and guard is enough to ensure that *NextQCtrl* does not loop infinitely, and indeed *BankSystemControllers*(*version*3) is livelock-free (and hence *BankSystem* \ ($A \cup B$) is livelock-free). It is also necessary to show that this version of the controllers, with a guard in place of the assumption, is still consistent with the controlled machines. This is straightforward to achieve: it essentially includes within the *CLI* that some queue between *queueNo* and *lastQueueNo* is non-empty. Having established this, we can then drop the guard completely, obtaining a controller whose behaviour does not depend on the value of *lastQueueNo* at all, and which is equivalent to Version 2. **Result 6** then allows this part of the state to be dropped, arriving back at (the equivalent) Version 2 of *BankSystemControllers* again. Thus, the system controlled by Version 2 must also be livelock-free.

This completes the verification of the case study and so to summarise - Version 1 was fine if we were only concerned with deadlock freedom but if we wanted to show that the system exhibited some more interesting properties and also livelock freedom we needed Version 2. Version 3 was only introduced to assist in the verification of Version 2.

5 Discussion

The paper identified general development steps so that our (CSP‖B) approach can be adopted more widely. The immediate benefit of adoption is the availability of tool support for almost all of these steps. Ongoing research is being conducted to provide tool support for **Step 3** of the development process.

In this paper we demonstrated the use of hiding for the first time so that a main external interface of a combined system can be identified, and also showed that desired liveness and safety properties of a combined system can be verified automatically. In the case study we demonstrated how state needed to be filtered up from the B into a CSP description so that this verification was successful. As a by-product, we showed that the architecture could be streamlined to contain only complex data-rich B components. We also showed that a B component is essential when complex state is involved because such state cannot be described easily within CSP. We noted that these extensions to our approach are underpinned by our existing CSP ‖ B framework.

To the best of our knowledge there are only two other approaches which aim to verify that a communicating specification meets some abstract specification. Circus [2] is one such approach which begins with an abstract specification and by applying strict refinement laws a combined specification (using Z and CSP) can be defined. Hence, they elegantly show by construction that a combined specification meets an abstract specification. Muntean and Rolland [7] take a similar approach but all the communicating interaction is expressed purely within B.

Both approaches are tool supported but do not allow model checking of behavioural properties.

Acknowledgements. Thanks to Lok Yeung for his careful reading of earlier drafts, and to Jim Woodcock and Anna Cavalcanti for a useful discussion which helped to clarify some issues regarding Circus.

References

1. Abrial J. R.: *The B Book: Assigning Programs to Meaning*, CUP (1996).
2. Cavalcanti A., Sampaio A., and Woodcock J.: *Refinement of Actions in Circus*, In REFINE'02, FME Workshop, Copenhagen (2002).
3. Hoare C. A. R.: *Communicating Sequential Processes*, Prentice Hall (1985).
4. Morgan C. C.: *Of wp and CSP*. In W.H.J. Feijen, A.J.M. van Gasteren, D. Gries and J. Misra, editors, *Beauty is our business: a birthday salute to Edsger W. Dijkstra*. Springer (1990).
5. Formal Systems (Europe) Ltd.: *Failures-Divergences Refinement: FDR2 User Manual* (1997), http://www.formal.demon.co.uk
6. Neilson D., Sorensen I. H.: *The B-Technologies: a system for computer aided programming*, B-Core (UK) Limited, Kings Piece, Harwell, Oxon, OX11 0PA (1999), http://www.b-core.com
7. Muntean T., Rolland O.:*Distributed Refinement: application to the B Method*, RCS'02, International Workshop on Refinement of Critical Systems: Methods, Tools and Experience, Grenoble (2002),
8. Schneider S.: *Concurrent and Real-time Systems: The CSP approach*, Wiley (2000).
9. Schneider S.: *The B-Method: An Introduction*, Palgrave, 2001.
10. Schneider S.,Treharne H.: *Communicating B Machines*. ZB2002, Grenoble, LNCS 2272, Springer, January (2002).
11. Schneider S.,Treharne H.: *CSP Theorems for Communicating B Machines*. Technical Report CSD-TR-02-12, Dept. of Computer Science, Royal Holloway (2002).
12. Treharne H., Schneider S.: *Using a Process Algebra to control B OPERATIONS*. In K. Araki, A. Galloway and K. Taguchi, editors, IFM'99, York, Springer (1999).
13. Treharne H., Schneider S.: *How to drive a B Machine*. ZB2000, York, LNCS 1878, Springer, September (2000).
14. Treharne H.: *Controlling Software Specifications*. PhD Thesis, Royal Holloway, University of London (2000).
15. Treharne H., Schneider S.: *Communicating B Machines (full version)*. Technical Report, RHUL (2001).

When Concurrent Control Meets Functional Requirements, or Z + Petri-Nets[*]

Frédéric Peschanski[1] and David Julien[2]

[1] University of Tokyo
pesch@yl.is.s.u-tokyo.ac.jp
[2] Laboratoire d'Informatique de Paris 6
David.Julien@lip6.fr

Abstract. It is our belief that the formal design of real-world concurrent systems does not fit well with model/state-oriented specification languages such as the Z notation. The problem with such systems is that they not only expose complex functional requirements but also critical control-level aspects such as concurrency. On the other hand, the most widely-spread formal languages dealing with concurrency, namely Petri-nets, reveal weaknesses (mostly state-space explosion) when dealing with complex functional requirements. In this paper, we propose a hybrid methodology, based on the traditional Z notation for the functional part of the system and using Petri-nets to model its concurrent control. We describe a simple method to derive new proof obligations in case of possible concurrent activation of Z operations, as modeled by the associated Petri-nets. By keeping the interface between both worlds as thin as possible, we do not put into question the interesting properties of the Z language: expressiveness, modularity and support for refinement. Moreover, our petri-based concurrent activation networks only address concurrency issues. Hence, it is likely that they remain manageable in term of state-space and so analyzable using existing Petri-net tools. We experimented this exploratory method on a real application, a research middleware kernel, which is now fully operational.

1 Introduction

The Z notation [11] supports the formal specification of computer systems with great freedom thanks to its modular and open design. However, most of Z-based industrial-strength specifications have been done on sequential systems, using models of states and transitions of the systems. Our research interest is focused on the design and implementation of concurrent and distributed systems and languages. Our main project is a component-based middleware system called Comet [8]. The problem with such systems is that they expose not only various and complex functional requirements but also critical control-level aspects. These aspects —we will focus on *concurrency* in this paper— do not fit well with

---

[*] This work is supported by the Japan Society for the Promotion of Science (JSPS) under research grand #14-02748.

standard state/transition models. As a matter of fact, we think that traditional Z-based methodologies fail to both (1) provide expressive abstractions to model concurrent control and (2) guide system designers regarding proof obligations when concurrency is involved.

Petri-nets and related formal languages [10], on the contrary, provide abstractions that are generally considered as very simple (denotationally speaking) and expressive to model concurrent systems. Formal techniques and support tools allow the relatively easy (and often automated) conduction of proof regarding concurrency such as finding deadlocks or starvation conditions and so on. However, despite the important research advances in the domain [4], it seems still difficult to model and analyze large specifications with complex functional requirements using only Petri net-based languages because of the large state-space these denote.

Therefore, we propose in this paper a hybrid methodology employing Z schemas to fulfill the functional requirements of the systems and *concurrent activation nets*, based on Petri-nets, to model concurrency as well as deriving new proof obligations at the functional level.

Sect. 2 of the paper presents our case study: the kernel of an operational research middleware platform. We present some extracts of the Z-based functional specification of this system. We then describe in Sect. 3 the issues raised by the concurrent nature of the case study. To address these issues, we model using Petri-nets a set of concurrent activation networks for the related functional specifications. We also explain our method to derive, from the activation nets, the new proof obligations for the specification designers. We design in Sect. 4 an extension of our middleware kernel showing that Z-based modular specifications and refinement techniques are not compromised by our approach. We then overview some related work and conclude the paper.

2 Case-Study: The Comet Kernel

The Comet middleware is a research experiment attempting to support highly dynamic component-based distributed systems based on an asynchronous model of communication [9]. One advantage of such asynchronous form of communication is its implicit concurrent nature resulting in a great autonomy of the involved components in term of control. The second most fundamental property of the system is that the deployed components do not make explicit reference to other components, they can only be related at runtime using connections. They then can exchange information in the form of asynchronous emissions of events. We thus enforce in Comet an explicit coupling relation among components, both in structural (explicit references) and behavioral (asynchronous control) terms so that the systems can be built dynamically and incrementally. In this paper, we are mainly interested by the control-level aspects —mostly concurrency— of the component internals.

From the previous discussion we can state that a component, in our middleware, is basically an *asynchronous software entity*. As in other concurrent models (such as actor languages [1] or active objects [2]), this implies a decoupling between the communication system and the execution layer. In our event-based approach, we distinguish:

- the reception of the events by a given component,
- the corresponding execution stage, and
- the potential resulting emission of output events.

Fig. 1 shows the various functional requirements of our asynchronous management of events within component boundaries. First, the *Receive* and *Send* functionalities explain the links between the components and the underlying communication system. Events, when received, are queued in the *InQueue* structure and then fetched concurrently by the *InFetch* operation. The execution phase is handled by *Exec* and output events are emitted asynchronously through *OutQueue*. The *OutFetch* phase is also decoupled in term of control from the other phases (except *Send*). We also define other structures and operations to describe the communication layer as well as other higher-level considerations (e.g. connection models).

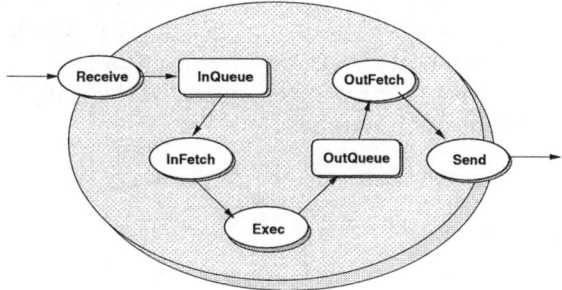

Fig. 1. Functional requirements (operation schemas)

All these structures and operations, namely the *functional requirements* of the system, have been specified and refined using the Z notation. The whole abstract (i.e. not refined) specification is composed of about one hundred schemas, resulting in a middle-sized model. Of course, we will only present a small subsets of these schemas, considering only (and partially) the operations involved within component boundaries.

2.1 Component State

The state manipulated within a component is composed of a set of input and output channels as well as two queuing systems. The corresponding Z-schema is given below:

```
┌─ Behavior ─────────────────────────────┐
│ in_channels : ℙ CommChannel            │
│ out_channels : ℙ CommChannel           │       ┌─ CommChannel ──────────┐
│ in_queue : seq Event                   │       │ id : IDENTIFIER        │
│ out_queue : seq Event                  │       │ type : ℙ TYPE          │
│ local_id : ℕ                           │       │ events : seq Event     │
├────────────────────────────────────────┤       └────────────────────────┘
│ local_id ≥ 0                           │
└────────────────────────────────────────┘
```

To remain concise, we don't show here the whole state and invariant, pointing only the essential aspects for event management. The only condition we expose is that the *local_id* counter should be positive[1]. This counter ensures that currently processed events have different local identifications. This invariant condition is not expressed exactly under these terms in our real system but this will be helpful to show some issues regarding concurrent activation later on. The *CommChannel* structure corresponds to an event channel between two components. It mainly exposes a seq *Event* data, that is, a sequence of events actually exchanged among the components. The *in_queue* and *out_queue* are also represented as sequences of events.

We will suppose that the component state is initially empty so that all sequences are empty ($\langle\rangle$) and the local identifier is zero. Another hypothesis is that some input and output channels have been set up in the initial configuration so that we don't have to go into the details of the complex establishment and removal of communication channels.

2.2 Operations

The reception of an event is a two-steps process. First, a particular input channel conveying new events must be chosen. This can be done by fetching an element c of *in_channels* non-deterministically, under the condition that $c.events \neq \langle\rangle$. Then, we have to extract one event from the channel and output it. The emission phase will consist in the converse operation (pushing an event into a channel). The *Receive* and *Send* operations are defined below:

```
┌─ Receive ──────────────────┐        ┌─ Send ─────────────────────────┐
│ ΔCommChannel               │        │ ΔCommChannel                   │
│ ev! : Event                │        │ ev? : Event                    │
├────────────────────────────┤        ├────────────────────────────────┤
│ events ≠ ⟨⟩                │        │ events' = ⟨ev?⟩ ⌢ events       │
│ ev! = last events          │        └────────────────────────────────┘
│ events' = front events     │
└────────────────────────────┘
```

---

[1] This condition could be omitted since we declare *local_id* as a natural number but it is sometimes worthy to explicit such implicit conditions.

In the *Receive* schema, we just pop an event (*ev*!) from a given and non-empty input channel without forgetting to remove it effectively. The *Send* schema takes as input an event (*ev*?) and pushes it in front of the output channel event queue[2].

When received effectively, the events must be queued for later (asynchronous) treatment using the *InQueue* facility. Concurrently, events can be fetched at any (non-deterministic) time by the *InFetch* operation. The corresponding schemas are as follows:

InQueue
$\Delta Behavior$
$ev? : Event$

$in\_queue' = \langle ev? \rangle \frown in\_queue$

InFetch
$\Delta Behavior$
$ev! : Event$

$in\_queue \neq \langle \rangle$
$ev! = last\ in\_queue$
$in\_queue' = front\ in\_queue$
$local\_id' = local\_id + 1$

Queuing consists simply in pushing the new event at the beginning of the queue (here, *in_queue*). Since we are, in the case of the *InQueue* schema, working at the *Behavior* level, the *Receive* schema shown previously must of course be promoted since communication channels are subparts of the considered state space. However, the promotion in this case does not impact on the concurrency issues we are discussing in this paper. The fetching phase can only be performed when the queue is not empty. The corresponding *InFetch* operation simply outputs the last event in the queue before removing it. From the previous schemas we can easily describe the output queuing system:

OutQueue
$\Delta Behavior$
$ev? : Event$

$out\_queue' = \langle ev? \rangle \frown out\_queue$
$local\_id' = local\_id - 1$

OutFetch
$\Delta Behavior$
$ev! : Event$

$out\_queue \neq \langle \rangle$
$ev! = last\ out\_queue$
$out\_queue' = front\ out\_queue$

The other operation involved in the process, *Exec*, has a more complex definition, mostly unrelated to our discussion. We will mainly retain that it serves as an interface between the input and output queuing systems, as depicted on Fig. 1. This execution phase denotes a finite sequence of four different kind of internal actions: functional action, side-effect, explicit as well as implicit event emissions. We are especially interested in the two last categories of actions concerning event communications. We will take into account that whenever an event is received and handled, then it denotes one or many resulting event emissions. This is captured by the signature $Exec \stackrel{\wedge}{=} [\Delta Behavior;\ evs! : seq\ Event]$ where all the events in *evs*! must be "passed" to *OutQueue* for effective emission.

---

[2] These simplified schemas denote unfair FIFO channels whereas our model also support alternative transport semantics with fairness restrictions.

2.3 Proof Obligations

In traditional Z-based specification methodologies, designers must conduct a set of formal proofs to verify incrementally the consistency of the system being modeled. In state/transition approaches like ours (or almost any Z-based model of our knowledge), this mostly consists in (1) *initialization theorems* to ensure that initializations preserve state invariants and (2) *precondition calculations* to enforce the consistency of the operations modifying the state space. We are mainly interested here in the potentially concurrent activation of operation schemas so that we will only address the issues concerning precondition calculations. These calculations must be done for each *Delta*-operation[3] defined on a given state. Establishing the list of all preconditions ensures that either the state invariant is completely preserved by the operation "effects" or that some other condition must be fulfilled. Depending on the context, this may lead to incrementally change the specification (by modifying the state definition) or just inform the system designers that the specification is somewhat incomplete (which occurs most of the time in complex systems where all the details cannot be taken into account).

For example, we can calculate the preconditions of *InQueue* as follows:

$$\text{pre } InQueue \Leftrightarrow \exists \, Behavior' \bullet InQueue \qquad \text{[def. of pre]}$$
$$\Leftrightarrow \exists \, in\_queue, in\_queue' : \text{seq } Event \bullet$$
$$\exists \, ev? : Event \bullet$$
$$in\_queue' = \langle ev? \rangle \frown in\_queue \qquad \text{[def. of } InQueue\text{]}$$

We use here the regular definition expansion technique to rewrite the proof obligation, using the concerned state and operation schemas. Then, we simplify our calculation by putting all conditions at the same level (i.e. removing the local existential quantifiers) and replacing the dotted variables by their values (unique point rule) to obtain the following condition:

$$\langle ev? \rangle \frown in\_queue \in \text{seq } Event$$

This is a theorem since *in_queue* is in essence a sequence of events. Consequently, there is no implicit precondition attached to the operation. The next step would be to explain what happen when the preconditions are not matched, in order to complete the operation.

3 Concurrent Control Model

As emphasized in [11] (Chap. 5), the Z notation provides great freedom regarding the operational interpretation of schemas. In consequence, any kind of system

---

[3] *Delta*-operation is our terminology for denoting an operation that modifies some system's state.

can virtually be conceived using Z-schemas. However, as time went by, the notation has been tightly connected to a well-tried methodology for the design and refinement of sequential systems.

In the previous section, we intuitively "imagine" from the state and operation schemas an operational model of our queuing system for components. The problem is that these schemas and the associated proof obligations only ensure a "correct" operationalization of the system as a sequential abstract machine. However, we are mainly concerned in our middleware research by the concurrent and distributed operationalization of such systems. Consequently, we propose in this section to somewhat change the intuitive interpretation of Z-based specifications by completing the functional requirements with a concurrent control model. This control model allows the description of *concurrent activations* of Z operations using *concurrent activation networks* represented by Petri-nets.

3.1 Petri-Nets

Using the Petri-net terminology, we find within such activation networks : *places*, *markings* (using discrete *tokens*), *transitions* and *arcs* to link the places to the transitions (and vice-versa). More formally, a Petri-net N is defined as a quadruplet $N = (P, T, Pre, Post)$ where:

- P is the set of places,
- T is the set of transitions,
- $Pre : P \times T \to \mathbb{N}$ is the function of preconditions,
- $Post : P \times T \to \mathbb{N}$ is the function of postconditions,

The *marking state* of a Petri-net is described by a vector M of naturals counting the number of tokens inside places (the vector length is hence equivalent to the number of places in the net). We distinguish the *initial* marking at time 0 since the Petri-nets will evolve discretely over time with tokens going on and through transitions from places to places. A *place marking* for place p is the integer valued function, noted $m(p)$, counting the number of tokens at place p over time.

Fig. 2 shows two simple nets with similar properties, each one of them consisting in 3 places and 4 transitions. We will now describe the top network (input processing) in more formal terms. The places and transitions are defined as follows :

- $P = \{InQueue, InLock, InFetch\}$
- $T = \{ql, qr, fl, fr\}$

The initial marking state of this net is $M_{init} = [\,0\ 1\ 0\,]$ since only the *InLock* place is marked at time 0 (i.e. $m(InLock) = 1$).

The *Pre* function explains, for each transition and each place, how many tokens must be consumed so that it can be crossed. We usually represent it as a matrix. The *Post* vector explain complementarily the number of tokens produced when a transition is crossed. In our case, they are defined as:

$$Pre = \begin{bmatrix} 1 & 0 & 0 & 0 \\ 0 & 1 & 1 & 0 \\ 0 & 0 & 0 & 1 \end{bmatrix} \quad Post = \begin{bmatrix} 0 & 1 & 0 & 0 \\ 1 & 0 & 0 & 1 \\ 0 & 0 & 1 & 0 \end{bmatrix}$$

In these matrices, transitions are aligned in columns and places in rows. Suppose for example that we want to cross transition *fl* (third column) from the initial marking. In order to find the next marking state M', we calculate:

$$M' = M_{init} - Pre_3 + Post_3 = [\,0\ 1\ 0\,] - [\,0\ 1\ 0\,] + [\,0\ 0\ 1\,] = [\,0\ 0\ 1\,]$$

Hence, after crossing transition *fl*, *InLock* "gave" its token to *InFetch*[4]. The most seducing aspect of such Petri-nets, in addition to their simplistic denotation, concerns their implicit non-deterministic behavior. We only define here a set of preconditions and postconditions for transitions, without telling which of them will or will not get crossed effectively at a certain time. This is where the non-deterministic nature of Petri-nets appear.

3.2 Activation Networks

Concurrent activation nets are introduced to design the control model of systems. They are refinements of traditional Petri-nets. We distinguish in such networks (1) the *utility* places which are standard Petri-net places and (2) the *ZPlaces* representing potential activations of operations in the Z-part of the specification. In the top network of Fig. 2, *InQueue* and *InFetch* places are *ZPlaces* whereas *InQueueLock* is a utility place. It has no direct impact on the functional specification but involves control-level changes that will have repercussions on the proof obligations.

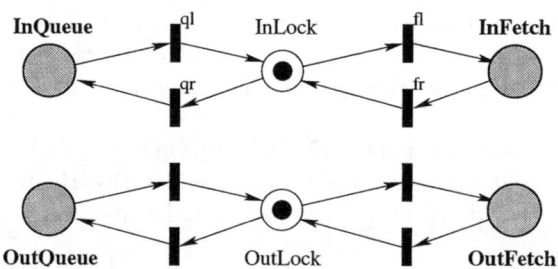

Fig. 2. Queuing phase concurrent activation networks

The basic rule of our concurrent activation network model is that if a given ZPlace contains a token, then, in the current state of the system, the corresponding operation (described by a Z schema) becomes *enabled*: its preconditions must

---

[4] Regarding the denotation, giving a token corresponds in fact to consuming a token and producing a new token.

be verifiable and the state changes it denotes (through its postconditions) must be taken into account.

For example, on the top network of Fig. 2, if the *fl* transition is crossed, then the *InFetch* operation becomes enabled so that, in Z terms, pre *InFetch* must be verifiable. We can also see that pre *InQueue* must be proven since this operation is also enabled (through transition *qr*) in the network. As a matter of fact, we can formally prove (either by simple flow analysis or, automatically, using one of the several available tools for Petri-nets analysis) on our example that the network is 1-bounded (there is at most one token in the system or $\| M \| \leq 1$) so that only one place can be marked at a certain time.

In consequence, there is no concurrency involved and no new proof obligation emerges from the given model. The case is similar for the bottom network of Fig. 2 : we can prove formally that operations *OutQueue* and *OutFetch* are *mutually exclusive*, thanks to the use of a locking mechanism (the *OutLock* places and transitions).

3.3 Concurrency Issues

The concurrent model we began to design is composed, for the moment, out of the two networks depicted on Fig. 2. Thus, these are not separated networks, they both are part of the *complete* concurrent control model of our system. Therefore, it is obvious in the resulting network that these two independent subnets are *parallel* in essence and, as so, denote concurrent activities. For example, it is likely that *InQueue* and *OutQueue* may become simultaneously enabled once the system is effectively operationalized. The same situation arises with operations *InFetch* and *OutFetch*, as well as *InQueue* and *OutFetch* and finally *InFetch* and *OutQueue*. The most important property of such concurrency constraints is that they can be automatically found using Petri-net analysis tools; the list of added proof obligations do not have to be established by hand[5].

All these concurrent activations must of course be taken into account at the functional level, under the form of new obligation proofs. For example, for operations *InQueue* and *OutQueue* to become enabled concurrently (and then noted *InQueue* $\|$ *OutQueue*), we must first calculate their independent preconditions pre *InQueue* and pre *OutQueue* but also their dependent ones which, in this case, correspond to pre (*InQueue* $\wedge$ *OutQueue*). The problem with the latter condition is that it does not capture well the postcondition effects when shared variables are involved. In that case, any order sequential composition must be established so that the generic form of the needed precondition calculation is the following one:

$$\text{pre } Op_1 \parallel Op_2 \,\widehat{=}\, \text{pre } Op_1 \wedge \text{pre } Op_2 \wedge \text{pre } (Op_1 \,\raise.2ex\hbox{$\scriptstyle\circ$}\, Op_2) \wedge \text{pre } (Op_2 \,\raise.2ex\hbox{$\scriptstyle\circ$}\, Op_1)$$

In our case, we simply have to calculate pre *InQueue* $\wedge$ pre *OutQueue* $\wedge$ pre (*InQueue* $\wedge$ *OutQueue*) since there is no postcondition sharing involved.

---

[5] Automated Petri-net analysis becomes complex and thus CPU-intensive when *model checking* is involved. As we can see in this paper, (fast) structural analysis is generally sufficent to deal with concurrent activation networks.

Moreover, we can note that both operations are also independent in term of preconditions. Hence, in that particular case : $pre\,(InQueue \land OutQueue) = pre\,InQueue \land pre\,OutQueue$. In consequence, there is no added proof obligation since we have already proven this in the functional specifications and its implicit sequential control model.

The same might be concluded about almost all the pairs of operations the two networks reference but this is not the case for the *InFetch* and *OutQueue* operations which seem to be coupled (in term of control) because of the shared *local_id* variable. The calculation of $pre\,InFetch \,\mathring{,}\, OutQueue$, when removing the details except the shared conditions leads to the following statements:

$pre\,InFetch \,\mathring{,}\, OutQueue \Rightarrow \exists\,local\_id, local\_id', local\_id'' : \mathbb{N} \bullet$
$\quad local\_id' = local\_id + 1 \land$ [from *InFetch*]
$\quad local\_id' \geq 1 \land local\_id'' = local\_id' - 1 \land$ [from *OutQueue*]
$\quad local\_id \geq 0 \land local\_id' \geq 0 \land local\_id'' \geq 0$ [*Behavior* invariant]

In order to prove the consistency of these conditions, we simply use the fact that $(local\_id \geq 0 \land local\_id' = local\_id + 1) \Rightarrow local\_id' \geq 1$.

However, the converse can not be proved that simply :

$pre\,OutQueue \,\mathring{,}\, InFetch \Rightarrow \exists\,local\_id, local\_id', local\_id'' : \mathbb{N} \bullet$
$\quad local\_id \geq 1 \land local\_id' = local\_id - 1 \land$ [from *OutQueue*]
$\quad local\_id'' = local\_id' + 1 \land$ [from *InFetch*]
$\quad local\_id \geq 0 \land local\_id' \geq 0 \land local\_id'' \geq 0$ [*Behavior* invariant]

The problem is easy to figure out: if *local_id* equals to 0, then the preconditions for *OutQueue* can not be verified. This introduces a control-level dependency between the two operations, *InFetch* having to come always before *OutQueue* when the value of the local identifier is zero. In other terms, the concurrent activation of the two functionalities can not be verified *in general*. To solve this problem, we both should try to work at the control and functional levels of our specification. At the functional level, we can use the precondition $local\_id \geq 1$ of operation *OutQueue* as a "marker" for the sequential dependency. At the control level, this would involve the connection, in some way or another, between the two activation networks, whose realization is shown in the next section.

4 Modularity and Refinement

The key aspect of our proposal is that, added to its relatively small impact on the standard Z-based methodology, it has been mainly designed to support (and, in some way, enforce) the most important methodological tools conveyed by the Z schema-based notation : *modularity* and *refinement*.

4.1 Modular Specifications

In the preceding sections, we described the activation network of the two concurrent queuing/fetching systems underlying the Comet middleware communication subtract. We haven't shown yet the reception process whose concurrent model is presented on Fig. 3.

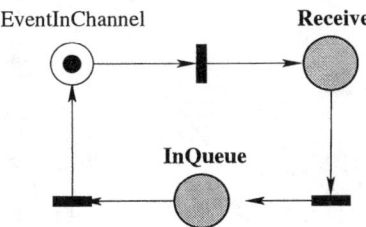

Fig. 3. Receiving phase concurrent activation network

It seems clear in this network that the *Receive* and *InQueue* operations are exclusive, the former having to be active at least once before the latter. This fact can be formally analyzed, automatically proving that for every marking m of this network, we have:

- mutual exclusion: $m(Receive) + m(InQueue) \leq 1$

Thus, we do not raise any new proof obligation using our formerly explained "discovery" method. It is now possible, from the networks of Fig. 2 and Fig. 3, with some extra information added, to deduce a global activation network, as shown on Fig. 4.

Of course, the resulting network adds some more transitions and places and is not just the concurrent composition of the modularly-defined subnetworks. The impact on the preconditions and postconditions functions is in that case purely *additive* : only *new* proof obligations may result from such assembly. Moreover, sequential proofs are particular cases (and sub-proofs) of concurrent ones so that all the local proofs will be *at least* used in the global network.

Table 1 summarizes all the proof obligations we finally raised using our method on the network shown on Fig. 4. Network invariants are obtained by classical flow analysis and lead to a set of inequalities. Two scenarios are also possible:

1. Atomic activations: there is only one possible mark for a set of places (first part of our table), so only one place in this set could be activated, which means that only one operation may be activated at a given time. In that case, all we have to do is to calculate each operation preconditions separately and merge them ($\wedge$ operator).

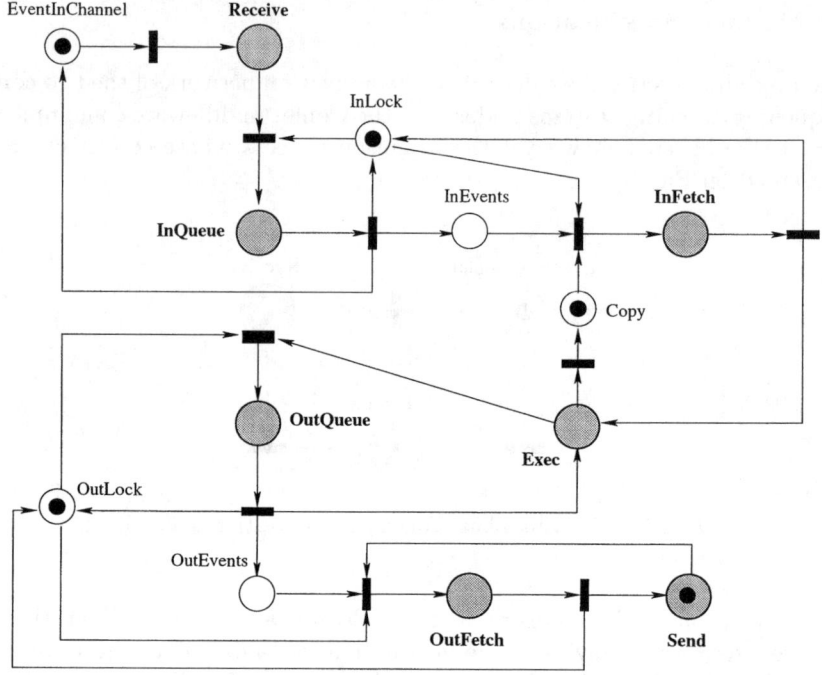

Fig. 4. Complete concurrent activation

2. Concurrent activations: there are multiple marks for a set of places (rest of the table), so several places could be activated, which means that several operations may become enabled simultaneously. In that case, we can't separate each operation preconditions evaluation.

At the functional level, the only impact of the activation networks concerns the new proof obligations. If a precondition calculus leaves holes in the specification, then this can lead to the modification of some functional aspect. However, except in the case of particularly inadequate specifications (regarding concurrency), only local state or operation schema modifications will be required to meet the concurrency model (e.g. synchronizations variables, timestamps, etc.). It is our belief that the general structure of the specification will be, most of the time, preserved even if the functional and control-level requirements are addressed separately (which should not be, in our opinion, the standard process).

Another interesting result we can draw out of the analysis of the whole activation network is that if there is only one event in the system, then the *InFetch* and *OutQueue* cannot be activated simultaneously. In simple terms, it is obvious that in order to have one token in the *OutQueue* ZPlace, then it has to be the "one" which "passed" through *InFetch* and *Exec* before. More formally, we can prove (automatically) that:

$$\| M \| \leq 4 \Rightarrow m(InFetch) + m(OutQueue) \leq 1$$

Table 1. Concurrent activation proofs

Network invariant	Proof obligation
Atomic activations	
$m(Receive) + m(InQueue) \leq 1$	pre $Receive \land$ pre $InQueue$
$m(InQueue) + m(InFetch) \leq 1$	pre $InQueue \land$ pre $InFetch$
$m(InFetch) + m(Exec) \leq 1$	pre $InFetch \land$ pre $Exec$
$m(OutQueue) + m(OutFetch) \leq 1$	pre $OutFetch$
$m(OutFetch) + m(Send) \leq 1$	pre $Send$
Concurrent activations	
$m(Receive) + m(InFetch) \leq 2$	pre $(Receive \parallel InFetch)$
$m(Receive) + m(Exec) \leq 2$	pre $(Receive \parallel Exec)$
$m(Receive) + m(OutQueue) \leq 2$	pre $(Receive \parallel OutQueue)$
$m(Receive) + m(Send) \leq 2$	pre $(Receive \parallel Send)$
$m(InQueue) + m(Exec) \leq 2$	pre $(InQueue \parallel Exec)$
$m(InQueue) + m(OutQueue) \leq 2$	pre $(InQueue \parallel OutQueue)$
$m(InQueue) + m(Send) \leq 2$	pre $(InQueue \parallel Send)$
$m(InFetch) + m(OutFetch) \leq 2$	pre $(InFetch \parallel OutFetch)$
$m(InFetch) + m(OutQueue) \leq 2$	pre $(InFetch \parallel OutQueue)$
$m(InFetch) + m(Send) \leq 2$	pre $(InFetch \parallel Send)$
$m(Exec) + m(Send) \leq 2$	pre $(InFetch \parallel Send)$
$m(OutQueue) + m(Send) \leq 2$	pre $(OutQueue \parallel Send)$

This invariant shows that the "unexpected" precondition we calculated at the end of Sect. 3.3, $local\_id \geq 1$, is "satisfied" by the above invariant if there is only one event in the system (which was the conflicting issue).

4.2 Refinement

The Z notation generally denotes a top-down specification process from abstract models of requirements to the resulting implementation of the system. The mediation of a *refinement calculus* allows this incremental implementation of the specified system. Refinement, in the case of Z, can be used to produce more concrete states and/or operations from more abstract ones. [11] is in our opinion a good source of information for the use of refinement in the framework of the Z notation and tools.

An important aspect of state or operation refinements is that they generally concern a reduced set of well localized schemas so that, once again, the modularity of the specification at the more abstract level is not put into question by the refinement needs. In our case, the main consequence is that the added proof obligations regarding a given activation network remain the same but must be redone in two situations:

1. The proof obligation references an operation that has a new refined version, or
2. the state referenced by the operation has been itself refined.

Unsurprisingly, this has some impact on the proof part of the specification. First, the refinement proofs must be conducted, which is in its own a complex process. Thereafter, concurrently activable operations must be checked against the refined state. We do think, however, that the overall structure of the specification remains unchanged in the refinement case. The operations preserve, in a way, their "locality" in the model so that the rules for concurrent activability do still apply in the refined case. Without an explicit denotation for the interface between the functional and control models, it is however necessary to consider the refined cases as "fresh" ones.

On the concurrent side, it is of course possible to refine an activation network to match the refined functional requirements. In the case of our middleware system, we propose various refinements. We will describe in this section an alternative *multi-session* behavior model for components. A multi-session controlled component allows internal concurrency, which means in our system the parallel handling of events. At the functional level, this leads to both the refinement of the component *Behavior* schema, as well as of most of the operations involved in the process of input and output events. For example, the following schema denotes the refinement of the main state schema:

$$
\begin{array}{l}
\underline{MSessionBehavior} \\
Behavior \\
ssessions : (TYPE \times IDENTIFIER) \nrightarrow MSession \\
gsessions : TYPE \nrightarrow MSession \\
\hline
\#(\text{ran } ssessions) + \#(\text{ran } gsessions) \leq MSession\_max \\
\forall\, s : \text{dom } ssessions \bullet \exists\, in : in\_channels \bullet \\
\quad \exists\, ct : in.type \bullet \{first(s) \mapsto ct\} \subseteq subtype \wedge second(s) = in.id
\end{array}
$$

This new state schema refines the more abstract *Behavior* state by adding concurrent sessions, either *specific* or *generic*, in the event management system. Specific sessions distinguish event sources and types whether generic ones only use event types (and are thus shared by all sources). Without going in too detailed explanations, the intention here is that if an event of the given type (or a subtype[6]) is received and if the source matches (specific sessions only), then it will be processed concurrently. There exists several sub-state schemas to define this whole state refinement. We will only give the *MSession* state which describes a local session:

---

[6] The subtyping relation we use is a relation *subtype* whose signature is $\mathbb{P}\, TYPE \times TYPE$.

$SESSION\_TYPE ::= specific \mid generic \mid none$

```
┌─────────────────────────────
│ EmptySession : MSession
├─────────────────────────────
│ EmptySession.stype = none
```

```
┌──── MSession ────────────────
│ stype : SESSION_TYPE
│ in_queue : seq Event
│ out_queue : seq Event
```

```
┌─────────────────────────────
│ MSession_max : ℕ
├─────────────────────────────
│ MSession_max = 10
```

These schemas show that sessions are composed out of a categorical type (either *specific*, *generic* or *none*) as well as an independent pair of queuing systems. Using this refinement (easily promoted to the independant global behavior), we can provide session-specific versions of the event management facilities such as the input queuing phase:

```
┌──── MSessionInQueueSession ────
│ ΔMSession
│ event? : Event
│ session? : MSession
├────────────────────────────────
│ session? ≠ EmptySession
│ in_queue' = ⟨event?⟩ ⌢ in_queue
│ out_queue' = out_queue
```

```
┌──── MSessionInQueueDefault ────
│ Receive
│ ΞMSession
│ session? : MSession
├────────────────────────────────
│ session? = EmptySession
```

The left schema describes the case when an event is matched positively with a session so that it is handled specifically (i.e. in parallel). When it is not matched, then the *MSessionInQueueDefault* operation tells the system the event has to be processed at a higher state level than the session one. There are of course several new proof obligations raised by this refinement of the more abstract specification. But we know from the previous sections how to find them.

There is however one aspect we haven't yet given a real meaning: the concurrent handling of event in sessions. We only shown yet functional support for concurrency but the concurrent model itself lacks concurrency. Our proposal here is to refine this concurrent model, giving a refinement of the more abstract activation network of Fig. 4. For clarity, we only show the result in term of input queuing, fetching and dispatch on Fig. 5.

We introduce here a way to link the functional and concurrent models more tightly using natural number globals. The *MSession_max* variable (which has of course to be a natural) is related to the homonymous place (called an *NPlace* in our terminology) of the activation network. The trivial network invariant $m(MSessionInQueueSession) \leq m(MSession\_max)$ induces that the *MSessionInQueueSession* operation in the functional specification can be simultaneously activated N times (if the marking is exactly N). That is, multiple instances of the same operations may be active at a certain time. It is of course

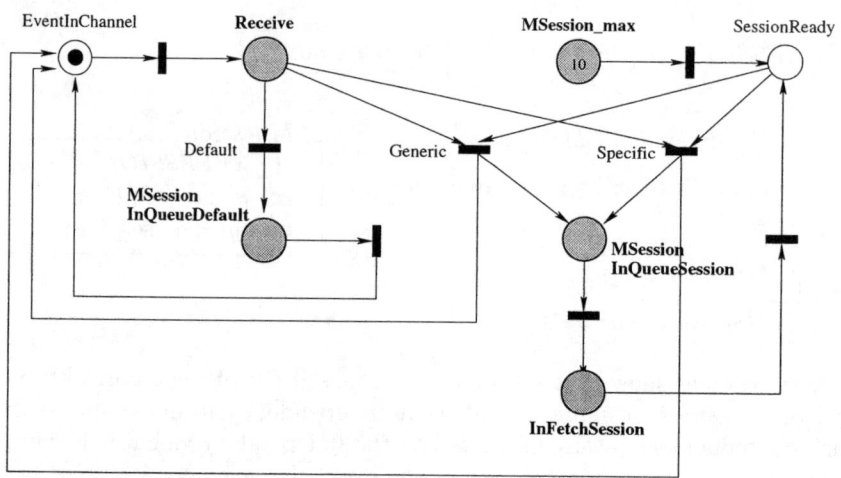

Fig. 5. Refined activation network (input only)

insufficient to prove that one activated instance fulfills the invariant requirements. We denote each different activation of the same operation by an integer subscript so that we have to check the following concurrent activation:

$$InQueueSession_1 \parallel InQueueSession_2 \parallel ... \parallel InQueueSession_N$$

From the local point of view, each instance of the operation takes is own state as the *session?* variable. They are thus completely independent with each other for any given session (i.e. the scope of $\Delta MSession$ is local) so that finally, no new proof obligation is needed in this particular case.

Let us now consider the *InFetchSession* operation and an extract of its promotion to the global state:

$$\begin{array}{|l}\hline \_InFetchSession_____ \\ \Delta MSession \\ ev! : Event \\ \hline in\_queue \neq \langle\rangle \\ ev! = last\ in\_queue \\ in\_queue' = front\ in\_queue \\ \hline \end{array}$$

$$\begin{array}{|l}\hline \_InFetchSessionPromote\_\_\_\_\_ \\ \Delta Behavior \\ \hline local\_id' = local\_id + 1 \\ \hline \end{array}$$

Here, we see that the promoted operation has an impact on the local identifier. So, it is not so simple to prove the consistency of:

$$InFetchSession_1 \parallel InFetchSession_2 \parallel ... \parallel InFetchSession_N$$

However, all sequential interleaving of these concurrent activations only concern the shared *local_id* variable and thus denote the following condition:

$\exists \, local\_id : \mathbb{N} \bullet$
$\quad (\exists \, local\_id_1 : \mathbb{N} \bullet local\_id_1 = local\_id + 1 \wedge local\_id_1 \geq 1) \wedge$
$\quad \ldots \wedge$
$\quad (\exists \, local\_id_N : \mathbb{N} \bullet local\_id_N = local\_id_{N-1} + 1 \wedge local\_id_N \geq N)$

It is not difficult to see that this is a theorem, but this clearly shows that the concurrency point of view has, as expected, some repercussions on the process to establish the consistency of the system, if compared to the standard sequential point of view.

5 Related Work

To our knowledge, while there exist specifications of concurrent programs in Z, there were only few attempts to address concurrency issues from a methodological point of view. Most of the time, concurrency proofs must be established completely by hand which is a tedious practice. Predicative notation has been integrated with Z in [7] to allow the design of concurrent and communicating protocols as well as deriving proof methods for concurrent aspects. Despite the interesting results of this approach, its use of a somewhat new and not very spread extension language may explain its relatively reduced impact on the Z community. Combinations of process algebras with Z [3] or Object-Z , as in TCOZ [6], seem to have received more audience. These approaches integrates fine-grain parallelism constructs (as found in CSP and CCS) with state-based functional specifications. Of course, the impact of the extra-features for concurrency and communication on the full-featured Z notation (or object-oriented extensions) is important. New and somewhat complex design and proof techniques must be introduced. This also reveals that concurrency is in essence a cross-cutting concern in presence of complex functional requirements. We diverge here since our concurrent constructs (activation networks) do not belong to the functional specification; they are kept separate. Therefore, the concurrency issues are designed (and partially verified) independently, which is not the case with integration techniques. Moreover, we do not introduce communication since we focus on shared-memory models. We then think process algebras may be used complementarily for aspects dealing with distribution.

The first attempt to bring closer the Z and Petri-net languages seems to be [5]. In order to preserve the advantages of both formal methods in their respective domains (in our opinion complex functional requirements on one side and complex concurrent models on the other side), the authors propose to maintain a synchronized model in both languages. The synchronizations points are transitions of the Petri-net which are associated to operation schemas so that the state of both specifications can be synchronized (the transitions are the same). Some proof techniques can be derived from this model but it seems difficult to maintain a clean separation at that level. Moreover, the Petri-nets can become very large because they have to reflect properly the functional requirements expressed in the Z part of the model. In our approach, we wanted to limit as much as possible the size of the networks (so that automated proof could be conducted as often as possible) and also limit the impact of the concurrent aspects on the specification. Thus, we only model activation rules in the network —as synchronized places— whereas functional requirements are only expressed in the Z part of the specification. The impact is then restricted to the proof level because concurrent activations only denote new proof obligations.

6 Conclusion

We have presented in this study a method we employed in a *real*, middle-sized software development process to support the traditional Z formal method when *concurrency* is involved. The first contributing aspect of our approach is its focus on having a minimal impact on the notation and method itself. We do not extend the schema-based notation and only add one operator for precondition calculations of concurrently enabled operations. In consequence, the full power of Z can be used to model the functional requirements of the systems, namely its state and operations. Modularity and support for refinement are not compromised and can be freely used.

However, concurrent systems are *in essence* different (and somewhat more complex) from sequential ones. Hence, an expressive and efficient (i.e. easily analyzable) language to model concurrency is needed. We think that Z-extensions for concurrency, despite their interest, are more complex and more intrusive than ours. Our contribution, here, is not to propose a new language (or extension) but simply to *reuse* an existing and widely spread language, *specifically aimed* at modeling concurrent systems, namely Petri-nets. We only show how to interpret such networks in the framework of the Z method. This allows system designers to inherit a large palette of tools for automated invariant calculations as well as work from a large and well established community.

The clean separation between functional and control-level concerns, as proposed by this hybrid formal method, also ensures that the concurrent activation networks remain "manageable". By removing all the purely functional aspects of the specifications, we limit in great proportions the state-space of the Petri-nets so that the usual analysis tools can be used even in the case of fairly complex specifications. In our case study, we only manipulated low-level Petri-nets with arcs of weight 1 and sizes of never more than dozens of places and transitions. Of course, our confidence in the resulting concurrent system must be tempered by the fact we conducted all Z proofs by hand.

This points out the main drawback of our approach: we support the automated analysis of the concurrent side of the model only. Some automation can be obtained at the functional-level of the specification, using existing Z-based tools. But at the interface between the two models, synchronization is done by hand. Moreover, the denotation of this interface is not easy to figure out, given the different essence of set-based theories (underlying Z proofs) and linear algebras (Petri-net analysis). Our approach here was to give a simple denotation of Petri-nets using the Z notation. But in order to obtain a complete and consistent denotation, we should be able to conduct all the proofs using the same framework, a task hardly manageable in our opinion. For example, it is arguable that despite the fact that our network are dead-lock and live-lock free, the Z schemas themselves can introduce functional-level dependencies that have an impact in term of concurrency. This, however, will be exposed when concurrent activation proofs will be conducted, resulting in new preconditions. And so forth, we surely cannot use automation tools at that level. But in practice, the pragmatic point of view we conveyed throughout the experiment led to an operational system, fulfilling our requirements; this showing that the method, if not mature, is valuable.

References

1. G. Agha. *Actors: A Model of Concurrent Computation in Distributed Systems.* Series in Artificial Intelligence. MIT Press, 1986.
2. J.-P. Briot. *Actalk: a Testbed for Classifying and Designing Actor Languages in the Smalltalk-80 Environment.* In S. Cook, editor, *Proceedings of ECOOP'89*, pages 109–129. Cambridge University Press, July 1989.
3. C. Fischer. How to combine z with a process algebra. In *Proceedings of ZUM'98*, volume LNCS 1493. Springer-Verlag, September 1998.
4. M. Heiner. Petri net based system analysis without state explosion. In *Proceedings of High Performance Computing'98*, April 1998.
5. M. Heiner and M. Heisel. Modeling safety-critical systems with z and petri-nets. In *Proceedings of Computer Safety, Reliability and Security*, volume LNCS 1698. Springer-Verlag, 1999.
6. B. Mahony and J. S. Dong. Timed communicating object z. *IEEE Transactions on Software Engineering*, 26(2):150–177, 2000.
7. R. F. Paige. Specification and refinement using a heterogeneous notation for concurrency and communication. Technical report, York University, October 1998.
8. F. Peschanski. A reflective middleware architecture for adaptive, component-based disitrubted systems. *IEEE DS Online*, 1(7), 2001.
9. F. Peschanski. A versatile event-based communication model for generic distributed interactions. In *Proceedings of DEBS'02 (ICDCS International Workshop on Distributed Event-based Systems)*. IEEE, July 2002.
10. J. L. Peterson. *Petri Net Theory and the Modeling of Systems.* Prentice-Hall, 1981.
11. J. M. Spivey. *The Z Notation: a reference manual.* http://spivey.oriel.ox.ac.uk/~mike/zrm/, 2001.

How to Diagnose a Modern Car with a Formal B Model?

Guilhem Pouzancre

ClearSy, Europarc de Pichaury, 1330 Av. J.R. G. Gautier de la Lauziere,
F-13856 Aix-en-Provence Cedex 3, France
guilhem.pouzancre@clearsy.com

1 Introduction

We introduce a modern method to diagnose vehicles. The method has been studied for Automobiles Peugeot. The classical methods to diagnose a car are based on technician's experience and failure knowledge (e.g., diagnostic trees). However cars become more and more complex and failures less and less predictable.

The modern cars are increasingly complex due to electronic components and services: lights and wipers turn on automatically, engine controller manages efficiently the torque and car radio manages the sound depending on the car speed.

Therefore, diagnostic of deficient components is complex, because of the car complexity and distributed functionalities: for example wheel sensors deficiency can induce effects on the car radio. On the other hand, deficiencies are mostly unpredictable, due to a wide variety of suppliers, car options and the short component life-cycle. Furthermore, garage mechanics have to diagnose bugs, which are, by definition, unpredictable.

However, all failures have a similar characteristic: a functional component does not respect its nominal specification. In our diagnosis method, event B models formalize the nominal functional specification and a B model interpreter (BI) checks which component does not match its specification.

To diagnose a car with this method we need:

- Correct and complete description of every vehicle component (vehicle B model)
- A rigourous link between the concrete car and the B models (dictionaries)
- A method to compare the components behaviour with their specification (record analysis)

2 Vehicle B Model

We build the vehicle model with the event B method, because BI requires a non-ambiguous language and automatic proofs. Moreover, refinement and proof obligations guide model engineers in building corrects models. The model only addresses the nominal behaviour of the components.

A car is described by 50 B models, 7000 events and 2000 abstract variables. Actually 98 percent of the proof obligations are discharged automatically, but invariant and abstract models are weak, so the correctness of the model is not suffisant to make a fully automatic diagnostic. Anymay progress in this way.

We build independent models for each vehicle component, because the vehicle component is the smallest unit of repair. Thus BI will signal defects at the smallest granularity that is relevant for repairing.

3 Dictionaries

To find the deficient component, BI compares vehicle parameters with abstract B variables and abstract B events. This comparison is possible only if a link is specified with a rigorous precision.

So, first, we introduce the notion of *observable parameters* of vehicle components. These parameters correspond to physical measures or input values that are relevant to a description of the component behaviour. Their value can be either quantitative (e.g., car speed) or qualitative (e.g., "Normal", "Absent", "Important").

Their counterpart in the B model are some variable declarations. The dictionary gives an informal but rigorous definition for those B variables. That definition describes the link between the variable value and some observable parameter value. Moreover, those definitions must be such that from any set of observable parameter values, one can either deduce the values of the B variables or conclude that the vehicle is deficient.

In addition, the event dictionary is used to synchronise the observable parameters evolution with the B variable evolution. We define an event with observable parameters value. A B event definition sounds like: "B event Alert occurs when the oil temperature gets above 120°".

BI uses the variable and event definitions to compare the evolution of observable parameters with the B model, which specify the expected evolution.

4 Record Analysis

It would take too much time to check all components in all contexts. Therefore, the technician reproduces the failure effect in a scenario. BI would then record all concrete event occurence and observable parameter values continually during the scenario (vehicle recording). BI would use the technician observations for subjective and non-recorded parameters.

But, it would still take too much time and resources to record all observable parameter values, so we defined specific rules to deduce, from the B event guard and body, the significant variables, and thus a list of parameters to record. This point is very important because B models allow to differentiate simulation (which needs to affect a value for each parameter) and animation (which only asks the value of relevant parameters).

To diagnose the deficient components, BI checks the vehicle recording. BI searches abnormal observable parameter values, unexpected B variable modifications or unexpected component reactions.

BI finds abnormal observable parameters value when the variable definition specifies a deficient situation. It finds an unexpected B variable modification when a B variable value changes but no concrete event is recorded. An unexpected component reaction corresponds to the case where an event is recorded but its guard is false or its substitution does not match to the evolution of observable parameters.

5 Conclusion

Currently, two vehicles have been fully modeled and a third is being worked on. The BI theory has been completely studied and it is owned by PSA.

Intermediate tools and methods have been derived from that theory to assist Peugeot expert to define diagnosis tests. The B models (translated into french) are also used everyday by the experts of the second level hotline of PSA.

Some more investigation is particularily needed in the following directions:

- Reduce the development cost of B models.
- Increase the B models correctness.
- Implement BI as an integrated application.

In the end, the use of the B interpreter will allow garage employees to diagnose directly hidden causes of failure and bugs, thus reducing the burden on the second level experts.

Parallel Hardware Design in B

Stefan Hallerstede*

KeesDA, 2, avenue de Vignate, 38610 Gières, France
stefan@keesda.com

We present the design of a parallel synchronous hardware component from a purely functional description of its behaviour. Starting from an abstract specification of a linear time-invariant (LTI) system in Event-B a pipelined implementation is developed. The presented approach is applicable to LTI systems that can be represented as linear constant-coefficient difference equations.

In the development of embedded systems space requirements and performance of used circuits are often the two most important constraints. To achieve high performance a high degree of parallelism is needed. At the same time, space requirements demand the use of as few components as possible. In this study we show how the B method may be used to design systems that meet these requirements. We use a variant of the B method called Event-B. Event-B has been conceived particularly for the modelling of abstract systems. Such systems are closed in the sense that they do not interact with some kind of environment. The environment is part of the specification. Event-B has been used to construct proved circuits [1]. We follow a similar approach in this study.

The target of the development process we propose is a synchronous circuit. A synchronous circuit is executed in units of clock cycles. During each cycle it reads input values a, produces output values b, and changes its state which is invisible to its environment (see figure 1). One way to specify such a system is to

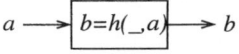

Fig. 1. Schema of a Synchronous Circuit

state a stream of input values, $x(n)$, and a stream of output values, $y(n)$, and a relationship $R(x, y)$ between them (see figure 2) as customary in signal processing [3]. It may be counterproductive to think of n as a time index though this

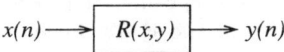

Fig. 2. Specification of a Discrete System

---

* We acknowledge the support of the EU (IST-2000-30103) for the PUSSEE project (project homepage: http://www.keesda.com/pussee/).

may be the case in some models. In signal processing, index n is usually referred to as time. Time may then also represent spatial coordinates, for instance. It is admissible if R relates an input value $x(n+k)$, $k > 0$, to an output value $y(n)$. There is however no guarantee that an implementation of such a system is feasible, i.e. there may exist no physical implementation of the system. Starting from $R(x, y)$ one can construct a circuit as shown in figure 1 for which x and y (read as sequences of values) satisfy in some sense $R(x, y)$. The use of sequences (or streams) to specify hardware components is not new (see e.g. [2,3]). In fact, it is a standard model in discrete-time signal processing [3]. Our contribution is the formal construction of a circuit beginning with a specification in terms of streams. Thus, the resulting circuit is proven to satisfy $R(x, y)$. The relation $R(x, y)$ may be specified like this:

$$y[1\mathinner{.\,.} N{-}1] = \{0\} \wedge$$
$$\forall n \cdot (n \geq N \Rightarrow y(n) = \sum j \cdot (j \in 0\mathinner{.\,.} N{-}1 \mid x(n{-}j)*v(j)) - w*y(n{-}1))$$

where v, w are weights and $N > 1$ is a constant. The resulting description of the circuit in B after the recomposition of the events that model the circuit is shown below. The state of the circuit is modelled by the variables rs, cn, and rz which correspond to hardware registers.

```
BEGIN
    FORALL r WHERE
        r ∈ 1 .. N
    THEN
        rs(r) := rs(r−1) + a*v(N−r)
    END;
    ss := rs(N);
    IF cn > 0 THEN
        rz, cn := 0, cn−1
    ELSE
        rz := ss − w*rz
    END;
    b := rz
END
```

References

1. Jean-Raymond Abrial. Event Driven Electronic Circuit Construction, 2001. http://www.matisse.qinetiq.com/links.htm.
2. Max Fuchs and Michael Mendler. A Functional Semantics for Delta-Delay VHDL Based on FOCUS. In C. D. Kloos and P. T. Breuer, editors, *Formal Semantics for VHDL*, pages 9–42. Kluwer Academic Publishers, 1995.
3. Alan V. Oppenheim and Ronald W. Schafer. *Discrete-Time Signal Processing*. Prentice Hall Signal Processing Series. Prentice Hall, Englewood Cliffs, NJ, USA, 1989.

Operation Refinement and Monotonicity in the Schema Calculus

Moshe Deutsch[1], Martin C. Henson[1], and Steve Reeves[2]

[1] Department of Computer Science, University of Essex, UK.
[2] Department of Computer Science, University of Waikato, New Zealand.
{mdeuts, hensm}@essex.ac.uk, stever@cs.waikato.ac.nz

Abstract. The schema calculus of Z provides a means for expressing structured, modular specifications. Extending this modularity to program development requires the monotonicity of these operators with respect to refinement. This paper provides a thorough mathematical analysis of monotonicity with respect to four schema operations for three notions of operation refinement. The mathematical connection between the equational schema logic and monotonicity is discussed and evaluated.

1 Introduction

One of the most important characteristics of Z is the facility it offers to structure large scale specifications in a modular fashion from smaller components using the wide spectrum of schema calculus operators [20,26,4].

Stepwise design from an initial abstract formal specification is an underlying notion of formal program development. It is known by different terms in the software engineering literature, one of which is the *transformational software process model*, in which design decisions are gradually incorporated into the initial abstract mathematical specification of the system, deriving a more concrete specification at each level. This process is also known as *refinement*.

Refinement in Z is discussed, for example, in [4,26,19,8]. However, none of this work successfully combines the modularity Z offers together with refinement. Consequently, refinement takes place on operations expressed as a single schema: the schema calculus operators are removed (essentially by using an equational logic) before applying refinement. The reason, as is quite well-known, is that the Z schema calculus has poor monotonicity properties, with respect to refinement, in the standard partial relational model for schemas. As a consequence many authors have developed case studies in Z without employing refinement at all (*e.g.* [12]) or hoping that their work will underlie software development using verification techniques (*e.g.* [16]). Other authors have addressed this by proposing methods for transforming Z specifications into fully monotonic frameworks such as Morgan's refinement calculus (*e.g.* [17,25,2,3]) or other notations based on Dijkstra's guarded command language (*e.g.* [27]); unfortunately, these require either the elimination of the schema operators prior to the process or the utilisation of exceedingly strong sideconditions. Others advocate substituting Z with a more powerful version of refinement calculus, which enriches the language with

Z-like specification constructors in order to equip it with modularity capabilities (*e.g.* [23,18,9]); ironically, the major disadvantage of this method is that, in many cases, the additional specification constructors re-introduce non-monotonicity. A radically different approach is taken in [14] and [15], where the semantics of both operation schemas (but not state schemas) and the schema calculus is modified in order to attain a language that is both modular and fully monotonic with respect to refinement. This yields a Z-like system in which, however, the schema operators no longer express exactly their usual informal semantics. Unlike the other methods discussed above, this work takes place entirely within the specification language and its logic.

In this paper, we undertake a comprehensive analysis of the monotonicity properties of four standard schema calculus operators, each of which is investigated with respect to three notions of operation refinement in Z (section 2). Unlike [14] and [15], this paper pursues its investigation of monotonicity in Z as it is informally understood in, for example, [20] and [26]. Such an investigation becomes possible in virtue of the logic for Z reported in, for example, [13] and a novel and simple technique of rendering all the theories of refinement in a proof-theoretic form: as sets of introduction and elimination rules. This leads to a uniform and simple method for proving the various monotonicity results in section 3.

A related analysis was presented in [10]. That investigation was fairly informal and was not extended beyond an analysis of monotonicity for schema conjunction and schema disjunction with respect to refinement. Section 3 also explores schema existential hiding and schema composition in this context. Additionally, some of the sideconditions used in [10] for attaining monotonicity are very strong. We improve on that, following a consideration of both intuitive and mathematical investigations.

We provide some essential notational conventions in appendix A[1] and a complete formal account of the precondition of compound operations in appendix B; this is an important precursor to the mathematical investigation presented in section 3. Our paper concludes with a summary and an agenda for further investigation (section 4).

2 Operation Refinement

Operation refinement concerns the derivation of a more concrete operation from a given abstract one, without changing the specification of the underlying state. It is sometimes called *algorithm design* [27]. The partial relation semantics of operation schemas in Z raises an immediate question: what does it mean for one operation schema to refine another? More generally: what does it mean for one partial relation to refine another? The standard answer involves some sort of lifted-totalisation of the underlying partial relations (see *e.g.* [26] and [4]). In [5] it is shown that the relational completion notion is equivalent to various other

---

[1] This is included for convenience. The reader may need to consult our previous work ([13] and [5]) in order to fully understand our notational and meta-notational conventions.

approaches, one of which, S-refinement (and its relatives), is much simpler and more intuitive. Therefore, in this paper we shall work entirely within the simpler S-refinement framework. This permits us to work directly with the language, rather than with a semantic interpretation (lifted totalised relations) involving additional semantic elements.

We begin by introducing[2] three distinct notions of operation refinement in Z, based on three distinct answers to the questions above.

2.1 S-Refinement

In this section, we introduce a pure proof theoretic characterisation of refinement, which is closely connected to sufficient refinement conditions introduced by Spivey (hence "S"-refinement) in, for example, [20] and as discussed in [17, 19,27,26].

This notion is based on two basic observations regarding the properties one expects in a refinement: first, that a refinement may involve the reduction of nondeterminism; second, that it may also involve the expansion of the domain of definition. Put another way, we have a refinement providing that *postconditions do not weaken* (we do not permit an increase in nondeterminism in a refinement) and that *preconditions do not strengthen* (we do not permit requirements in the domain of definition to disappear in a refinement).

This notion can be captured by forcing the refinement relation to hold *exactly* when these conditions apply. S-refinement is written $U_0 \sqsupseteq_s U_1$ (U_0 S-refines U_1) and is given by the definition that leads directly to the following rules:

Proposition 1. *Let z, z_0, z_1 be fresh variables.*

$$\frac{Pre\ U_1\ z \vdash Pre\ U_0\ z \quad Pre\ U_1\ z_0, z_0 \star z_1' \in U_0 \vdash z_0 \star z_1' \in U_1}{U_0 \sqsupseteq_s U_1} \ (\sqsupseteq_s^+)$$

$$\frac{U_0 \sqsupseteq_s U_1 \quad Pre\ U_1\ t}{Pre\ U_0\ t} \ (\sqsupseteq_{s_o}^-) \qquad \frac{U_0 \sqsupseteq_s U_1 \quad Pre\ U_1\ t_0 \quad t_0 \star t_1' \in U_0}{t_0 \star t_1' \in U_1} \ (\sqsupseteq_{s_1}^-)$$

□

We prove in [5] and [6] that S-refinement is equivalent to other characterisations of refinement, such as $W_\bullet$-refinement based on Woodcock's *chaotic* relational completion model (see, for example, [26] and [4]). As we remarked above, S-refinement deals directly with the language, rather than indirectly in terms of an interpretation as a (lifted-totalised) relation, and is therefore a simpler both as a theory and in terms of the analysis we undertake.

---
[2] We provide some notational conventions and the notion of *precondition* in appendix A.

2.2 SP-Refinement

This is an alternative proof theoretic characterisation of refinement, which is closely connected to refinement in the *behavioural* [4] or *firing condition* [21] approach. This special case of S-refinement may involve reduction of nondeterminism but insists on the *stability of the precondition* during the refinement step. SP-refinement is written $U_0 \sqsupseteq_{sp} U_1$ and is given by the definition that leads directly to the following rules:

Proposition 2. *Let z, z_0, z_1 be fresh variables.*

$$\frac{Pre\ U_1\ z \vdash Pre\ U_0\ z \quad z_0 \star z_1' \in U_0 \vdash z_0 \star z_1' \in U_1}{U_0 \sqsupseteq_{sp} U_1} \ (\sqsupseteq_{sp}^+)$$

$$\frac{U_0 \sqsupseteq_{sp} U_1 \quad Pre\ U_1\ t}{Pre\ U_0\ t} \ (\sqsupseteq_{sp_0}^-) \qquad \frac{U_0 \sqsupseteq_{sp} U_1 \quad t_0 \star t_1' \in U_0}{t_0 \star t_1' \in U_1} \ (\sqsupseteq_{sp_1}^-)$$

□

Likewise, we show in [6] that SP-refinement is equivalent to other characterisations of refinement. For example, $W_\square$-refinement is based on the *abortive* relational completion model, as discussed in [1] and [4].

2.3 SC-Refinement

SC-refinement is our third alternative proof theoretic characterisation of refinement. It is written $U_0 \sqsupseteq_{sc} U_1$ and is given by the definition that leads directly to the following rules:

Proposition 3. *Let z_0, z_1 be fresh variables*

$$\frac{z_0 \star z_1' \in U_1 \vdash z_0 \star z_1' \in U_0 \quad Pre\ U_1\ z_0, z_0 \star z_1' \in U_0 \vdash z_0 \star z_1' \in U_1}{U_0 \sqsupseteq_{sc} U_1} \ (\sqsupseteq_{sc}^+)$$

$$\frac{U_0 \sqsupseteq_{sc} U_1 \quad t_0 \star t_1' \in U_1}{t_0 \star t_1' \in U_0} \ (\sqsupseteq_{sc_0}^-) \qquad \frac{U_0 \sqsupseteq_{sc} U_1 \quad Pre\ U_1\ t_0 \quad t_0 \star t_1' \in U_0}{t_0 \star t_1' \in U_1} \ (\sqsupseteq_{sc_1}^-)$$

□

Lemma 1. *The following extra rule is derivable for SC-refinement:*

$$\frac{U_0 \sqsupseteq_{sc} U_1 \quad Pre\ U_1\ t}{Pre\ U_0\ t}$$

□

SC-refinement is introduced for technical reasons which inform the analysis to follow. This notion, in which the precondition may weaken, but in which the postcondition is stable, is not otherwise of much pragmatic interest.

3 Combining Operation Refinement with the Schema Calculus

A schema calculus operator is monotonic with respect to refinement if the schema expression denoted by its application to the individual (and independent) refinements of each of its arguments constitutes a refinement of the entire schema expression.

It is well known that, and in contrast to other paradigms such as the refinement calculus and even B, the most powerful characteristic of Z, as a specification language, is its potential for expressing modular specifications using schema operators. In order to properly take advantage of modularity, in particular to undertake specification refinement, it is vital that the various schema operators of the language are monotonic: when monotonicity holds, the components of a composite specification can be refined independently of the rest of the specification [10]. Refinement can also then be performed in a modular manner. Unfortunately it is well known that the Z schema calculus operators have very poor monotonicity properties. This has a major effect on their usefulness in the context of program development from Z specifications.

In this section, we analyse the monotonicity properties of four of the most interesting schema calculus operators[3] (conjunction, disjunction, existential hiding and composition) with respect to each one of the refinement theories presented in section 2. We provide informal intuitions and examples of monotonicity or non-monotonicity in each case. Additionally, we establish a formal account which enables us to employ several sideconditions as "healthiness conditions" of the specification, in order to attain monotonicity. Furthermore, we discuss the usefulness of these sideconditions in the context of the various refinement theories we consider.

3.1 Refinement for Conjunction

We do not get an introduction rule for the precondition of conjoined operations (see section B.1). Consequently, schema conjunction is *not monotonic* with respect to S-refinement.

Here is a counterexample. Consider the following schemas:

$$U_0 \mathrel{\hat=} [\,x, x' : \mathbb{N} \mid x' = 8\,] \quad U_1 \mathrel{\hat=} [\,x, x' : \mathbb{N} \mid x' < 10\,] \quad U_2 \mathrel{\hat=} [\,x, x' : \mathbb{N} \mid x' = 2\,]$$

We can note that U_1 is a nondeterministic operation that can be refined by strengthening its postcondition (*i.e.* losing nondeterminism), which is precisely what U_0 does. Therefore, by using ($\sqsupseteq_s^+$) we can easily prove that $U_0 \sqsupseteq_s U_1$. Conversely, when conjoining the operations we have the following schemas:

$$U_0 \wedge U_2 = [\,x, x' : \mathbb{N} \mid \mathit{false}\,] \quad U_1 \wedge U_2 = [\,x, x' : \mathbb{N} \mid x' = 2\,]$$

---

[3] Groves [10] claims that schema conjunction and schema disjunction have the most interesting properties. As we shall see in the sequel, schema composition and existential hiding are also very interesting.

In [5] and [6], we define a chaotic specification as: $Chaos =_{df} [T \mid false]$. A chaotic specification cannot constitute a refinement of any other specification because this would signify *augmentation of undefinedness* and therefore violate any notion of refinement presented in section 2^4. Thus, $U_0 \wedge U_2 \not\sqsupseteq_s U_1 \wedge U_2$.

Not only does the above counterexample show that monotonicity of conjunction does not hold with respect to S-refinement, it also shows the reason: strengthening the postcondition might create a chaotic specification, due to both the "postcondition only" approach Z takes, and the essence of schema conjunction. This motivates the following rule which has a sidecondition. It is perhaps not surprising that the following sidecondition is precisely the missing introduction rule for the precondition of conjoined operations.

Proposition 4. *Let U_0, U_1 and U_2 be operation schemas with the property that:*

$$\forall z \bullet Pre\ U_0\ z \wedge Pre\ U_2\ z \Rightarrow Pre\ (U_0 \wedge U_2)\ z$$

Then the following rule is derivable:

$$\frac{U_0 \sqsupseteq_s U_1}{U_0 \wedge U_2 \sqsupseteq_s U_1 \wedge U_2}$$

Proof

$$\cfrac{U_0 \sqsupseteq_s U_1 \quad \cfrac{\cfrac{\overline{Pre\ (U_1 \wedge U_2)\ z}\ {}^{(1)}}{Pre\ U_1\ z} \quad \cfrac{\overline{Pre\ (U_1 \wedge U_2)\ z}\ {}^{(1)}}{Pre\ U_2\ z}}{Pre\ U_0\ z \wedge Pre\ U_2\ z} \\ \vdots \\ \cfrac{Pre\ (U_0 \wedge U_2)\ z \qquad \delta}{U_0 \wedge U_2 \sqsupseteq_s U_1 \wedge U_2}}{}\quad \cfrac{z_0 \star z_1' \in U_1 \wedge U_2}{}\ {}^{(1)}$$

Where δ is:

$$U_0 \sqsupseteq_s U_1 \quad \cfrac{\overline{Pre\ (U_1 \wedge U_2)\ z_0}\ {}^{(1)}}{Pre\ U_1\ z_0} \quad \cfrac{\overline{z_0 \star z_1' \in U_0 \wedge U_2}\ {}^{(1)}}{z_0 \star z_1' \in U_0} \\ \cfrac{}{z_0 \star z_1' \in U_1} \quad \cfrac{\overline{z_0 \star z_1' \in U_0 \wedge U_2}\ {}^{(1)}}{z_0 \star z_1' \in U_2} \\ z_0 \star z_1' \in U_1 \wedge U_2$$

□

Much the same observation can be made for SP-refinement: again, since non-monotonicity follows in this case by a permissible reduction of nondeterminism, SP-refinement and S-refinement coincide in this respect. Hence, proposition 4 with $\sqsupseteq_s$ substituted by $\sqsupseteq_{sp}$ holds for SP-refinement. The proof is similar.

SC-refinement guarantees that no reduction of nondeterminism takes place, suggesting that, in general, schema conjunction is monotonic with respect to SC-refinement.

---

[4] See [5, section 4.4] for further detail.

Proposition 5. *The following rule is derivable:*

$$\frac{U_0 \sqsupseteq_{sc} U_1}{U_0 \wedge U_2 \sqsupseteq_{sc} U_1 \wedge U_2}$$

Proof

$$\frac{U_0 \sqsupseteq_{sc} U_1 \quad \dfrac{\overline{z_0 \star z_1' \in U_1 \wedge U_2}\ (1)}{z_0 \star z_1' \in U_1}}{\dfrac{z_0 \star z_1' \in U_0}{z_0 \star z_1' \in U_0 \wedge U_2}} \quad \dfrac{\overline{z_0 \star z_1' \in U_1 \wedge U_2}\ (1)}{z_0 \star z_1' \in U_2} \quad \begin{array}{c} \delta \\ \vdots \\ z_0 \star z_1' \in U_1 \wedge U_2 \end{array}$$
$$\overline{U_0 \wedge U_2 \sqsupseteq_{sc} U_1 \wedge U_2}\ (1)$$

Where δ is identical to δ branch in the proof of proposition 4 (with $\sqsupseteq_s$ substituted by $\sqsupseteq_{sc}$). □

A number of observations may be made from the proofs in this section. Firstly note that, although the non-monotonicity of conjunction with respect to S-refinement and SP-refinement is a direct consequence of the ability to strengthen the postcondition, the sidecondition used in proposition 4 is applied in the proof branch concerning the precondition. This is not surprising because if one attempts to formally prove the refinement of the conjoined schemas given in the counterexample, one discovers that the branch for the postcondition is provable, due to *false* in the antecedent of the implication; whereas the branch for the precondition fails for the opposite reason (*false* in the consequent). Thus, one can expect an application of a sidecondition in this branch at some point.

We would like to highlight the value of insights gained from a less formal analysis (the counterexample) for planning the proof strategy of the formal account. One of the benefits of a precise investigation is the ability to deduce or motivate various results as a direct consequence of proof attempts. An example of this is the sidecondition used in proposition 4. Groves [10], as we noted in section B.1, introduces a strong sidecondition guaranteeing monotonicity of conjunction which insists that the alphabets of (what we denote as) U_0 and U_2 are disjoint. We have established a weaker sidecondition. Moreover, this was devised through the attempt to prove proposition 4.

3.2 Refinement for Disjunction

Schema disjunction is *not monotonic* with respect to S-refinement. In contrast to the analysis of schema conjunction in section 3.1, the reason for non-monotonicity in this case is the fact that S-refinement enables us to extend the domain of specifications, that is, to weaken the precondition of the specification. Weakening the precondition of (at least) one constituent operation might extend the domain of specification of the disjunction of the two operations, leading to an increase in nondeterminism and a failure of refinement.

For example, consider the following schemas:

$$U_0 \triangleq [x, x' : \mathbb{N} \mid x' = 2] \qquad U_1 \triangleq [x, x' : \mathbb{N} \mid x = 0 \wedge x' = 2]$$

$$U_2 \triangleq [x, x' : \mathbb{N} \mid x = 1 \wedge x' = 3]$$

The specification U_1 constitutes a partial operation and therefore can be refined by weakening its precondition. Indeed, using $(\sqsupseteq_s^+)$ we can prove that $U_0 \sqsupseteq_s U_1$. However, respectively disjoining the above yields the following specifications:

$$U_0 \vee U_2 = [x, x' : \mathbb{N} \mid x' = 2 \vee x = 1 \wedge x' = 3]$$

$$U_1 \vee U_2 = [x, x' : \mathbb{N} \mid x = 0 \wedge x' = 2 \vee x = 1 \wedge x' = 3]$$

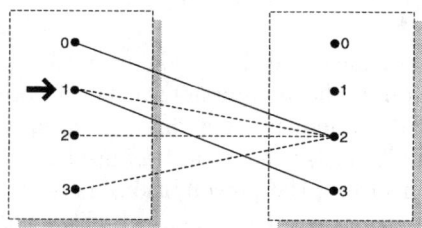

Fig. 1. The entire set of lines represent the schema $U_0 \vee U_2$. The solid lines represent the partial relation denoted by the schema $U_1 \vee U_2$, and the dotted lines represent the behaviours *added* by the schema $U_0 \vee U_2$. Note the point (marked with a right arrow) which represents *weakening of the postcondition* with respect to $U_1 \vee U_2$. Hence $U_0 \vee U_2 \not\sqsupseteq_s U_1 \vee U_2$.

Clearly $U_0 \vee U_2 \not\sqsupseteq_s U_1 \vee U_2$. This is because the schema $U_0 \vee U_2$ permits the behaviour $(\!| x \Rightarrow 1, x' \Rightarrow 2 |\!)$, which is prohibited by $U_1 \vee U_2$. In fact, this is a representative example: the only reason why S-refinement might not hold is an augmentation of nondeterminism with respect to the abstract disjunction; this is shown in Fig. 1. The analysis suggests that the sidecondition will be required in the proof branch concerning the postcondition, as we will now see.

Proposition 6. *Let U_0, U_1 and U_2 be operation schemas with the property that:*

$$\forall z \bullet \text{Pre } U_0 \, z \wedge \text{Pre } U_2 \, z \Rightarrow \text{Pre } U_1 \, z$$

Then the following rule is derivable:

$$\frac{U_0 \sqsupseteq_s U_1}{U_0 \vee U_2 \sqsupseteq_s U_1 \vee U_2}$$

Operation Refinement and Monotonicity in the Schema Calculus

Proof

$$\cfrac{\cfrac{}{Pre\,(U_1 \vee U_2)\,z}\,(1) \quad \cfrac{\cfrac{U_0 \sqsupseteq_s U_1 \quad \overline{Pre\,U_1\,z}\,(2)}{Pre\,U_0\,z}}{Pre\,(U_0 \vee U_2)\,z} \quad \cfrac{\overline{Pre\,U_2\,z}\,(2)}{Pre\,(U_0 \vee U_2)\,z}\,(2) \quad \cfrac{\delta_0 \atop \vdots}{z_0 \star z_1' \in U_1 \vee U_2}\,(1)}{U_0 \vee U_2 \sqsupseteq_s U_1 \vee U_2}$$

Where δ_0 stands for the following branch:

$$\cfrac{\cfrac{}{z_0 \star z_1' \in U_0 \vee U_2}\,(1) \quad \cfrac{\cfrac{U_0 \sqsupseteq_s U_1 \quad \overline{Pre\,U_1\,z_0} \quad \overline{z_0 \star z_1' \in U_0}\,(3) \atop \vdots \atop \delta_1}{z_0 \star z_1' \in U_1}}{z_0 \star z_1' \in U_1 \vee U_2} \quad \cfrac{\overline{z_0 \star z_1' \in U_2}\,(3)}{z_0 \star z_1' \in U_1 \vee U_2}\,(3)}{z_0 \star z_1' \in U_1 \vee U_2}$$

and δ_1 is:

$$\cfrac{\cfrac{}{Pre\,(U_1 \vee U_2)\,z_0}\,(1) \quad \cfrac{\overline{Pre\,U_1\,z_0}\,(4)}{Pre\,U_1\,z_0}}{Pre\,U_1\,z_0} \quad \cfrac{\cfrac{\overline{z_0 \star z_1' \in U_0}\,(3)}{Pre\,U_0\,z_0} \quad \overline{Pre\,U_2\,z_0}\,(4)}{Pre\,U_0\,z_0 \wedge Pre\,U_2\,z_0} \atop \vdots \atop Pre\,U_1\,z_0}\,(4)$$

The situation with SC-refinement is very similar since, as the counterexample illustrates, the critical factor leading to non-monotonicity in this case is weakening of the precondition. SC-refinement sanctions this property and therefore proposition 6 holds with $\sqsupseteq_s$ substituted by $\sqsupseteq_{sc}$. The proof, given this substitution, is similar.

We may conclude that schema disjunction is, generally, monotonic with respect to SP-refinement because weakening of the precondition is prohibited. The following rule is derivable:

Proposition 7.

$$\cfrac{U_0 \sqsupseteq_{sp} U_1}{U_0 \vee U_2 \sqsupseteq_{sp} U_1 \vee U_2}$$

Proof

$$\cfrac{\cfrac{\delta \atop \vdots}{Pre\,(U_0 \vee U_2)\,z} \quad \cfrac{\cfrac{}{z_0 \star z_1' \in U_0 \vee U_2}\,(1) \quad \cfrac{\cfrac{U_0 \sqsupseteq_{sp} U_1 \quad \overline{z_0 \star z_1' \in U_0}\,(3)}{z_0 \star z_1' \in U_1}}{z_0 \star z_1' \in U_1 \vee U_2} \quad \cfrac{\overline{z_0 \star z_1' \in U_2}\,(3)}{z_0 \star z_1' \in U_1 \vee U_2}\,(3)}{z_0 \star z_1' \in U_1 \vee U_2}\,(1)}{U_0 \vee U_2 \sqsupseteq_{sp} U_1 \vee U_2}$$

Where δ is identical to the precondition branch in the proof of proposition 6 (with $\sqsupseteq_s$ substituted by $\sqsupseteq_{sp}$). □

3.3 Refinement for Existential Quantification

It is well known that there is an intimate relationship between disjunction and existential quantification. We might then expect the monotonicity properties of schema existential quantification with respect to refinement to be similar to those for schema disjunction. Indeed, schema existential quantification is *not monotonic* with respect to S-refinement because weakening of the precondition might admit behaviours to the concrete operation that are unacceptable to the abstract one. The reason is that schema existential quantification can hide any arbitrary observation and in particular observations that can lead to an augmentation of nondeterminism. This is shown by the counterexample in Fig. 2.

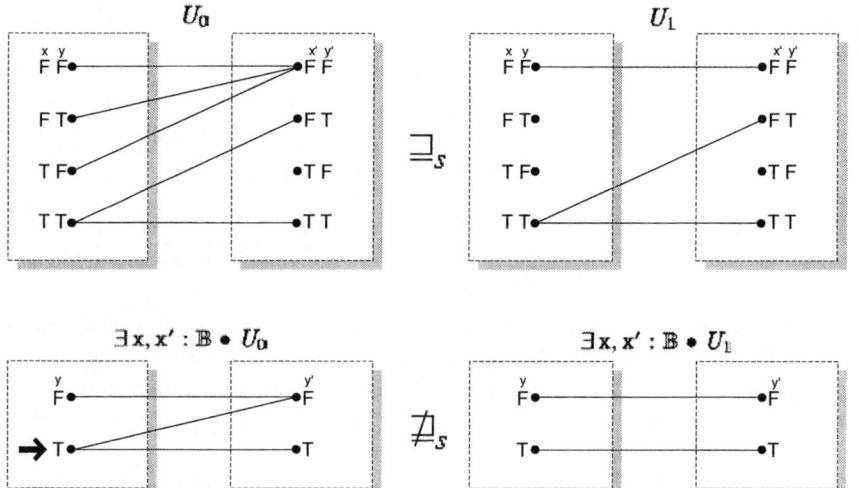

Fig. 2. A counterexample: schema existential quantification is not monotonic with respect to S-refinement.

In this case, we provide a pictorial representation of the operation schemas since that clearly illustrates the effect that existential hiding of observations has on S-refinement. We present the specifications U_0 and U_1, whose alphabets comprise the boolean observations x, x', y and y'. The specifications $\exists\, x, x' : \mathbb{B} \bullet U_0$ and $\exists\, x, x' : \mathbb{B} \bullet U_1$ hide the pair of observations x and x' from U_0 and U_1. Note that the schema U_1 denotes a partial operation, thus U_0 S-refines it by weakening the precondition. Indeed, this is provable by ($\sqsupseteq_s^+$). Nevertheless, hiding those observations introduces *weakening of the postcondition* (marked with a right arrow in Fig. 2) of $\exists\, x, x' : \mathbb{B} \bullet U_0$ with respect to $\exists\, x, x' : \mathbb{B} \bullet U_1$. Hence, S-refinement fails.

Like schema disjunction, the above counterexample also suggests that, in order to prove monotonicity of existential hiding with respect to S-refinement, a sidecondition is required in the proof branch concerning the postcondition. The sidecondition here is stronger than the one used for disjunction because, unlike schema disjunction, we do not have the additional disjoined schema.

Proposition 8. *Let U_0 and U_1 be operation schemas with the property that:*

$$\forall\, z \bullet Pre\ U_0\ z \Rightarrow Pre\ U_1\ z$$

Then the following rule is derivable:

$$\frac{U_0 \sqsupseteq_s U_1}{\exists\, z, z' : T^z \bullet U_0 \sqsupseteq_s \exists\, z, z' : T^z \bullet U_1}$$

Proof

$$\cfrac{\cfrac{Pre\,(\exists\, z,z':T^z \bullet U_1)\, z}{Pre\,(\exists\, z,z':T^z \bullet U_0)\, z}\ (1) \quad \cfrac{\cfrac{\cfrac{U_0 \sqsupseteq_s U_1 \quad \overline{Pre\ U_1\, y}\ (2)}{Pre\ U_0\, y}}{\cfrac{Pre\,(\exists\, z,z':T^z \bullet U_0)\, y \quad y \doteq z}{Pre\,(\exists\, z,z':T^z \bullet U_0)\, z}\ (2)} \quad \cfrac{\delta_0}{z_0 \star z_1' \in \exists\, z,z':T^z \bullet U_1}}{\exists\, z,z' : T^z \bullet U_0 \sqsupseteq_s \exists\, z,z' : T^z \bullet U_1}}\ (1)$$

Where δ_0 is:

$$\cfrac{Pre\,(\exists\, z,z':T^z \bullet U_1)\, z_0 \ (1) \quad \cfrac{\cfrac{\cfrac{U_0 \sqsupseteq_s U_1 \quad \overline{Pre\ U_1\, w}\ (3)}{Pre\ U_0\, w}}{\cfrac{Pre\,(\exists\, z,z':T^z \bullet U_0)\, w \quad w \doteq z_0}{Pre\,(\exists\, z,z':T^z \bullet U_0)\, z_0}\ (3)} \quad \cfrac{\delta_1}{z_0 \star z_1' \in \exists\, z,z':T^z \bullet U_1}}{z_0 \star z_1' \in \exists\, z,z':T^z \bullet U_1}\ (4)}{z_0 \star z_1' \in \exists\, z,z':T^z \bullet U_1}$$

δ_1 is:

$$\cfrac{z_0 \star z_1' \in \exists\, z,z':T^z \bullet U_0\ (1) \quad \cfrac{\cfrac{\delta_2}{\vdots}}{\cfrac{y_1 \in U_1}{y_1 \in \exists\, z,z':T^z \bullet U_1} \quad y_1 \doteq z_0 \star z_1'}{z_0 \star z_1' \in \exists\, z,z':T^z \bullet U_1}\ (5)}{z_0 \star z_1' \in \exists\, z,z':T^z \bullet U_1}\ (5)$$

and δ_2 is:

$$\cfrac{U_0 \sqsupseteq_s U_1 \quad \cfrac{\cfrac{}{Pre\ U_0\ y_0}\ (4) \quad \cfrac{\cfrac{}{y_0 \mathrel{\dot{=}} z_0}\ (4) \quad \cfrac{}{y_1 \mathrel{\dot{=}} z_0 \star z_1'}\ (5)}{y_0 \mathrel{\dot{=}} y_1}}{Pre\ U_0\ y_1} \quad \vdots \quad \cfrac{}{Pre\ U_1\ y_1} \quad \cfrac{}{y_1 \in U_0}\ (5)}{y_1 \in U_1}$$

□

Note that the above sidecondition forces a "fixed precondition" refinement, which is precisely SP-refinement. So it is an immediate consequence that schema existential hiding is monotonic with respect to SP-refinement, as expressed by the following proposition:

Proposition 9. *The following rule is derivable:*

$$\cfrac{U_0 \sqsupseteq_{sp} U_1}{\exists\, z, z' : T^z \bullet U_0 \sqsupseteq_{sp} \exists\, z, z' : T^z \bullet U_1}$$

□

The proof is essentially identical to proposition 8.

The situation with SC-refinement is very different from what we have seen so far. *Prima facie*, one might deduce that S-refinement and SC-refinement coincide, as far as monotonicity behaviour of existential hiding is concerned. Indeed, the same sidecondition as in proposition 8 is required for proving monotonicity of schema existential hiding with respect to SC-refinement. However, this is far too strong, since SC-refinement guarantees stability of the postcondition (as mapped from the original precondition). Since the sidecondition guarantees stability of the precondition, the result is provable only when the the abstract and concrete operations are *equivalent* which is, of course, far from useful.

3.4 Refinement for Composition

It is not surprising that schema composition is *not monotonic* with respect to S-refinement because composition in Z can be expressed in terms of conjunction and existential quantification. Following the results of sections 3.1 and 3.3, this suggests that both weakening the precondition and strengthening the postcondition of the underlying operations will cause a problem. This is fairly intuitive as, first, reduction of nondeterminism is *demonic* with respect to schema composition (since strengthening the postcondition on the *left* of the composition might demonically choose those after states that do not share any reference point with the precondition of the operation to the right of the composition). This results in losing requirements from the domain of specification. Secondly, weakening the precondition on the *right* of the composition might demonically extend the specification domain in such a way that composition will introduce unacceptable behaviours mapped from the original precondition.

The following counterexample not only shows the problem of combining schema composition and refinement, but it also motivates a solution by suggesting a sidecondition that is sufficient for attaining the monotonicity result. Consider the following specifications:

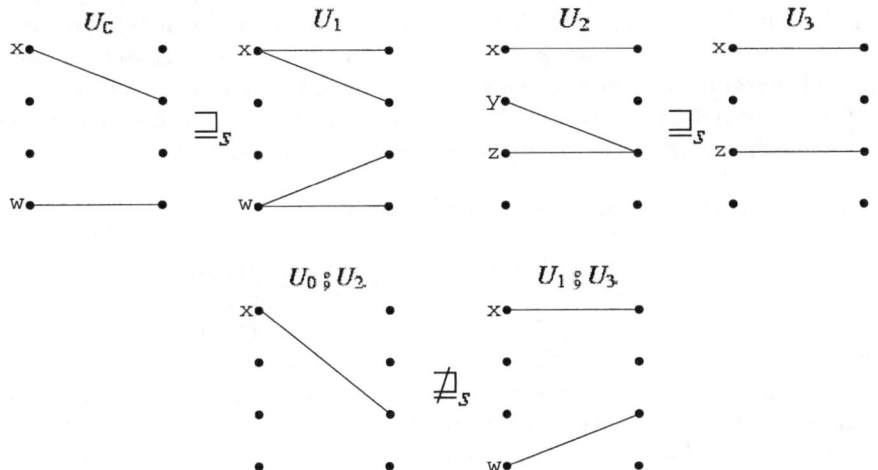

Fig. 3. A counterexample: schema composition is not monotonic with respect to refinement.

We introduce two abstract specifications, U_1 and U_3, and their respective S-refinements U_0 and U_2. We then show that the composition of the underlying concrete specifications does not constitute a refinement of the composition of their abstract counterparts. We label the input states of each specification using the labels x, y, z and w (from the top).

The specification U_1 has two instances of nondeterminism and U_0 S-refines it by reducing both of these. However, this is demonic, so that the after state mapped from w in U_0 does not compose with anything in the precondition of U_2; we therefore lose the input state w from the domain of $U_0 \mathbin{\raise.2ex\hbox{$\scriptstyle\circ$}} U_2$, whereas it still exists in the domain of $U_1 \mathbin{\raise.2ex\hbox{$\scriptstyle\circ$}} U_3$. This is one of the reasons for non-refinement[5]. U_2 S-refines U_3 by weakening its precondition so, in conjunction with the demonic reduction of nondeterminism by U_0, the after state mapped from x in U_0 is composed with the initial state y in U_2. This introduces a state mapped from x in $U_0 \mathbin{\raise.2ex\hbox{$\scriptstyle\circ$}} U_2$ which does not exist in $U_1 \mathbin{\raise.2ex\hbox{$\scriptstyle\circ$}} U_3$, yet x is in the precondition of $U_1 \mathbin{\raise.2ex\hbox{$\scriptstyle\circ$}} U_3$. This is the second reason for non-refinement. The fact that $(\sqsupseteq_s^+)$ fails for reasons concerning both the precondition and postcondition suggests that, in

---

[5] Note that had the precondition of U_3 not been weakened by U_2, we would have also lost the input x from the precondition of $U_0 \mathbin{\raise.2ex\hbox{$\scriptstyle\circ$}} U_2$. This would have induced a chaotic specification $U_0 \mathbin{\raise.2ex\hbox{$\scriptstyle\circ$}} U_2$.

contrast to our previous investigation, neither of the other refinement theories at our disposal can guarantee this monotonicity result. Furthermore, it suggests that a sidecondition which is sufficient for proving monotonicity will be needed in both precondition and postcondition branches of the monotonicity proof, and as we shall see in the sequel, this is indeed the case.

The counterexample above and [11, p.39-40][6] suggest a remedy for the problem: if we insist that every after state in U_1 is mapped onto at least one value in the precondition of U_3, then, not only can strengthening the postcondition (on the left) by U_0 never be demonic (as, in the presence of refinement, the precondition of U_2 is at least as large as the one of U_3), but also weakening the precondition (on the right) by U_2 can never introduce an after state in $U_0 \mathbin{\raise0.3ex\hbox{$\mathchar"9$}} U_2$ that is connected via an intermediate value that was not in the precondition of U_3[7]. We call this property *strong connectivity* and it is defined as follows:

Definition 1 (Strong Connectivity).

$$Sc\ U_0\ U_1 =_{df} \forall z_0, z_1 \bullet z_0 \star z_1' \in U_0 \Rightarrow Pre\ U_1\ z_1$$

Indeed, reconsidering Fig. 3, we can prove that schema composition is monotonic with respect to all of the refinement theories at our disposal, providing $Sc\ U_1\ U_3$ holds. In fact we can do better than that. Although strong connectivity is a very intuitive sidecondition, it is a relatively strong one: there is a weaker sidecondition which is also sufficient. This can be motivated by considering further counterexamples. We call it *forking connectivity*. Informally, two specifications comply with this property if, for every nondeterministic initial state (forking point) in the first specification, either *all* the after states mapped from it coincide with some initial state in the *precondition* of the the second specification, or *none* of them does.

Definition 2 (Forking Connectivity).

$$Fc\ U_0\ U_1 =_{df} \forall z_0, z_1, z_2 \bullet (z_0 \star z_1' \in U_0 \wedge z_0 \star z_2' \in U_0 \wedge Pre\ U_1\ z_1) \Rightarrow Pre\ U_1\ z_2$$

Obvious introduction and elimination rules follow from this.

With this in place, we can now prove the monotonicity result. We shall only provide the proof for S-refinement.

Proposition 10. *Let U_0, U_1, U_2 and U_3 be operation schemas with the property that:*

$$Fc\ U_1\ U_3$$

---

[6] Grundy proposes a modified *definition* of composition, in which strong connectivity is embedded.

[7] Unless, of course, this is as a result of composing an after state in U_0 that constitutes a new behaviour (outside the precondition of U_1) with an initial state in U_2 that accounts for a point of weakening the precondition of U_3. Such a case is not relevant in the present context.

Operation Refinement and Monotonicity in the Schema Calculus 117

Then the following rule is derivable.

$$\frac{U_0 \sqsupseteq_s U_1 \quad U_2 \sqsupseteq_s U_3}{U_0 \, \mathring{,} \, U_2 \sqsupseteq_s U_1 \, \mathring{,} \, U_3}$$

Proof

$$\cfrac{U_0 \sqsupseteq_s U_1 \quad \cfrac{\overline{Pre\,(U_1 \, \mathring{,} \, U_3)\,z}\,(1)}{Pre\,U_1\,z} \quad \overline{z \star y'_0 \in U_0}\,(2) \quad \cfrac{U_2 \sqsupseteq_s U_3 \quad \overset{\alpha_0}{\vdots}}{Pre\,U_2\,y_0}}{\cfrac{Pre\,U_0\,z \quad Pre\,(U_0 \, \mathring{,} \, U_2)\,z}{Pre\,(U_0 \, \mathring{,} \, U_2)\,z}\,(2) \quad \cfrac{\delta_1 \atop \vdots}{z_0 \star z'_1 \in U_1 \, \mathring{,} \, U_3}\,(1)}{U_0 \, \mathring{,} \, U_2 \sqsupseteq_s U_1 \, \mathring{,} \, U_3}$$

Where α_0 stands for the following branch:

$$\cfrac{\overline{Pre\,(U_1 \, \mathring{,} \, U_3)\,z}\,(1) \quad \cfrac{Fc\,U_1\,U_3 \quad \overline{z \star y'_0 \in U_1} \quad \cfrac{\overset{\beta_0}{\vdots}}{z \star w'_0 \in U_1}\,(3) \quad \overline{Pre\,U_3\,w_0}\,(3)}{Pre\,U_3\,y_0}\,(3)}{Pre\,U_3\,y_0}$$

and β_0 stands for the following branch:

$$\cfrac{U_0 \sqsupseteq_s U_1 \quad \overline{z \star y'_0 \in U_0}\,(2) \quad \cfrac{\overline{Pre\,(U_1 \, \mathring{,} \, U_3)\,z}\,(1)}{Pre\,U_1\,z}}{z \star y'_0 \in U_1}$$

and δ_1 is:

$$\cfrac{\overline{z_0 \star z'_1 \in U_0 \, \mathring{,} \, U_2}\,(1) \quad \cfrac{U_0 \sqsupseteq_s U_1 \quad \cfrac{\overline{Pre\,(U_1 \, \mathring{,} \, U_3)\,z_0}\,(1)}{Pre\,U_1\,z_0} \quad \overline{z_0 \star y'_1 \in U_0}\,(4) \quad \overset{\alpha_1}{\vdots}}{z_0 \star y'_1 \in U_1 \quad y_1 \star z'_1 \in U_3}}{z_0 \star z'_1 \in U_1 \, \mathring{,} \, U_3}\,(4)$$

Where α_1 stands for the following branch:

$$\cfrac{U_2 \sqsupseteq_s U_3 \quad \cfrac{\overline{Pre\,(U_1 \, \mathring{,} \, U_3)\,z_0}\,(1) \quad \overset{\beta_1}{\vdots}}{Pre\,U_3\,y_1}\,(5) \quad \overline{y_1 \star z'_1 \in U_2}\,(4)}{y_1 \star z'_1 \in U_3}$$

Where β_1 stands for the following branch:

$$\frac{Fc\ U_1\ U_3 \quad U_0 \sqsupseteq_s U_1 \quad \dfrac{\overline{Pre\ (U_1 \mathbin{\text{\usefont{U}{msa}{m}{n}\char"39}} U_3)\ z_0}\ {}^{(1)}}{\dfrac{Pre\ U_1\ z_0}{z_0 \star y'_1 \in U_1}} \quad \dfrac{z_0 \star y'_1 \in U_0\ {}^{(4)}}{\ } \quad \dfrac{z_0 \star w'_1 \in U_1}{\ }{}^{(5)} \quad \dfrac{\overline{Pre\ U_3\ w_1}}{\ }{}^{(5)}}{Pre\ U_3\ y_1}$$

□

Finally, it is interesting to note that, since weakening the precondition causes a problem on the right and strengthening the postcondition causes a problem on the left, it is an immediate consequence that schema composition is *monotonic on the right* with respect to SP-refinement (because the precondition is fixed), and is *monotonic on the left* with respect to SC-refinement (because postcondition is fixed). Hence, the following rules are derivable:

Proposition 11.

$$\frac{U_0 \sqsupseteq_{sp} U_1}{U_2 \mathbin{\text{\usefont{U}{msa}{m}{n}\char"39}} U_0 \sqsupseteq_{sp} U_2 \mathbin{\text{\usefont{U}{msa}{m}{n}\char"39}} U_1} \qquad \frac{U_0 \sqsupseteq_{sc} U_1}{U_0 \mathbin{\text{\usefont{U}{msa}{m}{n}\char"39}} U_2 \sqsupseteq_{sc} U_1 \mathbin{\text{\usefont{U}{msa}{m}{n}\char"39}} U_2}$$

Proof We only provide the proof for SP-refinement.

$$\frac{\delta_0 \qquad \delta_1}{\dfrac{Pre\ (U_2 \mathbin{\text{;}} U_0)\ z \quad z_0 \star z'_1 \in U_2 \mathbin{\text{;}} U_1}{U_2 \mathbin{\text{;}} U_0 \sqsupseteq_{sp} U_2 \mathbin{\text{;}} U_1}}\ {}^{(1)}$$

Where δ_0 is:

$$\frac{\overline{Pre\ (U_2 \mathbin{\text{;}} U_1)\ z}\ {}^{(1)} \quad \dfrac{z \star y' \in U_2\ {}^{(2)}}{\dfrac{Pre\ (U_2 \mathbin{\text{;}} U_0)\ z}{Pre\ (U_2 \mathbin{\text{;}} U_0)\ z}\ {}^{(2)}} \quad \dfrac{U_0 \sqsupseteq_{sp} U_1 \quad \overline{Pre\ U_1\ y}\ {}^{(2)}}{Pre\ U_0\ y}}{}$$

and δ_1 is:

$$\frac{\overline{z_0 \star z'_1 \in U_2 \mathbin{\text{;}} U_0}\ {}^{(1)} \quad \dfrac{\overline{z_0 \star y' \in U_2}\ {}^{(3)}}{\dfrac{z_0 \star z'_1 \in U_2 \mathbin{\text{;}} U_1}{z_0 \star z'_1 \in U_2 \mathbin{\text{;}} U_1}\ {}^{(3)}} \quad \dfrac{U_0 \sqsupseteq_{sp} U_1 \quad \overline{y \star z'_1 \in U_0}\ {}^{(3)}}{y \star z'_1 \in U_1}}{}$$

□

4 Conclusions and Future Work

In this paper, we have introduced three operation refinement theories for Z: S-refinement, SP-refinement and SC-refinement. These refinement theories were presented in entirely proof-theoretic form, characterising refinement directly in terms of the language and the behaviour of the various predicates involved. S-refinement, for example, is modelled and motivated by the two conditions proposed originally by Spivey (corresponding to the premises of our introduction rule for S-refinement). By reformulating these as theories, rather than as sufficient conditions, we have established a mathematical framework, based on a logic for Z, which underlies the analysis of monotonicity that we have presented. By adopting the S-family of refinement relations, rather than refinement based on a lifted totalisation semantics, our formal and informal analysis is very simple, does not require a semantic extension to the language, and it is easier to comprehend the technical intuitions.

We have provided a systematic analysis of monotonicity for schema conjunction, schema disjunction, schema existential hiding and schema composition with respect to the three refinement theories at our disposal. This has been undertaken by first shedding some light on the intuitive reasons for the lack of monotonicity in each case and then supporting these by mathematical results. We have shown that none of the operators is monotonic with respect to S-refinement, yet some operators are monotonic with respect to other characterisations of refinement (*e.g.* disjunction and existential hiding are monotonic with respect to SP-refinement). Nevertheless, the combination of both intuitive and mathematical investigations has directly motivated the set of sideconditions which constitute sufficient conditions for monotonicity of the various operators we have examined. We concluded, in particular, that the natural sidecondition for composition is too strong and have introduced a weaker sufficient condition for the purpose. Likewise, we have demonstrated that the sidecondition for conjunction suggested by Groves [10] is too strong, whereas a weaker condition is possible in this case.

Naturally, there are advantages and disadvantages in using a system with sideconditions. A major asset is that these sideconditions can be used as "healthiness conditions" on a Z specification, in order to enjoy the benefits of modular refinement. However, it could be argued that these sideconditions are expedient only if they refer *exclusively* to either the abstract or the concrete specifications [22]. In this way the true spirit of *abstraction* (in which the internal structure of the abstract specification is not to be disclosed) is upheld. Fortunately, the sideconditions for both conjunction and composition do comply with this requirement, whereas those for disjunction and existential hiding do not. This is not immensely problematic as these two conditions allude only to the precondition of the abstract operation (as well as to the precondition of the concrete one); thus, it is only the precondition of the abstract operation which has to be disclosed, rather than its entire structure.

Finally, if we take the results in this paper together with those in [5] and [6], our results demonstrate that the poor monotonicity properties of the Z schema calculus is not a special feature of the total relational model of refinement to be found in, for example, [26]. In [5] and [6] various alternative refinement theories including the *chaotic* relational completion, and a weakest precondition semantics are all shown to be equivalent to S-refinement. So, these poor properties are a direct consequence of the underlying partial relation semantics of Z. Recall that this semantics does permit the derivation of an *equational* logic for the schema calculus (as reported in, for example, [13]). Indeed such equations have often been used in informal guides to Z almost as *definitions* of the schema operations.[8] This equational logic means that there is, for any schema expression, a logically unique normal form (atomic schema). This is a very strong result and occupies part of the theory of Z which is *logically prior to any notion of refinement*. In that sense, in the context of normalisation, refinement takes place between single (unstructured) atomic schemas. No refinement theory can gainsay this observation and monotonicity must fail in order to maintain it.

So the pragmatic question that the mathematics suggests is this: *which is more important, the equational logic or monotonicity of the schema connectives?* The untutored answer is clear: the equational logic. But is this motivated by the relative importance of that over monotonicity? Or is it simply an accident of circumstance and the lack of a mathematical context in which the issue could be debated? We do not wish to answer this question; indeed there may quite reasonably be different pragmatic reasons for preferring one answer over the other in a variety of practical contexts. We have however, in this paper, provided a mathematical investigation which lays the issues out clearly, and from which an informed debate could begin.

Taking monotonicity, rather than the equational logic, to be the critical issue opens up some interesting lines for research. We could establish a semantics for Z by taking Woodcock's chaotic lifted-totalisation as the semantics for atomic schemas and then introducing interpretations for compound operation schema expressions by recursion over their structure using (almost) the standard relational operations. In this way, refinement could then be the subset relation on the semantics and the schema calculus would be fully monotonic. Naturally, the *nature* of the schema algebra would change, but those changes would be very interesting to explore. Similar projects (all leading to fully monotonic schema calculi) could be based on alternative semantics for atomic schemas using the other approaches (such as weakest precondition) detailed in [5]. In this case, significantly different semantics for the schema operators would be required. In fact, the model described in [15] is an example of this where the interpretation of atomic operation schemas is taken to be *sets of permissible implementations* and [9] is closely related to an example in which the underlying semantics for atomic operation schemas is given by a weakest precondition semantics. Naturally, in any such model, we would lose the usual equational logic for the operation schema calculus, trading this for a number of refinement *inequations* (see [15] for examples of this).

Acknowledgements. We would like to thank the New Zealand Foundation for Research, Science and Technology (grant reference: UOWX0011) and the Royal Society of Great Britain, for financially supporting this research. Moshe Deutsch is supported by the British Council through an ORS award.

---

[8] See *e.g.* [26, Chapter 12, pages 165-6 and 174].

This work has been influenced in its development by too many people to name explicitly. However, special thanks for particularly important discussions and comments go to Eerke Boiten, John Derrick, Lindsay Groves, Ralph Miarka, Greg Reeve, David Streader, Ray Turner, Mark Utting and Jim Woodcock.

References

[1] C. Bolton, J. Davies, and J. C. P. Woodcock. On the refinement and simulation of data types and processes. In K. Araki, A. Galloway, and K. Taguchi, editors, *Integrated Formal Methods (IFM'99)*. Springer, 1999.

[2] A. Cavalcanti. *A Refinement Calculus for Z*. PhD thesis, University of Oxford, 1997.

[3] A. Cavalcanti and J. C. P. Woodcock. ZRC – a refinement calculus for Z. *Formal Aspects of Computing*, 10(3):267–289, 1998.

[4] J. Derrick and E. Boiten. *Refinement in Z and Object-Z: Foundations and Advanced Applications*. Formal Approaches to Computing and Information Technology – FACIT. Springer, May 2001.

[5] M. Deutsch, M. C. Henson, and S. Reeves. An analysis of total correctness refinement models for partial relation semantics I. *University of Essex, technical report CSM-362*, 2001. To appear in the Logic Journal of the IGPL.

[6] M. Deutsch, M. C. Henson, and S. Reeves. Results on formal stepwise design in Z. In *9th Asia Pacific Software Engineering Conference (APSEC 2002)*, pages 33–42. IEEE Computer Society Press, December 2002.

[7] M. Deutsch, M. C. Henson, and S. Reeves. Operation refinement and monotonicity in the schema calculus. *University of Essex, technical report CSM-381*, February 2003.

[8] A. Diller. *Z: An Introduction to Formal Methods*. J. Wiley and Sons, 2nd edition, 1994.

[9] L. Groves. *Evolutionary Software Development in the Refinement Calculus*. PhD thesis, Victoria University, 2000.

[10] L. Groves. Refinement and the Z schema calculus. In *REFINE 2002: Refinement Workshop*. BCS FACS, July 2002.

[11] J. Grundy. *A Method of Program Refinement*. PhD thesis, University of Cambridge, 1993.

[12] I. Hayes. *Specification Case Studies*. Prentice Hall, 2nd edition, 1993.

[13] M. C. Henson and S. Reeves. Investigating Z. *Logic and Computation*, 10(1):43–73, 2000.

[14] M. C. Henson and S. Reeves. Program development and specification refinement in the schema calculus. In J. P. Bowen, S. Dunne, A. Galloway, and S. King, editors, *ZB 2000: Formal Specification and Development in Z and B*, volume 1878 of *Lecture Notes in Computer Science*, pages 344–362. Springer, 2000.

[15] M. C. Henson and S. Reeves. A logic for schema-based program development. *University of Essex, technical report CSM-361*, 2001. To appear in the Journal of Formal Aspects of Computing.

[16] J. Jacky. Formal specification of control software for a radiation therapy machine. *Radiation Oncology Department, University of Washington, technical report 94-07-01*, 1994.

[17] S. King. Z and the Refinement Calculus. In D. Bjørner, C. A. R. Hoare, and H. Langmaack, editors, *VDM '90 VDM and Z - Formal Methods in Software Development*, volume 428 of *Lecture Notes in Computer Science*, pages 164–188. Springer-Verlag, April 1990.

[18] B. P. Mahony. The least conjunctive refinement and promotion in the refinement calculus. *Formal Aspects of Computing*, 11:75–105, 1999.

[19] B. Potter, J. Sinclair, and D. Till. *An Introduction to Formal Specification and Z*. Prentice Hall, 2nd edition, 1996.

[20] J. M. Spivey. *The Z Notation: A Reference Manual*. Prentice Hall, 2nd edition, 1992.

[21] B. Strulo. How firing conditions help inheritance. In J. P. Bowen and M. G. Hinchey, editors, *ZUM '95: The Z Formal Specification Notation*, volume 967 of *Lecture Notes in Computer Science*, pages 264–275. Springer Verlag, 1995.

[22] M. Utting. Private communication. Department of Computer Science, University of Waikato, Hamilton, New Zealand, June 2002.

[23] N. Ward. Adding specification constructors to the refinement calculus. In J. C. P. Woodcock and P. G. Larsen, editors, *Formal Methods Europe (FME '93)*, volume 670 of *Lecture Notes in Computer Science*, pages 652–670. Springer-Verlag, 1993.

[24] J. C. P. Woodcock. Calculating properties of Z specifications. *ACM SIGSOFT Software Engineering Notes*, 14(5):43–54, 1989.

[25] J. C. P. Woodcock. Implementing promoted operations in Z. In C. B. Jones, R. C. Shaw, and T. Denvir, editors, *5th Refinement Workshop*, Workshops in Computing, pages 367–378. Springer-Verlag, 1992.

[26] J. C. P. Woodcock and J. Davies. *Using Z: Specification, Refinement and Proof*. Prentice Hall, 1996.

[27] J. B. Wordsworth. *Software Development with Z - A Practical Approach to Formal Methods in Software Engineering*. Internalional Computer Science Series. Addison-Wesley, 1992.

A Specification Logic - A Synopsis

In this appendix, we will revise a little Z logic, settling our notational conventions in the process. The reader may wish to consult [13] and [5] for a more leisurely treatment of our notational and meta-notational conventions.

Our analysis takes place in the "Church-style" version of the Z-logic due to Henson and Reeves, namely $\mathcal{Z}_C$ [13]. This provides a convenient basis, in particular a satisfactory logical account of the schema calculus of Z as it is normally understood, upon which the present work can be formalised.

A.1 Schemas

$\mathcal{Z}_C$ is a typed theory in which the types of higher-order logic are extended with *schema types* whose values are unordered, label-indexed tuples called *bindings*. For example, if the T_i are types and the z_i are labels (constants) then:

$$[\cdots z_i : T_i \cdots]$$

is a (schema) type. Values of this type are bindings, of the form:

$$(\!|\cdots z_i \Rrightarrow t_i \cdots |\!)$$

where the term t_i has type T_i.

The symbols $\preceq$, $\curlywedge$, $\curlyvee$ and $-$ denote the *schema subtype* relation, and the operations of *schema type intersection* and (compatible) *schema type union* and *schema type subtraction*. We let U (with diacriticals when necessary) range over operation schema expressions. These are sets of bindings linking, as usual, before observations with after observations. This captures the informal account to be found in the literature (*e.g.* [8], [26]). We can always, then, write the type of such operation schemas as $\mathbb{P}(T^{in} \curlyvee T^{out'})$ where T^{in} is the type of the input sub-binding and $T^{out'}$ is the type of the output sub-binding. We also permit *binding concatenation*, written $t_0 \star t_1$, when the alphabets of t_0 and t_1 are disjoint. This is, in fact, exclusively used for partitioning bindings in operation schemas into before and after components, so the terms involved are necessarily disjoint. We lift this operation to sets (of appropriate type):

$$C_0 \star C_1 =_{df} \{z_0 \star z_1 \mid z_0 \in C_0 \wedge z_1 \in C_1\}$$

The same restriction obviously applies here: the types of the sets involved must be disjoint. In this way reasoning in Z becomes hardly more complex than reasoning with binary relations.

We introduce two notational conventions in order to avoid the repeated use of filtering in the context of membership and equality propositions.

Definition 3. $t^{T_0} \dot{\in} C^{\mathbb{P} T_1} =_{df} t \upharpoonright T_1 \in C \qquad (T_1 \preceq T_0)$.

Definition 4. $t_0^{T_0} \dot{=} t_1^{T_1} =_{df} t_0 \upharpoonright (T_0 \curlywedge T_1) = t_1 \upharpoonright (T_0 \curlywedge T_1) \qquad (T_1 \preceq T_0$ or $T_0 \preceq T_1)$.

Moreover, in many contexts we need to compare bindings over a common restricted type.

Definition 5. $t_0^{T_0} =_T t_1^{T_1} =_{df} t_0 \upharpoonright T = t_1 \upharpoonright T \qquad (T \preceq T_0$ and $T \preceq T_1)$.

In [13] we showed how to extend $\mathcal{Z}_C$ to the schema calculus. For example:

$$[S \mid P] =_{df} \{z^T \mid z \in S \wedge z.P\}$$

defines atomic schemas, and:

$$S_0^{\mathbb{P} T_0} \vee S_1^{\mathbb{P} T_1} =_{df} \{z^{T_0 \curlyvee T_1} \mid z \dot{\in} S_0 \vee z \dot{\in} S_1\}$$
$$S_0^{\mathbb{P} T_0} \wedge S_1^{\mathbb{P} T_1} =_{df} \{z^{T_0 \curlyvee T_1} \mid z \dot{\in} S_0 \wedge z \dot{\in} S_1\}$$

respectively define schema disjunction and schema conjunction.

A.2 Preconditions

We can formalise the idea of the *precondition* of an operation schema (domain of the relation between the before and after states that the schema denotes) to express the partiality involved.

Definition 6. $\text{Pre } U \ x^V =_{df} \exists z \in U \bullet x =_{T^{in}} z \qquad (T^{in} \preceq V).$

Proposition 12. *Let y be a fresh variable, then the following introduction and elimination rules are immediately derivable for preconditions:*

$$\frac{t_0 \in U \quad t_0 =_{T^{in}} t_1}{\text{Pre } U \ t_1} \qquad \frac{\text{Pre } U \ t \quad y \in U, y =_{T^{in}} t \vdash P}{P}$$

□

Clearly, the precondition of an operation schema, in general, will not be the whole of T^{in}. In this sense operation schemas denote partial relations.

B The Precondition of Compound Operations

A key to reasoning about the monotonicity properties of the various schema calculus operators with respect to operation refinement is the necessity of reasoning about the precondition of operations defined by schema operations. This topic has been investigated informally in, for example, [24] and [27]. However, no systematic investigation has been presented or published before, nor does it appear to have been extended beyond the analysis of the preconditions of conjoined and disjoined operation schemas.

In this section, we provide complete precondition theories for schema conjunction, schema disjunction, schema existential hiding and schema composition. We shall not provide the proofs for the various results; should the reader be interested, a complete account for these is provided in [7].

B.1 The Precondition for Conjunction

In general, the precondition of a conjunction of operations is not the conjunction of the preconditions of the individual constituents [24]. This is a direct consequence of the underlying "postcondition only" approach Z takes (in contrast to other notations such as B or the refinement calculus).

In fact, we can be more precise: the usual form of a conjunction introduction rule fails, whereas the elimination rules hold. An example, which embodies this result, can be found in [24]. This can be remedied using a very strong sidecondition, insisting that the alphabets of the operations are disjoint (see, for example, [10] and [27, p.214]). We shall not formalise this result, as we believe it is too strong and as such does not cover the interesting cases of schema conjunction.

Proposition 13. *Let $i \in 2$, then the following elimination rules are derivable for the precondition of conjoined schemas:*

$$\frac{Pre\,(U_0 \wedge U_1)\,t}{Pre\,U_i\,t}\ (Pre^-_{\wedge_i})$$

□

B.2 The Precondition for Disjunction

The analysis of the precondition of disjoined operations is far less intricate than the one of conjoined operations. This is due to the mathematical fact that existential quantification is disjunctive; that is, fully distributes over disjunction (see [24], [26, p.210] and [27, p.125]). Hence, we get the following results:

Proposition 14. *Let $i \in 2$, then the following introduction and elimination rules for the precondition of the disjunction of schemas are derivable:*

$$\frac{Pre\,U_i\,t}{Pre\,(U_0 \vee U_1)\,t}\ (Pre^+_{\vee_i}) \qquad \frac{Pre\,(U_0 \vee U_1)\,t \quad Pre\,U_0\,t \vdash P \quad Pre\,U_1\,t \vdash P}{P}\ (Pre^-_{\vee})$$

□

With these in place, we can easily prove the full distributivity of the precondition over disjunction.

Theorem 1. $Pre\,(U_0 \vee U_1)\,t \Leftrightarrow Pre\,U_0\,t \vee Pre\,U_1\,t$ □

B.3 The Precondition for Existential Quantification

We now provide a theory for the precondition of an existentially quantified operation schema. In order to do that we first need to develop a theory for existentially hiding observations of an operation schema. We confine our investigation to deal solely with hiding a pair of observations together: a certain input observation and its output (primed) counterpart.

Firstly, for convenience reasons, we define a schema type[9] T_z whose alphabet comprises exactly those observations to be hidden from the operation.

Definition 7. *(i)* $T_z =_{df} T_z^{in} \curlyvee T_z^{out'}$ *(ii)* $T_z^{in} =_{df} [z : T^z]$ *(iii)* $T_z^{out'} =_{df} [z' : T^z]$

With this in place, the type of a schema expression of the form $\exists z, z' : T^z \bullet U$ will always have the type $\mathbb{P}(T - T_z)$; thus, we can omit the type superscripts when analysing schema existential hiding in the paper.

The following introduction and elimination rules for schema existential hiding are based on proposition 4.8 from [13].

---
[9] Notice that T_z constitutes a schema type, whereas T^z is the type of the hidden observations z and z'.

Proposition 15. *Let $T_z \preceq T$, then the following rules are derivable:*

$$\frac{t \in U}{t \mathrel{\dot\in} \exists z, z' : T^z \bullet U} \; (U_\exists^+) \qquad \frac{t \mathrel{\dot\in} \exists z, z' : T^z \bullet U \quad y \in U, y \mathrel{\dot=} t \vdash P}{P} \; (U_\exists^-)$$

The usual sideconditions apply to the eigenvariable y. □

We can now provide the theory for the precondition of an existentially quantified schema:

Proposition 16. *The following rules are derivable:*

$$\frac{Pre\ U\ t}{Pre\ (\exists z, z' : T^z \bullet U)\ t} \; (Pre_\exists^+) \qquad \frac{Pre\ (\exists z, z' : T^z \bullet U)\ t \quad Pre\ U\ y, y \mathrel{\dot=} t \vdash P}{P} \; (Pre_\exists^-)$$

Note that the usual sideconditions apply to the eigenvariable y. □

B.4 The Precondition for Composition

We will deal with instances of composition where the operation schema expression $U_0 \mathbin{\raisebox{0.2ex}{\scriptsize$\circ$}} U_1$ has the type $\mathbb{P}(T_0 \curlyvee T_1')$ and where U_0 is of type $\mathbb{P}(T_0 \curlyvee T_2')$ and U_1 is of type $\mathbb{P}(T_2 \curlyvee T_1')$. With this simplification in place we can omit the type superscripts when analysing schema composition in the paper. Secondly, we can reduce the introduction and elimination rules for schema composition (provided in [13]) as follows:

Proposition 17. *The following rules are derivable:*

$$\frac{t_0 \star t_2' \in U_0 \quad t_2 \star t_1' \in U_1}{t_0 \star t_1' \in U_0 \mathbin{\raisebox{0.2ex}{\scriptsize$\circ$}} U_1} \; (U_\circ^+) \qquad \frac{t_0 \star t_1' \in U_0 \mathbin{\raisebox{0.2ex}{\scriptsize$\circ$}} U_1 \quad t_0 \star y' \in U_0, y \star t_1' \in U_1 \vdash P}{P} \; (U_\circ^-)$$

The usual sideconditions apply to the eigenvariable y. □

We can now prove the following introduction and elimination rules for the precondition of composed operation schemas.

Proposition 18.

$$\frac{t_0 \star t_1' \in U_0 \quad Pre\ U_1\ t_1}{Pre\ (U_0 \mathbin{\raisebox{0.2ex}{\scriptsize$\circ$}} U_1)\ t_0} \; (Pre_\circ^+) \qquad \frac{Pre\ (U_0 \mathbin{\raisebox{0.2ex}{\scriptsize$\circ$}} U_1)\ t_0 \quad Pre\ U_1\ y, t_0 \star y' \in U_0 \vdash P}{P} \; (Pre_\circ^-)$$

The usual sideconditions apply to the eigenvariable y. □

Lemma 2. *The following additional rule is derivable for the precondition of composition:*

$$\frac{Pre\ (U_0 \mathbin{\raisebox{0.2ex}{\scriptsize$\circ$}} U_1)\ t_0}{Pre\ U_0\ t_0}$$

□

Using Coupled Simulations in Non-atomic Refinement

John Derrick[1] and Heike Wehrheim[2]

[1] Computing Laboratory, University of Kent, Canterbury, Kent, CT2 7NF, UK
[2] Universität Oldenburg, Fachbereich Informatik, 26111 Oldenburg, Germany

Abstract. Refinement is one of the most important techniques in formal system design, supporting stepwise development of systems from abstract specifications into more concrete implementations. *Non-atomic refinement* is employed when the level of granularity changes during a refinement step, i.e., whenever an abstract operation is refined into a *sequence* of concrete operations, as opposed to a single concrete operation. There has been some limited work on non-atomic refinement in Z, and the purpose of this paper is to extend this existing theory. In particular, we strengthen the proposed definition to exclude certain behaviours which only occur in the concrete specification but have no counterpart on the abstract level. To do this we use *coupled simulations*: the standard simulation relation is complemented by a second relation which guarantees the exclusion of undesired behaviour of the concrete system. These two relations have to agree at specific points (coupling condition), thus ensuring the desired close correspondence between abstract and concrete specification.

Keywords: Non-atomic refinement, action refinement, Z, coupled simulations.

1 Introduction

Refinement is one of the most important techniques in formal system design. Refinement supports the development on specifications on different levels of abstraction by supplying correctness criteria for moving between these levels. Thus a design may start with an abstract specification and use refinement to prove correctness of transformations to more concrete levels, which are closer to an actual implementation. In a state-based setting like Z [17], B [1] or VDM [11], refinement is concerned with proving correctness of changes made to either the state space or the operations within a specification, and is usually termed *data refinement* [5]. These data refinements are usually verified by using downward and upward simulations, which form a sound and jointly complete methodology for verifying refinements. In a process algebraic setting, like CSP [10], refinement (e.g., failure divergence refinement) compares the dynamic behaviour of processes: an implementation may not exhibit behaviour that the specification did not allow.

The basic assumption behind both data and failure divergence refinement is the *atomicity* of operations: during a refinement step the granularity of operations should be preserved; an abstract operation is always refined into *one* concrete operation. This assumption is, however, not always realistic. The necessity to split operations into a number of smaller steps naturally arises in system design. System models are developed at different levels of abstraction, and what seems to be atomic on an abstract level later often turns out to be composed out of several entities.

To tackle this a certain amount of existing work has been undertaken on *non-atomic refinement*, especially in the area of process algebras (therein called action refinement). Action refinement [2] allows the refinement of one operation (or action) into a complex process. Usually action refinement is defined via an *operator* in the process algebra as opposed to a *relation* between specifications. As a consequence the majority of work has been into considering whether a semantic equivalence which is a congruence with respect to action refinement can be found [3,21,20,14].

There has also been limited work on non-atomic refinement in the state-based context [6]. In these approaches an abstract operation AOp is always refined into a sequence of concrete operations, say $COp_1 \mathbin{\fatsemi} COp_2$. The simplest technique for treating such non-atomic refinements is to add a new operation *skip* to the abstract specification, and require that, apart from one, every concrete operation in the sequence refines *skip* and that the remaining operation refines AOp. This is, however, not possible in all cases. The effect of executing AOp may be distributed onto the whole sequence, for instance, inputs may be split onto several operations and outputs may have to be collected throughout the complete sequence.

Our starting point in this paper is therefore the definition of non-atomic refinement in [6] which also defines a downward simulation method to verify them. It already allows the more general case: neither COp_1 nor COp_2 have to match an abstract *skip* operation. Essentially, the (downward) simulation that is defined requires the following conditions to hold. (1) The execution of the sequence $COp_1 \mathbin{\fatsemi} COp_2$ is equivalent (modulo a retrieve relation) to an execution of AOp; (2) Whenever the precondition of AOp is true so is that of COp_1, and (3) (immediately) after executing COp_1 the precondition of COp_2 is true. This guarantees that AOp is simulated by $COp_1 \mathbin{\fatsemi} COp_2$ without requiring that any of the concrete operations matches an abstract *skip*.

However, there are also some limitations in this first approach to a truly non-atomic refinement. For some specifications the conditions are too liberal (and we will see examples of such specifications throughout the paper), and allow concrete specifications which show certain behaviours that lack an abstract counterpart. The two main difficulties which are not captured yet are the following: the sequence $COp_1 \mathbin{\fatsemi} COp_2$ may be started "in the middle" (i.e., COp_2 can be executed without COp_1 having occurred) and it may not be completed (i.e. no COp_2 after a COp_1). The second case seems to be excluded by condition (3) of non-atomic refinement. However, this condition does not require that COp_2's precondition remains true until the actual execution.

In this paper, we therefore propose a new definition of *coupled* non-atomic refinement for Z which settles these issues. The basic idea is to complement the existing simulation relation for non-atomic refinement with a second simulation relation which excludes undesired behaviours. These two relations have to be *coupled* (i.e., agree) at specific points, thus ensuring a tight correspondence of concrete and abstract specification. The idea of using coupled simulations (originally from Parrow and Sjödin [12]) for non-atomic refinement (or, for the opposite direction, *contraction*) has been proposed by Rensink [13]. While there are technical differences to our definition (e.g., concerning the semantic model: state-based formalism vs. transition system) the basic principle is the same. The second simulation relation avoids incomplete sequences and starts in the middle, and it is coupled with the first relation on *idle* states, i.e., states, in which all refinement sequences of abstract operations are completed.

The ultimate aim of this work is to link these ideas to those arising in a behaviour-oriented setting. That is, the definition of non-atomic refinement can be related to action refinement as occurring in a failure-divergence semantics. The aim will then be to define non-atomic refinement for specifications written in a combination of CSP and a state-based language such as Z or Object-Z. There are a number of proposals for semantic integrations of these specification languages [15,8,9,19,16], and there has been much interest in definitions of refinement for these integrations, and ultimately we see our work as contributing to this study. However, here we will concentrate on the basic definition in a state-based language, leaving these additional issues for the future.

The paper is structured as follows. In Section 2 we discuss the basics of both standard and non-atomic refinement as verified by simulations. In Section 3 we introduce the idea of a coupled simulation and present a schema calculus formulation of it. Section 4 extends this formulation with input and output transformation, necessary for the most general case of non-atomic refinement. Finally, in Section 5 we conclude.

2 Background

The setting in which our work is placed is that provided by a state-based language such as Z or Object-Z. We will, in fact, use the syntax and schema calculus as provided by Z, but crucially we will assume a 'blocking' model of operation preconditions. That is, we assume an operation is not possible outside its precondition, thus the precondition acts as a guard. This is also the interpretation of operations in Object-Z[1].

---

[1] We make this assumption because it is convenient to fix a single interpretation, and this interpretation is consistent with a process algebraic model, e.g., as in CSP. This is desirable since we are ultimately interested in combinations of notations across paradigms.

Refinement is a development methodology that allows one to move from abstract specifications towards an eventual implementation. Refinement is based upon the idea that valid developments are those that reduce non-determinism present in an abstract specification. In state-based languages such as Z, Object-Z, VDM etc, the standard approach to making verification tractable is to use *simulations*, see, for example, the use of upward and downward simulations in Z and Object-Z as described in [22,7].

In an upward or downward simulation, a retrieve relation R links the abstract state (*AState*) and the concrete state (*CState*), and requires that the concrete specification simulates the abstract specification. The advantage of these simulation methods is that they allow refinements to be verified on a step-by-step basis, i.e., there are individual conditions for the operations and the initialisation and, in particular, consideration of the complete program behaviour is not required.

The standard conditions [7] for a downward simulation (using a blocking model) are as follows. (Throughout the paper we assume specifications consist of a state space *State*, an initialisation *Init* together with a collection of operations.)

Definition 1. *Downward simulation*
A specification C is a downward simulation of the specification A if there is a retrieve relation R such that every abstract operation AOp is recast into a concrete operation COp and the following hold.

$\forall\, CInit \bullet (\exists\, AInit \bullet R)$
$\forall\, AState;\ CState;\ CState' \bullet R \wedge COp \implies (\exists\, AState' \bullet R' \wedge AOp)$
$\forall\, AState;\ CState \bullet R \implies (pre\, AOp \iff pre\, COp)$

As we have already discussed there is interest in defining a correct notion of non-atomic refinement where an abstract operation is refined by not one, but by a sequence of concrete operations thus allowing a change of granularity when we develop a specification. Such non-atomic refinements are useful since they allow an abstract specification to be described independently of the structure of the eventual implementation.

It is a relatively simple task to adapt Definition 1 to such a situation. Instead of a single concrete operation COp we refine into a sequence $COp_1 \mathbin{\fatsemi} COp_2$. Clearly, the equivalent of the above conditions must hold, it is also sensible to require that immediately after executing COp_1 the precondition of COp_2 is true. We are thus led to the following conditions (which are justified and derived formally from a relational semantics in [7]).

Definition 2. *Non-atomic downward simulation without IO transformations*
A specification C is a non-atomic downward simulation of the specification A if there is a retrieve relation R such that every abstract operation AOp is recast into a sequence of concrete operations $COp_1 \mathbin{\fatsemi} COp_2$ and, in addition to the initialisation, the following hold.

$\forall\, AState;\ CState;\ CState' \bullet R \wedge (COp_1 \mathbin{\fatsemi} COp_2) \implies \exists\, AState' \bullet R' \wedge AOp$
$\forall\, AState;\ CState \bullet R \implies (pre\, AOp \iff pre\, COp_1)$
$\forall\, AState;\ CState;\ CState' \bullet R \wedge COp_1 \implies (pre\, COp_2)'$

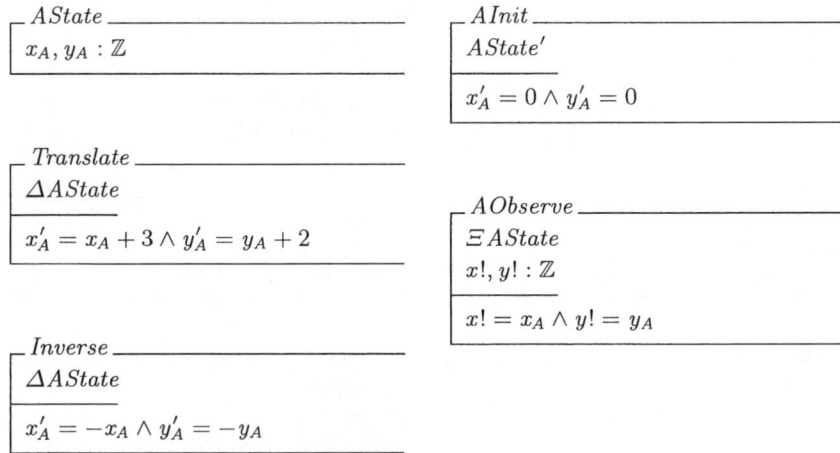

Fig. 1. *ATranslate*

The conditions reflect the intuition described in the introduction. The first condition says that the effect of $COp_1 \fatsemi COp_2$ is consistent with that of AOp (but can of course reduce any non-determinism in AOp). The second says that COp_1 can be invoked whenever AOp can, and the third says that when COp_1 has been completed COp_2 can be invoked (we write (pre COp_2)' so the before-state matches the after-state of COp_1). Informally these are clearly the correct[2] conditions for a refinement of AOp into $COp_1 \fatsemi COp_2$.

As an example, consider the abstract specification containing inverse and translate operations on coordinates x and y given in Figure 1. Then according to Definition 2, the specification in Figure 2 is a valid non-atomic refinement, and it is trivial to check that the required conditions hold. However, this specification, viewed as a non-atomic refinement, has some shortcomings. In particular, the concrete components $TransX_0$ and $TransY_0$ can be invoked an arbitrary number of times in any order. In other words, we have failed to capture the requirement that we can't do $TransY_0$ unless $TransX_0$ has already happened at some point in the past. This deficiency we will rectify in the definition we derive below (Definition 4).

There are other potential deficiencies though. For example, suppose we tackle the above problem by inserting Booleans (we assume the existence of a Boolean type) to control applicability. This is depicted in Figure 3, where we have also decomposed the inverse operation. The problem is solved. The non-atomic components can only be invoked in the correct order, although clearly it would still be possible to construct a specification where after $TransX_1$ it wasn't *always* possible to do $TransY_1$ (by adding another operation that disables it).

---

[2] These conditions generalise to a non-atomic refinement with an arbitrary number of concrete operations in the obvious manner.

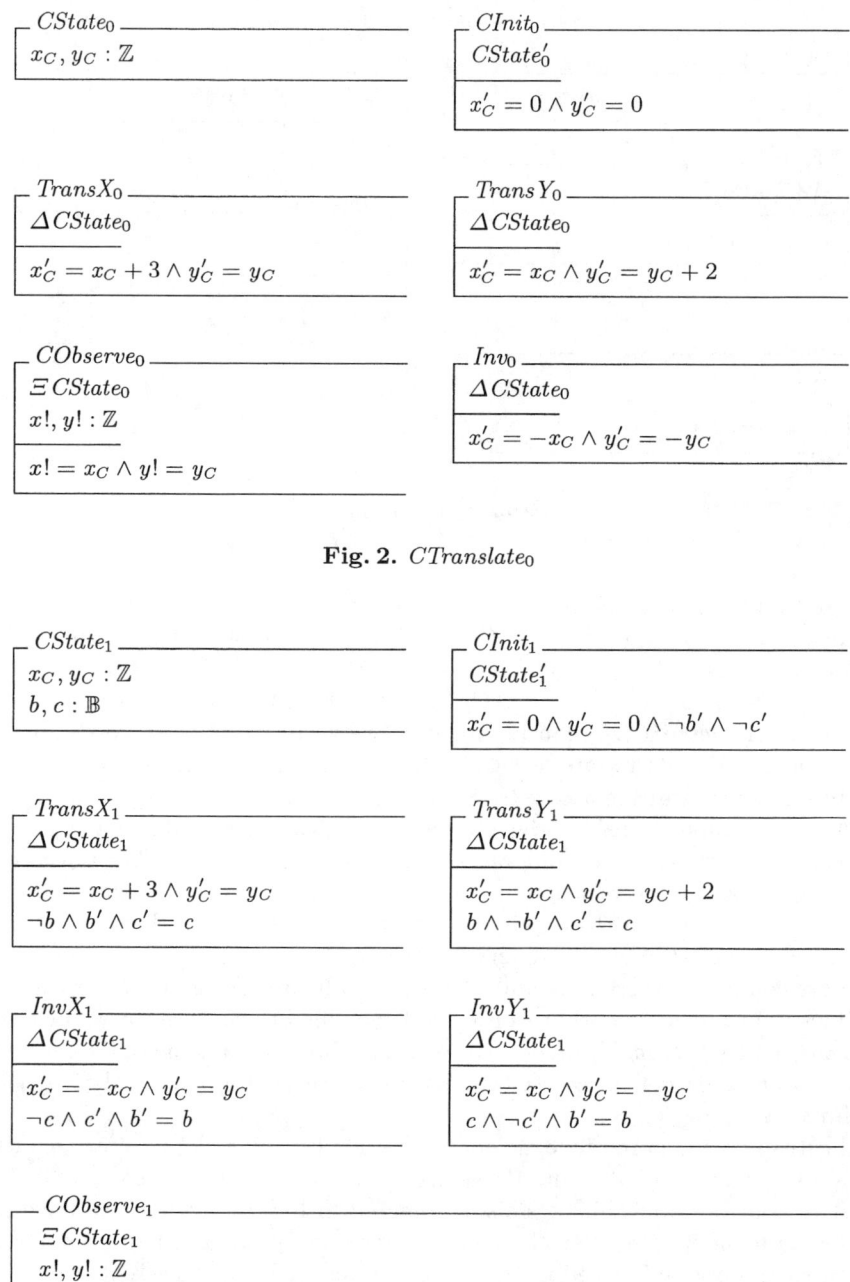

Fig. 2. $CTranslate_0$

Fig. 3. $CTranslate_1$

However, we now have an additional problem: the concrete non-atomic operations can be interleaved in such a way that they do not match any sequence of abstract operations. For example, $TransX_1 \mathbin{\raise0.5ex\hbox{$\scriptscriptstyle\circ$}} InvX_1 \mathbin{\raise0.5ex\hbox{$\scriptscriptstyle\circ$}} TransY_1 \mathbin{\raise0.5ex\hbox{$\scriptscriptstyle\circ$}} InvY_1$ is a valid sequence in the concrete specification, as is $TransX_1 \mathbin{\raise0.5ex\hbox{$\scriptscriptstyle\circ$}} InvX_1 \mathbin{\raise0.5ex\hbox{$\scriptscriptstyle\circ$}} InvY_1 \mathbin{\raise0.5ex\hbox{$\scriptscriptstyle\circ$}} TransY_1$. Whereas the first sequence refines *Translate* $\mathbin{\raise0.5ex\hbox{$\scriptscriptstyle\circ$}}$ *Inverse* the second sequence has no abstract counterpart (using a retrieve relation R which relates x_C with x_A and y_C with y_A).

The problem arises because the concrete specification has allowed interleavings which weren't possible in the abstract specification. *Translate* and *Inverse* are not independent since they modify the same variables. Thus a "concurrent" execution of their refinements, i.e., an interleaving of the concrete operations, may in principle lead to states with no matching abstract counterpart. This we will also seek to remedy in Definition 4 below.

Nevertheless, non-atomic refinement should not completely forbid interleavings on the concrete level. The next example shows a non-atomic refinement with acceptable interleavings. This example specifies a simple protocol between two users sending and receiving messages. A message consists of the actual text and a time-stamp, where $Time == \mathbb{N}$ and $M == Time \times Text$

─ *AState* ─────────────
$q : \text{seq } M$

─ *AInit* ─────────────
$AState'$

$q' = \langle \rangle$

─ *Send* ─────────────
$\Delta AState$
$m? : M$

$q' = q \mathbin{\frown} \langle m? \rangle$

─ *Receive* ─────────────
$\Delta AState$
$m! : M$

$q' = tail\ q$
$m! = head\ q$

This specification can be considered as a description of a protocol on a certain layer in the ISO/OSI reference model. Next we look at the protocol on a lower layer and develop a more concrete specification. In this layer, the send and receive operations are split: *Send* into *PrepareToSend* $\mathbin{\raise0.5ex\hbox{$\scriptscriptstyle\circ$}}$ *Transmit* and *Receive* into *PrepareToRec* $\mathbin{\raise0.5ex\hbox{$\scriptscriptstyle\circ$}}$ *Deliver*. *PrepareToSend* stores the message to be sent in a sequence *inStore* which contains just a single place. The time-stamp is only added when the message is actually transmitted to the link between the users. The transmission adds additional information to the message, in our case a *checksum*. Before delivering a message this additional information has to be removed (and for this the message is first stored in *outStore*).

─ *CState* ─────────────
$inStore : \text{seq } Text$
$outStore : \text{seq } M$
$link : \text{seq}(M \times \mathbb{N})$

$\#inStore \leq 1 \wedge \#outStore \leq 1$

─ *CInit* ─────────────
$CState'$

$inStore' = \langle \rangle \wedge link' = \langle \rangle$
$outStore' = \langle \rangle$

$$\begin{array}{l}\rule{6cm}{0.4pt}\ PrepareToSend\ \rule{6cm}{0.4pt}\\ \Delta CState \\ text?:Text \\ \rule{3cm}{0.4pt} \\ inStore = \langle\,\rangle \\ inStore' = inStore \frown \langle text?\rangle \end{array}$$

$$\begin{array}{l}\rule{6cm}{0.4pt}\ PrepareToRec\ \rule{6cm}{0.4pt}\\ \Delta CState \\ \rule{3cm}{0.4pt} \\ outStore = \langle\,\rangle \\ outStore' = head\ link \end{array}$$

$$\begin{array}{l}\rule{6cm}{0.4pt}\ Transmit\ \rule{6cm}{0.4pt}\\ \Delta CState \\ t?:Time \\ \rule{3cm}{0.4pt} \\ inStore \neq \langle\,\rangle \\ inStore' = tail\ inStore \\ link' = link \frown \langle((t?, head\ inStore), checksum(t?, head\ inStore))\rangle \end{array}$$

$$\begin{array}{l}\rule{6cm}{0.4pt}\ Deliver\ \rule{6cm}{0.4pt}\\ \Delta CState \\ msg!:M \\ \rule{3cm}{0.4pt} \\ outStore \neq \langle\,\rangle \\ outStore' = tail\ outStore \\ msg! = (first\ head\ outStore, second\ head\ outStore) \end{array}$$

The concrete specification is a non-atomic refinement of the abstract, where q is related to *link* projected down to the first and second component of the triples, as is documented via the retrieve relation R.

$$\begin{array}{l}\rule{6cm}{0.4pt}\ R\ \rule{6cm}{0.4pt}\\ AState \\ CState \\ \rule{3cm}{0.4pt} \\ \#q = \#link \\ \forall i:1..\#q \bullet q.i = (link.i.1.1, link.i.1.2) \\ inStore = \langle\,\rangle \\ outStore = \langle\,\rangle \end{array}$$

Now all possible concrete interleavings are valid. For example, *PrepareToSend* ⨾ *PrepareToRec* ⨾ *Transmit* ⨾ *Deliver* yields, if started with a non-empty *link*, the same as *PrepareToSend* ⨾ *PrepareToRec* ⨾ *Deliver* ⨾ *Transmit*. This is due to the fact that abstract sends and receives can be interleaved, that is, with non-empty q, *Send* ⨾ *Receive* is the same as *Receive* ⨾ *Send*.

Thus our definition of non-atomic refinement will have to distinguish when such interleavings are permissible, or when they are not.

Notice that this refinement is also general in other respects:

- none of the concrete non-atomic components (e.g., *PrepareToSend*) are a simple stuttering step (i.e., equal to *skip*).
- the ordering between the concrete non-atomic components is achieved by use of a common sequence which the first operations fills and the second empties.
- the input in *Send* is split into two inputs distributed onto *PrepareToSend* and *Transmit*.

To deal with the latter point we need to use the notion of IO transformations. Indeed, Definition 2 is labelled 'without IO transformations' because it requires that any inputs or outputs in the abstract operation are not distributed across the concrete operations. Again this is not always realistic, and often we need to verify a non-atomic refinement where, for example, the inputs or outputs in the abstract operation are split across the individual concrete operations (e.g., as in the above example). To support such a scenario in the schema calculus we need to use *IO transformers*.

2.1 Using IO transformers

IO transformers are a mechanism to alter the input and output in an IO refinement. IO refinement [7,4,18] is a generalisation of the standard simulation rules, which require identities between the concrete and abstract operations' inputs and outputs. In order to allow the types of inputs and outputs to change, IO refinement replaces these identities with arbitrary relations IT and OT between the input and output elements respectively. IT and OT act as retrieve relations between the inputs and outputs, hence allowing these to change under a refinement in a similar way to changing the state space.

IT and OT are written as schemas and called *input and output transformers*. An input transformer for a schema is an operation whose outputs exactly match the schema's inputs, and whose signature is made up of input and output components only; similarly for output transformers. These are applied to the abstract and concrete operations using piping ($\gg$). To do so we use (in Definition 3) an overlining operator, which extends componentwise to signatures and schemas: $\overline{x?} = x!, \overline{x!} = x?$. Thus $\overline{IT}$ denotes the schema where all inputs become outputs with the same basename, and all outputs inputs.

IO refinement allows inputs and outputs to be refined in a controlled manner. Controlled because since inputs and outputs are observable we must be able to reconstruct the original behaviour from a concrete refinement. This reconstruction is achieved by using the input and output transformers which act as wrappers to a concrete operation, converting abstract inputs to concrete ones and similarly for the output.

To use IO transformers in a non-atomic setting we use mappings from an abstract input to a sequence of concrete inputs representing the inputs needed in the decomposition.

The following definition expresses the refinement of AOp into a fixed sequence $COp_1 \, \S \, COp_2$. In the definition we assume, without loss of generality, that COp_1 and COp_2 are distinct operations with distinct parameter names in order to simplify the presentation.

Definition 3. *Non-atomic downward simulation with IO transformations*
A specification C is a non-atomic IO downward simulation of the specification A if there is a retrieve relation R such that every abstract operation AOp is recast into a sequence of concrete operations $COp_1 \, \S \, COp_2$, and for every $COp_1 \, \S \, COp_2$ there is an input transformer IT which is total on the abstract inputs, for every AOp there is a total injective output transformer OT, and, in addition to initialisation, the following hold.

$\forall AState;\ CState;\ CState' \bullet$
$\quad R \wedge (IT \gg COp_1 \, \S \, COp_2) \Rightarrow \exists AState' \bullet R' \wedge (AOp \gg OT)$
$\forall AState;\ CState \bullet R \Rightarrow (pre(\overline{IT} \gg AOp) \iff pre\ COp_1)$
$\forall AState;\ CState \bullet R \wedge COp_1 \Rightarrow (pre\ COp_2)'$

As an example, consider adding some input to our translate operation. Starting with the same $AState$ and $AInit$ (i.e., as in Figure 1) we specify *Translate* as follows.

─── *Translate* ───────────────────────
$\Delta AState$
$val?: \mathbb{Z} \times \mathbb{Z}$
─────────────
$x'_A = x_A + first\ val? \wedge y'_A = y_A + second\ val?$
──────────────────────────────

Using concrete state space $CState_0$ (c.f., Figure 2) we now wish to decompose *Translate* into the following:

─── *TransX* ──────────────
$\Delta CState_0$
$x_C?: \mathbb{Z}$
─────────
$x'_C = x_C + x_C?$
$y'_C = y_C$
─────────────────

─── *TransY* ──────────────
$\Delta CState_0$
$y_C?: \mathbb{Z}$
─────────
$x'_C = x_C$
$y'_C = y_C + y_C?$
─────────────────

Now, for $TransX \, \S \, TransY$ to be a non-atomic refinement of *Translate*, we need a suitable mapping between the input of the abstract operation and the inputs of the concrete operations. Thus we use an input transformer IT which takes the input of *Translate* and transforms it into inputs for the concrete sequence $TransX \, \S \, TransY$. IT will be the following.

─── *IT* ──────────────────────
$val?: \mathbb{Z} \times \mathbb{Z}$
$x_C!, y_C!: \mathbb{Z}$
──────────
$first\ val? = x_C! \wedge second\ val? = y_C!$
──────────────────────────

Due to absence of outputs no output transformer is needed here, it is the identity and the retrieve relation R is the obvious. Definition 3 can then be applied, checking, for example,

$$\forall AState;\ CState_0;\ CState'_0 \bullet$$
$$R \wedge (IT \gg TransX \mathbin{\raisebox{0.5ex}{,}\!\raisebox{-0.5ex}{,}} TransY) \Rightarrow \exists AState' \bullet R' \wedge Translate$$

which upon expansion is seen to be true. The purpose of the input transformer is to take in the input $val?$ for $Translate$ and turn them into outputs $x_C!, y_C!$ to be used as inputs for $TransX$ and $TransY$.

3 Coupled Simulations

In this section we explain how coupled simulations can be used to overcome the problems identified above. Remember that the intuition we want to capture is the following.

1. AOp is simulated by $COp_1 \mathbin{\raisebox{0.5ex}{,}\!\raisebox{-0.5ex}{,}} COp_2$.
2. After COp_1 it is always possible to do COp_2 (*completion* of refinement).
3. It is not possible to do COp_2 unless the beginning of the non-atomic operation has already started, i.e., COp_1 has already happened at some previous point (no starts "in the middle").
4. At the concrete level refinements of two (or more) abstract operations may only be interleaved if the interleaving matches a sequence of abstract operations.

We first deal with the situation where IO transformations are not needed. The generalisation to IO considerations is surprisingly easy, and we discuss this in Section 4 below.

For the sake of simplicity of presentation we assume a single abstract operation AOp is decomposed into a concrete sequence $COp_1 \mathbin{\raisebox{0.5ex}{,}\!\raisebox{-0.5ex}{,}} COp_2$ and that the non-atomic operations are used uniquely (i.e., not in two separate decompositions). We also assume IO names are distinct across operations in a decomposition. For example, it is not allowed to split $Translate$ into $TransX$ and $TransY$ and use the same name for the input in $TransX$ and $TransY$ (e.g. replace both $x_C?$ and $y_C?$ by $z?$). Furthermore, we do not allow *autoconcurrency*: once a refinement of an abstract operation has been started, we may not start another refinement unless the first is completed. All of these restrictions can, however, be omitted (at the price of a large amount of technical overhead).

For convenience of presentation we furthermore use the notation $s \in S$ (for a sequence S) to stand for $s \in \operatorname{ran} S$ and $S \setminus s$ to stand for the sequence S with the first occurrence of s removed.

Intuition (1) from above is covered by Definition 2, thus the purpose of the remainder of the definition we derive is to add the restrictions 2-4. It is clear from these requirements that one must somehow record whether the first part of a non-atomic sequence has commenced. This the coupled simulation does by being indexed with a sequence of concrete operations - those which have been started but not completed.

For instance, if we have two abstract operations AOp and BOp, being refined into $COp_1 \, \raisebox{0.2ex}{\scriptsize$\circ$}\hspace{-0.5ex}\raisebox{-0.4ex}{\scriptsize$\circ$}\, COp_2$ and $DOp_1 \, \raisebox{0.2ex}{\scriptsize$\circ$}\hspace{-0.5ex}\raisebox{-0.4ex}{\scriptsize$\circ$}\, DOp_2$, respectively, a simulation relation $R^{\langle DOp_1, COp_1\rangle}$ records the fact that both refinements have been started (first the one of BOp and afterwards that of AOp) but not yet completed. Upon completion of a sequence the corresponding start operation is removed from the index. The coupling condition then requires that the indexed simulation relation agrees with the standard retrieve relation when the sequence is empty, which is exactly the case when refinements that have been started are completed.

For a sequence of concrete operations S we write the coupled simulations as R^S. Coupledness thus requires that

$$R^{\langle\rangle} = R$$

Coupledness (together with the conditions on R^S) guarantees requirement 4 to hold.

The next condition records which non-atomic sequences have been started but not yet completed:

$$\forall \mathit{AState}, \mathit{CState}, \mathit{CState}' \bullet R^S \wedge COp_1 \Rightarrow \exists \mathit{AState}' \bullet \Xi \mathit{AState} \wedge (R^{S^\frown \langle COp_1\rangle})'$$

This says that whenever an operation COp_1 (which begins a non-atomic decomposition) is executed the resulting concrete state should be related to the same abstract state as before, however, not using R^S but instead $R^{S^\frown \langle COp_1\rangle}$.

The requirement embodied in (2) is then simply

$$\forall \mathit{AState}, \mathit{CState} \bullet R^S \wedge COp_1 \in S \Rightarrow \mathrm{pre}\, COp_2$$

The third requirement that one can't do COp_2 unless the beginning of the non-atomic operation has already started, can be checked by inspecting the current index S ($COp_1 \in S$). Thus the third requirement is covered by the following

$$\forall \mathit{AState}, \mathit{CState}, \mathit{CState}' \bullet$$
$$R^S \wedge COp_2 \Rightarrow COp_1 \in S \wedge \exists \mathit{AState}' \bullet AOp \wedge (R^{S\setminus \langle COp_1\rangle})'$$

This says that to perform COp_2 from a particular point one must have already done a COp_1, that is, $COp_1 \in S$, and that once the system has completed COp_2 it should be able to match this with the abstract AOp and link the states appropriately (i.e., via R^T with T being S with COp_1 removed). Note that COp_1 might not just have occurred, sometimes other concrete operations will be interleaved as we saw in the example above.

Taken together the rules lead to the following definition of non-atomic coupled simulation (without IO transformers).

Definition 4. *Non-atomic coupled downward sim. without IO transformations*
A specification C is a non-atomic coupled downward simulation of the specification A if there is a retrieve relation R showing that C is a non-atomic downward simulation of A, and there is a family of simulation relations R^S such that the following hold.
C $R^{\langle\rangle} = R$
S1 $\forall AState, CState, CState' \bullet R^S \wedge COp_1 \Rightarrow \exists AState' \bullet \Xi AState \wedge (R^{S^\frown \langle COp_1 \rangle})'$
S2 $\forall AState, CState \bullet R^S \wedge COp_1 \in S \Rightarrow pre\ COp_2$
S3 $\forall AState, CState, CState' \bullet R^S \wedge COp_2 \Rightarrow COp_1 \in S \wedge \exists AState' \bullet AOp \wedge (R^{S\setminus\langle COp_1\rangle})'$

Note that this in particular requires that for every initial state of C there is an initial state of A related by $R^{\langle\rangle}$.

Next, we take another look at the (problematic) translate and invert example (without inputs). We should now be able to show that the concrete specification $CTranslate_1$ from Figure 3 is not a non-atomic coupled simulation of the abstract specification $ATranslate$ from Figure 1, at least not when we use the same R as before. Here R is:

```
┌─ R ─────────────
│ AState
│ CState₁
├─────────────────
│ x_A = x_C
│ y_A = y_C
│ ¬b ∧ ¬c
└─────────────────
```

We set $R^{\langle\rangle}$ to be R thereby fulfilling the coupling condition C. There are now four (nonempty) sequences S which are relevant when checking the remaining conditions: $\langle TransX_1\rangle$, $\langle InvX_1\rangle$, $\langle TransX_1, InvX_1\rangle$ and $\langle InvX_1, TransX_1\rangle$. The corresponding retrieve schemas R^S can, in fact, be calculated from the (normal) retrieve relation R. For example, we find we need the following.

```
┌─ R^⟨TransX₁⟩ ───       ┌─ R^⟨InvX₁⟩ ────
│ AState                  │ AState
│ CState₁                 │ CState₁
├─────────────────        ├─────────────────
│ x_A = x_C − 3           │ x_A = −x_C
│ y_A = y_C               │ y_A = y_C
│ b ∧ ¬c                  │ ¬b ∧ c
└─────────────────        └─────────────────
```

To see this, note that whenever $TransX_1$ or $InvX_1$ are executed in a concrete state which is related to an abstract state via $R = R^{\langle\rangle}$, the resulting concrete state should be related to the *same* abstract state via $R^{\langle TransX_1\rangle}$ or $R^{\langle InvX_1\rangle}$, respectively. This can only be achieved when we require x_A to be equal to $x_C - 3$ or $-x_C$.

In a similar fashion we can derive $R^{\langle TransX_1, InvX_1\rangle}$ and $R^{\langle InvX_1, TransX_1\rangle}$. After execution of $TransX_1$, $InvX_1$ is enabled and after its execution the resulting concrete state still has to be related to the same abstract state. This is achieved by now equating x_A with $-x_C - 3$. In a similar way we can derive the retrieve relation needed after $InvX_1$ followed by $TransX_1$.

$$\begin{array}{|l|}\hline R^{\langle TransX_1, InvX_1\rangle} \\ AState \\ CState_1 \\ \hline x_A = -x_C - 3 \\ y_A = y_C \\ b \wedge c \\ \hline \end{array} \qquad \begin{array}{|l|}\hline R^{\langle InvX_1, TransX_1\rangle} \\ AState \\ CState_1 \\ \hline x_A = -x_C + 3 \\ y_A = y_C \\ b \wedge c \\ \hline \end{array}$$

This seems to be fine so far. Conditions C and S1 hold for all sequences S considered above. Condition S2 is fulfilled as well: when $TransX_1$ is in the index S then b is always true and thus $TransY_1$ is enabled; analogously for $InvX_1$ and $InvY_1$. However, a problem arises when we finish sequences that have already been started. As we have seen before there are some interleavings which do not have a matching abstract counterpart and for these interleavings condition S3 fails. Figure 4 shows such an interleaving.

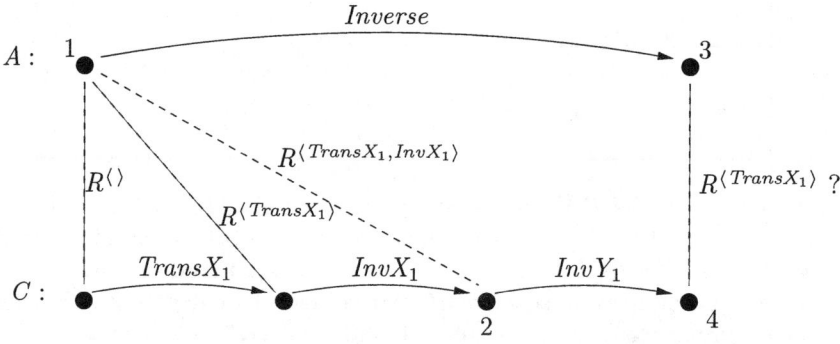

Fig. 4. Matching an interleaved concrete decomposition with its abstract counterpart

Starting with a pair of $R = R^{\langle\rangle}$-related states the concrete specification executes $TransX_1$ and then $InvX_1$. The two states reached via this execution still have to be related to the same abstract state. This is required by condition S1 and is indeed fulfilled. However, the completion of the now started refinement of *Inverse* causes problems. States 1 and 2 are related via $R^{\langle TransX_1, InvX_1\rangle}$, thus $x_A = -x_C - 3$. In the abstract state 3 coordinate x is changed: $x'_A = -x_A$, whereas in concrete state 4 x remains the same as in 2: $x'_C = x_C$. Thus we get: $x'_A = x'_C + 3$ which is in contrast with relation $(R^{\langle TransX_1\rangle})'$ requiring $x'_A = x'_C - 3$. Thus condition S3 is not met.

This completes the proof that $CTranslate_1$ is not a non-atomic refinement of $ATranslate$ (similar problems arise with other choices of retrieve relations).

The translate example can be adapted into a coupled non-atomic refinement that can be verified. Consider an abstract translate with a count operation (assuming the necessary variables have been declared).

$\underline{\quad Translate \quad\quad\quad\quad\quad\quad\quad\quad}$
$\Delta AState$
$x_A?, y_A? : \mathbb{Z}$
$\overline{\rule{0pt}{0.5ex}}$
$x'_A = x_A + x_A? \wedge y'_A = y_A + y_A?$
$a \wedge \neg a'$

$\underline{\quad CntTrans \quad\quad\quad\quad\quad\quad\quad}$
$\Delta AState$
$\overline{\rule{0pt}{0.5ex}}$
$cnt' = cnt + 1$
$\neg a \wedge a'$

Assume $Translate$ is not decomposed in the refinement, but that $CntTrans$ is decomposed into

$\underline{\quad CntTransStart \quad\quad\quad\quad\quad}$
$\Delta CState$
$\overline{\rule{0pt}{0.5ex}}$
$cnt' = cnt + 0.5$
$\neg a \wedge \neg d \wedge d'$

$\underline{\quad CntTransEnd \quad\quad\quad\quad\quad\quad}$
$\Delta CState$
$\overline{\rule{0pt}{0.5ex}}$
$cnt' = cnt + 0.5$
$d \wedge \neg d' \wedge a'$

Now, in this decomposition the variables modified as a direct result of the decomposition are independent from those in $Translate$. Hence any amount of interleaving of this with $Translate$ (or indeed any non-atomic refinement of it) is a valid coupled simulation (using the obvious coupled retrieve relations).

These two examples illustrate a general point: non-atomic coupled simulations allow either a fully sequential model or a fully concurrent model, but nothing in-between. That is, if some interleavings are allowed then all will be, and conversely, if some interleavings are not allowed, then none will be.

4 Coupled simulations with IO transformation

As a last step we add input and output transformers to our definition. This requires only a small change in the definition. Basically there are two differences: the first concerns the relations R^S which now have to record the inputs and outputs of the operations in S. The second difference is in the formulation of condition S3: the input and output transformers have to be applied when completing a sequence and matching it with the abstract operation AOp.

Definition 5. *Non-atomic coupled downward simulation with IO transformation A specification C is a non-atomic coupled downward simulation of the specification A if there is a retrieve relation R and there are input and output transformers IT and OT showing that C is a non-atomic downward simulation of A, and there is a family of simulation relations R^S such that the following hold.*

C $R^{\langle\rangle} = R$
S1 $\forall AState, CState, CState' \bullet R^S \wedge COp_1 \Rightarrow \exists AState' \bullet \Xi AState \wedge (R^{S^\frown \langle COp_1 \rangle})'$
S2 $\forall AState, CState \bullet R^S \wedge COp_1 \in S \Rightarrow pre\ COp_2$
S3' $\forall AState, CState, CState' \bullet IT \gg (R^S \wedge COp_2) \Rightarrow$
$COp_1 \in S \wedge \exists AState' \bullet (AOp \gg OT) \wedge (R^{S \backslash \langle COp_1 \rangle})'$

To see this definition in action, consider the translate example with inputs as described in Section 2.1. As before R^S records the effects of part of the concrete operation. With inputs in the concrete operation this necessitates the input being part of the coupled simulation. Thus, for example, $R^{\langle TransX \rangle}$ will be the following

$R^{\langle TransX \rangle}$
─────────────
$AState$
$CState_0$
$x_C? : \mathbb{Z}$
─────────────
$x_A = x_C - x_C?$
$y_A = y_C$

We use the same input and output transformers as before (see Section 2.1). Then it is clear by comparison with the example without outputs how this generalises the previous definition. It is also easy to check that the conditions required in Definition 5 hold. For example, calculating $IT \gg (R^{\langle TransX \rangle} \wedge TransY)$ we find it simplifies to

─────────────
$AState$
$\Delta CState_0$
$val? : \mathbb{Z} \times \mathbb{Z}$
─────────────
$y'_C = y_C + second\ val?$
$x_A = x_C - first\ val?$
$y_A = y_C$
$x'_C = x_C$

which matches with $Translate \wedge R'$.

A slightly more complicated example is provided by the protocol implementation. We need two transformers: an input transformer for $PrepareToSend\ \raisebox{2pt}{$\circ$}\!\!\raisebox{-2pt}{$\circ$}\ Transmit$ and an output transformer for $Receive$.

$ITPrepTrans$
─────────────
$m? : M$
$text! : Text$
$t! : Time$
─────────────
$text! = first\ m?$
$t! = second\ m?$

$OTReceive$
─────────────
$m? : M$
$msg! : M$
─────────────
$m? = msg!$

Using $R^{\langle\rangle} = R$ (as given in Section 2) as a starting point we get the following simulation relations R^S:

$\boxed{\begin{array}{l} R^{\langle PrepareToSend \rangle} \\ \hline AState \\ CState \\ text? : Text \\ \hline \#q = \#link \\ \forall i : 1..\#q \bullet \\ \qquad q.i = (link.i.1.1, link.i.1.2) \\ inStore = \langle text? \rangle \\ outStore = \langle\rangle \end{array}}$
$\boxed{\begin{array}{l} R^{\langle PrepareToReceive \rangle} \\ \hline AState \\ CState \\ \hline \#q = \#(outStore \frown link) \\ q.1 = (outStore.1.1, outStore.1.2) \\ \forall i : 2..\#q \bullet \\ \qquad q.i = (link.i.1.1, link.i.1.2) \\ inStore = \langle\rangle \\ outStore \neq \langle\rangle \end{array}}$

Note that the input which is used in operation *PrepareToSend* is now recorded in the simulation relation. When completing the refinement of *Send* the input transformer will relate it (together with the input of *Transmit*) to the input of *Send* (condition S3').

The simulation relations for $S = \langle PrepareToSend, PrepareToReceive \rangle$ and $S = \langle PrepareToReceive, PrepareToSend \rangle$ are equal (since the two operations modify different variables of *CState*). This is already a strong indication that all interleavings will have a matching abstract behaviour.

$\boxed{\begin{array}{l} R^{\langle PrepareToSend, PrepareToReceive \rangle} \\ \hline AState \\ CState \\ text? : Text \\ \hline \#q = \#(outStore \frown link) \\ q.1 = (outStore.1.1, outStore.1.2) \\ \forall i : 2..\#q \bullet q.i = (link.i.1.1, link.i.1.2) \\ inStore = \langle text? \rangle \\ outStore \neq \langle\rangle \end{array}}$

We check some of the conditions for non-atomic coupled simulation with IO transformation. Condition C is fulfilled by definition. For condition S1 consider the case that COp_1 is *PrepareToSend*. Since the precondition of *PrepareToSend* is $inStore = \langle\rangle$ it can only be executed in states related by $R^{\langle\rangle}$ or $R^{\langle PrepareToReceive \rangle}$. Execution of *PrepareToSend* leaves variable *link* unchanged and reads in an input which is stored in *inStore*. Thus the reached state is related to the same abstract state via $R^{\langle PrepareToSend \rangle}$ or $R^{\langle PrepareToReceive, PrepareToSend \rangle}$, respectively.

Condition S2 is easily seen to be fulfilled since the preconditions of *Transmit* and *Deliver* require *inStore* and *outStore*, respectively, to be nonempty. Condition S3' involves the application of input and output transformers. For instance, we have to check that

$\forall\, AState, CState, CState' \bullet ITPrepTrans \gg (R^{\langle PrepareToSend \rangle} \wedge Transmit) \Rightarrow$
$\exists\, AState' \bullet Send \wedge (R^{\langle\rangle})'$

holds. Here, the input transformer takes in the input $m?$ of $Send$ and relates it to the inputs $text?$ (recorded in the simulation relation) and $t?$ of operation $Transmit$. Thus, in effect $R^{\langle PrepareToSend \rangle}$ records both simulation information (i.e., which states need to be linked up) as well as the effect of performing $PrepareToSend$, condition S3' then checks whether this information is consistent with ending the operation (i.e., $Transmit$) and performing an abstract $Send$.

4.1 Calculating coupled simulations

The conditions required in Definition 5 ask for the existence of an appropriate coupled simulation R^S. However, it should be clear that in the worked examples we have looked at so far, we have in effect calculated R^S using the base retrieve relation R. This, in fact, is a general strategy which can be made precise.

As hinted at before the relations R^S record the effect of the concrete components present in S. We can use this information in the calculation. Consider the translate example given at the start of Section 2.1 (i.e., the one with inputs). R, $R^{\langle TransX \rangle}$ and $TransX$ were

R
$AState$
$CState_0$
$x_A = x_C$
$y_A = y_C$

$R^{\langle TransX \rangle}$
$AState$
$CState_0$
$x_C? : \mathbb{Z}$
$x_A = x_C - x_C?$
$y_A = y_C$

$TransX$
$\Delta CState_0$
$x_C? : \mathbb{Z}$
$x'_C = x_C + x_C?$
$y'_C = y_C$

and we notice that $R^{\langle TransX \rangle}$ is $(R[x'_C/x_C, y'_C/y_C]\,\S\, TransX)[x_C/x'_C, y_C/y'_C]$. This holds in general. Thus we can define $R^{\langle\rangle}$ to be R and

$$R^{S^\frown \langle COp_1 \rangle} \,\widehat{=}\, (R^S[CState'/CState]\,\S\, COp_1)[CState/CState'] \qquad (1)$$

where $[CState'/CState]$ represent the obvious global substitutions.

This definition allows one to compute R^S for all sequences S with started but unfinished refinements. The conditions in Definition 5 then need verifying. Obviously condition C holds automatically, as does condition S1. To see the latter note that in $R^{S^\frown \langle COp_1 \rangle}$ the abstract state remains unchanged (compared to R^S) and is related to the concrete state reached after executing COp_1.

Condition S2 then still requires checking (which is easy) as does S3' (in which lies some complexity). To check S3' we define the effect of finishing a concrete non-atomic operations. We let IT and OT be the input and output transformers, and assume In to be a list of inputs of AOp and Out to be a list of outputs of $COp_1\,\S\,COp_2$. We then define:

$R^S \blacktriangledown \langle COp_1 \rangle \,\widehat{=}\,$
$\bigl(((IT \gg (R^S[CState'/CState]\,\S\,COp_2)[AState'/AState])\,\S\,(AOp \gg OT))$
$[AState/AState', CState/CState']\bigr) \setminus (In, Out)$

This is the relation between abstract and concrete state which is reached when finishing a concrete sequence together with executing the corresponding abstract operation. The inputs and outputs are hidden since we do not care about their actual values anymore once both concrete and abstract operations have finished. Condition S3' then requires to check that $R^S \blacktriangledown \langle COp_1 \rangle$ is equal to $R^{S \backslash \langle COp_1 \rangle}$.

To understand the definition and what is required to be verified, we calculate $R^{\langle TransX \rangle} \blacktriangledown \langle TransX \rangle$ in the above example. That is we calculate

$$(IT \gg ((R^{\langle TransX \rangle})[x'_C/x_C, y'_C/y_C] \mathbin{\raisebox{0.5ex}{\scalebox{0.7}{\S}}} TransY)[x'_A/x_A, y'_A/y_A] \mathbin{\raisebox{0.5ex}{\scalebox{0.7}{\S}}} Translate)$$
$$[x_A/x'_A, y_A/y'_A, x_C/x'_C, y_C/y'_C] \setminus (val?)$$

which is

$$\begin{array}{|l} \underline{R^{\langle TransX \rangle} \blacktriangledown \langle TransX \rangle} \\ AState \\ CState_0 \\ \hline \exists val? : \mathbb{Z} \times \mathbb{Z} \bullet \\ \quad x_C - \text{first } val? = x_A - \text{first } val? \\ \quad y_C - \text{second } val? = y_A - \text{second } val? \end{array}$$

which is equivalent to R.

In practice the best approach seems to be to use (1) to calculate the expected values of R^S from a given R. S1 will hold by construction, leaving it necessary to check C, S2 and S3'. If one of the conditions fails then there is no coupled simulation with base relation R. However, the concrete system could still be a coupled non-atomic refinement, namely, under a different relation R.

5 Conclusions

In this paper we have adapted the idea of coupled simulations to a state-based setting. This allowed a derivation of a set of conditions which augment the existing definition of non-atomic downward simulations. The purpose of these additional conditions were to strengthen the downward simulation definition in a number of important ways.

Although the new conditions add complexity, we also showed how the additional coupled simulations that were needed could, in fact, be calculated from the base retrieve relation. Of course, how feasible this will be in practice remains to be seen. This has to be left for further work, as does the integration with process algebraic definitions which we discussed in the introduction.

References

1. J.-R. Abrial. *The B-Book: Assigning Programs to Meanings.* CUP, 1996.
2. L. Aceto. *Action Refinement in Process Algebras.* CUP, London, 1992.
3. L. Aceto and M. Hennessy. Towards action-refinement in process algebras. *Information and Computation*, 103:204–269, 1993.
4. E. A. Boiten and J. Derrick. IO-refinement in Z. In A. Evans, D. J. Duke, and T. Clark, editors, *3rd BCS-FACS Northern Formal Methods Workshop*. Springer-Verlag, September 1998. http://www.ewic.org.uk/.
5. W.-P. de Roever and K. Engelhardt. *Data Refinement: Model-Oriented Proof Methods and their Comparison.* CUP, 1998.
6. J. Derrick and E. Boiten. Non-atomic refinement in Z. In J. Woodcock and J. Wing, editors, *FM'99, World Congress on Formal Methods*, number 1709 in LNCS, pages 1477–1496. Springer, 1999.
7. J. Derrick and E. A. Boiten. *Refinement in Z and Object-Z.* Springer-Verlag, 2001.
8. C. Fischer. CSP-OZ - a combination of CSP and Object-Z. In H. Bowman and J. Derrick, editors, *Second IFIP International conference on Formal Methods for Open Object-based Distributed Systems*, pages 423–438. Chapman & Hall, July 1997.
9. C. Fischer. How to combine Z with a process algebra. In *ZUM'98: The Z Formal Specification Notation*, volume 1493 of *Lecture Notes in Computer Science*, pages 5–23. Springer-Verlag, September 1998.
10. C. A. R. Hoare. *Communicating Sequential Processes.* Prentice Hall, 1985.
11. C. B. Jones. *Systematic Software Development using VDM.* Prentice Hall, 1989.
12. J. Parrow and P. Sjödin. Multiway Synchronisation Verified with Coupled Simulation. In R. Cleaveland, editor, *CONCUR '92, Concurrency Theory*, number 630 in LNCS, pages 518–533. Springer, 1992.
13. A. Rensink. Action Contraction. In C. Palamidessi, editor, *CONCUR 2000 - Concurrency Theory*, number 1877 in LNCS, pages 290–304. Springer, 2000.
14. A. Rensink and R. Gorrieri. Action refinement as an implementation relation. In M. Bidoit and M. Dauchet, editors, *TAPSOFT '97: Theory and Practice of Software Development*, volume 1214 of *Lecture Notes in Computer Science*, pages 772–786, 1997.
15. G. Smith. A semantic integration of Object-Z and CSP for the specification of concurrent systems. In J. Fitzgerald, C. B. Jones, and P. Lucas, editors, *FME'97: Industrial Application and Strengthened Foundations of Formal Methods*, volume 1313 of *Lecture Notes in Computer Science*, pages 62–81. Springer-Verlag, September 1997.
16. G. Smith and J. Derrick. Specification, refinement and verification of concurrent systems - an integration of Object-Z and CSP. *Formal Methods in Systems Design*, 18:249–284, May 2001.
17. J. M. Spivey. *The Z Notation: A Reference Manual.* International Series in Computer Science. Prentice Hall, 2nd edition, 1992.
18. S. Stepney, D. Cooper, and J. C. P. Woodcock. More powerful data refinement in Z. In J. P. Bowen, A. Fett, and M. G. Hinchey, editors, *ZUM'98: The Z Formal Specification Notation*, volume 1493 of *Lecture Notes in Computer Science*, pages 284–307. Springer-Verlag, September 1998.
19. H. Treharne and S. Schneider. Using a process algebra to control B operations. In K. Araki, A. Galloway, and K. Taguchi, editors, *International Conference on Integrated Formal Methods 1999 (IFM'99)*, pages 437–456, York, July 1999. Springer.

20. R. van Glabbeek and U. Goltz. Equivalence notions for concurrent systems and refinement of actions. In A. Kreczmar and G. Mirkowska, editors, *Mathematical Foundations of Computer Science 1989*, volume 379 of *LNCS*, pages 237–248. Springer, 1989.
21. Walter Vogler. Failure semantics based on interval semiwords is a congruence for refinement. *Distributed Computing*, 4:139–162, 1991.
22. J. C. P. Woodcock and J. Davies. *Using Z: Specification, Refinement, and Proof*. Prentice Hall, 1996.

An Analysis of Forward Simulation Data Refinement

Moshe Deutsch and Martin C. Henson

Department of Computer Science, University of Essex, UK.
{mdeuts, hensm}@essex.ac.uk

Abstract. This paper investigates data refinement by forward simulation for specifications whose semantics is given by *partial* relations. The most well-known example of such a semantics is that for Z. The standard model-theoretic approach is based on totalisation and lifting. The paper examines this model, exploring and isolating the precise roles played by lifting and totalisation in the standard account by introducing a simpler, normative theory of forward simulation data refinement (SF-refinement) which captures refinement directly in the language and in terms of the natural properties of preconditions and postconditions. This theory is used in conjunction with four other model-theoretic approaches to determine the extent to which the standard approach is canonical, and the extent to which it is arbitrary.

1 Introduction

This paper investigates data refinement by forward simulation for specifications whose semantics is given by *partial* relations. The most well-known example of such a semantics is that for Z, in which schemas denote sets of bindings which establish, in general, a partial relation between before and after states.

In order to formulate a theory of data refinement for this underlying semantics, the standard approach is as described in [20] (Chapter 16, *et seq.*). This is a *model-theoretic* approach, in which the specifications (partial relations) are both *completed* (made total) and *extended* (by means of an additional semantic value). This modelling also involves extending the simulation relations, though not completing them. As is often the case with a model-based approach, the technical machinery raises a number of questions: why must the specifications and simulations be extended? Why extended in the manner presented? Why must the specifications be completed in the manner presented? In other words, one is interested in ensuring that there is a very clear motivation for what might otherwise appear to be rather arbitrary technical devices.

In this paper, we consider six data refinement theories, confining attention to refinement by means of forward simulation. These constitute generalisations of various operation refinement theories explored in [6] and [7] of which two are related to previous work [20, 5]. We will prove that three of these theories are equivalent and show that five of them are *acceptable* as refinement characterisations. In exploring these issues we integrate a mathematical with an informal analysis, using a variety of examples and counterexamples. Our results shed some light on the standard model-theoretic approach, in particular precisely explaining the extent to which it is canonical and the extent to which it is arbitrary.

We begin by introducing the notion of data simulation that underlies the forward and backward simulation refinement techniques (section 2), including the *lifted* simulations used in refinement based on relational completion operators (discussed in, for example, [20, 5] and investigated in detail in [6, 7]). These involve an additional distinguished element, called *bottom* and written $\bot$. We then define three alternative characterisations of data refinement (section 3) based on two distinct relational completion models discussed in [6] (see also appendix B, section B.1). We show that all three are *sound* with respect to a purely proof theoretic characterisation of forward simulation refinement, but only two of these are *complete* with respect to it (section 4). This fourth theory, SF-refinement, captures forward simulation data refinement directly in terms of the language, the relationship between the data types involved, and the concept of precondition. It is a more abstract, less constructive notion, not involving the introduction of either an auxiliary semantics, nor the introduction of an auxiliary element. We regard it as the *normative* theory for exploring the validity of refinement approaches that are based on forward simulation.

Our approach sheds light on the role of *lifting* in data refinement based on relational completion models by investigating a forward simulation refinement characterisation based on the non-lifted totalisation discussed in [6] (see also appendix B, section B.2). We show that this is an unacceptable refinement theory (section 5) and explain the reasons why the non-lifted totalisation is an adequate model for operation refinement [6] but not data refinement, emphasising the significance of $\bot$ in ensuring validity of model-theoretic approaches (section 6).

For technical convenience, our investigation takes place in $\mathcal{Z}_C$, the logic for Z reported in [13] and a simple *conservative extension* $\mathcal{Z}_C^\bot$ [6] which incorporates $\bot$ into the types of $\mathcal{Z}_C$. We summarise this, and additional notational conventions, in appendix A; further information is provided in appendix A of our companion paper, [8] (this volume). This allows us to work with Z schemas as easily as with abstract relations. Nothing we show here is specifically confined to Z: we use it as a convenient linguistic vehicle for state-based specification. We employ a novel technique of rendering all the theories of refinement as sets of introduction and elimination rules. This leads to a uniform and simple method for proving the various results in the sequel. As such, it contrasts with the more semantic based techniques employed in [3].

2 Data Simulations

The methods of data refinement in state-based systems are well established. The conditions under which a transformation is a correct refinement step can be summarised by two simulation based refinement techniques: *forward simulation* and *backward simulation* [4]. In this section we revise these and introduce some essential material underlying our investigation.

A data simulation [20, 22] is a relation between an abstract data space and a concrete counterpart. Data simulations[1] underly two refinement techniques which enable us to verify data refinement, as shown by the two semi-commuting diagrams in Fig. 1. Both

---

[1] The notion of simulation is overloaded in the literature. Various authors use it to denote a certain refinement technique, whereas others use it to denote the *retrieve relation* used in a

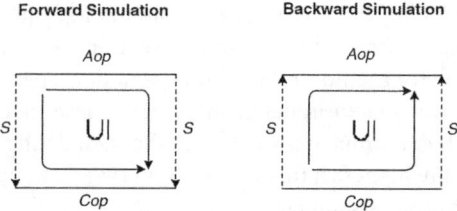

Fig. 1. Forward simulation and backward simulation refinement techniques. *Aop* and *Cop* represent the abstract and concrete operations (respectively), whereas *S* represents the simulation. Note that a forward simulation is oriented (by composition) from the abstract to the concrete data space and, in a backward simulation, in the opposite direction.

forward and backward simulation[2] refinement techniques are known to be sound but neither of them is singly complete. However, they are known to be *jointly complete* [21].

We will use the meta-variables[3] U_0 and U_1 to range over operation schemas. In this paper U_0 will always be concrete and U_1 abstract. We adopt the approach taken in [3]: our concrete type is $\mathbb{P}(T_0 \vee T_0')$ and the abstract type is $\mathbb{P}(T_1 \vee T_1')$. A forward simulation (abstract to concrete) is of type $\mathbb{P}(T_1 \vee T_0')$. In this way a simulation is modelled as a set of bindings like any other operation schema.

We will need to incorporate the $\bot$ element in a simulation used with lifted-totalised operations (see appendix B and [6,7]). Naturally, Woodcock's chaotic totalisation [20] is unacceptable here, as this might enforce a link between abstract and concrete states that are not supposed to be linked. The conventional approach [20,5] is to (non-strictly) lift[4] $\bot$ in the input set of the simulation, thus retaining its partiality. This leads to the following definition:

Definition 1 (Non-Strictly Lifted Forward Simulation).

$$\overset{\circ}{S}{}^{\mathbb{P}(T_1 \vee T_0')} =_{df} \{ z_1 \star z_0' \in T_{1_\bot} \star T_{0_\bot}' \mid z_1 \neq \bot \Rightarrow z_1 \star z_0' \in S \}$$

Then the following introduction and elimination rules are derivable:

Proposition 1.

$$\frac{t_1 \star t_0' \in T_{1_\bot} \star T_{0_\bot}' \quad t_1 \neq \bot \vdash t_1 \star t_0' \in S}{t_1 \star t_0' \in \overset{\circ}{S}} \ (\circ^+) \qquad \frac{t_1 \star t_0' \in \overset{\circ}{S} \quad t_1 \neq \bot}{t_1 \star t_0' \in S} \ (\circ_0^-)$$

$$\frac{t_1 \star t_0' \in \overset{\circ}{S}}{t_1 \star t_0' \in T_{1_\bot} \star T_{0_\bot}'} \ (\circ_1^-)$$

□

---

certain refinement technique. In this paper we use the word "simulation" to specifically denote a retrieve relation. It will be explicitly stated when used in other contexts.

[2] Forward and backward simulations are also respectively known as *downward* and *upward* simulations [4, 5, 10] due to their directions in the commuting diagrams in Fig. 1.

[3] We provide some notational conventions in appendix A and in appendix A of [8].

[4] Lifting signifies mapping $\bot$ of the input set of the relation onto all the states of its output set. In general, the notion of strictness discussed in this paper is with respect to $\bot$; therefore, strict lifting denotes mapping $\bot$ onto only its output counterpart.

Lemma 1. *The following additional rules are derivable for non-strictly lifted simulations:*

$$\frac{}{S \subseteq \overset{\circ}{S}}\ (i) \qquad \frac{}{\bot \in \overset{\circ}{S}}\ (ii) \qquad \frac{t' \in T'_{0_\bot}}{\bot \star t' \in \overset{\circ}{S}}\ (iii) \qquad \frac{t_1 \star \bot' \in \overset{\circ}{S}}{t_1 = \bot}\ (iv)$$

□

Lemmas 1(i – iv) demonstrate that definition 1 is consistent with the intentions described in [20] and [5]: the underlying partial relation is contained in the lifting; the ⊥ element is present in the relation and is mapped onto every after state, and no other initial state is so. This raises an immediate question: why does the lifting of the simulation have to be non-strict with respect to ⊥? This issue was not explored in [20, 5], where the non-strict lifting of the simulation is taken as self-evident. We will gradually provide an answer to this question in the sequel. For that, we will need the definition of a strictly lifted simulation:

Definition 2 (Strictly Lifted Forward Simulation).

$$S^{\mathbb{P}(\overrightarrow{T_1 \vee T'_0})} =_{df} \{z_1 \star z'_0 \in T_{1_\bot} \star T'_{0_\bot} \mid (z_1 \neq \bot \Rightarrow z_1 \star z'_0 \in S) \wedge (z_1 = \bot \Rightarrow z'_0 = \bot')\}$$

Obvious introduction and elimination rules follow from this.

Lemma 2. *The following additional rules are derivable for strictly lifted simulations:*

$$\frac{}{S \subseteq \overrightarrow{S}}\ (i) \qquad \frac{}{\overrightarrow{S} \subseteq \overset{\circ}{S}}\ (ii) \qquad \frac{}{\bot \in \overrightarrow{S}}\ (iii)$$

$$\frac{t_1 \star \bot' \in \overrightarrow{S}}{t_1 = \bot}\ (iv) \qquad \frac{t_1 \star t'_0 \in \overrightarrow{S} \quad t'_0 \neq \bot'}{t_1 \star t'_0 \in S}\ (v)$$

□

Lemmas 2(iv – v) embody the strictness captured by definition 2: if the after state is ⊥ then the initial state must also be ⊥, and if it is not ⊥ then the initial state was not either.

3 Four Theories for Data Refinement

In [6] and [7] we investigated operation refinement (that is the degenerate case of data refinement in which simulations are identity functions) for specifications whose semantics is given by partial relation semantics (again using Z as an example). We compared three characterisations of *operation refinement*: S-refinement, a proof theoretic characterisation closely connected to refinement as introduced by Spivey [17]; $W_\bullet$-refinement, based on Woodcock's relational completion operator [20]; and $W_\ominus$-refinement based on a strict relational completion operator (see appendix B, section B.1). We proved that all these refinement theories are equivalent. The investigation also illuminated the crucial role of ⊥ in total correctness operation refinement.

In this section, we provide four distinct notions of data refinement, based on the notions of operation refinement described above and generalised to forward simulation data refinement. We will then go on to compare them, thus providing a complementary investigation to that given in [6] and [7].

3.1 SF-Refinement

In this section, we introduce a purely proof theoretic characterisation of forward simulation refinement, which is closely connected to sufficient refinement conditions introduced by, for example, Josephs [14], King [15], Woodcock [20, p.260] (indicated as "F-corr") and Derrick and Boiten [5, p.90]. These conditions correspond to the premises of our introduction rule for SF-refinement.

This generalisation of S-refinement [6, 7] is based on two properties expected in a refinement: that *postconditions do not weaken* (we do not permit an increase in non-determinism in a refinement) and that *preconditions do not strengthen* (we do not permit requirements in the domain of definition to disappear in a refinement). In this case these two properties must hold in the presence of a simulation.

The notion can be captured by forcing the refinement relation to hold *exactly* when these conditions apply. SF-refinement is written $U_0 \sqsupseteq_{sf}^{s} U_1$ (U_0 SF-refines U_1 with respect to the simulation S)[5] and is given by the following $\mathcal{Z}_C$ definition:

Definition 3.

$$U_0 \sqsupseteq_{sf}^{s} U_1 =_{df} (\forall z_0, z_1 \bullet z_1 \star z_0' \in S \land Pre\ U_1\ z_1 \Rightarrow Pre\ U_0\ z_0) \land$$
$$(\forall z_2, x_0, x_1 \bullet Pre\ U_1\ x_1 \land x_0 \star z_2' \in U_0 \land x_1 \star x_0' \in S$$
$$\Rightarrow \exists y \bullet x_1 \star y' \in U_1 \land y \star z_2' \in S)$$

This leads directly to the following rules:

Proposition 2. *Let* x_0, x_1, z_0, z_1, z_2 *be fresh variables.*

$$\frac{\begin{array}{l} z_1 \star z_0' \in S, Pre\ U_1\ z_1 \vdash Pre\ U_0\ z_0 \\ Pre\ U_1\ x_1, x_0 \star z_2' \in U_0, x_1 \star x_0' \in S \vdash x_1 \star t' \in U_1 \\ Pre\ U_1\ x_1, x_0 \star z_2' \in U_0, x_1 \star x_0' \in S \vdash t \star z_2' \in S \end{array}}{U_0 \sqsupseteq_{sf} U_1} \ (\sqsupseteq_{sf}^{+})$$

$$\frac{U_0 \sqsupseteq_{sf} U_1 \quad Pre\ U_1\ t_1 \quad t_1 \star t_0' \in S}{Pre\ U_0\ t_0} \ (\sqsupseteq_{sf_0}^{-})$$

$$\frac{U_0 \sqsupseteq_{sf} U_1 \quad Pre\ U_1\ t_1 \quad t_0 \star t_2' \in U_0 \quad t_1 \star t_0' \in S \quad t_1 \star y' \in U_1, y \star t_2' \in S \vdash P}{P} \ (\sqsupseteq_{sf_1}^{-})$$

The usual sideconditions apply to the eigenvariable y. □

This theory does not depend on, and makes no reference to, the $\perp$ value; it is formalised in the theory $\mathcal{Z}_C$. We take SF-refinement as *normative*: this is our prescription for data refinement, and another theory is acceptable providing it is at least sound with respect to it.

---

[5] We will omit the superscript S from now on, in this and other notions of refinement that depend upon a simulation.

3.2 Relational Completion Based Refinement

We now introduce three forward simulation refinement theories in the extended framework $\mathcal{Z}_C^\perp$. These are based on the two distinct notions of the schema lifted-totalisation set out in section B.1 of appendix B. Each of them captures, schematically, the forward simulation commuting diagram in Fig. 1 and is based on *schema* or, more generally, *relational composition* (see [8], proposition 17).

WF$_\bullet$-Refinement. This notion of refinement is also discussed in [20, p.246] and [4]. It is written $U_0 \sqsupseteq_{wf_\bullet}^s U_1$ and is defined as follows:

Definition 4. $U_0 \sqsupseteq_{wf_\bullet}^s U_1 =_{df} \overset{\circ}{S} \mathrel{\raise.2ex\hbox{$\scriptstyle;$}} \overset{\bullet}{U_0} \subseteq \overset{\bullet}{U_1} \mathrel{\raise.2ex\hbox{$\scriptstyle;$}} \overset{\circ}{S}$

The following introduction and elimination rules are immediately derivable for WF$_\bullet$-refinement:

Proposition 3. *Let z_0, z_1 be fresh.*

$$\frac{z_1 \star z_0' \in \overset{\circ}{S} \mathrel{\raise.2ex\hbox{$\scriptstyle;$}} \overset{\bullet}{U_0} \vdash z_1 \star z_0' \in \overset{\bullet}{U_1} \mathrel{\raise.2ex\hbox{$\scriptstyle;$}} \overset{\circ}{S}}{U_0 \sqsupseteq_{wf_\bullet} U_1} \; (\sqsupseteq_{wf_\bullet}^+) \qquad \frac{U_0 \sqsupseteq_{wf_\bullet} U_1 \quad t_1 \star t_0' \in \overset{\circ}{S} \mathrel{\raise.2ex\hbox{$\scriptstyle;$}} \overset{\bullet}{U_0}}{t_1 \star t_0' \in \overset{\bullet}{U_1} \mathrel{\raise.2ex\hbox{$\scriptstyle;$}} \overset{\circ}{S}} \; (\sqsupseteq_{wf_\bullet}^-)$$

□

WF$_\phi$-Refinement. The natural generalisation of W$_\ominus$-refinement [6] (at least in the light of the standard literature) is to use strict-lifted totalised operations, yet a non-strict lifted simulation. We name this WF$_\phi$-refinement; it is written $U_0 \sqsupseteq_{wf_\phi}^s U_1$ and defined as follows:

Definition 5. $U_0 \sqsupseteq_{wf_\phi}^s U_1 =_{df} \overset{\circ}{S} \mathrel{\raise.2ex\hbox{$\scriptstyle;$}} \overset{\ominus}{U_0} \subseteq \overset{\ominus}{U_1} \mathrel{\raise.2ex\hbox{$\scriptstyle;$}} \overset{\circ}{S}$

Obvious introduction and elimination rules follow from this.

WF$_\ominus$-Refinement. Our third characterisation of refinement is motivated by the query raised in section 2. Establishing a refinement theory, in which both the operations and the simulation are strictly lifted, provides a point of reference which will aid us in investigating two important matters: firstly, whether the strict and non-strict relational completion operators are still interchangeable underlying generalisations of data refinement; secondly, whether the non-strict lifting of the simulation is an essential property. We name this theory WF$_\ominus$-refinement; it is written $U_0 \sqsupseteq_{wf_\ominus}^s U_1$ and defined as follows:

Definition 6. $U_0 \sqsupseteq_{wf_\ominus}^s U_1 =_{df} \vec{S} \mathrel{\raise.2ex\hbox{$\scriptstyle;$}} \overset{\ominus}{U_0} \subseteq \overset{\ominus}{U_1} \mathrel{\raise.2ex\hbox{$\scriptstyle;$}} \vec{S}$

Obvious introduction and elimination rules follow from this definition.

4 Three Equivalent Theories

In this section we demonstrate that three of the refinement theories are equivalent, whereas the fourth theory, $WF_\bullet$-refinement, is sound (but not complete) with respect to the others. We will clearly see the critical role that the $\bot$ value plays in model-theoretic refinement, in general, and the consequences of strict lifting, in particular.

Methodologically, we shall be showing that all judgements of refinement in one theory are contained among the refinements sanctioned by another. Such results can always be established proof-theoretically because we have expressed even our model-theoretic approaches as theories. Specifically, we will show that the refinement relation of a theory T_0 satisfies the elimination rule (or rules) for refinement of another theory T_1. Since the elimination rules and introduction rules of a theory enjoy the usual symmetry properties, this is sufficient to show that all T_0-refinements are also T_1-refinements. Equivalence can then be shown by interchanging T_0 and T_1.

4.1 $WF_\bullet$-Refinement and SF-Refinement Are Equivalent

We begin by showing that $WF_\bullet$-refinement implies SF-refinement by proving that $WF_\bullet$-refinement satisfies both SF-refinement elimination rules. Firstly the rule for preconditions.

Proposition 4. *The following rule is derivable:*

$$\frac{U_0 \sqsupseteq_{wf_\bullet} U_1 \quad Pre\ U_1\ t_1 \quad t_1 \star t'_0 \in S}{Pre\ U_0\ t_0}$$

Proof

$$\frac{\dfrac{\dfrac{t_1 \star \bot' \in \overset{\circ}{U_1} \, \overset{\circ}{\S}\, \overset{\circ}{S}}{\vdots}\ \delta}{\dfrac{\dfrac{\dfrac{\overline{t_1 \star y' \in \overset{\bullet}{U_1}}\ (2) \quad \dfrac{y \star \bot' \in \overset{\circ}{S}}{y = \bot}\ (L.\ 1(iv))}{t_1 \star \bot' \in \overset{\bullet}{U_1}}\quad Pre\ U_1\ t_1}{\dfrac{t_1 \star \bot' \in \overset{\bullet}{U_1}}{false}\ (L.\ 4)}{\dfrac{false}{Pre\ U_0\ t_0}\ (1)}\ (2)}$$

where δ is:

$$\dfrac{U_0 \sqsupseteq_{wf_\bullet} U_1 \quad \dfrac{\dfrac{t_1 \star t'_0 \in S}{t_1 \star t'_0 \in \overset{\circ}{S}}\ (L.\ 1(i)) \quad \dfrac{\neg Pre\ U_0\ t_0\ (1) \quad \dfrac{t_1 \star t'_0 \in S \quad t_0 \in T_0}{t_0 \in T_{0_\bot}}}{t_0 \star \bot' \in \overset{\bullet}{U_0}}\ (L.\ 5(iii))}{t_1 \star \bot' \in \overset{\circ}{S}\, \overset{\circ}{\S}\, \overset{\bullet}{U_0}}}{t_1 \star \bot' \in \overset{\circ}{U_1}\, \overset{\circ}{\S}\, \overset{\circ}{S}}$$

$\square$

Notice the explicit use of $\bot$ in the proof. This is reminiscent of our earlier investigation of operation refinement, in which the explicit use of $\bot$ is critical for proving that W$_\bullet$-refinement satisfies the precondition elimination rule for S-refinement (see, for example, proposition 4.11 of [6]). Much the same observation can be made here, only that the use of lemmas 5(iii) and 1(iv) in the proof suggests that *both* the lifted-totalisation of the operations and the lifting of the simulation are essential for showing that WF$_\bullet$-refinement guarantees that preconditions do not strengthen in the presence of the simulation.

Turning now to the second elimination rule in SF-refinement.

Proposition 5. *The following rule is derivable:*

$$\frac{U_0 \sqsupseteq_{wf\bullet} U_1 \quad \text{Pre } U_1 \, t_1 \quad t_0 \star t_2' \in U_0 \quad t_1 \star t_0' \in S \quad t_1 \star y' \in U_1, y \star t_2' \in S \vdash P}{P}$$

Proof

$$\frac{U_0 \sqsupseteq_{wf\bullet} U_1 \quad \dfrac{\dfrac{t_1 \star t_0' \in S}{t_1 \star t_0' \in \overset{\circ}{S}} \,(L.\,1(i)) \quad \dfrac{t_0 \star t_2' \in U_0}{t_0 \star t_2' \in \overset{\bullet}{U_0}} \,(L.\,5(i))}{t_1 \star t_2' \in \overset{\circ}{S} \,\overset{\bullet}{;} \,\overset{\bullet}{U_0}} \quad \dfrac{\delta}{\vdots} \\ \dfrac{t_1 \star t_2' \in \overset{\bullet}{U_1} \,\overset{\circ}{;} \,\overset{\circ}{S}}{P}}{P} \,(I)$$

where δ is:

$$\frac{\dfrac{\overline{t_1 \star y' \in \overset{\bullet}{U_1}} \,(I) \quad \text{Pre } U_1 \, t_1}{t_1 \star y' \in U_1} \quad \dfrac{\overline{y \star t_2' \in \overset{\circ}{S}} \,(I) \quad \dfrac{\overline{t_1 \star y' \in \overset{\bullet}{U_1}} \,(I) \quad \text{Pre } U_1 \, t_1}{\dfrac{t_1 \star y' \in U_1}{y \neq \bot} \,(L.\,4)}}{y \star t_2' \in S}}{\dfrac{t_1 \star y' \in U_1 \wedge y \star t_2' \in S}{\vdots \\ P}}$$

□

Theorem 1. $U_0 \sqsupseteq_{wf\bullet} U_1 \Rightarrow U_0 \sqsupseteq_{sf} U_1$

Proof This follows immediately, by ($\sqsupseteq_{sf}^+$), from propositions 4 and 5[6].□

We now show that SF-refinement satisfies the WF$_\bullet$-elimination rule.

Proposition 6. *The following rule is derivable:*

$$\frac{U_0 \sqsupseteq_{sf} U_1 \quad t_1 \star t_0' \in \overset{\circ}{S} \,\overset{\bullet}{;} \,\overset{\bullet}{U_0}}{t_1 \star t_0' \in \overset{\bullet}{U_1} \,\overset{\circ}{;} \,\overset{\circ}{S}}$$

---

[6] The proofs of such theorems are always automatic by the structural symmetry between introduction and elimination rules. We shall not give them in future.

Proof

$$
\cfrac{t_1 \star t_0' \in \overset{\circ}{S} \, \overset{\circ}{,} \, \overset{\bullet}{U_0} \qquad \cfrac{\overline{Pre\ U_1\ t_1 \vee \neg Pre\ U_1\ t_1}\ (LEM) \qquad \overset{\delta_0}{\vdots} \qquad \overset{\delta_1}{\vdots}}{t_1 \star t_0' \in \overset{\bullet}{U_1} \, \overset{\circ}{,} \, \overset{\circ}{S}}\ (1)}{t_1 \star t_0' \in \overset{\bullet}{U_1} \, \overset{\circ}{,} \, \overset{\circ}{S}}
$$

Where δ_0 is:

$$
\cfrac{U_0 \sqsupseteq_{sf} U_1 \quad \overline{Pre\ U_1\ t_1}\ (2) \quad \cfrac{\overset{\beta_0}{\vdots}}{y \star t_0' \in U_0} \quad \cfrac{\overline{t_1 \star y' \in \overset{\circ}{S}}\ (1) \quad \overline{Pre\ U_1\ t_1}\ (2)}{t_1 \star y' \in S}\quad t_1 \neq \bot \quad \overset{\beta_1}{\vdots}}{t_1 \star t_0' \in \overset{\bullet}{U_1} \, \overset{\circ}{,} \, \overset{\circ}{S}}\ (3)
$$

Where β_0 stands for the following branch:

$$
\cfrac{\overline{y \star t_0' \in \overset{\bullet}{U_0}}\ (1) \quad U_0 \sqsupseteq_{sf} U_1 \quad \overline{Pre\ U_1\ t_1}\ (2) \quad \cfrac{\overline{t_1 \star y' \in \overset{\circ}{S}}\ (1) \quad \overline{Pre\ U_1\ t_1}\ (2) \quad t_1 \neq \bot}{t_1 \star y' \in S}\ (L.\ 4)}{\cfrac{Pre\ U_0\ y}{y \star t_0' \in U_0}}
$$

and β_1 is:

$$
\cfrac{\cfrac{\overline{t_1 \star w' \in U_1}\ (3)}{t_1 \star w' \in \overset{\bullet}{U_1}}\ (L.\ 5(i)) \quad \cfrac{\overline{w \star t_0' \in S}\ (3)}{w \star t_0' \in \overset{\circ}{S}}\ (L.\ 1(i))}{t_1 \star t_0' \in \overset{\bullet}{U_1} \, \overset{\circ}{,} \, \overset{\circ}{S}}
$$

δ_1 stands for the following branch:

$$
\cfrac{\overline{\neg Pre\ U_1\ t_1}\ (2) \quad \cfrac{\cfrac{\overline{t_1 \star y' \in \overset{\circ}{S}}\ (1)}{t_1 \star y' \in T_{1_\bot} \star T_{0_\bot}'}}{t_1 \in T_{1_\bot}}\ (L.\ 5(iii)) \quad \cfrac{\cfrac{\overline{y \star t_0' \in \overset{\bullet}{U_0}}\ (1)}{y \star t_0' \in T_{0_\bot} \star T_{0_\bot}'}}{t_0' \in T_{0_\bot}'} \blacklozenge (L.\ 1(iii))}{\cfrac{t_1 \star \bot' \in \overset{\bullet}{U_1} \qquad \bot \star t_0' \in \overset{\circ}{S}}{t_1 \star t_0' \in \overset{\bullet}{U_1} \, \overset{\circ}{,} \, \overset{\circ}{S}}}
$$

□

Notice that this proof depends on the use of the *law of excluded middle* (see, for example, [19]). We suspect that this result is strictly classical, and there appear to be many other examples of this in refinement theory, so abandoning the *constructive approach* that was taken in [12] may be inevitable.

Theorem 2. $U_0 \sqsupseteq_{sf} U_1 \Rightarrow U_0 \sqsupseteq_{wf_\bullet} U_1$ □

Theorems 1 and 2 together establish that the theories of SF-refinement and WF$_\bullet$-refinement are equivalent.

4.2 WF$_\phi$-Refinement and SF-Refinement Are Equivalent

We now show that WF$_\phi$-refinement and SF-refinement are equivalent.

Proving that WF$_\phi$-refinement satisfies both SF-elimination rules leads to proofs identical to propositions 4 and 5, modulo a substitution of $\sqsupseteq_{wf_\phi}$ for $\sqsupseteq_{wf_\bullet}$, $\overset{\ominus}{U}$ for $\overset{\bullet}{U}$, applications of $(\ominus_0^-)$ for $(\bullet_0^-)$ and lemmas 6(iv) and 6(i) in place of lemmas 5(iii) and 5(i) (respectively). Likewise, proving that SF-refinement satisfies WF$_\phi$-elimination rule is very similar to the proof of proposition 6. In this case, we require the same general substitutions as above, in addition to applications of $(\ominus_1^-)$ for $(\bullet_1^-)$. From this we immediately get implication in both directions:

Theorem 3. $U_0 \sqsupseteq_{wf_\phi} U_1 \Leftrightarrow U_0 \sqsupseteq_{sf} U_1$ □

Despite their superficial dissimilarity, SF-refinement, WF$_\bullet$-refinement and WF$_\phi$-refinement are all equivalent to one another. This reinforces the results from [6] and [7] showing clearly the significance of ⊥ (proposition 4). In addition we have shown that strict lifting of the operations is sufficient for introducing a model based refinement theory that preserves the very natural properties of SF-refinement.

The fact that, given the appropriate substitutions, the proofs in this section are identical to the ones in section 4.1 suggests that the *minimal* mathematical properties of the lifted-totalised models, which are essential for establishing theorems 1 and 2 are the ones of $\overset{\ominus}{U}$. To be more specific, the use of lemma 5(iii) (propositions 4 and 6) indicates that everything outside the precondition of the underlying operation, *including* ⊥, should be mapped onto ⊥ of the output state space. This observation is precisely the property of strictly-lifted totalised relations within a non-strict framework, as there is no evidence requiring a property which expresses the non-strict lifting of the operations.

4.3 WF$_\ominus$-Refinement Is Sound with Respect to SF-Refinement

Section 4.2 and [6] demonstrate that the strict and non-strict relational completion operators are interchangeable. In order to examine whether a similar observation can be made for strict and non-strict lifting of the simulation, we need to investigate the relationship between WF$_\ominus$-refinement and SF-refinement.

In order to show that WF$_\ominus$-refinement implies SF-refinement, we need to make use of the same substitutions and amendments to the proofs of propositions 4, 5 as we did in theorem 3, except that $\sqsupseteq_{wf_\ominus}$ replaces $\sqsupseteq_{wf_\bullet}$, $\vec{S}$ replaces $\overset{\circ}{S}$ and we apply lemmas 2(i) and 2(iv) in place of lemmas 1(i) and 1(iv) (respectively). Moreover, applications of $(\overset{\rightarrow}{_0})$ replace $(\circ_0^-)$. From this we have:

Theorem 4. $U_0 \sqsupseteq_{wf_\ominus} U_1 \Rightarrow U_0 \sqsupseteq_{sf} U_1$ □

The other direction of implication (completeness) fails. In fact, given the above substitutions to the proof of proposition 6, we can see exactly why: it fails in the proof step labelled ♠ (δ_1 branch): the application of lemma 1(iii) does not have a counterpart substitution in a strict framework because it involves the non-strict lifting of the simulation. This unsuccessful proof attempt aids us in devising the representative counterexample shown in Fig. 2. This complements the mathematical analysis and clearly illustrating the failure.

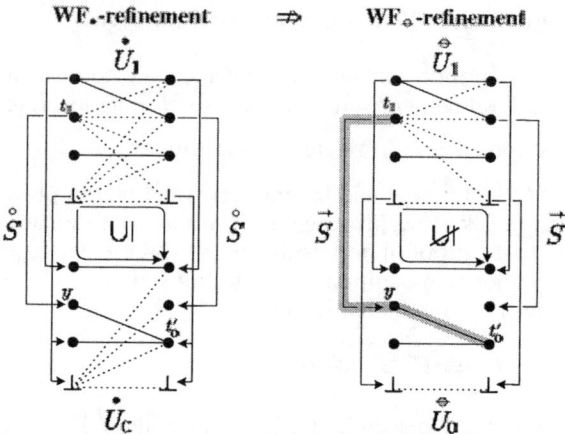

Fig. 2. A counterexample: $WF_\ominus$-refinement is not complete with respect to SF-refinement.

Each of the diagrams in Fig. 2 constitutes an extension of the forward simulation commuting diagram in Fig. 1, showing the (lifted-totalised) operations and the (lifted) simulation. Since a model theoretic refinement can be captured diagrammatically, $WF_\bullet$-refinement represents SF-refinement (to which it is equivalent: theorems 1, 2 in section 4.1). Both diagrams capture the data we have in the δ_1 branch of proposition 6. In the case of $WF_\bullet$-refinement, we have three pieces of information: $t_1 \star y' \in \overset{\circ}{S}$, $y \star t_0' \in \overset{\bullet}{U_0}$ (which denotes a path from t_1 to t_0' through the simulation via an intermediate state y) and $\neg\ Pre\ U_1\ t_1$, from which we need to establish a commuting path in the other direction. As shown in the proof, and illustrated in the diagram on the left, the fact that t_1 (being outside the precondition of U_1) is (also) mapped onto $\bot$ and that the simulation is non-strictly lifted, allows a commuting path from t_1 through $\bot$ in $\overset{\bullet}{U_1}$ and then, via the simulation, to t_0'. This is not the case with $WF_\ominus$-refinement, because the highlighted path is not associated with a path in the other direction: the subset relation fails.

Abstractly, we can observe that both diagrams illustrate a classic case of *weakening the precondition* in the presence of forward simulation: t_1 is outside the precondition of the abstract operation, yet its concrete counterpart y is in the precondition of the concrete operation, and they are both linked by the simulation. This is, naturally, a valid case of $WF_\bullet$-refinement, but not of $WF_\ominus$-refinement precisely because of the strict lifting of the simulation, as we can see in the diagram on the right. This illuminates the significance of $\bot$ in sanctioning preconditions to weaken as well as in preventing them from strengthening (proposition 4) throughout forward simulation refinement (we will reinforce this observation in section 5). Furthermore, we can easily see, from both the mathematical analysis and the counterexample, that the strictly-lifted totalisation of the operations has nothing to do with the fact that SF-refinement fails to imply $WF_\ominus$-refinement.

In conclusion, $WF_\ominus$-refinement is an acceptable theory of refinement because it is sound with respect to SF-refinement (theorem 4). However, it is not complete because the strict lifting of forward simulation has a restrictive effect: under certain circumstances $WF_\ominus$-refinement *prevents weakening of preconditions* and hence narrows the diversity of possible design decisions.

5 The Non-lifted Totalisation Underlying Data Refinement

In [6] we presented Pre_1 as a distinct semantics for the notion of the precondition of an operation. This notion underlies $W_\circ$-refinement, a model-theoretic operation refinement theory based on *non-lifted totalisation*[7] (denoted $\mathring{U}$) of the underlying operations. We demonstrated that $W_\circ$-refinement is equivalent to S_1-refinement, a *normative* characterisation of refinement which is identical to S-refinement [6,7] with all occurrences of Pre_0 substituted by Pre_1. This allows us to obtain an acceptable model-theoretic characterisation of operation refinement, without having to use $\bot$ values.

In this section we will show that this is not the case under the generalisation to data refinement, highlighting the inevitability of using $\bot$ values in both lifting (of the simulation) and relational completion models (of the operations) underlying forward simulation refinement.

We begin by introducing $WF_\circ$-refinement as a generalisation of $W_\circ$-refinement [6] with forward simulation. Since the totalisation of the operations is not lifted, we do not lift the simulation either; nor do we totalise it for reasons discussed in section 2. Therefore, $WF_\circ$-refinement is defined as follows:

Definition 7. $U_0 \sqsupseteq^s_{wf_\circ} U_1 =_{df} S \mathbin{\mathring{,}} \mathring{U}_0 \subseteq \mathring{U}_1 \mathbin{\mathring{,}} S$

Obvious introduction and elimination rules for $WF_\circ$-refinement follow from this definition.

In [6] we proved that $W_\circ$-refinement and $W_\bullet$-refinement are equivalent for bindings that range over the *natural carrier set*[8]. We can make a similar observation in forwards refinement because the following proposition is provable using the same sidecondition.

Proposition 7. *Let $t_1 \star t'_0$ be a binding with the property that: $t_1 \star t'_0 \in T$ Then the following rule is derivable:*

$$\frac{U_0 \sqsupseteq_{wf_\circ} U_1 \quad t_1 \star t'_0 \in \mathring{S} \mathbin{\mathring{,}} \dot{U}_0}{t_1 \star t'_0 \in \dot{U}_1 \mathbin{\mathring{,}} \mathring{S}}$$

□

From this we can easily establish soundness of $WF_\circ$-refinement with respect to $WF_\bullet$-refinement for all bindings that range over the natural carrier set, and therefore conclude that $WF_\circ$-refinement is an acceptable refinement theory. But it would be inappropriate to base our judgement on the observation above, because at this stage we do not know what exactly the sidecondition in proposition 7 means. In [6] we concluded that a similar sidecondition means that the (chaotic) lifted-totalisation and the non-lifted totalisation coincide in a "$\bot$-less" framework, under the interpretation of Pre_1. However that followed noting that $W_\circ$-refinement is an acceptable refinement theory: it is sound (as well as complete) with respect to the normative theory S_1-refinement. Clearly we need to take the same approach here: SF_1-refinement (that is SF-refinement with all

---

[7] The definitions of Pre_1 and the non-lifted totalisation can be found in appendix B, section B.2. Moreover, in this section, we will refer to the standard definition of preconditions as Pre_0 in order to distinguish it from the new notion.

[8] Natural carrier sets in $\mathcal{Z}_C^\bot$ explicitly exclude bindings that contain at least one observation bound to $\bot$ (see appendix A for further detail).

instances of Pre_0 substituted by Pre_1) would be our normative characterisation, guaranteeing the two properties expected in a forward simulation refinement (section 3.1), under the interpretation of Pre_1. Notice that we can prove that SF-refinement satisfies both SF_1-refinement elimination rules. This is a straightforward consequence of lemma 7 (appendix B, section B.2). From this we immediately get the following theorem:

Theorem 5. $U_0 \sqsupseteq_{sf} U_1 \Rightarrow U_0 \sqsupseteq_{sf_1} U_1$ □

We start with completeness: $WF_\circ$-refinement is *not complete* with respect to SF_1-refinement since SF_1-refinement fails to satisfy the $WF_\circ$-elimination rule. The proof attempt is essentially very similar to the one that leads to the counterexample in Fig. 2; thus it fails for similar reasons. This induces the counterexample shown in Fig. 3.

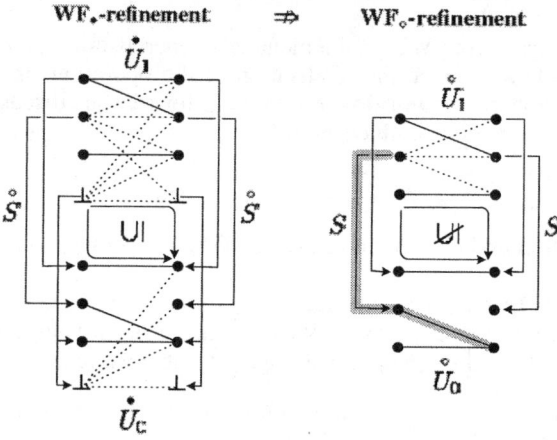

Fig. 3. A counterexample: $WF_\circ$-refinement is not complete with respect to SF_1-refinement[9].

Notice that the refinement case presented in Fig. 3 is very similar to the one in Fig. 2 because it depicts a similar observation: under certain circumstances $WF_\circ$-refinement *prevents weakening of preconditions*.

A more severe phenomenon is that $WF_\circ$-refinement is *not sound* with respect to SF_1-refinement. Employing the same proof strategy involving elimination rules, we start by proving that $WF_\circ$-refinement satisfies the SF_1-elimination rule for postconditions.

Proposition 8. *The following rule is derivable:*

$$\frac{U_0 \sqsupseteq_{wf_\circ} U_1 \quad Pre_1\ U_1\ t_1 \quad t_0 \star t_2' \in U_0 \quad t_1 \star t_0' \in S \quad t_1 \star y' \in U_1, y \star t_2' \in S \vdash P}{P}$$

The structure of the proof is very similar to the one of proposition 5. □

From this we can deduce that $WF_\circ$-refinement *guarantees that postconditions do not weaken*. Nevertheless, it cannot guarantee that *preconditions do not strengthen* because it fails to satisfy the SF_1-elimination rule for preconditions. If we attempt to prove

---

[9] We can use $WF_\bullet$-refinement to represent an SF_1-refinement in the counterexample, because we have theorem 5 and we know that SF-refinement and $WF_\bullet$-refinement are equivalent.

proposition 4 with $\sqsupseteq_{wf_\circ}$ replacing $\sqsupseteq_{wf_\bullet}$ and Pre_1 in place of Pre_0, we immediately learn that, unlike the proof of proposition 4, we cannot derive a contradiction from the assumption that t_0 is *not* in the precondition of U_0. This is precisely because the non-lifted totalisation does not involve $\bot$ values which, ultimately, lead to the contradiction in proposition 4. We exhibit a counterexample in Fig. 4, which manifests this observation. This is a classic case of *strengthening the precondition* in the presence of forward

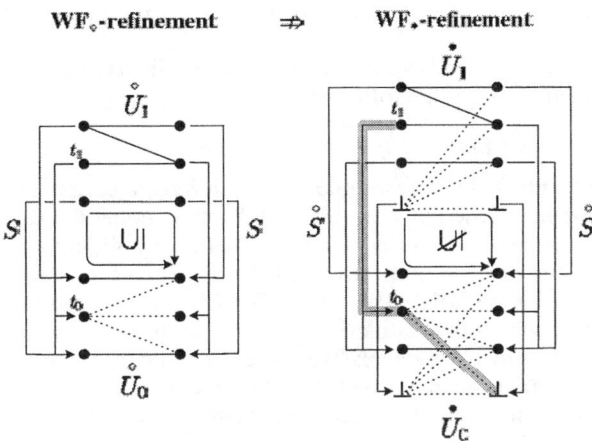

Fig. 4. A counterexample: $WF_\circ$-refinement is not sound with respect to SF_1-refinement.

simulation, something that is naturally prohibited by $WF_\bullet$-refinement (again, representing the normative theory) due to a path (highlighted in the diagram on the right) linking t_1 to $\bot$ via t_0, which is not associated to a path in the other direction, because t_1 is in the precondition of U_1 and thus is not mapped onto $\bot$. As we can see in the diagram on the left, this is not the case in $WF_\circ$-refinement, which allows requirements to disappear from the domain of specification.

In conclusion, the fact that $WF_\circ$-refinement is not sound with respect to SF_1-refinement is a sufficient argument for stipulating that it is an unacceptable refinement theory. We would like to highlight the significance of using a normative refinement characterisation as a common ground in such investigations: not only does it enable us to pinpoint the source of the problem in terms of the two basic properties concerning preconditions and postconditions (*e.g.* Fig. 4), it also overrules excessively strong results (*e.g.* proposition 7) that, in contrast to [6], constitute a very partial picture when a generalisation to forward simulation data refinement is involved. Moreover, it is interesting to observe that, since $WF_\circ$-refinement is also incomplete with respect to the normative theory, Fig. 3 and Fig .4 jointly demonstrate that under certain circumstances $WF_\circ$-refinement guarantees that *preconditions do not weaken*. This is, of course, the converse of the basic property permitted in a refinement.

6 Discussion

The non-lifted totalisation underlying refinement introduces a variety of problems. Woodcock [20, p.237-238] motivates an explanation to some extent. We discussed that thoroughly in [6] (section 4.4), where we, ultimately, raised a question: why is there a distinction between *implicit* (*Chaos*) and *explicit* (*True*) permission to behave in a lifted totalised framework and not in a non-lifted totalised one? In this section we will gradually answer this question, and secure the observations we made in section 5.

A useful way to examine the essence of a relational completion model is by scrutinising it under *extreme specifications* (see, for example, [9], chapter 3). This enables us to observe and explain phenomena that might not emerge otherwise. In this spirit we define two such specifications which respectively denote explicit and implicit "permission to behave":

Definition 8. *(i)* $True =_{df} [T \mid true]$ *(ii)* $Chaos =_{df} [T \mid false]$

By applying the (chaotic) lifted-totalisation and the non-lifted totalisation to these specifications we immediately get the following:

Lemma 3. *(i)* $\overset{\circ}{True} = \overset{\circ}{Chaos}$ *(ii)* $\overset{\bullet}{True} \neq \overset{\bullet}{Chaos}$ □

Lemma 3(i) represents a counterexample, in which *augmentation of undefinedness* is possible in a refinement based on non-lifted totalisation, under the standard interpretation of preconditions [8, definition 6]. This is remedied by $W_{\bullet}$-refinement [6] because the Woodcock-completion [20] imposes a distinction between *implicit* and *explicit* permission to behave (lemma 3(ii)). The alternative Pre_1 interpretation of preconditions (section B.2), under which the distinction between implicit and explicit permission to behave collapses, leads to a Woodcock-like operation refinement theory, $W_{\circ}$-refinement [6], in which the relations need not be lifted. This theory is simply defined as a subset relation of the (non-lifted) totalised relations, where the subset *prevents augmentation of nondeterminism* and the non-lifted totalisation, in conjunction with the subset, plays the same role as its lifted counterpart in *preventing augmentation of undefinedness*. Therefore, $W_{\circ}$-refinement is an acceptable refinement theory that guarantees these two elementary properties without utilising $\perp$ values. So why does the non-lifted totalisation have no future underlying model-theoretic refinement? More specifically, we are asking: why does it not work for data refinement?

The answer concerns the data simulations and the properties of *composition*. Consider the example in Fig. 5, where we present the specification $True^{10}$ as a refinement of a certain specification U_1, under both $WF_{\circ}$-refinement and $WF_{\bullet}$-refinement.

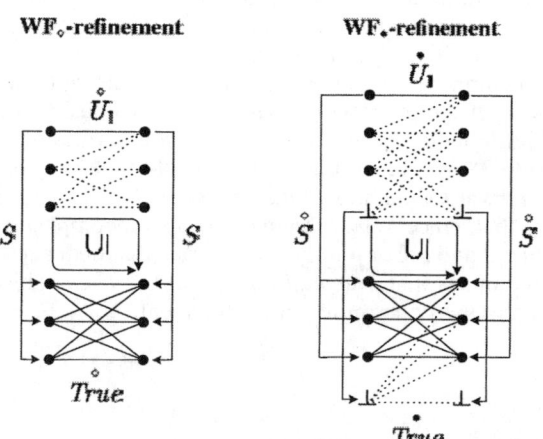

Fig. 5. An example: the specification $True$ refines the specification U_1.

---

[10] As usual, $True$ is of type $\mathbb{P}(T_0 \vee T_0')$ and U_1 is of type $\mathbb{P}(T_1 \vee T_1')$.

This is *not* a case of weakening the postcondition because the simulation links the first output state in U_1 with *all* the output states in $True$[11]; thus, it is a sensible case of data refinement. Yet in a non-lifted totalised operation, it is impossible to indicate whether an input state is mapped onto *all* output states as a result of not being mapped onto anything, or being mapped onto everything in the underlying operation. For this reason, the specifications $True$ and $Chaos$ are *indistinguishable* in this model and therefore the $WF_\circ$-refinement case in Fig. 5 also holds for $Chaos$, as we can see in Fig. 6. Naturally

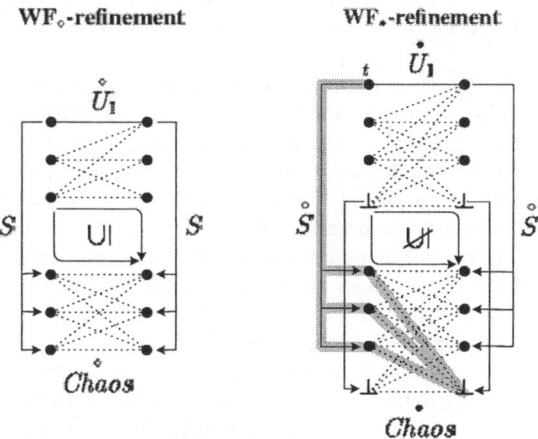

Fig. 6. A counterexample: the specification $Chaos$ constitutes a valid $WF_\circ$-refinement case of the specification U_1.

it is unacceptable that a chaotic specification refines some other specification that is *not chaotic*. This means that undefinedness has been augmented, as a result of *strengthening preconditions*. Indeed, as we have seen in section 5, $WF_\circ$-refinement sanctions this feature and is therefore unacceptable as a refinement theory. This case is prohibited by $WF_\bullet$-refinement, precisely because the lifted-totalisation maps input states outside the precondition of the underlying operation onto $\bot$, as well as everything else in the output set. Thus, $WF_\bullet$-refinement fails in Fig. 6 since all the highlighted paths leading to $\bot$ are not associated with paths in the other direction. Notice that the only way to establish these paths is through a link between t and $\bot$ in $\overset{\bullet}{U_1}$: this does not exist, because t is in the precondition of U_1.

In conclusion, $\bot$ underlies the *distinction* between $True$ and $Chaos$ in the lifted totalised framework. This prevents imprudent cases of refinement such as the one in Fig. 6 by prohibiting a strengthening of preconditions *in the presence of the simulation*. For this reason we prefer to refer to $\bot$ simply as the "distinguished" value, rather than "undefined" [20] or "non-termination" [9, 16, 2, 11], or even our own previous suggestion, the "abortive" value [6].

---

[11] Recall that, although $WF_\circ$-refinement is unacceptable as a refinement theory, it still guarantees that postconditions do not weaken (proposition 8). This is certainly the case for $WF_\bullet$-refinement, being as it is, equivalent to SF-refinement.

7 Conclusions and Future Work

In this paper, we introduced six distinct notions of (forward simulation) data refinement. By reformulating these as theories, rather than as sufficient conditions, we established a mathematical framework, based on the logic for Z, which underlies our analysis. We demonstrated in section 4 that what look like different models of specification and refinement are, in fact, intimately related. Having a non-model-theoretic benchmark (SF-refinement) allows us to scrutinise the role of the $\bot$ value in the model-theoretic approaches and evaluate the essence of the relational lifted-totalisation found in the literature.

The SF-refinement theory is entirely proof-theoretic, characterising refinement directly in terms of the language and the behaviour of preconditions and two basic observations regarding the properties one expects in a refinement: preconditions do not strengthen and postconditions do not weaken in the presence of (forward) simulation. We advocate a different approach to [20] and [5] by taking SF-refinement to be the fundamental characterisation of refinement, rather than (what we have denoted as) $WF_\bullet$-refinement. Such an approach has two major advantages: first, we establish a clear normative framework based on unquestionable properties. We have seen in section 5 that whenever a potential theory fails to be sound with respect to the normative theory, we can pinpoint the grounds for that failure, in terms of the two basic properties concerning preconditions and postconditions. This aids us in isolating the problem and in constructing representative counterexamples that illuminated relational completion, in general, and the non-lifted totalisation in particular. Secondly, as we reported in section 4, having a normative theory for investigating the relationships amongst various candidate theories not only simplifies the process (for example, as we have seen: many similarities in the proofs), it also enables us to compare the details of the proofs. In this paper we have been led to the conclusion that the strict and non-strict relational completion models are interchangeable in the context of forward simulation refinement, but that the strict lifting of the simulation has a restrictive effect, by prohibiting preconditions to weaken under certain circumstances.

In this paper we have not provided an analysis of backward simulation data refinement. We will, in future work, show that in backward simulation all the model-theoretic approaches based on lifted totalisation, including $WB_\ominus$-refinement (the backward simulation counterpart of $WF_\ominus$-refinement), are equivalent to SB-refinement (the normative theory in this case). Consequently, in this framework, the strict and non-strict lifting of the simulation are interchangeable, as well as the strict and non-strict relational completion models of the operations. The non-lifted totalisation has the same impact in backwards refinement: $WB_\circ$-refinement (the backward simulation counterpart of $WF_\circ$-refinement) is an unacceptable refinement theory because it permits strengthening of preconditions and is, therefore, not sound with respect to the normative theory SB_1-refinement.

There is much more to say about data refinement, particularly generalising results we have detailed in [6] in the context of operation refinement, *e.g.* formulating forward and backward simulation refinement theories based on a *sets of implementations* model or data refinement theories based on weakest preconditions, and then exploring their relationships with SF and SB-refinement. There is an additional interesting dimension, in which we explore generalisations of *firing conditions* refinement [7, 5, 18] underlying forward and backward simulation techniques. We can investigate their relationships with a variety of data refinement theories based on the *abortive relational completion* model as given in [7], [5] and [1].

Acknowledgements

Moshe Deutsch is supported by the British Council through an ORS award. Special thanks for particularly important discussions and comments go to Steve Reeves, Ray Turner, Eerke Boiten, John Derrick, Lindsay Groves, Ralph Miarka, Greg Reeve, David Streader, Jim Woodcock and Rob Arthan.

References

1. C. Bolton, J. Davies, and J. C. P. Woodcock. On the refinement and simulation of data types and processes. In K. Araki, A. Galloway, and K. Taguchi, editors, *Integrated Formal Methods (IFM'99)*. Springer, 1999.
2. A. Cavalcanti and J. C. P. Woodcock. A weakest precondition semantics for Z. *Technical Monograph PRG-TR-16-97. Oxford University Computing Laboratory*, 1997.
3. W. P. de Roever and K. Engelhardt. *Data Refinement: Model-Oriented Proof Methods and Their Comparison*. Prentice Hall International, 1998.
4. J. Derrick and E. Boiten. Calculating upward and downward simulations of state-based specifications. *Information and Software Technology*, 41:917–923, July 1999.
5. J. Derrick and E. Boiten. *Refinement in Z and Object-Z: Foundations and Advanced Applications*. Formal Approaches to Computing and Information Technology – FACIT. Springer, May 2001.
6. M. Deutsch, M. C. Henson, and S. Reeves. An analysis of total correctness refinement models for partial relation semantics I. *University of Essex, technical report CSM-362*, 2001. To appear in the Logic Journal of the IGPL.
7. M. Deutsch, M. C. Henson, and S. Reeves. Results on formal stepwise design in Z. In *9th Asia Pacific Software Engineering Conference (APSEC 2002)*, pages 33–42. IEEE Computer Society Press, December 2002.
8. M. Deutsch, M. C. Henson, and S. Reeves. Operation refinement and monotonicity in the schema calculus. In D. Bert, J. Bowen, S. King, and M. Walden, editors, *ZB 2003: Formal Specification and Development in Z and B*, volume 2651 of *Lecture Notes in Computer Science*, this volume. Springer-Verlag, June 2003.
9. J. Grundy. *A Method of Program Refinement*. PhD thesis, University of Cambridge, 1993.
10. J. He, C.A.R Hoare, and J.W. Sanders. Data refinement refined. In G. Goos and J. Hartmanis, editors, *European Symposium on Programming (ESOP '86)*, volume 213 of *Lecture Notes in Computer Science*, pages 187–196. Springer-Verlag, 1986.
11. J. He, C.A.R Hoare, and J.W. Sanders. Prespecification in data refinement. *Information Processing Letters*, 25(2):71–76, 1987.
12. M. C. Henson and S. Reeves. New foundations for Z. In J. Grundy, M. Schwenke, and T. Vickers, editors, *Proc. International Refinement Workshop and Formal Methods Pacific '98*, pages 165–179. Springer, 1998.
13. M. C. Henson and S. Reeves. Investigating Z. *Logic and Computation*, 10(1):43–73, 2000.
14. M. B. Josephs. The data refinement calculator for Z specifications. *Information Processing Letters*, 27:29–33, 1988.
15. S. King. Z and the Refinement Calculus. In D. Bjørner, C. A. R. Hoare, and H. Langmaack, editors, *VDM '90 VDM and Z – Formal Methods in Software Development*, volume 428 of *Lecture Notes in Computer Science*, pages 164–188. Springer-Verlag, April 1990.
16. R. Miarka, E. Boiten, and J. Derrick. Guards, preconditions, and refinement in Z. In J. P. Bowen, S. Dunne, A. Galloway, and S. King, editors, *ZB2000: Formal Specification and Development in Z and B*, volume 1878 of *Lecture Notes in Computer Science*, pages 286–303. Springer-Verlag, August 2000.
17. J. M. Spivey. *The Z Notation: A Reference Manual*. Prentice Hall, 2nd edition, 1992.
18. B. Strulo. How firing conditions help inheritance. In J. P. Bowen and M. G. Hinchey, editors, *ZUM '95: The Z Formal Specification Notation*, volume 967 of *Lecture Notes in Computer Science*, pages 264–275. Springer Verlag, 1995.

19. N. W. Tennant. *Natural Logic*. Edinburgh University Press, 2nd edition, 1990.
20. J. C. P. Woodcock and J. Davies. *Using Z: Specification, Refinement and Proof*. Prentice Hall, 1996.
21. J. C. P. Woodcock and C. C. Morgan. Refinement of state-based concurrent systems. In D. Bjørner, C. A. R. Hoare, and H. Langmaack, editors, *VDM '90 VDM and Z – Formal Methods in Software Development*, volume 428 of *Lecture Notes in Computer Science*, pages 340–351. Springer-Verlag, April 1990.
22. J. B. Wordsworth. *Software Development with Z – A Practical Approach to Formal Methods in Software Engineering*. Internalional Computer Science Series. Addison-Wesley, 1992.

A $\mathcal{Z}_C^\perp$ - A Synopsis

Our mathematical account takes place in a simple conservative extension $\mathcal{Z}_C^\perp$ of $\mathcal{Z}_C$, the core Z-logic of [13]. This provides a convenient basis, in particular a satisfactory logical account of the schema calculus, upon which the present work can be formalised. In this appendix, we will revise $\mathcal{Z}_C^\perp$, settling some notational conventions in the process. This is included for convenience only and the reader may need to consult [13] and [6] at least in order to fully understand our notational and meta-notational conventions[12].

The only modification we need to make in $\mathcal{Z}_C^\perp$ is to include the new distinguished terms which are explicitly needed in the approach taken in [20]. Specifically: the types of $\mathcal{Z}_C$ are extended to include terms $\perp^T$ for every type T. There are, additionally, a number of axioms which ensure that all the new $\perp^T$ values interact properly, e.g.

$$\perp^{[z_0:T_0 \cdots z_n:T_n]} = \langle\!\langle z_0 \Rrightarrow \perp^{T_0} \cdots z_n \Rrightarrow \perp^{T_n} \rangle\!\rangle$$

In other words, $\perp^{[z_0:T_0 \cdots z_n:T_n]}.z_i = \perp^{T_i}$ ($0 \leq i \leq n$). Note that this is the *only* axiom concerning distinguished bindings, hence, binding construction is *non-strict* with respect to the $\perp^T$ values.

Finally, the extension of $\mathcal{Z}_C^\perp$ which introduces schemas as sets of bindings and the various operators of the schema calculus is undertaken as usual (see [13]) but the carrier sets of the types must be adjusted to form what we call the *natural carrier sets* which are those sets of elements of types which *explicitly exclude* the $\perp^T$ values:

Definition 9. Natural carriers *for each type are defined by closing:* $\mathbb{N} =_{df} \{z^\mathbb{N} \mid z \neq \perp^\mathbb{N}\}$ *under the operations of cartesian product, powerset and schema set.*[13]

As a result the schema calculus is *hereditarily $\perp$-free*:

Definition 10 (Semantics for atomic schemas). $[T \mid P] =_{df} \{z \in T \mid z.P\}$

Note that this definition draws bindings from the *natural carrier* of the type T. As a consequence, writing $t(\perp)$ for a binding satisfying $t.\mathbf{x} = \perp$ for some observation $\mathbf{x}$, we have:

Lemma 4. $t(\perp) \in U \Rightarrow false$ □

We will also need the *extended carriers*. These are defined for all types as follows:

Definition 11. $T_\perp =_{df} T \cup \{\perp^T\}$

B   Relational Completion

In this appendix, we review the chaotic relational completion operators discussed in [6] and [7].

---
[12] Further information regarding $\mathcal{Z}_C$ and the notion of the *precondition* of an operation schema is provided in appendix A of [8] (this volume).
[13] The notational ambiguity does not introduce a problem, since only a set can appear in a term or proposition, and only a type can appear as a superscript.

B.1 Lifted Totalisation

Firstly, we define the non-strict-lifted totalisation in line with the intentions described in [20], chapter 16. We will write $T^\star$ for the set $T_\perp^{in} \star T_\perp^{out'}$.

Definition 12. $\overset{\bullet}{U} =_{df} \{z_0 \star z_1' \in T^\star \mid Pre\ U\ z_0 \Rightarrow z_0 \star z_1' \in U\}$

Then the following introduction and elimination rules are derivable:

Proposition 9.

$$\frac{t_0 \star t_1' \in T^\star \quad Pre\ U\ t_0 \vdash t_0 \star t_1' \in U}{t_0 \star t_1' \in \overset{\bullet}{U}} (\bullet^+) \quad \frac{t_0 \star t_1' \in \overset{\bullet}{U} \quad Pre\ U\ t_0}{t_0 \star t_1' \in U} (\bullet_0^-) \quad \frac{t_0 \star t_1' \in \overset{\bullet}{U}}{t_0 \star t_1' \in T^\star} (\bullet_1^-)$$

□

Lemma 5. *The following extra rules are derivable for lifted-totalised sets:*

$$\frac{}{U \subseteq \overset{\bullet}{U}} (i) \quad \frac{}{\perp \in \overset{\bullet}{U}} (ii) \quad \frac{\neg Pre\ U\ t \quad t \in T_\perp^{in}}{t \star \perp' \in \overset{\bullet}{U}} (iii) \quad \frac{\neg Pre\ U\ t_0 \quad t_0 \in T_\perp^{in} \quad t_1' \in T_\perp^{out'}}{t_0 \star t_1' \in \overset{\bullet}{U}} (iv)$$

□

The strict-lifted totalisation is defined as follows:

Definition 13. $\overset{\ominus}{U} =_{df} \{z_0 \star z_1' \in T^\star \mid (Pre\ U\ z_0 \Rightarrow z_0 \star z_1' \in U) \wedge (z_0 = \perp \Rightarrow z_1' = \perp')\}$

We obtain obvious introduction and elimination rules, which in this case we will not state explicitly. In addition, we have fairly standard properties:

Lemma 6.

$$\frac{}{U \subseteq \overset{\ominus}{U}} (i) \quad \frac{}{\overset{\ominus}{U} \subseteq \overset{\bullet}{U}} (ii) \quad \frac{}{\perp \in \overset{\ominus}{U}} (iii)$$

$$\frac{\neg Pre\ U\ t \quad t \in T_\perp^{in}}{t \star \perp' \in \overset{\ominus}{U}} (iv) \quad \frac{\neg Pre\ U\ t_0 \quad t_0 \in T^{in} \quad t_1' \in T_\perp^{out'}}{t_0 \star t_1' \in \overset{\ominus}{U}} (v)$$

Notice that in (v) t_0 ranges over the natural carrier set, rather than the extended carrier. □

B.2 Non-lifted Totalisation

In [6], we defined a non-lifted totalisation operator based on a revised notion of preconditions. According to this notion, an input state is in the precondition of the operation *iff* it is mapped (by the operation) onto some output state(s) but not onto all of them. We name this Pre_1[14], given by the following definition:

Definition 14. Let $T^{in} \leq V$.

$$Pre_1\ U\ z^V =_{df} \exists x_0', x_1' \in T^{out'} \bullet z \upharpoonright T^{in} \star x_0' \notin U \wedge z \upharpoonright T^{in} \star x_1' \in U$$

It is evident that the new notion of preconditions implies the standard one.

Lemma 7. $Pre_1\ U\ t \Rightarrow Pre_0\ U\ t$ □

Then the *non-lifted totalisation* of a set of bindings is given by the following $\mathcal{Z}_C^\perp$ definition. We will write T for the set $T^{in} \star T^{out'}$.

Definition 15. $\overset{\circ}{U} =_{df} \{z_0 \star z_1' \in T \mid Pre_1\ U\ z_0 \Rightarrow z_0 \star z_1' \in U\}$

Obvious introduction and elimination rules follow from this definition. Notice that the values in this completion range over the natural carrier set of the type T, thus $\perp$ values do not play any role here.

---

[14] In this section we refer to the standard definition of preconditions as Pre_0 in order to distinguish it from the new one.

$B^\#$: Toward a Synthesis between Z and B

Jean-Raymond Abrial

Consultant, Marseille, France
jr@abrial.org

Abstract. In this paper, I present some ideas and principles underlying the realization of a new project called $B^\#$. This project follows the main ideas and principles already at work in B, but it also follows a number of older concepts developed in Z. In $B^\#$, the intent is to have a formal system to be used to *model* complex system in general, not only software systems.

1 Introduction

In this short paper, I present some ideas and principles underlying the realization of a new project called $B^\#$. This project certainly follows the main ideas and principles already at work in B [1], but it also follows a number of older concepts developed in Z [8].

From B, it borrows the idea of *refinement, proof and tool* (such as Atelier B). But B was a formal system initially developed for constructing software systems. In $B^\#$, the intent is to have a formal system to be used to *model* complex system in general, not only software systems. This is the reason why in $B^\#$ a central idea is to use the general paradigm of *events* (borrowed from Action System [4] and less directly from TLA [5]) in order to model discrete transition systems.

From Z, it borrows the important concept of *generic extensions* (a concept that is also present in many formal systems such as PVS [6], Isabelle [7], etc). This concept of genericity is very important in that it gives the possibility to enlarge at will a given kernel of mathematical types and operators. It is also very interesting for developing very general models (with many refinements and proofs), which can be further reused in special cases, without paying the price of redoing all the proofs (since they are also generic).

The paper is organized around three directions. First the mathematical language and its possible generic extension mechanism (§2), second the formal language used to model complex transition systems (§3), and third a brief overview of the tools (§4). In what follows, I do not present any linguistic construct, I prefer to concentrate on the concepts and their rationales.

2 Simplifying and Extending the Mathematical Language

In this section, I first briefly sketch the mathematical language we shall use in $B^\#$ (§2.1). It is a simplified version of that presented in the B-Book. Then I will explain how statements written in this language can be proved (§2.2) using a first order sequent calculus based prover, and also validated (§2.3). Next, I will present an extension mechanism (§2.4) and finally I explain how one can still prove statements while remaining "first order" (§2.5).

2.1 Expressing Mathematical Statements

The kernel mathematical language contains three embedded languages, that of predicate logic, that of set theory, and finally that of arithmetic.

1. The *Logical Language* remains that of the *First Order* Predicate Calculus with equality and pairs.
2. The *Set-Theoretic Language* is rather simplified with comparison to that proposed in the B-Book. It is essentially made of the following:
   a) The three "given" *set constructs*, namely cartesian product, power set, and set comprehension, are first introduced. They are "defined" by means of three *translation axioms* transforming corresponding set memberships into First Order Predicate Calculus statements (still containing however some more elementary set memberships). They are given together with the *extensionality axiom* defining set equality.
   b) The elementary *set operators* (union, intersection, difference, inclusion) are then defined as mere linguistic extensions. All such operators are clearly *total*.
   c) Likewise, the definitions of various *relational and functional operators* are also defined by similar linguistic extensions. Among these, one operator is *partial*, namely that of partial function application. The precondition for using that operator requires that the term parameter of the function application in question lies within the domain of the function.
3. The *Arithmetic Language* is defined by means of the set of integers and basic arithmetic operations. This is introduced with, say, the Peano's axioms.

2.2 Proving Mathematical Statements

A *Prover* has been developed for Predicate Calculus with equality and pairs. It is "generic" in that it can handle predicates and terms which are uninterpreted. It is called the Predicate Prover (PP for short): this is essentially a Sequent Calculus based prover.

1. Statements belonging exclusively to the Logical Language can thus be potentially directly handled by PP.
2. Statements involving the Set-Theoretic Language are not treated directly by PP. In fact, a *Translator* has been constructed which transforms any set-theoretic statement $\mathcal{S}$ into a corresponding Predicate Calculus statement $\Pi(\mathcal{S})$ containing uninterpreted set memberships. This is done by applying systematically the above definitions and axioms until no more transformations are possible. The resulting statement $\Pi(\mathcal{S})$ is then proved (if possible) by using PP.

3. Statements involving the Arithmetic Language are treated accordingly. The Translator and PP have been extended in order to have some possibility to handle statements involving the Arithmetic Language.

2.3 Validating Mathematical Statements

When translating a set-theoretic statement $\mathcal{S}$, nothing guarantees that it is "meaningful": it may contain occurrences of function application operators, say $f(E)$, which are used outside their precondition (i.e. E not within $\mathsf{dom}(f)$). In that case, the Translator cannot replace $f(E)$ by a dummy x such that the pair $E \mapsto x$ belongs to f. In other words nothing can be said about the expression $f(E)$.

In order to treat such a potentially meaningless statements $\mathcal{S}$, a number of extra statements, $\Delta(\mathcal{S})$ are thus generated by the Translator together with $\Pi(\mathcal{S})$. Statements $\Delta(\mathcal{S})$ are called the *validating statements* of $\mathcal{S}$.

Such statements, once proved, guarantee that partial operator occurrences that can be found within $\mathcal{S}$ are indeed used within their preconditions, and this at the very place where they happen to be present. This is done according to the study made in [2]. Of course, such statements $\Delta(\mathcal{S})$ can be assumed as extra hypotheses within the proof of $\Pi(\mathcal{S})$.

2.4 Generic Extension Mechanisms

Besides the kernel mathematical language and proof system alluded above, B$^\#$ contains a mechanism by which new types and new operators can be freely defined within *libraries of mathematical extensions*. Most of the time, these types and operators are *generic* in that they are parameterized by some type variables. Such generic parameters can be instantiated with type expressions: that is type variables, cartesian products of types, power of types, or instantiated generic types.

1. *Types* are defined in a way that seems to look like abstract data types although the analogy is only apparent. In fact, they are not at all abstract: their corresponding mathematical definitions are given explicitly as is traditional in any mathematical textbook. More precisely, a type is defined by means of some *fields* glued together by a *type axiom*.

   For instance, a generic type, $\mathsf{seq}(|S|)$, of sequences of type S is defined by means of two fields: first a size field which is a member of $\mathbb{N}$ (the set of natural numbers), and second a fnc field which is a partial function from $\mathbb{N}$ to S. The field values are related by the type axiom, which says that the domain of fnc is exactly the interval 1..size.

2. New generic and usually parameterized partial *operators* are defined by means of: (1) a precondition (acting on the values of the parameters), and (2) an explicit definition using either the basic operators or other already defined generic operators.

For instance a generic operator remove($|S|$)(s) can be defined on sequences s of type seq($|S|$). The precondition is obviously that the sequence s is not empty (that is size($|S|$)(s) $\neq 0$).

Notice that the field names of a type can be used as generic *projection operators* acting on expressions of the corresponding type. For instance, in a scope where there exists a variable s of type seq($|S|$), one can then speak of size($|S|$)(s) and fnc($|S|$)(s).

Conversely, to each generic type is associated a *constructing operator*, which yields an expression defining a specific element of the type. This (partial) operator is parameterized by the values of the fields of the type. Its precondition is clearly given by the axiom of the type instantiated by the given values of the fields.

2.5 How to Remain "First Order"

Statements involving the extended language briefly defined in previous sections are clearly not "first order" any more. This is due to the genericity: when a generic type or operator is used in a mathematical statement S, the generic instantiation is still explicitly written. It seems then that we cannot use the PP proof system in order to prove such statements.

The solution to this problem is, again, translation. In fact, a preliminary transformation is performed on a statement S, which removes the genericity by *renaming* in a flat manner (with dummies) all the generic instantiations of the various types and operators to be found in S. In doing so, the definitions and properties of the various types and operators are also instantiated and renamed accordingly. This yields a statement S', which is then again "first order". The translation of previous section can then take place on S'. The various preconditions (properly instantiated) of the operators are then used in order to generate the corresponding statements $\Pi(S')$ and $\Delta(S')$.

3 Reshaping the B Language

In $B^\#$, the formal Language is highly simplified by comparison to that in B. The presentation starts by introducing the basic components of a $B^\#$ text: the model (§3.1) and the refinement (§3.2). Then the concept of decomposition (§3.3) is introduced which allows one to cut a model into almost independent sub-models which can be further refined and decomposed. Two other categories of components are then introduced: the context (§3.4) and the project (§3.5). Finally the notion of generic instantiation of a project (§3.6) is presented.

3.1 Model

The basic component of a $B^\#$ text is called a *model*. It essentially contains the description of a *state transition system*. The state is represented by a number of *variables* together with an *invariant*. The transitions are described by means of a number of *events*. Each of them is made of a *guard* (the necessary enabling condition) and of an *action* which describes, in a possibly non-deterministic way, how the event modifies the state. The guard can be a simple predicate or a quantified predicate with the quantification ranging over the action. The action is essentially described by means of a before-after predicate sometimes syntactically reshaped. Note that there is no action operator, that is no conditional action, no explicit choice action, no sequential action, no loop action etc. Besides this, a model can contain some *modalities* expressing certain reachability conditions for the events [3]. Libraries of mathematical extensions can be referenced from within a model.

3.2 Refinement

A formal model can mention another model which it is supposed to *refine*. In this case, the former is called a *refinement*, and the latter is called its *abstraction*. A refinement may enlarge the state of its abstraction by adding new variables to it. It can also change completely the state variables (data refinement). In that case a, so-called, gluing invariant is provided which links both abstract and concrete states.

Each event in a refinement bearing the same name as one in its abstraction is supposed to refine it. But a refinement may also contain events with no counterpart in the abstraction. Such "new" events are supposed to refine an implicit event which "does nothing" (skip). There exists a third category of events bearing names which do not correspond to any event in the abstraction. Such an event contains in its definition the name of an event of the abstraction which it is supposed to refine. This gives the possibility to have *several* events in the refinement refining the same abstract event. The proof obligations guaranteeing that a refinement indeed refines its abstraction are the classical ones. Two special rules are added: the first one guarantees that the new events cannot take control forever (a variant is provided for this), and the second one ensures relative deadlock-freeness (that is, the refinement does not deadlock more often than its abstraction).

3.3 Decomposition

A model $\mathcal{M}$ can be *decomposed* into several independent sub-models. In first approximation, the events of $\mathcal{M}$ are partitioned among the sub-models. Likewise, the state variables of $\mathcal{M}$ are also partitioned among the sub-models. There exists however in each sub-model $\mathcal{N}$ some extra variables and events pertaining to some neighbor sub-models $\mathcal{P}$: they constitute the *interface* of $\mathcal{N}$ with $\mathcal{P}$. Each interface event in $\mathcal{N}$ must be proved to be refined by the corresponding event in $\mathcal{M}$. The interface variables and events must not themselves be refined in further developments.

On Figure 1, you first see a model $\mathcal{M}_1$ refined by $\mathcal{M}_2$. The latter is then decomposed into models $\mathcal{N}_1$ and $\mathcal{P}_1$, which are further respectively refined by models $\mathcal{N}_2$ and $\mathcal{P}_2$. An arrow from $\mathcal{X}$ to $\mathcal{Y}$ indicates that $\mathcal{Y}$ refines $\mathcal{X}$.

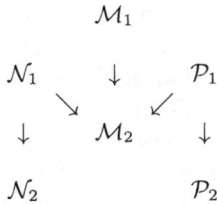

Fig. 1. A typical refinement and decomposition situation.

3.4 Context

Besides models, one may find some other kinds of components in a B# development. Such components are called *contexts*. A context contains some *parametric elements* for a development. These are some generic set parameters together with a number of constants and corresponding properties. Such a context can be "seen" from a model. It can also be refined. Refining a context simply means adding more generic sets or constants. Libraries of mathematical extensions can be referenced from within a context.

On Figure 2, you first see a model $\mathcal{M}_1$ refined by $\mathcal{M}_2$ and then by $\mathcal{M}_3$. Model $\mathcal{M}_1$ "sees" context $\mathcal{C}_1$, which is refined by context $\mathcal{C}_2$. Models $\mathcal{M}_2$ and $\mathcal{M}_3$ "see" context $\mathcal{C}_2$.

$$
\begin{array}{ccc}
\mathcal{C}_1 & \leftarrow & \mathcal{M}_1 \\
\downarrow & & \downarrow \\
\mathcal{C}_2 & \leftarrow & \mathcal{M}_2 \\
& \nwarrow & \downarrow \\
& & \mathcal{M}_3
\end{array}
$$

Fig. 2. Models and their contexts.

3.5 Project

Another kind of component in a $B^\#$ development is called a *project*. It contains a summary of the contents of some of the various models and contexts that are related by the refinement and visibility relationships in a formal development. A project has a name, and first contains the list of involved models and contexts. Such a list must be coherent in that the presence of a refined model or context must involve that of its abstraction, and the presence of a model must involve that of the context it sees. It also contains a list of the various parameters of a development, namely the generic sets and constants that can be found in the most refined context of the project and a list of the various variables and events that can be found in the most refined model of the project. The sets and constants of a project are its *formal parameters*.

For instance, from the development shown on figure 2, one may extract a project, shown on figure 3, involving models $\mathcal{M}_1$ and $\mathcal{M}_2$ and contexts $\mathcal{C}_1$ and $\mathcal{C}_2$. It must also contain the generic sets and constants that are defined in context $\mathcal{C}_2$, and the variables and events that are defined in model $\mathcal{M}_2$.

$$
\begin{array}{ccc}
\mathcal{C}_1 & \leftarrow & \mathcal{M}_1 \\
\downarrow & & \downarrow \\
\mathcal{C}_2 & \leftarrow & \mathcal{M}_2
\end{array}
$$

Fig. 3. A project $\mathcal{P}$ extracted from the development shown on Fig. 2.

3.6 Generic Instantiation of a Project

Refinement and decomposition introduced above are *structuring mechanisms* whose rôle is to make easier the construction of large models. In other words, they help in the construction of some *solution* to a given problem. The third structuring mechanism we introduce now, that of a *project generic instantiation*, is somewhat different in nature. Its rôle is not directly concerned with the construction of a solution to a given problem. It is rather concerned with the problem itself. The idea is to try to take advantage of the fact that a given problem might be a special case of a more general one. Once this is recognized, the solution of the latter might be specialized accordingly thus saving the cost of re-developing a solution that has already been developed in a more general framework. For instance, on Fig. 4, you can see a certain complete development.

Now suppose it can be recognized that the middle part of this development, namely that involving models $\mathcal{N}_2$ and $\mathcal{N}_3$, is a *special case* of the project $\mathcal{P}$ shown on Fig. 3, then it would be quite convenient to *incorporate* this specialization of $\mathcal{P}$ directly in our development without rewriting and re-proving it.

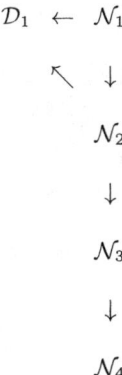

Fig. 4. A certain development.

The first thing to do is to instantiate project $\mathcal{P}$ to obtain, say, project $\mathcal{P}'$. This is done by giving values to the formal parameters of $\mathcal{P}$, namely its generic sets and constants. The values in question are expressions defined within the context $\mathcal{D}_1$. In doing this instantiation, models, variable and events of $\mathcal{P}$ can also be renamed. This is shown on Fig. 5.

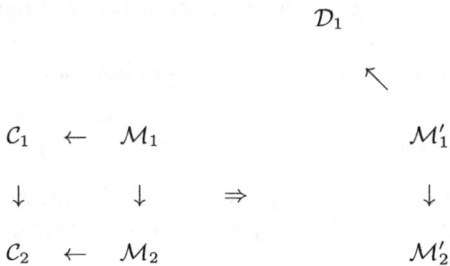

Fig. 5. Instantiating from context $\mathcal{D}_1$ project $\mathcal{P}$ into project $\mathcal{P}'$.

The second step is to incorporate project $\mathcal{P}'$ into our current development. This is shown on Fig. 6. The proof obligation consists in proving that model $\mathcal{M}'_1$, the instantiation of $\mathcal{M}_1$, is a genuine refinement of $\mathcal{N}_1$. Notice that refinement $\mathcal{N}_4$ now refines model $\mathcal{M}'_2$ which is part of the instantiated project $\mathcal{P}'$.

4 Tools

In this short section, I briefly present the various tools which are envisaged within the B$^\#$ project (some of them already exist). I make a distinction between the main tools (§4.1) and the peripheral tools (§4.2).

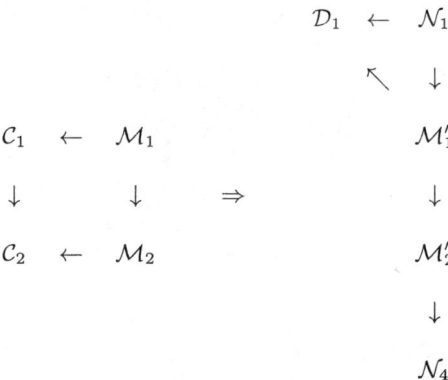

Fig. 6. Incorporation of $\mathcal{P}'$ into the current development.

4.1 Main Tools

These comprise three categories of tools organized around three "chains":

1. **The Upper Chain**: it contains the classical tools and analyzers. Lexical analyzer, syntactic analyzer, type checker.
2. **The Middle Chain**: it contains the Proof Obligation Generator including the "delta" tool able to generate validation proof obligations alluded above in section 2.3.
3. **The Lower Chain**: it contains the provers both automatic and interactive.

4.2 Peripheral Tools

A number of other tools can be freely added to the previous ones. They could be developed as needed. Here is an open list of such tools:

1. **Graphical Viewer**: produces a graphical representation of the formal text corresponding to a certain B$^\#$ development
2. **Editor-Navigator**: able to dynamically move along a B$^\#$ development in order to interrogate and possibly modify it.
3. **Simulator-Animator**: able to animate and visualize the behavior of an event model.
4. **Sequential Program Synthesiser**: transforms an event model into a sequential program. This is done by putting together various events (according to certain syntactic rules) in order to progressively build the various constructs of sequential programming: conditional operator, sequential operator, loop operator, procedure call, assignment statement.
5. **Distributed Program Synthesiser**: transforms an event model into a distributed program. This is essentially a generalization of the previous tool. Its outcome consists of several sequential programs linked by messages sent over a network.

6. **Translators**: transforms an event model (probably already treated by the two previous tools) into programs written in C, Java or even VHDL.
7. **Failure Analysis Tool**: able to analyze the possible "failures" of a complex system represented by an event model simulating its behavior.
8. etc.

5 Conclusion

The main ideas at work in the project $B^\#$ have been presented in this paper. Many of them have already been experimented with B in some indirect way. The project $B^\#$ is still in its infancy at the moment, but it might be operational within a few years.

Acknowledgements. I would like to warmly thank D. Bert, D. Cansell, D. Méry, and L. Voisin for numerous very helpful discussions on these matters.

References

1. J.-R. Abrial. *The B-Book: Assigning Programs to Meanings*. Cambridge University Press (1996).
2. J.-R. Abrial and L. Mussat. On Using Conditional Definitions in Formal Theories. In *ZB2002: Formal Specification and Development in Z and B, LNCS 2272*, pages 242–269. Springer-Verlag, 2002.
3. J.-R. Abrial and L. Mussat. Introducing Dynamic Constraints in B. In *B'98: Recent Advances in the Development and Use of the B Method, LNCS 1393*, pages 83–128. Springer-Verlag, april 1998.
4. R. J. R. Back and R. Kurki-Suonio. *Decentralization of Process Nets with Centralized Control*. 2nd ACM SIGACT-SIGOPS Symp. on Principles of Distributed Computing, 1983.
5. L. Lamport. The Temporal Logic of Actions. *ACM Trans. Program. Lang. Syst.*, 16(3):872–923, 1994.
6. S. Owre, J. M. Rushby and N. Shankar. PVS: A Prototype Verification System. In *11th Int. Conf. on Automated Deduction (CADE), LNCS 607*, pages 748–752, Springer-Verlag, 1992.
7. L. C. Paulson. Newblock Isabelle: A Generic Theorem Prover. In *LNCS 828*. Springer-Verlag, 1994.
8. J. M. Spivey. *Understanding Z*. Cambridge University Press, 1988.

Introducing Backward Refinement into B

Steve Dunne

School of Computing and Mathematics, University of Teesside
Middlesbrough, TS1 3BA, UK
s.e.dunne@tees.ac.uk

Abstract. The B Method exploits a direct first-order wp predicate-transformer formulation of downward simulation to generate its proof obligations for a refinement, so B's notion of refinement is restricted to that of forward refinement. Therefore some refinements we would intuitively recognise as valid cannot be proved so in B. While relational formulations of upward simulation abound in the refinement literature, the only predicate-transformer formulations proposed hitherto have been higher-order ones quantified over all postconditions, which cannot be conveniently exploited by the B Method. Here, we propose a new first-order predicate-transformer formulation of upward simulation suitable to be adopted by B for backward refinement.

1 Introduction

The incompleteness of the data refinement rules employed by the B Method [2] is well known, as is that of their counterparts in, for example, Z [16] or the Refinement Calculus [13] too. It means that not all refinements we would recognise intuitively as being valid can in fact be proved to be so from the rules. Fortunately, the rules do cover most practical applications of refinement, although industrial practitioners of formal methods have occasionally been known to encounter situations where their inadequacy has been exposed [17].

Data refinement is essentially based on the notion of one abstract data type simulating another. Hoare, He and Sanders [12] reduce the general problem of simulation of one abstract data type by another, in the absence of unbounded nondeterminism, into the two special cases they call *downward* and *upward* simulation. The subject is also comprehensively described by de Roever and Engelhardt [3], who show that forward refinement is based on a downward or L-simulation, while backward refinement is based on an upward or L^{-1}-simulation.

B uses a direct first-order formulation of the forward refinement proof rules to generate its refinement proof obligations syntactically from the text of an abstract operation and its refining concrete counterpart [2,15]. In order to introduce backward refinement into B a similar first-order formulation of the backward refinement proof rules is required. Most presentations of these proof rules are formulated relationally [19,3,4]. In both [20] and [18], on the other hand, predicate-transformer formulations of the backward refinement proof rules are offered, but these are higher-order formulations quantifying over all postconditions. The contribution of this paper is to discover a suitable set of first-order proof rules for backward refinement, so that backward refinement proof obligations can be generated syntactically from the texts of the abstract machine specification and its refinement machine.

The rest of the paper is organised as follows. After dealing with certain preliminaries in Section 2 we present some motivating examples for backward refinement in a B context in Section 3. Next we develop some necessary extra predicate-transformer machinery in Section 4. In Section 5 we develop our general technique for formulating simulation rules, and then vindicate it by applying it to the case of a downward simulation to derive the ordinary forward refinement rules of B. In section 6 we apply the same general technique to the case of an upward simulation and so derive the corresponding rules for a backward refinement.

2 Preliminaries

2.1 Notation

Syntactic substitution. When Q is a predicate, x a variable (or list of variables)[1] and E an expression (or list of expressions) of appropriate type, we will write $Q(x/E)$ to denote the predicate derived from Q by replacing all its free occurrences of (any component of) x by (the corresponding component of) E.

Universal implication. We use the symbol $\Rrightarrow$ to denote universal implication over all state variables in scope. Thus if w signifies this bunch of variables $P \Rrightarrow Q$ means $\forall w \,.\, P \Rightarrow Q$. Sometimes we want to limit a universal implication to a specific bunch of state variables; in such a case we subscript the $\Rrightarrow$ with the bunch concerned. Thus $P \Rrightarrow_y Q$ means $\forall y \,.\, P \Rightarrow Q$.

Precedence. We adopt the syntactic convention throughout this paper that each of the predicate transformers we introduce has a higher precedence than the ordinary logical connectives. So our predicate transformers will bind more tightly to predicates than the logical connectives between predicates. For example, $[S]\,Q \wedge R$ means $([S]\,Q) \wedge R$ rather than $[S]\,(Q \wedge R)$, and $\neg\,R\,\langle S\rangle^{o}$ means $\neg\,(R\,\langle S\rangle^{o})$ rather than $(\neg\,R)\,\langle S\rangle^{o}$.

2.2 Refining one Abstract Machine Specification by Another

Strictly speaking in B one cannot talk of one abstract machine specification refining another, since a refinement machine is a separate syntactic entity quite distinct from an abstract machine specification. However, Robinson [14] shows how we can express such a refinement relationship between two abstract machine

---

[1] We will often, as here, use a single variable to signify a list or bunch of basic variables. A bunch is essentially a flattened set. In contrast to set theory, bunch theory [9] makes no distinction between an element a and the singleton bunch comprised by a.

specifications by what he calls *reconciliation through implementation*: if two abstract machine specifications A and B have identical operation signatures and A can be implemented simply by importing B and promoting all its operations, then we are justified in saying that A is refined by B.

3 Some Examples

We present three examples of varying complexity, each of which illustrates the incompleteness of B's refinement rules.

3.1 The Limited Counter

The following two abstract machine specifications are B adaptations of the pair of modules given as an example by Gardiner and Morgan [8], which they in turn attribute originally to Abadi and Lamport [1]. First we consider the machine

> MACHINE $Acounter$
> VARIABLES ii, jj
> INVARIANT $ii \in 0..10 \;\land\; jj \in 0..10 \;\land\; ii + jj \in 0..10$
> INITIALISATION $ii := 0 \;\|\; jj :\in 0..10$
> OPERATIONS
>   **inc** $\;\hat{=}\;$ IF $jj > 0$ THEN $ii, jj := ii + 1, jj - 1$ END ;
> $rr \longleftarrow$ **report** $\;\hat{=}\;$ $rr := ii$
> END

Notice that the state variable jj in $Acounter$ is initialised nondeterministically. If it happens to be initialised to n, say, then the first n calls of operation inc will increment ii but subsequent calls will have no effect. But now we consider the machine

> MACHINE $Bcounter$
> SEES $Bool\_TYPE$
> VARIABLES ii, bb
> INVARIANT $ii \in 0..10 \;\land\; bb \in BOOL$
> INITIALISATION $ii := 0 \;\|\; bb :\in BOOL$
> OPERATIONS
>   **inc** $\;\hat{=}\;$
>   CHOICE
>   SELECT $bb = FALSE \;\land\; ii < 10$
>   THEN $ii := ii + 1$ END
>   OR $bb := TRUE$ END ;
> $rr \longleftarrow$ **report** $\;\hat{=}\;$ $rr := ii$
> END

in which our integer variable jj has been replaced by the boolean variable bb. As long as bb is false calls of *inc* might or might not increment ii, but once bb becomes true subsequent calls have no effect. Any implementation which imports *Acounter* might just as well import *Bcounter*, and *vice versa*, since only the value of ii, and not that of jj or bb, is visible to the implementation through the operation *report*. No importing implementation could possibly distinguish between the two machines. This suggests that the two machines mutually "refine" each other.

And indeed, using Robinson's technique of reconciliation through implementation, the implementation

    IMPLEMENTATION   *BcounterI*
    REFINES   *Bcounter*
    IMPORTS $Bool\_TYPE$, *Acounter*
    PROMOTES   *inc*, *report*
    INVARIANT $bb = TRUE \Rightarrow jj = 0$
    END

can easily be proved using the existing refinement rules of B, which vindicates half of our conjecture. But the reciprocal implementation

    IMPLEMENTATION   *AcounterI*
    REFINES   *Acounter*
    IMPORTS $Bool\_TYPE$, *Bcounter*
    PROMOTES   *inc*, *report*
    INVARIANT $bb = TRUE \Rightarrow jj = 0$
    END

is problematic. It cannot be proved by B's existing refinement rules.

3.2 The Casino

It is quite possible to find simpler examples than the limited counter which expose B's incomplete approach to refinement equally effectively. The following, which simply models the spinning of a roulette wheel, must be among the most trivial. The machine

    MACHINE   *Acasino*
    VARIABLES ii
    INVARIANT $ii \in 0..36$
    INITIALISATION $ii :\in 0..36$
    OPERATIONS
        $rr \longleftarrow$ **spin** $\;\widehat{=}\;$ BEGIN $rr := ii \;\|\; ii :\in 0..36$ END
    END

always "decides" nondeterministically but in advance what the outcome of the next spin of the wheel will be. In contrast, the machine

MACHINE $Bcasino$
OPERATIONS
    $rr \longleftarrow$ **spin** $\widehat{=}$ $rr :\in 0..36$
END

simply "decides" the outcome of each spin as it occurs. Again, it is intuitively clear that these machines would be indistinguishable to any importing implementation, yet using B's ordinary refinement rules we can only prove refinement between them in one direction: the $Acasino$ can certainly be proved by them to refine the $Bcasino$ but not the other way round.

3.3 Schrödinger's Cat

Our last example is inspired, somewhat whimsically perhaps, from the famous physicist's well-known illustration of the perplexities of Quantum Theory. A cat is put in a box and later taken out again, upon which we learn whether it has survived or expired during its confinement. First we introduce a machine declaring relevant types:

MACHINE $Globals$
SETS
    $BOXSTATE = \{empty, occupied\}$
    $CATSTATE = \{alive, expired\}$
END

Then in our $Acat$ machine underneath, the cat's fate –although only reported when it is taken out– is actually decided when it is placed in the box.

MACHINE $Acat$
SEES $Globals$
VARIABLES $thecat, thebox$
INVARIANT $thebox \in BOXSTATE \wedge thecat \in CATSTATE$
INITIALISATION $thebox := empty \parallel thecat :\in CATSTATE$
OPERATIONS
    put $\widehat{=}$ PRE $thebox = empty$
            THEN $thebox := occupied \parallel thecat :\in CATSTATE$
            END ;
    $rr \longleftarrow$ **get** $\widehat{=}$
            PRE $thebox = occupied$
            THEN $thebox, rr := empty, thecat \parallel thecat :\in CATSTATE$
            END
END

On the other hand, in the following *BCat* machine the cat's fate is not decided
until it is taken out of the box:

    MACHINE   *Bcat*

    SEES   *Globals*

    VARIABLES   *thebox*

    INVARIANT   *thebox* $\in BOXSTATE$

    INITIALISATION   *thebox* := *empty*

    OPERATIONS

        put $\hat{=}$ PRE *thebox* = *empty*
                    THEN *thebox* := *occupied*
                    END ;

        rr ⟵ **get** $\hat{=}$
                PRE *thebox* = *occupied*
                THEN *thebox* := *empty* || *rr* :$\in CATSTATE$
                END

    END

Although a user of these machines would not be able to distinguish between them, under the ordinary forward refinement rules of B *Acat* refines *Bcat* but not *vice versa*.

The common thread between all three examples is that in each of them one machine postpones resolution of nondeterminism while the other resolves it earlier. The earlybird machine forward-refines the procrastinating machine because it downward-simulates it. The procrastinating machine, on the other hand, upward-simulates the former, and so doesn't satisfy the ordinary B refinement rules which are based only on forward refinement.

4 Semantics of Generalised Substitutions

The semantics of generalised substitutions [2,7] are usually expressed by interpreting each substitution S as a wp predicate transformer, the weakest precondition for S to establish a postcondition Q conventionally being denoted by $[S]\,Q$. Below we explain how the same semantics can be expressed instead by means of wlp and trm. Important to this approach is the notion of the active frame s of a substitution S, which denotes the bunch of state variables which could be changed by S [7].

4.1 A trm-wlp Semantics for Substitutions

We denote the weakest liberal precondition (wlp) [5,6,10] predicate-transformer effect of a substitution S by $[S]^\circ\_$. Thus $[S]^\circ Q$ denotes the weakest precondition for S to establish a postcondition Q providing it terminates at all. In Table 1

Table 1. The trm-wlp semantics of generalised substitutions

S	$\mathrm{trm}(S)$	$[S]^\circ Q$
$skip$	true	Q
$x := E$	true	$Q(E/x)$
$P \mid S$	$P \wedge \mathrm{trm}(S)$	$(P \vee \forall s \,.\, Q) \wedge [S]^\circ Q$
$P \Longrightarrow S$	$P \Rightarrow \mathrm{trm}(S)$	$P \Rightarrow [S]^\circ Q$
$S \;[]\; T$	$\mathrm{trm}(S) \wedge \mathrm{trm}(T)$	$[S]^\circ Q \wedge [T]^\circ Q$
$@z \,.\, S$	$\forall z \,.\, \mathrm{trm}(S)$	$\forall z \,.\, [S]^\circ Q$
$S \,;\, T$	$\mathrm{trm}(S) \wedge [S]^\circ \mathrm{trm}(T)$	$[S]^\circ [T]^\circ Q$

we define the semantics of a substitution S in terms of its termination predicate $\mathrm{trm}(S)$, representing $[S]$true, and its wlp predicate-transformer effect $[S]^\circ Q$. We note in particular in Table 1 that the frame s of S appears in the definition of $[P \mid S]^\circ Q$. This captures the fact that invoking a generalised substitution outside its precondition is unpredictable and may lead to any resulting final state.

A wp/wlp pairing rule. The following rule, *cf.* [6, ch. 7 formula (2)] and [10, ch. 3 formula (3)], relates wp, trm and wlp for a substitution S:

$$[S]\,Q \;=\; \mathrm{trm}(S) \wedge [S]^\circ Q \qquad\qquad \text{Pairing Rule}$$

It ensures that the standard wp semantics of generalised substitutions can easily be recovered from Table 1.

4.2 Strongest Postcondition

In Table 2, as an alternative to wlp, we present an equivalent characterisation of generalised substitutions, based on the rather less familiar strongest-postcondition (sp) predicate transformer [6,10]. We denote the strongest postcondition delivered by S from a given precondition R by $R\,[S]^\circ$. This characterises those states which may be reached by execution of S from a state satisfying R. Our choice of such a postfix notation is partly motivated by the pleasingly simple form it lends to the sp effect of a sequential composition. As in Table 1, we note that here in Table 2 the frame s of S appears in the definition of $R\,[P \mid S]^\circ$. Again, this captures the fact that invoking a generalised substitution outside its precondition is unpredictable and may lead to any resulting final state.

Table 2 doesn't give any more meaning to generalised substitutions than Table 1, since wlp and sp are semantically equivalent. They both convey a substitution's partial-correctness semantics. The $^\circ$ superscripts in $[S]^\circ\_$ and $\_[S]^\circ$ are intended to remind us of this.

Table 2. Strongest postcondition semantics of generalised substitutions

S	$R[S]^o$
$skip$	R
$x := E$	$\exists x' .\ R(x'/x) \wedge x = E(x'/x)$
$P \mid S$	$(\forall s .\ R \Rightarrow P) \Rightarrow R[S]^o$
$P \Longrightarrow S$	$(P \wedge R)[S]^o$
$S \;[\!]\; T$	$R[S]^o \vee R[T]^o$
$@z . S$	$\exists z .\ R[S]^o$
$S\,;\,T$	$R[S]^o[T]^o$

4.3 A Rule Relating wlp and sp

Hesselink's formula (10) in [10, ch. 5] expresses the relationship between wlp and sp for programs; it is also implied by Dijkstra and Scholten's formula (3) in [6, ch. 6]. In the context of generalised substitutions the same relationship can be expressed as the following general rule for any generalised substitution S with frame s, any precondition R and any postcondition Q, where S is regarded as an abstract program over a state space characterised by the bunch s of state variables:

$$R \;\Rrightarrow_s\; [S]^o Q \quad \equiv \quad R[S]^o \;\Rrightarrow_s\; Q \qquad\qquad \text{Slide Rule}$$

The name reflects the $[S]^o$ "sliding" freely to either end of the $\Rrightarrow_s$ without changing the meaning of the proposition in which it appears. Note the use of universal implication over the bunch s of state-variables. Universal rather than ordinary implication is essential to the rule; it is certainly not the case that for any generalised substitution S, precondition R and postcondition Q, the predicate $R \Rightarrow [S]^o Q$ is always equivalent to the predicate $R[S]^o \Rightarrow Q$.

A nice intuition as to the validity of the rule can readily be gained by recognising that $R \Rrightarrow_s [S]^o Q$ and $R[S]^o \Rrightarrow_s Q$ are respective wlp and sp formulations of the same Hoare triple [11]

$$\{R\}\ S\ \{Q\}$$

asserting that any execution of S from an initial state satisfying R will, if it terminates, yield a final state satisfying Q.

4.4 Conjugate Predicate Transformers

For any predicate transformer PT, which transforms predicates Y into corresponding ones $PT(Y)$, we define its conjugate PT^* as

$$PT^*(Y) \;=_{df}\; \neg\, PT(\neg\, Y)$$

In particular for any generalised substitution S we will write the conjugate of its wp transformer $[S]\_$ as $\langle S \rangle \_$ and that of its sp transformer $\_[S]^o$ as $\_\langle S \rangle^o$. Again, we adopt the convention that these bind more tightly to predicates than logical connectives between predicates. For any postcondition Q or precondition R we have

$$\langle S \rangle Q \quad =_{df} \quad \neg\, [S]\,\neg\, Q \qquad\qquad \text{Conjugate wp}$$
$$R\,\langle S \rangle^o \quad =_{df} \quad \neg\, (\neg\, R)\,[S]^o \qquad\qquad \text{Conjugate sp}$$

Our operational intuitions of these two conjugate predicate transfomers are that:

- $\langle S \rangle Q$ characterises those before-states from which execution of S is either not guaranteed to terminate, or may deliver an after-state satisfying Q;
- $R\,\langle S \rangle^o$ characterises those after-states for which all executions of S reaching them must have started in a before-state satisfying R.

We use the two above definitions to calculate conjugate wp and conjugate sp explicitly in Table 3 for each basic construct of the generalised substitution language.

Table 3. Conjugate wp and sp for generalised substitutions

S	$\langle S \rangle Q$	$R\,\langle S \rangle^o$
$skip$	Q	R
$x := E$	$Q(E/x)$	$\forall\, x'\,.\ x = E(x'/x) \Rightarrow R(x'/x)$
$P \mid S$	$P \Rightarrow \langle S \rangle Q$	$(\forall\, s\,.\ P \vee R)\ \wedge\ R\,\langle S \rangle^o$
$P \Longrightarrow S$	$P\ \wedge\ \langle S \rangle Q$	$(P \Rightarrow R)\,\langle S \rangle^o$
$S\ [\!]\ T$	$\langle S \rangle Q\ \vee\ \langle T \rangle Q$	$R\,\langle S \rangle^o\ \wedge\ R\,\langle T \rangle^o$
$@\,z\,.\,S$	$\exists\, z\,.\ \langle S \rangle Q$	$\forall\, z\,.\ R\,\langle S \rangle^o$
$S\,;\,T$	$\langle S \rangle\langle T \rangle Q$	$R\,\langle S \rangle^o\,\langle T \rangle^o$

4.5 About the Tables

Tables 1,2 and 3 testify that the various predicate-transformer characterisations of generalised substitutions they exhibit can be syntactically calculated for any given GSL expression and postcondition or precondition expression. This is, of course, very important if we are to envisage our refinement approach ever being adopted by one of the B development toolkits.

However, the refinement theory we will develop in sections 5 and 6 does not rely on the specific definitions the tables contain, but rather only on the two semantic rules we have given relating wp, trm, wlp and sp, and the definition of conjugacy for predicate transformers. Thus, the development of our refinement theory which follows is essentially an axiomatic one, not depending on the specific trm, wlp and sp definitions for the GSL constructs in Tables 1 and 2 and their conjugates in Table 3. Indeed, an interesting exercise in validation of Tables 1 and 2 is to prove that their respective wlp and sp definitions for each GSL construct are consistent with our Slide Rule.

5 Forward Refinement

Suppose we have an abstract data type whose states are characterised by a (bunch of) variable(s) a and a concrete data type whose states are characterised by a (bunch of) variable(s) c, where a and c are disjoint. Let R be the abstraction relation between the abstract and concrete states, expressed in "alphabetised" form – that is, as a predicate over variables a, c – and let the abstract and concrete state invariants I and J be subsumed into R, so that $R \Rrightarrow I \wedge J$. Then we can deduce the standard forward refinement rules used by the B method, as shown in the next two subsections.

5.1 Forward Initialisation

For a downward simulation each possible initial concrete state must be related through R to an initial abstract state. Let AI be a substitution with frame a and CI a substitution with frame c, representing respectively the abstract and concrete initialisations[2] of a downward simulation, as represented in Figure 1. The concrete initial states are then characterised by $\text{true}\,[CI]^o$ while the concrete states related by the abstraction relation R to the initial abstract states are characterised by $\langle AI \rangle R$.

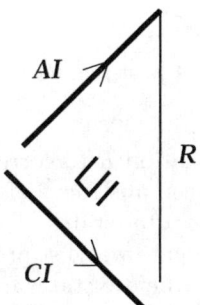

Fig. 1. Downward simulation initialisation

---

[2] We assume that AI and CI have already been syntactically checked as having no preconditions, so they are guaranteed to terminate.

Noting that $\Rrightarrow$ in this context indicates quantification over a and c, we can therefore express the requirement illustrated in Figure 1 by

$\quad$ true $[CI]^o \Rrightarrow \langle AI \rangle R$
$\equiv \qquad$ {Slide Rule}
$\quad$ true $\Rrightarrow [CI]^o \langle AI \rangle R$
$\equiv \qquad$ {logic}
$\quad [CI]^o \langle AI \rangle R$
$\equiv \qquad$ {CI being an initialisation means trm(CI) is always true}
$\quad$ trm(CI) $\wedge$ $[CI]^o \langle AI \rangle R$
$\equiv \qquad$ {Pairing Rule}
$\quad [CI] \langle AI \rangle R$ $\hfill$ InitFwdRef

which we recognise as the familiar B forward refinement initialisation rule.

5.2 Forward Refinement of Operations

Figure 2 shows an abstract operation represented by a generalised substitution A with frame a from abstract before-states to abstract after-states, where the latter

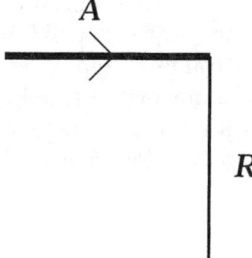

Fig. 2. An abstract operation A post-related by R to the concrete state-space

are related by the abstraction relation R to corresponding concrete after-states. The indicated relationship between abstract before-states at the upper left and potential corresponding concrete after-states at the bottom right of Figure 2 is characterised by $\langle A \rangle R$, the conjugate weakest precondition for A to establish R. In particular, this relates abstract before-states from which A may not terminate to every concrete after-state, in accordance with the total-correctness notion of a potentially non-terminating computation being capable of delivering any result.

Conversely, Figure 3 shows a concrete operation represented by a generalised substitution C with frame c from concrete before-states to concrete after-states, the former being related by the abstraction relation R to corresponding abstract before-states. This time we can express the indicated relationship between

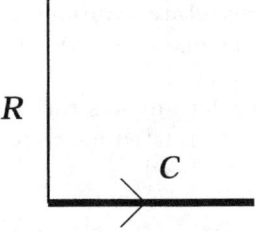

Fig. 3. A concrete operation C pre-related by R to the abstract state-space

abstract before-states at the upper left and potential corresponding concrete after-states at the bottom right of Figure 3 by the predicate $R[C]^o$. Again in accordance with the total-correctness interpretation of non-termination, this in particular relates abstract before-states linked through R to a concrete before-state from which C may not terminate, to every concrete after-state.

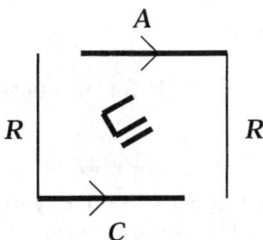

Fig. 4. Downward simulation of A by C

Operations without outputs. For the moment we will assume A and C don't have outputs. The standard forward data refinement rules for B correspond to the downward simulation illustrated in Figure 4, where every possible related pair of abstract before- and concrete after-states in Figure 3 has to be admitted also by Figure 2. In particular, any abstract state related by R to a concrete state from which there is a non-terminating execution of C, must itself admit a non-terminating execution of A. Noting again that $\Rightarrow\!\!\!\Rightarrow$ indicates quantification over a and c, we therefore need

$$R \wedge \neg\,\mathrm{trm}(C) \;\;\Rightarrow\!\!\!\Rightarrow\;\; \neg\,\mathrm{trm}(A)$$
$$\equiv \quad\{\mathrm{logic}\}$$
$$\mathrm{trm}(A) \wedge R \;\;\Rightarrow\!\!\!\Rightarrow\;\; \mathrm{trm}(C) \hspace{4em} \text{OpFwdRef 1}$$

Remembering that the abstract state invariant is already subsumed in R, we recognise OpFwdRef 1 above as one of the two familiar existing rules in B for refinement of an operation.

We also have to ensure that for any abstract before-state from which termination of A is guaranteed, all its related concrete after-states via Figure 3 are admitted also via Figure 2, so we need

$\quad \mathrm{trm}(A) \wedge R[C]^\circ \;\Rrightarrow\; \langle A \rangle R$

$\equiv \quad$ {since c is non-free in $\mathrm{trm}(A)$}

$\quad \mathrm{trm}(A) \;\Rrightarrow\; (\, R[C]^\circ \;\Rrightarrow_c\; \langle A \rangle R \,)$

$\equiv \quad$ {Slide Rule}

$\quad \mathrm{trm}(A) \;\Rrightarrow\; (\, R \;\Rrightarrow_c\; [C]^\circ \langle A \rangle R \,)$

$\equiv \quad$ {logic}

$\quad \mathrm{trm}(A) \wedge R \;\Rrightarrow\; [C]^\circ \langle A \rangle R$

$\equiv \quad$ {assuming OpFwdRef 1}

$\quad \mathrm{trm}(A) \wedge R \;\Rrightarrow\; \mathrm{trm}(C) \wedge [C]^\circ \langle A \rangle R$

$\equiv \quad$ {Pairing Rule}

$\quad \mathrm{trm}(A) \wedge R \;\Rrightarrow\; [C] \langle A \rangle R \qquad\qquad\qquad\qquad\qquad$ OpFwdRef 2a

which is the other refinement rule in B for an operation without outputs.

Operations with outputs.[3] Now suppose A and C output the (bunch of) variable(s) r. We need to distinguish C's output from A's, so we modify C into C' to write to r' rather than r. The corresponding downward simulation is shown in Figure 5, in which the right-hand appearance of the abstraction invariant R is strengthened by the predicate $r = r'$, which captures the requirement that A and C' must concur about values they can output. Once again, in particular any abstract state related by R to a concrete state from which there is a non-terminating execution of C', must itself admit a non-terminating execution of A, and so, since $\mathrm{trm}(C') = \mathrm{trm}(C)$, OpFwdRef 1 in Section 5.2 still holds without modification here in the context of operations with outputs.

We do have to modify OpFwdRef 2a, however, to take an operation's outputs into account. The corresponding modified form is

$\quad \mathrm{trm}(A) \wedge R \;\Rrightarrow\; [C'] \langle A \rangle (R \wedge r = r') \qquad\qquad\qquad$ OpFwdRef 2

Remembering that the abstract state invariant I is already subsumed in the abstraction relation R, we recognise OpFwdRef 2 as the other familiar B refinement rule for operations.

---

[3] The reader might wonder if we ought also to give operations with inputs a similar special consideration to that we give here to those with outputs. Fortunately, this isn't necessary, since an operation with inputs can simply be regarded as providing a template for a family of individual operations, one for each possible value of the input.

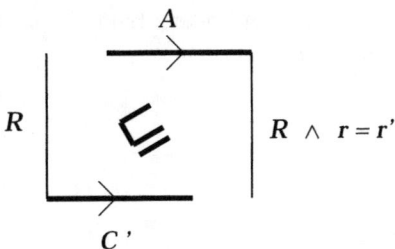

Fig. 5. Downward simulation of an operation with outputs

6 Backward Refinement

We can derive analogous refinement rules for backward refinement by considering, in the context of an upward simulation, the abstract and concrete initialisations in Figure 6, and the abstract and concrete operations in Figure 7.

6.1 Backward Initialisation

From Figure 6 we see the requirement for upward simulation is expressed by

$$\langle CI \rangle R \;\Rrightarrow\; \text{true}\,[AI]^o$$
$$\equiv \quad \{\; \langle CI \rangle R \;=_{df}\; \neg\,[CI]\neg\,R \;\}$$
$$\neg\,[CI]\neg\,R \;\Rrightarrow\; \text{true}\,[AI]^o$$
$$\equiv \quad \{\text{logic}\}$$
$$\neg\,\text{true}\,[AI]^o \;\Rrightarrow\; [CI]\neg\,R$$
$$\equiv \quad \{\text{Pairing Rule}\}$$
$$\neg\,\text{true}\,[AI]^o \;\Rrightarrow\; \text{trm}(CI) \wedge [CI]^o\neg\,R$$

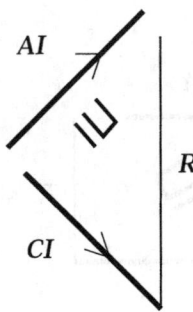

Fig. 6. Upward simulation initialisation

$$
\begin{aligned}
&\equiv \quad \{CI \text{ being an initialisation means } \mathrm{trm}(CI) \text{ is always true}\} \\
&\quad \neg\, \mathrm{true}\,[AI]^o \;\Rrightarrow\; [CI]^o \neg\, R \\
&\equiv \quad \{\text{Slide Rule}\} \\
&\quad (\neg\, \mathrm{true}\,[AI]^o)[CI]^o \;\Rrightarrow\; \neg\, R \\
&\equiv \quad \{\text{logic}\} \\
&\quad R \;\Rrightarrow\; \neg\,(\neg\, \mathrm{true}\,[AI]^o)[CI]^o \\
&\equiv \quad \{\text{defn of } \_\,\langle CI \rangle^o\} \\
&\quad R \;\Rrightarrow\; \mathrm{true}\,[AI]^o \langle CI \rangle^o \qquad\qquad\qquad\qquad\qquad\quad \text{InitBwdRef}
\end{aligned}
$$

6.2 Backward Refinement of Operations

Figure 7 shows an abstract operation A being upwards simulated by a concrete operation C, where as usual R represents the abstraction relation of the simulation and r is the common output of A and C. In fact, C' rather than C appears, this being a variant of C modified to write to r' rather than r. The requirement is that every pair of concrete before- and abstract after-states related through the right-hand bottom path in Figure 7 must be admitted by the left-hand upper path too. In particular, every concrete state from which there is a non-terminating execution of C' must be related by R to an abstract state from which there is a non-terminating execution of A. Thus we need

$$
\begin{aligned}
&\quad \neg\, \mathrm{trm}(C) \;\Rrightarrow_c\; \exists\, a\,.\, R \wedge \neg\, \mathrm{trm}(A) \\
&\equiv \quad \{\text{logic}\} \\
&\quad (R \Rrightarrow_a \mathrm{trm}(A)) \;\Rrightarrow_c\; \mathrm{trm}(C) \qquad\qquad\qquad\qquad \text{OpBwdRef 1}
\end{aligned}
$$

We must also ensure that every terminating right-hand bottom path in Figure 7 is matched by a left-hand upper path. This gives the following condition:

$$
\begin{aligned}
&\quad \langle C' \rangle^o (R \wedge r = r') \;\Rrightarrow\; R[A]^o \\
&\equiv \quad \{\text{defn of } \langle C' \rangle^o\_ \text{ and logic}\} \\
&\quad \neg\, R[A]^o \;\Rrightarrow\; [C']^o \neg\,(R \wedge r = r')
\end{aligned}
$$

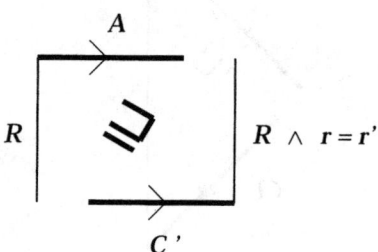

Fig. 7. Upward simulation of an operation with outputs

$$
\begin{array}{rl}
\equiv & \{\text{Slide Rule}\} \\
& (\neg\, R\,[A]^{\circ})[C']^{\circ} \;\Rrightarrow\; \neg\,(R \,\wedge\, r = r') \\
\equiv & \{\text{logic}\} \\
& R \,\wedge\, r = r' \;\Rrightarrow\; \neg\,(\neg\, R\,[A]^{\circ})[C']^{\circ} \\
\equiv & \{\text{defn of } \_\,\langle C'\rangle^{\circ}\} \\
& R \,\wedge\, r = r' \;\Rrightarrow\; R\,[A]^{\circ}\,\langle C'\rangle^{\circ} \hfill \text{OpBwdRef 2}
\end{array}
$$

6.3 Finalisation

In Hoare, He and Sander's data-type simulations [12] and those in [3], the notion of initialisation is complemented by that of finalisation. Yet B has no explicit forward-refinement finalisation proof obligation which mirrors its one for initialisation. This is because operation outputs have already been catered for in the operation refinement proof obligations, so finalisation in B is trivial in that it simply "throws away" the local states of a machine and its refinement. Thus the

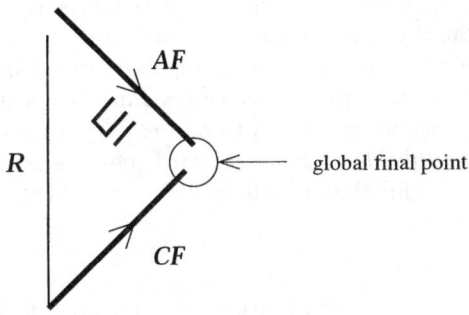

Fig. 8. Downward simulation finalisation

diagram in Figure 8 trivially commutes, since the abstract and concrete finalisations AF and CF map respectively all abstract states a and all concrete states c to the same unique final global point.

The situation for backward-refinement finalisation is rather different, as can be seen in Figure 9. Here the diagram only commutes if R covers all valid concrete states c. Recalling that J is our concrete state invariant, it seems, therefore, we have acquired the following finalisation proof obligation concerning R:

$$J \;\Rrightarrow_c\; \exists\, a\,.\, R \hfill \text{FinBwdRef}$$

But now B's way of actually expressing a refinement machine comes to our assistance. In B we never actually write the concrete machine N which refines a given abstract machine M. Instead we write what Abrial [2, ch. 11] calls the *differential*, DN, which can be combined syntactically with M to yield N. If the

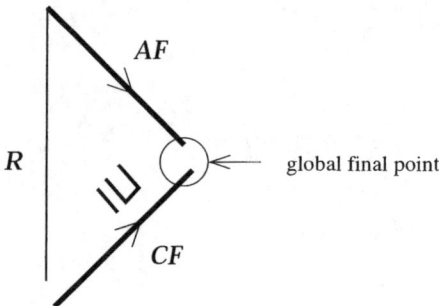

Fig. 9. Upward simulation finalisation

invariant of M is I and that of DN is R then the invariant J of the imputed concrete machine N is defined by

$$J \quad =_{df} \quad \exists\, a\,.\, I \wedge R$$

In other words, every valid concrete state c satisfying the concrete state invariant J is by definition related by R to a valid abstract state a satisfying the abstract state invariant I. Hence, our putative proof obligation FinBwdRef above will inevitably always be satisfied in a concrete machine N constructed in this way.

So as long as we restrict ourselves to expressing our backward refinements differentially as we already do in B for forward refinements, FinBwdRef will be automatically satisfied, and therefore needn't be explicitly stated or proved.

6.4 Summary of the Rules

In Table 4 we summarise the initialisation rules for both forward and backward refinement so these may be conveniently compared. Similarly, in Table 5 we

Table 4. Initialisation rules for forward and backward refinement

Forward Refinement	Backward Refinement
$[CI]\,\langle AI \rangle\, R$	$R \;\Rightarrow\; \mathrm{true}\,[AI]^{\circ}\,\langle CI \rangle^{\circ}$

summarise the rules for an operation refinement in both forward and backward refinement.

It is interesting to observe the near-duality of the two sets of rules. It seems as though in backward refinement the conjugate strongest postcondition $\langle C' \rangle^{\circ}$ is a sort of dual to the weakest precondition $[C']$ in forward refinement, while the strongest postcondition $[A]^{\circ}$ in backward refinement acts as the dual of conjugate weakest precondition $\langle A \rangle$ in forward refinement.

Table 5. Operation refinement rules for forward and backward refinement

Forward Refinement	Backward Refinement
$\mathrm{trm}(A) \wedge R \;\Rrightarrow\; \mathrm{trm}(C)$	$(R \Rrightarrow_a \mathrm{trm}(A)) \Rrightarrow_c \mathrm{trm}(C)$
$\mathrm{trm}(A) \wedge R \;\Rrightarrow\; [C']\langle A \rangle (R \wedge r = r')$	$R \wedge r = r' \;\Rrightarrow\; R[A]^\circ \langle C' \rangle^\circ$

7 Conclusion

We have formulated first-order predicate-transformer proof obligations for backward refinement which could conveniently be incorporated by the toolkits supporting the B method to support a new BACKREFINES category of machine refinement. We have so far only manually tested our new backward refinement rules on the smaller two examples we presented in Section 3. Trying out our rules on our more elaborate first example, the limited counter, awaits the incorporation of our new rules into one of the B toolkits.

In this paper we haven't addressed the twin fundamental issues of the soundness and completeness of our new backward refinement rules, although we believe their soundness is guaranteed by the nature of our direct derivation of the rules, designed to ensure the commutivity of the relevant diagrams. The question of completeness is more problematic. Indeed, have we given B a complete refinement method, in the sense that any valid refinement can now be proved so, by resolving it into a backward intermediate refinement of the specification, itself in turn forward-refined by the original refinement? The answer is: not quite. Our backward refinement rules will not necessarily enable us to prove that a loop-employing refinement of an unboundedly nondeterministic abstract operation is correct, even when it is in fact valid. However, this is a well-known fundamental limitation of backward refinement [8,3] rather than a shortcoming specifically of our approach.

Acknowledgements. I am indebted to the three anonymous reviewers and Colin Fidge for helpful comments on the draft version of this paper.

References

[1] M. Abadi and L. Lamport. The existence of refinement mappings. *Theoretical Computer Science*, 82(2):253–284, 1991.
[2] J.-R. Abrial. *The B-Book: Assigning Programs to Meanings*. Cambridge University Press, 1996.
[3] W.-P. de Roever and K. Engelhardt. *Data Refinement: Model-Oriented Proof Methods and their Comparison*. Number 47 in Cambridge Tracts in Theoretical Computer Science. Cambridge University Press, 1998.

[4] J. Derrick. A single complete refinement rule for Z. *Journal of Logic and Computation*, 10(5):663–675, 2000.
[5] E.W. Dijkstra. *A Discipline of Programming*. Prentice-Hall International, 1976.
[6] E.W. Dijkstra and C.S. Scholten. *Predicate Calculus and Program Semantics*. Springer Berlin, 1990.
[7] S.E. Dunne. A theory of generalised substitutions. In D. Bert, J.P. Bowen, M.C. Henson, and K. Robinson, editors, *ZB2002: Formal Specification and Development in Z and B*, number 2272 in Lecture Notes in Computer Science, pages 270–290. Springer-Verlag, 2002.
[8] P.H.B. Gardiner and Carroll Morgan. A single complete rule for data refinement. *Formal Aspects of Computing*, 5:367–382, 1993.
[9] E.C.R. Hehner. Bunch theory: a simple set theory for computer science. *Information Processing Letters*, 12(1):26–30, 1981.
[10] Wim H. Hesselink. *Programs, Recursion and Unbounded Choice*. Number 27 in Cambridge Tracts in Theoretical Computer Science. Cambridge University Press, 1992.
[11] C.A.R. Hoare. An axiomatic basis for computer programming. *Communications of the ACM*, 12(10):576–583, 1969.
[12] C.A.R. Hoare, He Jifeng, and J.W. Sanders. Data refinement refined. Number 213 in Lecture Notes in Computer Science, pages 187–196. Springer-Verlag, 1986.
[13] C.C. Morgan. *Programming from Specifications (2nd edn)*. Prentice Hall International, 1994.
[14] K. Robinson. Reconciling axiomatic and model-based specifications using the B Method. In Jonathan P. Bowen, Steve Dunne, Andy Galloway, and Steve King, editors, *ZB2000: Formal Specification and Development in B and Z*, number 1878 in Lecture Notes in Computer Science, pages 95–106. Springer, 2000.
[15] Steve Schneider. *The B Method: an introduction*. Cornerstones of Computing. Palgrave, 2001.
[16] J.M. Spivey. *The Z Notation: a Reference Manual (2nd edn)*. Prentice Hall, 1992.
[17] Susan Stepney, David Cooper, and Jim Woodcock. More powerful Z data refinement: pushing the state of the art in industrial refinement. In Jonathan P. Bowen, Andreas Fett, and Michael G. Hinchey, editors, *ZUM '98: The Z Formal Specification Notation, 11th International Conference of Z Users, Berlin, September, 1998, Proceedings*, number 1493 in Lecture Notes in Computer Science, pages 284–307. Springer, 1997.
[18] J. von Wright. The lattice of data refinement. *Acta Informatica*, 31(2):105–135, 1994.
[19] J. Woodcock and J. Davies. *Using Z: Specification, Refinement and Proof*. Prentice Hall, 1996.
[20] J.C.P. Woodcock and Carroll Morgan. Refinement of state-based concurrent systems. In Dines Bjørner, C. A. R. Hoare, and Hans Langmaack, editors, *VDM '90, VDM and Z - Formal Methods in Software Development, Third International Symposium of VDM Europe, Kiel, FRG, April 17-21, 1990, Proceedings*, number 428 in Lecture Notes in Computer Science, pages 340–351. Springer, 1990.

Expression Transformers in B-GSL

Bill Stoddart and Frank Zeyda

School of Computing and Mathematics, University of Teesside, Middlesbrough, U.K.
{bill, f.zeyda}@tees.ac.uk

Abstract. The B concept of generalised substitutions is applied to expressions as well as predicates to obtain "expression transformers", which formalise the idea of speculative computation and form part of the executable subset of our language. We define expression transformers over the syntactic constructs of B-GSL, and show this definition is equivalent to an alternative based on before-after predicates. The use of expression transformers is illustrated by example programs which combine functional and imperative programming styles and exploit backtracking.

Keywords: Expression transformers, term transformers, predicate transformers, B, combining functional and imperative programming, backtracking, reversible computation.

1 Introduction

Abrial's "Generalised Substitution Language"[1] uses the mechanism of syntactic substitution to describe updates to a system's state in terms of predicate transformers. Thus the weakest pre-condition for $x := F$ to guarantee a post condition Q, (written $[x := F]Q$) is obtained by substituting F for each free occurrence of x in Q. For example:

$$[x := x+1]x < 10 \;\equiv\; x+1 < 10 \;\equiv\; x < 9$$

interpreted as: to guarantee that $x := x + 1$ will deliver a state in which $x < 10$, we must start from a state in which $x < 9$. This form of substitution in a predicate converts a post-condition to a pre-condition: one might say it works "backwards".

We can apply the same mechanical substitution in *expressions*, but what would that mean? Consider:

$$[x := x+1]x+10 \;=\; x+1+10 = x+11$$

with the interpretation: the value of expression $x + 10$ after executing $x := x + 1$ would be $x + 11$. It appears that applying substitutions to expressions might form a basis for describing the effects computations would have *were they to be carried out*. Substitution in an expression converts it into another expression representing the value the original expression would have after the substitution. It works in a *forward* direction.

GSL generalises the idea of predicate transformer to cover all the syntactic constructs of an abstract command language (pre-conditions, guards, choice, sequence and local variables). We will do the same with expression transformers to arrive at the definition of $S \diamond E$ which will be an expression on the current state space which gives the possible values that could be taken by E after the execution of S.

We will see later that the language of expression transformers is equivalent in power to that of predicate transformers, but in terms of development method we propose to use them in very different ways. Whereas predicate transformers form the basis of the B development method, based on invariant preservation and refinement, expression transformers are part of the executable subset of the language. As such, they can provide a number of benefits, including succinct expression of search algorithms and integration of imperative and functional programming.

An aspect of GSL which will be essential to our approach is the separation between guards and choice, which enables GSL to describe conditional execution in terms of these two more primitive constructs. With the notations: $g \Longrightarrow S$ for "t guards S" and $S \;[\!]\; T$ for "S choice T", the construct:

if t then A else B end

can be expressed as:

$t \Longrightarrow A \;[\!]\; \neg\, t \Longrightarrow B$

The separation of guard and choice allows a succinct and elegant description of language properties, but also allows for constructs which are not generally considered to be executable when used in isolation, for example:

$t \Longrightarrow A$

or

$t \Longrightarrow A \;[\!]\; u \Longrightarrow B$

the problem being that we may be offering a list of choices for which none of the guards are true. There is, however, an operational interpretation for such commands. In this interpretation any choice which is not forced by the guards is considered to be provisional. If execution reaches a point at which no choice is feasible (all guards are false) it backtracks to the previous point of choice, and tries a different choice. If no further choices remain at that point, it again backtracks. This provides an execution mechanism which will search for a feasible path through a computation. It may also, of course, report that a program *cannot* be executed.

This interpretation is well known, having been mentioned, for example, in Greg Nelson's seminal paper [10] from 1989. However, it is not generally considered as a useful phenomenon since the target architecture for most formal software development does not support backtracking. In a previous paper the first author has argued that an efficient execution platform for the form of backtracking exhibited by GSL can be implemented through a *reversible virtual machine* [11].

Allowing provisional choice gives us an expressive language for solving problems in which definitive information on which to base choices is not necessarily available at the point where the choice must be made. For example in resource allocation problems such as constructing a university time table. But this form of backtracking has a disadvantage. It does not allow us to remember any results obtained during the execution of a provisional choice. For example in a game playing program we might want to play through all possible choices for the next n moves and evaluate all the resulting positions for use in a minimax algorithm which will select the best move. In fact we can easily adjust our reversible virtual machine to do this, but we would seem to be distancing ourselves from the formal semantics of GSL. Whilst looking for a solution to this problem we became aware of the work of Morris and Bunkenburg on "Term Transformers" which provided us with the idea of formalising *speculative computation*. The original aspects of our own approach as described in this paper are to incorporate this idea within B-GSL and apply it to a language featuring partial commands and backtracking. We also look at integrating imperative and functional programming, which is the central motivation of Morris and Bunkenburg's work[9,8].

The paper is structured as follows. In section 2 we recall the predicate transformer semantics of GSL, and illustrate its "backtracking" properties using the "knight's tour" problem.

In section 3 we present some notations, including an integration of bunches and GSL. Bunches are Eric Hehner's lightweight alternative to sets, and will allow a less cluttered presentation of our theory.

In section 4 we introduce the notation $S \diamond E$ to represent "the bunch of possible values that can be taken by expression E after execution of program S". We define $S \diamond E$ in terms of "expression transformers" over the syntactic constructs of GSL. We also give a closed form, prove the two definitions are equivalent, and derive a number of simple but important results.

In section 5 we illustrate the use of expression transformers in implementations, where they allow succinct expression of searching and a style which combines aspects of functional and imperative programming.

In section 6 we summarise developments in our reversible virtual machine implementation. In section 7 we comment on related work, and compare expression transformers with term transformers. In section 8 we draw our conclusions and outline future work.

2 B-GSL and Backtracking

B has a programming notation, the "Abstract Machine Notation", AMN, with a semantics given in the "Generalised Substitution Language", GSL. In this paper, which is not generally about concrete syntax but about the expressive power of an abstract command language equipped with backtracking and expression transformers, our notation is based on GSL. A slight notational variation is that we use equals between predicates, which is not usual B style. $P = Q$ will mean P and Q have the same truth value over all instantiations of their free variables. We also write $P \equiv Q$ with precisely the same meaning, but with $\equiv$ having lower precedence than $=$.

We first remind the reader of the predicate transformer semantics of GSL expressions, as defined over the syntactic forms in the language. In the following discussions, $[S]Q$ is the weakest pre-condition for operation S to establish predicate Q. We express state changes in terms of a meta-variable x, which may be a variable list, so that the form $x := E$, for example, could be matched by, e.g. $a, b := 4, 2$. The notation $(\lambda x.Q)E$ represents a re-writing of Q which replaces every occurrence of the components of x in Q by the related components of E.

Name	Notation	Rule
Skip	$skip$	$[skip]Q \equiv Q$
Assignment	$x := E$	$[x := E]Q \equiv (\lambda x.Q)E$
Pre-Condition	$P \mid S$	$[P \mid S]Q \equiv P \wedge [S]Q$
Guard	$g \Longrightarrow S$	$[g \Longrightarrow S]Q \equiv g \Rightarrow [S]Q$
Choice	$S \mathbin{[\!]} T$	$[S \mathbin{[\!]} T]Q \equiv [S]Q \wedge [T]Q$
Unbounded Choice	$x :\in A$	$[x :\in A]Q \equiv \forall a.(a \in A \Rightarrow [x := a]Q)$ if $a \backslash Q$
Sequential Composition	$S; T$	$[S; T]Q \equiv [S][T]Q$
Local Variable	$@z.S$	$[@z.S]Q \equiv \forall z.[S]Q$ if $z \backslash Q$

The "backtracking" nature of GSL can be demonstrated as follows. Consider the operation:

$$(S \mathbin{[\!]} T); g \Longrightarrow U$$

and suppose the "execution" of T will cause g to be false, i.e. assume:

$$[T]\neg g$$

Then we can prove that the availability of choice T is irrelevant to any final result, as expressed in the property:

$$[(S \mathbin{[\!]} T); g \Longrightarrow U]Q \;=\; [S; g \Longrightarrow U]Q$$

Two possible interpretations of this result are (1) that the choice between S and T is made by a clairvoyant demon which can look ahead and will avoid potential infeasibility, or (2) that a backtracking mechanism is used such that if the choice of T is made, on finding continuation infeasible, execution will backtrack and try the alternative choice S.

Expression Transformers in B-GSL 201

Our proof will need the GSL monotonicity property that given an operation S and predicates Q and R, then $(Q \Rightarrow R) \Rightarrow ([S]Q \Rightarrow [S]R)$.
Proof

$$\neg g \Rightarrow \neg g \vee [U]Q \qquad \text{logic}$$

Hence $[T]\neg g \Rightarrow [T](\neg g \vee [U]Q)$ monotonicity

Thus, since we are given $[T]\neg g$, we can assume the truth of $[T](\neg g \vee [U]Q)$

Now $[(S \,[]\, T); \; g \Longrightarrow U]Q$

$$\begin{aligned}
&= [S \,[]\, T][g \Longrightarrow U]Q & &\text{Sequential Composition}\\
&= [S][g \Longrightarrow U]Q \wedge [T][g \Longrightarrow U]Q & &\text{Choice}\\
&= [S][g \Longrightarrow U]Q \wedge [T](g \Rightarrow [U]Q) & &\text{Guard}\\
&= [S][g \Longrightarrow U]Q \wedge [T](\neg g \vee [U]Q) & &\text{Logic}\\
&= [S][g \Longrightarrow U]Q \wedge true & &\text{Shown above}\\
&= [S][g \Longrightarrow U]Q & &\text{Logic}\\
&= [S; \; g \Longrightarrow U]Q & &\text{Sequential Composition}
\end{aligned}$$

□

For a more substantial example consider the problem of the "knight's tour". From a given starting square on the chess board, we have to find a sequence of 63 moves which takes a knight to every other square on the board. We can solve this problem with a loop which proposes moves, verifies them and records them. Full details of the loop invariant are omitted. Assuming some simple subsidiary operations, an operation to solve the problem could be defined as:

$tour(s) \mathrel{\widehat{=}} s \in SQUARE \;|$
    $position := s;$
    $moves := 0;$
    WHILE
        $moves < 63$
    DO
        $propose\_move;$
        $verify\_unvisited;$
        $record\_move;$
        $moves := moves + 1$
    INVARIANT
        $moves \in 0..63$
        ... further details omitted
    VARIANT
        $63 - moves$
    END

After placing the knight at an initial position we enter a loop. The loop body consists of the following operations:

- Propose a move, selecting non-deterministically from the possible knight moves available at the current position.
- Verify. If the proposed move is to an unvisited square, this operation is equivalent to *skip*. Otherwise it is infeasible and provokes backtracking.
- Perform the proposed move, add it to a recorded sequence of successful moves and mark the new position as visited.
- Increment the count which records the number of moves that have been made.

The program relies on the angelic nature of demonic choice which is subjected to subsequent feasibility checks. "The demon abhors a miracle", even one that will occur some millions of operations later. In operational terms, of course, miracles provoke backtracking, so the number of attempted moves is far higher than the number which are finally retained. When implemented on our reversible virtual machine, a run which required approximately 5 million attempted moves took 35 seconds to execute on a 1.2GHz P4.

3 Bunches

Bunches have been proposed by Eric Hehner [2,3] as a light weight alternative to sets. A bunch is the contents of a set without the packaging that allows set representation to build up complex structures. We can have sets of sets, but we cannot have bunches of bunches. Bunches are self flattening, and that property will simplify our presentation of expression transformers.

A second property of bunches that will be useful is that any value is an elementary bunch or element. For example 2 is a bunch. In set theory we must distinguish between 2 and $\{2\}$, i.e. between an element and a set containing just that element. In bunch theory there is no such distinction.

The empty bunch is written as *null*. If A and B are bunches then their union, written A, B is also a bunch. We write $A : B$ to say A is a sub-bunch of B. As with sets, the repetition and order of elements has no significance. Some examples:

$2, 3 : 1, 2, 3, 4$
$2 : 2$
$A : A, B$

What follows is a simple and limited incorporation of bunches into GSL. We write bunch comprehension as $\S D \mid P \bullet E$. This is the bunch of all values of expression E that can be generated using the values of variables declared in D and satisfying predicate P. P may be omitted if it is *true* and E may be omitted if it is the variable (or variable list) D. An example of bunch comprehension is:

$\S n \mid n \in \mathbb{N} \wedge n < 3 \bullet n * n \quad = \quad 0, 1, 4$

Whereas some texts which employ bunches use the notation $[a;\ b]$ for an ordered pair, we keep the standard B notation (a, b). Bunches are of written without brackets, or by using bunch brackets ($\S$ ..) where context is insufficient to distinguish bunches from tuples.

Incorporating bunches in GSL will not add any new types to our system. Instead, we have the following typing rules.

- all elements of a bunch must be of the same type
- the type of a bunch is the type of its elements

Identifiers always represent elements. If E is an expression, replacing x in E by the bunch B gives a new expression which denotes $\S\, b \mid b : B \bullet (\lambda\, x.E)\, b$. Two obvious consequences of this rule are:

- Function application distributes over bunch union, e.g.
  $f(\S\, x, y) = f(x), f(y)$
  and
  $1, 2 + 3, 4 = 4, 5, 6$
- set operations distribute over bunch union, e.g. for sets A, B, C of the same type we have: $A \cup B, C = (A \cup B), (A \cup C)$

If P is a predicate, replacing x in P by the bunch B gives the new predicate: $\forall\, b . b : B \Rightarrow [x := b] P$

We will use, without proof, the following bunch lemmas:

L1. Under the condition y not free in E:

$$\S\, x \mid \exists\, y . P(x, y) \bullet E \quad = \quad \S\, x, y \mid P(x, y) \bullet E$$

L2. Under the condition y not free in P:

$$\S\, x, y \mid P \wedge Q \bullet E \quad = \quad \S\, x \mid P \bullet (\S\, y \mid Q \bullet E)$$

L3. Given a function f such that $f \in T \to U$, and an expression E of type T, then:

$$f(\S\, x \mid P \bullet E) \quad = \quad \S\, x \mid P \bullet f(E)$$

L4. (Bunch property) Under the assumption that y is an element:

$$(y : \S\, x \mid P \bullet E) \quad = \quad (\exists\, x . P \wedge y : E)$$

L5. Under the assumption that y is an element

$$(y : \S\, x \mid Q) \quad = \quad [x := y] Q$$

L6. $(\forall\, x . x : A \Rightarrow x : B) \quad = \quad A : B$

4 Expression Transformers

An abstract command language with backtracking will search for a feasible path of program execution, but will not tell us if more than one such path exists. Nor, within the semantics of predicate transformers, can we easily express a desire for it to find an answer and then backtrack, whilst remembering the answer. These are not difficult to arrange on our reversible virtual machine, but would hold little interest if we could not relate them to a tractable mathematical semantics.

To attempt to solve these problems let $S \diamond E$ represent the bunch of values that could be taken by expression E after executing S. Note that $S \diamond E$ is an expression on the current state space, and its evaluation does not change the current state space. It is implemented by executing all feasible paths through S, recording the resulting value of E each time, and backtracking to try another path until all paths are exhausted. If S is not feasible, then $S \diamond E$ will be equal to the empty bunch. The operator $\diamond$ is necessarily right associative. It has a lower precedence than the GSL connectives $:=, \Longrightarrow, |, [\!]$ which in turn have a lower precedence than expression connectives.

4.1 The Open Form

As with the predicate transformer $[S]Q$ we can describe $S \diamond E$ by a set of rules over the syntactic constructs of GSL. Note that there is no rule for pre-condition, since we suppose that we protect ourselves from invoking an operation outside its pre-condition by discharging the relevant proof obligations.

Name	Rule
Skip	$skip \diamond E = E$
Assignment	$x := F \diamond E = [x := F]E$
Guard	$g \Longrightarrow S \diamond E =$ if g then $S \diamond E$ else $null$ end
Choice	$S [\!] T \diamond E = (S \diamond E), (T \diamond E)$
Unbounded Choice	$(x :\in A) \diamond E = \S a \mid a \in A \bullet [x := a]E$
Sequential Composition	$S; T \diamond E = S \diamond T \diamond E$
Local variable	$@z.S \diamond E = \S z \bullet S \diamond E$

To illustrate the use of these rules let us consider the possible values taken by the expression $2 * x$ after running the program:

$(x := 0 [\!] x := 1); x := x + 1$

Intuitively we can see that these values will be 2 and 4. We can derive this result formally as follows:

$$(x := 0 \,[\!]\, x := 1); \; x := x + 1 \diamond 2 * x$$
$$= (x := 0 \,[\!]\, x := 1) \diamond x := x + 1 \diamond 2 * x \qquad \text{Sequential Composition}$$
$$= (x := 0 \,[\!]\, x := 1) \diamond 2 * (x + 1) \qquad \text{Assignment}$$
$$= x := 0 \diamond 2 * (x+1), x := 1 \diamond 2 * (x+1) \qquad \text{Choice}$$
$$= 2, 4 \qquad \text{Assignment}$$

We have defined expression transformation by a set of rules over the syntactic constructs of GSL. We will refer to this as the "open form" of the definition since if new basic constructs are added to the language, new rules would be required to handle these. We can use the open form to derive additional properties for various forms of substitution. For example:

$$S; \; x := E \diamond x \quad = \quad S \diamond E$$

Proof

$$S; \; x := E \diamond x$$
$$= S \diamond x := E \diamond x \qquad \text{sequential composition}$$
$$= S \diamond E \qquad \text{assignment}$$

□

4.2 The Closed Form

We can also formulate a "closed form" for expression transformation, as follows. For a machine with state variable (or variable list) x, let us write the predicate which relates new and old values of state with respect to some operation S as $prd_S(x, x')$.[1] Then the bunch of values comprising $S \diamond E$ can be given by replacing x in E by each value x' which is a possible after state with respect to S. That is:

Theorem 1.

$$S \diamond E \quad = \quad \S\, x' \mid prd_S(x, x') \bullet [x := x']E$$

Proof is by structural induction over the syntactic forms of substitutions in GSL. There are two base cases:

Skip: when S has the form *skip*, then: $prd_S(x, x') \equiv x' = x$, hence
$$\S\, x' \mid prd_S(x, x') \bullet [x := x']E =$$
$$\S\, x' \mid x' = x \bullet [x := x']E \quad = \quad E \quad = \quad skip \diamond E$$

Assignment: when S has the form $x := F$, then $prd_S(x, x') \equiv x' = F$ hence
$$\S\, x' \mid prd_S(x, x') \bullet [x := x']E =$$
$$\S\, x' \mid x' = F \bullet [x := x']E \quad = \quad [x := F]E \quad = \quad x := F \diamond E$$

---
[1] we choose a notation slightly different from the standard B $prd_x(S)$ to focus attention on the arguments x and x'.

We now consider the inductive cases:
Guard: when S has the form $g \Longrightarrow T$, then $prd_S(x, x') = \neg\, [g \Longrightarrow T]x' \neq x$
$= \neg\, (g \Rightarrow [T]x' \neq x)$
$= \neg\, (\neg\, g \vee [T]x' \neq x)$
$= g \wedge \neg\, [T]x' \neq x$
$= g \wedge prd_T(x, x')$
We consider two cases, g and $\neg\, g$
For case g we have: $\quad g \wedge prd_T(x, x') \equiv prd_T(x, x')\quad$, hence

$\S\, x' \mid prd_S(x, x') \bullet [x := x']E\ =$

$\S\, x' \mid prd_T(x, x') \bullet [x := x']E\ =$

$T \diamond E$

For case $\neg\, g$, $g \wedge prd_T(x, x') \equiv false$ hence

$\S\, x' \mid prd_S(x, x') \bullet [x := x']E\ =$

$\S\, x' \mid false \bullet [x := x']E\ =$

$null$

Thus combining cases with a conditional expression:

$\S\, x' \mid prd_S(x, x') \bullet [x := x']E\ =$

$\quad$ if g then $T \diamond E$ else $null$ end $\quad = \quad g \Longrightarrow T \diamond E$

Choice: when S has the form $T \,[\!]\, U$, then $prd_S(x, x') = \neg\, [T \,[\!]\, U]x' \neq x$
$= \neg\, ([T]x' \neq x \wedge [U]x' \neq x)$
$= \neg\, [T]x' \neq x \vee \neg\, [U]x' \neq x$
$= prd_T(x, x') \vee prd_U(x, x')\quad$ hence

$\S\, x' \mid prd_S(x, x') \bullet [x := x']E\ =$

$\S\, x' \mid prd_T(x, x') \vee prd_U(x, x') \bullet [x := x']E\ =$

$\S\, x' \mid prd_T(x, x') \bullet [x := x']E\, , \S\, x' \mid prd_U(x, x') \bullet [x := x']E\ =$

$(T \diamond E), (U \diamond E)\ =$

$T \,[\!]\, U \diamond E\quad$ by induction assumption, definition of choice

Unbounded choice: when S has the form $x :\in A$, then $prd_S(x, x') = x' \in A$, hence:

$\S\, x' \mid prd_S(x, x') \bullet [x := x']E\ =$

$\S\, x' \mid x' \in A \bullet [x := x']E\ =$

$\quad$ choosing a new bound variable name a which is not free in E

$\S\, a \mid a \in A \bullet [x := a]E\ =$

$x :\in A \diamond E$

Sequence: when S has the form T; U, then $prd_S(x, x') = \exists x''.prd_T(x, x'') \wedge prd_U(x'', x')$ (where x'' is "fresh" with respect to $prd_T(x, x')$ and $prd_U(x, x')$)

Hence $\S\, x' \mid prd_S(x, x') \bullet [x := x']E$

$= \S\, x' \mid \exists x''.prd_T(x, x'') \wedge prd_U(x'', x') \bullet [x := x']E$

which by L1

$= \S\, x', x'' \mid prd_T(x, x'') \wedge prd_U(x'', x') \bullet [x := x']E$

which by L2

$= \S\, x'' \mid prd_T(x, x'') \bullet (\S\, x' \mid prd_U(x'', x') \bullet [x := x']E)$

$= \S\, x'' \mid prd_T(x, x'') \bullet [x := x''](\S\, x' \mid prd_U(x, x') \bullet [x := x']E)$

which by induction

$= \S\, x'' \mid prd_T(x, x'') \bullet [x := x'']U \diamond E$

which with a change of bound variable name

$= \S\, x' \mid prd_T(x, x') \bullet [x := x']U \diamond E$

which by a further inductive step

$= T \diamond U \diamond E$

Local variables: Let $T = @z.S$, then[2] $prd_T(x, x') = \exists z, z'.prd_S((x, z), (x', z'))$. We assume the arbitrary name z is chosen so that z is not free in E.

Then $\S\, x' \mid prd_T(x, x') \bullet [x := x']E$

$= \S\, x' \mid \exists z, z'.prd_S((x, z), (x', z')) \bullet [x := x']E$

which since z is not free in E

$= \S\, x' \mid \exists z, z'.prd_S((x, z), (x', z')) \bullet [x, z := x', z']E$

which by lemma 1

$= \S\, z, x' \mid \exists z'.prd_S((x, z), (x', z')) \bullet [x, z := x', z']E$

which by lemma 2

$= \S\, z \bullet (\S\, x' \mid \exists z'.prd_S((x, z), (x', z')) \bullet [x, z := x', z']E)$

which by lemma 1

$= \S\, z \bullet (\S\, x', z' \mid prd_S((x, z), (x', z')) \bullet [x, z := x', z']E)$

$= \S\, z \bullet S \diamond E$

□

We present some properties that can be derived as corollaries. The first of these is referred to by Morris and Bunkenburg as the "fundamental law". They comment:

---

[2] See The B Book, page 294

"The closest analogue in predicate transformers to the fundamental law is the collection of basic properties known as healthiness conditions".

Corollary 1. *Given a function f such that $f \in T \to U$, and an expression E of type T, then:*
$$f(S \diamond E) = S \diamond f(E)$$

Proof

$$\begin{array}{rll}
S \diamond E & = \; \S\, x' \mid prd_S(x, x') \bullet [x := x']E & \text{closed form} \\
f(S \diamond E) & = f(\S\, x' \mid prd_S(x, x') \bullet [x := x']E) & \text{Leibnitz} \\
& = \; \S\, x' \mid prd_S(x, x') \bullet f([x := x']E) & \text{lemma 3} \\
& = \; \S\, x' \mid prd_S(x, x') \bullet [x := x']f(E) & \text{since } x \text{ not free in } f \\
& = \; S \diamond f(E) & \text{closed form}
\end{array}$$

□

Remark The proof needs the condition x not free in f, which can be derived from the fact that x is a variable or variable list and f is a constant. Syntactic restrictions prevent a variable being used to describe the properties of a constant.

The next result gives the expression transformer form of the "before-after predicate". This is more intuitive than the predicate transformer equivalent, with its use of double negation in $prd_S(x, x') = \neg\, [S]x \neq x'$. Using expression transformers we can just say that the new state x' must be a possible result of S.

Corollary 2. $prd_S(x, x') = x' : S \diamond x$

Proof

$$\begin{array}{rl}
& x' : S \diamond x \\
= & x' : \S\, x' \mid prd_S(x, x') \bullet [x := x']x \hspace{1cm} \text{closed form} \\
= & x' : \S\, x' \mid \neg\, [S]x \neq x' \bullet x' \hspace{1cm} \text{applying substitution} \\
= & x' : \S\, u \mid \neg\, [S]x \neq u \bullet u \hspace{1cm} \text{change of bound variable name} \\
= & \exists\, u \bullet u = x' \wedge \neg\, [S]x \neq u \hspace{1cm} \text{lemma 4 (bunch property)} \\
= & [u := x']\neg\, [S]x \neq u \hspace{1cm} \text{one point rule} \\
= & \neg\, [S]x \neq x' \hspace{1cm} \text{applying substitution}
\end{array}$$

□

Our final corollary concerns the equivalent expressive power of expression transformers and predicate transformers. However, since we have limited our interest in $S \diamond E$ to a world in which $trm(S)$ is guaranteed to hold, we can only prove the present result under the same assumption. This is not a fundamental limitation, but to transcend it we need to give some meaning to $S \diamond E$ when $trm(S)$ is false, and, as well as giving a more clumsy theory, this seems contrary to the spirit of B.

Since the closed form for $S \diamond E$ is defined using the predicate transformer properties of S, we know already that predicate transformers are as expressive as expression transformers. We now prove the converse, by showing how to express $[S]Q$ in terms of the expression transformer properties of S (under the restriction mentioned above).

We make use of Abrial's normal form for a generalised substitution:

$$S = (trm(S) \mid @\, x'.prd_S(x, x') \Longrightarrow x := x')$$

Corollary 3. $trm(S) \Rightarrow ([S]Q = (S \diamond x) : \S\, x \mid Q)$

Proof

$$\begin{aligned}
trm(S) &\Rightarrow [S]Q = [\,@\, x'.prd_S(x, x') \Longrightarrow x := x']Q & \text{normal form} \\
&= \forall x'.[prd_S(x, x') \Longrightarrow x := x']Q & \text{@ rule} \\
&= \forall x'.prd_S(x, x') \Rightarrow [x := x']Q & \text{guard} \\
&= \forall x'.prd_S(x, x') \Rightarrow x' : \S\, x \mid Q & \text{lemma 5} \\
&= \forall x'.x' : (S \diamond x) \Rightarrow x' : \S\, x \mid Q & \text{corollary 2} \\
&= S \diamond x : \S\, x \mid Q & \text{lemma 6}
\end{aligned}$$

□

Remark An equivalent formulation of this corollary is:
$[S]Q \;=\; (S \diamond Q) : true$

5 Applications

Although we have used bunches for theory presentation, they do not form part of our implementation language. So in these example applications, any expression of the form $S \diamond E$ that could denote a plurality of elements or none will be packaged within set brackets.

5.1 Evaluating Set Expressions, Feasibility, and Quantifications

We present some executable constructs which illustrate the expressive capabilities of expression transformers. First the expression transformer evaluations of set union, intersection, and set difference. We assume the existence of a variable e of suitable type, and A and B are finite sets represented in the state space of our machine:

$$A \cup B = \{(e :\in A) [\!] (e :\in B) \diamond e\}$$

$$A \cap B = \{e :\in A;\; e \in B \Longrightarrow skip \diamond e\}$$

$$A \setminus B = \{e :\in A;\; e \notin B \Longrightarrow skip \diamond e\}$$

We can evaluate whether an operation is feasible:

$$fis(S) = (\{S \diamond x\} \neq \{\})$$

The set operations are reasonably efficient, but the expression for $fis(S)$ evaluates all execution paths of S whereas it only needs to find one such path to know S is feasible.[3] We can also evaluate quantifications as binary expressions:

$$(\exists x. x \in A \land P) \quad = \quad fis(x :\in A; \; P \Longrightarrow skip)$$

$$(\forall x. x \in A \Rightarrow P) \quad = \quad (card(A) = card(\{x :\in A; \; P \Longrightarrow skip \diamond x\}))$$

5.2 Recursion in Implementations

An operation with output parameter a and input parameter b has a definition of the form:

$$a \leftarrow OP(b) \triangleq S$$

When OP is subsequently invoked as say $c \leftarrow Op(E)$ its effect can be described by the simple syntactic replacement $[a, b := c, E]S$, that is by rewriting S with a replaced by c and b replaced by E. Thus $a \leftarrow OP(b) \triangleq a := b + 1$ invoked as $c \leftarrow Op(E)$ becomes $[a, b := c, E]a := b + 1$ i.e. $c := E + 1$.

Recursively defined operations cannot, however, be handled in this way, and are not supported in classical B development tools. Abrial and Lafitte have developed a treatment of recursion in implementations based on set transformers, which is presented in chapter 12.5 of the B Book [1]. Here we present a treatment based on expression transformers.

Consider the problem of specifying and implementing an operation to find the maximum element in a non empty set of n integers. In the specification we might have constants $max2$, max with properties:

$max2 \in \mathbb{Z} \times \mathbb{Z} \to \mathbb{Z} \land max \in \mathbb{P}\,\mathbb{Z} \nrightarrow \mathbb{Z}$

$\forall(i,j).$ if $(i > j)$ then $max2(i,j) = i$ else $max2(i,j) = j$ end

$\forall(s).s \in \mathbb{P}\,\mathbb{Z} \land card(s) > 0 \Rightarrow$

    if $card(s) = 1$ then $max(s) = choice(s)$

    else $max(s) = max2(choice(s), max(s \setminus choice(s)))$ end

With the help of the constant max we can specify an operation:

$n \leftarrow MAX(A) \triangleq A \in \mathbb{P}\,\mathbb{Z} \land A \neq \{\} \mid n := max(A)$

---

[3] In fact all these expressions are implemented directly as primitives of our virtual machine, as described in our previous papers [11], [13].

In this specification the constants are not thought of as being "executed" or "implemented", they are just mathematical objects which form part of our descriptive apparatus. We do feel, however, that the way they have been defined could guide us in writing an implementation.

A first problem in doing this has been alluded to above: the incompatibility between B's treatment of i/o parameters by syntactic rewriting, and the use of recursion. A second problem is that in a recursively defined constant we can just write a function application to obtain its value, since a function application is an expression defined on the state space. A B operation, however, is not such an expression; it is a predicate transformer. It does not denote any value: rather, it describes how values change.

We can overcome these discrepancies with the help of expression transformers and definitions. We name operations in upper case, and definitions in lower case.

We will need to revise our abstract specification so that its operations leave their results in a *VARIABLE*. Assume an integer variable *answer* is available for this purpose, and with the constants *max* and *max2* defined as above, let the abstract operations be:

$MAX2(x, y) \triangleq x \in \mathbb{Z} \land y \in \mathbb{Z} \mid$

$\qquad answer := max2(x, y)$ end

$MAX(A) \triangleq \quad A \in \mathbb{P}\,\mathbb{Z} \land A \neq \{\} \mid answer := max(A)$

In our implementation we re-use the names *max2* and *max*. These now appear as definitions:

DEFINITIONS

$\qquad max2(i, j) == MAX2(i, j) \diamond answer$

$\qquad max(A) == MAX(A) \diamond answer$

They represent expressions that can be used in a similar way to the abstract constants with the same names. Thus to reason about the *MAX* and *MAX2* operations we can refer to the definitions of *max* and *max2* given at the specification level as mathematical constants, whilst their executional behaviour is given by these definitions.

Finally we have the concrete operations:

OPERATIONS

$\qquad MAX2(i, j) \triangleq i \in \mathbb{Z} \land j \in \mathbb{Z} \mid$

$\qquad\quad$ if $i > j$ then $answer := i$ else $answer := j$ end

$\qquad MAX(A) \triangleq A \in \mathbb{P}\,\mathbb{Z} \land \text{card}(A) > 0 \mid$

$\qquad\quad$ if $\text{card}(A) = 1$ then $answer := choice(A)$

$\qquad\quad$ else $answer := max2(choice(A), max(A \setminus \{choice(A)\}))$ end

Depositing a result in a global variable may seen an unlikely strategy to adopt when writing a recursive program, so we ask the reader to recall at this point that $MAX(A) \diamond answer$ is an expression whose evaluation *does not affect the machine state*. Thinking in operational terms, the value of *answer* is only temporarily changed during the evaluation of the expression $MAX \diamond answer$ and is restored by reverse execution. The different values taken by the variable at various levels of recursion are held on the history stack, a component in the reversible virtual machine architecture which is used to incrementally record state changes and thus to hold the information required for reversing a computation.

The example we have chosen here is amenable to expression in a purely functional style of programming, but the method we have introduced allows free use of state during function evaluation, whilst guaranteeing that function evaluation has no side effects. We see an example of this in the next section.

5.3 Extending the Functional Style: A Simple Mini-Max Algorithm

We are now able to adopt a functional style of programming, whilst remaining in, and making use of, a state based language. We present a mini-max algorithm to illustrate our approach to using state in a purely functional setting. We can make use of state, as when updating the position of the game after a move, but the expressions that perform such state updates are evaluated without side effects.

We remind the reader that the mini-max algorithm for two player games requires that there should be some heuristic to "score" any game position, such that a high score indicates an advantage to player A and a low score an advantage for player B.

We assume variables which represent the state of the game, an expression *score* which applies the heuristic to the current state of the game and returns a value, and operations $AMOVE$ and $BMOVE$ which non-deterministically choose and play a move for players A and B respectively. We code the algorithm from the point of view of player A, assuming that A has just made a provisional move and wishes to evaluate the resulting position.

$$EVAL(n) \cong$$
$$\quad \text{if } n = 0 \text{ then } mark := score$$
$$\quad \text{else } mark :=$$
$$\qquad min($$
$$\qquad\quad \{BMOVE \diamond$$
$$\qquad\qquad max($$
$$\qquad\qquad\quad \{AMOVE \diamond eval(n-1)\}$$
$$\qquad\qquad)$$
$$\qquad\quad \}$$
$$\qquad)$$
$$\quad end$$

Where $eval(n)$ is given in the DEFINITIONS clause as:

$$eval(n) == EVAL(n) \diamond mark$$

Now we can use *eval(n)* as a function to provide the minimax score for the current board position based on a $2 * n$ move look ahead. As in pure functional programming it is an expression which represents a value. Unlike pure functional programming *we can carry state with us*. Some examples: neither *eval* nor *score* need to be passed the state of the game, since they can access its representation in state variables; likewise *AMOVE* and *BMOVE* have their effect by *changing the current state*. There is a guarantee of "no side effects" even though we are able to change the current state of the game during our minimax search.

6 The Implementation Architecture

In "An Implementation Architecture for B-GSL"[11] we proposed a reversible virtual machine as a platform for implementing backtracking. The virtual machine has three modes. In normal forward mode it executes as a conventional computer. In conservative mode it preserves, on a history stack, the information it might later need to retrace its steps. The final mode is reverse mode, which is entered when forward execution is infeasible, and which returns to the previous point of choice whilst undoing any state changes made since that point. Whilst still maintaining this general approach, we have made significant progress in matching our implementation to the behaviour of contemporary processor architectures, which typically use instruction pre-fetch and instruction pipelines. Conversion from virtual machine to native code now takes place at compile time, eliminating the use of branch via register instructions which have found to be particularly expensive on pipelined architectures. We have also discovered a more efficient implementation of backtracking: conservative execution pushes any data needed to restore the previous state onto a history stack, followed by a pointer to the native code fragment that will perform the restoration. When reverse mode is entered, the history stack is exchanged with the system stack and a "return" machine code instruction is executed. This enters the last restoration routine to be left on the history stack, which now, very conveniently, finds the data it needs on the system stack. It removes and uses this data then terminates with a "return" instruction, which immediately enters the next restoration routine. The final return in this sequence is to code which re-exchanges the history stack and the system stack and re-establishes forward execution. Full details of this mechanism and its integration with bounded choice are given in our paper "Efficient Reversibility with Guards and Choice" [12]. Details of our implementation of sets is given in "Implementing Sets for Reversible Computation" [13].

7 Related Work

Our idea of expression transformers is taken directly from the "term transformers" of Morris and Bunkenburg [9],[8]. They work with a "term language" in which there is no fundamental difference between commands, predicates and expressions. This allows term transformers to be treated as a generalisation of predicate transformers (thinking of predicates as boolean terms). This approach to formal language is very different to that of B, where we distinguish between expressions (which denote values), predicates (which are subject to proof) and operations (which transform predicates). Expression transformers are therefore very limited in scope in comparison to term transformers, and in consequence do not raise the same semantic issues.

M & B's work on term transformers concentrates mainly on the deterministic executable subset of their term language, and many results, including the fundamental law, are introduced before non-determinism is mentioned. However, the term language itself accomodates non-determinism and indeed admits non-deterministic values as well as non-deterministic operations. A bottom element is introduced to denote the result of evaluating a term transformation when the pre-condition of its operation is false.

A primary motivation for Morris and Bunkenburgs interest in term transformers is an integration of state into functional programming. They compare term transformers with "Monads" [6] [14], which are used in Haskell [4], a lazy evaluation language. Another technique that can be mentioned in this respect is "Effects" which is typically associated with strict languages [5]. Although we have given some limited examples which use expression transformers to incorporate recursion and a functional programming style into B, we can expect our approach to encounter some limitations when we try to generalise it, e.g. to the treatment of executable "functions" as "first class objects".

8 Conclusions

We have taken the syntactic constructs of B-GSL and have defined the expression transformer effect of each such construct, giving an "open form" semantics[4] of expression transformers. To verify the intuition embodied in these definitions and to relate our semantics to the existing predicate transformer semantics of B-GSL, we have introduce a "closed form" definition for expression transformers based on the before-after-predicate derived for each syntactic construct in the language from its predicate transformer rules. We have shown the two definitions are equivalent and derived some additional properties.

Like many formalisms for sequential programming, B-GSL already includes a semantics of backtracking. Expression transformers help us to exploit this, and allow the integration of functional and state based programming. These features can be supported at the execution level by a reversible virtual machine.

This paper has incorporated expression transformers into B-GSL, but not into the B development method. Our future work will address this.

Acknowledgements. Steve Dunne engaged with us in many extended conversations relating to this paper and brought to our attention the work of Joe Morris and Alexander Bunkenburg on term transformers. Professor Joe Morris

---

[4] Some readers may object to the term "semantics" in this context. It is intended in the same sense as "predicate transformer semantics".

provided a pre-publication copy of his paper. Jean-Raymond Abrial suggested the "closed form" definition. The referees offered perceptive and helpful comments. We extend our warmest thanks to them all.

References

[1] Jean-Raymond Abrial. *The B Book*. Cambridge University Press, 1996.
[2] E C R Hehner. Bunch theory: A simple set theory for computer science. *Information Processing Letters*, 12.1 pp26-31, 1981.
[3] E C R Hehner. *A Practical Theory of Programming*. Springer Verlag, 1993.
[4] http://www.haskell.org. Haskell98, a non-strict purely functional language. Technical report, 1998.
[5] J M Lucassen. *Types and Effects, towards the integration of functional and imperitive programming*. PhD thesis, MIT laboratory for computer science, 1987.
[6] E Moggi. Notions of Computation and Monads. *Information and Computation 93(1)*, 1991.
[7] J Morris and A Bunkenburg. A theory of bunches. *Acta Informatica*, 37(8).
[8] J M Morris. An easy route from functional to imperative programming. Presented at the 5th Irish Formal Methods Workshop, Trinity College, Dublin, July 2001.
[9] J M Morris and A Bunkenburg. Term transformer semantics. Submitted to ACM Transactions on Programming Languages and Systems, 1999.
[10] Greg Nelson. A Generalization of Dijkstra's Calculus. *ACM Transactions on Programming Languages and Systems, Vol 11, No. 4*, 1989.
[11] W J Stoddart. An Execution Architecture for B-GSL. In Bowen J and Dunne S E, editors, *ZB2000*, Lecture Notes in Computer Science, no 1878, 2000.
[12] W J Stoddart. Efficient reversibility with guards and choice. In M A Ertl, editor, *18th EuroForth*, 2002. Available from:
www.complang.tuwien.ac.at/anton/euroforth2002/papers/bill.rev.ps.gz.
[13] W J Stoddart and F Zeyda. Implementing sets for reversible computation. In M A Ertl, editor, *18th EuroForth*, 2002. Available from:
www.complang.tuwien.ac.at/anton/euroforth2002/papers/bill.sets.ps.gz.
[14] P Wadler. Monads for functional programming. In J Jeuring and E Meijer, editors, *Advanced Functional Programming*, Lecture notes in Computer Science, no 925, 1995.

Probabilistic Termination in B

Annabelle McIver[1], Carroll Morgan[2], and Thai Son Hoang[2]

[1] Dept. of Computing, Macquarie University, NSW 2109 Australia;
anabel@ics.mq.edu.au
[2] Dept. Comp. Sci. & Eng., University of New South Wales, NSW 2052 Australia;
{carrollm, htson}@cse.unsw.edu.au

Abstract. The B Method [1] does not currently handle probability. We add it in a limited form, concentrating on "almost-certain" properties which hold with probability one; and we address briefly the implied modifications to the programs that support B.

The *Generalised Substitution Language* is extended with a binary operator $\oplus$ representing "abstract probabilistic choice", so that the substitution $prog_1 \oplus prog_2$ means roughly "choose between $prog_1$ and $prog_2$ with some probability neither one nor zero". We then adjust B's proof rule for loops — specifically, the variant rule — so that in many cases it is possible to prove "probability-one" correctness of programs containing the new operator, which was not possible in B before, while remaining almost entirely within the original Boolean logic.

Applications include probabilistic algorithms such as the IEEE 1394 Root Contention Protocol ("FireWire") [9] in which a probabilistic "symmetry-breaking" strategy forms a key component of the design.

1 Introduction

A coin is "almost certain" to come up heads eventually, if flipped often enough; mathematically, we say that heads will eventually appear *with probability one*. Such "coin flips" have many applications in computer programming, in particular in the many symmetry-breaking protocols found in distributed systems.

An example is the IEEE 1394 FireWire protocol [9], in which a leader is elected from a collection of processes executing identical code over an acyclic connected network. At its final "root-contention" stage, two processes can enter livelock while each tries repeatedly to elect the other. The protocol breaks the livelock by having the processes flip two coins, one each, continuing until the outcomes differ; at that stage, the process with "heads" becomes the leader, and the one with "tails" concedes. Because it is almost certain that the outcomes will eventually differ, the contention is resolved.

Using *standard* (i.e. non-probabilistic) B, we cannot express such protocols exactly. The closest we can come is to use demonic choice for coin flips, along the lines of Fig. 1. We cannot prove termination of that program, however: the demonic choices $\square$ could choose to make xx and yy equal every time... forever. Thus any standard B presentation of this protocol [2] would have to include an *informal* termination argument at this point.

$xx, yy := heads, heads;$
WHILE $xx = yy$ DO
  $xx := heads \square xx := tails;$
  $yy := heads \square yy := tails$
END

Program 1a: *Demonic coin-flips*

In Prog. 1a, the binary operator $\square$ is B's demonic choice.[1] Variable xx represents the coin of some process X, and yy is the coin of process Y. The loop body — representing one "round" of attempting to break the livelock — is executed until the two processes make different choices. At that stage, if it is ever reached, the process whose variable holds *heads* becomes the new leader.

Fig. 1. Demonic abstraction of FireWire's symmetry-breaking *root-contention protocol*

The contribution of this paper is to show how to give a *formal* argument, for such situations, without much extra complexity in the logic: we augment the syntax of *GSL* with an "abstract probabilistic choice" operator $\oplus$; we extend the distribution laws of *GSL* to deal with it; we adjust the proof obligations for loops so that they are sound for loop bodies containing the new operator, carefully identifying any limitations; and we provide the justification for the soundness of all the above.

Our main technical result is Thm. 1 (Sec. 6). It states roughly that as long as *some* probability is used in programs like Prog. 1a, rather than demonic choice, termination occurs with probability one *no matter what probability was used* (provided certain general conditions are met, which we later explain). We write the loop as in Fig. 2, using $\oplus$ for the unknown probability, and we use a modified WHILE-loop proof obligation to show its correctness. We call $\oplus$ "abstract" because we do not know the precise value it uses.

For soundness, it is sufficient (Sec. 7) that the abstract choices $\oplus$ are implemented by "concrete" probabilistic choices $_p\oplus$ that are "bounded away from zero and one" — that is, that there is a fixed constant $\varepsilon > 0$ for the *whole execution* such that all actual probabilistic choices $_p\oplus$ used to implement $\oplus$ satisfy $\varepsilon \leq p \leq 1-\varepsilon$ at the moment they are executed. The p-values can vary dynamically — we allow demonic choice from a range of probabilities — provided

---

[1] We are ignoring several practical details of some B realisations, in particular that WHILE-loops and demonic choice do not usually appear together, since the former are restricted to implementation machines while the latter is banned there; and we leave out the INVARIANT and VARIANT sections of the loop. Also, we move freely between *GSL* (e.g. $\square$) and *AMN* (e.g. WHILE).

$$xx, yy := heads, heads;$$
$$\text{WHILE } xx = yy \text{ DO}$$
$$xx := heads \oplus xx := tails;$$
$$yy := heads \oplus yy := tails$$
$$\text{END}$$

Program 2a: *Abstract coin-flips*

In Prog. 2a, the binary operator $\oplus$ is the proposed "abstract" probabilistic choice. Provided the actual probability used is neither zero nor one, the loop will almost-certainly terminate and a new leader will be elected.

Fig. 2. Probabilistic abstraction of FireWire's symmetry-breaking protocol

---

they remain within the inverval $[\varepsilon, 1-\varepsilon]$ for the chosen ε. We call that a *proper* implementation of $\oplus$.[2]

The two adjustments we make to the WHILE proof-obligations are (A) to change the termination argument so that the variant must be bounded *above* as well as below; and in proving its strict decrease (B) to interpret $\oplus$ "angelically" rather than "demonically" — that is, we require only that the body *can* decrease the variant, not that it must. For all other uses — for example, (C) to prove preservation of the invariant — operator $\oplus$ is interpreted demonically.

The full rule is given at Thm. 1 (p231), where (A), (B) and (C) are labelled.

In Sec. 2 we briefly recall the details[3] of *pGSL* [11], the fully probabilistic version of *GSL*; in Sec. 3 we explain the role of "almost-certain" properties, and how the standard variant rule fails to deal with them; in Sec. 4 we appeal to the "zero-one" law from probability theory that underlies our approach, and we adapt it to *pGSL*; in Sec. 5 we give the modified variant rule that arises from it. Section 6 assembles the pieces into a single rule, and Sec. 7 shows how it can all be expressed in our original Boolean domain. The remaining sections describe an example — the root-contention protocol — and discuss implementation issues.

---

[2] It is a slightly stronger condition than just lying strictly between zero and one, analogous to the use of *uniform-* rather than simple continuity of functions in analysis.

[3] One detail is that, because *GSL* allows "naked guarded commands" [15,20], our *pGSL* as defined earlier [11] allows infinite expectations, generated by guards and by the miraculous substitution MAGIC. However, the theory [17] on which the current paper rests is itself based on *pGCL* [18], extending the original "Dijkstra-style" *GCL* [3] which is miracle-free — and so its expectations lie in the interval [0, 1] (that is, without ∞). We finesse this slight mismatch by excluding infeasible substitutions in our treatment here, in particular by treating IF $\cdots$ END as a whole.

2 Full Probabilistic Reasoning in $pGSL$

To explain and justify our approach, we must temporarily appeal to the fully explicit probabilistic B logic $pGSL$, where $prog_1\ {}_p\!\oplus prog_2$ means "choose program $prog_1$ with probability p, and program $prog_2$ with probability $1-p$". Although the justification is somewhat detailed, the results are simple; and once they are re-inserted into the simpler Boolean domain (Sec. 7), no arithmetic is required.

A comprehensive introduction to $pGSL$ is given elsewhere [11].

2.1 Brief Introduction to $pGSL$

The numeric program logic $pGSL$ uses real- rather than Boolean-valued expressions to describe program behaviour: the numbers represent "expected values" rather than the normal predicates that definitely do, or do not hold. Given a state space S, let the predicates over S be $\mathcal{P}S$, and let the *expectations* over S be $\mathcal{E}S$.

Consider the simple program

$$xx := -yy \quad {}_{\frac{1}{3}}\!\oplus \quad xx := +yy \,, \tag{1}$$

over integer variables xx, yy, using a construct ${}_{\frac{1}{3}}\!\oplus$ which we interpret as "choose the left branch with probability $1/3$, and choose the right branch with probability $1 - 1/3$". Recall that for any predicate *post* over *final* states, and a standard GSL substitution *prog*, the predicate $[prog]post$ acts over *initial* states: it holds just in those initial states from which *prog* is guaranteed to reach *post*. If *prog* is probabilistic, as Prog. (1) is, what can we say about the *probability* that $[prog]post$ holds in some initial state?

It turns out that the answer is just $[prog]\langle post\rangle$, where we use angle brackets $\langle \cdot \rangle$ to convert predicates to expectations, whose values here are restricted to the unit interval: $\langle false\rangle$ is 0 and $\langle true\rangle$ is 1, and in general $\langle post\rangle$ is the characteristic function of (the set denoted by) *post*.

Now in fact we can continue to use substitution, once we generalise $[prog]$ itself to expectations instead of predicates: to emphasise the generalisation, however, we use the slightly different notation $[\![prog]\!]$ for it. We begin with the two definitions

$$[\![xx := E\,]\!]\, exp \quad \widehat{=}^4 \quad \text{"exp with xx replaced everywhere by E"} \tag{2}$$

$$[\![prog_1\ {}_p\!\oplus prog_2]\!]\, exp \quad \widehat{=} \quad p \times [\![prog_1]\!]\, exp + (1-p) \times [\![prog_2]\!]\, exp \,, \tag{3}$$

in which *exp* is an expectation; and for Prog. (1) we now calculate the probability that the predicate

$$\text{the final state will satisfy } xx \geq 0 \tag{4}$$

holds in a given initial state. We have

---
[4] We use "$\widehat{=}$" for "is defined to be".

$$[\![xx:=-yy \quad {}_{\frac{1}{3}}\oplus \quad xx:=+yy]\!]\langle xx \geq 0\rangle$$

$$\equiv^5 \quad \begin{aligned}&(1/3) \times [\![xx:=-yy]\!]\langle xx \geq 0\rangle \\ &+ (2/3) \times [\![xx:=+yy]\!]\langle xx \geq 0\rangle\end{aligned} \qquad \text{using (3)}$$

$$\equiv \quad (1/3)\langle -yy \geq 0\rangle + (2/3)\langle +yy \geq 0\rangle \qquad \text{using (2)}$$
$$\equiv \quad (1/3)\langle yy \leq 0\rangle + (2/3)\langle yy \geq 0\rangle \,. \qquad \text{arithmetic}$$

Our answer is the final arithmetic formula above — call it a "pre-expectation" — and the probability we seek is found by reading off the formula's value for various initial values of yy:

When yy is initially negative, $\langle true\rangle/3 + 2\langle false\rangle/3$
(4) holds finally with probability $= 1/3 + 2(0)/3$
$= 1/3$

When yy is initially zero, $1/3 + 2(1)/3$
$= 1$

When yy is initially positive, $0/3 + 2(1)/3$
$= 2/3 \,.$

Those results correspond with our operational intuition about the effect of probabilistic choice ${}_{\frac{1}{3}}\oplus$ in Prog. (1); note in particular how in the "initally zero" case the two branches' probabilities are automatically summed to one, since both establish the postcondition.

2.2 Concise Summary of *pGSL*

The rest of *pGSL* is not much more than the above: the definitions of the remaining substitutions are given in Fig. 3.

Implication-like relations between expectations are

$$\begin{aligned}exp_1 \Rrightarrow exp_2 &\;\widehat{=}\; exp_1 \text{ is everywhere no more than } exp_2 \\ exp_1 \equiv exp_2 &\;\widehat{=}\; exp_1 \text{ is everywhere equal to } exp_2 \\ exp_1 \Lleftarrow exp_2 &\;\widehat{=}\; exp_1 \text{ is everywhere no less than } exp_2.\end{aligned}$$

Note that $\models pred_1 \Rightarrow pred_2$ exactly when $\langle pred_1\rangle \Rrightarrow \langle pred_2\rangle$, and so on; that is the motivation for the symbols chosen.

In its full generality, an expectation is a function describing how much each program state is "worth". The special case of an embedded predicate $\langle pred\rangle$ assigns to each state a worth of 0 or of 1: states satisfying *pred* are worth 1, and states not satisfying *pred* are worth 0. The more general expectations arise when one estimates, in the *initial* state of a probabilistic program, what the worth of its *final* state will be. That estimate, the "expected worth" of the final state, is obtained by summing over all final states

---
[5] Later we explain the use of '$\equiv$' rather than '='.

The probabilistic generalised substitution language *pGSL* acts over "expectations" rather than predicates: *expectations* take values in $[0, 1] \cup \{\infty\}$.

$[\![xx := E]\!] exp$	The expectation obtained after replacing all free occurrences of xx in exp by E, renaming bound variables in exp if necessary to avoid capture of free variables in E.
$[\![pre \mid prog]\!] exp$	$\langle pre \rangle \times [\![prog]\!] exp$, where $0 \times \infty \hat{=} 0$.
$[\![prog_1 \,\square\, prog_2]\!] exp$	$[\![prog_1]\!] exp$ min $[\![prog_2]\!] exp$
$[\![pre \rightarrow prog]\!] exp$	$1/\langle pre \rangle \times [\![prog]\!] exp$, where $\infty \times 0 \hat{=} \infty$.
$[\![\text{SKIP}]\!] exp$	exp
$[\![prog_1 \,{}_p\!\oplus prog_2]\!] exp$	$p \times [\![prog_1]\!] exp + (1-p) \times [\![prog_2]\!] exp$
$[\![@xx \cdot pred \implies prog]\!] exp$	(min $xx \mid pred \cdot [\![prog]\!] exp$), where xx does not occur free in exp.
$prog_1 \sqsubseteq prog_2$	$[\![prog_1]\!] exp \Rightarrow [\![prog_2]\!] exp$ for all exp

- exp is an expectation (possibly but not necessarily $\langle pred \rangle$ for some predicate $pred$);
- pre is a predicate (not an expectation);
- $\times$ is multiplication;
- $prog, prog_1, prog_2$ are probabilistic generalised substitutions;
- p is an expression over the program variables (possibly but not necessarily a constant), taking a value in $[0, 1]$; and
- (min $xx \mid pred \cdot [\![prog]\!] exp$) is the infimum over all xx satisfying $pred$ of the value (in this case) $[\![prog]\!] exp$.
- xx is a variable (or a vector of variables).

We give the definitions including infeasible or "miraculous" commands [16, Sec. 1.7], but in the main text will avoid them by treating IF $\cdots$ END as a whole, thus effectively restricting our expectations to $[0, 1]$ (that is, without ∞).

Fig. 3. *pGSL* — the probabilistic Generalised Substitution Language [11]

---

the worth of the final state multiplied by the probability the program "will go there" from the initial state.

Naturally the "will go there" probabilities depend on "from which initial state", and so the expected worth is a function of the initial state.

When the worth of final states is given by $\langle pred \rangle$, the expected worth of the initial state turns out to be just the probability that the program will reach *pred*, as we saw in the previous section. That is because

	expected worth of initial state
$\equiv$	(probability *prog* reaches *pred*) $\times$ (worth of states satisfying *pred*)
	$+$ (probability *prog* does not reach *pred*) $\times$ (worth of states not satisfying *pred*)
$\equiv$	(probability *prog* reaches *pred*) $\times$ 1 $+$ (probability *prog* does not reach *pred*) $\times$ 0
$\equiv$	probability *prog* reaches *pred* ,

where matters are simplified by the fact that all states satisfying *pred* have the same worth.

2.3 Some *pGSL* Idioms

More generally, analyses of programs *prog* in practice lead to conclusions of the form

$$p \quad \equiv \quad [\![prog]\!]\langle post \rangle \tag{5}$$

for some p and *post* — that is, where the pre-expectation is not of the form $\langle pre \rangle$. Given the above, we can interpret in two equivalent ways:

1. the expected worth $\langle post \rangle$ of the final state is at least[6] the value of p in the initial state; or
2. the probability that *prog* will establish *post* is at least p.

Each interpretation is useful, and in the following example we see them both — we look at one round of the root-contention protocol (much idealised in Fig. 2, and with explicit probabilities included) and ask for the probability that the coins will differ after that round:

$$\left[\!\!\left[\begin{array}{l} xx := heads \; {}_{\frac{1}{2}}\!\oplus\; xx := tails \; ; \\ yy := heads \; {}_{\frac{1}{2}}\!\oplus\; yy := tails \end{array} \right]\!\!\right] \langle xx \neq yy \rangle$$

$\equiv$ ${}_{\frac{1}{2}}\!\oplus$, :=, and sequential composition
$[\![xx := heads \; {}_{\frac{1}{2}}\!\oplus\; xx := tails]\!](\langle xx \neq heads \rangle/2 + \langle xx \neq tails \rangle/2)$

$\equiv$ $(1/2)(\langle heads \neq heads \rangle/2 + \langle heads \neq tails \rangle/2)$ ${}_{\frac{1}{2}}\!\oplus$ and :=
     $+ (1/2)(\langle tails \neq heads \rangle/2 + \langle tails \neq tails \rangle/2)$

$\equiv$ $(1/2)(0/2 + 1/2) + (1/2)(1/2 + 0/2)$ definition $\langle \cdot \rangle$
$\equiv$ $1/2$.   arithmetic

---

[6] We must say 'at least' in general, because of possible demonic choice in S; and some analyses give only the weaker $p \Rightarrow [\![prog]\!]\langle post \rangle$ in any case.

We can then use the second interpretation above to conclude that the faces differ with probability (at least[7]) 1/2.

But half-way through the above calculation we find the more general expression

$$[\![xx := \text{heads} \, {}_\frac{1}{2}\oplus\, xx := \text{tails}]\!](\langle xx \neq \text{heads}\rangle/2 + \langle xx \neq \text{tails}\rangle/2) \;,$$

and what does that mean on its own? It must be given the first interpretation, since its post-expectation is not of the form $\langle pred \rangle$, and it means

the expected value of

$$\langle xx \neq \text{heads}\rangle/2 + \langle xx \neq \text{tails}\rangle/2$$

after executing $xx := \text{heads} \, {}_\frac{1}{2}\oplus\, xx := \text{tails}$,

which the calculation goes on to show is in fact 1/2. But for our overall conclusions we do not need to think about the intermediate expressions — they are only the "glue" that holds the overall reasoning together.

Finally — a generalisation of (5) — we mention an idiom we will need later; it is

$$p \times \langle pre \rangle \quad \Rrightarrow \quad [\![prog]\!]\langle post \rangle \;, \tag{6}$$

which means "the probability that $prog$ will establish $post$ is at least p from any initial state satisfying pre". If pre holds then $p \times \langle pre \rangle$ is just p; and if it does not hold then $p \times \langle pre \rangle$ is zero, making (6) trivially true.

2.4 Treating Standard Programs Probabilistically

Although we have used the double brackets $[\![\;]\!]$ for probabilistic substitution, to distinguish it from the ordinary standard substitution (single brackets), if $prog$ is standard then in fact there is little distinction to make: an important property of our approach is that if we choose to deal with standard programs within the extended probabilistic framework, we incur no penalty since — as the following lemma shows — the calculations are effectively the same.

Lemma 1. *Embedding of standard programs* — *If prog is a standard and feasible program — that is, one which contains no probabilistic choices and is non-miraculous — then for any postcondition post we have*

$$[\![prog]\!]\langle post \rangle \quad \equiv \quad \langle [prog]post \rangle \;.$$

That is, it is immaterial whether one calculates the precondition $[\cdot]$ or pre-expectation $[\![\cdot]\!]$ for a standard program with respect to a standard postcondition: although one uses true/false in the first case, and 1/0 in the second, the same calculations are performed either way.

---

[7] Knowing there is no demonic choice in the program, we can say it is exactly 1/2.

Less formally, recall that in (standard) *GSL* we typically deal with conclusions of the form $pre \Rightarrow [prog]post$, which means "the final state is guaranteed to satisfy *post* if the initial state satisfied *pre*". In *pGSL*, instead we have conclusions $preE \Rrightarrow \llbracket prog \rrbracket postE$, which means "the expected value of *postE* in the final state is at least the expected value of *preE* in the initial state".

If we use *pGSL* for standard reasoning, i.e. our pre- and post-expectations are of the form $\langle pre \rangle$ and $\langle post \rangle$ and our program contains no $_p\oplus$, then we are dealing with $\langle pre \rangle \Rrightarrow \llbracket prog \rrbracket \langle post \rangle$ which, interpreted as above, means "the expected value of $\langle post \rangle$ in the final state is at least the expected value of $\langle pre \rangle$ in the initial state". But we know from elementary probability that the expected value of a characteristic function of a predicate[8] is just the probability that the predicate holds: so we have really said "the probability that *post* holds in the final state is at least the probability that *pre* held in the initial state".

For standard ($_p\oplus$-free) programs however, predicates either hold (probability 1) or they do not (probability 0). And for x, y in $\{0, 1\}$, to say $x \leq y$ is only to say "y is 1 if x was 1". Thus for standard programs specifically, we have said "the probability that *post* holds in the final state is 1 if the probability that *pre* held in the initial state was 1" — and this is just the usual interpretation in standard *GSL*.

Thus we can use probabilistic substitutions $\llbracket \cdot \rrbracket$ for all cases.

3 Almost-Certain Properties, and the Failure of the Standard Variant Rule

3.1 Absolute-versus Almost-Certain Correctness

We saw that $\llbracket prog \rrbracket \langle post \rangle$ is the greatest guaranteed probability that predicate *post* will hold after execution of *prog*. When that probability is one, we say that *post* is established almost-certainly:

> Probabilistic program *prog* establishes postcondition *post* from precondition *pre almost-certainly* just when
>
> $$\langle pre \rangle \quad \Rrightarrow \quad \llbracket prog \rrbracket \langle post \rangle \ .$$

Although almost-certain properties can be crucial to the correctness of many programs, the standard *GSL* $[\cdot]$-logic is too weak to be able to verify them in most cases: it is not defined for probabilistic choice, whether abstract $\oplus$ or concrete $_p\oplus$. In effect, the best the standard logic can do is to treat the probabilistic behaviour as *demonic* nondeterminism, as we did in Fig. 1.[9]

---

[8] The *characteristic function* of a predicate returns 1 for states satisfying the predicate, and 0 otherwise — thus our $\langle \cdot \rangle$ merely converts a predicate into its characteristic function.

[9] A useful way — though approximate — of looking at the benefit probabilistic choice offers beyond demonic choice is to regard it as a kind of "fairness". Although a demonic coin can come up tails every time, no matter how often it is flipped, a probabilistic coin must eventually give heads (and tails, too) provided its probabilistic bias is proper.

$n := 2;$
WHILE $n \neq 0$ DO
　　$n := n - 1$
END

Program 4a:
Absolute correctness

$n := 1;$
WHILE $n \neq 0$ DO
　　$n := n - 1 \;_{0.5}\oplus\;$ SKIP
END

Program 4b:
Almost-certain correctness

Prog. 4a terminates absolutely after exactly two iterations.

Prog. 4b terminates almost-certainly: although one cannot predict the number of iterations, the chance that it runs forever is zero. (In fact, it terminates after an "expected", rather than exact, two iterations: if the program were run many times and the number of iterations averaged, that average would be two.)

Fig. 4. Absolute- versus almost-certain correctness

$n := 1;$
WHILE $n \neq 0$ DO
　　$n := n - 1 \;\oplus\;$ SKIP
END

Program 5a:
Almost-certain correctness

$n := 1;$
WHILE $n \neq 0$ DO
　　$n := n - 1 \;\square\;$ SKIP
END

Program 5b:
Demonic <u>in</u>correctness

Like Prog. 4b, the abstract-probabilistic Prog. 5a terminates almost-certainly: although without knowing the actual probabilities used to implement $\oplus$ at runtime we cannot pre-calculate an expected number of iterations, that makes termination no less certain.

In Prog. 5b, the abstract probabilistic choice has been replaced by demonic choice. Because *in principle* that choice could be resolved to SKIP on all iterations, our logic does not prove termination of the loop at all.

Fig. 5. Almost-certain correctness versus "demonic" incorrectness

---

We say that a property holds *absolutely* if it can be proved using techniques of the standard *GSL* logic, e.g. $pre \Rrightarrow [prog]\,post$.[10] Figure 4 contrasts absolute- and almost-certain correctness.

---

[10] We overload "$\Rrightarrow$" deliberately, because in both guises it expresses essentially the same idea: we now have $\langle pred_1 \rangle \Rrightarrow \langle pred_2 \rangle$ iff $pred_1 \Rrightarrow pred_2$.

3.2 The Failure of the Standard Variant Rule

The standard variant rule is not strong enough to prove almost-certain termination of probabilistic loops.

In Prog. 4b the loop terminates almost-certainly because, to avoid termination, the SKIP branch must be chosen every time. That is, since the probability of choosing the second branch i times in succession is $1/2^i$, the probability of choosing it "forever" is $1/2^\infty$, effectively zero. Thus the chance that the first branch is eventually selected — leading to immediate termination — is one.

Consider now an attempt to prove the termination of Prog. 4b using the standard variant rule. Although the variant of Prog. 4a is just n, we cannot use n for Prog. 4b, since if SKIP is selected then n does not decrease. In fact, for that reason, we cannot establish that *any* variant V will surely decrease: no matter what expression it is, SKIP will leave it unchanged.

And no other existing form of standard *GSL* reasoning can show that such loops terminate, either. Consider the more general loop Prog. 5a. In a technical sense (which we make precise below), the "closest" standard program to it is the demonic Prog. 5b: it is the "best behaved" standard program that behaves "no better than" Prog. 5a. Thus no standard technique can attribute more properties to Prog. 5a than it attributes to Prog. 5b — and since Prog. 5b is indeed *not* certain to terminate, no standard technique can establish termination for Prog. 5a.

The important step is therefore to understand how *pGSL* allows us to strengthen the standard variant technique to exploit the special connection between abstract probability and almost-certain correctness. It turns out that the key lies in probability theory's so-called "zero-one" laws, to which we now turn.

4 A Probabilistic *Zero-One* Law for Loops

4.1 Direct Calculation of Almost Certainties

A naive way to determine the probability of termination of a probabilistic WHILE-loop is by direct calculation. In Prog. 4b, for instance, the probability that eventually $n = 0$ can be computed as the infinite sum over the disjoint probabilities that the assignment "$n := n - 1$" causes termination on the i-th iteration:

$$\sum_{i:=1}^{\infty} 1/2^i \quad = \quad 1/2 + 1/2^2 + 1/2^3 + \cdots \quad = \quad 1 \;. \tag{7}$$

Unfortunately the computation of infinite limits in general is not practical — often the limit can be finessed by fixed-point methods, but even that is not straightforward.

Fortunately we can do better by appealing to probability theory's so-called *zero-one* laws in combination with *pGSL*'s logic. In Sec. 4.3 below we give a simple zero-one law, essentially transcribed from a probability text [5], but couched in terms of probabilistic WHILE-loops; first, however, we introduce the "demonic retraction", convenient for expressing the law in *pGSL*.

4.2 Demonic Retractions of Probabilistic Programs

In our discussion above of the failure of the standard variant rule, we remarked that in fact *no* standard rule would be sufficient, and we referred to the "closest" standard program. We now make that more precise.

Recall that $[\![prog]\!]\langle post \rangle$ is the greatest guaranteed probability that *post* is established by execution of the probabilistic program *prog*. If *prog* were a refinement of some standard program $prog_d$ (writing "d" for "demonic"), then we would necessarily have

$$[\![prog_d]\!]\langle post\rangle \quad \Rrightarrow \quad [\![prog]\!]\langle post\rangle \ . \tag{8}$$

That is because *prog* — being a refinement $\sqsubseteq$ of $prog_d$ (recall Fig. 3) — must establish any postcondition at least as probably as $prog_d$ does. But the left-hand side of (8) can take values only in $\{0,1\}$, since it is a standard program applied to a standard postcondition, and thus (8) is equivalent to

$$[\![prog_d]\!]\langle post\rangle \quad \Rrightarrow \quad \lfloor [\![prog]\!]\langle post\rangle \rfloor \ ,$$

where $\lfloor \cdot \rfloor$ is the mathematical *floor*[11] function. That leads us to the following definition.

Definition 1. <u>Demonic retraction</u> — *Let prog be a probabilistic program in pGSL, and let post and pre be predicates in $\mathcal{PS}$. Since $\langle pre \rangle$ is $\{0,1\}$-valued, we note that post is almost-certainly established under execution of prog from any initial state satisfying pre just when*

$$\langle pre \rangle \quad \Rrightarrow \quad \lfloor [\![prog]\!]\langle post \rangle \rfloor \ . \tag{9}$$

As a syntactic convenience, we therefore make the definition

$$\lfloor prog \rfloor post \quad \widehat{=} \quad ([\![prog]\!]\langle post\rangle = 1) \ ,$$

in which — note — program prog may be probabilistic but $\lfloor prog \rfloor post$ is Boolean-valued, and therefore is a predicate (not an expectation). That allows us to write (9) as simply

$$pre \quad \Rrightarrow \quad \lfloor prog \rfloor post \ ,$$

where as noted above we write $\Rrightarrow$ for Boolean as well as "numeric" implication. We call $\lfloor prog \rfloor$ the demonic retraction *of $[\![prog]\!]$.*

4.3 A Zero-One Law

Demonic retraction allows a convenient statement of our zero-one law, that if the probability of a loop's termination is bounded away from zero, then in fact it is one.

---

[11] The *floor* of a real number is the greatest integer that does not exceed it.

Lemma 2. *Zero-one law for loops* — *Let* WHILE G DO *prog* END *be a loop, let I be a predicate (its invariant), and let δ be strictly greater than zero. If both*

$$I \wedge G \;\;\Rightarrow\;\; \lfloor prog \rfloor I \qquad (10)$$

$$and \quad \delta \times \langle I \rangle \;\;\Rightarrow\;\; [\![\text{WHILE } G \text{ DO } prog \text{ END}]\!]\langle true \rangle \qquad (11)$$

hold, then in fact $I \Rightarrow \lfloor \text{WHILE } G \text{ DO } prog \text{ END} \rfloor (I \wedge \neg G)$.

Proof. It is a standard result from Markov-process theory; a proof specialised to our context can be found elsewhere [17].

Informally, the lemma says that if I is almost-certainly invariant, and if the probability of termination everywhere in I is at least some positive constant δ, then in fact the loop almost-certainly establishes both the invariant and the negated guard from any initial state satisfying the invariant.[12] (Recall (6) for the idiom $\delta \times \langle I \rangle$.)

4.4 Distribution of Demonic Retraction

We shall use Lem. 2 to construct a variant rule for almost-certain termination. Part of its suitability is that its first antecedent (10) can be established in the usual induction-over-the-syntax style of *pGSL* reasoning: in fact, $\lfloor \cdot \rfloor$ distributes just as $[\cdot]$ does, except that it is defined for $\;_p\!\oplus$ as well. Especially important is that the distribution takes place in the *Boolean* domain — the arithmetic $\;_p\!\oplus$ is converted to a Boolean $\wedge$ by $\lfloor \cdot \rfloor$-distribution, being treated effectively as demonic choice □.

Lemma 3. *Demonic distributivity* — *Demonic retraction has the same*[13] *distributivity properties as the standard substitution $[\cdot]$, and extends it as follows: if $0<p<1$ then*

$$\lfloor prog_1 \;_p\!\oplus\; prog_2 \rfloor post \;\equiv\; \lfloor prog_1 \rfloor post \;\wedge\; \lfloor prog_2 \rfloor post \;.$$

Proof. If $0<p<1$ and $0 \leq x,y \leq 1$ then $px + (1-p)y$ is one iff x,y are both 1.

Note that there is no rule for distributing $\lfloor \cdot \rfloor$ through WHILE.[14] Dealing with $\lfloor \text{WHILE } G \text{ DO } prog \text{ END} \rfloor$ is after all the purpose of Lem. 2 (in its eventual formulation as Thm. 1), and we must now turn to its second antecedent (11).

5 Probabilistic Variants for Almost-Certain Termination

To establish (11) we formulate a probabilistic variant rule. Before stating it, we need several definitions.

---

[12] It's called a "zero-one" law because it says that the probability of correctness must be either zero or one — it cannot be somewhere in between.

[13] Recall (Footnote 3) we do not treat infeasible substitutions directly: the relevant distribution law here would be for IF $\cdots$ END as a whole.

[14] That does not mean that $\lfloor \text{WHILE} \cdots \rfloor$ is undefined; rather it means that it cannot be expressed in terms of $\lfloor \cdot \rfloor$ alone applied to the body.

5.1 Angelic Retraction and Definiteness

"Angelic" retraction is the dual of demonic: it expresses "not almost-certain not to succeed".

Definition 2. <u>Angelic *retraction*</u> — *Let prog be a probabilistic program in pGSL, and let post and pre be predicates in $\mathcal{PS}$. We note that post has "some chance" of being established under execution of prog from any initial state satisfying pre if*

$$\langle pre \rangle \quad \Rightarrow \quad \lceil [\![prog]\!] \langle post \rangle \rceil \, , \tag{12}$$

where $\lceil \cdot \rceil$ is the mathematical ceiling[15] *function.*

As a syntactic convenience, we make the definition

$$[\![prog]\!] post \quad \widehat{=} \quad ([\![prog]\!] \langle post \rangle \neq 0) \, ,$$

in which — again — program prog may be probabilistic but $[\![prog]\!] post$ is a predicate. That allows us to write (12) as simply

$$pre \quad \Rightarrow \quad [\![prog]\!] post \, .$$

We call $[\![prog]\!]$ the angelic retraction *of $[\![prog]\!]$.*

We will also need a stronger form of "some chance", since in some cases we cannot allow that chance to be arbitrarily small.

Definition 3. <u>Definiteness</u> — *A probabilistic program prog is said to be "definite" if there is some positive constant Δ so that, for all postconditions post, if prog establishes post with some non-zero probability, then in fact it establishes it with probability at least Δ — that is, program prog is* definite *iff there is a $\Delta > 0$ such that for all post*

$$\Delta \times \lceil [\![prog]\!] \langle post \rangle \rceil \quad \Rightarrow \quad [\![prog]\!] \langle post \rangle \, . \tag{13}$$

Further, we say that a family of programs is uniformly definite *if there is a single Δ with respect to which all members of the family are definite.*

In Sec. 7 we state simple sufficient conditions for a program to be definite; App. A gives examples of programs that are not.

5.2 A Probabilistic Variant Rule

We can now formulate a rule for establishing the second antecedent (11) of Lem. 2.

Lemma 4. <u>*Probabilistic variant rule*</u> — *In the loop* WHILE G DO $prog$ END, *with its invariant I, suppose we have an integer-valued expression V over the state space such that*

---
[15] The *ceiling* of a real number is the least integer that it does not exceed.

- *V is bounded above and below:* There are integer constants L, H such that
$$I \wedge G \quad \Rightarrow \quad L \leq V \leq H \ ; \text{ and} \tag{14}$$
- *V has some chance of decrease:* For all N,
$$I \wedge G \wedge (V=N) \quad \Rightarrow \quad [\![prog]\!](V < N) \ . \tag{15}$$

Provided the loop body prog is definite, there is a positive δ — as required by (11) — such that the loop terminates with at least that probability from any state satisfying I; that is, we have
$$\delta \times \langle I \rangle \quad \Rightarrow \quad [\![\text{WHILE } G \text{ DO } prog \text{ END}]\!]\langle true \rangle \ , \tag{16}$$
as required in Lem. 2.

Proof. Suppose the loop has not terminated, thus that $I \wedge G$ holds in the current state. By (14) the probability of termination from the current state cannot be less than the probability of $H-L+1$ successive decreases of V; by (15) we know that each decrease occurs with some non-zero probability; because prog is definite we know that probability is at least Δ for some $\Delta > 0$; and the overall probability of termination is therefore no less than Δ^{H-L+1}.

Thus we satisfy our conclusion (16) with $\delta := \Delta^{H-L+1}$.

Now we have reduced the second antecedent (11) of Lem. 2 to the angelic property (15), and for that we can use distribution properties analogous to those of Sec. 4.4.

5.3 Distribution of Angelic Retraction

Angelic distributivity is — like demonic distributivity — almost the the same as normal $[\cdot]$-distributivity; it has however an extra restriction.

Lemma 5. *Angelic distributivity* — Angelic retraction has the same[16] distributivity properties as the standard substitution $[\cdot]$ except as follows:

- If $0<p<1$ then
$$[\![prog_1 \ {}_p\!\oplus\ prog_2]\!]post \quad \equiv \quad [\![prog_1]\!]post \ \vee \ [\![prog_2]\!]post \ .$$

- Provided the family prog of programs determined by values of xx satisfying pred is uniformly definite, we have
$$[\![@xx \cdot (pred \implies prog)]\!]post \quad \equiv \quad (\forall xx \cdot \ pred \Rightarrow \ [\![prog]\!]post) \ .$$

Proof. The proof of the first case is by arithmetic, as for the demonic case. In the second case, the only difficulty is that an infinite set of non-zero probabilities can nevertheless have infimum zero; but that is excluded by the uniform definiteness provision.

Note that in the crucial case of probabilistic choice we have the angelic $\vee$ instead of the demonic $\wedge$. Again there is no distribution rule for WHILE.

---
[16] Recall Footnote 13.

6 Re-assembling the Proof Rule for Loops

If we draw together all the material from above, we can state in summary that to prove almost-certain correctness of a WHILE-loop whose body is definite, we must find an invariant and variant and proceed as usual, except that

- We ensure the variant is bounded above (as well as below);
- In proving "safety" properties, such as preservation of the invariant, we interpret probabilistic choice demonically using $\lfloor \cdot \rfloor$; and
- In proving "liveness" properties, such as decrease of the variant, we interpret probabilistic choice angelically using $\lceil \cdot \rceil$.

The crucial point is that in the above we do not refer to the *values* of the probabilities, except (see Sec. 7) in checking the provisos. Stating that formally, we have our main theorem:

Theorem 1. *Almost-certain correctness of loops* — Suppose we have a loop WHILE G DO *prog* END, *where prog is definite. Furthermore let I be a predicate and V be an integer-valued expression over the program variables; and let L and H be constant integers. Then*

If	$G \wedge I$	$\Rightarrow$	$L \leq V \leq H$	(A)[17]
and, for all N,	$G \wedge I \wedge (V{=}N)$	$\Rightarrow$	$\lceil prog \rceil (V{<}N)$	(B)
and	$G \wedge I$	$\Rightarrow$	$\lfloor prog \rfloor I$,	(C)

then $\qquad\qquad\qquad\qquad\qquad I \;\Rightarrow\; \lfloor \text{WHILE } G \text{ DO } prog \text{ END} \rfloor I$.

For establishing the antecedents involving $\lfloor \cdot \rfloor$ and $\lceil \cdot \rceil$ we use their distribution laws, which are almost the same as for standard substitution $[\cdot]$. Using them effectively is the subject of our final technical section.

7 Returning to Purely-Boolean Reasoning

7.1 Using Abstract Choice $\oplus$; Ensuring Definiteness

To establish the ($0{<}p{<}1$)-provisos of the distribution laws (Sections 4.4 and 5.3), and to ensure that a loop body is definite, the following are sufficient:

1. Ensure that the probabilities used in choices are *proper* over the whole execution of the program: that is, find a positive constant ε such that every p in any choice ${}_p\oplus$ satisfies $\varepsilon \leq p \leq 1{-}\varepsilon$ every time the choice is executed; and
2. Do not allow (nested) WHILE-loops in loop bodies.

---

[17] Recall Page 218 for these labels.

Condition 1 trivially establishes the ($0<p<1$)-provisos of the distribution laws for $_p\oplus$, so in their use we may simply ignore the p altogether. We are then in effect using "quasi distribution-laws"

$$\begin{array}{ll} \lfloor prog_1 \oplus prog_2 \rfloor post & \equiv \quad \lfloor prog_1 \rfloor post \wedge \lfloor prog_2 \rfloor post \\ \lceil prog_1 \oplus prog_2 \rceil post & \equiv \quad \lceil prog_1 \rceil post \vee \lceil prog_2 \rceil post \,, \end{array} \quad (17)$$

obtained from the actual $_p\oplus$-laws simply by ignoring the p.[18]

That the two conditions together are sufficient for loop bodies to be definite can be seen as follows. If $prog$ contains no loops, then there is a single upper bound K on the number of $_p\oplus$'s executed by it from any initial state. If $prog$ is guaranteed to establish $post$ with any non-zero probability, then in fact that probability must be at least ε^K, where ε is the constant with respect to which its $_p\oplus$'s are proper (Condition 1). Simply take $\Delta \hat{=} \varepsilon^K$ in (13).

Nested loops are "not allowed" in B, in any case, so the restriction is no hardship: if the effect of a nested loop is needed, it is encapsulated in a separate machine and its specification is used instead.[19]

The two conditions are sufficient also to ensure that the family of programs within any specification is uniformly definite.

7.2 An Example

With Prog. 5a we can give a simple example of purely Boolean reasoning for almost-certain correctness: the program is shown to terminate almost-certainly using the invariant $0 \leq n \leq 1$ and the variant n. For decrease of the variant we refer to (15), and calculate

	$\lceil n := n-1 \oplus \text{SKIP} \rceil (n < N)$	
if	$\lceil n := n-1 \rceil (n < N) \vee \lceil \text{SKIP} \rceil (n < N)$	using (17)
if	$\lceil n := n-1 \rceil (n < N)$	take left-hand disjunct
if	$n-1 < N$	assignment
if	$(n \neq 0) \wedge (0 \leq n \leq 1) \wedge (n = N)\,,$	

which is the required antecedent. Note no explicit probabilities are used.

8 Application to Root Contention

In the final *root-contention* stage of the FireWire protocol it is possible for two processes to send "you be leader" messages to each other, creating a potential livelock; each process detects this by receiving such a message from the process

---

[18] We write "quasi" because $prog_1 \oplus prog_2$ is not actually a program, nor even a class of programs: for example, we cannot tell by looking at $_{1/n}\oplus$ on its own whether it is proper or not — it depends on the context, in particular on whether the surrounding program allows n to be arbitrarily large. That is why we must formulate our "real" laws with the p present.

[19] See Appendix A.

to which it has just sent one. The livelock is broken by each process separately choosing, with probability 1/2, either to resend the message after a "short" time or a "long" time; almost certainly one process will eventually choose "short" while the other chooses "long"; and then the "short" process becomes leader, because its message arrives before the other's has been sent. (This is idealised: the actual protocol allows a range of times.)

In Fig. 2 we gave an abstraction of root contention, using *heads* and *tails* for the two choices; here (compare Sec. 2.2) is the calculation showing that the loop satisfies criterion (B) of Thm. 1. The variant is $\langle xx = yy \rangle$, bounded above and below by 1 (criterion (A), using the loop guard), and the invariant is just *true*, trivially maintained (criterion (C)). We have

$$\left[\!\!\left[\begin{array}{l} xx := \mathit{heads} \;\oplus\; xx := \mathit{tails} \;; \\ yy := \mathit{heads} \;\oplus\; yy := \mathit{tails} \end{array} \right]\!\!\right] (\langle xx = yy \rangle < N)$$

$\equiv$ $\qquad\qquad\qquad\qquad\qquad\qquad\qquad\qquad\qquad\qquad\quad \oplus, := \text{, sequential composition}$
$\qquad\qquad [\![xx := \mathit{heads} \oplus xx := \mathit{tails}]\!] (\langle xx = \mathit{heads} \rangle < N)$
$\vee \qquad [\![xx := \mathit{heads} \oplus xx := \mathit{tails}]\!] (\langle xx = \mathit{tails} \rangle < N)$

$\Leftarrow \qquad [\![xx := \mathit{heads} \oplus xx := \mathit{tails}]\!] (\langle xx = \mathit{heads} \rangle < N)$ $\qquad\qquad$ drop disjunct
$\Leftarrow \qquad \langle \mathit{tails} = \mathit{heads} \rangle < N$ $\qquad\qquad\qquad\qquad\qquad\qquad\qquad\qquad$ as above
$\equiv \qquad 0 < N$ $\qquad\qquad\qquad\qquad\qquad\qquad\qquad\qquad\qquad\qquad\qquad$ definition $\langle \cdot \rangle$
$\Leftarrow \qquad 1 = N$
$\Leftarrow \qquad xx = yy \;\wedge\; \mathit{true} \;\wedge\; (\langle xx = yy \rangle = N) \;,\qquad$ if $xx = yy$ then $\langle xx = yy \rangle$ is 1

which is the antecedent of (B).

9 Implementation Issues

The introduction of the $\oplus$ operator into *GSL* requires changes in the *B* implementation, where the developer writes the programs (usually called machines) in the Abstract Machine Notation *AMN*; only after analysis is the program translated into the more concise *GSL* form. We introduce a construct ACHOICE into *AMN* for that purpose, so that

$\qquad$ ACHOICE
$\qquad\qquad prog_1$
$\qquad$ OR $\qquad\qquad\qquad$ corresponds to $\qquad\qquad prog_1 \oplus prog_2$.
$\qquad\qquad prog_2$
$\qquad$ END

Because we have to prove that variants are bounded above as well as below, a new clause BOUND is introduced to declare the upper bound of a variant. (We assume that the lower bound is zero.) Thus a WHILE-loop now appears

> WHILE G DO
> *prog*
> INVARIANT I
> VARIANT V
> BOUND H
> END .

To calculate $[\![\cdot]\!]$ for the loop as a whole, any abstract $\oplus$ in the body is simply treated as $\Box$, generating $\wedge$, except within variant-decrease proof obligations where it generates $\vee$ instead. To implement this behaviour, we split the proof obligations for WHILE into two parts:

1. Obligations for partial correctness, including preserving the invariant of the loop: $\oplus$ treated as $\Box$; and
2. Obligations for decrease of the variant: $\oplus$ treated angelically.

Unfortunately, this split might result in duplicated proof obligations elsewhere. Consider the following example, where an occurence of $\oplus$ followed by an operation with a precondition:

$$prog_1 \oplus prog_2; \quad pre \mid prog_3$$

While proving the preservation of the invariant I, we treat $\oplus$ as $\Box$, i.e. we have to prove that both $prog_1$ and $prog_2$ establish pre. But the proof of decrease of the variant must be handled separately, because of the angelic interpretation of $\oplus$; and in that case we find that we must prove that *either* $prog_1$ or $prog_2$ establishes pre.

This repetition of $[prog_1]pre$ and $[prog_2]pre$ is clearly not a problem in theory, but it is certainly inconvenient in practice if the proofs require manual assistance — since it will have to be given twice. A possible solution is to rely more heavily on the theory of probabilistic loops [17], where we find that only partial correctness is required for preservation of the invariant by the loop body: partial correctness applied to preconditions allows them simply to be discarded.

10 Summary and Conclusions

Our contribution has been to observe that for a program all of whose probabilistic choices are proper — are bounded away from zero and one — many interesting almost-certain properties do not depend on the probabilities' actual values, and to specialise that observation to the context of the B method.

To use these results:

1. Specify and refine a system "as normal", introducing $\oplus$ as required.
2. Use ordinary substitution rules $[\cdot]$ except when treating $\oplus$; in those cases, treat $\oplus$ as demonic choice *except* when proving decrease of loop variants, where it is treated angelically.

3. Bound variants above as well as below, if the associated loop bodies contain $\oplus$.[20]
4. If the final program contains abstract choices $\oplus$, implement them (outside of B, in the target language/hardware) with proper concrete choices $_p\oplus$, and do not use nested WHILE-loops.

A simple technique to ensure proper implementation of $\oplus$ (Item 4) is to use random devices (whether hardware or software) whose probabilities vary between *fixed*[21] neither-zero-nor-one bounds; since the number of such devices in any program is finite, proper implementation is assured. Choice at runtime within the fixed bounds can be demonic, as for example it would be in the actual root-contention protocol where the delays can be selected demonically from a range.

To calculate expected time to termination, also important, full (numeric) *pGSL* is required, because the answer sought is a number (of e.g. iterations). The "slightly extended" *GSL* we've used here achieves a separation of concerns: prove termination (alone) using a simple logic; use a more complex logic for more discriminating results. Interesting also is *pGSL*'s expressivity, for example the formula (13) which concisely captures a subtle property.

11 Related and Future Work

We have focussed broadly on the practical verification and refinement of probabilistic programs. The mathematical foundations are explained in earlier, more general work [14] which specialises a quantitative formulation of the temporal logic $qM\mu$ [12] to the "almost-certain" fragment.

Rao [23] takes a similar approach to the almost-certain verification of Unity programs; his results incorporate a Unity-style fairness assumption, which ours do not.

Hurd [7] and Paulin [21] have investigated the verification of probabilistic programs in higher-order logic; their concern so far has been the proof of particular programs, rather than to establish general techniques appropriate for a sequence of program refinements as might occur in an extended development.

Earlier work [6] in probabilistic program verification already makes use of the zero-one laws from probability theory in an "operational" rather than a program-logic setting. The quantitative program logic used here is a generalisation of Kozen's (determinstic) probabilistic PDL [8], where we have incorporated demonic [18] and angelic [10] choice.

Stoelinga [24] gives a nice summary of other work relating to to the verification of FireWire; Fidge and Shankland, and Abrial use probabilistic- and standard predicate transformers respectively.

---

[20] In fact, for simplicity require upper bounds for variants in all cases, since in non-probabilistic loops the variant's initial value is trivially respected as an upper bound.
[21] By "fixed" we mean not a function of the state.

Fidge and Shankland, going beyond "almost-certain", address the question of "how long?" To analyse the expected time-to-consensus of FireWire and similar algorithms in this style, rather than simply termination, one must use "full" numeric logic instead of the probability-one abstraction. They did this [4] using the *Probabilistic Guarded Command* langauge *pGCL* [13], which is essentially *pGSL* in the original (Dijkstra-) style.

It was Abrial's development of the protocol [2] that provided the target for specialisation of our almost-certain temporal logic [14] and led directly to this presentation. He used Event- rather than "original" *B*, and that introduces some new concerns which could be addressed in future work.

In *Event-B* there is no explicit loop construct — there are only naked guarded commands (i.e. *events*). An abstract event system can be refined by a concrete one where we have more events; and each old (but concrete) event must then refine its abstract counterpart in the usual way. On the other hand, the new events generate different obligations; they must be proved

1. to refine SKIP; and
2. together to decrease a variant.

We must also prove that the overall concrete event system does not deadlock more often than the abstract one — if the abstract one is live then the new one must be; and if the abstract one terminates, then the new one must not terminate "earlier".

Rule (1) would be verified using the "demonic" $\lfloor \cdot \rfloor$. Rule (2) above ensures that the new events must eventually deadlock (if left alone); that is in order to give the old events the possibility to be "executed" as in the abstraction. Thus in "probabilistic Event-B" the second rule would have to be changed so that the new events are ensured probabilistically to decrease the (bounded) variant on every step (under its guard and the invariant, of course): here we would find $\lceil \cdot \rceil$ used in some form.

In our example of Sec. 8, we would end up at some point with the following new events:

$$xx = yy \implies (xx := heads \oplus xx := tails) \parallel (yy := heads \oplus yy := tails)$$
$$xx < yy \implies \text{"Process } X \text{ is the leader"}$$
$$xx > yy \implies \text{"Process } Y \text{ is the leader"} \, ,$$

where for convenience we introduce the order $heads < tails$.

Of course, the above is still far too abtract. In the real protocol, we have no "coins" such as xx, yy (although, as Stoelinga points out [24], introducing them might be an improvement). And the last two events (daemons) do not exist as such: instead there are some timings and watchdogs. But that system could be considered a faithful abstraction (for the time being).

Acknowledgements. This work was begun by McIver and Jean-Raymond Abrial while they attended a meeting of *IFIP WG 2.3* hosted by the Turku Institute for Computer Science in Finland, for which we thank the organisers.

We thank Colin Fidge and Ken Robinson for their comments, and Abrial both for the interesting discussions that continued after the meeting and for his direct contributions to the paper, especially the remarks concerning *Event-B* in Sec. 11.

Morgan, together with Ken Robinson, thanks the Australian Research Council for its 3-year grant *A00103115* for research into *pGSL*. They and Hoang are grateful also for the kind assistance of *B-Core (UK)* with implementation issues.

References

[1] J.-R. Abrial. *The B Book: Assigning Programs to Meanings*. Cambridge University Press, 1996.
[2] J.-R. Abrial, D. Cansell, and D. Mery. A mechanically proved and incremental development of the IEEE 1394 Tree Identify Protocol. *Formal Aspects of Computing*, 14(3), 2002.
[3] E.W. Dijkstra. *A Discipline of Programming*. Prentice Hall International, Englewood Cliffs, N.J., 1976.
[4] C. J. Fidge and C. Shankland. But what if I don't want to wait forever? *Formal Aspects of Computing*, 2002. To appear.
[5] G. Grimmett and D. Welsh. *Probability: an Introduction*. Oxford Science Publications, 1986.
[6] S. Hart, M. Sharir, and A. Pnueli. Termination of probabilistic concurrent programs. *ACM Transactions on Programming Languages and Systems*, 5:356–380, 1983.
[7] Joe Hurd. A formal approach to probabilistic termination. In *Proceedings 15th International Conference on Theorem Proving and Higher Order Logic, 20–23 August 2002. Hampton, Virginia*, volume 2410 of *LNCS*. Springer Verlag, 2002.
[8] D. Kozen. A probabilistic PDL. In *Proceedings of the 15th ACM Symposium on Theory of Computing*, New York, 1983. ACM.
[9] S. Maharaj, J.M.T. Romijn, and C. Shankland. An introduction to the IEEE 1394 FireWire. *Formal Aspects of Computing*, 2002. To appear.
[10] A.K. McIver and C. Morgan. Demonic, angelic and unbounded probabilistic choices in sequential programs. *Acta Informatica*, 37:329–354, 2001.
[11] Carroll Morgan. The generalised substitution language extended to probabilistic programs. In *Proc. 2nd International B Conference B'98*, volume 1393 of *LNCS*, 1998. Also available at [22, B98].
[12] Carroll Morgan and Annabelle McIver. An expectation-based model for probabilistic temporal logic. *Logic Journal of the IGPL*, 7(6):779–804, 1999. Also available at [22, MM97].
[13] Carroll Morgan and Annabelle McIver. *pGCL*: Formal reasoning for random algorithms. *South African Computer Journal*, 22, March 1999. Also available at [22, pGCL].
[14] Carroll Morgan and Annabelle McIver. Almost-certain eventualities and abstract probabilities in the quantitative temporal logic *qTL*. In *Proceedings CATS '01*. Elsevier, 2000. Also available at [22, PROB-1]; to appear in *Theoretical Computer Science*.
[15] C.C. Morgan. The specification statement. *ACM Transactions on Programming Languages and Systems*, 10(3), July 1988. Reprinted in [19].

[16] C.C. Morgan. *Programming from Specifications.* Prentice-Hall, second edition, 1994. At web.comlab.ox.ac.uk/oucl/publications/books/PfS.
[17] C.C. Morgan. Proof rules for probabilistic loops. In He Jifeng, John Cooke, and Peter Wallis, editors, *Proceedings of the BCS-FACS 7th Refinement Workshop,* Workshops in Computing. Springer Verlag, July 1996. At www.springer.co.uk/ewic/workshops/7RW; also available at [22, M95].
[18] C.C. Morgan, A.K. McIver, and K. Seidel. Probabilistic predicate transformers. *ACM Transactions on Programming Languages and Systems,* 18(3):325–353, May 1996.
[19] C.C. Morgan and T.N. Vickers, editors. *On the Refinement Calculus.* FACIT Series in Computer Science. Springer Verlag, Berlin, 1994.
[20] G. Nelson. A generalization of Dijkstra's calculus. *ACM Transactions on Programming Languages and Systems,* 11(4):517–561, October 1989.
[21] C. Paulin-Mohring. Randomized algorithms in type theory. Presentation at Daghstuhl Workshop, August 2001.
[22] PSG. Probabilistic Systems Group: Collected reports. At web.comlab.ox.ac.uk/oucl/research/areas/probs/bibliography.html.
[23] J.R. Rao. Reasoning about probabilistic parallel programs. *ACM Transactions on Programming Languages and Systems,* 16(3), May 1994.
[24] M.I.A. Stoelinga. Fun with FireWire: Experiments with verifying the IEEE 1394 Root Contention Protocol. In S. Maharaj, C. Shankland, and J.M.T. Romijn, editors, *Formal Aspects of Computing,* 2002. To appear.

A Definiteness is Necessary in Thm. 1

The loop *BadLoop*, defined

$$BadLoop \ \widehat{=} \quad kk := 1; \\ \text{WHILE } kk \neq 0 \text{ DO} \\ \quad kk := 0 \ _{1/2^{kk}}\oplus \ kk := kk+1 \\ \text{END},$$

fails to terminate with probability $\prod_{kk:=1}^{\infty}(1-1/2^{kk})$, which is about .29: that is, it is "quite likely" to terminate (probability .71), but does not terminate almost-certainly. Its body contains an improper probabilistic choice $_{1/2^{kk}}\oplus$: for any $\varepsilon > 0$ there is a possible execution in which the choice is executed with kk so large than $1/2^{kk} < \varepsilon$. As a result, the body is not definite: consider the postcondition $kk = 0$, which the body can establish with arbitrarily small but still non-zero probability.

Yet *BadLoop* satisfies all the antecedents of Thm. 1 except the restriction that the body be definite; in particular, the variant $\langle kk \neq 0 \rangle$ (recall the variant of Sec. 8) is decreased on every iteration with some non-zero (but ever smaller) probability. Without that restriction, therefore, we could conclude incorrectly that *BadLoop* terminates almost-certainly.

The same can occur even with proper choices, if a (nested) loop is used. The WHILE-program *CountHeads*, defined as an operation

$$CountHeads \;\;\widehat{=}\;\; \begin{array}{l} xx := heads;\; nn := 0; \\ \text{WHILE}\; xx = heads\; \text{DO} \\ \quad xx := heads \;{}_{1/2}\!\oplus\; xx := tails; \\ \quad nn := nn + 1 \\ \text{END}\;, \end{array}$$

contains only proper choices — choice $_{1/2}\oplus$ for the flip — and yet it is not definite: we have $[\![CountHeads]\!]\langle nn > N\rangle \equiv 1/2^N$, which for large-enough N is less than any $\Delta > 0$. If we use it within *WorseLoop*, defined

$$WorseLoop \;\;\widehat{=}\;\; \begin{array}{l} CountHeads;\; kk := 1; \\ \text{WHILE}\; nn \leq kk\; \text{DO} \\ \quad CountHeads; \\ \quad kk := kk + 1 \\ \text{END}\;, \end{array}$$

we see the same effect as before: termination is with probability .71, and all antecedents of Thm. 1 are satisfied except definiteness. (And this time all choices are proper.) Again definiteness saves us, in this case excluding *CountHeads* from the loop body.

To use *CountHeads* within the body of *WorseLoop* we would, by the rules of B, have to use a specification instead: the tightest we could get would be along the lines of ($@nn' \cdot nn' \in \mathbb{N}^+ \implies nn := nn'$). That specification is definite, but does not satisfy (B): the variant is not guaranteed to decrease with any non-zero probability, and thus soundness is preserved.

Probabilistic Invariants for Probabilistic Machines

Thai Son Hoang[1], Zhendong Jin[1], Ken Robinson[1],
Annabelle McIver[2], and Carroll Morgan[1]

[1] School of Computer Science & Engineering, University of New South Wales,
NSW 2052 Australia;
{htson, zjin, kenr, carrollm}@cse.unsw.edu.au
[2] Department of Computing, Macquarie University,
NSW 2109 Australia;
anabel@ics.mq.edu.au

Abstract. Abrial's *Generalised Substitution Language* (*GSL*) [4] can be modified to operate on arithmetic expressions, rather than Boolean predicates, which allows it to be applied to probabilistic programs [13]. We add a new operator $_p\oplus$ to *GSL*, for probabilistic choice, and we get the *probabilistic Generalised Substitution Language* (*pGSL*): a smooth extension of *GSL* that includes random algorithms within its scope.

In this paper we begin to examine the effect of *pGSL* on *B*'s larger-scale structures: its *machines*. In particular, we suggest a notion of *probabilistic* machine invariant. We show how these invariants interact with *pGSL*, at a fine-grained level; and at the other extreme we investigate how they affect our general understanding "in the large" of probabilistic machines and their behaviour.

Overall, we aim to initiate the development of *probabilistic B* (*pB*), complete with a suitable *probabilistic AMN* (*pAMN*). We discuss the practical extension of the *B-Toolkit* [5] to support *pB*, and we give examples to show how *pAMN* can be used to express and reason about probabilistic properties of a system.

Keywords: Probability, program correctness, generalised substitutions, weakest preconditions, *the B Method* (*B*), probabilistic algorithms.

1 Introduction

Abrial's *Generalised Substitution Language* (*GSL*) [4] is a weakest-precondition based method of describing computations and their meaning; it is complemented by the structures of *Abstract Machines*, together with which it provides a framework for the development of mathematically verified systems.

GSL can be extended to the *probabilistic Generalised Substitution Language* (*pGSL*), in which the standard Boolean values—representing certainty—are replaced by real values—representing probabilities. In principle, the *standard* machines of *the B Method* (*B*) can be extended to *probabilistic B* (*pB*) machines, which would allow us to implement random algorithms, or to model faulty (unreliable) operations. For practical use, we need to extend the standard toolkit to be able to generate proof obligations for the probabilistic constructs, and to enable proofs to be conducted in the standard set of Booleans extended by the set of reals.

This paper is concerned with the development and tool support of probabilistic machines based on *pGSL*. There are many foundational issues on probabilistic computational models that are not the subject of this paper and are not addressed here; more complete references may be found elsewhere [13]. The theory on which this paper is based [9] requires that those real values—which we call "expectations"—are non-negative and bounded. To avoid clutter in the exposition, however, our examples below do not necessarily adhere to those constraints.

The contribution of this paper is to extend the concept of *invariant* to probabilistic machines, based on the theory of *pGSL*: we define probabilistic invariants; we set out the proof obligations for maintaining such invariants by extending the current rules in the B; we give informal interpretations of the meaning of those invariants in practice; we develop a machine construct and give examples of how to use it; we highlight possible pitfalls; and we suggest approaches to correct them.

2 An Introduction to Probability and *pGSL*

2.1 Elementary Probability Theory

We briefly review and define some elementary concepts in probability theory [6]: the principal concepts we need are distribution and expectation.

> **Experiment:** Any process of observation or measurement.
> **Outcomes:** The results obtained from an experiment.
> **Sample space:** The set of all possible outcomes of an experiment.
> **Event:** A subset of the sample space.
> **Probability distribution** (discrete): A normalised function from the sample space to $[0, 1]$ giving the probability of each outcome.
> **Random variable:** Any function from the sample space into the reals.
> **Characteristic function:** The *characteristic function* of an event is a random variable that takes value 1 for outcomes in the event, and 0 otherwise. Given an event *pre* (written as a predicate) the expression $\langle pre \rangle$ is the characteristic function of that event.
> **Expected value** (discrete): If f is a bounded random variable and μ is a discrete distribution, both over sample space S, then the expected value of f over μ is defined:
> $$\sum_{s \in S} f(s) * \mu(s) .$$

This simplified presentation is sufficient for our purpose here.

As a consequence of the above definitions, it can be shown that the expected value of a characteristic function over a distribution is equal to the probability assigned to its underlying set by the distribution.

2.2 Brief Introduction to *pGSL*

pGSL is a logic for reasoning about programs operating over a computational model in which initial states are taken to final distributions over states (or, in the case of demonic programs, to *sets* of final distributions). The details of that model can be found elsewhere [10].

For the details of *pGSL* itself we first refer the reader to our companion paper [11, Sec. 2.1 and Sec. 2.2]. Fig. 1 gives a summary of substitutions in *pGSL*.

2.3 Probabilistic *pGSL* Extends Standard *GSL*

Recall that in (standard) *GSL* we typically deal with conclusions of the form $pre \Rightarrow [prog]post$, which means "the final state is guaranteed to satisfy *post* if the initial state satisfied *pre*". In *pGSL*, instead we have conclusions of the form $preE \Rrightarrow [prog]postE$, which means "the expected value of *postE* in the final state is at least the expected value of *preE* in the initial state". In fact, the *pGSL* interpretation generalises the standard interpretation, as we now show.

Suppose our pre- and post-expectations are "standard", that is they are of the form $\langle pre \rangle$ and $\langle post \rangle$. In that case, our second interpretation becomes "the expected value of $\langle post \rangle$ in the final state is at least the expected value of $\langle pre \rangle$ in the initial state". But we know from elementary probability theory (Sec. 2.1) that the expected value of a characteristic function of a predicate (for us, a predicate is the same as a subset of state space—that is, it is an event) is just the probability that the predicate holds: so we have really said "the probability that *post* holds in the final state is at least the probability that *pre* held in the initial state".

For standard programs, predicates either hold (probability 1) or they do not (probability 0). And for x, y in $\{0, 1\}$ to say $x \leq y$ is only to say "y is 1 if x was 1". Thus, for those specifically, we have said "the probability that *post* holds in the final state is 1 if the probability that *pre* held in the initial state was 1"—and this is just the usual interpretation in standard *GSL*.

2.4 Some *pGSL* Idioms

In this paper, we will be dealing with conclusions of the form

$$exp \equiv [prog]exp \qquad (1)$$

for some expectation *exp* and probabilistic substitution *prog*. By analogy with the standard case,

$$pred \equiv [prog]pred,$$

we call *exp* an *invariant* of *prog*.

The probabilistic generalised substitution language *pGSL* acts over "expectations" rather than predicates. Expectations are bounded, non-negative, real-valued functions of the state space; with the exception that when dealing with miracles they can take a formal value ∞.

$[x := E] \, exp$	The expectation obtained after replacing all free occurrences of x in exp by E, renaming bound variables in exp if necessary to avoid capture of free variables in E.
$[y, x := F, E] \, exp$	The expectation obtained after replacing all free occurrences of y and x in exp by F and E respectivley, renaming bound variables in exp if necessary to avoid capture of free variables in F and E.
$[pre \mid prog] \, exp$	$\langle pre \rangle \times [prog] \, exp$, where $0 \times \infty \mathrel{\hat{=}} 0$.
$[prog_1 \,\|\, prog_2] \, exp$	$[prog_1] \, exp \, \min \, [prog_2] \, exp$
$[pre \Longrightarrow prog] \, exp$	$1/\langle pre \rangle \times [prog] \, exp$, where $\infty \times 0 \mathrel{\hat{=}} \infty$.
$[\text{SKIP}] \, exp$	exp
$[prog_1 \,{}_p\oplus\, prog_2] \, exp$	$p \times [prog_1] \, exp \, + \, (1{-}p) \times [prog_2] \, exp$
$[@y \cdot pred \Longrightarrow prog] \, exp$	$(\min y \mid pred \cdot [prog] \, exp)$, where y does not occur free in exp.
$prog_1 \sqsubseteq prog_2$	$[prog_1] \, exp \Rrightarrow [prog_2] \, exp \quad$ for all exp

- exp is an expectation (possibly but not necessarily $\langle pred \rangle$ for some predicate $pred$);
- pre is a predicate (not an expectation);
- $\langle pre \rangle$ denotes the predicate pre converted to an expectation, here restricted to the unit interval: $\langle false \rangle$ is 0 and $\langle true \rangle$ is 1.
- $\times$ is multiplication;
- $prog, prog_1, prog_2$ are probabilistic generalised substitutions;
- p is an expression over the program variables (possibly but not necessarily a constant), taking a value in $[0, 1]$; and
- x is a variable.
- y is a variable, or a vector of variables.
- E is an expression.
- F is an expression, or a vector of expressions

We give the definitions including infeasible or "miraculous" commands [12, Sec. 1.7], but omit them in the main text for brevity. Also, with these definitions, monotonicity is maintained; instead of conjuntivity, we have a more general property *sublinearity* [13]. We do not use sublinearity here.

Fig. 1. *pGSL*—the probabilistic Generalised Substitution Language [13]

For example, we toss a fair coin and want to estimate the number of heads that turn up. Let nn be the number of times that we toss the coin and cc be the number of times that head turns up. Considering the expectation $nn - 2 \times cc$, we calculate

$$\begin{bmatrix} cc := cc+1 \\ nn := nn+1 \end{bmatrix} {}_{\frac{1}{2}}\oplus\; cc := cc \;\|\; \end{bmatrix} (nn - 2 \times cc)$$

$\equiv$
$$\left[{}_{\frac{1}{2}}\oplus \begin{array}{l} (cc := cc+1 \;\|\; nn := nn+1) \\ (cc := cc \quad\;\|\; nn := nn+1) \end{array} \right] (nn - 2 \times cc)$$
parallel substitution[1]

$\equiv$
$$(1/2)((nn+1) - 2 \times (cc+1)) \\ + (1/2)((nn+1) - 2 \times cc)$$
${}_{\frac{1}{2}}\oplus$ and :=

$\equiv \quad nn - 2 \times cc$
arithmetic

According to our interpretation (Sec. 2.3) of *pGSL*, this calculation shows that the expected value of $nn - 2 \times cc$ is never decreased by this operation. If we initialise nn and cc both to 0 then that expectation is initially 0—then we have shown that the expected value of $nn - 2 \times cc$ is never negative. In other words, the expected value of cc is never greater than $nn/2$.

Such interpretations will be crucial to our understanding of "probabilistic invariant".

3 Using *pGSL*: Probabilistic Machines

In earlier sections we introduced *pGSL* and explained its use of expectations to interpret individual probabilistic substitutions. Here we focus on our main topic: the meaning of these expectations when used as "invariants" for a *pB* machine.

We begin with a standard specification—the well-known "library" example—and use that as a basis against which we can contrast a probabilistic version. Our aim is, first, to show how probabilistic invariants capture its probabilistic properties and, second, to highlight some of the unexpected and subtle issues that can arise.

3.1 A Simple Library in *B*

Consider the specification of a simple Library in Fig. 2. The state of the machine contains three variables, namely *booksInLibrary*, *loansStarted* and *loansEnded*

---

[1] Here we apply the simple rule to integrate parallel substitution ($\|$) with probabilistic choice substitution (${}_{pp}\oplus$):
Provided S, T, U are all standard, we have:

$$(S \;{}_p\oplus\; T) \;\|\; U = (S \;\|\; U) \;{}_p\oplus\; (T \;\|\; U).$$

```
MACHINE  StandardLibrary ( totalBooks )
VARIABLES
    booksInLibrary , loansStarted , loansEnded
INVARIANT
    booksInLibrary ∈ ℕ ∧ loansStarted ∈ ℕ ∧ loansEnded ∈ ℕ ∧
    loansEnded ≤ loansStarted ∧
    booksInLibrary + loansStarted − loansEnded = totalBooks
INITIALISATION
    booksInLibrary := totalBooks  ‖  loansStarted := 0  ‖  loansEnded := 0

OPERATIONS
    StartLoan ≙
        PRE  booksInLibrary > 0  THEN
            booksInLibrary := booksInLibrary − 1  ‖
            loansStarted := loansStarted + 1
        END ;

    EndLoan ≙
        PRE  loansEnded < loansStarted  THEN
            booksInLibrary := booksInLibrary + 1  ‖
            loansEnded := loansEnded + 1
        END
END
```

Fig. 2. Standard specification of a Library

representing: the number of books in the library; the number of book loans initiated by the library; and the number of book loans completed by the library, respectively. To keep the example simple, we ignore other functions of the library. Initially, *booksInLibrary* has value *totalBooks* (a parameter of the machine). Both *loansStarted* and *loansEnded* are assigned 0 initially.

We have two operations that can modify the state of the machine, START-LOAN, for starting a loan of a book, and ENDLOAN, for ending the loan of a book. The STARTLOAN operation has a precondition that there are books available for loan; it decrements the books held and increments the book loans. The ENDLOAN operation is complementary in the obvious way.

The (standard) invariant of this machine is

$$booksInLibrary + (loansStarted - loansEnded) = totalBooks , \qquad (2)$$

in which the term *loansStarted* − *loansEnded* is an abstraction of the number of books that are in the on-loan database of the library—that is, books that are recorded as on loan.

MACHINE *ProbabilisticLibrary* (*totalBooks*)
SEES *Real_TYPE*
CONSTANTS *pp*
PROPERTIES $pp \in REAL \wedge pp \leq real\ (\ 1\ ) \wedge real\ (\ 0\ ) \leq pp$
VARIABLES
  booksInLibrary , *loansStarted* , *loansEnded* , *booksLost*
INVARIANT
  $booksInLibrary \in \mathbb{N} \wedge loansStarted \in \mathbb{N} \wedge loansEnded \in \mathbb{N} \wedge booksLost \in \mathbb{N} \wedge$
  $loansEnded \leq loansStarted \wedge$
  $booksInLibrary + booksLost + loansStarted - loansEnded = totalBooks$
EXPECTATIONS
  $real\ (\ 0\ ) \Rightarrow pp \times real\ (\ loansEnded\ ) - real\ (\ booksLost\ )$
INITIALISATION
  $booksInLibrary\ ,\ loansStarted\ ,\ loansEnded\ ,\ booksLost := totalBooks\ ,\ 0\ ,\ 0\ ,\ 0$

OPERATIONS
  StartLoan $\widehat{=}$
    PRE *booksInLibrary* > 0 **THEN**
      booksInLibrary := *booksInLibrary* − 1 ∥
      loansStarted := *loansStarted* + 1
    END ;

  EndLoan $\widehat{=}$
    PRE *loansEnded* < *loansStarted* **THEN**
      PCHOICE *pp* **OF**
        booksLost := *booksLost* + 1
      OR
        booksInLibrary := *booksInLibrary* + 1
      END ∥
      loansEnded := *loansEnded* + 1
    END
END

Fig. 3. Simple probabilistic Library

3.2 Adding Probabilistic Properties

In the Boolean world of standard *B*, the operations and invariants express certainty: books are either in the library or they are on loan; they can't be anywhere else. In a real library, books are occasionally lost. In this section, we discuss how that can be modelled in *pB*.

One approach might be to add a *Lose* operation of the form

$$Lose \quad \widehat{=} \quad booksInLibrary := booksInLibrary - 1\ , \quad\quad (3)$$

and to arrange that every so often LOSE is invoked, with some probability. The problem with this is that we have no way in B (or in pB for that matter) of modelling a probabilistically invoked operation.

We can however model operations with probabilistic *effects* in pB, and so we take that approach.

The loss of a book will be modelled by altering the ENDLOAN operation so that, with some probability pp, the user fails to return a book to the library; in that case the effect of ENDLOAN is to consider the book lost.

With the introduction of probabilistic-choice substitution (in Sec. 2), we can specify this behaviour within the ENDLOAN operation. The *PCHOICE* construct is the *probabilistic AMN* (*pAMN*) counterpart of $_p\oplus$. In this operation, the chance of a book being lost is pp—where *booksInLibrary* fails to increase; the other $1-pp$ of the time, *booksInLibrary* increases as normal. The variable *booksLost* is introduced to record the number of books lost and is initialised to 0. In the case of losing a book, *booksLost* will increase accordingly. We replace the standard substitution $booksInLibrary := booksInLibrary + 1$ with

> **PCHOICE** pp **OF**
> $booksLost := booksLost + 1$
> **OR**
> $booksInLibrary := booksInLibrary + 1$
> **END**

With the introduction of the variable *booksLost*, we must of course adjust the standard invariant, to include the new variable:

$$\begin{aligned} & (booksInLibrary + booksLost) \\ + \;& (loansStarted - loansEnded) \\ = \;& totalBooks \;. \end{aligned} \qquad (4)$$

The first term on the left-hand side is the number of books not in the on-loan database; the second term is the number of books that are in the on-loan database. This specification is simply modelling the effect of loss, without attempting to identify where it occurs. In practice, loss could be the consequence of a faulty (unreliable) loan or return operation. At some point, "loss" needs to be recognised and that is modelled by the probabilistic $booksLost := booksLost+1$.

3.3 The *EXPECTATIONS* Clause

In Fig. 1 we introduced a new *EXPECTATIONS* clause into $pAMN$ for declaring the probabilistic invariant. It gives an expression V over the program variables, denoting the random-variable invariant, and an initial expression e which is evaluated over the program variables when the machine is initialised. We write it $e \Rrightarrow V$. Its interpretation is that the expected value of V, at any point, is always at least the value of e initially. The value of e can be dependent on the context of the machine (machine's parameters, constants, etc.), but often e will just be a constant.

3.4 What Do Probabilistic Invariants Guarantee?

We answer that by analogy with standard invariants, which we review first.

Suppose a machine has initialisation INIT and two operations OPX and OPY. If we satisfy the standard proof obligations with respect to some invariant I, viz.

$$\text{true} \Rrightarrow [\text{INIT}]I$$
$$I \Rrightarrow [\text{OPX}]I$$
$$I \Rrightarrow [\text{OPY}]I, \tag{5}$$

then we are assured that

$$\text{true} \Rrightarrow [\text{INIT; OP?; OP?; ...; OP?}]I \tag{6}$$

holds for any (finite) sequence of operations OP? each chosen from $\{\text{OPX, OPY}\}$. It doesn't matter when the choice between "do OPX now", "do OPY now" and "stop now" is made—that is whether the sequence of operations is chosen in advance or whether it is evolved "on-the-fly" on the basis of the machine state and/or outputs produced so far by the operations already executed.

The fact that (5) assures (6) is in fact the *soundness* of the (standard) invariant technique.

For soundness of the probabilistic invariant technique clearly there must be a similar situation—that is a probabilistic version of (5) and (6)—with the first implying the second: it is that if

$$E \Rrightarrow [\text{INIT}]I$$
$$I \Rrightarrow [\text{OPX}]I$$
$$I \Rrightarrow [\text{OPY}]I, \tag{7}$$

then we are assured that

$$E \Rrightarrow [\text{INIT; OP?; OP?; ...; OP?}]I \tag{8}$$

for any finite sequence OP?; OP?; ...; OP? of operations, no matter when or how chosen. (Recall that E is some "initial" expression, possibly depending on parameters to the machine.)

It might be surprising that in the probabilistic case the "when/how" makes a crucial difference; we show by example that it does.[2] Consider the *Counter* machine shown in Fig. 4

This machine *fails* to satisfy our probabilistic proof obligations (7) even though

$$0 \Rrightarrow [\text{INIT; OP?; OP?; ...; OP?}](count) \tag{9}$$

---

[2] It can be shown that it makes no difference in the standard case whether the operations are chosen beforehand or on-the-fly—the proof obligations are the same.

```
MACHINE  Counter
SEES
    Int_TYPE , Real_TYPE
VARIABLES
    count
INVARIANT
    count ∈ INT
INITIALISATION
    count := 0

OPERATIONS
    cc ⟵ OpX ≘
        PCHOICE  frac ( 1 , 2 )  OF
            count := count + 1  ∥
            cc := count
        OR
            count := count − 1  ∥
            cc := count
        END ;

    OpY ≘ count := 0

END
```

Fig. 4. The Counter Machine

is trivially true, for any finite sequence OP?; OP?; ...; OP? of operations *chosen in advance*.

The machine fails to satisfy (7) because $count \Rightarrow [\text{OpY}](count)$ cannot be proved. And the reason that it *must* fail is that (9) is not true—for this machine—if the operations can be chosen on-the-fly: consider for example the program fragment

$$Prog \triangleq \text{INIT};$$ (10)
$$c \longleftarrow \text{OpX};$$
$$\textbf{IF } c = 1 \textbf{ THEN } \text{OpY } \textbf{ELSE } \text{OpX } \textbf{END}.$$

The IF-statement represents a choice, on-the-fly, of whether to execute OpX or OpY as the second operation; and it is readily verified that the expected value of count after (10) is -0.5, which fails the instantiation (9) of the general (8) for this machine. That is, we do *not* have $0 \Rightarrow [Prog](count)$.

Thus the answer to the title of this section is that

probabilistic invariants guarantee (8) provided (7) holds.

The strong constraint "no matter how the operations are chosen" in (4) is absolutely necessary: the (usual) situation is that our machine must behave correctly no matter what environment makes use of it. A system containing code like (10) is a perfectly reasonable use of MACHINE Counter—and any such system, if it depended on the expected value of count being non-negative afterwards, would fail.

3.5 A Probabilistic Invariant for the Library

In this section, we try to find the probabilistic invariant for a probabilistic library (Fig. 3) by "informal" reasoning.

With the introduction of probabilistic choice substitution in the new END-LOAN operation, we want an estimated upper bound for the number of books lost. Informally, we believe that $pp * loansEnded$ is the expected value of the number of books actually lost. That informal reasoning leads to:

the expected value of $pp * loansEnded - booksLost$ is at least 0.

Thus we define $V \cong pp * loansEnded - booksLost$ to be the expected-value invariant of the probabilistic library machine. The initial value for V is 0 (established by the initialisation).

When we claim that V is an expected-value invariant for this machine, we mean that, if we check the value of V many times during the running of operations of the Library, then the average of our observation of V will be at least 0. As explained in Sec. 3.4 that is the intended meaning of our probabilistic invariant. From that we can conclude for our probabilistic library machine, the expected number of books lost (value of $booksLost$) is bounded above by $pp * loansEnded$.

3.6 Proof Obligations

Recall that the proof obligations for a non-probabilistic machine are:

N1: The initialisation needs to establish the invariant given the context of the machine (information about sets and constants)

$$[Init]I .$$

N2: The operations need to maintain the invariant

$$I \Rightarrow [Op]I .$$

For probabilistic machines, the same ideas will be applied, except that the invariant now may take *real* values instead of Boolean. In order to prove that the *real* invariant is bounded below, we have to prove the following:

P1: The initialisation needs to establish the lower bound of the probabilistic invariant, given the context of the machine (information about sets and constants)

$$e \Rrightarrow [Init]\, V \ .$$

P2: The operations do not decrease the expected value of the probabilistic invariant, i.e. the expected value of the invariant after the operation is at least the expected value before the operation

$$V \Rrightarrow [Op]\, V \ .$$

We have to prove the above for each *real-valued* invariant. The standard (Boolean) invariants can be treated the same as before (with probabilistic choice substitution being treated as demonic). Consequently, proof obligations for the *probabilistic* (expectation) and Boolean invariants may be generated, and proved, separately.

3.7 Proving the Obligations

Here we only discuss the proof of maintenance of the probabilistic invariant:

$$V \ \widehat{=} \ pp * loansEnded - booksLost \ . \tag{11}$$

In the example in Fig. 3, consider the proof obligation for the initialisation $(P1)$.[3] We have to prove that

$$0 \Rrightarrow [Initialisation]\, V \ .$$

Consider the right-hand side of the inequality:

$[Initialisation]\, V$

$$\equiv \begin{bmatrix} booksInLibrary, loansStarted, \\ loansEnded, booksLost \end{bmatrix} := totalBooks, 0, 0, 0 \Bigg]\, V$$

$$\equiv \begin{bmatrix} booksInLibrary, loansStarted, \\ loansEnded, booksLost \end{bmatrix} := totalBooks, 0, 0, 0 \Bigg] \begin{pmatrix} pp * loansEnded \\ - booksLost \end{pmatrix}$$

$\equiv \ pp * 0 - 0$ \hfill substitution
$\equiv \ 0$ \hfill arithmetic

So we have shown that the initialisation establishes the initial lower bound for the probabilistic invariant.

For operation STARTLOAN, since the operation both increases *loansStarted* and decreases *booksInLibrary* deterministically, and since the expected-value invariant does not contain *loansStarted* and *booksInLibrary*, we can easily prove that the operation maintains the invariant.

We have to do similar reasoning with operation ENDLOAN, i.e. to prove that $V \Rrightarrow [EndLoan]\, V$ (proof obligation *P2*). We calculate

---
[3] All calculations use real numbers, but we will omit any type casting.

$[EndLoan]\,V$

$\equiv \left[\begin{array}{l}\begin{pmatrix}(booksLost := booksLost + 1\\ {}_{pp}\oplus\\ booksInLibrary := booksInLibrary + 1)\end{pmatrix}\\ ||\\ loansEnded := loansEnded + 1\end{array}\right]V$

$\equiv \left[\begin{array}{l}\begin{pmatrix}(booksLost := booksLost + 1\\ ||\\ loansEnded := loansEnded + 1)\end{pmatrix}\\ {}_{pp}\oplus\\ \begin{pmatrix}(booksInLibrary := booksInLibrary + 1\\ ||\\ loansEnded := loansEnded + 1)\end{pmatrix}\end{array}\right]\begin{pmatrix}pp * loansEnded\\ -booksLost\end{pmatrix}$

parallel substitution with ${}_{pp}\oplus$

$\equiv pp * \left[\begin{array}{l}booksLost := booksLost + 1\\ ||\\ loansEnded := loansEnded + 1\end{array}\right]\begin{pmatrix}pp * loansEnded\\ -booksLost\end{pmatrix}$

$+\,(1-pp) * \left[\begin{array}{l}booksInLibrary := booksInLibrary + 1\\ ||\\ loansEnded := loansEnded + 1\end{array}\right]\begin{pmatrix}pp * loansEnded\\ -booksLost\end{pmatrix}$

${}_{pp}\oplus$

$\equiv pp * (pp * (loansEnded + 1) - (booksLost + 1))$
$\quad + (1-pp) * (pp * (loansEnded + 1) - booksLost)$

parallel substitution and :=

$\equiv pp * loansEnded - booksLost$ \hfill arithmetic
$\equiv V$

So we have shown that $V \Rrightarrow [EndLoan]\,V$. (In fact, the expectation is unchanged since there is no demonic nondeterminism).

In this example, we have specified a library system that includes the chance of books being lost. From the probabilistic invariant, we can estimate the cost of maintaining the library (the number of books lost). Furthermore, we have discussed how we can reason about the specification and how to write it in pB.

3.8 What the Invariant Means

With the two calculations of the previous section we have established the mathematical validity of the invariant V for the machine of Fig. 3, in the sense that the proof obligations are satisfied. How do we interpret that validity?

Recall Sec. 3.4: it means that over a large number of tests of the machine, carried out by an adversary, who can choose to resolve demonic choice within

$totalCost \longleftarrow$ **StockTake** $\hat{=}$
BEGIN
  $totalCost := cost \times booksLost \parallel$
  $booksInLibrary := booksInLibrary + booksLost \parallel$
  $loansStarted := loansStarted - loansEnded \parallel$
  $loansEnded := 0 \parallel$
  $booksLost := 0$
END

Fig. 5. STOCKTAKE operation

operations any way he wishes (although there is none in our example), and who can choose to invoke operations in any order, we will observe that the average value of V is at least the stated value.

In the machine of Fig. 3, we conclude therefore that the expected value of $pp * loansEnded - booksLost$ is at least 0; no matter what the adversary does. We wrote the invariant that way so that we could give an expected upper bound for $booksLost$—it is $pp * loansEnded$.

In general, we might wish to establish several such average-case inequalities. For each one we would formulate a suitable probabilistic invariant and lower bound; and each would generate its own proof obligations $(P1)$, $(P2)$ as above.

4 Pitfalls: Mixing Demonic and Probabilistic Choice

The validity of a probabilistic invariant assures us of a lower bound for its average value over many sequences of machine-operation invocations. In this section we show by example just how strong a requirement that is, given an adversarial tester who has complete freedom in choosing which operations to invoke. We show how the mathematical constraint of having to prove the invariant's validity guides us in the design of machines that are well-behaved even against such adversaries.

4.1 StockTake Breaks the Probabilistic Invariant

Imagine that every year, the library needs to do a stocktake: update the number of book lost, and reset the information about the status of the library. The library wants to estimate the cost for doing such operations annually. Assuming that the cost for replacing a book is a constant, $cost$, the operation STOCKTAKE is defined in Fig. 5.

The STOCKTAKE operation is very similar to the initialisation, but with an extra output to represent the cost for replacing the books lost. One can easily prove that the operation maintains the standard invariant. The surprise comes when trying to prove the obligation for maintaining the probabilistic invariant by this operation. We have to prove that $V \Rrightarrow [StockTake]\,V$. Consider the right-hand side of that inequality (considering the effect of variables *loansEnded* and *booksLost* only):

$$[StockTake]\,V$$
$$\equiv\quad [loansEnded, booksLost := 0, 0]\,V$$
$$\equiv\quad [loansEnded, booksLost := 0, 0]$$
$$(pp * loansEnded - booksLost)$$
$$\equiv\quad 0\,.$$

So to show the invariant does not decrease we must prove that

$$pp * loansEnded - booksLost \;\Rrightarrow\; 0\,, \tag{12}$$

which we cannot prove in this context. The question here is what did we do wrong in the above operation.

4.2 Surprising Interaction of Demonic and Probabilistic Choice

To understand the failure to maintain the probabilistic invariant we will discuss a number of aspects.

Initialisation is not forever It is first worth reviewing why we might have expected the STOCKTAKE operation to be satisfactory. We might have observed that STOCKTAKE is very similar to the machine initialisation. In standard B it is obvious that we can repeat the initialisation whenever we wish, and the standard invariant will be maintained. However, maintaining the probabilistic invariant means not decreasing the expected value. If the standard B invariant is viewed in this light, it is a Boolean expression that is expected to evaluate to true (1) after the initialisation. This represents a monotonic increase over its value before initialisation, which was either false (0) or true (1). If the initialisation is re-run as an operation it starts from an expected value of true (1) and so guarantees not to decrease the expected value.

It is obvious that when we move to real-valued expectations, the obligation of maintaining the expected value is stronger, and some notions taken from the simpler Boolean context will fail.

The initialisation of a pB machine establishes the probabilistic invariant on the assumption of a lower bound of the expectation; for the probabilistic library machine this was 0. Since a sequence of operations monotonically increases the probabilistic invariant it is presumptuous to expect that the initialisation, if run again at an arbitrary time would maintain the invariant. Thus, in general, there is no guarantee that an operation that duplicates the initialisation will maintain the probabilistic invariant.

The effect of demonic nondeterminism It is worth reminding ourselves that the choice of operations for a machine is demonically nondeterministic. As a consequence the machines must be designed to ensure that undesirable operation sequences do not lead to the violation of critical properties of machine behaviour. It is precisely for this reason that we use invariance in both non-probabilistic and probabilistic machines to establish that such critical properties are maintained regardless of the choice of operation sequence.

The probabilistic library machine is intended to achieve an upper bound of $pp * loansEnded$ for $booksLost$. Before the addition of the STOCKTAKE operation this was being controlled by the probabilistic choice in the ENDLOAN operation. STOCKTAKE now provides an opportunity for demonic nondeterminism to subvert that expectation, according to the following scenario. Suppose a malevolent library administrator wishes to show that library loan system is "broken": that the rate of book loss is higher than the advertised claim of pp. If the administrator adopts a policy of running STOCKTAKE whenever $booksLost$ is large relative to $pp * loansEnded$, then the library managers will indeed see that system is "broken".

Notice that in a probabilistic machine there can be times when loss rate will be higher than expected. The problem with the above scenario is that the operation is chosen demonically to run only at those times. Consider the testing of a system. We might suggest that a machine-tester, in selecting what operation to run next, should not be able to see the current state of the machine.[4] We say that the demonic choice (taken by the tester), of which operation to run next, is *omniscient* if he is allowed to see the machine's state, and *oblivious* if he is not. Omniscient testing is clearly more severe than oblivious; so our proof obligations, which are sufficient to guarantee correct behaviour under omniscient testing, are stronger than alternative obligations we might formulate to guarantee survival under oblivious testing. (In fact, operation STOCKTAKE would probably be admitted by proof obligations designed for oblivious testing.[5])

Finally, we note that there is no difference between omniscient and oblivious testing of standard machines: if a standard machine is guaranteed to survive oblivious testing, then it is also guaranteed to survive omniscient testing. Only for probabilistic[6] machines does the omniscient/oblivious distinction matter.

4.3 Capturing Long-Term Behaviour

In our failure to satisfy the proof obligation for STOCKTAKE, the mathematics is in fact suggesting what we should do. *Formally* we introduce a new variable—call

---

[4] That this is reasonable can be seen by testing a coin: it would be wrong to flip the coin until heads shows, and then say "look, it always gives heads".

[5] We do not pursue the mathematical formulation of oblivious testing here, as the notion of what "can be seen" and what cannot turns out to be surprisingly complex. But we recognise it as a fruitful line of further research.

[6] In fact, adding angelic choice also reveals the distinction: any two of probabilistic/angelic/demonic are sufficient.

it "*fix*" for now—with the sole purpose of being able to satisfy that obligation. Routine calculation shows that we must modify the machine as follows: *fix* is given the value 0 initially; the value of *fix* is unchanged in all other operations; but in STOCKTAKE, we use *fix* to maintain information that is critical to the expectation:

$$fix := pp * loansEnded - booksLost + fix \ . \tag{13}$$

The expectation invariant is modified as follows:

$$V' \ \widehat{=} \ pp * loansEnded - booksLost + fix \ . \tag{14}$$

The new expectation invariant has the lower bound 0 established by the initialisation. Since the operations STARTLOAN and ENDLOAN do not change the value of *fix*, they will maintain invariant V' (in those cases *fix* acts as a constant). For the STOCKTAKE operation, we can prove that it maintains the probabilistic invariant V' (considering the changes for *loansEnded*, *booksLost* and *fix* only):

$\qquad [StockTake] V'$

$\equiv \quad [loansEnded, booksLost, fix := 0, 0, pp * loansEnded - booksLost + fix] V'$

$\equiv \quad [loansEnded, booksLost, fix := 0, 0, pp * loansEnded - booksLost + fix]$

$\qquad (pp * loansEnded - booksLost + fix)$

$\equiv \quad pp * loansEnded - booksLost + fix \ .$

So $V' \Rrightarrow [StockTake] V'$—that is, the STOCKTAKE operation does not decrease the expected value of V'.

But what is the interpretation of *fix*? It is in fact a "running" long-term surplus/deficit indicator of books lost compared with what we expected to lose; and our new invariant tells us that we expect that indicator to be zero.

More abstractly, we see that the invariant is forcing us not to "lose information" as the original version of STOCKTAKE did. The reason—we can now see—is that meaningful statements about long-term behaviour can only be made if there are variables which record it; and operations that somehow "erase" the long-term behaviour will fail proof obligations.

In this specific case, we can say that—without *fix*—a hostile library administrator could decide (demonic choice) to run STOCKTAKE only when the rate of stolen books was "running high", and so give a false picture in that "snapshot" of the long-term behaviour of the library. Including *fix* makes sure that the snapshot includes *all* the behaviour up to that point.

5 Modifying the *B-Toolkit*

The *B-Toolkit* is a configuration management tool that assists a developer to produce a logically consistent set of *B* machines. Some of the important services provided by the tool are: analysis including syntax and type checking;

proof obligation generation; proof assistance (both automatic and interactive); and machine markup. The replacement of *GSL* by *pGSL*—with the consequent replacement of *Abstract Machine Notation* (*AMN*) by *pAMN* obviously affects those processes. The changes required to adapt the *B-Toolkit* consisted of

Introduction of Real numbers: We use a read-only (seen) machine to introduce a REAL type. Currently this type is the set of non-negative rational numbers, with numbers being denoted by a constructor $frac(m, n)$.

Acceptance of *pAMN*: The parser had to be modified to accept the new *pAMN* constructs of: *EXPECTATIONS* clause, probabilistic choice construct (*PCHOICE*)

Analyser: The type and construct analysis had to be modified or extended. The analyser produces a canonic, (abstract) syntactic parse and separate canonic type information for each machine. Every process after analysis will use the canonic information rather than using the raw *AMN*.

Proof obligation generator: The *B-Toolkit* needed to generate proof obligations for the new *PCHOICE* clause and for the probabilistic invariant. For the normal invariant, the *PCHOICE* substitution is treated as a non-deterministic *CHOICE* substitution; for the new expectation invariant, the proof obligations must follow the *pGSL* as stated in figure Fig. 1. Notice that while normal Boolean expressions could be converted to numeric expressions, we leave Boolean expressions unchanged. This has the effect of ensuring that the proof of all Boolean goals or sub-goals will proceed using the standard proof rules.

Provers: No change was required for the provers, but we needed to add new rules to support real number evaluations that arise as a consequence of expectations.

Mark-up: Small changes were required to mark-up the new *EXPECTATIONS* and *PCHOICE* constructions and the $\Rrightarrow$ expectation order.

The *B-Toolkit* is implemented on top of a theorem prover (the *B-Tool* prover), so every toolkit process is driven by a set of proof rules. A consequence of the separation of canonic (abstract) parse and type information by the analyser for each machine is that, after the analysis phase all other phases can be based purely on syntax. This considerably simplified the conversion of the *B-Toolkit* to handle numeric, rather than Boolean, logic, since proof obligations and proof rules are typeless. Some existing proof rules had to be modified and new rules added to support the the new syntax and proof theory of *pAMN* and *pGSL*. Currently, the probabilistic analysis (of expectations) of a machine is stored separately from the unaltered standard (non-probabilistic) analysis, but they could be merged.

It should be noted that the ProbabilisticLibrary machine has been: analysed; proof obligations have been generated; proof obligations have been discharged; and the machine marked up using the modified *B-Toolkit*. The marked-up text of machines appearing in this paper have been included directly from the *B-Toolkit*.

6 Further Work

The loss of conjunctivity—to be replaced by sublinearity—brings some complicated problem when it comes to refinement under $pGSL$. In general, refinement is a second-order property, but with the interpretation from Gries [7], we get an equivalent first-order refinement rule for the standard case of B (using GSL). Unfortunately, the introduction of probabilistic choice substitution does not preserve the necessary condition for the maintenance of the first-order equivalence. A current challenge is the development of a suitable strategy for refinement under $pGSL$. A possible solution might be the use of auxiliary variables and additional special rules for maintaining the meaning of refinement using first-order logic. It should be noted that first-order rules offer considerable advantages for the implementation of tools.

7 Conclusions

In this paper, we have presented a practical approach to extending the B to include probabilistic choice. We have extended pB machines to include a probabilistic choice construct and a probabilistic state invariant. New proof obligations for the establishment and maintenance of the probabilistic invariant have been described. A simple case study of a library, in which books may be lost, has been used to illustrate how we can use pB and how we can reason formally about expected outcomes of the system. We have shown that there are significant differences between standard B operations and pB operations.

The *B-Toolkit* has been modified to incorporate the new $pAMN$ constructs and also to provide the generation and proof of proof obligations. In some cases, we have had to strike a balance between the theoretical and practical ideas to accommodate probability successfully into the *B-Toolkit*. Further investigation is required on refinement and machine composition using the pB.

Beyond a guarantee of "absolute" correctness, other major aspects of system/software design are essentially quantitative. Often the operating conditions provide an environment whose behaviour can only be estimated to within a "probabilistic margin of error". But even in these situations useful information about the operating "performance" of the implemented system can still be guaranteed. Other situations call for probability to be deliberately "programmed into the system" when standard methods fail to produce a guarantee of termination.

The main case study of this paper provides an example of the former situation, whilst there are many instances of the latter situation in distributed computing, with the FireWire protocol [14] and Rabin's distributed consensus [2] providing typical examples. In both situations the quantitative specification can be expressed as a numeric constraint and validated by the techniques set out in this paper. We have a complete development—through to implementation using probabilistic termination [11]—of Rabin's distributed consensus algorithm in pB.

Indeed many more performance-style specifications lend themselves to an approach based on invariants including "the expected time to achieve a stated goal" [8] or the "probability that a goal will be achieved within a specific time". Expected times to achieve "stability" for instance are of particular importance when systems use probability as an "in-built" facility.

Other tools such as the model checker PRISM [1] can also deal with these problems, however the model-checking approach contrasts fundamentally with the B in that model checkers are analysis- rather than design tools.

Acknowledgements. We wish to acknowledge the assistance of B-Core[5] for the modification of the *B-Toolkit*. We thank the anonymous reviewers for comments that we have used to improve the paper.

The authors at University of New South Wales gratefully acknowledge the support of the Australian Research Council under the large grant A00103115.

References

[1] Probabilistic symbolic model checker.
http://www.cs.bham.ac.uk/~dxp/prism/publications.html.
[2] Specification and development of probabilistic systems.
http://web.comlab.ox.ac.uk/oucl/research/areas/probs/.
[3] *Proceeding of the 3rd International Conference of B and Z Users*. Springer, 2003.
[4] J-R. Abrial. *The B-Book*. Cambridge University Press, 1996.
[5] B-Core(UK) Ltd. B Toolkit. http://www.b-core.com.
[6] John E. Freund. *John E. Freund's Mathematical Statistics*. Prentice Hall International, Inc., 6 edition, 1999.
[7] D. Gries and J. Prins. A new notion of encapsulation. In *Symposium on Language Issues in Programming Environments*. SIGPLAN, June 1985.
[8] A. K. McIver. Quantitative program logic and counting rounds in probabilistic distributed algorithms. In *Proc. 5th Intl. Workshop ARTS '99*, volume 1601, 1999.
[9] A. K. McIver and C. C. Morgan. Demonic, angelic and unbounded probabilistic choices in sequential programs. *Acta Informatica*, 37:329–354, 2001.
[10] C. C. Morgan, A. K. McIver, and K. Seidel. Probabilistic predicate transformers. *ACM Transactions on Programming Languages and Systems*, 18(3):325–353, May 1996.
[11] A. K. McIver, C. C. Morgan, and Thai Son Hoang. Probabilistic termination in B. In *Proceeding of the 3rd International Conference of B and Z Users* [3].
[12] C. C. Morgan. *Programming from Specifications*. Prentice-Hall, second edition, 1994. At web.comlab.ox.ac.uk/oucl/publications/books/PfS.
[13] C. C. Morgan. The generalised substitution language extended to probabilistic programs. In *Proceedings B'98: the 2nd International B Conference*, volume 1393 of *LNCS*, Montpelier, April 1998. Also available at [2, B98].
[14] Stoelinga and Vaandrager. Root contention in IEEE 1394. In *Proceedings of the 5th AMAST workshop on real time and probabilistic systems Bamberg, Germany, ARTS' 1999*, volume 1061 of *LNCS*.

Proving Temporal Properties of Z Specifications Using Abstraction

Graeme Smith and Kirsten Winter

Software Verification Research Centre
University of Queensland 4072, Australia
{smith, kirsten}@svrc.uq.edu.au

Abstract. This paper presents a systematic approach to proving temporal properties of arbitrary Z specifications. The approach involves (i) transforming the Z specification to an abstract *temporal structure* (or state transition system), (ii) applying a model checker to the temporal structure, (iii) determining whether the temporal structure is too abstract based on the model checking result and (iv) refining the temporal structure where necessary. The approach is based on existing work from the model checking literature, adapting it to Z.

1 Introduction

Specifications in Z [Spi92], and related languages such as Object-Z [Smi00], often involve predicates of arbitrary complexity and have infinite state spaces. Consequently, tool support for proving properties of such specifications has focussed on theorem proving [KSW96,Saa97,TM95], rather than automated techniques such as model checking [CGP00] which are limited with respect to the notation supported and the size of the state space of the specification.

To extend the limits of model checking, much research in the past decade has focussed on *abstraction* as a means of state space reduction [CGL94,LGS+95]. A system model with a large, or infinite, state space is transformed to one with a reduced state space suitable for model checking. This is done based on the notion of *abstract interpretation* (originally developed to derive abstract semantics of programming languages [CC79]). In essence, abstraction is the inverse of downward simulation data refinement [DB01]. Hence, any properties which are preserved by such refinement and can be proved true for the abstract model are also true for the concrete model. Properties preserved by downward simulation are of the form that something is true on all abstract behaviours. A property which states something is true on one, or a limited number, of abstract behaviours is not, in general, preserved.

For abstraction to be practically useful, two further issues need to be addressed. Firstly, the derivation of the abstract model needs to be at least systematic, and at best automatic. Otherwise, we are left with a significant intellectual task and lose the primary benefit of model checking. Secondly, we need to deal with the case where a property of interest is proved false for the abstract model.

In this case, nothing can be deduced about the concrete model which (like a refinement) may have additional properties due to a decrease in nondeterminism. These issues have been addressed by the model checking community (e.g., [GS97,SS99,CGJ+00]) and, in this paper, we draw on these results to provide a practical approach to abstraction for Z.

Our goal is to present a systematic approach to abstraction of Z specifications that could be supported by a theorem prover. The approach is not specific to any particular theorem prover, nor is the abstract model produced aimed at any particular model checker. The approach could be used with any suitable combination of such tools. We begin in Section 2 with a summary of the relevant results from the model checking community. In Section 3, we present an approach to abstraction for Z specifications and illustrate it by an example in Section 4. In Section 5, we show, via the example, how to deal with properties that are proved false for the abstract system. Future directions are discussed in Section 6.

2 Background

Abstraction as a means of state space reduction has been a topic of research in the model checking community for some time. Early work provided a theoretical framework for abstraction. For example, Clarke, Grumberg and Long [CGL94] provide a method for transforming finite state programs to an abstract transition system. They prove that the properties of the abstract model expressed in a restricted temporal logic which only allows properties that state that something is true on all abstract behaviours (namely the universal fragment of CTL*, ∀CTL*) are also properties of the program, and hence that the abstract model can be used to verify the program. A similar approach is described by Loiseaux et al. [LGS+95] for a slightly more expressive temporal logic (a restricted version of the μ-calculus).

The general idea is to group states in the concrete model into equivalence classes and map these via an abstraction function, **Abs**, to states of the abstract model (see Figure 1).

2.1 Finding the Abstraction Function

The abstraction function should be chosen in such a way that the property of interest can easily be proved in the abstract model. A number of papers, including that of Clarke, Grumberg and Long [CGL94], suggest guidance for finding such functions (e.g., [Jac94,WVF97]). For example, Jackson [Jac94] in his approach for abstracting Z specifications, suggests using the properties to be proved as a basis for defining a suitable abstraction function. Assume we want to prove that a variable $y : \mathbb{N}$ is less than 10. Of course, we could split the state space into the equivalence classes $y < 0$, $y = 0$ and $y > 0$. However, for this property it is more useful to use the equivalence classes $y < 10$, $y = 10$ and $y > 10$.

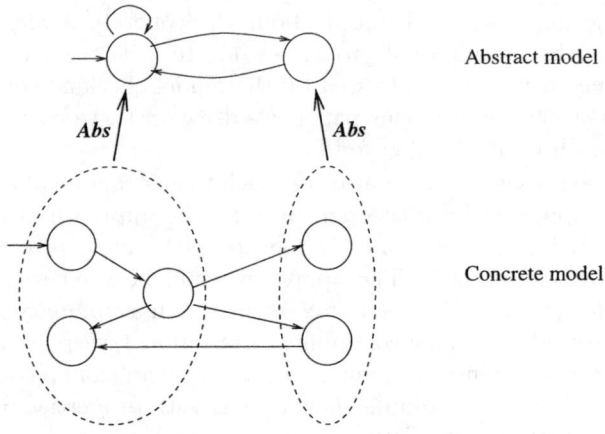

Fig. 1. Abstraction using equivalence classes of states

However, none of the approaches mentioned above provide a systematic way of defining an abstraction function. This problem is overcome by Graf and Saïdi [GS97]. They present an automated approach to abstraction which does not require an abstraction function to be defined in advance. Instead, it requires a set of predicates on which to base the abstraction process.

From these predicates, Graf and Saïdi form a set of *monomials*. A monomial is a conjunction of, for each predicate, either the predicate or its negation. For example, given the predicates p_1 and p_2, the monomials are $p_1 \wedge p_2$, $p_1 \wedge \neg p_2$, $\neg p_1 \wedge p_2$ and $\neg p_1 \wedge \neg p_2$. Since the monomials partition the complete concrete state space, they can be used as the equivalence classes of the concrete states.

Choosing the predicates can be based on the user's understanding of the system. However, Graf and Saïdi offer general guidance for choosing them.

- Using predicates which appear in the property to be proved results in an abstract model where states either satisfy these predicates or not.
- Using the predicates in the guards of transitions simplifies the abstraction process. Since the information of enabledness of transitions is encoded in the abstract state space the possible transitions of the abstract model are easily determined.
- In general, *atomic predicates*, e.g., $x = 2$ and $y = 3$ rather than $x = 2 \Rightarrow y = 3$, result in a better level of abstraction.

The second point listed above, using the predicates in the guards, is essential. Otherwise, properties proved for the abstract model may not be true for the concrete model, i.e., we do not have a proper abstraction. For example, in Figure 2 since the equivalence class containing concrete states s_1 and s_2 does not reflect the guard of the transition, we are able to prove that the abstract model always progresses to state t_2. The corresponding property on the concrete model, that it always progresses to state s_3, is however not true.

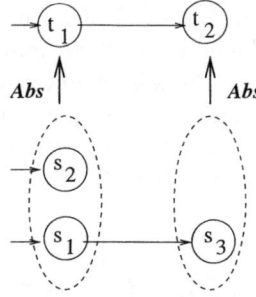

Fig. 2. Equivalence classes not reflecting transition guards

2.2 False Counter-Example Detection and Refinement

When we model-check an abstract model, the model checker might successfully prove the property of interest. In this case, we know the property holds for our concrete model as well. However, if the model checker disproves the property by producing a counter-example, we cannot determine anything about the concrete model. The model checker has effectively proved that something is not true on at least one abstract behaviour. Such properties on one, or a limited number of behaviours, are not necessarily true of our concrete model. Hence, the counter-example may also be a counter-example of the concrete model, or it may only be a counter-example of the less deterministic abstract model. In the latter case, we call it a *false counter-example*.

The counter-examples produced by most existing model checkers are a sequence of states starting from an initial state. These sequences are either finite or, if infinite, involve a loop back to a previous state (see Figure 3).

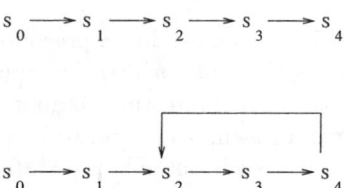

Fig. 3. Finite and infinite (looping) counter-examples

If we get a false counter-example, the abstract model needs to be refined closer to the concrete model. Clarke et al. [CGJ+00] introduce algorithms for automatically detecting false counter-examples of the kinds in Figure 3. This is done based on the fact that a false counter-example contains an abstract state whose corresponding concrete state is not reachable in the concrete model.

Given a false counter-example, they also automatically derive a refinement of the abstract model in which the false counter-example is avoided. This is done by finding the last abstract state in the false counter-example whose corresponding equivalence class of concrete states is reachable in the concrete model. This equivalence class is split based on whether or not a state is reachable via the counter-example (see Figure 4 in which s_4 and s_5 are separated from s_6).

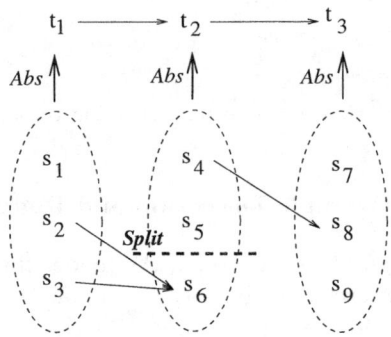

Fig. 4. Splitting of equivalence classes

For deriving the abstract model, Clarke et al. follow the approach of Graf and Saïdi [GS97] of using a set of predicates. However, rather than using them to generate an abstract model, they use them to generate an abstraction function which is then used to compute the abstract model.

3 Abstraction of Z Specifications

An operation in Z does not have a guard, but a precondition outside of which the operation can occur changing the state arbitrarily. Such arbitrary state changes make it impossible to prove most interesting temporal properties (over all behaviours). We restrict our approach, therefore, to Z specifications where operations are *totalised*. That is, for each possible pre-state, the operation explicitly specifies a post-state which in some cases may be an error state.

The precondition of such a totalised operation is equivalent to true. Hence, whether the operation is interpreted as having a precondition (in the Z sense) or guard is irrelevant (the operation can occur from any pre-state). In this work, we choose to treat them as having guards. This is done to extend the applicability of our approach to Object-Z (where operations are guarded [Smi00]) as well as non-standard (behavioural) interpretations of Z with guarded operations [DB01].

We follow the approach of using a set of predicates to derive an abstract Z specification. Since all operation guards are true, we use only the atomic predicates in the property to be proved. (For Object-Z or guarded interpretations of Z, we would also need to use the atomic predicates in the operation guards to avoid the problem illustrated in Figure 2.) Using the monomials of these atomic predicates, we form equivalence classes of the state space of the concrete model. An explicit abstraction function then relates these equivalence classes to single abstract states. This abstraction function is used to derive an abstract model. The soundness of our process will be proven with respect to Z downward simulation laws [DB01].

For expressing system properties, we adopt Linear Temporal Logic (LTL) [Eme90], the temporal operators of which are explained below.

G ϕ Now and at all points in the future, it is the case that ϕ is true.
F ϕ At some point in the future, it will be the case that ϕ is true.
X ϕ In the next state, it will be the case that ϕ is true.
ϕ **U** ψ At some point in the future, it will be the case that ψ is true, and from now until then it is always the case that ϕ is true.

An LTL property holds for a specification, if it holds for all *paths*, i.e., sequences of states, that the specified system can undergo.

3.1 The Abstraction Process

Properties expressed in LTL are preserved by downward simulation data refinement [DB01]. This is because the properties have to hold for all paths that the specified system can undergo. Since downward simulation only eliminates paths (by reducing nondeterminism) and does not allow new ones to be added, properties which are true on all paths of an abstract specification, will be true on all paths of a refinement of that specification.

Hence, a suitable abstraction will be one that can be refined to the original specification using downward simulation. Under a guarded interpretation of operations, a Z specification with state schema *CState*, initial state schema *CInit* and operations $COp_1 \ldots COp_n$ is a downward simulation of an abstract specification with state schema *AState*, initial state schema *AInit* and operations $AOp_1 \ldots AOp_n$, if there is a retrieve relation *Retr* such that the following conditions hold [DB01].

Initialisation $\forall \textit{CInit} \bullet \exists \textit{AInit} \bullet \textit{Retr}$
Applicability $\forall \textit{AState}; \textit{CState} \bullet$
$\textit{Retr} \Rightarrow (\text{pre } AOp_i \Leftrightarrow \text{pre } COp_i) \quad \text{for } i \in 1..n$
Correctness $\forall \textit{AState}; \textit{CState}; \textit{CState}' \bullet$
$\textit{Retr} \wedge COp_i \Rightarrow (\exists \textit{AState}' \bullet \textit{Retr}' \wedge AOp_i) \quad \text{for } i \in 1..n$

These conditions are used to show the soundness of our abstraction process below.

Assume the monomials, built from the atomic predicates of the property to be proved, are $p_1, \ldots, p_n$. Then the state schema of the abstract specification is:

$\begin{array}{|l}\hline \_AState_____ \\ \quad s : State \\ \hline\end{array}$

where $State ::= s_1 \mid \ldots \mid s_n$, and the abstraction function is defined by a schema:

$\begin{array}{|l}\hline \_Abs_____ \\ \quad AState \\ \quad CState \\ \hline \quad p_1 \Rightarrow s = s_1 \\ \quad \ldots \\ \quad p_n \Rightarrow s = s_n \\ \hline\end{array}$

Informally, the abstraction function is a mapping $\{p_1 \mapsto s_1, \ldots, p_n \mapsto s_n\}$.

The initial state schema and operations of the abstract system are derived such that the original specification refines the abstract specification under a retrieve relation which is the inverse of the abstraction function (and hence defined by the same schema, i.e., $Retr = Abs$).

The initialisation condition for downward simulation requires that there is an abstract initial state related to each concrete initial state. Since the monomials partition the concrete state space, they represent all concrete states. Therefore, there will be an abstract state corresponding to each concrete initial state. To ensure that this abstract state is also an abstract initial state, we define the abstract initial state schema as:

$\begin{array}{|l}\hline \_AInit_____ \\ \quad AState \\ \hline \quad \exists\, CInit \bullet Abs \\ \hline\end{array}$

With this definition of $AInit$, the initialisation condition becomes:

$$\forall\, CInit \bullet \exists\, AState \mid (\exists\, CInit \bullet Abs) \bullet Abs$$
$$\equiv \forall\, CInit \bullet \exists\, AState \bullet (\exists\, CInit \bullet Abs) \land Abs$$
$$\Leftarrow \forall\, CInit \bullet \exists\, AState;\ CInit \bullet Abs \land Abs$$
$$\equiv \forall\, CInit \bullet \exists\, AState;\ CInit \bullet Abs$$

If there are no initial concrete states then the above is immediately true. If there is a concrete initial state then there is an abstract state related to it due to the abstraction function being based on monomials (and hence $\exists\, AState;\ CInit \bullet Abs$ is true).

For each operation, we require that the applicability and correctness conditions hold. This will be true when an abstract operation starts and ends only in states which are related to those equivalence classes containing concrete states that serve as start and end points of the corresponding concrete operation[1]. Hence, an abstract operation AOp_i is defined as:

$$
\begin{array}{|l}
\_AOp_i_____ \\
\Delta AState \\
\hline
\exists\, CState;\ CState' \bullet COp_i \land Abs \land Abs'
\end{array}
$$

The applicability condition becomes:

$\forall\, AState;\ CState \bullet Abs \Rightarrow$
$\quad\quad ((\exists\, AState' \bullet \exists\, CState;\ CState' \bullet COp_i \land Abs \land Abs') \Leftrightarrow \mathrm{pre}\, COp_i)$
$\equiv \forall\, AState;\ CState \bullet Abs \Rightarrow$
$\quad\quad ((\exists\, CState;\ CState' \bullet COp_i \land Abs \land (\exists\, AState' \bullet Abs')) \Leftrightarrow \mathrm{pre}\, COp_i)$

Since there is an abstract state related to each concrete state due to the abstraction function being based on monomials, the above is equivalent to:

$\forall\, AState;\ CState \bullet Abs \Rightarrow$
$\quad\quad ((\exists\, CState;\ CState' \bullet COp_i \land Abs) \Leftrightarrow \mathrm{pre}\, COp_i)$
$\equiv \forall\, AState;\ CState \bullet Abs \Rightarrow$
$\quad\quad ((\exists\, CState \bullet Abs \land (\exists\, CState' \bullet COp_i)) \Leftrightarrow \mathrm{pre}\, COp_i)$
$\equiv \forall\, AState;\ CState \bullet Abs \Rightarrow$
$\quad\quad ((\exists\, CState \bullet Abs \land \mathrm{pre}\, COp_i) \Leftrightarrow \mathrm{pre}\, COp_i)$

Since $\mathrm{pre}\, COp_i$ is true under our restriction that operations be totalised, the above is trivially true. (For Object-Z or guarded interpretations of Z, $\mathrm{pre}\, COp_i$ would not necessarily be true. In this case, since the monomials defining the abstraction function would be based on atomic predicates in the operation guards, the same operations would be enabled from any two concrete states related to the same abstract state. Hence, the above would be true.)

The correctness condition becomes:

$\forall\, AState;\ CState;\ CState' \bullet Abs \land COp_i \Rightarrow$
$\quad\quad (\exists\, AState' \bullet Abs' \land (\exists\, CState;\ CState' \bullet COp_i \land Abs \land Abs'))$
$\Leftarrow \forall\, AState;\ CState;\ CState' \bullet Abs \land COp_i \Rightarrow$
$\quad\quad (\exists\, AState' \bullet Abs' \land COp_i \land Abs \land Abs')$
$\equiv \forall\, AState;\ CState;\ CState' \bullet Abs \land COp_i \Rightarrow$
$\quad\quad Abs \land COp_i \land (\exists\, AState' \bullet Abs' \land Abs')$
$\equiv \forall\, AState;\ CState;\ CState' \bullet Abs \land COp_i \Rightarrow (\exists\, AState' \bullet Abs')$
$\Leftarrow \forall\, CState' \bullet (\exists\, AState' \bullet Abs')$

Since there is an abstract state related to each concrete state due to the abstraction function being based on monomials, the above is true.

---

[1] However, not all of the concrete states in the equivalence class need to satisfy this condition.

3.2 Handling Inputs and Outputs

The approach as presented so far only works for specifications without inputs and outputs. We could have accounted for inputs and outputs by basing our abstraction function on a refinement definition which included them [DB01]. Instead, we embed them in the specification state. Since LTL properties only involve state variables, this embedding allows us to prove properties about inputs and outputs in our approach.

The embedding is done in such a way that no new properties are introduced on the existing state variables. Each input and output variable appears as a distinct state variable whose name is the same as that of the original variable[2] and whose type is the declared type of the input or output variable extended with an undefined element $\bot$.

Initially, all outputs are equal to $\bot$ and the values of inputs are unconstrained. For each operation, if an input or output is declared by the operation (before the embedding) then no additional constraints are placed on it. In the case of an output, the originally declared variable is renamed to a post-state (primed) variable. If an input or output is not declared by an operation, its value in the pre-state, in the case of inputs, and post-state, in the case of outputs, is $\bot$. This will be illustrated in the example in the next section.

The new specification after the embedding has no new paths modulo the embedded variables. Nor does it have fewer paths than the original specification. Although inputs are set to particular (unspecified) values initially and after each operation, post-states exist for all possible values allowing the specification to proceed as before. The unspecified nature of the inputs models the fact that it is the environment of the specified system that is choosing them. Hence, it only makes sense to use inputs in assumptions of a property we wish to prove, e.g., on the left-hand side of an implication.

4 Unique Number Allocator Example

To illustrate our approach, we introduce a simple example of an infinite state system. The system is a unique number allocator which accepts requests for a strictly positive number and sends them to the requester. It is specified as having two variables: *used* denoting the numbers that it has already allocated, and *alloc* denoting the number, if any, it has allocated but not yet sent.

─── *Allocator* ───────────────────────────────
 used : $\mathbb{P}\,\mathbb{N}_1$
 alloc : $\mathbb{F}\,\mathbb{N}_1$
 ─────────────
 $\#alloc \leqslant 1$
──

Initially, no numbers have been allocated.

---
[2] The original specification must not use the same name for inputs or outputs in different operations unless they have the same type.

```
┌─ Init ─────────────────────────────────
│ used = ∅
│ alloc = ∅
└────────────────────────────────────────
```

The operation *Request* specifies that whenever *alloc* is empty and *used* $\neq$ $\mathbb{N}_1$, a request for a new number can be made. A new number (not previously allocated) is placed in *alloc* and added to *used*. When *alloc* is not empty or *used* = $\mathbb{N}_1$, the operation leaves the state unchanged.

```
┌─ Request ──────────────────────────────
│ ΔAllocator
│
│ alloc = ∅ ∧ used ≠ ℕ₁ ⇒
│   (∃ n : ℕ₁ • n ∉ used ∧ alloc' = {n} ∧ used' = used ∪ {n})
│ alloc ≠ ∅ ∨ used = ℕ₁ ⇒ alloc' = alloc ∧ used' = used
└────────────────────────────────────────
```

The operation *Send* specifies that whenever *alloc* is not empty, its element may be sent (and removed from *alloc*). When *alloc* is empty the operation outputs the value zero to indicate an error and leaves the state unchanged.

```
┌─ Send ─────────────────────────────────
│ ΔAllocator
│ n! : ℕ
│
│ alloc = {n!} ⇒ alloc' = ∅ ∧ used' = used
│ alloc = ∅ ⇒ n! = 0 ∧ alloc' = alloc ∧ used' = used
└────────────────────────────────────────
```

We embed the inputs and outputs, in this case just the output $n! : \mathbb{N}$, in the specification as follows.

```
┌─ Allocator_IO ─────────┐   ┌─ Init_IO ──────────┐
│ Allocator              │   │ Init               │
│ n! : ℕ^⊥               │   │ n! = ⊥             │
└────────────────────────┘   └────────────────────┘

┌─ Request_IO ───────────┐   ┌─ Send_IO ──────────┐
│ Request                │   │ Send[n!'/n!]       │
│ n!' = ⊥                │   └────────────────────┘
└────────────────────────┘
```

where $\mathbb{N}^\perp$ is the set of natural numbers extended with the undefined value $\perp$. Note that we only restrict the value of $n!$ initially and *after* operations. Hence, $n!$ is renamed to $n!'$ in the operation *Send* above.

One property that we want for the unique number allocator is that we never send a given value $v : \mathbb{N}_1$ twice. This can be expressed in LTL as follows.

$$\mathbf{G}\ (n! \neq v \vee \mathbf{X}\ (\mathbf{G}\ n! \neq v))$$

That is, it is always the case that either $n! \neq v$ or (if $n! = v$) in the next state, it will always be the case that $n! \neq v$.

The property only has one atomic predicate $n! \neq v$ and hence the set of monomials is $\{n! \neq v, n! = v\}$. Following the process in Section 3 gives the abstract state schema:

$$
\begin{array}{|l}
\hline
AState \\
\hline
s : State \\
\hline
\end{array}
$$

where $State ::= s_1 \mid s_2$ and abstraction function:

$$
\begin{array}{|l}
\hline
Abs \\
\hline
AState \\
Allocator_{IO} \\
\hline
n! \neq v \Rightarrow s = s_1 \\
n! = v \Rightarrow s = s_2 \\
\hline
\end{array}
$$

The initial state schema is:

$$
\begin{array}{|l}
\hline
AInit \\
\hline
AState \\
\hline
\exists\, used, alloc : \mathbb{P}\,\mathbb{N}_1;\; n! : \mathbb{N}^\perp \mid \#alloc \leqslant 1 \wedge n! = \perp \bullet \\
\quad n! \neq v \Rightarrow s = s_1 \wedge \\
\quad n! = v \Rightarrow s = s_2 \\
\hline
\end{array}
$$

which simplifies to:

$$
\begin{array}{|l}
\hline
AInit \\
\hline
AState \\
\hline
s = s_1 \\
\hline
\end{array}
$$

The abstract operations similarly simplify to:

$$
\begin{array}{|l}
\hline
ARequest \\
\hline
\Delta AState \\
\hline
s' = s_1 \\
\hline
\end{array}
\qquad
\begin{array}{|l}
\hline
ASend \\
\hline
\Delta AState \\
\hline
true \\
\hline
\end{array}
$$

Finally, the property is also abstracted to:

$\mathbf{G}\ (s = s_1 \vee \mathbf{X}\ (\mathbf{G}\ s = s_1))$

The entire abstraction process is systematic and potentially automatable. The simplifications of the abstract schemas could be done using a theorem prover either automatically, or in the case of more complicated specifications, with some user guidance. The conversion of the abstract specification into the input format of a model checker is also potentially automatable since its state schema comprises a single variable with a finite set of values (representing possible states) and its operations define transitions between these values. In other words, the abstract specification defines a simple *temporal structure* (or state transition system) as shown in Figure 5.

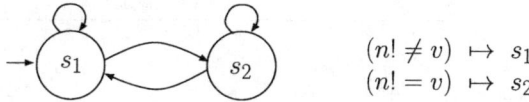

Fig. 5. Temporal structure of the abstract specification of the unique number allocator

Hence, we should be able to model check the abstract specification to see if our desired property holds. What we will find, and what will become evident from Figure 1, is that our abstract specification is too abstract to prove this property. Hence, the model checker will return a counter-example for the abstract system which is not a counter-example for our original specification. Dealing with such counter-examples is the topic of the next section.

5 False Counter-Example Detection and Refinement

As we are targeting the use of standard model checkers, we assume counter-examples returned by model checking are either a finite or infinite (looping) sequence of states as shown in Figure 3. To determine whether or not they are false counter-examples, we follow an approach that is inspired by the work of Clarke et al. [CGJ+00]. We show here the process to follow for finite sequences of states. Clarke et al. argue that the process for infinite (looping) sequences of states is a minor variation on that for finite sequences.

5.1 False Counter-Example Detection

Assume our counter-example is a sequence of states $\langle t_0, \ldots, t_m \rangle$ where $t_0, \ldots, t_m :$ *State*. We need to find a sequence of operations in the original (concrete) specification that passes through concrete states related to the abstract states in the counter-example. If such a sequence of operations cannot be found we can conclude that the corresponding states are not reachable in the concrete model and thus, the counter-example is a false counter-example.

The initial concrete states related to the abstract state t_0 are given by the schema C_0.

$$\begin{array}{|l}\hline C_0 \\ \hline CInit \\ \hline \exists\, s : State \bullet s = t_0 \wedge Abs \\ \hline \end{array}$$

The concrete states related to t_1 that can be reached from a state in C_0 are given by the schema C_1.

$$\begin{array}{|l}\hline C_1 \\ \hline CState \\ \hline \exists\, s : State \bullet s = t_1 \wedge Abs \\ \exists\, CState' \bullet (\exists\, C_0 \bullet COp_1 \vee \ldots \vee COp_n) \wedge \theta CState = \theta CState' \\ \hline \end{array}$$

This schema defines the states that are related to t_1 and which are post-states of one of the operations $COp_1, \ldots, COp_n$ when the pre-state is C_0. Note that the final conjunct of the second predicate equates the post-state variables to the variables of the schema's declaration part. The conjunct is out of the scope of the existentially quantified variables satisfying C_0.

Following this pattern, for any abstract state t_i $(1 \leqslant i \leqslant m)$ the concrete states related to t_i that can be reached from the initial state via concrete states related to $t_1, \ldots, t_{i-1}$ are given by the schema C_i.

$$\begin{array}{|l}\hline C_i \\ \hline CState \\ \hline \exists\, s : State \bullet s = t_i \wedge Abs \\ \exists\, CState' \bullet (\exists\, C_{i-1} \bullet COp_1 \vee \ldots \vee COp_n) \wedge \theta CState = \theta CState' \\ \hline \end{array}$$

If such a schema evaluates to false, there is no reachable concrete state related to the abstract state and hence we have a false counter-example.

5.2 The Example Revisited

The abstract specification of the unique number allocator in Section 4 is too abstract. It does not have the property that s can never equal s_2 twice (corresponding to the concrete property that $n!$ can never equal some $v : \mathbb{N}_1$ twice). Hence, if we tried to check this property with a model checker a counter-example would be returned. Model checkers generally return the counter-example that is found first (i.e., the shortest one). In the example, this is $\langle s_1, s_2, s_2\rangle$ (see Figure 5).

Applying the above process to this counter-example, schema C_0 would be:

$$
\begin{array}{|l}
C_0 \\\hline
Init_{IO} \\\hline
\exists\, s : State \bullet \\
\quad s = s_1 \land \\
\quad n! \neq v \Rightarrow s = s_1 \land \\
\quad n! = v \Rightarrow s = s_2
\end{array}
$$

which simplifies to:

$$
\begin{array}{|l}
C_0 \\\hline
Init_{IO}
\end{array}
$$

since $n!$ does not equal v in $Init_{IO}$; it equals $\bot$.

Schema C_1 would then be:

$$
\begin{array}{|l}
C_1 \\\hline
Allocator_{IO} \\\hline
\exists\, s : State \bullet \\
\quad s = s_2 \land \\
\quad n! \neq v \Rightarrow s = s_1 \land \\
\quad n! = v \Rightarrow s = s_2 \\
\exists\, Allocator'_{IO} \bullet \\
\quad (\exists\, Init_{IO} \bullet Request_{IO} \lor Send_{IO}) \land \theta Allocator'_{IO} = \theta Allocator_{IO}
\end{array}
$$

which simplifies to:

$$
\begin{array}{|l}
C_1 \\\hline
Allocator_{IO} \\\hline
false
\end{array}
$$

since initially (when $alloc = \varnothing$), $Request_{IO}$ requires $n!'$ to equal $\bot$ and $Send_{IO}$ requires that it equals 0. Hence, $\langle s_1, s_2, s_2 \rangle$ is a false counter-example.

This process is again potentially automatable using a theorem prover to perform the simplifications either automatically or with some user guidance. False counter-example detection would also be possible using the algorithms underlying a Z animator such as Possum [DHT97].

5.3 Abstraction Refinement

Once a false counter-example has been detected, we need to refine the abstract model to avoid this counter-example during subsequent model checking. Similarly to the approach of Clarke et al. [CGJ[+]00], we need to split the abstract state that is related (via the abstraction function) to the last reachable concrete state (see Figure 4). We separate those states of the corresponding equivalence class that can perform a transition to the next equivalence class from those that cannot. This separation results in two new equivalence classes which are then mapped into two new abstract states.

In our approach, the last reachable concrete state is defined by the schema C_i where C_{i+1} is the first schema whose predicate simplifies to false. We split the corresponding abstract state t_i into two: one state where there is a transition to the state t_{i+1} and another where there is no transition to the state t_{i+1}.

This manifests itself as replacement of the value of t_i by two new values s_{n+1} and s_{n+2} in type $State$, and a change in the abstraction function. The predicate $p \Rightarrow s = t_i$ will be replaced by two new predicates:

$$p \wedge (\exists\, CState' \bullet (COp_1 \vee \ldots \vee COp_n) \wedge q) \Rightarrow s = s_{n+1}$$

and

$$p \wedge (\nexists\, CState' \bullet (COp_1 \vee \ldots \vee COp_n) \wedge q) \Rightarrow s = s_{n+2}$$

The first predicate models the case where the concrete state satisfies the monomial p corresponding to abstract state t_i and there is a transition via a concrete operation to a concrete state satisfying the monomial q corresponding to abstract state t_{i+1}. The second predicate models the case where there is no such transition.

Given this new abstraction function, the refined abstract specification and property can then be constructed as before.

5.4 Refining the Example

If we apply the above to our example and the counter-example of Section 5.2, the last reachable state is defined by the schema:

$$\begin{array}{|l}\hline C_0 \\ \hline Init_{IO} \\ \hline\end{array}$$

and we need to split the abstract state $s = s_1$ by changing the definition of $State$ to:

$$State ::= s_3 \mid s_4 \mid s_2$$

and replacing the predicate $n! \neq v \Rightarrow s = s_1$ in Abs by:

$$n! \neq v \wedge (\exists\, Allocator'_{IO} \bullet (Request_{IO} \vee Send_{IO}) \wedge n = v) \Rightarrow s = s_3$$

which simplifies to $n! \neq v \wedge alloc = \{v\} \Rightarrow s_3$ and:

$$n! \neq v \wedge (\nexists\, Allocator'_{IO} \bullet (Request_{IO} \vee Send_{IO}) \wedge n = v) \Rightarrow s = s_4$$

which simplifies to $n! \neq v \wedge alloc \neq \{v\} \Rightarrow s_4$.

Following the abstraction process as before, the abstract initial state schema will simplify to:

$$
\begin{array}{|l}
Ainit \\
\hline
AState \\
\hline
s = s_4 \\
\end{array}
$$

and the operations to:

$$
\begin{array}{|l}
ARequest \\
\hline
\Delta AState \\
\hline
s = s_3 \Rightarrow s' = s_3 \\
s \in \{s_2, s_4\} \Rightarrow s' \in \{s_3, s_4\} \\
\end{array}
\qquad
\begin{array}{|l}
ASend \\
\hline
\Delta AState \\
\hline
s = s_3 \Rightarrow s' = s_2 \\
s = s_4 \Rightarrow s' = s_4 \\
\end{array}
$$

This abstract specification defines the temporal structure in Figure 6.

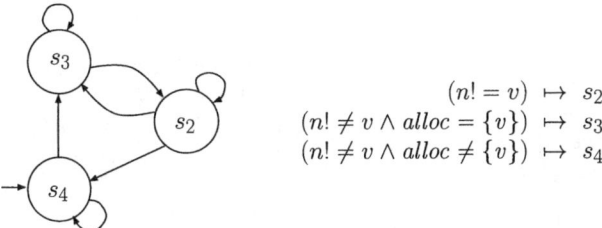

Fig. 6. First refinement of the abstract specification of the unique number allocator

This structure avoids the above counter-example by not allowing a transition from the initial state s_4 to s_2. A transition to s_2 can only occur from s_3 which is related to concrete states where $alloc = \{v\}$. However, the property, now abstracted to:

$$\mathbf{G}\ (s \in \{s_3, s_4\} \vee \mathbf{X}\ (\mathbf{G}\ s \in \{s_3, s_4\}))$$

can still not be proved. In fact, three more refinements are necessary.

The first refinement, in response to the false counter-example $\langle s_4, s_3, s_2, s_2 \rangle$, results in splitting s_2 into states s_5 and s_6 related to the concrete states where $n! = v \wedge alloc = \{v\}$ and $n! = v \wedge alloc \neq \{v\}$ (the former of which is unreachable, i.e., has no ingoing transitions). The reachable sub-graph of the temporal structure is shown in Figure 7.

The second refinement, in response to the false counter-example $\langle s_4, s_3, s_6, s_3, s_6 \rangle$, results in splitting s_6 into states s_7 and s_8 related to the concrete states where $n! = v \wedge alloc \neq \{v\} \wedge v \in used$ and $n! = v \wedge alloc \neq \{v\} \wedge$

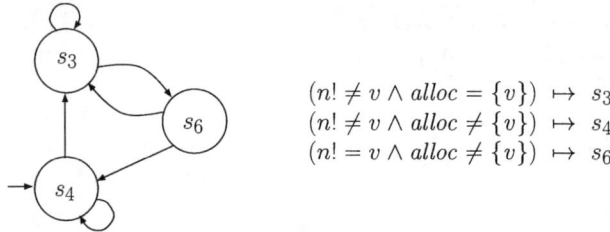

$(n! \neq v \wedge alloc = \{v\}) \mapsto s_3$
$(n! \neq v \wedge alloc \neq \{v\}) \mapsto s_4$
$(n! = v \wedge alloc \neq \{v\}) \mapsto s_6$

Fig. 7. Second refinement of the abstract specification of the unique number allocator

$v \notin used$ (the latter of which is unreachable). The reachable sub-graph of the temporal structure is shown in Figure 8.

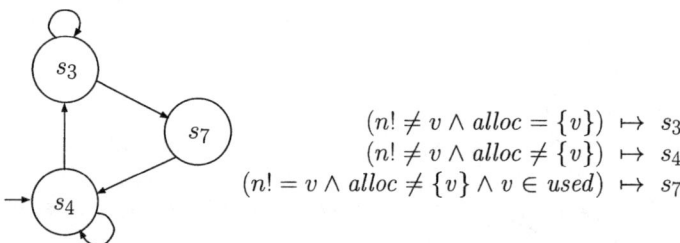

$(n! \neq v \wedge alloc = \{v\}) \mapsto s_3$
$(n! \neq v \wedge alloc \neq \{v\}) \mapsto s_4$
$(n! = v \wedge alloc \neq \{v\} \wedge v \in used) \mapsto s_7$

Fig. 8. Third refinement of the abstract specification of the unique number allocator

The final refinement, in response to the false counter-example $\langle s_4, s_3, s_7, s_4, s_3, s_7 \rangle$, results in splitting s_4 into states s_9 and s_{10} related to the concrete states where $n! \neq v \wedge alloc \neq \{v\} \wedge v \notin used$ and $n! \neq v \wedge alloc \neq \{v\} \wedge v \in used$. The reachable sub-graph of the corresponding temporal structure is shown in Figure 9.

The abstracted property:

$$\mathbf{G}\ (s \in \{s_3, s_9, s_{10}\} \vee \mathbf{X}\ (\mathbf{G}\ s \in \{s_3, s_9, s_{10}\}))$$

can be proved in this case and hence the process terminates.

As the example shows, a number of refinements may be required before a property can be proved (or a real counter-example found). However, the process of false counter-example detection and refinement is systematic and hence potentially automatable with theorem prover support for simplifying predicates.

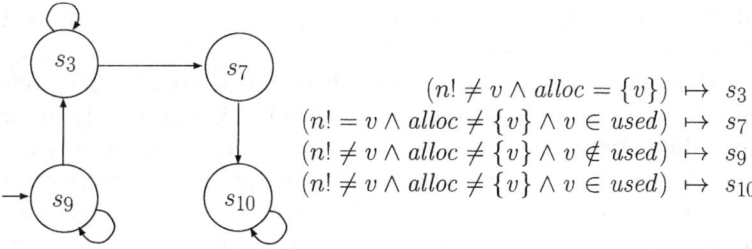

Fig. 9. Final refinement of the abstract specification of the unique number allocator

6 Conclusion and Future Work

In this paper, we have suggested a methodology for model checking Z specifications through an iterative process that employs abstraction and stepwise refinement of large or even infinite models. As the first step of this process, we derive an abstraction function from the set of atomic predicates given in the property to be proved. This abstraction function allows us to generate an abstract model which can be treated by a model checker. By means of Z downward simulation laws, we proved that the derived abstraction function satisfies the conditions for a retrieve relation. Therefore, the generation of the abstract model is sound, i.e., all properties preserved by downward simulation and that hold in the abstract model are also properties of the concrete model.

However, if a property is not satisfied in the abstract model the output counter-example indicating the violation might be a false counter-example having no corresponding execution in the concrete model. In this case, the false counter-example is used to refine the abstract model into a model closer to the concrete model. This refined model will avoid the false counter-example and can be model checked again. We iterate these last two steps of model checking and refining the model until the property is either satisfied by the model or a real counter-example is found.

Other work on abstraction techniques for Z or related languages has been published. Jackson [Jac94] (for Z) as well as Wehrheim [Weh99] (for CSP-OZ), suggest some general user guidance on how to find a suitable abstraction function. However, they do not provide any systematic support for the generation of such an abstraction function. Mota et al. [MBS02] go further in that they suggest an algorithm for generating an abstraction function for the language CSP_Z. Whereas our approach for this generation works syntactically based on a combination of Z predicates, their approach is based on comparing states and the enabledness of operations in all executable paths of a given specification. States with the same operations enabled are considered as belonging to the same equivalence class. This procedure immediately raises the question of efficiency for more complex examples in which arbitrarily many executions, or executions that do not show any behavioural pattern that repeatedly occurs, have to be analysed. Moreover, Mota et al. do not handle false counter-example detection and the corresponding refinement of the abstract model.

The techniques we have adapted have been automated in the model checking community. We claim that our approach for Z is potentially automatable. The major difficulty arising is that arbitrarily complex predicates need to be simplified. While in many cases this could be done automatically with the aid of theorem prover tactics, there may still be a need for some user guidance. In any case, we need to consider modifications aimed at producing better abstractions and abstraction refinements and also examine the general efficiency of our approach.

Our approach is restricted to Z specifications with totalised operations since, without totalisation, arbitrary state changes result in specifications without many interesting temporal properties. This restriction allowed us to treat operations as being guarded, rather than as having preconditions outside of which their occurrence can change the state arbitrarily. This means our approach can also be used with guarded interpretation of Z [DB01] and with Object-Z [Smi00]. Using a structured notation like Object-Z would allow us to additionally use specification decomposition as a means of reducing complexity. This has been examined by Winter and Smith [WS03] and could be combined with this work to increase its effectiveness in dealing with large specifications.

Acknowledgements. This work was supported by a University of Queensland External Support Enabling Grant.

References

[CC79] P. Cousot and R. Cousot. Systematic design of program analysis framework. In *6th ACM Symposium on Principles of Programming Languages*, 1979.

[CGJ+00] E. Clarke, O. Grumberg, S. Jha, Y. Lu, and H. Veith. Counterexample-guided abstraction refinement. In A.P. Sistla E.A. Emerson, editor, *Computer Aided Verification (CAV'00)*, volume 1855 of *LNCS*. Springer-Verlag, 2000.

[CGL94] E. Clarke, O. Grumberg, and D. Long. Model checking and abstraction. *ACM Transactions on Programming Languages and Systems*, 16(5):1512–1542, 1994.

[CGP00] E. Clarke, O. Grumberg, and D. Peled. *Model Checking*. MIT Press, 2000.

[DB01] J. Derrick and E. Boiten. *Refinement in Z and Object-Z, Foundations and Advanced Applications*. Springer-Verlag, 2001.

[DHT97] P. Strooper D. Hazel and O. Traynor. Possum: An animator for the SUM specification language. In W. Wong and K. Leung, editors, *Asia Pacific Software Engineering Conference (APSEC 97)*, pages 42–51. IEEE Computer Society, 1997.

[Eme90] E. A. Emerson. Temporal and modal logic. In J. van Leeuwen, editor, *Handbook of Theoretical Computer Science*, volume B, pages 996–1072. Elsevier Science Publishers, 1990.

[GS97]   S. Graf and H. Saïdi. Construction of abstract state graphs with PVS. In *Int. Conf. on Computer Aided Verification (CAV 97)*, volume 1254 of *LNCS*, pages 72–83. Springer-Verlag, 1997.

[Jac94]   D. Jackson. Abstract model checking of infinite specifications. In M. Naftalin, T. Denvir, and M. Bertran, editors, *Formal Methods Europe (FME'94)*, volume 873 of *LNCS*, pages 519–531. Springer-Verlag, 1994.

[KSW96]   Kolyang, T. Santen, and B. Wolff. A structure preserving encoding of Z in Isabelle/HOL. In J. von Wright, J. Grundy, and J. Harrison, editors, *Theorem Proving in Higher Order Logics (TPHOLs 96)*, volume 1125 of *LNCS*, pages 283–298. Springer-Verlag, 1996.

[LGS+95]   C. Loiseaux, S. Graf, J. Sifakis, A. Bouajjani, and S. Bensalem. Property preserving abstractions for the verification of concurrent systems. *Formal Methods in System Design*, 6(1), 1995.

[MBS02]   A. Mota, P. Borba, and A. Sampaio. Mechanical abstraction of CSP_Z processes. In L.-H. Eriksson and P. Lindsay, editors, *Formal Methods Europe (FME'2002)*, volume 2391 of *LNCS*, pages 163–183. Springer-Verlag, 2002.

[Saa97]   M. Saaltink. The Z-Eves system. In J. Bowen, M. Hinchey, and D. Till, editors, *International Conference of Z User (ZUM 97)*, volume 1212 of *LNCS*, pages 72–85. Springer-Verlag, 1997.

[Smi00]   G. Smith. *The Object-Z Specification Language*. Advances in Formal Methods. Kluwer Academic Publishers, 2000.

[Spi92]   J.M. Spivey. *The Z Notation: A Reference Manual*. Prentice Hall, 2nd edition, 1992.

[SS99]   H. Saïdi and N. Shankar. Abstract and model check while you prove. In N. Halbwachs and D. Peled, editors, *Computer Aided Verification (CAV 99)*, volume 1633 of *LNCS*, pages 443–454. Springer-Verlag, 1999.

[TM95]   I. Toyn and J. McDermid. CADiZ: An architecture for Z tools and its implementation. *Software - Practice and Experience*, 25(3):305–330, 1995.

[Weh99]   H. Wehrheim. Data abstraction for CSP-OZ. In J. Woodcock and J. Wing, editors, *World Congress on Formal Methods (FM'99)*, volume 1709 of *LNCS*. Springer-Verlag, 1999.

[WS03]   K. Winter and G. Smith. Compositional verification for Object-Z. In *3rd International Conference of Z and B Users (ZB 2003)*, LNCS. Springer-Verlag, 2003. This volume.

[WVF97]   J. M. Wing and M. Vaziri-Farahani. A case study in model checking software systems. *Science of Computer Programming*, 28:273–299, 1997.

Compositional Verification for Object-Z

Kirsten Winter and Graeme Smith

Software Verification Research Centre
University of Queensland 4072, Australia
{kirsten, smith}@svrc.uq.edu.au

Abstract. This paper presents a framework for compositional verification of Object-Z specifications. Its key feature is a proof rule based on decomposition of hierarchical Object-Z models. For each component in the hierarchy local properties are proven in a single proof step. However, we do not consider components in isolation. Instead, components are envisaged in the context of the referencing super-component and proof steps involve assumptions on properties of the sub-components. The framework is defined for Linear Temporal Logic (LTL).

1 Introduction

Object-Z [Smi00,Smi92] is an extension to Z [Spi92] which facilitates modelling in an object-oriented style through the addition of classes. Thus, an Object-Z specification models a system in a natural way by means of its components. It seems quite obvious to suggest a *compositional* approach for the analysis of such specifications that exploits this compositional structure. This raises the questions: Is it possible to split the proof task for the whole system into smaller sub-tasks in which we consider only a single sub-component at a time? Are these sub-tasks suited to being solved by model checking?

Smith [Smi95b] suggests an approach for modular reasoning by means of an axiomatic semantics which provides a deductive system based on the logic W [WB92]. This semantics allows single state and operation schemas to be analysed enabling class invariants to be proved by structural induction. When a class is used as an object within another class, its invariants can be used to help prove invariants of the incorporating class. Arbitrary properties on the behaviour of classes, however, cannot be proven.

Similarly, Griffiths [Gri97] introduces an approach for modular reasoning for Object-Z facilitating proof-steps for single classes. As in [Smi95b], this work is based on a reference semantics for Object-Z. Griffiths adopts a particular view on the reference semantics that allows for *strict modularity*. Strict modularity renders classes semantically independent of the rest of the specification. The semantic properties of an object are thus independent of its environment and can be proven in isolation (in contrast to system properties which must be proven for a particular specification as a whole). To achieve this independence, operations involving calls to operations in other components are considered to consist of an internal transition and an external interaction. Similarly, an independence of the object's state is achieved by viewing attributes of other components as referenced variables which do not influence the local state semantically. The effect is that components are treated as *open* systems whose environment is unknown, and hence unconstrained.

Both approaches were developed for use with an interactive theorem prover (e.g., [SKS02]). Theorem provers have no limitation in terms of the model's state space and its environment. However, as soon as model checking is considered for the verification task, the complexity of the state space of targeted components becomes a vital criterion for applicability. Model checkers, as automated tools, handle finite systems that are *closed*. That is, the component has to be considered together with its environment. If the environment is unrestricted (as in the approach of Griffiths [Gri97]), this leads to an explosion of the state space and makes model checking infeasible.

In this paper we present an approach for modular verification of Object-Z specifications aimed at using model checking. It does not consider single components of a system in isolation but *maximal restrictions* of components. A maximal restriction of a component represents an object in the *specific* context in which it is used. The environment is thus restricted to the conditions of the actual specification. This notion allows us to treat the smallest possible entity of a complex system at each step. Since the context imposes restrictions on the behaviour of a component, impossible behaviour is cut out.

The components in our approach are objects, not classes. Classes could also be considered as components since they can be incorporated into other classes via inheritance. However, the flexibility of inheritance in Object-Z, and especially the ability to cancel and redefine operations [Smi00], means that behavioural properties are not in general shared between a class and the classes it inherits. Hence, the potential for modular reasoning is limited.

Maximally restricted components can only be defined for hierarchical object systems without circularities. Therefore, our approach focuses on Object-Z specifications with fixed object hierarchies and with value semantics [Smi92] rather than reference semantics. As shown recently by Smith [Smi02], Object-Z specifications with value semantics can be refined to those with reference semantics. Hence, our approach does not limit the potential for transformation of specifications to object-oriented code. It does, however, focus reasoning on the functionality of the specified system rather than the lower-level details of the object-oriented design.

Restrictions on components are not only given through the context of the super-component but also through the properties of the sub-components. For instance, not much can be proven about the behaviour of a component without any knowledge of the effect of operations of its sub-components that are involved in the behaviour. To solve this problem we adopt the *assume-guarantee style* reasoning that is suggested for the verification of parallel processes and hardware designs (e.g., [Pnu85,GL94]).

Within the assume-guarantee paradigm, assumptions about the environment are employed when verifying properties of a process. Properties are stated as a triple of the form $\langle\varphi\rangle M\langle\psi\rangle$, where φ and ψ are temporal logic formulas and M is a process. This triple is satisfied if M satisfies ψ whenever the environment of M satisfies φ. A typical proof rule of this paradigm supports compositional reasoning, e.g.:

$$\frac{\langle true \rangle \quad M \quad \langle \varphi \rangle \qquad \langle \varphi \rangle \quad M' \quad \langle \psi \rangle}{\langle true \rangle \; M \parallel M' \; \langle \psi \rangle}$$

The overall system consists of the sub-process M and M' running in parallel. Properties on each sub-process are proven in single steps where property φ, proven for process M, is used as an *assumption* to prove property ψ on process M'. From these two proof steps it can be concluded that property ψ also holds for the system as a whole.

We adopt the assume-guarantee paradigm for a compositional proof rule for Object-Z. The parallel composition of two processes $M \parallel M'$ is replaced by the concept of *incorporating* maximal restrictions of Object-Z components. We base the formal definition of incorporating components and maximal restrictions of components on *OZ structures*. An OZ structure defines the semantics of an Object-Z component in terms of a temporal structure (or Kripke structure). This provides the foundation for the compositional proof strategy for Object-Z and allows us to prove soundness of the corresponding proof rule for Linear Temporal Logic (LTL) [Eme90].

Section 2 introduces our compositional strategy in terms of maximal restrictions of system components. The underlying concept of OZ structures and their corresponding operations are formally defined in Section 3 and Section 4. This formalisation is used in Section 5 to formalise our proof rule in order to prove its soundness. We conclude in Section 6 with a discussion of future directions.

2 Decomposition of an Object-Z Class Hierarchy

Our work is based on a value semantics for Object-Z [Smi95a]. As a consequence, an Object-Z model does not specify any object references. Instead, a class may instantiate other objects, which are then part of the class. Therefore, we are able to give a *hierarchy of components* that is free of circularities. Each component is instantiated by one *super-component*, i.e., this super-component is unique, and it can only refer to *sub-components* that are strictly lower in the hierarchy (see Figure 1 where unsuitable relations between classes are crossed out). The hierarchy is given in terms of *levels*. The

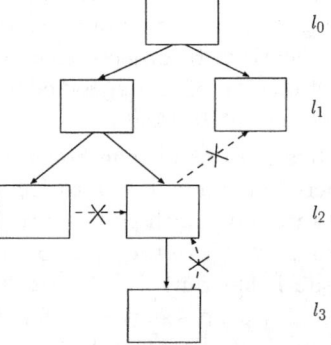

Fig. 1: Hierarchy of components for value semantics

example in Figure 1 comprises levels l_0, l_1, l_2, and l_3. We exclude models in which one operation evokes more than one operation on the same sub-component (since this violates Object-Z's history semantics [Smi95a]).

Semantically, every super-component together with its sub-components can be considered as an object of an ordinary Object-Z class in which the class definition of each sub-component is simply *incorporated* into the class definition of the super-component.

Example. We present a simple example of a super-component incorporating its sub-component. Assume we define two classes D and A as follows:

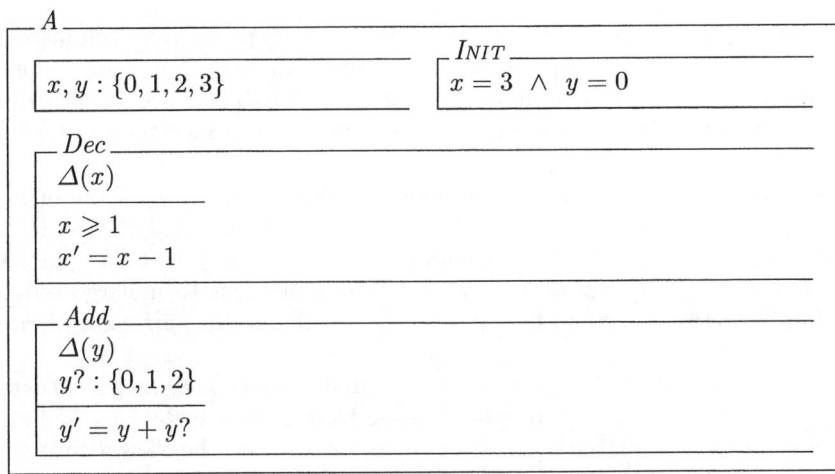

Class D, the class of the super-component, contains an object a of class A, the sub-component. The full system of A incorporated into D can be modelled as an Object-Z class B below. The operations incorporated from class A are not included in B's visibility list. The operation $a.Dec$ is called from D's operation Dec. The operation $a.Add$ is not used by D and so can never occur.

```
┌─ B ─────────────────────────────────────────────────────┐
│ ↾(n, a.x, a.y, INIT, Inc, Dec, Both)                    │
│ ┌─────────────────────────┐  ┌─ INIT ──────────────────┐│
│ │ n : {0, 1, 2}           │  │ a.x = 3 ∧ a.y = 0 ∧ n = 0││
│ │ a.x, a.y : {0, 1, 2, 3} │  └─────────────────────────┘│
│ ├─────────────────────────┤                             │
│ │ a.x > n                 │                             │
│ └─────────────────────────┘                             │
│ ┌─ a.Dec ─────────────────┐  ┌─ a.Add ─────────────────┐│
│ │ Δ(a.x)                  │  │ Δ(a.y)                  ││
│ │                         │  │ y? : {0, 1, 2}          ││
│ ├─────────────────────────┤  ├─────────────────────────┤│
│ │ a.x ⩾ 1                 │  │ a.y' = a.y + y?         ││
│ │ a.x' = a.x − 1          │  └─────────────────────────┘│
│ └─────────────────────────┘                             │
│ Inc ≙ [ Δ(n) | n' = n + 1 ]                             │
│ Dec ≙ [ a.x > 1 ] ∧ a.Dec                               │
│ Both ≙ Inc ∧ Dec                                        │
└─────────────────────────────────────────────────────────┘
```

Note that B is self-contained with respect to all definitions of state variables and operations that are used within the class. The object declaration $a : A$ has been replaced by declarations of two new variables representing its state variables x and y. To avoid name clashes, the names of these variables include the prefix '$a.$' (i.e., $a.x$, $a.y$).

2.1 Maximally Restricted Components

While proving properties, however, we would like a stepwise approach instead of targeting a component incorporating all its sub-components. We want to be able to consider only the smallest sub-system at each step. Therefore, we are aiming at the *maximal restriction* for each component within a hierarchy of Object-Z components.

The maximal restriction of a component is defined in terms of the operator *driven by*: A component a of class A is *driven by* a component d of class D. This operator captures the notion of a component operating within the particular context of its super-component. It allows the component to undergo only the subset of its class's behaviour that is actually possible in the particular hierarchy that is given.

We define the driven-by operator more formally based on temporal structures in Section 4.1. In terms of Object-Z classes, we can derive the class definition for a sub-component driven by its super-component from the class definitions of sub-component and super-component (classes A and D in our example) in four steps:

1. Replace the initial conditions of A with those initial conditions given in D that concern A (i.e., that contain state variables of A). Note that sub-components must be explicitly initialised in Object-Z using the notation $a.\textsc{Init}$ if this is intended. This is necessary since it is also possible that a

sub-component is not in its initial state when its super-component is in its initial state.
2. Add all state invariants of D to A which concern state variables of A. If such an invariant involves a state variable x of D then all occurrences of x must be replaced by a local variable which can take on any value of x's type.
3. Remove all operations from A that are never called in D.
4. Add all preconditions that occur on A's operations within D to the operations in A.

The following example shows how to apply this simple procedure to a given Object-Z model.

Example revisited. Given the class definitions of D and A as above, then the driven sub-component a is an object of a class C which can be modelled as shown below. Note that all attributes in class C are referred to using the prefix 'a.', i.e., $a.x$ and $a.y$.

Class C contains only the operation Dec whose precondition is further restricted by the precondition $(a.x > 1)$, the precondition on the operation call in class D. Furthermore C adopts the state invariant on variable $a.x$ from D, ensuring that $a.x > 0$. To get this invariant we have to replace n, which is a state variable within class D, by its possible values and therefore have the expression $\exists\, m : \{0,1,2\} \bullet a.x > m$. The initial state remains unchanged since it coincides with the initial condition in class D.

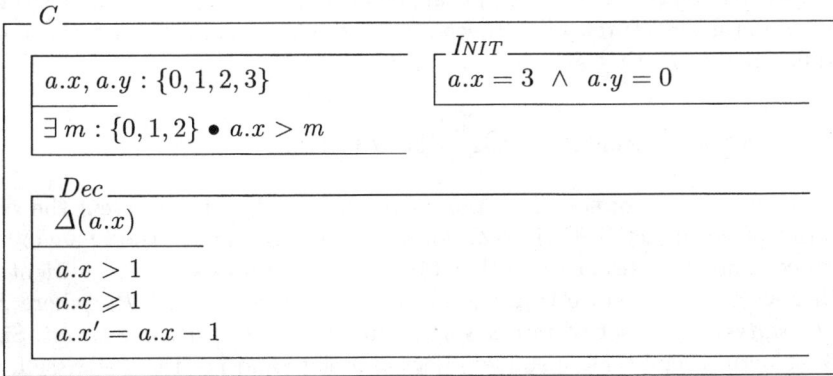

The *maximal restriction* of a component is given as the component driven by its maximally restricted super-component. We adopt the notation $\widetilde{[\,\_\,]}$ for the driven-by operator. Assume $c(i)$ is a sub-component on level i of the given hierarchy and $c(i-1)$ is the super-component of $c(i)$ on level $i-1$. Then the maximal restriction of $c(i)$ is denoted as $\widetilde{c(i)} = \bigl[\,c(i)\,\bigr]_{\widetilde{c(i-1)}}$. On the top-most level of a hierarchy $\widetilde{c(0)} = c(0)$.

2.2 Compositional Proof Strategy

With the definition of a maximal restriction of a component we can now introduce a proof strategy that relies on a decomposition of a hierarchy of components.

Assume we have levels $l_0, l_1, \ldots, l_n$ in the hierarchy of the given system specification. We start with the lowest level in this hierarchy, namely l_n.

1. For all maximally restricted components on level l_n, $\widetilde{c(n)}$, we prove some properties $\{\varphi_n\}$ that are *observable* in $\widetilde{c(n)}$. Properties are observable in a component if all free variables contained in the property are local state variables in the component.
2. We use the properties $\{\varphi_n\}$ which are proved on the components $\widetilde{c(n)}$ as *assumptions* for proving properties on the maximal restriction of the super-component $\widetilde{c(n-1)}$.
3. We repeat the last step until we reach the component on the highest level, $\widetilde{c(0)}$.

For this stepwise proof procedure the user has to find for each level the necessary observable properties that can be proven locally on a maximally restricted component and will be helpful to prove properties on the next higher level. The benefit of this approach is that at each step only the local behaviour of an entity has to be considered. We observe that the maximally restricted components on each level are smaller than components that incorporate all sub-components of all lower levels.

In the remainder of this paper, we formalise this procedure in order to prove it sound. We introduce a simple proof rule for temporal logic properties which is formally defined in terms of temporal structures. The next sections introduce these temporal structures for Object-Z, called *OZ structures*, and the corresponding operations that are used in our context.

3 A Z Specification of OZ Structures

In this section, we introduce the notion of an *OZ structure* to represent the value semantics of an object in Object-Z. An OZ structure models the behaviour of one object and its interface to other objects. It comprises a unique identifier together with a single state transition system of the form $\langle S, I, R \rangle$, where S is a set of *states*, I is a set of *initial states*, and R is a *transition relation*. Since an OZ structure represents a single object of a class and not the class itself, the identifier is needed in order to refer to the object from OZ structures of other objects in the specification.

Each OZ structure covers the information that is observable at its own level. Thus, the OZ structure of each component includes information about the interface to its sub-components, i.e., input variables, operation calls and the existence of output variables, but not definitions from its sub-components.

Inputs and output variables are embedded into the state space following the approach of Smith and Winter [SW03]. Special variables are included in the state to denote the component and sub-component events which occurred in the transition to the current state. A component may also refer to state variables of sub-components for the sake of restricting them, e.g., within state invariants. This allows state variables from the sub-component to be related to the local variables. Hence, such referenced variables are also included in the states of an OZ structure.

3.1 OZ Structure

A *state* of an OZ structure maps a finite set of (variable) names to their current values.

$[Name, Value]$

$State == Name \nrightarrow Value$

For notational convenience, we assume names comprise identifiers such as n, a, etc., denoting local state variables; $a.x$, $a.y$, etc., denoting sub-component state variables; and the special names ev and $a.ev$, etc., denoting the names of the operation last called locally and on sub-components respectively.

Values comprise allowable Z values as well as operation names. The latter are assigned only to names ev, $a.ev$, etc., and include the values *none*, which models that no operation was called, and *init*, which models that initialisation has just happened.

An OZ structure is defined as follows.

─── *OZStruct* ─────────────────────────
$Ident : Name$
$S : \mathbb{P}\, State$
$I : \mathbb{P}\, State$
$R : \mathbb{P}(State \times State)$
─────────────
$\forall s_1, s_2 : S \bullet \operatorname{dom} s_1 = \operatorname{dom} s_2$
$I \subseteq S$
$R \subseteq (S \times S)$
$\forall s : S \bullet \exists s' : S \bullet (s, s') \in R$
─────────────────────────────────

Apart from the identifier, OZ structures are defined similarly to *temporal structures* (Kripke structures) [Eme90]: Each state refers to the same variable names, i.e., the set of state variables cannot be increased or decreased in an OZ structure. The set of initial states is a subset of all states in the structure, i.e., $I \subseteq S$. The transition relation R is total, which is a characteristic of temporal structures. That is, each state in S has an outgoing edge. When deriving an OZ structure from an Object-Z class, this completeness can be achieved by adding to each state s without an outgoing edge (i.e., each state that is not a valid pre-state to any of the available operations) a transition back into itself such that no operation is called. However, since the event variable ev is part of the state space, we have to introduce a copy of the state in which we modify the event variable to *none* (i.e., all state variables remain unchanged except ev).

Usually, a labelling function L is defined for temporal structures which maps each state of the structure to a set of satisfied atomic propositions AP, i.e., $L : S \rightarrow AP$. In OZ structures, this information is encoded into the states themselves: The mapping from variable names to their current evaluation in a state provides the set of atomic propositions that are satisfied in the state.

The example revisited To illustrate our notion of structures we describe the structure of an object d of the class D of the example introduced in Section 2 in terms of its state graph (see Figure 2).

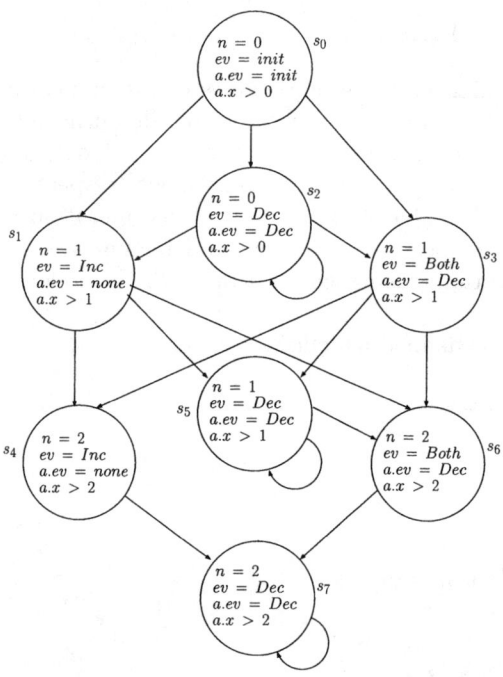

Fig. 2. Structure of object d of class D.

To keep the representation finite for the figure, we refer to the value of $a.x$ "symbolically" by means of the given state invariant stating that $a.x$ is greater than n. The states, in fact, represent sets of states that form a sub-graph whose behaviour is not distinguishable on the level of d.

Note that on the level of d the effect of operation Dec, and $a.Dec$ respectively, is not observable. Therefore, states s_2, s_5, and s_7 can loop forever. These looping transitions also help to provide a *total* transition relation between the states. Therefore, we do not have to introduce additional states in which no event occurs (i.e., $ev = none$). To prove properties in D, we obviously have to employ assumptions on the effect of $a.Dec$ on variable $a.x$.

3.2 Auxiliary Functions on OZ Structures

To allow for a relation between states of sub-components and super-components, we define an auxiliary *dot* operator as a meta-relation on states. This operator changes the names of a state to include a prefix reflecting the sub-component to which the state belongs. That is, given that id is the identifier of a sub-component and $x_1, \ldots, x_n$ are names in the domain of the state of that sub-component then:

$$id \underline{\ dot\ } \{x_1 \mapsto v_1, \ldots, x_n \mapsto v_n\} = \{id.x_1 \mapsto v_1, \ldots, id.x_n \mapsto v_n\}$$

We also define a notion of agreement between states. A state s_1 *agrees with* another state s_2, $s_1 \approx s_2$, if it has the same value for any name the two states have in common.

$$\begin{array}{|l}
\_ \approx \_ : State \leftrightarrow State \\
\hline
\forall s_1, s_2 : State \bullet \\
\quad s_1 \approx s_2 \Leftrightarrow (\forall n : \mathrm{dom}\, s_1 \cap \mathrm{dom}\, s_2 \bullet s_1(n) = s_2(n))
\end{array}$$

Additionally, we define a function *names* for retrieving the *domain* of a structure. The domain of a structure is the set of state variable names occurring in the domain of its states:

$$\begin{array}{|l}
names : OZStruct \to \mathbb{F}\, Name \\
\hline
\forall m : OZStruct \bullet \\
\quad \forall s : m.S \bullet names(m) = dom(s)
\end{array}$$

4 Operations on OZ Structures

We now define operations on OZ structures that correspond to the operations on Object-Z classes which are informally introduced in Section 2, namely *A driven by D* and *D incorporating A*.

4.1 A Driven by D

An OZ structure a can be seen in the environment of another OZ structure d, $[a]_d$. That is, we look at a within the context of d. This imposes those restrictions on states and initial states of a that are defined in d. Especially, the possible operations are reduced to those which are actually called by d.

This restriction is specified using the relation $\approx$ between states of the driven component and states of the driving component.

We define the OZ structure of a driven sub-component as follows:

$$\begin{array}{|l} [\_]\_ : (\mathit{OZStruct} \times \mathit{OZStruct}) \nrightarrow \mathit{OZStruct} \\ \hline \forall\, a : \mathit{OZStruct};\ d : \mathit{OZStruct}\ \bullet \\ (a, d) \in \mathrm{dom}\,[\_]\_ \Leftrightarrow a.\mathit{Ident} \in \mathit{names}(d)\ \wedge \\ (a, d) \in \mathrm{dom}\,[\_]\_ \Rightarrow \\ \quad (\mathbf{let}\ c == [\,a\,]_d;\ id == a.\mathit{Ident}\ \bullet \\ \quad c.\mathit{Ident} = id\ \wedge \\ \quad c.S = \{s : \mathit{State} \mid s \in a.S \wedge (\exists\, ds : d.S\ \bullet\ (id\ \underline{dot}\ s) \approx ds) \\ \qquad\qquad \bullet\ id\ \underline{dot}\ s\}\ \wedge \\ \quad c.I = \{i : \mathit{State} \mid i \in \mathrm{ran}\, a.R^{*}(\!|\, a.I\, |\!)\ \wedge (\exists\, di : d.I\ \bullet\ (id\ \underline{dot}\ i) \approx di) \\ \qquad\qquad \bullet\ id\ \underline{dot}\ i\}\ \wedge \\ \quad c.R = \{s : \mathit{State},\ s' : \mathit{State} \mid (s, s') \in a.R\ \wedge \\ \qquad\qquad (\exists\, ds : \mathit{State};\ ds' : \mathit{State} \mid (ds, ds') \in d.R\ \bullet \\ \qquad\qquad\quad (id\ \underline{dot}\ s) \approx ds \wedge (id\ \underline{dot}\ s') \approx ds') \\ \qquad\qquad \bullet\ ((id\ \underline{dot}\ s), (id\ \underline{dot}\ s'))\})\end{array}$$

All names in the domain of the states in a are substituted in $[\,a\,]_d$ by names with the appropriate prefix. For example, the variable name x is replaced by $a.x$ in our example in Section 2. This applies to all state variables, including the variable ev.

The set of states of a driven sub-component includes only those states of the sub-component that agree with a state in the super-component. That is, identical variable names carry the same value in these states. We use the dot operator to gain identical names, i.e., $(id\ \underline{dot}\ s) \approx ds$.

Similarly, the set of initial states collects all reachable states of the sub-component that agree with an initial state in the super-component. If the initial condition of the sub-component does not coincide with the initial condition of the super-component then the latter condition is adopted. That is, the initialisation of the driven structure is overwritten by the driving environment. However, initially the driven sub-component must be in a state reachable within the structure, i.e., in the range of the reflexive-transitive closure of relation R on initial states ($\mathrm{ran}\, a.R^{*}(\!|\, a.I\, |\!)$). This is required by the history semantics of Object-Z [Smi95a].

The transition relation of a driven structure is defined as a set of pairs of states of the sub-component that have a matching pair of states in the super-component. That is, for each transition (s, s') there is a corresponding transition in the super-component such that pre- and post-state agree with s and s' (modulo name prefixes).

4.2 Stuttering Components

If we consider components in the environment of super-components, we have to allow for non-active behaviour in which the super-component is active but not referring to the local operations of the driven sub-component. In terms of structures, this forces us to introduce *stuttering* behaviour of sub-components.

Stuttering is represented in a structure by stuttering states. A stuttering state leaves all state variables unchanged except the event ev which becomes *none*. The structure may stay arbitrarily long in a stuttering state before it becomes active again. Infinite stuttering is not excluded.

We formalise these additions to states and transitions in the following way. (Note that $id.ev$ denotes a name in this definition and not an expression.)

$$
\begin{array}{|l}
stutt : OZStruct \twoheadrightarrow OZStruct \\
\hline
\forall\, c : OZStruct \bullet \\
\quad c \in \mathrm{dom}\, stutt \Leftrightarrow (\exists\, a, d : OZStruct \bullet c = [\,a\,]_d) \land \\
\quad c \in \mathrm{dom}\, stutt \Rightarrow \\
\qquad \textbf{let}\ \ e == stutt(c);\ id == c.Ident \bullet \\
\qquad e.Ident = id\ \land \\
\qquad e.S = c.S \cup \{s : State \mid \mathrm{dom}\, s = names(c) \land s(id.ev) = none\ \land \\
\qquad\qquad\quad (\forall\, p : (names(a) \setminus \{id.ev\})\bullet (\exists\, cs : c.S \bullet s(p) = cs(p)))\} \land \\
\qquad e.I = c.I\ \land \\
\qquad e.R = c.R\ \cup \{s : e.S, s' : e.S \mid s'(id.ev) = none\ \land \\
\qquad\qquad\qquad (\forall\, p : (names(a) \setminus \{id.ev\}) \bullet s(p) = s'(p))\} \\
\qquad\qquad \cup \{t : e.S, t' : e.S \mid t(id.ev) = none \land t = t'\} \\
\qquad\qquad \cup \{q : e.S, q' : e.S \mid q(id.ev) = none\ \land \\
\qquad\qquad\qquad (\exists\, cs : c.S \mid (cs, q') \in c.R \bullet \\
\qquad\qquad\qquad\quad (\forall\, p : (names(c) \setminus \{id.ev\}) \bullet cs(p) = q(p)))\}
\end{array}
$$

An example of a stuttering component is given in Figure 3 where a and d are objects of classes A and D, respectively, of the example given in Section 2. The structure $[\,a\,]_d$ consists of the states s_0, s_1, and s_2. To get the structure $stutt([\,a\,]_d)$ we have to extend the set of states by s_{0B}, s_{1B}, and s_{2B}, in which the structure is passive. These states, although not important on the level of a, are necessary for generating a correct incorporating structure (see Section 4.3).

Again, this graph only shows events locally observable to a. Operation *Add* is never active in this structure since within the environment of d it is never called. Since the state variable $a.y$ does not occur in a delta-list of any of the operations of $[\,a\,]_d$, it remains unchanged in every state.

4.3 D Incorporating A

A system comprising an OZ structure d *incorporating* an OZ structure a is denoted by $d \ll \{a\}$. Since d may incorporate several objects, the right-hand argument is modelled as a (finite) set of the corresponding OZ structures. To be self-contained, $d \ll aset$ incorporates all definitions of state variables and operations that are referred to in the super-component d but leaves out non-referenced definitions and operations of the sub-components. The definition of $\_ \ll \_$ coincides with our suggested Object-Z model of class B in the example in Section 2 and is formalised as follows.

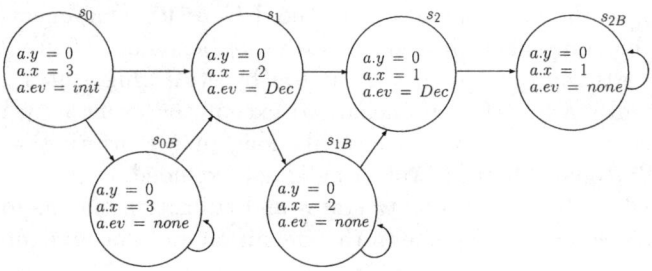

Fig. 3. Structure of the object $stutt([a]_d)$.

$$\begin{array}{l}
\_ \ll \_ : (\mathit{OZStruct} \times \mathbb{F}\, \mathit{OZStruct}) \to \mathit{OZStruct} \\
\hline
\forall\, d : \mathit{OZStruct};\ aset : \mathbb{F}\, \mathit{OZStruct} \bullet \\
(d, aset) \in \mathrm{dom}\_ \ll \_ \Leftrightarrow (\forall\, a : aset \bullet a.\mathit{Ident} \in \mathit{names}(d)) \wedge \\
(d, aset) \in \mathrm{dom}\_ \ll \_ \Rightarrow \\
\quad (\mathbf{let}\ b = d \ll aset;\ aset' = \{a : aset \bullet stutt([\,a\,]_d)\} \bullet \\
\quad b.\mathit{Ident} = d.\mathit{Ident} \\
\quad b.S = \{s : \mathit{State} \mid \mathrm{dom}(s) = (\mathit{names}(d) \setminus \{a : aset \bullet a.\mathit{Ident}\}) \\
\qquad\qquad\qquad\qquad\qquad\quad \cup \bigcup\{a : aset' \bullet \mathit{names}(a)\} \\
\qquad \wedge (\exists\, ds : d.S \bullet ds \approx s) \\
\qquad \wedge (\forall\, a : aset' \bullet \exists\, as : a.S \bullet as \approx s)\} \\
\quad b.I = \{is : b.S \mid (\exists\, di : d.I \bullet di \approx is) \\
\qquad\qquad\qquad \wedge (\forall\, a : aset' \bullet \exists\, ai : a.I \bullet ai \approx is)\} \\
\quad b.R = \{s : b.S, s' : b.S \mid \\
\qquad\qquad (\mathit{names}(d) \triangleleft s, \mathit{names}(d) \triangleleft s') \in d.R \\
\qquad \wedge\ \forall\, a : aset' \bullet \\
\qquad\qquad (\mathit{names}(a) \triangleleft s, \mathit{names}(a) \triangleleft s') \in a.R\})
\end{array}$$

The definition relies on restricting all sub-components a in $aset$ to stuttering components driven by the super-component, i.e., to the form $stutt([\,a\,]_d)$. As a consequence, the restrictions from the super-component are already included. All state variable names in the sub-components are given with an appropriate prefix (see definition of $[\_]\_$). The initial states do not necessarily agree with the initial states of each of the sub-components a but need only agree with one of their reachable states (see the definition of initial states in a driven structure in Section 4.1). Also, the sub-components include passive behaviour (when none of their operations are called).

This assumption keeps the definition of the operator $\ll$ very simple: Each state of the incorporating structure $d \ll aset$ contains those names that are names of the super-component d except the identifiers of the sub-components (i.e., $\{a : aset \bullet a.\mathit{Ident}\}$) and the names of the sub-components which are annotated with the identifier of the sub-component through prefixing (e.g., $a.x$).

Moreover, for each state in the state space of $d \ll aset$ there exists a matching state in the super-component as well as a matching state in the sub-components. This is defined by means of the relation $\approx$. Accordingly, each initial state of the incorporating structure has a matching initial state in the super-component as well as in each of the sub-components.

The definition of the transition relation ensures that each pair of pre- and post-states has a matching pair of states in the super-component and in the sub-components. The inclusion of stuttering states in the sub-components in $aset$ enables this definition of the transition relation to be satisfied.

5 Compositional Proofs

Based on the definition of OZ structures in Section 3 and operations thereof in Section 4, we are now able to formally define our proof strategy employing decomposition.

Following the strategy informally given in Section 2.2, a proof of a temporal property of a large hierarchical system is divided into smaller proof-steps. In each of these steps, we prove a *locally observable* property for a maximally restricted component on a single level. For proving local properties, we employ properties proven for the sub-components on the next lower level as *assumptions*. For the system depicted in Figure 4, three proof step are suggested: proof-step 1 involves component E and assumptions proven on sub-component F, proof-step 2 involves component B and assumptions proven on sub-components D and E, proof-step 3 involves component A and assumptions proven on B and C.

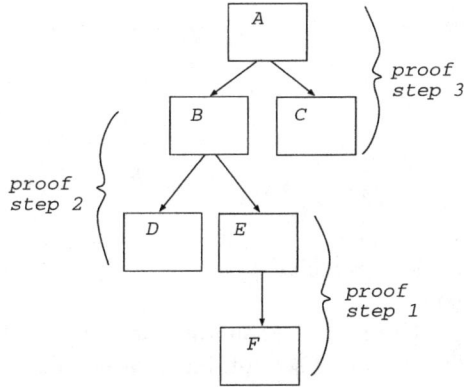

Fig. 4: Proof steps for a hierarchical system

To argue that this stepwise procedure is sound, we introduce the following proof rule on OZ structures.

Definition 5.1: Proof rule for hierarchical OZ structures

Let φ_e, φ, ψ be temporal logic properties and A and B be two OZ structures, where B is a sub-component of A. Then the following proof rule can be assumed:

$$\frac{\langle true \rangle \quad stutt([\,B\,]_A) \quad \langle \varphi \rangle}{\langle \varphi_e \rangle \quad A \ll \{B\} \quad \langle \psi \rangle}$$

If $\langle true \rangle$ $stutt([\,B\,]_A)\langle \varphi \rangle$ and $\langle \varphi_e \wedge \varphi \rangle A \langle \psi \rangle$ can be proven, we can deduce that $\langle \varphi_e \rangle$ $A \ll \{B\}$ $\langle \psi \rangle$ is satisfied as well. (Property $true$ represents that no assumption is made. φ_e represents any arbitrary assumption on the environment of the overall system.)

Using the proof rule above, our proof steps are simplified to local proofs on the smaller components $stutt([\,B\,]_A)$ and A instead of the incorporating structure $A \ll \{B\}$ as a whole. Structure $stutt([\,B\,]_A)$ reduces B to that part that is used within the context of A. Structure A does not incorporate attributes and state variables of B (other than those that are already referred to in A itself), instead the proof step relies on assumptions on the behaviour of B, namely φ.

The list of proof steps in our proof rule can easily be extended if we consider larger hierarchies of components (e.g., as shown in Figure 4):

$$
\begin{array}{lll}
\langle true \rangle & stutt([\,F\,]_E) & \langle \varphi_1 \rangle \\
\langle \varphi_1 \rangle & stutt([\,E\,]_B) & \langle \varphi_2 \rangle \\
\langle true \rangle & stutt([\,D\,]_B) & \langle \varphi_3 \rangle \\
\langle \varphi_2 \wedge \varphi_3 \rangle & stutt([\,B\,]_A) & \langle \varphi_4 \rangle \\
\langle true \rangle & stutt([\,C\,]_A) & \langle \varphi_5 \rangle \\
\langle \varphi_e \wedge (\varphi_4 \wedge \varphi_5) \rangle & A & \langle \psi \rangle \\
\hline
\langle \varphi_e \rangle \quad A \ll \{B \ll \{D, \{E \ll \{F\}\}\}, C\} & & \langle \psi \rangle
\end{array}
$$

Note that each single proof step targets a much smaller component than the overall system $A \ll \{B \ll \{D, \{E \ll \{F\}\}\}, C\}$ which incorporates six components.

We prove the soundness of our proof rule for Linear Temporal Logic (LTL). The following section introduces LTL and its semantics.

5.1 The Temporal Logic LTL

LTL is a temporal logic for which model checking algorithms exist. It is defined on *paths*, i.e., sequences of states of a temporal structure, in the following way [GL94,Eme90]:

Definition 5.2: Linear Temporal Logic (LTL)

LTL formulas are those which can be generated by the following rules
- each atomic proposition $n = v$ is a formula, where n is variable name and v a value in the domain (i.e., type) of n
- if φ and ψ are formulas, then $\neg \varphi$ and $\varphi \wedge \psi$ are formulas
- if φ and ψ are formulas, then $\varphi \mathbf{U} \psi$ and $\mathbf{X} \varphi$ are formulas

These rules allow us to derive formulas of the form $\varphi_1 \vee \varphi_2$, $\varphi_1 \rightarrow \varphi_2$ (implication), the Boolean constants $true$ and $false$, as well as $\mathbf{F}\,\varphi = true\,\mathbf{U}\,\varphi$ ("eventually φ") and $\mathbf{G}\,\varphi = \neg \mathbf{F}\,\neg \varphi$ ("always φ").

The semantics of LTL is given in terms of temporal structures (or OZ structures as defined in Section 3). A *path* of a temporal structure $M = (S, I, R)$ is an infinite sequence of states $\pi = s_0 s_1 s_2 \ldots$ such that $(s_i, s_{i+1}) \in R$ for all indices $0 \leq i$. The notation π_i is used for the suffix of path π starting at index i, i.e., $\pi_i = s_i s_{i+1} s_{i+2} \ldots$

Definition 5.3: Semantics of LTL

Assume M is a temporal structure, $\pi = s_0 s_1 s_2 \ldots$ a path of M, and $\varphi, \varphi_1, \varphi_2$ are LTL formulas.

$M, \pi \models (n = v)$ if and only if $(n \mapsto v) \in s_0$
$M, \pi \models \neg \varphi$ if and only if $M, \pi \not\models \varphi$
$M, \pi \models \varphi_1 \wedge \varphi_2$ if and only if $M, \pi \models \varphi_1$ and $M, \pi \models \varphi_2$
$M, \pi \models \mathbf{X}\,\varphi$ if and only if $M, \pi_1 \models \varphi$
$M, \pi \models \varphi_1 \mathbf{U}\, \varphi_2$ if and only if $\exists j (M, \pi_j \models \varphi_2)$ and $\forall k < j (M, \pi_k \models \varphi_1)$

A formula φ is called *valid* in structure M, if $M, \pi \models \varphi$ for any path π of M that starts in an initial state of M. That is, to satisfy an LTL property *every* possible behaviour of our system or sub-component has to satisfy the property. We lift the operator $\models$ to a relation on structures and formulas in order to denote *validation* of a formula in a structure which is then denoted by $M \models \varphi$.

5.2 Soundness of Compositional Proofs

Since the semantics of LTL is given in terms of the relation $\models$ we reformulate the proof rule given in Definition 5.1. The statement $\langle \varphi_1 \rangle M \langle \varphi_2 \rangle$ can be formulated in the following way: φ_2 is valid in M under the assumption that φ_1 holds if any path π from an initial state in M satisfies $\varphi_1 \rightarrow \varphi_2$, i.e., $M, \pi \models (\varphi_1 \rightarrow \varphi_2)$ for all π and therefore $M \models (\varphi_1 \rightarrow \varphi_2)$.

To ensure soundness of the proof rule, we have to prove the following theorem for all LTL formulas.

Theorem 1

$$\forall \varphi, \varphi_e, \psi \bullet stutt(\lfloor B \rfloor_A) \models \varphi \;\wedge\; A \models (\varphi_e \wedge \varphi) \rightarrow \psi$$
$$\Rightarrow \; (A \ll \{B\}) \models \varphi_e \rightarrow \psi.$$

With the two following lemmas the proof of Theorem 1 becomes straightforward.

Lemma 1 $\forall \varphi \bullet stutt(\lfloor B \rfloor_A) \models \varphi \;\Rightarrow\; (A \ll \{B\}) \models \varphi$

If a property is valid in structure $stutt(\lfloor B \rfloor_A)$ then it is also valid in structure $A \ll \{B\}$.

Lemma 2 $\forall \varphi \bullet A \models \varphi \;\Rightarrow\; (A \ll \{B\}) \models \varphi$

If a property is valid in structure A then it is also valid in structure $A \ll \{B\}$.

Intuitively, these lemmas are true since the structure $A \ll \{B\}$, the full system, is more restricted than structures A or $stutt([\,B\,]_A)$.

Proof of Theorem 1: Let φ, φ_e, and ψ be any LTL formulas. Assume $stutt([\,B\,]_A) \models \varphi$ and $A \models (\varphi_e \wedge \varphi) \to \psi$. With Lemma 1 and Lemma 2 it follows that $A \ll \{B\} \models \varphi$ and $A \ll \{B\} \models (\varphi_e \wedge \varphi) \to \psi$. According to the semantics of LTL, this implies $A \ll \{B\} \models \varphi \wedge ((\varphi_e \wedge \varphi) \to \psi)$ from which it follows that $A \ll \{B\} \models \varphi_e \to \psi$. □

For the proof of Lemma 1 and Lemma 2, we introduce two additional Lemmas, Lemma 3 and Lemma 4 later on.

In the following, we refer to S_A, S_B and S_{AB} as the sets of states of the corresponding structures A, $stutt([\,B\,]_A)$, and $A \ll \{B\}$ according to the definitions in Sections 3.1, 4.1, 4.2, and 4.3. A similar notation is used for sets of initial states I_A, I_B and I_{AB}, and transition relations R_A, R_B and R_{AB}. Recall also that function *names* provides the set of state variables of a structure (as defined in Section 3.2, note that $names(stutt([\,B\,]_A)) = names([\,B\,]_A)$).

Lemma 3 *For all paths $\pi^{AB} = t_0 t_1 \ldots$ in structure $A \ll \{B\}$ there exists a path $\pi^B = s_0 s_1 \ldots$ in structure $stutt([\,B\,]_A)$ such that $\forall\, i \geq 0 \bullet t_i \approx s_i$.*

For every path in the incorporating structure $A \ll \{B\}$ there exists a *corresponding* path in the *stuttering* driven sub-component $stutt([\,B\,]_A)$. That is, every state in the path of the incorporating structure has a corresponding state (i.e., a state that agrees with it) in the path of the driven component. This lemma holds only for sub-components which include stuttering states as defined in Section 4.2. They allow the sub-component to remain unchanged while the super-component calls operations outside the sub-component.

Proof: $\forall\, t_i$ in path $\pi^{AB} = t_0 t_1 \ldots$ in $A \ll \{B\}$ there exists a state $s_i \in S_B$ such that $(names([\,B\,]_A) \lhd t_i) \in S_B$ and $\forall\, i \geq 0 \bullet (s_i, s_{i+1}) \in R_B$ (per definition of R_{AB} in Section 4.3). It follows that there exists a path $\pi^B = s_0 s_1 \ldots$ in structure $stutt([\,B\,]_A)$. □

Using Lemma 3 we are now able to prove Lemma 1. The proof is given inductively over the structure of LTL formulas.

Proof of Lemma 1:

- Assume $\varphi = (n = v)$ and $stutt([\,B\,]_A) \models \varphi$.
  Proof by contradiction:
    Assume $A \ll \{B\} \not\models \varphi$

$\Rightarrow$ $\exists \pi^{AB} = t_0^{ab} t_1^{ab} \ldots$ of $A \ll \{B\}$ such that
$(A \ll \{B\}), \pi^{AB} \not\models (n = v)$
$\Rightarrow$ $\exists t_0^{ab} \in I_{AB} \bullet (n,v) \notin t_0^{ab}$
$\Rightarrow$ $\exists s_0^b \in I_B \bullet (n,v) \notin s_0^b$ (by definition of I_{AB})
$\Rightarrow$ $\exists \pi^B = s_0^b \ldots$ of $stutt([\,B\,]_A)$ such that
$stutt([\,B\,]_A), \pi^B \not\models (n = v)$
$\Rightarrow$ $stutt([\,B\,]_A) \not\models \varphi$ (by definition of $\models$)

- Assume $\varphi = \mathbf{X}\,\varphi_1$ and $stutt([\,B\,]_A) \models \varphi$.
  Proof by contradiction:
  Assume $A \ll \{B\} \not\models \varphi$
  $\Rightarrow$ $\exists \pi^{AB} = t_0^{ab} t_1^{ab} \ldots$ of $A \ll \{B\}$
  such that $(A \ll \{B\}), \pi_1^{AB} \not\models \varphi_1$
  $\Rightarrow$ $\exists \pi^B = s_0^b s_1^b \ldots$ of $stutt([\,B\,]_A)$ such that $\forall j \geq 0 (s_j^b \approx t_j^{ab})$ and
  $stutt([\,B\,]_A), \pi_1^B \not\models \varphi_1$ (by Lemma 3)
  $\Rightarrow$ $\exists \pi^B$ of $stutt([\,B\,]_A)$ such that $stutt([\,B\,]_A), \pi^B \not\models \varphi$
  $\Rightarrow$ $stutt([\,B\,]_A) \not\models \varphi$ (by definition of $\models$)

- Assume $\varphi = \varphi_1 \mathbf{U}\,\varphi_2$ and $stutt([\,B\,]_A) \models \varphi$.
  Proof by contradiction:
  Assume $A \ll \{B\} \not\models \varphi$
  $\Rightarrow$ $\exists \pi^{AB} = t_0^{ab} t_1^{ab} \ldots$ of $A \ll \{B\}$ such that
  $\nexists j (A \ll \{B\}, \pi_j^{AB} \models \varphi_2)$ or
  $(\exists j (A \ll \{B\}, \pi_j^{AB} \models \varphi_2)$ and $\exists k < j (A \ll \{B\}, \pi_k^{AB} \not\models \varphi_1))$
  $\Rightarrow$ $\exists \pi^B = s_0^b s_1 \ldots$ of $stutt([\,B\,]_A)$ such that $\forall j \geq 0 (s_j^b \approx t_j^{ab})$ and
  $\nexists j (stutt([\,B\,]_A), \pi_j^B \models \varphi_2)$ or
  $(\exists j (stutt([\,B\,]_A), \pi_j^B \models \varphi_2)$ and $\exists k < j (stutt([\,B\,]_A), \pi_k^B \not\models \varphi_1))$
  (by Lemma 3)
  $\Rightarrow$ $\exists \pi^B$ of $stutt([\,B\,]_A)$ such that $\Rightarrow stutt([\,B\,]_A), \pi^B \not\models \varphi_1 \mathbf{U}\,\varphi_2$
  $\Rightarrow$ $stutt([\,B\,]_A) \not\models \varphi$ (by definition of $\models$)

- Assume $\varphi = \neg \varphi_1$ and $stutt([\,B\,]_A) \models \varphi$.
  Proof by contradiction:
  Assume $A \ll \{B\} \not\models \varphi$
  $\Rightarrow$ $\exists \pi^{AB} = t_0^{ab} t_1^{ab} \ldots$ of $A \ll \{B\}$ such that
  $(A \ll \{B\}), \pi^{AB} \models \varphi_1$
  $\Rightarrow$ $\exists \pi^B = s_0^b a_1^b \ldots$ of $stutt([\,B\,]_A)$ such that $\forall j \geq 0 (s_j^b \approx t_j^{ab})$ and
  $stutt([\,B\,]_A), \pi^B \models \varphi_1$ (by Lemma 3)
  $\Rightarrow$ $\exists \pi^B$ of $stutt([\,B\,]_A)$ such that $stutt([\,B\,]_A), \pi^B \not\models \varphi$
  $\Rightarrow$ $stutt([\,B\,]_A) \not\models \varphi$ (by definition of $\models$)

- Assume $\varphi = \varphi_1 \wedge \varphi_2$ and $stutt([\,B\,]_A) \models \varphi$.
  $\Rightarrow$ $stutt([\,B\,]_A) \models \varphi_1$ and $stutt([\,B\,]_A) \models \varphi_2$

$\Leftrightarrow \quad (A \ll \{B\}) \models \varphi_1$ and $(A \ll \{B\}) \models \varphi_2$
(following the results from above)

$\Leftrightarrow \quad (A \ll \{B\}) \models \varphi$

□

The proof for Lemma 2 follows the same induction. In fact, all proof steps are similar if we use the following Lemma 4 instead of Lemma 3.

Lemma 4 *For all path $\pi^{AB} = t_0 t_1 \ldots$ in structure $A \ll \{B\}$ there exists a path $\pi^A = s_0 s_1 \ldots$ in structure A such that $\forall i \geq 0 \bullet t_i \approx s_i$.*

All paths in the incorporating structure $A \ll \{B\}$ have a corresponding path in structure A which does not incorporate all restrictions of sub-component B.

Proof of Lemma 4:
For all paths $\pi^{AB} = t_0 t_1 \ldots$ in $A \ll \{B\}$ it holds that $\forall i \geq 0 \bullet \exists s_i, s_{i+1} \in S_A$ such that $(names(A) \triangleleft t_i) = s_i$ and $(names(A) \triangleleft t_{i+1}) = s_{i+1}$ and $(s_i, s_{i+1}) \in R_A$ (with definition of path and R_{AB} in Section 4.3). It follows that $\pi^A = s_0 s_1 \ldots$ is a path in A.

□

6 Conclusion and Future Work

This paper introduced a compositional proof strategy for Object-Z that is inspired by results for the verification of parallel processes and hardware design (e.g., [Pnu85,GL94]). Based on a value semantics for Object-Z, this approach allows us to prove temporal properties given in Linear Temporal Logic (LTL). It aims at the use of model checking for single proof steps on sub-components. OZ structures, a concept for temporal structures of Object-Z components, is introduced as a semantic foundation of the proof rule.

We adopt a value semantics for Object-Z in order to avoid circularities in the hierarchy of the system specification. However, referring to work by Smith [Smi02], we argue that a system specification on an abstract level given in a value semantics can be refined to a more concrete specification in a reference semantics. Compositional verification, as suggested in this paper, is to be applied on the abstract level focusing on properties of a system's functionality, rather than details of its object-oriented design.

The sub-components to be considered in a single proof step in the compositional strategy are still possibly infinite structures. Thus, to render our approach feasible for model checking, a suitable *abstraction technique* is needed. An abstraction relation over temporal structures maps an infinite structure to a finite (more abstract) one which preserves the properties to be shown. The work by Smith and Winter [SW03] introduces such an abstraction technique for Z. Future work will investigate how this abstraction technique can be adapted for Object-Z and how it can be combined with our compositional proof strategy.

Further investigation is also necessary to develop a proof strategy for systems with a non-fixed hierarchy in which the number of components on each level may change.

Acknowledgements. The authors wish to thank the anonymous referees for their detailed comments on this paper. This work was supported by a University of Queensland External Support Enabling Grant.

References

[Eme90] E. A. Emerson. Temporal and modal logic. In J. van Leeuwen, editor, *Handbook of Theoretical Coomputer Science*, volume B. Elsevier Science Publishers, 1990.

[GL94] O. Grumberg and D.E. Long. Model checking and modular verification. *ACM Transactions on Programming Languages and Systems*, 16(3):843–871, 1994.

[Gri97] A. Griffiths. Modular reasoning in Object-Z. In W. Wong and K. Leung, editors, *Proc. of the Joint 1997 Asia Pacific Software Engineering Conference and International Computer Science Conference*, IEEE, pages 140–149. Computer Society Press, 1997.

[Pnu85] A. Pnueli. In transition from global to modular temporal reasoning about programs. In K. R. Apt, editor, *Logics and Models of Concurrent Systems*, volume 13 of *NATO ASI Series*, pages 123–144. Springer-Verlag, 1985.

[SKS02] G. Smith, F. Kammüller, and T. Santen. Encoding Object-Z in Isabelle/HOL. In D. Bert, J.P. Bowen, M.C. Henson, and K. Robinson, editors, *Proc. of Int. Conf. of Z and B Users (ZB 2002)*, volume 2272 of *LNCS*, pages 82–99. Springer-Verlag, 2002.

[Smi92] G. Smith. *An Object-Oriented Approach to Formal Specification*. PhD thesis, Department of Computer Science, University of Queensland, 1992.

[Smi95a] G. Smith. A fully abstract semantics of classes for Object-Z. *Formal Aspects of Computing*, 7(3):289–313, 1995.

[Smi95b] G. Smith. Reasoning about Object-Z specifications. In *Proc. of the Asia-Pacific Software Engineering Conference (APSEC95)*, IEEE, pages 489–497. Computer Society Press, 1995.

[Smi00] G. Smith. *The Object-Z Specification Language*. Kluwer Academic Publishers, 2000.

[Smi02] G. Smith. Introducing reference semantics via refinement. In C. George and H. Miao, editors, *Proc. on Int. Conference on Formal Engineering Methods (ICFEM 2002)*, volume 2495 of *LNCS*, pages 588–599. Springer-Verlag, 2002.

[Spi92] J.M. Spivey. *The Z Notation - A Reference Manual*. Prentice Hall, 1992.

[SW03] G. Smith and K. Winter. Proving temporal properties of Z specificatons using abstraction. In *3rd International Conference of Z and B USers (ZB 2003)*, LNCS. Springer-Verlag, 2003. This volume.

[WB92] J.C.P. Woodcock and S.M. Brien. $\mathcal{W}$: A logic for Z. In *Z User Workshop (ZUM'92)*, Workshops in Computing, pages 77–98. Springer-Verlag, 1992.

Timed CSP and Object-Z

John Derrick

Computing Laboratory, University of Kent, Canterbury, CT2 7NF, UK.
J.Derrick@ukc.ac.uk.

Abstract. In this paper we discuss a simple integration of timed CSP and Object-Z. Following existing work, the components in such an integration are written as either Object-Z classes, or timed CSP processes, and are combined together using CSP parallel composition.
Here we discuss the approach in general, and describe how the semantics of timed CSP can be used as the semantics of the integrated notation. We briefly discuss verification and analysis for integrated descriptions, before providing a more in-depth discussion of refinement in this approach. We describe both refinement of individual components, as well as a two-event model which distinguishes between start and end events. The latter allows operation duration to be specified and we show how refinement in this model integrates into traditional state-based simulation rules.

Keywords: Timed CSP; Object-Z; Refinement.

1 Introduction

In this paper we discuss an integration of timed CSP [15] and Object-Z [18]. The motivation for such a combination is a recognition that some of the hardest implementation issues in computer science involve the correct real-time scheduling of complex interactions. This has led to considerable work on notations which support the specification of timing of events. These include timed process algebras, such as timed CSP, as well as alternatives, such as timed automata [12], which offer related but distinct approaches to concurrency, interaction and time.

There has also been relevant work on integrating notations in order to provide a suitably expressive medium supporting a range of concerns such as timing, temporal ordering as well as data handling. Examples of these include integrations of CSP [10] and Object-Z, such as those described by Smith [17], Fischer [6,8] and Mahony and Dong [13].

In this paper we extend work in this area by investigating combinations of timed CSP and Object-Z which builds upon the integration of untimed CSP and Object-Z due to Smith [17] and Smith and Derrick [19,20].

In [17,19,20] Object-Z is used to specify the component processes of a system, and CSP is used to describe how the components synchronise and interact. The failures-divergences semantics of CSP is used to provide the integration with a sound semantic basis. This approach can be extended [4] by using CSP processes to describe the desired temporal ordering, in addition to describing the component integration. Here we extend this in the obvious fashion by using *timed* CSP to describe timing requirements on the events in the component processes, which are again specified in Object-Z. We consider a number of ways in which this can be achieved as well as discussing verification and refinement strategies.

Section 2 describes this integration via a simple example, and in Section 3 we discuss the obvious semantic basis for such an integration, i.e., the timed failures semantics of timed CSP. This is achieved by embedding the failures-divergences of an Object-Z component (as derived in [17,19,20]) into the timed failures model consisting of timed traces and timed refusals.

Subsequently, in Section 4, we consider to what extent verification and analysis techniques from timed CSP can be used on the integrated notation as well as discussing the compositional refinement of components.

Thus far the integrated language will have been described in terms of a simple and obvious correlation between CSP events and Object-Z operations. This so called one-event model, takes an atomic view of operations and is satisfactory for a simple specification and analysis of a specification. However, occasionally a more complex model is necessary and Section 5 discusses a two-event model whereby we are explicit about the beginning and termination of operations, and thus each operation is mapped to two events. We discuss in some detail refinement in this model and its relation with refinement in the one event model. Finally, we conclude in Section 6.

2 Combining Timed CSP and Object-Z

Object-Z is an extension of Z designed to support an object-oriented specification style. Throughout this paper we assume the reader is familiar with the Object-Z notation, introductions are provided by [5] and [18]. CSP on the other hand is a process algebra which models a system as a collection of processes which run concurrently, communicate over unbuffered channels and synchronise on particular events. Both [14] and [15] provide comprehensive introductions to the language.

As indicated in the introduction, we can combine these two languages by using Object-Z to describe the components and CSP to describe their interaction. The integration is described in some depth in [17,19,20], and we illustrate its essence with an example based around the classic lift case study [9].

We have a number of floors defined by the following:

$minFloor, maxFloor : \mathbb{N}$

$minFloor < maxFloor$

$FLOOR == minFloor..maxFloor$

Two of the components are given as Object-Z classes: *Lift* and *Con*. *Con* represents the central controller, operations *Close* and *Open* work the doors, and users external to the lift can *Request* a floor to go to. To communicate which floor the lift should be sent to a *SetTarget* operation is used, and the lift communicates which floor it has arrived at when it stops by using the *Arrive* operation.

The lift on the other hand, also opens and closes its own doors, and can accept requests from those inside it. The movement of the lift is modelled by two operations: *MoveOneFloor* moves the lift one floor at a time, and *Arrive* halts the lift at the desired target. This target is chosen from either the requests inside the lift or from the requests made to the controller. This is achieved by using two operations: *InternalTarget* and *SetTarget*. Only one of these will be invoked per lift movement cycle, and in the case of the latter it will synchronise with the same named operation in the controller.

This gives two components, the final one is described directly as a CSP process, which we use simply to specify the correct cycle of door opening and lift movement. CSP serves much better for this purpose than using, for example, Boolean variables in the Object-Z classes. Our top level description will thus be $LiftSys = Order \| Lift \| Con$, where:

$STATUS ::= open \mid closed$

___Lift___
$pos, target : FLOOR$
$req : \mathbb{P}\, FLOOR$
$door : STATUS$

___INIT___
$pos = minFloor \land door = open \land req = \varnothing \land target = minFloor$

___RequestD___
$\Delta(req)$
$f? : FLOOR$

$req' = req \cup \{f?\}$

___Close___
$\Delta(door)$

$door = open \land door' = closed$

___Open___
$\Delta(door)$

$door = closed \land door' = open$

___SetTarget___
$\Delta(target)$
$f? : FLOOR$

$target' = f?$

___InternalTarget___
$\Delta(target)$

$target' \in req$

┌─ *MoveOneFloor* ──────────────┐ ┌─ *Arrive* ──────────────┐
│ $\Delta(pos)$ │ │ $\Delta(req)$ │
│ ───────────────────────────── │ │ $f! : FLOOR$ │
│ $pos \neq target$ │ │ ─────────────────────── │
│ $pos > target \Rightarrow pos' = pos - 1$ │ │ $pos = target \land f! = pos$ │
│ $pos < target \Rightarrow pos' = pos + 1$ │ │ $req' = req \setminus \{pos\}$ │
└───────────────────────────────┘ └─────────────────────────┘

┌─ *Con* ───┐
│ ┌───┐ │
│ │ $req : \mathbb{P}\, FLOOR$ │ │
│ │ $pos : FLOOR$ │ │
│ │ $doors : FLOOR \to STATUS$ │ │
│ │ ─── │ │
│ │ $\neg \exists i, j : FLOOR \bullet doors(i) = open \land doors(j) = open \land i \neq j$ │ │
│ └───┘ │
│ ┌─ *Init* ──┐ │
│ │ $req = \varnothing \land pos = minFloor \land doors(minFloor) = open$ │ │
│ └───┘ │
│ ┌─ *RequestE* ──────────────┐ ┌─ *SetTarget* ────────────┐ │
│ │ $\Delta(req)$ │ │ $f! : FLOOR$ │ │
│ │ $f? : FLOOR$ │ │ ──────────────────────── │ │
│ │ ──────────────────────── │ │ $f! \in req$ │ │
│ │ $req' = req \cup \{f?\}$ │ │   │ │
│ └───────────────────────────┘ └──────────────────────────┘ │
│ ┌─ *Open* ──┐ │
│ │ $\Delta(doors)$ │ │
│ │ ─── │ │
│ │ $doors' = doors \oplus \{pos \mapsto open\}$ │ │
│ └───┘ │
│ ┌─ *Close* ─────────────────┐ ┌─ *Arrive* ───────────────┐ │
│ │ $\Delta(doors)$ │ │ $\Delta(req, pos)$ │ │
│ │ ──────────────────────── │ │ $f? : FLOOR$ │ │
│ │ $doors' = doors \oplus \{pos \mapsto closed\}$ │ │ ──────────────────────── │ │
│ │   │ │ $req' = req \setminus \{f?\}$ │ │
│ │   │ │ $pos' = f?$ │ │
│ └───────────────────────────┘ └──────────────────────────┘ │
└───┘

$Order = InternalTarget \to Q$
$\qquad \Box$
$\qquad SetTarget \to Q$

$Q = Close \to R$

$R = MoveOneFloor \to R$
$\qquad \Box$
$\qquad Arrive \to Open \to Order$

This produces an elegant and simple style of specification (process instantiation is achieved via parameterised classes, see [17]), with an intuitive semantic basis (as discussed below). The CSP has been used to describe synchronisation between components and the (untimed) temporal ordering. It is an obvious extension to add any necessary timing information by using timed CSP.

Timed CSP is an extension of CSP which contains additional primitives designed to support real-time specification. To the standard CSP primitives a number of new timing constructs are added including, for example, timeout, delay and timed interrupt.

To illustrate these consider adding timing information to the lift case study. The timing requirements we use are taken from [13] (for comparison with another integrated notation). In particular, we require:

- Once the lift door is open, it must remain so for at least t_0 time units before closing.
- Lift travel time between two consecutive floors is a constant (given by time t_1), but there is a constant time delay (given by t_2) for acceleration and braking.
- Any passengers inside the lift are given a period of time, t_3, to make an internal request before the lift accepts any external requests.

These can be expressed within a timed CSP model by the process *TOrder*, defined by[1]:

$TOrder = P \| CD$

$P = InternalTarget \rightarrow Q$
$\square$
$\quad WAIT\ t_3;\ SetTarget \rightarrow Q$

$Q = Close \rightarrow R$

$R = MoveOneFloor \xrightarrow{t_1} R$
$\square$
$\quad Arrive \xrightarrow{t_2} Open \rightarrow P$

$CD = Open \rightarrow WAIT\ t_0;\ Close \rightarrow CD$

The process P illustrates the delay operator, and the behaviour of $WAIT\ t_3;\ SetTarget \rightarrow Q$ is such that it delays for precisely t_3 time units before evolving to the behaviour $SetTarget \rightarrow Q$. That is, after t_3 time units (and not before), $SetTarget$ will be enabled.

---
[1] To make the subsequent presentation easier, we have explicitly avoided issues concerned with hiding some of the events such as *MoveOneFloor*.

The process $Arrive \stackrel{t_2}{\rightarrow} Open \rightarrow P$ illustrates another sort of delay, i.e. a delay after the occurrence of an event. Here $Arrive$ happens at any point in time, but $Open$ is not enabled until t_2 time units have elapsed after the occurrence of $Arrive$. A full description of the operators is given in [15].

Having expressed our timing requirements very simply in timed CSP, we can offer the obvious integration with the Object-Z component processes to define a specification complete with timing requirements as follows:

$TLiftSys = TOrder \| Lift \| Con$

Postponing for the moment a discussion of the semantics, the informal meaning of this specification should be clear. The temporal *ordering*, communication and effect of this specification is identical to that of *LiftSys*, however, the use of *TOrder* has introduced some precision into the time that events are performed within the lift and the controller. To confirm that our intuition of the meaning of this specification we need to consider the semantics of such an integration, and the next section considers this point.

3 Semantics

The combined Object-Z and CSP notation has been given a semantics as described in more detail in [17,19]. Combined Object-Z and CSP specifications are given a well-defined meaning by giving the Object-Z classes a failures-divergences semantics identical to that of a CSP process. In a failures-divergences semantics a process is modelled by a triple (A, F, D) where A is its alphabet, F its failures and D its divergences. The failures of a process are pairs (t, X) where t is a finite sequence of events that the process may undergo, and X is a set of events the process may refuse to perform after undergoing t.

To integrate Object-Z components in a failures-divergences semantics, the failures of an Object-Z class are derived from its *histories semantics*, as defined for Object-Z classes in [16]. A history is a non-empty sequence of states together with a sequence of operations. Either both sequences are infinite or the state sequence is one longer than the operation sequence, and the histories of a class with states S and operations O can be represented as a set $H \subseteq S^\omega \times O^\omega$ such that a number of properties hold (e.g., the histories are prefixed closed).

In order to derive the failures of a class from its histories, Object-Z operations are mapped to CSP events using the following function which turns an operation op with assignment of values to its parameters p to the appropriate event:

$event((op, p)) = op.\beta(p)$

The meta-function β replaces each parameter name in p by its basename, i.e., it removes the ? or !. Thus the event corresponding to an operation (op, p) is a communication event with the operation name op as the channel and an assignment of values to the basenames of the operation's parameters as the value passed on that channel. For example, the event corresponding to an object of class *Lift* requesting a floor l is $RequestD.\{(f,l)\}$.

It is then possible to define the failures directly in terms of the histories, and [19,20] describes how this is done in detail. Since Object-Z does not allow hiding of operations (hiding is only possible at the CSP level), divergence is not possible within a component. Therefore, a class is represented by its failures together with empty divergences.

For example, we can calculate the failures of the *Lift* class. The traces would contain elements such as (assuming suitable values for l, k, n)

$$\langle Open, RequestD.\{(f,l)\}, RequestD.\{(f,k)\}, SetTarget.\{(f,n)\},$$
$$InternalTarget, Close, MoveOneFloor, Arrive.\{(f,l)\}\rangle$$

and failures such as

$(\langle\rangle, \{Open, InternalTarget, MoveOneFloor\})$
$(\langle Close, RequestD.\{(f,l)\}\rangle, \{Close, MoveOneFloor\})$

This approach can be extended in an obvious fashion, and we will give combined timed CSP / Object-Z specifications a similar semantics by embedding the failures derived from the Object-Z components into a timed failures model, which is the semantic basis for timed CSP.

3.1 The Timed Failures Semantic Model

Timed CSP adopts a model of time in which events are instantaneous, time is modelled by the reals and passes with respect to a single global clock. The meaning of a timed CSP process is given by its timed failures, where in a manner similar to the untimed failures model, the timed failures model consists of timed traces together with timed refusals.

A timed trace is a sequence of timed events, where a timed event consists of a time together with an event, in which the times are non-decreasing. For example, if $t_3 = 4$, then $\langle (4, SetTarget), (4.5, Close), (4.5, MoveOneFloor)\rangle$ is a timed trace of the process P given above. $ttrace(P)$ denotes the set of timed traces of a timed CSP process P, and $trace(Q)$ denotes the set of traces of a (untimed) CSP process Q.

A timed refusal is a record of which timed events were refused during an execution, and thus a refusal set $\aleph$ is a set of timed events. The refusal of an event a at time t means that a is not possible at the state reached at time t, where at any time the refusal information is subsequent to the events performed at that time. Refusal sets of well-founded processes are conveniently represented by combinations (in particular, finite unions) of refusal tokens, the latter being sets of the form $[t_1, t_2) \times A$, where A is a set of events.

The timed failures of a process can be derived from its executions, and as expected a trace in the timed failures will be a sequence of events occurring in an execution, and a timed refusal will be a set of timed events which could be refused during that execution.

For example, the timed failures of the process P include:

$(\langle\rangle, [0,\infty) \times \{Close\})$
$(\langle(t, InternalTarget)\rangle, ([0,t) \times \{Close\}) \cup$
$\qquad ([t,\infty) \times \{SetTarget, InternalTarget\}))$

A number of projection operators are defined on timed traces, including $\uparrow$ and $\restriction$, where $s \uparrow D$ projects the trace onto an interval (i.e., produces a subtrace of s whose timings belong to D), and $s \restriction t = s \uparrow [0,t]$. In addition, for finite traces, $end(s)$ returns the time of the last event in the trace s. $strip(s)$ is the sequence extracted from s by removing the timing information. Projections are also defined on refusals, e.g., $\aleph \restriction A$ restricts the refusal set to events contained in A. $\aleph \uparrow t$ is the refusal set at and after t, and $\aleph \mid \restriction t$ the refusal set strictly before t. $s \downarrow A$ denotes the number of A events in s.

The set of events that appear at some time in $\aleph$ is denoted $\sigma(\aleph)$, and Σ denotes the universal set of events.

The timed failures of a timed CSP process P are denoted $\mathcal{TF}[\![P]\!]$ and the (untimed) failures of a CSP process Q are denoted $\mathcal{F}[\![Q]\!]$.

In order to give a combined timed CSP and Object-Z specification a well-defined meaning, we embed the failures of an Object-Z component into the timed failures semantics of timed CSP. A complete specification such as $TLiftSys$ will therefore have a meaning in terms of timed failures.

In order to embed failures into timed failures we can use timed refinement relations which map untimed models into timed models (for an overview see [15]). There are a number of these *timewise refinement relations* that can be used depending upon whether one wants to preserve just trace information or, in addition, include refusal information, but in each case the essence is that a timewise refinement of a process will be consistent with the untimed description.

Trace information. If we wish to consider only trace information we can use trace timewise refinement. In this approach a process Q is a trace timewise refinement of P if, for any trace s of Q, $strip(s)$ is an allowed trace of P. This is defined (for an untimed process P and a timed process Q) as:

$$P_T \sqsubseteq_{TF} Q \quad = \quad \forall (s, \aleph) \in \mathcal{TF}[\![Q]\!] \bullet \#s < \infty \Rightarrow strip(s) \in traces(P)$$

The traces of an untimed process do not include infinite traces, so this definition places no restriction upon the infinite timed traces of Q. However, as discussed in [15] this does not mean that Q has arbitrary infinite traces since the downward closure of timed failures means that all finite prefixes of any infinite trace of Q must be consistent[2] with P.

We then define the timed interpretation (which we denote $[\![P]\!]_t$) of an untimed process or Object-Z component (since this generates untimed failures) to be any timed failures produced from valid timed trace refinement:

$$[\![P]\!]_t = \bigcup_i \mathcal{TF}[\![Q_i]\!] \quad \text{where } Q_i \text{ is any timed process such that } P_T \sqsubseteq_{TF} Q_i$$

---

[2] Strictly speaking this holds for processes which do not contain infinite non-determinism, however, for the purposes of this paper we restrict ourselves to processes which only contain finite non-determinism.

Since $\bigcup_i \mathcal{TF}[\![Q_i]\!] = \mathcal{TF}[\![\sqcap_i Q_i]\!]$, this is equivalent to viewing the embedding of an untimed process P as being given by the choice of all possible timed processes consistent with P.

Thus this definition offers an interpretation of an (untimed) Object-Z component in the timed failures model such that the timed traces are consistent with the temporal ordering defined within the Object-Z component.

For example, consider the *Lift* component. Its *timed* interpretation according to this model will consist of elements $(s, \aleph)$ such that s is consistent with the untimed traces. Since one such untimed trace is

$$\langle Open, RequestD.\{(f,l)\}, RequestD.\{(f,k)\}, SetTarget.\{(f,n)\},$$
$$InternalTarget, Close \rangle$$

a valid timed trace consistent with this is

$$\langle (0, Open), (1.2, RequestD.\{(f,l)\}), (1.3, RequestD.\{(f,k)\}),$$
$$(1.3, SetTarget.\{(f,n)\}), (2, InternalTarget), (7, Close) \rangle$$

The overall behaviour of *TLiftSys* is given by combining the behaviours of *Lift*, *Con* and *TOrder* according to the standard timed CSP definition of $\|$.

Refusal information. More interesting and useful, though, is an interpretation which also considers refusal information. In order to interpret an untimed process P in a timed failures model we use failures timewise refinement. This is based on the observation that a timed refusal $(s, \aleph)$ will be consistent with P if $strip(s)$ is the untimed trace, and that the timed refusal will contain refusal tokens of the form $[t, \infty) \times X \subseteq \aleph$. That is, an event being in X means, in the context of time, that it could eventually be refused for ever after the performance of the trace $strip(s)$.

Failures timewise refinement is defined as:

$$P_{SF} \sqsubseteq_{TF} Q =$$
$$\forall (s, \aleph) \in \mathcal{TF}[\![Q]\!] \bullet \#s < \infty \Rightarrow$$
$$strip(s) \in traces(P) \land$$
$$\forall X \subseteq \Sigma \bullet ((\exists t : \mathbb{R}^+ \bullet [t, \infty) \times X \subseteq \aleph) \Rightarrow (strip(s), X) \in \mathcal{F}[\![P]\!])$$

As before this leads to the following embedding of an untimed process P into a timed failures model:

$[\![P]\!]_f = \bigcup_i \mathcal{TF}[\![Q_i]\!]$ where Q_i is any timed process such that $P_{SF} \sqsubseteq_{TF} Q_i$

Thus in terms of the *Lift* component, since we know that

$(\langle \rangle, \{Open, InternalTarget, MoveOneFloor\})$ and
$(\langle Close, RequestD.\{(f,l)\} \rangle, \{Close, MoveOneFloor\})$

are valid untimed failures, it follows that

$(\langle \rangle, [0, \infty) \times \{Open, InternalTarget, MoveOneFloor\})$
$(\langle (1, Close), (3, RequestD.\{(f,l)\}) \rangle, [3, \infty) \times \{Close, MoveOneFloor\})$

are valid timed failures of *Lift*. Note that in this interpretation an untimed event being enabled corresponds in the timed framework to an eventual offer. That is, it might not be offered straight away, however, it cannot be refused forever. An illustration of this is the fact that $WAIT\ t_3; SetTarget \rightarrow STOP$ is a timed process that is consistent with the untimed process $SetTarget \rightarrow STOP$.

Thus $[\![P]\!]_f$ provides a mechanism by which we can interpret Object-Z components in the timed failures model, and hence calculate the overall timed failures of a specification such as $TLiftSys = TOrder \| Lift \| Con$ described above.

4 Analysis and Refinement

In order to analyse a combined Object-Z/timed CSP specification, we can verify properties by expressing them as constraints on timed failures. In general, there are at least three types of properties that one might consider trying to verify for an integrated specification (an extensive overview of the range of analysis available in timed CSP is contained in [15]):

- untimed properties,
- properties on timed traces, and
- properties on timed failures.

These properties are expressed as predicates on timed failures using the notation familiar from CSP: P **sat** $S(s, \aleph)$, meaning $\forall (s, \aleph) \in \mathcal{TF}[\![P]\!] \bullet S(s, \aleph)$. For an integrated specification of the form $P \| C$ we can verify properties componentwise by using the following result [15]:

$$\frac{P \text{ sat } S_1(s, \aleph) \quad C \text{ sat } S_2(s, \aleph)}{P \| C \text{ sat } \exists \aleph_1, \aleph_2 \bullet S_1(s, \aleph_1) \wedge S_2(s, \aleph_2) \wedge \aleph = \aleph_1 \cup \aleph_2}$$

Verification of the timed CSP components, e.g., P, proceeds as normal, and with the embeddings of untimed processes into timed models, properties can be translated from an untimed context to a timed context. For example, with the trace interpretation if an Object-Z component C satisfies a property expressed in terms of its traces, i.e., C **sat** $S(tr)$, then this property can be translated to a timed interpretation: $[\![C]\!]_t$ **sat** $\#s < \infty \Rightarrow S(strip(s))$.

In a similar fashion properties expressed on both traces and failures can be translated from an untimed context to a timed context. So, if C satisfies a property expressed in terms of its traces and failures, i.e., C **sat** $S = (S_t(tr), S_f(tr, X))$, then this property can be translated to a timed interpretation: $[\![C]\!]_f$ **sat** T where $T = (\#s < \infty \Rightarrow S_t(strip(s))) \wedge \forall t : \mathbb{R}^+; A \subseteq \Sigma \bullet ([t, \infty) \times A \subseteq \aleph \Rightarrow S_f(strip(s), A))$.

As an example of this, deadlock freedom is preserved by such a translation. Thus we can calculate deadlock freedom on the individual components in an integrated Object-Z / timed CSP specification, knowing that their timed interpretations will also be deadlock free (although obviously not necessarily their parallel composition).

There are further properties that we might wish to verify that are independent of time. For example, the property that the lift doors alternate between being opened and closed can be expressed as

$TLiftSys$ **sat** $s \downarrow \{Close\} \leq s \downarrow \{Open\} \leq s \downarrow \{Close\} + 1$

and this is verified by showing that $Lift$ **sat** $s \downarrow \{Close\} \leq s \downarrow \{Open\} \leq s \downarrow \{Close\} + 1$. This amounts to showing the corresponding untimed version is true, and this can be verified for an Object-Z component using methods explained in [20].

Not all properties hold for each component. For example, the timed requirement that external targets cannot be set initially until after t_3 time units have elapsed is the following:

$s = \langle \rangle \Rightarrow SetTarget \in \sigma(\aleph \upharpoonright t_3)$

The $Lift$ and Con components do not satisfy this property, since they place no constraints upon the timings of events. However, it is sufficient to show that this property is satisfied by the timed CSP process $TOrder$, and since this component refuses $SetTarget$, the synchronisation must also.

As another example, consider the requirement that $Close$ must be available after a certain time, t_5 say, after a target has been set. If $got\_target(s)$ represents a new target having been set and $door\_open(s)$ the lift door being open, this property can be expressed as:

$door\_open(s) \wedge got\_target(s) \Rightarrow$
$\qquad (Close \notin \sigma(\aleph \upharpoonright (end(s \upharpoonright InternalTarget) + t_5)) \vee$
$\qquad Close \notin \sigma(\aleph \upharpoonright (end(s \upharpoonright SetTarget) + t_5)))$

However, this property doesn't necessarily hold for all the components. In particular, since the timed interpretation of $Lift$ is to allow all possible timings, some of these will indeed refuse $Close$ after t_5 of having received a target.

The property still holds for the complete specification however. In effect the timed interpretation of $Lift$ offers a choice of all possible timings, and the synchronisation with $TOrder$ chooses those which are compatible with the timed requirements in that timed CSP process. Verification of this property, therefore, is still possible for the complete specification. To do so what we need to note is that in $Lift$ and Con

$door\_open(s) \wedge got\_target(s) \Rightarrow$ pre $Close$

That is, $Close$ will be available with unspecified timing, and since the timed property holds for $TOrder$, we can easily conclude that the property holds for the complete specification.

4.1 Refinement

Compositionality results can also be obtained for refinement in the integrated notation. In CSP, refinement is defined in terms of failures and divergences [2]: C is a refinement of A if *failures* $C \subseteq$ *failures* A and *divergences* $C \subseteq$ *divergences* A

In an integration of (untimed) CSP and Object-Z, this serves as a basis for refinement in the integrated notation [20] (since the divergences of an Object-Z component are empty, we in fact need only consider the failures).

Because state-based simulations are sound and jointly complete with respect to CSP failures-divergences refinement [11], they can be adapted for use on the Object-Z components, enabling component-wise refinements to be undertaken (e.g., see the use of downward simulations in [20]).

We can follow a similar approach when combining timed CSP with Object-Z. In the timed CSP semantics the natural refinement relation is sub-setting of timed failures. However, in addition to the timed CSP components, some of our components are untimed Object-Z classes. Thus the natural question to ask is whether state-based refinement for the Object-Z components implies timed failures refinement (i.e., sub-setting of timed failures). This we show now.

Because simulations are sound with respect to CSP failures-divergences refinement [11], the question reduces to whether failures-divergences refinement implies timed failures refinement for their timed interpretation. Suppose, therefore, that the process P_2 is a failures-divergences refinement of P_1. We wish to show that, interpreted as timed processes, the timed failures of P_2 are included in those of P_1, i.e., $[\![P_2]\!]_f \subseteq [\![P_1]\!]_f$.

Suppose $(s, \aleph) \in [\![P_2]\!]_f$. Since the timed interpretations are constructed to be the closure of finite failures, it suffices to consider just the finite ones. For example, consider a failure $(s, \aleph)$ of the form $(s, [t, \infty) \times X)$ for some t and $X \in \mathcal{F}[\![P_2]\!]$. Then since $\mathcal{F}[\![P_2]\!] \subseteq \mathcal{F}[\![P_1]\!]$, we have $X \in \mathcal{F}[\![P_1]\!]$. Thus $strip(s) \in traces(P_2) \subseteq traces(P_1)$, and hence $(s, \aleph) \in [\![P_1]\!]_f$.

The consequences of this is that we can refine the Object-Z components in the standard fashion, i.e., using state-based simulations, knowing that their timed interpretations are timed refinements of each other. The next section considers more consequences of refinement, this time in the context of a two-event model of operations.

5 The Two-Event Model

The standard assumption in CSP and Object-Z is that events and operations are instantaneous, i.e., they are atomic and take no duration. In a timed context, however, one sometimes wishes to reason about the duration of operations, e.g., in the *Lift* the *RequestD* operation can probably be assumed to be atomic, however, *MoveOneFloor* in reality certainly does take time to complete. There are a number of ways of dealing with operation and event duration, and one of the simplest is to adopt the, so-called, two-event model.

The two-event model [7] considers an operation to be defined by its beginning and end, and thus two events are used to model each operation, allowing us to reason about start and end times, and therefore duration. Thus in the integration described here, we will distinguish between start and finish events explicitly in the timed CSP part, and map each operation in the Object-Z components to two events. This will allow us to be explicit about start and end times in timed CSP, whilst specifying the effects of the operation in terms of state changes in a single description.

Subscripts s and f denote the start and finish events associated with a single operation, the absence of a subscript denoting an atomic event. Thus one might write the following in the timed CSP component:

$$R = MoveOneFloor_s \xrightarrow{d_1} MoveOneFloor_f \xrightarrow{t_1} R$$
$$\Box$$
$$Arrive \xrightarrow{t_2} Open_s \xrightarrow{d_2} Open_f \rightarrow P$$

where here $Arrive$ is instantaneous, but $MoveOneFloor$ and $Open$ have durations as specified.

To integrate Object-Z into this framework we need a model whereby operations are embedded into the semantics as two, instead of one, events. Since timings are absent from the Object-Z components, we work at the untimed level, and thus consider how to embed a two-event model into the Object-Z history semantics, and hence into the failures semantics.

There are a number of ways to split a single operation into two events. The choice we take here is that the start event determines when the operation is possible (and determines what inputs are used), and the end event determines the after state and the outputs, where the state space the end event works with is that identified by the start event.

We will thus split an operation Op into two events embedded in the history semantics. The two events are effectively an enabled and an effect part. The enabled part, called Op_s, is enabled on an instance of the precondition and does not change the state, i.e., $Op_s = Y \land \Xi State$ where Y is an instance of the precondition (this can be encoded as a schema in the schema calculus but we omit the details here).

The effect part, called Op_f, is the effect of the operation if we have chosen this particular instance (i.e., a particular set of bindings that satisfies the precondition) of the precondition, and this can be expressed as $\exists\, outputsof\,\overline{Y} \bullet \overline{Y}' \,\raisebox{0.1em}{$\mathrm{\scriptstyle 9}$}\, Op$. Here $\overline{Y}$ is an IO decoration [4] that turns all inputs in Y to outputs with the same basename. These outputs are then consumed by the operation Op (and hidden so that they are no longer visible), this ensures that Op is being applied using before states and inputs consistent with those chosen by the particular instance Y.

So, for example, for the operation

$\begin{array}{|l}\underline{\mathit{Op}}\\ \Delta(x) \\ n?, m! : \mathbb{N} \\ \hline n? \geq 2 \land x = 1 \land x' = 2 \\ m! = n? + 1 \\ \end{array}$

we have pre $Op \mathrel{\widehat{=}} [n? : \mathbb{N} \mid x = 1 \wedge n? \geq 2]$, and this will give rise to pairs of events in the history model. For example, one instance of the precondition is $[n? : \mathbb{N} \mid x = 1 \wedge n? = 3]$. If we call this Y, then $\overline{Y}$ will be $[n! : \mathbb{N} \mid x = 1 \wedge n! = 3]$, and thus $\overline{Y}'$ will be $[n! : \mathbb{N} \mid x' = 1 \wedge n! = 3]$. We can then form the composition $\exists\, outputsof\,\overline{Y} \bullet \overline{Y}' \mathbin{\raise.3pt\hbox{$\mathchar"203A$}} Op$ which will then be the end event associated with the start event given by Y:

$$\exists\, n! \bullet [n! : \mathbb{N} \mid x' = 1 \wedge n! = 3] \mathbin{\raise.3pt\hbox{$\mathchar"203A$}} Op = [\Delta(x)\, m! : \mathbb{N} \mid x' = 2 \wedge m! = 4]$$

Notice that we are splitting the operation into two events, rather than two operations, i.e., we have a single operation which gives rise to two events in the history semantics, and these events correspond to all instances $Y \wedge \Xi State$ and $\exists\, outputsof\,\overline{Y} \bullet \overline{Y}' \mathbin{\raise.3pt\hbox{$\mathchar"203A$}} Op$.

In embedding these events into the history semantics, we need to make sure that the histories of each component correspond to ones consistent with the interpretation of starting and finishing an operation. In particular, we require:

- operations must start before they finish;
- the termination of operations cannot be refused after they have started;
- operations must eventually terminate after they have started.

The histories derived from an Object-Z component using this two-event model will therefore be subject to a number of healthiness conditions that represent the points highlighted. The histories, remember, are sequences of states and operations which represent the evolution of an object. A history h is a tuple $(s, o) \in S^\omega \times O^\omega$, where O^ω is the set of sequences of operations (that an object could evolve through). The healthiness conditions are restrictions on the allowable histories, and reflect the structure of the operation sequence o. The first and third conditions can be written as:

- $(\neg \exists i \bullet o(i) = Op_f \wedge \forall j \leq i \bullet o(j) \neq Op_s) \wedge \#\{i \mid o(i) = Op_s\} = \#\{i \mid o(i) = Op_f\}$
- If $o \notin O^*$ then $\#\{i \mid o(i) = Op_s\} = \#\{i \mid o(i) = Op_f\}$

In the latter condition, O^* is the set of finite sequences of operations, and this condition thus formalises the requirement that operations must terminate if started. Note that an explicit condition for the second point is not necessary since by construction of the two events corresponding to an operation, Op_f can never be refused given Op_s has occurred.

The particular two-event model we have chosen uses the initial state for computation of the after state, and this has consequences for how operations can be interleaved.

Because the before state and inputs have been fixed by the start event, once the start event has occurred, the end event can never be refused (i.e., $Y \wedge \Xi State \vdash \mathrm{pre}(\exists\, outputsof\,\overline{Y} \bullet \overline{Y}' \mathbin{\raise.3pt\hbox{$\mathchar"203A$}} Op))$. In addition, it means that in any interleaving of operations, the result of an operation depends only upon when it was invoked, and the final state depends only upon the last operation to terminate. This guarantees that operations, once invoked, cannot be interfered with. Again we note that other choices of two-event model might take a different approach in this respect.

With start and finish events made explicit within the timed CSP part of the specification, a wider range of behaviours can be described. For example, we might wish to specify some fault tolerant behaviour, given by a process FTB, which is invoked if the doors do not close properly. This could be specified by:

$$Q = Close_s \rightarrow ((WAIT\ d_2;\ Close_f \rightarrow R) \triangleright^{d_3} FTB)$$

saying that it takes at least d_2 time units to close the doors, but if they haven't closed by d_3 then invoke the fault tolerant mechanism. Here, $\triangleright^{d_3}$ is the timeout operator. In general, the process $P \triangleright^d Q$ offers a time-sensitive choice between P and Q. Initially the process P is available, and if P performs some external event before d time has elapsed then the choice is resolved in favour of P. However, if P does not perform any external event before d time has elapsed then the choice is resolved in favour of Q.

The whole process of using a two-event model thus consists of the following. In an integrated specification $P \| C$, where P is a CSP process and C an Object-Z class, we first specify start and finish events in the CSP process for those events which we wish to have explicit duration. The correct synchronisation between components is found by determining the timed failures semantics of P and C and then calculating the composition. The timed failures semantics of C is often intuitive, but if not can be calculated via the history semantics of Object-Z.

When deriving the history semantics for C, we use a two-event interpretation for those events in P which use a two-event model. Histories which do not satisfy the healthiness conditions are removed. The failures semantics, and hence the timed failures semantics, is then derived from the remaining histories, and synchronisation between events in P and C then yields the complete specification with timing information embedded in it.

5.1 Refinement

By embedding a single operation as two events in the semantics, we have broken the original symmetry between operations and events. Since state-based simulations were used on Object-Z components, as they correspond to failures-divergences refinement at the semantic level, the natural question to ask is whether this result still holds for the two-event model. In fact, the result is still valid as we illustrate now.

To verify the result we need to work in the framework defined by Joseph [11] that provides a link between simulations and failures-divergences refinement. In this framework a process P is defined by a tuple $(A, S, \longrightarrow, R)$, where A is the set of events; S the set of states; $\longrightarrow \subseteq S \times A \times S$ its transition relation, and R its initial states. A transition under event e from state σ_1 to σ_2 is denoted by $\sigma_1 \stackrel{e}{\longrightarrow} \sigma_2$. In addition, the set of next possible events that a system P can undergo when in state σ is denoted $next_P(\sigma)$.

Simulations can be defined in this framework, e.g., the definition of downward simulation between two processes $P_i = (A, S_i, \longrightarrow_i, R_i)$, $(i = 1, 2)$ is as follows.

Definition 1 *Downward simulation*
P_2 *is a downward simulation of* P_1 *if there is a relation* $D \subseteq S_1 \times S_2$ *such that*

1. $\forall \sigma_1 \in S_1, \sigma_2 \in S_2 \bullet \sigma_1 \, D \, \sigma_2$ *implies* $next_{P_1}(\sigma_1) \subseteq next_{P_2}(\sigma_2)$
2. $\forall \sigma_1 \in S_1, \sigma_2, \sigma_2' \in S_2, e \in A \bullet$
   $\sigma_1 \, D \, \sigma_2 \wedge \sigma_2 \xrightarrow{e}_2 \sigma_2'$ *implies* $\exists \sigma_1' \in S_1 \bullet \sigma_1 \xrightarrow{e}_1 \sigma_1' \wedge \sigma_1' \, D \, \sigma_2'$
3. $\forall \sigma_2 \in R_2 \bullet \exists \sigma_1 \in R_1 \bullet \sigma_1 \, D \, \sigma_2$

As commented above, downward and upward simulations are sound and jointly complete with respect to CSP failures-divergences refinement [11]. What we show now is that the downward simulation conditions for a single event interpretation are equivalent to the downward simulation conditions for both start and finish events in the two-event model.

Consider the applicability condition:

$$\forall \sigma_1 \in S_1, \sigma_2 \in S_2 \bullet \sigma_1 \, D \, \sigma_2 \text{ implies } next_{P_1}(\sigma_1) \subseteq next_{P_2}(\sigma_2)$$

Now for any given event e we know two things. First, if $\sigma \xrightarrow{e}$ then $\sigma \xrightarrow{e_s e_f}$, and hence $\sigma \xrightarrow{e_s}$. Second, from $Y \wedge \Xi State \vdash \text{pre} \exists \text{outputsof} \, \overline{Y} \bullet \overline{Y}' \,\S\, Op$ we know that if e_s has occurred in a trace then e_f cannot be refused, and that if $\sigma \xrightarrow{e_f}$ then $\sigma \xrightarrow{e_s} \sigma \xrightarrow{e_f}$.

Putting these together means that the applicability condition is equivalent to the applicability condition for start events together with the applicability condition for finish events.

Correctness is similar. For example, given correctness for the single event interpretation:

$$\forall \sigma_1 \in S_1, \sigma_2, \sigma_2' \in S_2, e \in A \bullet \sigma_1 \, D \, \sigma_2 \wedge \sigma_2 \xrightarrow{e}_2 \sigma_2' \text{ implies}$$
$$\exists \sigma_1' \in S_1 \bullet \sigma_1 \xrightarrow{e}_1 \sigma_1' \wedge \sigma_1' \, D \, \sigma_2'$$

If $\sigma_2 \xrightarrow{e}_2 \sigma_2'$ then $\sigma_2 \xrightarrow{e_s}_2 \sigma_2 \xrightarrow{e_f}_2 \sigma_2'$. Correctness allows us to deduce that $\sigma_1 \xrightarrow{e_s}_1 \sigma_1 \xrightarrow{e_f}_1 \sigma_1'$. Correctness for e_s follows immediately from this. Correctness for e_f (and the reverse implication) follows for an arbitrary state if we again note that e_f is in a trace only if e_s precedes it. Thus if $\sigma_2'' \xrightarrow{e_f}_2 \sigma_2$ with $\sigma_1'' \, D \, \sigma_2''$, then $\sigma_2'' \xrightarrow{e_s}_2 \sigma_2'' \xrightarrow{e_f}_2 \sigma_2$, and correctness for e locates the necessary state in S_1 for correctness of e_f.

To summarise, we have shown that with the two-event embedding defined above, downward simulation for a single event model is equivalent to downward simulation for the two-event model. This is essentially due to the fact that applicability for the finish event and correctness for the start event are always true, thus the downward simulation for a single event splits into two conditions: applicability for the start events and correctness for the finish events.

The consequences of this is that even with this two-event model, state-based simulations are the correct refinement relations to use, since they generate simulations in the two-event model, and thus correspond to failures-divergences refinement in the two-event semantics. Another way to put this is to note that failures sub-setting of the two-event model can be verified by simulations for the single events.

This has important practical consequences. Because the correct state-based simulation rules are invariant with respect to the CSP model chosen, Object-Z components can be specified and developed independently without concern for whether the one or two-event model semantics will be used. This in itself is a good motivation for the use of this particular two-event model.

We can also explore the link with non-atomic refinement [3,4]. Non-atomic refinement is a generalisation of the standard Z and Object-Z simulation rules, and it deals with a change of granularity between specifications. In particular, non-atomic refinement defines simulation conditions for refinements where a *single* abstract operation is decomposed into a *sequence* of concrete operations. This has obvious links to the two-event model, since there a single event e has been decomposed to the sequence e_s; e_f.

In fact, it is easy to verify that in a relational setting the refinement between e and e_s; e_f corresponds to non-atomic refinement as defined in [3,4]. The link then to notions of action refinement in process algebras [1], however, remain to be made, and in particular the link to failure-divergences refinement has to be explored further.

6 Conclusions

We are not the first to consider integrations of timed CSP with state-based notations such as Z and Object-Z, nor are we the first to investigate a two-event model.

Integrations of timed CSP and state-based languages include those defined by Mahony and Dong [13] and Sühl [21]. The former produces a language called TCOZ, and is a monolithic integration which combines timed CSP and Object-Z in a rather non-compositional way. That is, the specification style involves writing a specification in a completely new notation rather than by combining components written in the individual languages as we have done here. A specification in [13] provided the basis for the lift example presented above, and comparing the two approaches and two examples it is clear that although TCOZ is very expressive, it perhaps lacks the simplicity of integration that we have achieved here.

The closest approach to our work is the language RT-Z as defined by Sühl in [21]. Indeed, the philosophy behind the two is close, although [21] uses Z as opposed to Object-Z. However, [21] does not provide a full discussion of the semantics as we have done here, nor does Sühl investigate the related notions of refinement.

RT-Z does, however, consider the two-event model, and an overview of the use of such models when combining process algebras with state-based systems is provided by Fischer in [7]. Indeed, [7] contains a useful comparison of single, double, and multi-event approaches to the granularity of operation decomposition.

As discussed by Fischer in [7] there is a potential problem with synchronisation in the two-event model. In particular, input parameters are included in the start event, and output parameters in the finish event. Then synchronisation via parallel composition is a potential problem, because the synchronisation needs to match input values with output values. The solution to this is to ensure that specifications which contain synchronisation on two-event events only have one way communication (indeed causality would suggest that synchronisation in an event with duration has to necessarily be one way). Then the first event of one component can synchronise with the second event of the other. However, the full consequences of this need to be explored further, and in fact we have restricted the use of two-events above to operations which needed no synchronisation.

The alternative approach is to adopt a multi-event model, with three events distinguished in general: start, finish and middle, and to ensure that all communication (which is hidden anyway) is achieved via the middle event which is introduced especially for this purpose. The usefulness of this model needs to be investigated.

References

[1] L. Aceto. *Action Refinement in Process Algebras*. CUP, London, 1992.
[2] S.D. Brookes and A.W. Roscoe. An improved failures model for communicating processes. In *Pittsburgh Symposium on Concurrency*, volume 197 of *Lecture Notes in Computer Science*, pages 281–305. Springer-Verlag, 1985.
[3] J. Derrick and E. A. Boiten. Non-atomic refinement in Z. In J. M. Wing, J. C. P. Woodcock, and J. Davies, editors, *FM'99 World Congress on Formal Methods in the Development of Computing Systems*, volume 1708 of *Lecture Notes in Computer Science*, pages 1477–1496, Berlin, 1999. Springer-Verlag.
[4] J. Derrick and E.A. Boiten. *Refinement in Z and Object-Z, Foundations and Advanced Applications*. Springer-Verlag, 2001.
[5] R. Duke and G. A. Rose. *Formal Object-Oriented Specification Using Object-Z*. Cornerstones of Computing. Macmillan, 2000.
[6] C. Fischer. CSP-OZ - a combination of CSP and Object-Z. In H. Bowman and J. Derrick, editors, *Second IFIP International conference on Formal Methods for Open Object-based Distributed Systems*, pages 423–438. Chapman & Hall, July 1997.
[7] C. Fischer. How to combine Z with a process algebra. In J. P. Bowen, A. Fett, and M. G. Hinchey, editors, *ZUM'98: The Z Formal Specification Notation*, volume 1493 of *Lecture Notes in Computer Science*, pages 5–23. Springer-Verlag, 1998.
[8] C. Fischer. *Combination and implementation of processes and data: from CSP-OZ to Java*. PhD thesis, University of Oldenburg, January 2000.
[9] C. Fischer and H. Wehrheim. Model checking CSP-OZ specifications with FDR. In K. Araki, A. Galloway, and K. Taguchi, editors, *International Conference on Integrated Formal Methods 1999 (IFM'99)*, pages 315–334, York, July 1999. Springer.

[10] C. A. R. Hoare. *Communicating Sequential Processes*. Prentice Hall, 1985.
[11] M.B. Josephs. A state-based approach to communicating processes. *Distributed Computing*, 3:9–18, 1988.
[12] N. A. Lynch and F. Vaandrager. Forward and backward simulations for timing-based systems. In J. W. de Bakker, W.-P. de Roever, C. Huizing, and G. Rozenberg, editors, *Real-Time: Theory in Practice (REX Workshop, Mook, The Netherlands, June 1991)*, LNCS 600, pages 397–446. Springer-Verlag, 1992.
[13] B. Mahony and J.S. Dong. Timed communicating Object-Z. *IEEE Transactions on Software Engineering*, 26(2):150–177, February 2000.
[14] A.W. Roscoe. *The Theory and Practice of Concurrency*. International Series in Computer Science. Prentice Hall, 1998.
[15] S. Schneider. *Concurrent and Real-Time Systems: The CSP Approach*. Wiley, 2000.
[16] G. Smith. A fully abstract semantics of classes for Object-Z. *Formal Aspects of Computing*, 7(3):289–313, 1995.
[17] G. Smith. A semantic integration of Object-Z and CSP for the specification of concurrent systems. In J. Fitzgerald, C. B. Jones, and P. Lucas, editors, *Formal Methods Europe (FME '97)*, LNCS 1313, pages 62–81, Graz, Austria, September 1997. Springer-Verlag.
[18] G. Smith. *The Object-Z specification language*. Kluwer Academic Publishers, 2000.
[19] G. Smith and J. Derrick. Refinement and verification of concurrent systems specified in Object-Z and CSP. In M. G. Hinchey and S. Liu, editors, *Formal Engineering Methods*, pages 293–302, Hiroshima, Japan, 12–14 November 1997. IEEE Computer Society Press.
[20] G. Smith and J. Derrick. Specification, refinement and verification of concurrent systems - an integration of Object-Z and CSP. *Formal Methods in System Design*, 18:249–284, May 2001.
[21] C. Sühl. RT-Z: An integration of Z and timed CSP. In K. Araki, A. Galloway, and K. Taguchi, editors, *International conference on Integrated Formal Methods 1999 (IFM'99)*, pages 29–48. Springer, July 1999.

Object Orientation without Extending Z

Mark Utting and Shaochun Wang

The University of Waikato, Hamilton, NZ.
{marku, sw19}@cs.waikato.ac.nz
http://www.cs.waikato.ac.nz/~marku

Abstract. The good news of this paper is that without extending Z, we can elegantly specify object-oriented systems, including encapsulation, inheritance and subtype polymorphism (dynamic dispatch). The bad news is that this specification style is rather different to normal Z specifications, more abstract and axiomatic, which means that it is not so well supported by current Z tools such as animators. It also enforces behavioural subtyping, unlike most object-oriented programming languages. This paper explains the proposed style, with examples, and discusses its advantages and disadvantages.

1 Introduction

Object orientation offers a technology for structuring large, complex software systems [Mey97], so many Z researchers have proposed different approaches for extending Z with an object-oriented structuring mechanism [SBC92]. These include attempts to use standard Z in a more object oriented style, and proposed extensions to Z to allow fully object oriented specifications. Some of them are being widely accepted, some are not.

One of the most popular extensions is Object-Z [DKRS91]. From our experience of Object-Z, we found that its state semantics in modelling objects is too complex. It is a better match for software implementation, rather than for software specification and design. In other words, its explicit state modelling is a structuring mechanism simulating object oriented programming (OOP), not emphasizing the abstract nature of object oriented analysis and design (OOAD). We believe that some of the mechanisms of object-oriented programming, such as non-monotonic inheritance and the use of reference semantics as the default paradigm, need to be specified abstractly in an object-oriented specification language and that OOAD can be supported with a simple but powerful semantics.

Our intension is to explore the semantics of object oriented concepts, and to specify object oriented systems in Z. The key insight of this paper is that by using an abstract model of objects, subtypes can be modelled as subsets; moreover, we can use subsets to model inheritance and dynamic dispatch. We also introduce an elegant encoding of objects into standard Z, which is described in Section 6.1.

The following sections illustrate the approach with a series of examples, gradually introducing more features and discussing their ramifications. Section 9 describes our conclusions and areas for future work. This paper uses a value semantics for objects, rather than reference semantics, but the conclusion briefly discusses how our approach can also support references and object identity.

2 Encoding Object-Orientation into Z

This section describes how we represent objects and methods in Z. The four key ideas, explained in the following subsections, are that:

1. **Objects are black boxes.**
2. **Subtypes are subsets.**
3. **Methods are functions/relations.**
4. **Observations allow model-oriented specification.**

2.1 Objects Are Black Boxes

Unlike most object-oriented extensions of Z, we do not specify a concrete model of objects. Instead we view each object as a black box whose internal details are hidden. In Z, we do this by defining a given type for each hierarchy of classes. An object is simply a member of this given type.

To model a single-rooted inheritance hierarchy where all classes inherit from the *Object* class (as in Java and Smalltalk), we define a single given type

   [*Object*]

To model a multi-rooted inheritance hierarchy (as in C++), we define one given type for each root class (e.g., [*Document, Window*]). With this multi-rooted approach, errors such as applying a method to an object of the wrong class can often be detected statically by the Z type system, whereas in the single-rooted approach, those errors would be caught by the domain checks of Z/EVES instead. The multi-rooted approach has the disadvantage (or advantage) that it is impossible to later define an object that inherits from two different hierarchies. For example, $x \in Document \cap Window$ is ill-typed in Z. In other words, the multi-rooted approach ensures that two class hierarchies with separate roots are *disjoint*. For this reason, when specifying a new system whose class hierarchies are likely to evolve, we usually commence with the single-rooted approach because it is more flexible.

2.2 Subsets Model Subtypes

This approach to inheritance and behavioural subtyping is refreshingly simple. To define a new type of objects, *Document*, which inherits from an existing type (say, *Object*), we simply define *Document* to be a subset of *Object*. To write *Document* $\subseteq$ *Object* as a declaration in Z, we must write this in the slightly less obvious form:

$\mid$ *Document* : $\mathbb{P}$ *Object*

This extends elegantly to multiple inheritance. For example, we might want to specify that an *Pane* is a *Document* that is displayed in a *Window*. That is, *Pane* $\subseteq$ *Document* and *Pane* $\subseteq$ *Window*. We write this in Z as:

$\mid$ *Window* : $\mathbb{P}$ *Object*

$\mid$ *Pane* : $\mathbb{P}(Document \cap Window)$

2.3 Methods Are Functions/Relations

In a programming language, a method call is written as:

```
outputs := object.method(inputs)
```

This method call typically changes the internal state of the object, and may have side-effects on other parts of the system such as the outputs.

Given *object*, *object'* $\in$ *Class*, *inputs* $\in$ *Inputs* and *outputs* $\in$ *Outputs*, we model the above method call by the Z predicate:

$(object', outputs) \in method(object, inputs)$

where *method* is a loosely defined axiomatic relation:

$\mid$ *method* : $(Class \times Inputs) \leftrightarrow (Class \times Outputs)$
$\overline{}$
$\mid$ *PreAx*
$\mid$ *PostAx*

When a method must modify other objects, these must be passed as inputs and returned as outputs of the method. For example, an execute method of Command in [GHJV94] on page 233-242, can be specified as:

$\mid$ *execute* : $(Command \times Document) \rightarrow Document$

The preconditions and postconditions give a partial specification of the behaviour of *method*. It is easy in Z to specify contradictions when writing arbitrary axioms, but we reduce the danger of this by writing precondition and postcondition axioms in a standard style: the *PreAx* above is written as:

($\forall$ *self* : *Class*; *in* : *Inputs*
  $\mid$ *Precondition*
    $\bullet$ $(self, in) \in$ dom *method*)

while *PostAx* is written as:

($\forall$ *self*, *self'* : *Class*; *in* : *Inputs*; *out* : *Outputs*
  $\mid$ $(self', out) \in method(self, in)$
    $\bullet$ *Postcondition*)

In this paper, all of our methods happen to be deterministic and total, so we use total functions rather than relations, and do not need to specify explicit preconditions. But in the general case, we use precondition axioms to specify lower bounds on the domain of the method, and postcondition axioms to specify the range.

Note that these pre and postcondition axioms often give a *partial* specification (that is, a *loose* specification) of *method* at the point it is declared. Then each subtype adds additional precondition or postcondition axioms to more tightly specify the behaviour of *method* on that subtype. For example, if we add a subtype $Class_2 \subseteq Class$, then we would specify the extra behaviour by adding an extra postcondition axiom:

$$(\forall\, self : Class_2;\ self' : Class;\ in : Inputs;\ out : Outputs$$
$$|\ (self', out) \in method(self, in)$$
$$\bullet\ ExtraPostcondition)$$

This has the effect of giving us *more* information about the possible outputs of *method* when the input object happens to belong to the subtype. (Note how the type of $self'$ is still the original supertype—this ensures that all possible outputs are constrained). If we combine the original axiomatic definition of *method* with the extra postcondition, we see that the effect is to *strengthen* the whole postcondition:

$$method : (Class \times Inputs) \leftrightarrow (Class \times Outputs)$$

$$(\forall\, self, self' : Class;\ in : Inputs;\ out : Outputs$$
$$|\ (self', out) \in method(self, in)$$
$$\bullet\ Postcondition\ \wedge$$
$$(self \in Class_2 \Rightarrow ExtraPostcondition))$$

So, in a complex hierarchy of subtypes, the final postcondition axiom for a method will typically contain one implication $(self \in SubClass_i \Rightarrow Post_i)$ for each class in the hierarchy—this models the effect of dynamic dispatch in an object-oriented language. If $Post_i$ and $Post_j$ are contradictory, they must belong to disjoint subtypes in the hierarchy. We discuss the issue of overriding a method with contradictory behaviour more in Section 5.

Preconditions are different. If we add an extra precondition axiom:

$$(\forall\, self : Class_2;\ in : Inputs$$
$$|\ ExtraPrecondition$$
$$\bullet\ (self, in) \in \mathrm{dom}\ method)$$

and combine this with the original axiomatic definition of *method* (showing only the precondition parts) we see that the whole precondition is actually *weakened*, because *more* values are now known to be in the domain of *method*.

$$method : (Class \times Inputs) \leftrightarrow (Class \times Outputs)$$
$(\forall\, self : Class;\ in : Inputs$
- $(Precondition \Rightarrow (self, in) \in \mathrm{dom}\ method) \wedge$
  $(self \in Class_2 \wedge ExtraPrecondition \Rightarrow (self, in) \in \mathrm{dom}\ method))$

Those readers who are familiar with the usual notions of Z refinement will recognise that this strengthening-postconditions and weakening-preconditions property means that the behaviour of *method* at a subtype (like $Class_2$) is a *refinement* of its behaviour at the supertype. In object-oriented circles, this is called *behavioural subtyping*. Our axiomatic style of specifying methods guarantees behavioural subtyping, and we will have more to say about this in later sections.

2.4 Observations Allow Model-Oriented Specification

Given that objects are just members of some given type, which has no internal structure, it is not clear how we *can* write preconditions and postconditions for a method. How can a postcondition compare $self'$ with $self$? We want to specify more than just equality or inequality!

To support model-oriented specification, we declare *observations* of each class, which effectively give us a partial view of the internal state of the object. An observation is simply a total function from the class to some other type. For example:

$$size : Class \to \mathbb{N}$$
$$count : Class_2 \to \mathbb{N}$$

Since $Class_2 \subseteq Class$, the *size* observation is applicable to $Class_2$ objects as well. So the further down the subtype hierarchy we go, the more observations we can make of an object.

These observations should not be regarded as part of the implementing of the object – an observation *may* be implemented by a data field, but could be implemented by a method which calculates and returns a value, or it may not be implemented at all, because it is defined only for specification purposes (in such cases, all uses of it will be refined into calls to other methods).

3 The MagicBall Example

In order to illustrate our approach on specifying objects and methods in value semantics, we start from a simple example of MagicBall.

3.1 MagicBall Specification

Let us say we have an object – a magic ball which has three different sizes: small, medium and large. The changes of sizes are observable.

A specification of such magic balls in Z is:

$[MagicBall]$

$Size ::= small \mid medium \mid large$

$\mid size : MagicBall \to Size$

$\begin{array}{|l}
inc : MagicBall \to (MagicBall \times Size) \\
dec : MagicBall \to (MagicBall \times Size) \\
\hline
\forall\, ball, ball' : MagicBall;\ s : Size \\
\quad \bullet\ (inc\ ball = (ball', s) \Rightarrow \\
\qquad size\ ball' = s\ \wedge \\
\qquad (size\ ball = small \Rightarrow s = medium)\ \wedge \\
\qquad (size\ ball = medium \Rightarrow s = large)\ \wedge \\
\qquad (size\ ball = large \Rightarrow s = large)) \\
\quad \wedge\ (dec\ ball = (ball', s) \Rightarrow \\
\qquad size\ ball' = s\ \wedge \\
\qquad (size\ ball = small \Rightarrow s = small)\ \wedge \\
\qquad (size\ ball = medium \Rightarrow s = small)\ \wedge \\
\qquad (size\ ball = large \Rightarrow s = medium))
\end{array}$

We call a set of related axioms like the above, which defines the object type MagicBall, an *object specification* or (informally) a *class specification* of MagicBall.

3.2 Implementations of MagicBall

As we pointed out in section 2.4, the MagicBall specification is a partial view of the internal state of an object. We can have many implementations for this specification, each of them may have different number of states, and each implementation must conform to the observations of its specification. These implementations are also called models of the specification in this paper.

Three *models* of the magic ball specification are shown in Fig. 1. For example, model *M1* could be defined in Z as:

$M1 ::= S \mid M \mid L$
$size_{M1} == \{S \mapsto small, M \mapsto medium, L \mapsto large\}$
$inc_{M1} == \{S \mapsto M, M \mapsto L, L \mapsto L\}$
$dec_{M1} == \{S \mapsto S, M \mapsto S, L \mapsto M\}$

Informally, we say that the state spaces of each of these models are subsets of *MagicBall* (or possible instantiations of *MagicBall*). However, we never equate *MagicBall* with an explicit concrete model like $M1$, $M2$ or $M3$, because we want

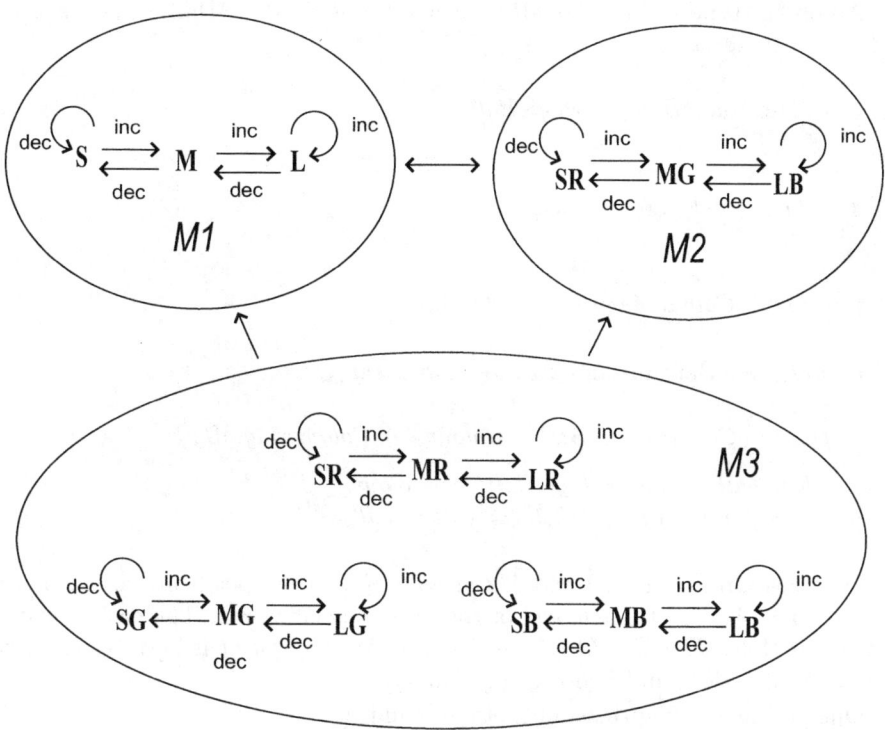

Fig. 1. Models of MagicBall

the freedom to continue making further subtypes, which specify more complex models. Hence, we always keep the *MagicBall* set abstract.

One thing we should notice here is that *all* models of the MagicBall specification must have at least three states, because the axioms specify observations of at least three distinct values.

4 Extending the MagicBall Example with Colour

An extended ColourMagicBall example is given here to show how to specify a subtype by *subsetting*, and how to deal with the frame problem.

4.1 ColourMagicBall Specification

A colour magic ball, in addition to its size attribute, has a colour which may be red, green or blue. The changes of colours are observable.

An object type ColourMagicBall as a subtype of MagicBall is specified as a *subset* of MagicBall:

$$\mid ColourMagicBall : \mathbb{P}\ MagicBall$$

$$Colour ::= red \mid green \mid blue$$

$$\mid colour : ColourMagicBall \to Colour$$

ColourMagicBall has an extra method *paint*.

$$\begin{array}{l} paint : (ColourMagicBall \times Colour) \to ColourMagicBall \\ \hline \forall\ ball, ball' : ColourMagicBall;\ c : Colour \\ \quad \bullet\ paint\,(ball, c) = ball' \Rightarrow colour\ ball' = c \end{array}$$

Obviously in Fig. 1, $M2$ and $M3$ are *models* of this specification. It is not so obvious that $M1$ is also a *model* of the above specification. The easiest way to prove it is that $M1$ and $M2$ are *isomorphic*. Method *paint* is non-deterministic in the specification, and is not displayed.

One possible $M2$ with paint method could be:

$$\begin{array}{l} M2 ::= SR \mid MG \mid LB \\ size_{M2} == \{SR \mapsto small, MG \mapsto medium, LB \mapsto large\} \\ colour_{M2} == \{SR \mapsto red, MG \mapsto green, LB \mapsto blue\} \\ inc_{M2} == \{SR \mapsto MG, MG \mapsto LB, LB \mapsto LB\} \\ dec_{M2} == \{SR \mapsto SR, MG \mapsto SR, LB \mapsto MG\} \\ paint_{M2} == \{(SR, red) \mapsto SR, (MG, red) \mapsto SR, (LB, red) \mapsto SR, \\ \qquad\qquad (SR, green) \mapsto MG, (MG, green) \mapsto MG, (LB, green) \mapsto MG, \\ \qquad\qquad (SR, blue) \mapsto LB, (MG, blue) \mapsto LB, (LB, blue) \mapsto LB\} \end{array}$$

The fact that $M2$ is a model of ColourMagicBall means that when we paint a ball, its size can change. This is perhaps a little surprising, but is simply because we forgot to specify that painting a ball should not change its size. We can do this by adding one more postcondition:

$$\begin{array}{l} \forall\ ball, ball' : ColourMagicBall;\ c : Colour \\ \quad \bullet\ paint\,(ball, c) = ball' \Rightarrow size\ ball' = size\ ball \end{array}$$

Note that $M3$ is the *model* of this revised ColourMagicBall specification, and neither $M1$ nor $M2$ anymore. This revised ColourMagicBall is a *subtype* of the MagicBall. Some models of MagicBall may not be models of ColourMagicBall, but all models of ColourMagicBall are models of MagicBall.

4.2 The Frame Problem

We should also notice that the *inc* and *dec* operation may behave weirdly, i.e. we don't know whether these methods will change the colour of the colour magic balls or not. In fact, our current axioms allow the *inc* method to mutate a Colour-MagicBall into a MagicBall! Most OO programming languages do not support such mutations, but Smalltalk does. We can specify that the type remains unchanged to advoid this:

$$\forall \, ball : ColourMagicBall;\ ball' : MagicBall;\ s : Size \bullet$$
$$(inc\ ball = (ball', s) \Rightarrow ball' \in ColourMagicBall) \land$$
$$(dec\ ball = (ball', s) \Rightarrow ball' \in ColourMagicBall)$$

Similarly, if we want these inherited methods to leave new observations unchanged (this is the default in most object-oriented programming languages), we can easily specify this by adding some restrictions on *inc* and *dec* for Colour-MagicBall:

$$\forall \, ball : ColourMagicBall;\ ball' : MagicBall;\ s : Size \bullet$$
$$(inc\ ball = (ball', s) \Rightarrow colour\ ball = colour\ ball') \land$$
$$(dec\ ball = (ball', s) \Rightarrow colour\ ball = colour\ ball')$$

This "frame problem" arises when we always want to constrain the inherited methods from changing subtype observations. Stating these no-change facts can be unwieldy and verbose. However, there are situations where inherited methods *do* need to change new attributes, so banning this possibility is undesirable. The verbosity problem could be easily solved by adding "macro" or structural syntax, which may result in an extended Z (same semantics, but extended syntax) or Z tools.

Fig. 2 shows a model of ColourMagicBall $M3$ with unchanged subtype observation inheritance. To make the figure more readable, we omitted the inputs of the paint method, and the bidirectional arrows of all *paint* transitions are not shown.

5 Behavioural Subtyping versus Inheritance

In this section, we discuss the differences between behavioural subtyping, as used in this paper, and inheritance, as used in typical object-oriented programming languages.

Informally, we say that type B is a *behavioural subtype* of type A iff [MRT98]:

- the interface of B conforms to that of A, and
- the methods of B have the same (or refined) behaviour as those of A.

Interface conformance means that B has methods with the same names, and compatible signatures, as the methods of A. It may have additional methods too.

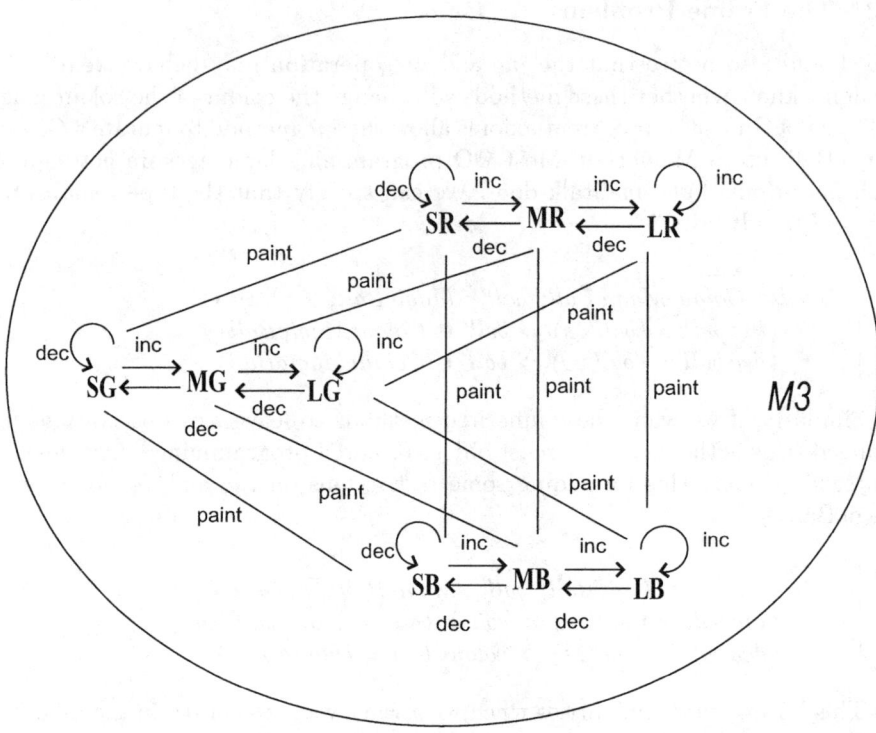

Fig. 2. A model of ColourMagicBall

In our approach, subtypes are always interface conformant with their supertypes, because the set of objects B is defined to be a subset of A, which means that all the methods of A are automatically applicable to B objects.

There are many different ways of defining behaviour, but one simple one is to view the behaviour of an object as being characterized by the set of all the properties (observations) that the behaviour satisfies. To ensure behavioural subtyping, subtypes must preserve all the properties of their supertypes. Typically, they add *more* properties. In our approach, the set of properties associated with a type is simply all the theorems that are derivable from its axioms. Since our subtypes *add* axioms (and cannot retract axioms–impossible in Z), our approach guarantees that subtypes enjoy all the properties of their supertypes if these subtypes exist. The pre/post refinement relationship discussed in Section 2.3 is simply a consequence of this axiomatic extension property.

We see that our approach ensures behavioural subtyping. However, it is common in programming languages to define inheritance hierarchies that are *not* behavioural subtypes, because subtype methods use dynamic dispatching to override the default behaviour of the corresponding supertype methods [LW94].

What happens if we try this in our approach? Is there any way of specifying such *non-monotonic* inheritance hierarchies?

5.1 The Bird/Emu Example

A classic example in the object-oriented literature is birds and emus. The *Bird* superclass has a *canFly* attribute that returns true, but the *Emu* subclass overrides this to return false, because emus are an exception to the default behaviour of birds, which is to fly. We can specify this as follows.

$[Bird]$

$CanFly ::= yes \mid no$

$\quad canfly : Bird \rightarrow CanFly$
$\quad \forall\, bird : Bird \bullet canfly\ bird = yes$

Now we add the Emu subtype, and try to override *canfly*.

$\quad Emu : \mathbb{P}\, Bird$
$\quad \forall\, emu : Emu \bullet canfly\ emu = no$

This might look okay, but attempting to 'create an emu' by proving an initialization theorem like $\exists\, e : Emu \bullet true$, fails. In fact, from the above axioms we can prove that $Emu = \emptyset$. This is the lesson, *if one specifies subtype behaviour that is inconsistent with the supertype behaviour, the subtype will be empty.* [1]

Nevertheless, we can obtain some of the desired effect if we are prepared to go back and change the *supertype* specification. Essentially, we must remove the contradiction by modifying the supertype to weaken the faulty assumption that all birds can fly, and instead allow for the possibility of non-flying birds.

$[Bird]$

$\quad canfly : Bird \rightarrow CanFly$
$\quad \forall\, bird : Bird \mid bird \notin Emu \bullet canfly\ bird = yes$

$\quad Emu : \mathbb{P}\, Bird$
$\quad \forall\, emu : Emu \bullet canfly\ emu = no$

---

[1] An alternative approach would be to specify subtypes using $\mathbb{P}_1$ rather than $\mathbb{P}$, to ensure that subtypes are non-empty. But this would make the whole specification inconsistent. We prefer the $\mathbb{P}$ approach, since it localizes the effects of inconsistency to the subtype that causes it.

Here we have the effect that is sometimes desired in object-oriented programs: the supertype-only objects (the ordinary, non-emu birds) have $canfly = yes$, whereas the subtype objects (the emus) have $canfly = no$. Effectively, the complete set of birds is a union partitioned by two subclasses: ordinary birds which can fly and emu-like birds which can't fly.

Note that the resulting system still satisfies behavioural subtyping, because at the *Bird* level, the value of the *canfly* attribute on emus is unknown, while the *Emu* level simply strengthens this by adding the property that $canfly = no$ for emus. The bird-only objects ($Bird \setminus Emu$) have different behaviour to the *Emu* subtype objects, but behavioural subtyping still holds between the whole *Bird* set and its *Emu* subset.

The lesson here is: *we can specify systems where the supertype-only objects have different behaviour to the subtype objects, but to do this, we must carefully specify the supertype behaviour to allow exceptions in the subtype.*

In object-oriented programming languages, this non-monotonic overriding effect can be implemented by late binding of methods, without modifying the supertype code. But in our strictly behavioural subtyping approach, the supertype specifications must be modified. This insistence on purity could be regarded as a disadvantage of our approach, but we prefer to regard it as a desirable discipline that leads to clearer specifications that are easier to reason about.

6 The Quadrilaterals Example

In this section, we specify the widely used quadrilaterals example [SBC92] for comparison with other styles of object orientation in Z.

We also introduce a more familiar object-oriented notation to specify the example. For instance, instead of using

$$method : (Class \times Inputs) \to (Class \times Outputs)$$

to declare an operation, we declare it as a special infix operator

$$\_ \bullet method(\_) : (Class \times Inputs) \to (Class \times Outputs)$$

so that the method can be called as $(x', o) = x \bullet method(in)$. This looks more like traditional object-oriented syntax for method calls. Note that $\bullet method$ is a legal *Word* in Standard Z: it is a subscripted bullet followed by an alphabetic name, and would be written in Unicode as '↘ • ↖ m e t h o d'. Similarly, we sometimes declare observation functions as postfix operators (and add the subscript bullet), so that we can write calls to them as $x \bullet size$.

6.1 The Quadrilaterals Example with OO-Like Syntax

The classes of quadrilaterals are shown in Fig. 3. It is assumed that readers are familiar with the context of this example from the specifications in [SBC92].

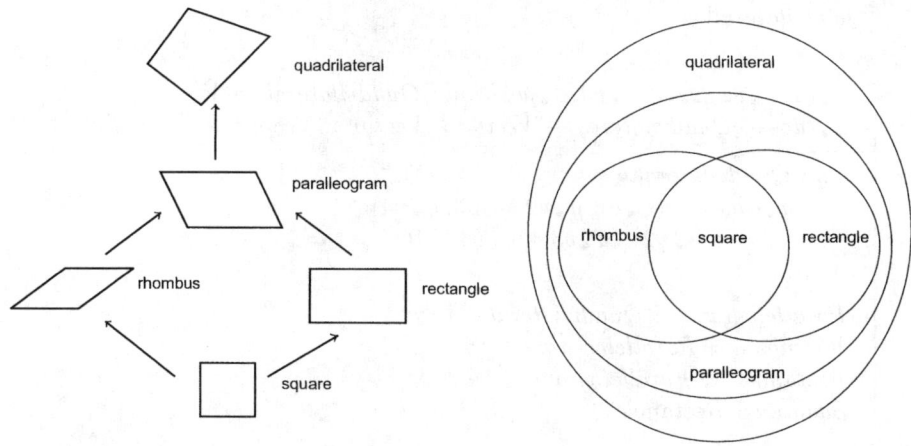

Fig. 3. Quadrilaterals

[*Vector*, *Scalar*]

Some operations of *vector* are defined as the following. Note that we use polar coordinate to represent an angle. In our approach, there is no difficulty to define cartesian and polar coordinates at the same time, because we treat them as observable properties rather than internal representations.

$$\begin{array}{l}
\_+\_ : Vector \times Vector \to Vector \\
\_._\_ : Vector \times Vector \to Scalar \\
\mathbf{0} : Vector \\
0, 1 : Scalar \\
\_+\_ : Scalar \times Scalar \to Scalar \\
\_-\_ : Scalar \times Scalar \to Scalar \\
\_/\_ : (Scalar \times Scalar) \nrightarrow Scalar \\
\_\times\_ : (Scalar \times Scalar) \to Scalar \\
\_\bullet x : Vector \to Scalar \\
\_\bullet y : Vector \to Scalar \\
\_\bullet \rho : Vector \to Scalar \\
\_\bullet \theta : Vector \to Scalar \\
tan(\_) : Scalar \nrightarrow Scalar
\end{array}$$

$\mathbf{0} \bullet \rho = 0$
$\forall q : Quadrilateral \bullet$
$\quad q \bullet \rho \times q \bullet \rho = q \bullet x \times q \bullet x + q \bullet y \times q \bullet y \wedge$
$\quad tan(q \bullet \theta) = q \bullet y / q \bullet x$
[definitions omitted]

Then we define the specification of quadrilaterals with four edges of $v1$, $v2$, $v3$, and $v4$:

[Quadrilateral]

$\_\bullet v1, \_\bullet v2, \_\bullet v3, \_\bullet v4, \_\bullet position : Quadrilateral \to Vector$
$\_\bullet edges : Quadrilateral \to Vector \times Vector \times Vector \times Vector$

$\forall\, q : Quadrilateral \bullet$
$\quad q\bullet edges = (q\bullet v1, q\bullet v2, q\bullet v3, q\bullet v4) \wedge$
$\quad q\bullet v1 + q\bullet v2 + q\bullet v3 + q\bullet v4 = \mathbf{0}$

$Parallelogram : \mathbb{P}\, Quadrilateral$
$Rhombus : \mathbb{P}\, Parallelogram$
$Rectangle : \mathbb{P}\, Parallelogram$
$Square : \mathbb{P}\, Rectangle$

$Square = Rectangle \cap Rhombus$
$\forall\, q : Quadrilateral \bullet$
$\quad q\bullet v1 + q\bullet v3 = \mathbf{0} \Leftrightarrow q \in Parallelogram$
$\forall\, p : Parallelogram \bullet$
$\quad p\bullet v1\bullet\rho = p\bullet v2\bullet\rho \Leftrightarrow p \in Rhombus\, \wedge$
$\quad (p\bullet v1).(p\bullet v2) = 0 \Leftrightarrow p \in Rectangle$

In short, a quadrilateral can be moved around by changing its position. For all except general quadrilaterals, the angle between two adjacent sides is well defined.

$\_\bullet move(\_) : (Quadrilateral \times Vector) \to Quadrilateral$
$\_\bullet angle : Parallelogram \to Scalar$
$\_\bullet shear(\_) : (Quadrilateral \times Scalar) \to Quadrilateral$

$\forall\, q, q' : Quadrilateral;\ v : Vector \bullet$
$\quad q' = q\bullet move(v) \Rightarrow$
$\qquad (q'\bullet position = q\bullet position + v \wedge q'\bullet edges = q\bullet edges)$
$\forall\, q : Parallelogram;\ angle : Angle \bullet$
$\quad q\bullet angle = q\bullet v2\bullet\theta - q\bullet v1\bullet\theta$
$\forall\, q, q' : Quadrilateral;\ angle : Scalar \bullet q' = q\bullet shear(angle) \Rightarrow$
$\quad (q'\bullet position = q\bullet position\, \wedge$
$\quad (q'\bullet v1\bullet x = q\bullet v1\bullet x + q\bullet v1\bullet y \times tan(angle) \wedge q'\bullet v1\bullet y = q\bullet v1\bullet y\, \wedge$
$\quad\ q'\bullet v2\bullet x = q\bullet v2\bullet x + q\bullet v2\bullet y \times tan(angle) \wedge q'\bullet v2\bullet y = q\bullet v2\bullet y\, \wedge$
$\quad\ q'\bullet v3\bullet x = q\bullet v3\bullet x + q\bullet v3\bullet y \times tan(angle) \wedge q'\bullet v3\bullet y = q\bullet v3\bullet y\, \wedge$
$\quad\ q'\bullet v4\bullet x = q\bullet v4\bullet x + q\bullet v4\bullet y \times tan(angle) \wedge q'\bullet v4\bullet y = q\bullet v4\bullet y))$

Here we give a clear and explicit definition for shearing method. Apart from the readability and completeness comparing with other proposed approaches (the definition of shearing is omitted in all other object-oriented Z approaches in [SBC92]), the shearing function defined here is obviously more intuitive and reasonable.

In our shearing function, any quadrilateral can be sheared. A square may become a rhombus after shearing, although the type conversion could make it harder to reason about. And many object oriented programming languages can not easily support this feature.

Like other approaches in [SBC92], in order to avoid type conversion problems, we can also limit the shearing function on quadrilaterals except squares, rhombi and rectangles.

$$\begin{array}{|l}
\_\bullet shear(\_) : (Quadrilateral \times Scalar) \nrightarrow Quadrilateral \\
\hline
\mathrm{dom}(\mathrm{dom}\ shear) = Quadrilateral \setminus (Rhombus \cup Rectangle)
\end{array}$$

6.2 A Drawing System of Quadrilaterals

A drawing system can be simply defined as a sequence of quadrilaterals:

$$DrawingSystem == \mathrm{seq}\ Quadrilateral$$

$$\begin{array}{|l}
\_\bullet add(\_) : (DrawingSystem \times Quadrilateral) \to DrawingSystem \\
\_\bullet delete(\_) : (DrawingSystem \times \mathbb{N}) \to DrawingSystem \\
\_\bullet move(\_,\_) : (DrawingSystem \times \mathbb{N} \times Vector) \to DrawingSystem \\
\_\bullet angle(\_) : (DrawingSystem \times \mathbb{N}) \to Scalar \\
\_\bullet shear(\_,\_) : (DrawingSystem \times \mathbb{N} \times Scalar) \to DrawingSystem \\
\hline
\forall ds : DrawingSystem;\ q : Quadrilateral;\ n : \mathbb{N};\ v : Vector \mid n \leq \#ds \bullet \\
\quad (ds' = ds\bullet add(q) \Rightarrow ds' = ds \frown \langle q \rangle\ \wedge \\
\quad ds' = ds\bullet delete(n) \Rightarrow ds' = ((\mathrm{dom}\ ds) \setminus \{n\}) \upharpoonright ds\ \wedge \\
\quad ds' = ds\bullet move(n, v) \Rightarrow \\
\quad\quad ds' = ((1\mathrel{..} n-1) \triangleleft ds) \frown (ds\ n)\bullet move(v) \frown ((n+1\mathrel{..} \#ds) \triangleleft ds)\ \wedge \\
\quad ds' = ds\bullet shear(n, v) \Rightarrow \\
\quad\quad ds' = ((1\mathrel{..} n-1) \triangleleft ds) \frown (ds\ n)\bullet shear(v) \frown ((n+1\mathrel{..} \#ds) \triangleleft ds)\ \wedge \\
\quad ds\bullet angle(n) = (ds\ n)\bullet angle)
\end{array}$$

Then we can *add* or *delete* quadrilaterals, inquiring *angles*, *move* and *shear* each quadrilateral in the drawing system respectively.

As a simple rule, if a class is a composition of objects without any other distinguishable observation properties, we can explicitly specify it as a sequence of objects. Otherwise, we must define it as a given set or a subset of a given set (Because the space limit in this paper, we will elaborate this problem in another paper). For instance, we declare the drawing system as:

[DrawingSystem]

and plus an attribute of composition:

$$\begin{array}{|l}
\_.comps : DrawingSystem \to \mathrm{seq}\ Quadrilateral
\end{array}$$

$\_\, .\, add(\_) : (DrawingSystem \times Quadrilateral) \rightarrow DrawingSystem$
$\_\, .\, delete(\_) : (DrawingSystem \times \mathbb{N}) \rightarrow DrawingSystem$
$\_\, .\, move(\_,\_) : (DrawingSystem \times \mathbb{N} \times Vector) \rightarrow DrawingSystem$
$\_\, .\, angle(\_) : (DrawingSystem \times \mathbb{N}) \rightarrow Scalar$
$\_\, .\, shear(\_,\_) : (DrawingSystem \times \mathbb{N} \times Scalar) \rightarrow DrawingSystem$

$\forall\, ds : DrawingSystem;\ q : Quadrilateral;\ n : \mathbb{N};\ v : Vector \mid n \leq \#ds \bullet$
$\quad (ds' = ds\, .\, add(q) \Rightarrow ds'\, .\, comps = ds\, .\, comps \frown \langle q \rangle\ \wedge$
$\quad ds' = ds\, .\, delete(n) \Rightarrow$
$\quad\quad ds'\, .\, comps = ((\text{dom}\, ds\, .\, comps) \setminus \{n\}) \upharpoonright ds\, .\, comps\ \wedge$
$\quad ds' = ds\, .\, move(n, v) \Rightarrow$
$\quad\quad ds'\, .\, comps = ((1\, ..\, n - 1) \lhd ds\, .\, comps) \frown$
$\quad\quad\quad (ds\, .\, comps\ n)\, .\, move(v) \frown$
$\quad\quad\quad ((n + 1\, ..\, \#ds\, .\, comps) \lhd ds\, .\, comps)\ \wedge$
$\quad ds' = ds\, .\, shear(n, v) \Rightarrow$
$\quad\quad ds'\, .\, comps = ((1\, ..\, n - 1) \lhd ds\, .\, comps) \frown$
$\quad\quad\quad (ds\, .\, comps\ n)\, .\, shear(v) \frown$
$\quad\quad\quad ((n + 1\, ..\, \#ds\, .\, comps) \lhd ds\, .\, comps)\ \wedge$
$\quad ds\, .\, angle(n) = (ds\, .\, comps\ n)\, .\, angle)$

7 Explicit Models for Animation and Proof

Using an abstract model of objects is convenient for specification, but makes it difficult to animate specifications (for validation and testing purposes), because there is no explicit finite model of objects. No existing Z animators are capable of animating abstract objects and axiomatic functions and methods over those objects, in the style that we have used.

In Section 3 we showed an explicit model for the *MagicBall* specification that could easily be animated. In this section, we briefly show how a specification of a hierarchy of classes could be converted into an explicit model, which would be more suitable for animation. Also, seeing one possible instantiation of the *Object* given type gives insight into how our specification style works.

First of all, we build a hierarchy of state spaces, in the same way that Object-Z does. Schema inclusion is useful here to model inheritance. Usually, the state space of each class contains just the attributes that were defined as observation functions, but it is possible to write specifications that require additional implicit attributes.

$MagicBallState \,\widehat{=}\, [size : Size]$
$ColourMagicBallState \,\widehat{=}\, [MagicBallState;\ colour : Colour]$

Next we define a free type that ranges over all the possible object types in the system. Note that we are assuming a closed, non-extensible system here!

$Object ::= mball \langle\!\langle MagicBallState \rangle\!\rangle$
$\quad\quad\quad\quad\ \mid cmball \langle\!\langle ColourMagicBallState \rangle\!\rangle$

Now we can define the hierarchy of subsets, starting from the bottom of the hierarchy and defining each supertype to be the union of all its subtypes plus its own members. This is like the *Class* ↓ type in Object-Z.

$ColourMagicBall == \mathrm{ran}\ cmball$
$MagicBall == ColourMagicBall \cup \mathrm{ran}\ mball$

Next we define the observation functions, so that they select the desired field out of a class state and out of all of its subclass states.

$size == (\lambda\ m : \mathrm{ran}\ mball \bullet m.size) \cup (\lambda\ cm : \mathrm{ran}\ cmball \bullet cm.size)$

$colour == (\lambda\ cm : \mathrm{ran}\ cmball \bullet cm.colour)$

Finally we can define each method as a relation that satisfies all the relevant preconditions and postconditions. Preconditions and postconditions that were added in a subtype are guarded by a membership constraint so that they are only applicable to that subtype. For example, *inc* can be defined as:

$inc == \{ball, ball' : MagicBall;\ s : Size\ |$
$\qquad size\ ball' = s\ \wedge$
$\qquad (size\ ball = small \Rightarrow s = medium)\ \wedge$
$\qquad (size\ ball = medium \Rightarrow s = large)\ \wedge$
$\qquad (size\ ball = large \Rightarrow s = large))\ \wedge$
$\qquad (ball \in ColourMagicBall \Rightarrow ball' \in ColourMagicBall)\ \wedge$
$\qquad (ball \in ColourMagicBall \Rightarrow colour\ ball = colour\ ball')\}$

We sometimes find it useful to think of this explicit model as we specify objects abstractly, but we do NOT propose that one should ever write such an explicit model. It is just one possible instantiation of the *Object* type. It is more verbose (the case analysis style explodes as more classes are added), and it is not extensible. We are not yet sure whether Z theorem provers work better with the abstract or explicit model, but we suspect the abstract model is preferable. On the other hand, it is clear that the explicit model is more suitable for animation than the abstract specification. It would be interesting to develop a tool that transformed the abstract style of specification into the explicit model for animation purposes.

8 Related Work

Our goal of formally specifying object-oriented systems in Z is to specify the object-oriented concepts in first order logic and set theory, and utilize the existing powerful tools of Z. This greatly reduces the burden of learning a new object-oriented formal specification language. The most important thing in our approach is that we give an abstract, concise and consistent perception of object types, subtyping and inheritance.

The abstract view of observable object behaviour closely relates to the research on algebraic specification of abstract data types [CGK+]. Most of the algbaic specification use the initial algebra for the semantics of a specification, but we use refinement theory for modelling and interpreting object-oriented constructs, and defining behavioural subtyping and inheritance.

Our approach is significantly different from any other object oriented approaches in Z. Firstly, we interpret object-oriented concepts in standard Z, rather than extending Z like Object-Z [DKRS91], MOOZ, OOZE, Z++, and ZEST [SBC92]. Secondly, most object-oriented Z extensions explicitly model object state (typically by state schemas, where Hall [Hal90] is an exception), whereas we use an abstract model of objects (given types or subsets of given types). Thirdly, we model methods using functions and relations, whereas most other object oriented styles use operation schemas. For example, Hall's style [Hal90] and ZERO [SBC92]. We use value semantics and separate object identity from its representation, which allows us to consolidate *object type* or *class* with Z *type*. It also makes it possible for us to use subsetting to model inheritance, and gives us an constructive way to build behavioural subtyping.

OOZE [AG91] is a Z-like notation, built on top of order-sorted algebras—a very different semantic basis to standard Z. It supports inheritance, sophisticated modularization and dynamic binding (including the ability for subtypes to override supertype behaviour in non-compatible ways). Its use of axiomatic specification style is similar to ours, but that is the only similarity. We map object-oriented constructs into standard Z sets and relations, which gives a simpler semantics and is more familiar to Z users.

[Rob00] shows how a loose axiomatic specification can be proved to be refined by a constructive concrete model.

9 Conclusions

We have shown that an elegant and simple object-oriented specification style is possible in Z. Modelling objects as black boxes makes it possible to specify subtype hierarchies using subset constraints. Our approach does not provide much in the way of hiding or encapsulation facilities, but this is a problem with Z and standard Z—the simple section mechanism is not sufficient to support modularity. Nevertheless, the way we define methods provides a limit encapsulation. We can group methods of an *object type* together by searching the whole specification for methods which take this *object type* as the first parameter. This could also enhance the extensibility of software specification by adding more methods in other parts of the specification later when it is needed.

Our style of specification is one that can be reasoned about using the standard Z theorem provers, but is not supported by existing animation tools, because of its abstractness. It would be an interesting challenge to try and develop animation support for this abstract style. One promising approach might be to develop a tool that translates our abstract style of object specification into an explicit object model that existing animators can handle.

Our approach uses value semantics rather than references, but again, we believe this is the most elegant approach for a specification language, and closest to the spirit of Z. It is easy to simulate (explicit) reference semantics in a value-semantics specification language (using seq *Quadrilateral* like in Sect. refsec:quads, or *Ref* ↛ *Object* mappings), but the converse is not true. Reference semantics is harder to reason about, due to the aliasing problems. An advantage of using explicit references is that the specifier can use them only where necessary, and in a controlled and localised way, thus preserving the ease of reasoning as much as possible.

An interesting, and intrinsic, feature of our approach is that subtypes preserve all the properties of their supertypes. In other words, our specification style enforces behavioural subtyping. This is a restriction that might be considered undesirable in a programming language, where the purpose of inheritance is often code reuse rather than behaviour specialization, so subclasses often override inherited methods with incompatible (non-monotonic) behaviour. With our approach, if one wants to override the behaviour of a supertype in a non-monotonic fashion, one must instead reorganise the hierarchy so that the supertype and subtype become siblings, and their common parent specifies just their common behaviour. This is often better style anyway, and we believe that in a specification language it is good discipline for subtype hierarchies to be behavioural hierarchies.

References

[AG91]   Antonio J. Alencar and Joseph A. Goguen. OOZE: An object-oriented Z environment. In P. America, editor, *Proceedings ECOOP'91*, LNCS 512, pages 180–199, Geneva, Switzerland, July 15-19 1991. Springer-Verlag.

[CGK+]   Maura Cerioli, Martin Gogolla, Hélène Kirchner, Bernd Krieg-Brückner, Zhenyu Qian, and Markus Wolf (Eds.). Algebraic system specification and development: Survey and annotated bibliography - second edition -.

[DKRS91] R. Duke, P. King, G. A. Rose, and G. Smith. The Object-Z specification language: Version 1. Technical Report 91-1, The University of Queensland, St. Lucia 4072, Australia, 1991.

[GHJV94] Erich Gamma, Richard Helm, Ralph Johnson, and John Vlissides. *Design Patterns: Elements of Reusable Object-Oriented Software*. Addison-Wesley Professional Computing Series. Addison-Wesley, 1994.

[Hal90]   J. A. Hall. Using Z as a specification calculus for object-oriented systems. In D. Bjørner, C. A. R. Hoare, and H. Langmaack, editors, *VDM and Z – Formal Methods in Software Development*, volume 428 of *LNCS*, pages 290–318. VDM-Europe, Springer-Verlag, 1990.

[LW94]   Barbara H. Liskov and Jeannette M. Wing. A behavioral notion of subtyping. *ACM Transactions on Programming Languages and Systems*, 16(6):1811–1841, November 1994.

[Mey97]   B. Meyer. *Object-Oriented Software Construction, Second Edition*. The Object-Oriented Series. Prentice-Hall, Englewood Cliffs (NJ), USA, 1997.

[MRT98]   N. Medvidovic, D. S. Rosenblum, and R. N. Taylor. A type theory for software architectures. Technical Report UCI-ICS-98-14, Department of Information and Computer Science, University of California, Irvine, April 1998.

[Rob00]   Ken Robinson. Reconciling axiomatic and model-based specification using the B method. In *ZB'2000 – International Conference of B and Z Users*, volume 1878 of *Lecture Notes in Computer Science (Springer-Verlag)*, pages 95–106, Helsington, York, UK YO10 5DD, August 2000. Department of Computer Science – University of York.

[SBC92]   S. Stepney, R. Barden, and D. Cooper. *Object Orientation in Z*. workshops in computing. Springer-Verlag, 1992.

Comparison of Formalisation Approaches of UML Class Constructs in Z and Object-Z

Nuno Amálio and Fiona Polack

Department of Computer Science, University of York, York, YO10 5DD, UK
{namalio, fiona}@cs.york.ac.uk

Abstract. UML, and other object-oriented approaches to system specification and design, are increasingly popular in industry. Many attempts have been made to formalise either the notations, the system models produced using these notations, or both. However, there have been no attempts to compare the expressiveness of the formal approaches. This paper compares Z and Object-Z approaches to object-oriented formalisation. The Z approaches reflect different formalisation goals (a formal model of the system, a formal model of a diagrammatic object-oriented model). The Object-Z approach produces compact formal models, but imposes a particular semantic interpretation on the UML notations.

Keywords: Z, Object-Z, UML, formalisation, specification.

1 Introduction

There have been many attempts to formalise object-oriented (OO) notations. However, there has been no independent attempt to compare the formalisations. This paper considers three Z and one Object-Z (OZ) approaches to formalisation of structural constructs of the Unified Modelling Language (UML), and suggests some extensions, and slight changes to the original approaches.

UML is widely used in industrial systems development. It provides a range of OO diagrammatic notations for expressing the structural and behavioural aspects of computer systems. There have been many versions of UML (e.g.[1, 2,3,4], and UML2.0 is in preparation). Various attempts have been made to formally define the syntax and semantics of the notations, in the UML definition documents [1,2,3] and by others [5,6,7,8], and to represent UML models in a formal notation [9,10]. The purpose of these attempts is to allow UML models to be rigorously checked, and to allow formal analysis of the modelled systems.

There are many approaches to formal specification. Z [11,12] and Object-Z [13,14] were selected as the target of our analysis because various formalisation approaches using these languages already exist.

OZ is an object-oriented extension of Z designed to represent OO properties.

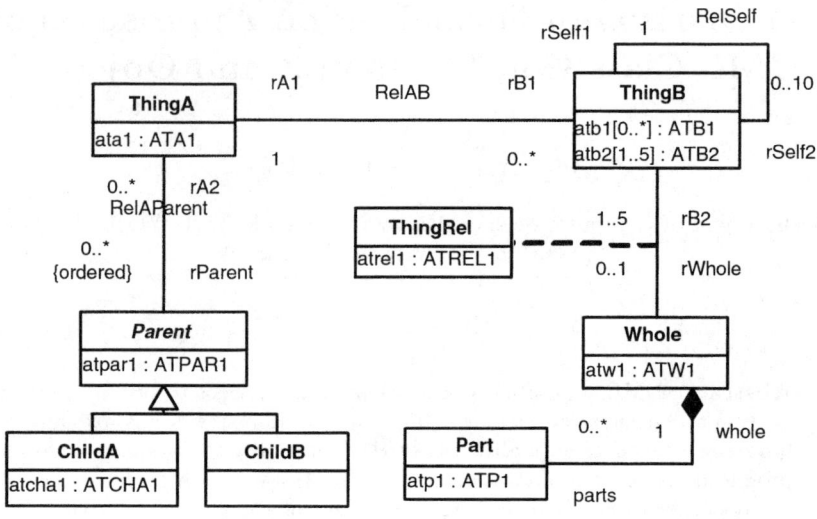

Fig. 1. Example UML class diagram

2 UML Constructs

The formalisation approaches are considered for the main structural components of UML class diagrams, focusing on features used to describe requirements. This excludes class operations, and constructs closer to design, such as navigability of associations and visibility of class properties. The UML definitions are based on the UML 1.4 specification [3].

Figure 1 is the UML class diagram used to illustrate the various formalisation approaches; it contains typical constructs of this kind of diagram. A UML *class* is represented by a box and is a descriptor for a set of objects. A class has a name (*ThingA*, *ThingB*, etc) and a set of attributes (*ata1*, *atb1*, etc); class operations would be added in a third compartment to the class box. An attribute may have a multiplicity property (see *atb1*, *atb2*); when the property is absent the attribute is single-valued. A UML class may be *abstract* meaning that it cannot have direct instances; *Parent* is an abstract class.

UML generalisation describes a relationship, where a more general class (*superclass*) is specialised by one or more classes (*subclass*es). It includes two different OO concepts: *inheritance* and *subtyping*. Inheritance means that a subclass comprises its own characteristics (attributes, operations and associations), plus all the characteristics of its superclass(es). In Fig. 1, an object of *ChildA* has two attributes, *atpar1* and *atcha1*. Subtyping means that subclass objects are indistinguishable from superclass objects [15]; a consequence of subtyping is *substitutability*: subclass objects may replace superclass objects whenever superclass objects are expected. By default generalisation relationships are *disjoint*. This constraint indicates that a superclass instance cannot be more than one subclass instance at a time. Alternatively, an *overlapping* constraint indicates that one subclass instance may be an instance of another subclass of the generalisation. The generalisation in Fig. 1 is disjoint.

A UML *association* describes a set of links among objects. A *binary association* connects objects of two classes; *n-ary* associations connect objects of n classes. Self-referencing associations (e.g. *RelSelf*), in which the linked objects are all from one class, are allowed. An association has an optional name (*RelAB*, etc). UML allows class characteristics to be attached to an association via an *association class*, such as *ThingRel* in Fig. 1. This allows the attribute, *atrel1*, to be associated to links between *ThingB* and *Whole*.

An association is composed of *association-ends*, which are connected to classes. An association-end may have several properties. The *rolename* indicates the role played by the connected class in the association (e.g. *rA1*, *rA2*). The *multiplicity* indicates the multiplicity of the connected class's participation in the association; in Fig. 1, for the association *RelAB*, one *ThingA* object must participate in each link of the association, whereas any number of *ThingB*'s objects ("0..*", indicating zero to any finite multiplicity) can participate in the association's links. For multiplicities greater than one, an *ordered* constraint may be attached to an association-end (see *rParent* end); it indicates that the objects of that end are ordered. An *aggregation* property (represented by a white diamond) indicates that the attached class is an aggregate of objects. Aggregation can be strong or weak; strong aggregation is termed *composition* (represented by a black diamond). In Fig. 1, *Whole* is a composition of *Part* objects.

Aggregation and composition are used to express a "part of" relationship among otherwise-distinct classes. This concept is clearly present in the real world, and thus needs to be representable in specification of requirements: doors and wheels are parts of cars, words and sentences are part of paragraphs, etc. Cars and doors have different characteristics, but changing the location of the car causes doors to relocate also. The UML semantics of this shared behaviour and ownership is not well defined [16]. The semantics of aggregation is left open, according to the application, but composition is given a slightly more precise meaning: the part must be included in at most one composite at a time (*unshared containment*); if a composite is destroyed the parts must also be destroyed (*deletion propagation*).

3 Analysis of Formalisation Approaches in Z

This paper focuses on the following formalisation approaches:

- Hall [17,18] predates UML, it aims to structure Z specifications in an OO style. Hall's work forms the basis for recent work, like the France approach, and, for instance, Hammond [19]'s work on Shlaer-Mellor diagrams and Z. The OO concepts supported include class, association and inheritance, but not association class, aggregation and composition.

[ATA1]
─────────────────────
ThingA
───────
ata1 : ATA1

ThingAExt
─────────
ThingAs : $\mathbb{F}$ ThingA

Fig. 2. Formalisation of classes and class attributes in the Dupuy approach

$orel[X, Y] == X \twoheadrightarrow \text{iseq } Y$

$[X, Y]$
─────────
$urel : orel[X, Y] \rightarrow (X \leftrightarrow Y)$
$\forall or : orel[X, Y] \bullet urel(or) = \{x : X;\ y : Y \mid x \in \text{dom } or \wedge y \in \text{ran}(or\ x) \bullet x \mapsto y\}$

Fig. 3. Z Generics for ordered association-ends

- France et al [20,9] (referred to as France), is UML-specific, and considers all class concepts except association class, and also presents specialisations of associations (not included here).
- Dupuy et al [10,21,22] (referred to as Dupuy), presents formalisations of OO concepts in Z[10,21] and in OZ[10,22].

Dupuy's Z approach does not formalise the concept of object identity (Fig. 2). This simplifies the formalisation of the class concept, but brings problems. Z has a value semantics; a variable declaration in Z represents a value rather than a reference to a value. This includes variables of types defined as schemas, containing assignment of values to its components (schema bindings). In Fig. 2 the schema *ThingAExt* contains a component, *ThingAs*, representing all instances of class *ThingA*; if two distinct instances of this class have the same value for the attribute *ata1* they get merged in the set *ThingAs* (same schema binding), which is not what is wanted. This constitutes a fundamental flaw in the approach, hence, we do not analyse it further here.

3.1 Z Generics Used in the Formalisations

In this section, we introduce some Z generics, not provided by the original approaches, to factor some commonality found in the formalisations, and to make the resulting specifications more readable.

The first group of generics (Fig. 3) provide support for *ordered* association ends, when the association is formalised as a relation between classes (discussed later). *orel* maps the objects of the unordered association-end to a sequence (injective to avoid object-repetitions) of objects of the ordered end. The function *urel* coverts the ordered association to an association with no ordering.

$$\begin{array}{|l|}\hline [X, Y] \\ \hline hasMult1\_ : \mathbb{P}((X \leftrightarrow Y) \times \mathbb{PN}) \\ \hline (hasMult1\_) = \{r : X \leftrightarrow Y;\ m : \mathbb{PN}\ |\ \\ (\forall x : \text{dom}\ r \bullet \#(r(\!|\ \{x\}\ |\!)) \in m)\} \\ \hline \end{array}$$

$$\begin{array}{|l|}\hline [X, Y] \\ \hline hasMult\_ : \mathbb{P}((X \leftrightarrow Y) \times \mathbb{PN} \times \mathbb{PN}) \\ \hline (hasMult\_) = \{r : X \leftrightarrow Y;\ m1, m2 : \mathbb{PN}|\ \\ hasMult1(r, m1) \wedge hasMult1(r^\sim, m2)\} \\ \hline \end{array}$$

Fig. 4. Z Generics for multiplicities of association-ends

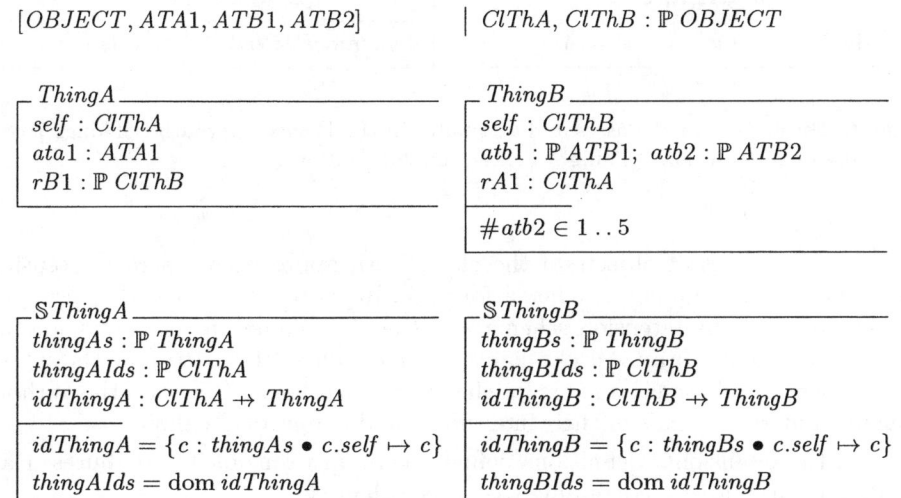

Fig. 5. Formalisation of classes, attributes, and associations as roles in the Hall approach ("Thing" intensional definitions; "$\mathbb{S}\,Thing$" extensional definitions)

The operator *hasMult* (Fig. 4) helps to define association multiplicities in the Hall approach for associations formalised as a relation between classes; it constrains the number of pairs of a relation between classes to the multiplicity of the corresponding association.

3.2 Classes and Attributes

Figures 5 and 6 present Z formalisations of the UML classes *ThingA* and *ThingB* using, respectively, the approaches of Hall and France. Other classes would follow a similar pattern.

Hall and France formalise the concept of object identity. Hall introduces object identities as the given set *OBJECT*, from which the specific object identities of each class are derived (e.g. *ClThA*, object identity of *ThingA*). France introduces a given set for each class (e.g. *CLTHA*).

A UML class has two related but distinct meanings. The *class intension* defines the properties that a set of objects have in common. The *class exten-*

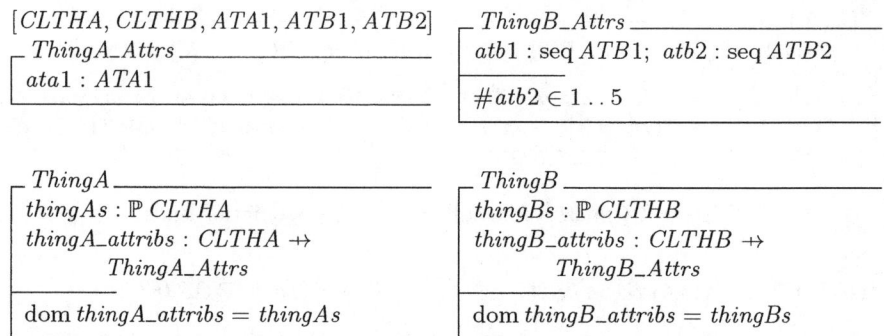

Fig. 6. Formalisation of classes and attributes in the France approach ("Thing_Attrs" is intensional definition; "Thing" is extensional definition.)

sion defines a set of objects of the class. Both approaches separate intension and extension; there is a Z schema for each. In terms of naming, Hall uses the class name for the intension schema and the class name prefixed by $\mathbb{S}$ for the extension schema; France uses the class name suffixed by _Attrs for the intension schema, and the class name for the extension schema. However, the authors include different details in their intensional and extensional definitions.

All the intensional definitions define a class in terms of its attributes. Hall adds the variable *self* containing the object identity.

Attribute types are defined abstractly in all approaches; actual attributes are defined in the class intension. Hall does not support explicitly the formalisation of UML class attributes in his work; intuitively they can be modelled as a variable of a set (single-valued attributes) or a variable of a power-set (multi-valued attributes); if required multiplicity constraints on attributes can be stated as predicates (see formalisation of *atb2*). France models multi-valued attributes as sequences, making the formalisation closer to the UML use, where the contents of a multi-valued attribute are expressed with an array-like syntax (we prefer sets as it makes the definitions more abstract); support for multiplicity constraints is provided (we prefer to write predicates in the form $\#A \in n_1 \ldots n_2$ rather than $n_1 \leq \#A \leq n_2$, as it is closer to the UML counter-part).

Hall's extension defines a set of instances of the class type (representing object identities existing in the system), and a set of instances of the intension (representing object values in the system). These are mapped by a function (e.g. *idThingA*). France's extension is simpler, defining the set of objects identities (e.g. *thingAs*) and mapping these to the class attributes (e.g. *thingA_attribs*).

Hall's intensional definitions (Fig. 5) also include the definition of associations, discussed in section 3.4.

3.3 Generalisation/Specialisations

Generalisation relationships are difficult to represent in Z because the language does not have *subtyping* (which makes type-checking easier). Thus, in Z, subclass objects must be represented as members of different sets (its own and all its superclasses) with distinct characteristics.

$$ClParent, ClChA, ClChB : \mathbb{P}\ OBJECT$$

$$\begin{array}{|l}\underline{Parent}\\ self : ClParent \\ atpar1 : ATPAR1 \end{array}$$

$$\begin{array}{|l}\underline{ChildA}\\ Parent;\ atcha1 : ATCHA1 \\ \hline self \in ClChA \end{array}$$

$$\begin{array}{|l}\underline{ChildB}\\ Parent \\ \hline self \in ClChB \end{array}$$

$$\begin{array}{|l}\underline{ParentHierarchy}\\ \mathbb{S}Parent;\ \mathbb{S}ChildA;\ \mathbb{S}ChildB \\ \hline childAIds = parentIds \cap ClChA \\ childBIds = parentIds \cap ClChB \\ \forall s : childAIds \bullet (\lambda\ ChildA \bullet \theta Parent)(idChildA\ s) = idParent\ s \\ \forall s : childBIds \bullet (\lambda\ ChildB \bullet \theta Parent)(idChildB\ s) = idParent\ s \\ \mathrm{disjoint}\langle childAIds, childBIds\rangle \\ parentIds = childAIds \cup childBIds \end{array}$$

Fig. 7. Formalisation of generalisation/specialisation in the Hall approach

Hall and France have identical definitions for the intensions of the classes involved in the inheritance hierarchy, except for Hall's *self* object identity. The class *Parent* (see Figs. 7 and 8) is defined as a normal class; the intension schema of the superclass is then included in each intensional subclass schema, allowing attribute inheritance.

The extensional definitions of the two approaches are slightly different. The superclass extension is defined like a normal class in both approaches. Hall also defines the extension of subclasses like normal classes. France provides alternative subclass extensional definitions (see Fig. 8), adding the necessary constraints on the hierarchy. The first predicate expresses the fact that the subclass identities are superclass identities, enforcing subtyping; the second predicate ensures that an object's state is consistent, whether the object is seen as a superclass instance or a subclass instance.

France and Hall complete the generalisation formalisation with a full hierarchy schema. France's (schema *ParentConfig*) includes the subclass extensions, and predicates expressing the *disjoint* property of the hierarchy, and the *abstract* property of the class *Parent*. Hall's (*ParentHierarchy*) includes predicates

$\boxed{\begin{array}{l}\textit{Parent\_Attrs}\\ \textit{atpar}1:ATPAR1\end{array}}$ $\boxed{\begin{array}{l}\textit{ChildA\_Attrs}\\ \textit{Parent\_Attrs}\\ \textit{atcha}1:ATCHA1\end{array}}$ $\boxed{\begin{array}{l}\textit{ChildB\_Attrs}\\ \textit{Parent\_Attrs}\end{array}}$

$\boxed{\begin{array}{l}\textit{ChildA}\\ \textit{Parent};\ \textit{childAs},\textit{ClChA}:\mathbb{P}\ \textit{CLPARENT}\\ \textit{childA\_attribs}:\textit{CLPARENT}\nrightarrow\textit{ChildA\_Attrs}\\\hline \textit{childAs}=\{x:\textit{parents}\mid x\in\textit{ClChA}\}\\ \forall s:\textit{childAs}\bullet(\textit{childA\_attribs}\ s).\textit{atpar}1=(\textit{parent\_attribs}\ s).\textit{atpar}1\\ \mathrm{dom}\ \textit{childA\_attribs}=\textit{childAs}\end{array}}$

$\boxed{\begin{array}{l}\textit{ParentConfig}\\ \textit{ChildA};\ \textit{ChildB}\\\hline \mathrm{disjoint}\langle\textit{childAs},\textit{childBs}\rangle\\ \bigcup\{\textit{childAs},\textit{childBs}\}=\textit{parents}\end{array}}$

Fig. 8. Formalisation of generalisation/specialisation in the France approach

equivalent to France's subclass extension schemas, enforcing subtyping and state consistency (but expressed using the schema binding operator, θ). The last two predicates enforce the *disjoint* property of the hierarchy, and the *abstract* property of the *Parent* class (not formalised in the original work), respectively.

Subclass extensional definitions in the France approach have a scalability problem, as a predicate is required for every superclass attribute to enforce attribute inheritance; this could be made more concise if the schema binding operator (θ) were used, as in the Hall approach.

3.4 Associations

Hall provides two alternative formalisations of associations. The first views an association as *roles* played by classes. Figure 5 presents the formalisation of the UML association *RelAB* using this alternative. A variable, holding references (object identities) to the objects of the class at the opposite end of the association, is introduced in the intension schema of each participant class (*rB1*, *rA1*). Depending on the multiplicity of the association-end, each variable holds one reference (expressed as a simple set; multiplicity "1") or many references (expressed as power-set; multiplicity "0..*"); more restricting multiplicity constraints, although not provided in the original approach, can be easily stated as predicates, like multiplicity of class attributes (see Fig. 5).

Hall's second alternative for handling associations considers an association to be a class of links, thus providing an exact parallel to the class formalisation.

```
┌─ RelAParent ──────────────────────────┐   ┌─ RelSelf ─────────────────────────┐
│ self : ClRelAPar                      │   │ self : ClRelSelf                  │
│ relAParent : orel[ClThA, ClParent]    │   │ relSelfB : ClThB ↔ ClThB          │
└───────────────────────────────────────┘   ├───────────────────────────────────┤
                                            │ hasMult(relSelfB, 1..1, 0..10)    │
                                            └───────────────────────────────────┘
```

Fig. 9. Hall's formalisation of associations as a class of links (intensional definitions)

```
┌─ RelAB ───────────────────────────┐   ┌─ RelAParent ──────────────────────────┐
│ ThingA; ThingB                    │   │ ThingA; Parent                        │
│ relAB : CLTHB ↔ CLTHA             │   │ relAParent : orel[CLTHA, CLPARENT]    │
├───────────────────────────────────┤   ├───────────────────────────────────────┤
│ relAB ∈ thingBs → thingAs         │   │ urel(relAParent) ∈ thingAs ↔ parent   │
└───────────────────────────────────┘   └───────────────────────────────────────┘

┌─ RelSelf ────────────────────────────────────────────────────────────────┐
│ ThingB; relSelf : CLTHB ↔ CLTHB                                          │
├──────────────────────────────────────────────────────────────────────────┤
│ relSelf ∈ {rel : thingBs → thingBs | (∀ x : thingBs • #(rel(| {x} |)) ∈ 0..10)} │
└──────────────────────────────────────────────────────────────────────────┘
```

Fig. 10. Formalisation of associations in the France approach

In Fig. 9, the schema *RelAParent* is the intension schema corresponding to the association with the same name; it includes the variable *self* holding the object identity and a relation between the participating classes. We use our generic *orel* (Fig. 3) to handle the *ordered* association-end. The extension schema would follow the rules of normal classes.

Hall's approach of modelling an association as a class of links does not capture exactly the UML semantics of associations, because links have a set semantics, but formalising them as a class gives them identity allowing repetitions. In order to enforce the correct behaviour a constraint is required on the system schema, stating that link repetitions cannot exist (Fig. 16, last three predicates).

Neither of Hall's alternatives is a complete specification; the full definition is made in a (sub)system-level schema that adds the relevant constraints among objects and links (Fig. 16). These formalisations all operate on object identities.

France (Fig. 10) does not treat associations as classes. Associations are defined in their own schema (e.g. *RelAB*), where the extension schemas of the participant classes are included, and there is a variable modelling the actual association as a relation between classes; multiplicity constraints are modelled as predicates (*RelAB* is a "1..∗" association, hence constrained to a total function from the side many to the side 1). These schemas are included in the system schema (Fig. 17) but without any extensional superstructure.

Self-referencing associations can be easily accommodated in Hall's and France's formalisation rules (definitions of *RelSelf* in Figs. 9 and 10). Support for

```
┌─ ThingRel ─────────────────────────────────
│ self : CLTHREL; atrel1 : ATREL1
│ relThingRel : CLTHB ↔ CLWH
├────────────────────────────────────────────
│ hasMult(relThingRel, 0..1, 1..5)
└────────────────────────────────────────────
```

Fig. 11. Extension to Hall's approach for association classes (intensional definition)

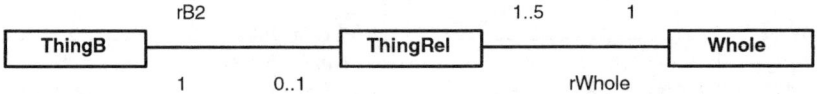

Fig. 12. Modelling trick of promoting the association-class to a class

```
┌─ ThingRelConfig ───────────────────────────
│ ThingRelCW; ThingRelCB
├────────────────────────────────────────────
│ ∀ r₁, r₂ : thingRels | thingRelCB r₁ = thingRelCB r₂
│   ∧ thingRelCW r₁ = thingRelCW r₂ • r₁ = r₂
└────────────────────────────────────────────
```

Fig. 13. Extension to the France approach for association classes

multiplicity constraints are absent in Hall's original work but they can be easily stated; we use our generic *hasMult* (Fig. 4) instantiated with the multiplicity values of the association.

3.5 Association Class

Although no explicit formalisation rules for the concept of association class are provided by Hall, they can be accommodated in the second alternative of associations (association as a class of links). For the association class *ThingRel*, the attribute is included in the intension schema, and the multiplicity constraint of the association is stated as a predicate using the *hasMult* generic (see Fig. 11); the class extension would follow the rules of normal classes.

France's formalisation does not have an approach for association classes. However, we can formalise this by following the common modelling trick of promoting the association-class to a class [23] (Fig. 12). Having said this, promoting the association-class to a class does not exactly capture the semantics of the construct. An association-class behaves like an association, in that link repetition is not allowed; by promoting the association-class, link repetitions become allowed as two distinct objects may contain the same tuple. To overcome this, we add an extra schema to France's formalisation (Fig. 13), where the association

$$\begin{array}{|l}\hline \textit{Whole} \\\hline self : ClWh \\ atw1 : ATW1 \\ parts : \mathbb{P}\ ClPart \\\hline\end{array} \quad \begin{array}{|l}\hline \textit{Part} \\\hline self : ClPart \\ atp1 : ATP1 \\ whole : ClWh \\\hline\end{array} \quad \begin{array}{|l}\hline \textit{WholeComp} \\\hline \mathbb{S}\ Whole;\ \mathbb{S}\ Part \\\hline \forall\ w_1, w_2 : wholes \mid w_1 \neq w_2 \bullet \\ \qquad disjoint\langle w_1.parts, w_2.parts\rangle \\\hline\end{array}$$

Fig. 14. Extension to Hall's approach for composition

$$\begin{array}{|l}\hline \textit{Whole\_Agg} \\\hline Whole \\ Part \\ whole\_agg : CLPART \rightarrowtail CLWH \\\hline whole\_agg \in parts \rightarrow wholes \\\hline\end{array} \quad \begin{array}{|l}\hline \textit{DelAgg} \\\hline \Delta\ Whole\_Agg \\ delaggs? : \mathbb{P}\ CLWH \\\hline delaggs? \subseteq wholes \\ wholes' = wholes \setminus delaggs? \\ parts' = parts \setminus \{p : parts;\ a : delaggs? \mid \\ \qquad whole\_agg(p) = a \bullet p\} \\\hline\end{array}$$

Fig. 15. Composition in the approach of France

schemas are included, stating that link repetitions are not allowed. In the Hall formalisation we add this constraint in the system state schema.

3.6 Aggregation and Composition

The UML concepts of aggregation and composition are difficult to formalise as their semantics is not well-defined [16].

Hall's original work did not consider composition and aggregation. Here, we extend the approach to handle composition, by using Hall's first association rule and by introducing a schema to state the extra properties (Fig. 14). In the schema *WholeComp* the property *unshared containment* is enforced, i.e., no two distinct composites (*Whole*'s objects) can have parts in common (*Part*'s objects). This extension supports only unshared containment, not deletion propagation.

France divides the formalisation of composition and aggregation into a static representation and a dynamic representation (Fig. 15). Essentially, on the static part, naming conventions are used to distinguish the formal representation of composition from simple associations; the difference amounts to replacing the relation by a partial function, this way restricting the possible multiplicities to "1" or "0..1". Note that the predicate of the schema *Whole_Agg*, requiring that the mapping of parts to composites is a total function, i.e., each part takes part in exactly one composition, would also be added for an ordinary association with multiplicity "1" at one of its ends. The dynamic representation is described as an operation to delete composites, where it is stated that when a composite is deleted so are its parts. This representation, however, would not handle compo-

―― System ―――――――――――――――――――――――――――――――――――――
S ThingA; S ThingB; WholeComp
S RelAParent; S RelSelf; S ThingRel; S ParentHierarchy
―――
$\forall a : thingAs \bullet a.rB1 \subseteq thingBIds$
$\forall b : thingBs \bullet b.rA1 \in thingAIds$
$\forall w : wholes \bullet w.parts \subseteq partIds$
$\forall p : parts \bullet p.whole \in wholeIds$
$\forall r : relAParents \bullet \mathrm{dom}(urel(r.relAParent)) \subseteq thingAIds \wedge$
    $\mathrm{ran}(urel(r.relAParent)) \subseteq parentIds$
$\forall rs : relSelfs \bullet \mathrm{dom}\, rs.relSelfB \subseteq thingBIds \wedge \mathrm{ran}\, rs.relSelfB \subseteq thingBIds$
$\forall th : thingRels \bullet \mathrm{dom}\, th.relThingRel \subseteq thingBIds \wedge \mathrm{ran}\, th.relThingRel \subseteq wholeIds$
$\forall r_1, r_2 : relAParents \bullet \exists a : thingAIds; \; p : parentIds \mid$
    $(a,p) \in urel(r_1.relAParent) \wedge (a,p) \in urel(r_2.relAParent) \bullet r_1 = r_2$
$\forall r_1, r_2 : relSelfs \bullet \exists b_1, b_2 : thingBIds \mid$
    $(b_1,b_2) \in r_1.relSelfB \wedge (b_1,b_2) \in r_2.relSelfB \bullet r_1 = r_2$
$\forall r_1, r_2 : thingRels \bullet \exists b : thingBIds; \; w : wholeIds \mid$
    $(b,w) \in r_1.relThingRel \wedge (b,w) \in r_2.relThingRel \bullet r_1 = r_2$

Fig. 16. Formalisation of the system state in the Hall approach

―― System ―――――――――――――――――――――――――――――――――――――
RelAB; RelAParent; Whole_Agg; ParentConfig; RelSelf; ThingRelConfig
―――

Fig. 17. Formalisation of the system state in the France approach

sition hierarchies with more than one level, i.e., if the part to delete would also be a composite.

Dupuy's otherwise flawed formalisation models the dynamic behaviour by defining delete operations and by adding a proof obligation on composition, to assert the deletion propagation semantics; composition hierarchies with more than one level are also not supported.

3.7 The System State

In Z, it is conventional to complete a specification with a schema representing the whole system state. Operations are defined on this schema, since a state element that is not explicitly updated may take any value after an operation.

Both approaches create complete system schemas, where the extensional definitions are included. Hall explicitly adds to the system state schema invariants of wider scope than the component schemas (Fig. 16); the formalisation of associations is completed in the state schema by stating dependency constraints of object references in associations (a reference to an object must be in the set of object identities of the referenced object). We also add constraints to enforce the correct association semantics (described above).

France forces additional constraints into the component schemas; the system state just includes those schemas (Fig. 17).

3.8 Conclusion of Z Comparison

Hall gives concise and rigorous formalisations of class-related concepts. These were not meant to cover UML explicitly, but we find that most UML concepts could be formalised by using Hall's original work; also what we need extra could be accommodated.

The work of France et al is more recent, and is written specifically for UML constructs. Not all of the model could be directly formalised by using the original rules, but what the approach didn't provide could be accommodated. The intent of stating as much as possible in "local-scope" schemas rather than more "globally-scope" (system or sub-system schemas) is to enhance scalability.

We prefer Hall's first alternative to handle associations as roles in objects, as it closely matches the OO paradigm. An object is its attributes, operations and associations.

4 Analysis of Formalisation in Object-Z

Object-Z (OZ) is a genuinely-OO formal notation. In OZ, one can make declarations of references to class schemas because the value stored is the value of the object identifier. This removes the problem of updating object references in Z; it also removes the need for explicit extension schemas. The built-in OZ *self* constant is the implicit identity of each object [13] (compared to Hall's explicit identity variable). The language also supports the concept of inheritance.

Three OZ approaches to the formalisation of UML concepts were considered:

- Araújo [24] is a simplistic approach, where a Z-style representation is presented in the OZ superstructure. This approach had inadequate formalisation guidelines, and did not exploit the OO features of OZ.
- Dupuy et al [10,22], whose Z approach is considered flawed, has an OZ variant which also captures the OO semantics; the OZ variant does not have the problems of the Z counter-part, as OZ supports implicit identity.
- Kim and Carrington[25] (KC) is the approach considered in detail here as it was written specifically for UML. (We have applied this approach to a case study [26]).

The formalisations use only the OZ class structure (outer schema box) and state clause (inner schema). In normal usage, further schema boxes are added to the class structure to represent the initialisation and operations of the class. UML features more suitable to design, such as visibility, are also directly expressible in the OZ notation, but are not explored here. We focus on features closer to requirements specification.

[$ATA1, ATB1, ATB2, ATW1, ATP1, ATPAR1, ATCHA1, ATREL1$]

―― ThingA ――――――――――――――――――
| $ata1 : ATA1$
| $rB1 : \mathbb{P}\ ThingB;\ rParent : \text{iseq}\ Parent$
|――――――――――――――――――――――
| $\forall\ rb : rB1 \bullet self = rb.rA1$
| $\forall\ rp : \text{ran}\ rParent \bullet self \in rp.rA2$

―― Parent ――――――――――――――――――
| $atpar1 : ATPAR1$
| $rA2 : \mathbb{P}\ ThingA$
|――――――――――――――――――――――
| $\forall\ ra : rA2 \bullet self \in \text{ran}\ ra.rParent$

―― ThingB ――――――――――――――――――
| $atb1 : \mathbb{P}\ ATB1;\ atb2 : \mathbb{P}\ ATB2$
| $rA1 : ThingA;\ rWhole : \mathbb{P}\ ThingRel;\ rSelf1 : ThingB;\ rSelf2 : \mathbb{P}\ ThingB$
|――――――――――――――――――――――
| $\#atb2 \in 1..5 \wedge \#rWhole \in 0..1 \wedge \#rSelf2 \in 1..10$
| $self \in rA1.rB1 \wedge self \in rSelf1.rSelf2$
| $\forall\ rs_2 : rSelf2 \bullet self = rs_2.rSelf1$
| $\forall\ rw : rWhole \bullet self = rw.rB2$

Fig. 18. UML classes, attributes, and associations in the Kim & Carrington approach

4.1 Classes, Attributes, and Associations

Figure 18 shows the formalisation of classes *ThingA*, *ThingB* and *Parent* of Fig. 1, using the KC approach.

Attribute types, as in Z, are defined abstractly as given sets. For each class there is a corresponding class schema. The static features of UML classes are expressed directly in the OZ state schema. The KC approach omits multi-valued attributes, but, as in Z, they can be represented using a power-set, and multiplicity constraints, if required, are formalised as predicates in the state schema, see definitions of *atb1* and *atb2* of class *ThingB*.

Like Hall's first Z association rule, KC formalise associations as roles played by classes; participation of a class in an association is modelled as a class attribute (it is legitimate in OZ to refer to a class before it has been defined). In applying KC's rules we again make slight changes. KC formalises every association as a power-set; if the multiplicity at the association-end is "1", a predicate is added restricting the size of the set to "1". This results in clumsy specifications, as it adds predicates in the state schema, and makes the attribute more difficult to handle. We consider multiplicity "1" a special case, and define a simple set (see definition of *rA1* in *ThingB*). In each class's state clause, the predicates with the term *self* express the fact that objects must reference each other in the

```
┌─ ChildA ─────────────────────    ┌─ ChildB ─────────────────────
│ Parent                            │ Parent
│                                   └──────────────────────────────
│ atcha1 : ATCHA1
└──────────────────────────────
```

Fig. 19. Generalisation in the Kim & Carrington's approach

context of an association. As in Z approaches, we prefer to express multiplicities in the form "$\#s \in n1..n2$" (the omission of predicates for role and multi-valued attribute multiplicities represents UML's "$0..*$" multiplicity.)

Self-referential associations can also be formalised nicely in this approach by using OZ's recursive definitions (see definitions *rSelf1* and *rSelf2* of *ThingB*).

This approach is true to the OO (and UML) paradigm in expressing all features of a class in one place. It also captures the meta-structure of the UML concept, by formalising the association as roles within each participant class.

4.2 Generalisation/Specialisations

Figure 19 presents the KC formalisation of *ChildA* and *ChildB*, subclasses of *Parent*. OO inheritance (includes attributes and operations) is supported by OZ; inheritance from the superclass, *Parent*, is expressed like schema inclusion in Z, but, unlike Z, if *Parent* had operations these would also be inherited.

OZ inheritance does not imply subtyping, hence additional statements are required to enforce the subtyping property of generalisation. KC achieves this by using OZ polymorphism. The formalisation is completed in the system class schema (Fig. 22) by declaring the set of *Parent* objects as polymorphic (*parents* : $\mathbb{P}\downarrow Parent$).

Unlike in the Z approaches, in OZ there is no need for extra predicates to enforce the *disjointness* among subclass objects; it is guaranteed by the language. The formalisation of the constraint *overlapping* would be difficult and would result in a non-intuitive solution; it is not included in the KC approach.

The abstract property of the class *Parent* is also expressed in the system class (Fig. 22).

4.3 Association Classes

The KC approach formalises association-class as a class, containing its attributes and two attributes representing the ends of the association (Fig. 20). The multiplicity of the association is modelled via roles on the association classes (see *ThingB* in Fig. 18). This shortens and simplifies the formalisation.

Like the Z counterparts, this formalisation does not capture the full semantics of association classes, as there can be repetitions of links. This problem was not considered in the original approach; to overcome it we enforce the correct semantics with a predicate in the system class schema (Fig. 22).

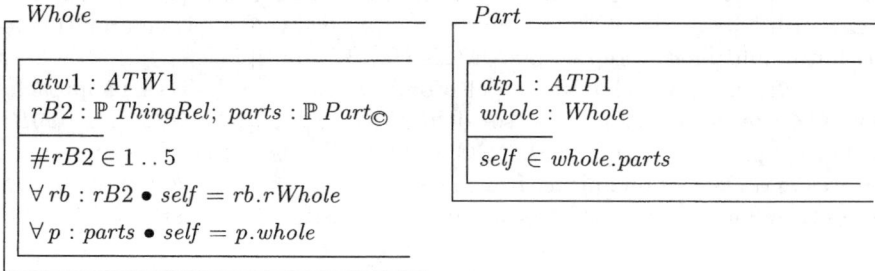

Fig. 20. Association class in the Kim & Carrington approach

┌─ *Whole* ─────────────────────────┐ ┌─ *Part* ────────────────┐
│ $atw1 : ATW1$ │ │ $atp1 : ATP1$ │
│ $rB2 : \mathbb{P}\, ThingRel;\ parts : \mathbb{P}\, Part_{©}$ │ │ $whole : Whole$ │
├───────────────────────────────────┤ ├─────────────────────────┤
│ $\#rB2 \in 1\,..\,5$ │ │ $self \in whole.parts$ │
│ $\forall\, rb : rB2 \bullet self = rb.rWhole$ │ └─────────────────────────┘
│ $\forall\, p : parts \bullet self = p.whole$ │
└───────────────────────────────────┘

Fig. 21. Composition in the Kim & Carrington approach

4.4 Aggregation and Composition

Figure 21 shows KC formalisation of the composition relationship of Fig. 1. The formalisation expresses the required role definitions. Both the part class, *Part*, and the composite class, *Whole*, are formalised according to the rules of classes and associations. The *parts* declaration is qualified by the OZ unshared containment symbol (©). This indicates that the parts are entirely contained within the structure represented by *Whole* (implying *deletion propagation*), and that no object of class *Part* is contained by two distinct objects of class *Whole* (*unshared containment*). OZ containment is a very reasonable compromise given the confusion surrounding the semantics of UML aggregation and composition. In fact, object containment expresses those properties of UML composition on which there seems to be some agreement.

Aggregation formalisation in KC would be the same as simple associations.

4.5 System State

In KC the whole system is defined in an OZ class schema, as a collection of class-instances (Fig. 22). The formalisation rules are as follows:

- Each OZ class is instantiated as a set in the system class.
- If the OZ class is a superclass, then the instantiation of that class must be a set of the polymorphic type of the class.

┌─ System ───┐
│ ┌───┐ │
│ │ $thingAs : \mathbb{P}\,ThingA$; $thingBs : \mathbb{P}\,ThingB$; $parents : \mathbb{P}\downarrow Parent$ │ │
│ │ $childAs : \mathbb{P}\,ChildA$; $childBs : \mathbb{P}\,ChildB$; $thingRels : \mathbb{P}\,ThingRel$ │ │
│ │ $wholes : \mathbb{P}\,Whole$; $parts : \mathbb{P}\,Part$ │ │
│ ├───┤ │
│ │ $\forall\, a : thingAs \bullet a.rB1 \subseteq thingBs \land \mathrm{ran}(a.rParent) \subseteq parents$ │
│ │ $\forall\, b : thingBs \bullet b.rA1 \in thingAs \land b.rWhole \subseteq thingRels$ │
│ │ $\land\ b.rSelf1 \in thingBs \land b.rSelf2 \subseteq thingBs$ │
│ │ $\forall\, p : parents \bullet p.rA2 \subseteq thingAs$ │ │
│ │ $\forall\, w : wholes \bullet w.rB2 \subseteq thingRels \land w.parts \subseteq parts$ │
│ │ $\forall\, p : parts \bullet p.whole \in wholes$ │ │
│ │ $\forall\, tr : thingRels \bullet tr.rB2 \in thingBs \land tr.rWhole \in wholes$ │
│ │ $\forall\, tr_1, tr_2 : thingRels \mid tr_1.rWhole = tr_2.rWhole \land tr_1.rB2 = tr_2.rB2 \bullet tr_1 = tr_2$ │
│ │ $childAs \subseteq parents \land childBs \subseteq parents$ │ │
│ │ $\forall\, p : parents \bullet p \notin Parent$ │ │
│ └───┘ │
└───┘

Fig. 22. Kim & Carrington's representation of the system state

– Constraints state that references of instances are existing instances and that the set of subclass instances is a subset of the superclass instances.

In the system state schema, we also add constraints to overcome missing features and make slight corrections to the original approach. The abstract property of the class *Parent* (missing in the original work) is stated at the end of the predicate. A constraint stating the correct behaviour of *ThingRel* as an association class (disallowing repetitions of links in its instances) is also enforced in the predicate of the system state schema (predicate before last).

5 Comparison and Conclusion

We have analysed different formalisation approaches of UML class constructs. None of the approaches provide full support for the features used in the example UML diagram. We have provided extensions, and made slight changes to the originals to allow a full, to some extent semantically correct, and more practical formalisation.

Hall's formalisation of association as classes of links, and KC's association class formalisation violate the semantics of UML associations, as link (tuple of object references) repetitions are not allowed in the UML. This was a recurring problem in the UML formalisation, that could be corrected by enforcing the correct behaviour in component or system schemas.

In general, Z is a more open language than OZ. The approaches show that Z can be used to approximate OO semantics, but in a cumbersome way.

OZ's inherent OO concepts invariably produce more concise formalisations of UML concepts. The specifications are also *lighter* and more intuitive, as they do not contain the many predicates enforcing OO semantics found on the Z counter-parts.

We found that the KC OZ approach provided good formalisations for the more problematic concepts of UML generalisation and composition, which do not have a precise semantics. The constraint *overlapping* of UML generalisation may not have an easy formalisation into OZ, but this constraint is seldom used. Due to the ambiguous definitions of some concepts in the UML, some compromises were required in order to formalise them. Both France and KC give the same interpretation to these concepts and made similar compromises.

The Z approaches are generally effective at capturing the OO semantics, but they result in cumbersome specifications, that do not provide enough abstraction from the details of OO semantics enforcement. Regarding the more problematic concepts of UML, the formalisation of generalisation is satisfactory, but composition needs further work. Another feature that may contribute to lack of abstraction and readability in Z is the description of behavioural properties (not considered here), as it will require more machinery to state semantically correct class operation behaviour.

We are currently working on a UML to Z formalisation approach based on Z generics and templates that corrects problems with the approaches analysed here, and that tries to improve the readability, abstraction, and conciseness of the resulting Z specifications.

The problems with formalising the semantic intent of composition and aggregation is partly a result of considering only the UML static concepts. Composition and aggregation constrain the behaviour of instances of associated classes rather than their static properties; the semantics can only be expressed in behavioural models, and enforced through theorems of behaviour.

The paper has not considered behavioural specification. Both the Z and OZ approaches facilitate the specification of class-level operations. In OZ, these are tightly bound to the class, and maintain the OO principles of encapsulation etc. In Z, these are simple operations on components of the state. An essential difference is that, unless the other classes are explicitly specified not to change, simple Z operations on one class leave undefined the effect on any other class. Z schema calculus allows simple operations to be built up into system functions or transactions; this is less easy in OZ, because of the need to access class-level operations through the class interface. The system state class defined by KC should assist this part of the specification.

The KC approach is most appropriate if the development is clearly sited in the OO paradigm with compatible semantics, but the Z approaches allow more flexibility in other development paradigms. The KC gives full traceability between UML and formal models, whereas the Hall and the France approaches give a Z model that is amenable to formal proof and development if required.

Z is more mature, having an ISO standard [11], a range of type-checking tools [27,28,29,30] and some proof assistants [30,31]. OZ has only a prototype type-checker [32]. Assuming that each language reaches maturity, choice of Z or OZ would depend on the intended development, and on whether the developer wishes to express formally the semantics of the modelled system or the semantics of the system models.

Despite the problems with the original approaches, we consider that there is substantial support in the literature for helping practitioners in the integration of UML and formal specification languages, thus, taking advantage of the added precision, rigour and verification mechanisms provided by formalisation [26]. We claim that UML integration with a formal specification language is currently, from a practical point of view, the most effective and pragmatic way of introducing rigour and precision in UML-based requirements specifications.

Acknowledgements. We would like to thank Susan Stepney for fruitful discussions and comments on this work. This research was supported for Amálio by the Portuguese Foundation for Science and Technology under grant 6904/2001.

References

1. OMG: Unified Modeling Language Specification, version 1.1. Object Management Group. (1997) Available at http://www.rational.com/uml.
2. OMG: Unified Modeling Language Specification, version 1.3. Object Management Group. (1999) Available at http://www.omg.org/uml.
3. OMG: Unified Modeling Language Specification, version 1.4. Object Management Group. (2001) Available at http://www.omg.org/uml.
4. Rumbaugh, J., Jacobson, I., Booch, G.: The Unified Modeling Language Reference Manual. Addison Wesley Longman, Reading, Mass. (1999)
5. Evans, A., France, R., Lano, K., Rumpe, B.: The UML as a formal modeling notation. [33] 336–348
6. Evans, A., Lano, K., France, R., Rumpe, B.: Meta-modeling semantics of UML. In Kilov, H., Rumpe, B., Simmonds, I., eds.: Behavioral Specifications of Businesses and Systems, Kluver Academic Publisher (1999)
7. Lano, K., Bicarregui, J., Evans, A.: Structured axiomatic semantics for UML models. Technical Report GR/K67311-2, BCS FACS/EROS ROOM Workshop, A. Evans and K. Lano eds, Dept. of Computing, Imperial College, London (2000)
8. Polack, F., Laleau, R.: A rigorous metamodel for UML static conceptual modelling of information systems. In: CAiSE 2001: Advanced Information Systems Engineering, Interlaken, Switzerland. Volume 2068 of LNCS., Springer (2001) 402–416
9. Bruel, J.M., France, R.B.: Transforming UML models to formal specifications. [33]
10. Dupuy, S.: Couplage de notations semi-formelles et formelles pour la spécification des systèmes d'information. PhD thesis, Université Joseph Fourier, Grenoble I (2000)
11. ISO: Information technology—Z formal specification notation—syntax, type system and semantics (2002) ISO/IEC 13568:2002, International Standard.
12. Spivey, J.M.: The Z Notation: A Reference Manual. 2nd edn. Prentice Hall (1992)

13. Smith, G.P.: The Object-Z Specification Language. Advances in Formal Methods. Kluwer Academic Publishers (2000)
14. Duke, R., Rose, G.: Formal Object-Oriented specification using Object-Z. Cornerstones of Computing. MacMillan Press Limited (2000)
15. Bourdeau, R.H., Cheng, B.H.: A formal Semantics for Object Model Diagrams. IEEE Transactions on Software Engineering **21** (1995) 799–821
16. Henderson-Sellers, B., Barbier, F.: Black and white diamonds. In France, R., Rumpe, B., eds.: UML'99. Beyond the Standard. 2nd International Conference, Fort Collins, CO, USA. Volume 1723 of LNCS., Springer (1999) 550–565
17. Hall, A.: Using Z as a specification calculus for object-oriented systems. In Hoare, C.A.R., Bjørner, D., Langmaack, H., eds.: VDM '90 VDM and Z– Formal Methods in Software Development. Volume 428 of LNCS., Springer (1990) 290–318
18. Hall, A.: Specifying and interpreting class hierarchies in Z. [34] 120–138
19. Hammond, J.: Producing Z specifications from object-oriented analysis. [34] 316–336
20. France, R.B., Grant, E., Bruel, J.M.: UMLtranZ: An UML-based rigorous requirements modeling technique. Technical report, Colorado State University, Fort Collins, Colorado, USA (2000)
21. Dupuy, S., Ledru, Y., Chabre-Peccoud, M.: Vers une intégration utile de notations semi-formelles et formelles: une expérience en UML et Z. L'Object, numéro thématique Méthodes formelles pour les objects **6** (2000)
22. Dupuy, S., Ledru, Y., Chabre-Peccoud, M.: Integrating OMT and Object-Z. In Evans, A., Lano, K., eds.: Proceedings of BCS FACS/EROS ROOM Workshop, London, UK (1997)
23. Fowler, M., Scott, K.: UML Distilled. 2nd edn. Addison-Wesley (2000)
24. Araújo, J.: Metamorphosis: An Integrated Object-Oriented Requirements Analysis and Specification Method. PhD thesis, Department of Computing, University of Lancaster (1996)
25. Kim, S.K., Carrington, D.: A formal mapping between UML models and Object-Z specifications. In Bowen, J., et al., eds.: ZB 2000: Formal Specification and Development in Z and B, York, UK. Volume 1878 of LNCS., Springer (2000) 2–21
26. Amálio, N.: Formalization of UML models in Object-Z for quality assurance and requirements specification. Master's thesis, Department of Computer Science, University of York, Heslington, York, YO10 5DD, UK (2001)
27. Spivey, J.: The Fuzz manual, 2nd edition. Computer Science Consultancy (1992)
28. Toyn, I.: CADiZ web pages. http://www-users.cs.york.ac.uk/~ian/cadiz/ (2001)
29. Stepney, S.: Formaliser Home Page. (http://public.logica.com/~formaliser/)
30. Saaltink, M.: The Z/EVES system. In: ZUM'97: The Z Formal Specification Notation. Volume 1212 of LNCS., Springer (1997)
31. Arthan, R.: The ProofPower web pages. (http://www.lemma-one.com/-ProofPower/index/index.html)
32. Johnston, W.: Wizard: A type checker for Object-Z. Technical report 96-24, Software Verification Research Centre, The University of Queensland, Brisbane, Australia (1996)
33. Bézivin, J., Muller, P.A., eds.: UML'98: Beyond the Notation, Mulhouse, France. Volume 1618 of LNCS., Springer (1998)
34. Bowen, J., Hall, A., eds.: Z User Workshop, Cambridge. Workshops in Computing, Springer (1994)

Towards Practical Proofs of Class Correctness

Bertrand Meyer

ETH Zürich, Chair of Software Engineering
http://se.inf.ethz.ch
(also Eiffel Software, Santa Barbara, and Monash University)

Abstract. Preliminary steps towards a theory, framework and process for proving that contract-equipped classes satisfy their contracts, including when the run-time structure involves pointers; and its application to correctness proofs of routines from a *LINKED_LIST* class, such as element removal and list reversal.

1 Scope

"Trusted Components" are reusable software elements with guaranteed quality properties. Establishing a base of trusted components is among the most promising approaches to improving the general state of software; the potential for widespread reuse justifies the effort necessary to get the components right [11].

The most ambitious guarantee of component properties is a mathematical proof. The present work is part of an effort to produce a library of object-oriented components, equipped with contracts in the Eiffel style, and accompanied with mathematical proofs – mechanically checked – that the implementations satisfy the contracts.

We introduce a theory for correctness proofs of classes, and apply it to proofs for a class describing linked lists.

Like any realistic example of object-oriented component, the linked list class produces run-time structures relying extensively on pointers. A related set of articles [13] propose a general proof framework for pointers. The present article uses their results, but can be read independently. For more details about pointer semantics please refer to the complete series.

The scope of the Trusted Components effort is, of course, much broader than the work reported here. A Component Quality Model, under development, addresses the evaluation of commercial grade components from various technologies other than O-O classes, for example .NET assemblies and Enterprise Java Beans. The present discussion focuses on a special case: proving the correctness of classes. It is not the fulll story, but it's an important story – or, in the current state of this work, the beginning of an important story – that a Trusted Components project cannot afford to skip.

2   Guidelines

This work is based on some distinctive decisions.

We focus on the *object* structure. In descriptions of object technology developing the method's contribution to software engineering [10], the emphasis is naturally on *classes*, the compile-time module and type unit mechanism. Many formal treatments of object-oriented programming, such as Abadi and Cardelli's *Theory of Objects* [1], accordingly start from classes. To study the semantics of O-O computation, it seems more productive to start by modeling the run-time object structure, and the associated operations such as feature call, then work our way up – in a second step of the effort, only sketched in the present article – to classes and other program-level mechanisms such as inheritance.

In our study of these run-time object structures we'll take it for granted that they may include *pointers* (also called "references"). Although this is true of all realistic O-O programs and libraries, pointers have not been at the center of O-O theories; Abadi and Cardelli largely ignore them. By using high-level functions and associated operators we can model pointers in a simple way.

A useful literature exists on the formal treatment of pointers [3,4,8,15,16, 17]. Some of it discusses this problem in a general context, whereas we will restrict the analysis to object-oriented programs. This means in particular that unlike many authors we won't concern ourselves with general pointer assignments *object.pointer_field := value* which, although still supported by recent languages from C++ and Java to C#, conflict with data abstraction principles. In O-O development one obtains the desired effect through a procedure call *object.set_pointer_field (value)* where *set_pointer_field* is a procedure of the corresponding class. Then the only legal form of assignment, and the only one we consider, is *field := value*, relative to the current object.

This notion of *current object* (*Current* in Eiffel, *self* or *this* in other languages) is central to the O-O method and to the model below. One of the most potent contributions of Simula 67, it is comparable in its depth to the notion of recursion in general programming. *Current* makes every operation relative: any variable, expression or operation is meaningful only in relation to the current object, which varies between successive executions of the same construct. To model this notion we will consider that any mathematical interpretation of a programming construct is a function whose single argument represents the current object. (The result of such a function is usually itself a function, representing for example a state transition.)

This reflects the actual behavior of object-oriented computation. In Eiffel the rule is explicit: executing a program is defined as creating one object, the *root*, and applying to it a specified *root procedure*. Upon execution, the root assumes the role of current object. If the procedure contains a call *x.proc* for some *x* of type *C* in the root's class, executing this call really means executing *root.x.proc*. If *proc* itself contains an assignment *field := value*, both *field* and *value* must also be interpreted relatively, as denoting *root.x.field* and *root.x.value*. This goes on: if *proc* contains a call *y.other_proc*, any operation in *op* in *other_pro* really means *root.x.y.op* etc.

Even though the execution of any O-O programming construct is relative to the root-originated chain *root.x.y....* which determines its run-time target, the text of the construct, in the class where it appears, cannot know that target. To account for this fundamental property, any theory of object-oriented computation must be a "general relativity" theory.

Another characteristic of this work is that its specification techniques do not hesitate to take advantage of *high-level functions* and operations such as composition; assertions using these mechanisms will figure prominently in contracts, giving a power of expression that seems hard to match through other means such as first-order predicate calculus. Perhaps the most visible effect of this approach is that we'll be able to model the fundamental operation of object-oriented computation, a feature call *x.f(a)*, through the mathematical expression $\bar{x}.\bar{f}(\bar{a})$ where $\bar{x}$ and $\bar{f}$ are mathematical functions directly modeling *x* and $\bar{f}$, $\bar{a}$ models the argument *a*, and "." is function composition.

The functions are *possibly partial* (abbreviated from now on to just "partial" if there is no ambiguity). Although many authors stay away from them, partial functions address many issues elegantly. For example we don't need any special concept to describe a void (null) pointer; it's simply a function applied outside of its domain. The reason for the common distrust of partial functions is the need to guard every function application *f*(*a*) by a proof that *a* belongs to **domain** (*f*). We dodge this by almost never applying a function directly to its arguments, but instead relying on operators which handle partiality gracefully such as *composition*.

A final characteristic is the role of *models*. We can only prove a class correct relative to some view of the intended behavior of its instances. Rather than relying on a pure algebraic approach, we'll define such views through a mathematical model for the instances, interpreting for example a list as a sequence. Then we can specify the effect of a routine as its mathematical effect on the model. Combined with the use of high-level functions and operators, this gives us all the expressiveness we need. We will see that this technique has important practical consequences on the proof process: a key part will be the building of an appropriate model for the structures under study.

3 What to Prove

Given classes that implement certain structures and associated operations, with contracts that specify the intended effect of the operations, the goal of the present effort is to prove that the implementations satisfy the contracts.

To understand the issues, let us start with an informal look at such a class and the kind of properties that will have to be proved.

A Routine

An example from the EiffelBase library is the following routine from the class *LINKED_LIST*[*G*]:

```
remove_front is
        -- Remove first element of list.
    require
        not_empty: first /= Void
    do
        first := first. right
    ensure
        one_less: count = old count – 1
            ... Other postcondition clauses (see text) ...
    end
```

Feature *first* is called *first_element* is the actual EiffelBase class.

The figure illustrates the underlying structure and the operation's effect. Class *LINKABLE[G]*, complementing *LINKED_LIST*, describes individual list cells, each with a reference field *right* leading to the next cell if any.

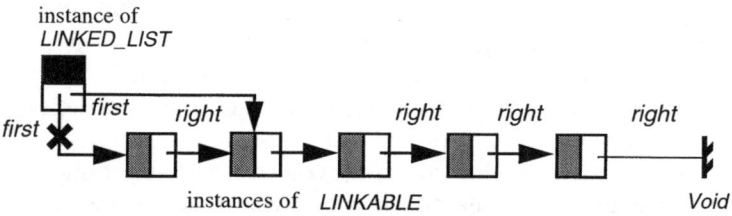

Fig. 1. Removing the front element

A property of such structures, which all public operations such as *remove_front* must maintain, is the absence of cycles; more precisely, starting from a *LINKED_LIST* instance and following *right* links zero or more times, we must never encounter a *LINKABLE* element twice, and end with a *Void*. The place to express such properties is the class invariant.

We must prove that, whenever the precondition (**require** clause) and the invariant both hold, executing the body (**do**) will lead to a state in which the postcondition (**ensure**) holds and the invariant holds again. Such proofs require a semantics for both the instructions and the assertions, as developed in the remaining sections.

Defining a Model

Besides a semantic theory, we will need *models* of the object structures.

The example highlights the issue: contract expressiveness. The postcondition of *remove_front* states that the routine must decrease *count*, the number of list elements, by one, but omits the key property that the remaining elements are the same as before, except for the first, in their original order.

Contrary to a commonly encountered view, the solution does not have to involve extending the assertion language with first-order predicate calculus, which would be inadequate anyway to state many properties of interest. An example where predicate calculus doesn't appear to help is the invariant identified earlier: the absence of cycles.

It is more effective to focus on the abstract structure that an implementation class such as *LINKED_LIST* represents, and on the effect that operations have on it. In other words we introduce a model, expressing the *abstraction function* [6] associated with the class. For *LINKED_LIST[G]* the model should be a sequence of values (each of type *G*, the formal generic parameter). So if we assume the corresponding type *SEQUENCE[G]* we will have, in the class, a feature

> *model*: SEQUENCE [*G*]
>   -- The sequence of values associated with this list

used for specification and proof purposes only. Another article [14] discusses in detail the use of such model features, showing in particular how to combine this notion with inheritance: if *LINKED_LIST* is just one of the descendants of a more general class *LIST*, whose other descendants such as *ARRAYED_LIST* provide alternative implementations, the *model* may be introduced in *LIST*, and [14] shows how to discharge much of the proof work in that higher-level class, so that the descendants only require a proof of implementation consistency. Here we limit ourselves to a simpler framework and do all the work in *LINKED_LIST*, ignoring inheritance. The immediate consequence is that we may now specify *remove_front* fully through the new postcondition

> **ensure**
>   *head_chopped_off*. *model* = **old** *model*. *tail*

where *tail* is a function on sequences, with the obvious meaning. Then we don't any more need the clause *one_less* (stating that *count* goes down by one) except as a theorem that will follow from the new clause *head_chopped_off* and the property of sequences that *s.tail.count = s.count − 1*.

It is easy to apply the same approach to a routine *put_front* (*x:G*) that inserts an element at the beginnning:

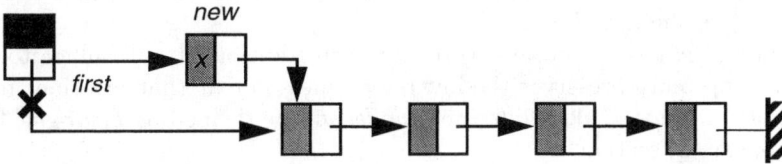

Fig. 2. Inserting at the front

The postcondition in this case is

> *extended*: **model** = <x> + **old** *model*

where + denotes sequence concatenation and <x> a singleton sequence.

Once we have given ourselves a few more operations on sequences, we will also be able to express invariant properties such as the absence of cycles.

Reversing a List

The use of a model enables us to specify sophisticated operations, such as this list reversal routine using the procedure *put_right* from *LINKABLE*, which sets the *right* link. (The following figure helps understand the invariant.)

```
reverse is
          -- Change list to have the same elements in reverse
    order.
       local
          previous, next: LINKABLE [G]
       do
          from
              next := first
          invariant                      -- See figure
              spliced: old model = [first. right**] □ mirror
                                              + next. right**
          variant
              next. right**. count
          until
              next = Void
          loop
              [previous, first, next] := [first, next, next. right]
              first. put_right (previous)
          end
       ensure
          reversed: model = old model □ mirror
       end
```

where $s \square$ *mirror* is the mirror image of a sequence s and f^{**}, for a partial function f, is the function that for any *obj* yields the sequence *obj*, f (*obj*), f (f (*obj*)) etc., going for as long as defined. This is a generalization of reflexive transitive closure, hence the notation.

To prove that the routine ensures its postcondition, it will suffice to prove that the loop body preserves the invariant, since on exit that invariant implies [*first.right***] *mirror* = **old** *model*, and *model* will be defined as *first.right***. The proof appears in section 10.

For brevity the invariant uses = instead of the object equality function *equal*. As in a postcondition, **old** *v* in the loop invariant denotes *v*'s value on entry to the routine. [*a*, *b*, ...] := [*x*, *y*, ...] denotes multiple simultaneous assignment.

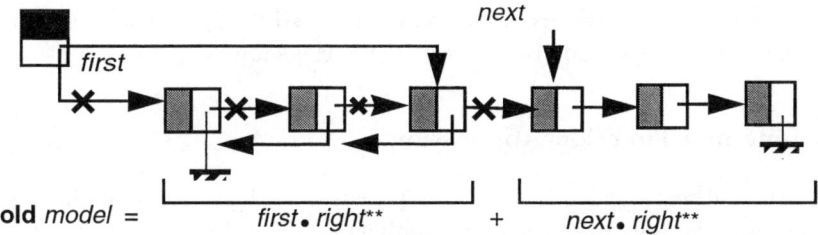

Fig. 3. List reversing: intermediate state

The specification techniques illustrated by these examples take advantage of:
- The notion of model.
- To define models, any well-defined mathematical concept: here sequences, elsewhere sets, functions, relations, graphs etc.
- High-level operators on these structures, such as +, *mirror* and **.

This appears to give us the modeling power that we need to express the specifications of all practiacally useful data structures.

It remains to devise the semantic description techniques that will enable us to prove that the implementations satisfy these specifications.

4 Notations

The following notations help keep the semantics and proofs simple.

Function Abstraction

function *a* | *expression* denotes a function *f* such that *f (a)* = *expression* for any applicable *a*. This is plain lambda notation with keyword syntax. Although the approach is strongly typed we'll leave the type of *a* implicit.

Basic Composition

The semantic models rely throughout on composition of relations and functions. Function composition will rely on the operator "$\circ$", used in the loop invariant and postcondition of *reverse*; $f \circ g$ is the **function** *a* | *g (f (a))*. The operands appear in the order of application:

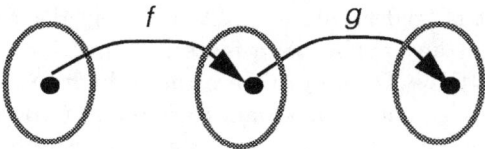

Fig. 4. Composition

The symbol differs slightly from the commonly used " ∘ " to avoid any confusion, since the order of operands is reversed: $f \square g$ is the same as $g \circ f$.

Grouping and Function Application

Ordinary mathematical notation uses parentheses both for grouping and for function application; this can cause confusion when the elements grouped are themselves functions. For that reason, we reserve parentheses for function application, as in $f(a)$, and use brackets for grouping, as in

$$[f \square g] \square h = f \square [g \square h]$$

which, true for any f, g and h, expresses associativity of composition; applied to an individual element a this gives

$$[[f \square g] \square h](a) = [f \square [g \square h]](a)$$

using both grouping (brackets) and function application (parentheses). Associativity lets us omit many brackets, as in $f \square g \square h$.

> Some functional formalisms write function application simply by juxtaposing the function and the argument, as in $f\ a$. This convention has not been retained here as it would cause confusion. Since our functions are partial, we will anyway, as noted in section 2, use function application as little as possible.

Partial Functions

$A \nrightarrow B$ is the set of partial functions from A to B; composition, defined for arbitrary relations, works well with partial functions.

When defining multi-level function spaces such as $A \nrightarrow [B \nrightarrow C]$, we may omit brackets associating from the right, writing $A \nrightarrow B \nrightarrow C$ in this example.

Rightmost Composition

We will use two variants of composition, which are fundamentally the same operation as "$\square$" but with different signatures, made necessary by the multi-level function spaces involved in the semantic models.

The first variant is "rightmost composition". Consider f in $A \nrightarrow [B \nrightarrow C]$, so that that $f(a)$ for any applicable a is itself a function. Given a function g similarly in $A \nrightarrow [C \nrightarrow D]$, we can't use the ordinary composition $f \square g$ (the signatures don't match), but we may want to compose $f(a)$ and $g(a)$ for a given a. The resulting function will be written $f \blacksquare g$. This can go over several levels, with functions in $A_1 \to ... A_n \nrightarrow X \nrightarrow Y$ and $A_1 \nrightarrow ... A_n \nrightarrow Y \nrightarrow Z$, for some sets X, Y and Z; the general definition then is

$$f \bullet g = \text{function } a_1 \mid [\text{ function } a_2 \mid [\ldots \mid [\text{function } a_n \mid \\ [[\ldots [[f(a_1)](a_2)]\ldots](a_n)] \square [[\ldots [[g(a_1)](a_2)]\ldots](a_n)]]\ldots]$$

We may similarly define the "rightmost inverse" f^{-1*} of such a function f as

$$\text{function } a_1 \mid [\ldots \mid [\text{function } a_n \mid \quad [\ldots [f(a_1)]\ldots](a_n)]^{-1}]\ldots]$$

and, when the rightmost target set is $\mathbb{B}$ (booleans), the "rightmost implication" $f \stackrel{*}{\Rightarrow} g$ as

$$\forall\ a_1, a_2, \ldots a_n \mid [\ldots [[f(a_1)](a_2)]\ldots](a_n)] \implies [\ldots [[g(a_1)](a_2)]\ldots](a_n)]$$

as well as the "rightmost conjunction" $\stackrel{*}{\wedge}$.

State-Curried Composition

The other variant of composition arises from the specific nature of our semantic functions which (as seen in the next sections) all have signatures of the form $A_1 \not\rightarrow \ldots A_n \not\rightarrow States \not\rightarrow Y$, where $States$ is the set of possible run-time states. We will use such functions to model a linked list structure by representing *first*

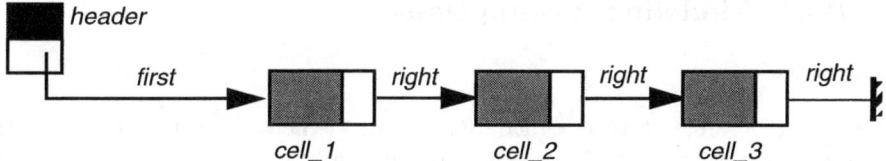

Fig. 5. Denoting successive list cells

and *right* as functions in $Objects \not\rightarrow States \not\rightarrow Objects$; given an object *header*, for example, [*first* (*header*)] (*s*) is the object to which its *first* link points in state *s*—*cell_1* on the figure. It's desirable to compose such functions *applied in the same state*, for example *first* and *right* so that the result, applied to *header*, gives us the object labeled *cell_2*. This is the kind of expressiveness we need to state properties of the current state, in particular class invariants, loop invariants and other assertions.

We cannot directly compose two such functions, f in $X \not\rightarrow States \not\rightarrow Y$ and g in $Y \not\rightarrow States \not\rightarrow Z$. Fixing the state, however, we may compose their two variants

$$\text{function } x \mid [f(x)](s)$$
$$\text{function } x \mid [g(x)](s)$$

for a given s, the same on both lines. This operation will simply use a period
".". The definition of f.g is

> **function** x ǀ [**function** s ǀ [g ([f (x)] (s))] (s)]

This choice of symbol works well for modeling the object structures created
by object-oriented programs: as the previous example indicates, the successive
items of a list will be given by the functions *first*, *first.right*, *first.right.right* etc.
all applied in the same state. It is indeed one of the results of this article that
we can understand *feature application*, the central operation of object-oriented
programming, as the mathematical notion of *function composition*. In the case
of an attribute, the composition operator is "." as just seen; in the case of a
routine it will be rightmost composition, "■".

Both of these operators are fundamentally the same as composition; they
simply massage the order of arguments to remove any signature mismatch. The
purpose is clear: express as many properties as possible through composition
operators. On first reading of the following discussion you may disregard the
differences between ".", "∘" and "■", just seeing them as composition tuned to
the required signature in each case. All the examples of this discussion and other
proofs based on the theory must be mechanically type-checked, to ensure use of
the proper variant in each case and justify this call for the reader's trust.

5 Basic Modeling Assumptions

The State

The set of possible state is called *States*. An element of *States* describes the
instantaneous state of an object-oriented program's execution, and is defined by
a set *Objects* and a collection of functions:

- *Objects* denotes of set of addresses hosting objects. *Objects* is a subset of
  Addresses, the set of possible (abstract) memory addresses [13]. Note that an
  element of *Objects* doesn't represent the contents of an object, but its location;
  this reflects the notion of *object identity*, making it possible to consider each
  object individually regardless of its contents.
- There's also a collection of functions in *Objects* ↛ *Objects* (the set of partial
  functions from *Objects* to itself) representing objects' reference fields. Class
  LINKABLE, for example, has an attribute *right*: *LINKABLE[G]* as illustrated
  next, which yields a function, also called *right*, in the model. When discussing
  the properties of such functions in general, we'll give them names like x, y, ...
- Objects may also have non-reference fields; for example class *LINKABLE[G]*
  has an attribute *item*: *G* representing the values in cells, shown as the shaded
  areas in the figure. For cells of type *LINKABLE[INTEGER]*, *item* fields denote
  integers. Such attributes are represented by functions in *Objects* ↛ *Expanded*,
  where *Expanded* is the set of possible non-reference values including booleans,
  integers, real numbers etc. General names for such functions are u, v, ...

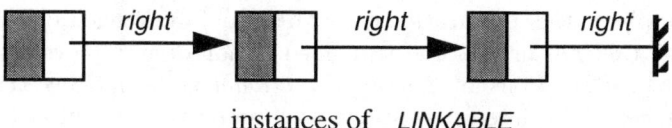

instances of LINKABLE

Fig. 6. "Right" links in *LINKABLE* objects

Values will denote the set of all possible values: *Objects* ∪ *Expanded*.

All the functions involved are partial (meaning, by the earlier convention, *possibly* partial). Partiality helps us in two different ways:

- It gives us a simple interpretation for *Void*: we model a void reference, such as the rightmost link on the last figure, simply by ensuring that the function, here *right*, is not defined for the corresponding object.
- We can also use partial functions to handle type rules of a statically typed O-O language, by defining a function such as *right* so that its domain is a subset of the set of *LINKABLE* objects.

Other Conventions

Names such as *f, g*, ... denote functions from *Objects* to either *Objects* or *Expanded*, representing fields that contain either references or other values. Names such as *obj, obj1*... denote objects; *a, b*, ... denote objects or values.

For elements of the software text: *i, j*, ... denote instructions; *r, s*, ... denote routines. All our routine calls will have exactly one argument, as in *r (a)* or *x.r(a)*; this causes no loss of generality if we assume that the set of values, as in Eiffel, includes a *TUPLE* type.

Assertions, for which we will use names such as *P, Q*, ..., denote boolean properties applicable to a certain object in a certain state. For example the assertion *n>0* is a function of the state, true in states for which *n*, evaluated on the current object, is positive. Accordingly, class invariants will be modeled as functions in *Objects* $\nrightarrow$ *States* $\nrightarrow$ $\mathbb{B}$, and pre- or postconditions of a routine with arguments as functions in *Values* $\nrightarrow$ *Objects* $\nrightarrow$ *States* $\nrightarrow$ $\mathbb{B}$.

Interpreting State Changes

The execution of an object-oriented program consists of a sequence of state changes reflecting execution of individual constructs, for example a procedure call *x.r (a)*.

The basic semantics defined below is of the *denotational* style; this means we define the meaning of a typical imperative construct as a function in $A_1 \nrightarrow ... A_n \nrightarrow$ *States* $\nrightarrow$ *States* where $A_1, ... A_n$ hold the parameters of the construct, and the resulting *States* $\nrightarrow$ *States* function describes the new state produced by the construct in terms of the previous state. This approach is mathematically simplest.

When applying the specification through a proof workbench such as Atelier B [3,5] we may take advantage of a predefined notion of event covering the *States* ↛ *States* transformations in a more *operational* style, making the functions implicit. Since we are interested in pre-post properties of routines, proofs will use a partly *axiomatic* style.

We may compose state transformations. In the denotational view this operation uses rightmost composition as defined in section 4; in a more *operational* interpretation it simply means executing events in sequence. The formal properties are in direct correspondence.

Possible State Changes

The state being defined by a set of objects and a collection of functions on these objects, an elementary state change will either

1● Change the set of *Objects* by adding or removing an object.
2● Change one of the functions; at the most basic level this means changing the value of one of the functions on one of its possible arguments.

There is no such thing as "changing an object" in this model. The model for an object is just an integer, representing its abstract "address". So we may add or remove an object (events of type 1), but to model the changing of a field in an existing object – what an O-O programmer would think of as changing the object – we use events of type 2, changing the corresponding function. Assume for example that class *EMPLOYEE* has an attribute *age*: *INTEGER*. If we execute *Jill*.*pass_birthday* where *pass_birthday* is a procedure of the class that performs

```
age := age + 1
```

the mathematical effect is to change function *age* so that its value for that object, *age* (*Jill*), is increased by one.

Events of type 1 correspond to object allocation (by the program) and deallocation (by the program or a garbage collector). They are studied in detail in the second part ("coarse-grain model") of [13]. For the present discussion we don't consider them: the set of objects is fixed, and all that happens is procedure calls that modify these objects – meaning, as we have just seen, changing some values of the applicable functions. The case of a procedure that may create an object will be handled by combining the two discussions.

Function Substitution

The basic operation, representing an event of type 2, modifies the value of a function for a single object. Given two functions *f* and *g* in *Objects* ↛ *Objects* or *Objects* ↛ *Values*, it will be written

```
f := g
```

and defined as the function in *Objects* ⇸ [*States* ⇸ *States*] that – informally – yields for any object *obj* the state transformation that changes nothing except the value of *f* (*obj*), which in the new state is the value of *g* (*obj*) in the original state, if defined, undefined otherwise (the functions involved are partial).

> Here is a more formal definition of this operation. The state, as we have seen, has two components: the set *Objects* representing object identities, and a set of functions in *Objects* ⇸ *Objects* or *Objects* ⇸ *Values*, each with a name such as *f, g, h*... We may denote these functions, for a given state *s*, as *s.f, s.g,* ... Then *f* := *g*, as noted, is a function in *Objects* ⇸ [*States* ⇸ *States*]; call it *assign*. For any object *obj* and state *s*, *assign* (*obj*) is a function from *States* to *States*, and so [*assign* (*obj*)] (*s*) is a new state, which we may call *s'*. Then *s'* is the same state as *s* except for its '*f*' component, the function we're calling *s'.f*. That function is the same as *s.f* except at *obj*:
> - *s'.f* (*obj'*) = *s.f* (*obj'*)   – For *obj'* other than *obj*
> - *s'.f* (*obj*) = *s.g* (*obj*)   – Or undefined if *obj* is not in the domain of *s.g*.

The := operator enjoys two characteristic properties

```
[A1]   [[ f := g ] ∎ f ]  = g
[A2]   [[ f := g ] ∎ h]  = h   -- For a function h other than f
```

where the use of composition (more precisely, rightmost composition "∎") avoids having to worry about the functions being defined or not.

> Properties are numbered in a single sequence, with different initial letters, A for axiom, S for semantics etc.

The := operator will, through these properties, enable simple proofs of attribute assignment instructions *x* := *y* in a class text. An advantage is that unlike traditional assignment axioms the rules do not involve textual substitutions or other transformations of the program text; they simply rely on function composition.

Unlike the Hoare assignment axiom, these properties work forward; but their practical application in the examples that follow leads to a backward style similar to weakest precondition calculus.

Note the signature *Objects* ⇸ [*States* ⇸ *States*] of *f* := *g*: the operation changes the state of a single function at a *single point*, denoted by the *Objects* argument. The B notation, for a specific *obj* in *Objects*, would be *f* (*obj*) := *g* (*obj*); the repetition of *obj* explains why we need a special notation where *obj* appears just once. This special role of *obj* illuminates the special role of the "current object" in O-O computation.

We may generalize function substitution to multiple sources and targets:

```
[f₁, f₂, ... fₙ] := [g₁, g₂, ... gₙ]
```

with the corresponding generalization of the characteristic properties, reflecting that the substitutions are simultaneous:

[A3] $[[f_1, \ldots f_n := g_1, \ldots g_n] \bullet f_i] = g_i$ -- For $1 \leq i \leq n$

[A4] $[[f_1, \ldots f_n := g_1, \ldots g_n] \bullet h] = h$ -- For h other than all f_i

6 The Semantic Rules

We are now ready to examine the semantics of the object-oriented mechanisms. The denotation of a programming language construct c – the mathematical model for c – will be written $\bar{c}$.

The following table, followed by an explanation of every entry, specifies the semantics of the core subset of an O-O language such as Eiffel. Each entry gives the denotation $\bar{c}$ of a different construct c; the last column gives the signature of that denotation, that is to say the set (of partial functions) to which it belongs. The last entry, [S19], gives the cumulative definition of the correctness of a routine having a pre- and postcondition.

The left-hand sides of the equalities cite constructs of an object-oriented programming language; the right-hand sides are their mathematical denotations. The rightmost column gives the signatures of these denotations – the mathematical sets to which they belong (sets of functions in all cases).

In case [S5] we simply prescribe that for any attribute f of the class the model will include a corresponding function. The rule $\bar{f} = f$ indicates that we use the same name for the function in the model as for the attribute in the software text.

Case [S6], $f := g$, is a standard assignment. The fields represented by f and g may be value fields, for example of type *INTEGER*, or reference fields leading to other objects or *Void*. The mathematical intepretation of such an assignment as an operation of the state is that it replaces the value of f, for any object *obj* to which the assignment is applied, by the value of g for that object.

> The operator := on the left-hand side is assignment, from the programming language; := on the right side is a mathematical operator, function substitution. Inventing a new operator for the latter purpose would avoid the risk of confusion but make the notation more complex.

This rule, [S6], captures the essence of the "current object" in object technology. The key is that we do not specify any particular object: $\bar{f} := \bar{g}$ is a function, applicable to an object. Both the target and the source of the assignment are themselves functions applicable to an object; the effect of the assignment is to replace the value of the target function on that object, whatever it is, by the value of the source for the same object.

Since in this discussion we do not consider such operations as object creation, all run-time events ultimately reduce to operations such as $f := g$ whose model is a function from *Objects* to state transformers.

Case [S7] is the generalization to multiple sources and targets.

Construct	Denotation	Signature
Basic constructs		
[S5] Name of attribute of class	$\overline{f} = f$	Objects $\nrightarrow$ States $\nrightarrow$ Values
[S6] Attribute assignment	$\overline{f := g} = \overline{f} := \overline{g}$	Objects $\nrightarrow$ States $\nrightarrow$ States
[S7] Multiple attr. assignment	$\overline{[f_1,...f_n] := [g_1,...g_n]} = [\overline{f_1},...\overline{f_n}] := [\overline{g_1},...\overline{g_n}]$	Objects $\nrightarrow$ States $\nrightarrow$ States
[S8] Instruction sequencing	$\overline{i ; j} = \overline{i} \bullet \overline{j}$	Objects $\nrightarrow$ States $\nrightarrow$ States
[S9] Attribute call	$\overline{x \cdot f} = \overline{x} \cdot \overline{f}$	Objects $\nrightarrow$ States $\nrightarrow$ Objects
Routine: $r(a)$ is require pre do $body$ ensure $post$ end		
[S10] Routine (overall semantics)	$\overline{r} = \textbf{function}\ a\ |\ \overline{body}$	Values $\nrightarrow$ Objects $\nrightarrow$ States $\nrightarrow$ States
[S11] Routine call, unqualified	$\overline{r(u)} = \overline{r}\,(\overline{u})$	Objects $\nrightarrow$ States $\nrightarrow$ States -- For procedure Objects $\nrightarrow$ States $\nrightarrow$ Values -- For function
[S12] Routine call, qualified	$\overline{x \cdot r(u)} = \overline{x} \bullet \overline{r}\,(\overline{u})$	Same as above entry [S11]
[S13] Unary expression (for operator §)	$\overline{\S\ a} = \overline{\S\ \overline{a}}$ (Use [S11], [S12])	Objects $\nrightarrow$ States $\nrightarrow$ Values
[S14] Binary expression (for operator §)	$\overline{a\ \S\ b} = \overline{\overline{a}\ \S\ \overline{b}}$ (Use [S11], [S12])	Objects $\nrightarrow$ States $\nrightarrow$ Values
Assertions and correctness (in routine $r(a)$)		
[S15] Class or loop invariant	Use [S11], [S12], [S13], [S14]	Objects $\nrightarrow$ States $\nrightarrow$ $\mathbb{B}$
[S16] Pre- or postcondition	Use [S11], [S12], [S13], [S14]	Values $\nrightarrow$ Objects $\nrightarrow$ States $\nrightarrow$ $\mathbb{B}$
[S17] Postcondition clause	$\overline{\textbf{ensure}\ Q} = \overline{r} \bullet \overline{Q}$	Values $\nrightarrow$ Objects $\nrightarrow$ States $\nrightarrow$ $\mathbb{B}$
[S18] "Old" equality assertion	$\overline{\textbf{ensure}\ f = \textbf{old}\ g} = \overline{r} \bullet \overline{f} = \overline{g}$	Objects $\nrightarrow$ States $\nrightarrow$ $\mathbb{B}$
[S19] Routine correctness	$\overline{[pre\ \overset{*}{\wedge}\ inv\ \overset{.}{\Rightarrow}}$ $\overline{r} \bullet [\overline{post\ \overset{*}{\wedge}\ inv}]]$	$\mathbb{B}$

In case [S8] *i; j* is the instruction sequence that executes *i* then *j*. As we model instructions by functions, the model for their sequence is the composition of their models. We must use rightmost composition "$\blacksquare$" rather than ordinary composition "$\circ$" since the denotations of *i* and *j* are not state transformers but functions from *Objects* to state transformers; recall that $i \blacksquare j$ is the function that, for any *obj*, yields *i* (*obj*) composed with (*j obj*).

Case [S9], "attribute call", applies an attribute to an object, and is written *x.f* in O-O notation; it is pleasant to model it through function composition as $\bar{x}.\bar{f}$. Calls to the other kind of feature, routines, will have a similar rule [S12].

Case [S10] defines the semantics of a routine *r* as being, for any argument *a*, the semantics $\overline{body}$ of the routine's body as applied to *a*. The name *r* is not by itself a construct, but defining a semantics for *r* helps define the model of the actual constructs involving *r*: calls to the routine.

Case [S11], *r(u)*, is the first kind of such call: **unqualified**, that is to say, executed from a routine of the same class and using the current object as target. The effect is simply to apply the function $\bar{r}$, the semantics of *r*, to the denotation $\bar{u}$ of *u*.

Case [S12] is the second kind of call, **qualified**: *x.r* (*u*) applies a certain feature to a certain explicitly named target with certain arguments. The observation here is that *x* as well as *u* are, mathematically, functions on objects; so is *r* with an extra degree of abstraction corresponding to the argument. The mathematical equivalent is simply $\bar{x} \blacksquare \bar{r} (\bar{u})$, closely mirroring the programming language notation as in attribute call [S9]. This rule shows feature application, the fundamental computational mechanism of object-oriented development, as function composition and function application.

Cases [S13] and [S14] acknowledge the property that (in Eiffel at least) an expression involving a unary or binary operator is just an abbreviation for a function call; for example *a + b* is formally a function call *a.plus* (*b*) where *plus* is the function **infix** "+" associated with the operator. So to handle these cases we just apply the function's model to the operands' model. The same approach will work for predefined equality and inequality operators: the model for $\overline{a = b}$ is $\bar{a} = \bar{b}$.

This also gives the model for a class or loop invariant [S15] since it's a boolean-valued expression. The signature is *Objects* $\not\rightarrow$ [*States* $\not\rightarrow$ $\mathbb{B}$]: applied to any object, the model is a boolean-valued function of the state.

The same holds of a routine's precondition or postcondition [S16] with an extra function level – the initial *Values* in the signature – corresponding to the argument of the enclosing routine *r*.

It is convenient to give a model [S17] to a postcondition clause **ensure** *Q*, the composition of the semantics of *r* and the semantics of *Q*. The signature of $\bar{r} \blacksquare \bar{Q}$ is *Values* $\not\rightarrow$ *Objects* $\not\rightarrow$ *States* $\not\rightarrow$ $\mathbb{B}$ (this is also the signature of $\bar{Q}$, and the signature of $\bar{r}$ is *Values* $\not\rightarrow$ *Objects* $\not\rightarrow$ *States* $\not\rightarrow$ *States*).

In such a postcondition, we may encounter a reference to **old** *f* where *f* is an expression, of signature *Objects* $\not\rightarrow$ *States* $\not\rightarrow$ *Values* (*f* may not involve the routine's arguments). This represents the value of *f* evaluated on the current object on entry to the routine r. The mathematical model must "unwind" the semantics of r; rule [S18] addresses the common case of a postcondition clause of the form $f = \mathbf{old}\ g$, which we interpret as $\bar{r}.\bar{f} = \bar{g}$, expressing that the value of f in the state resulting from executing r is the original value of g.

Case [S19] gives the basic proof obligation for a routine: that the precondition and invariant imply the postcondition and invariant evaluated in the state resulting from executing the routine. A similar rule will apply, for example, to the proof that a loop body satisfies the loop invariant.

Viewed as definitions of the semantics, these equalities are recursive; for example the denotation of $f := g$ refers to $\bar{g}$, the denotation of g. Since the routines may themselves be recursive, the equalities do not actually provide a proper definition of the semantics unless we use a fixpoint interpretation. We can avoid the issue by noting that the goal is to prove properties of routines through [S19]; if encountering a recursive call, we will assume the property to prove, in line with Hoare's axiomatics of routines [7].

7 Operator Properties

The proofs that follow will use some properties of the functional operators used in modeling object structures.

Sequence Closure

Introduced earlier, "sequence closure", f^{**} for a function $f : A \nrightarrow A$, is the function that for any $x : A$ yields the sequence $x, f(x), f(f(x))$ ..., up to the first value that is outside of the domain of f. (The formal definition is not included but poses no difficulty.) For all the examples of this article the structures are acyclic so the sequence is finite.

In light of the preceding discussion of the "." operator we may generalize the notation to a function f representing an attribute, and hence of signature *Objects* $\nrightarrow$ *States* $\nrightarrow$ *Objects* rather than just *Objects* $\nrightarrow$ *Objects*: we just take f^{**}, for a given state s, as denoting the application of $**$ to
   function *obj* | [**function** *s* | [*f* (*obj*)] (*s*)]
Here is an example:

In a given state, function *right*** applied to the first *LINKABLE* cell *cell_1*, yields the sequence of *LINKABLE* cells consisting of *cell_1*, *cell_2* and *cell_3*. Applying *first.right*** to the *header* object yields the same sequence.

Sequence Closure Properties

The following properties involve functions $f, g, ...$ in *Objects* $\nrightarrow$ *States* $\nrightarrow$ *Objects*. The state plays no explicit role – it is the same throughout – so the properties will also hold for functions in *Objects* $\nrightarrow$ *Objects* if we replace "." by plain composition "∘". By including *States* in the signature we cover the intended application to functions $f, g, ...$ representing reference attributes.

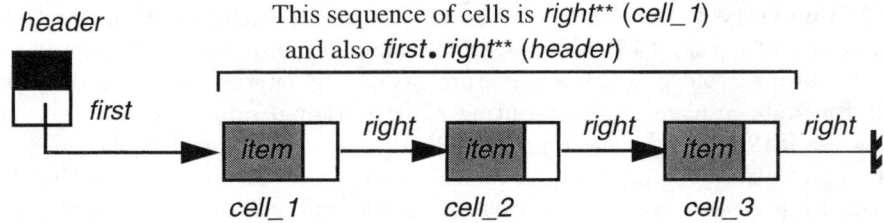

Fig. 7. Reflexive-transitive sequence closure

The first property relates sequence closure and composition:

$$[T20] \quad f \cdot f^{**} = f^{**} \cdot tail$$

In words – as illustrated below in the application of both sides to an argument *obj* in a given state – this states that if you start from an object and follow the *f* link once, the *f* sequence starting at the resulting object is the tail of the *f* sequence starting at the original object:

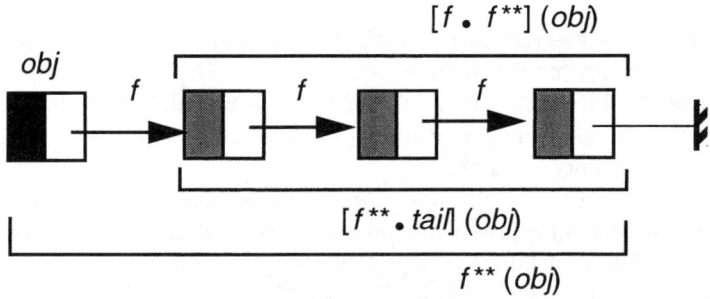

Fig. 8. Tail and composition

Two corollaries are

$$[T21] \quad f^{**} = <f> + f \cdot f^{**}$$
$$[T22] \quad f \cdot g^{**} = <f> + f \cdot g \cdot g^{**}$$

We may use the notation f^{++} for the expression $f.f^{**}$ that appears in both [T20] and [T21]; it yields for any x the sequence $f(x), f(f(x))...$, that is to say $f^{**}(x)$ deprived of its first element. [T21] indicates that $f^{**} = <f> + f^{++}$.

Sequence Closure and Function Substitution

A related property, involving the state, combines sequence closure and the function substitution:operator

[T23] $[f := f.g] \bullet [f.g^{**}] = f.g^{**}.\,tail$

which we may illustrate as follows:

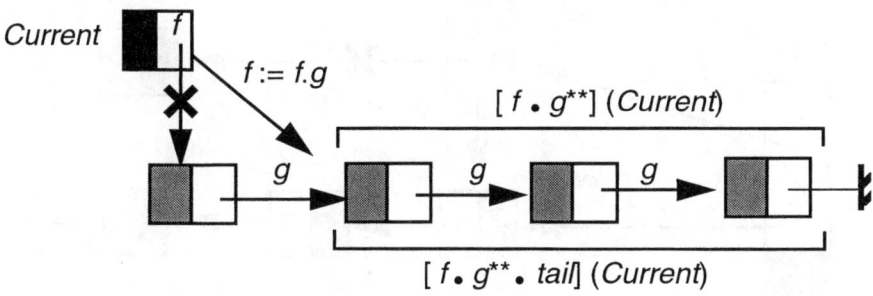

Fig. 9. Tail and composition

In words: consider the g sequence starting at the target of the f link from the current object. (It's $f.g^{**}$, appearing on both sides of [T23].) Replacing the f link of *Current* by $f.g$ implies replacing that sequence by its tail.

Proof of [T23]: the property [A1] of function substitution lets us simplify the left-hand side into

$f.g.g^{**}$

which, by applying [T20] to g, yields the right-hand side.

The next property, illustrated below, enables us to deal with the effect of remote assignments by deducing that after a call $f.set\_g\,(h)$, where $set\_g\,(a)$ performs $g := a$, the value of $f.g$ will be h:

[T24] $[f.[g:=h]] \bullet [f.g] = h$

Proof: apply both sides to an object *obj* and let $obj' = f(obj)$. From the definition of "$\bullet$" the left-hand side is $[[g := h]\,(obj')] \bullet [[f.g]\,(obj)]$, that is, $[[g := h]\,(obj')] \bullet [g\,(obj')]$, which from the definition of function substitution [A1] is $h\,(obj')$.

As a consequence:

[T25] $[f.[g:=h]] \bullet [f.g^{**}] = <f> + h.g^{**}$

Again an illustration may help.

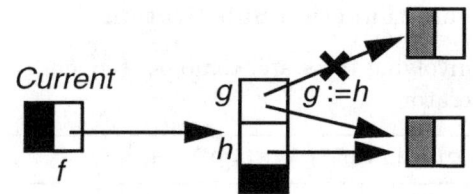

Fig. 10. Effect of remote assignment

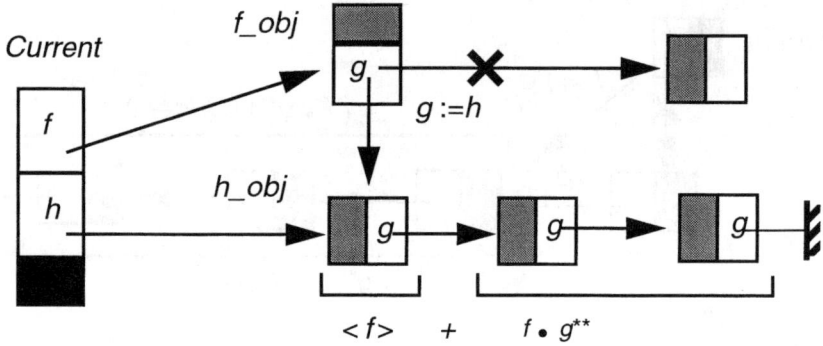

Fig. 11. Effect of remote assignment

In words: call *f_obj*, as illustrated, the target of the *f* link from the *Current* object. The left side of [T25] denotes the *g* sequence from *f_obj* – the sequence *f.g*** – evaluated in the state resulting from reattaching, in *f_obj*, the *g* link to the target *h_obj* of the *h* link. The right side is, in the original state, the sequence that starts with *f_obj* and continues with the *g* sequence beginning at *h_obj*.

Proof: from [T22] we write the left side as $[f.[g := h]] [<f> + f.g.g^{**}]$. Distributing over the concatenation operator + and applying [T24] gives the right side.

Finally, we will use the following elementary property, given without proof, of the *mirror* and concatenation operations on sequences:

[T26] (s1 + s2) □ mirror = s2 □ mirror + s1 □ mirror

8 Modeling Linked Lists

We will apply the preceding semantic rules to prove the correctness of LINKED_LIST routines *remove_front* and *reverse*. This requires expressing more precisely the properties of the model used for this class. The experience gained so far in proving properties of classes indicates that this step of devising a proper model is just as important as the task of performing the proofs once a model has been devised.

Sequences and Their Properties

As noted earlier, we associate with an instance of *LINKED_LIST* [G] a *model* of type *SEQUENCE* [G], representing the sequence of its values. The basic property of the *model* may be expressed as a class invariant, relative to the current state:

> **[A27]** *model* = *first . right** . item*

The decision to define a *SEQUENCE* model for every list object belongs in a higher-level class, *LIST*, of which *LINKED_LIST* is a descendant. The linked-list *model* is an implementation of the abstract *model* from *LIST*. This overall structure and the relation of the proof technique to inheritance are covered in [14]; in the present discussion we examine the implementation class independently of its ancestry.

As illustrated below, *first.right*** is the sequence of *LINKABLE* [G] cells making up the list; we could use it as the model, but what is of interest to users of the list is not the sequence of cells, it's the sequence of *G* values they host, which the definition [A27] gives us by composing *first.right*** with *item*.

This relies on the standard definition of a finite sequence *s* as a function from an integer interval starting at 1 to a set *X*, here *LINKABLE* [G]. If *f* is a function in $X \to G$ for some *G*, the composition *s.f* describes another sequence, with values in *G*, obtained by applying *f* to every element of *s*.

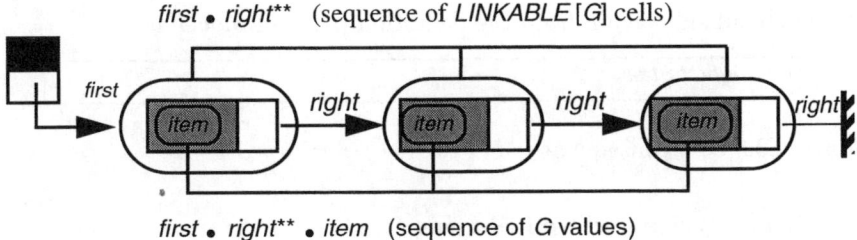

Fig. 12. Modeling a linked list as a sequence of values

The function *item* comes, like *right*, from class *LINKABLE*:

```
class LINKABLE [G] feature
    right: LINKABLE [G]
        -- Reference to next cell
    item: G
        -- Value stored in cell
    ... Routines (see below) ...
end
```

Like the above definition of *model*, all formulae of interest include the composition ".*item*" as their last element; as a result we can remove it in all equalities between such formulae. For brevity we will from now on ignore *item*, using for *model* the simplified version

> **[A28]** *model* = *first . right***

as if we were dealing with a sequence of *LINKABLE [G]* items rather than a sequence of *G* values. This simplification was already present in the loop invariant of the *reverse* procedure in section 3.

A property of the model is:

> **[T29]** [*first* := *first . right*] ▪ *model* = *model . tail*

Proof: the left-hand side, through the definition [A27] of *model*, is

> [*first* := *first . right*] ▪ [*first . right***]

The property [A1] of function substitution lets us simplify this into

> *first . right . right***

The right-hand side, again from the definition [A27] of *model*, is

> *first . right** . tail*

yielding [T29] as a consequence of [T20].

Prohibiting Cycles and Tail Sharing

Our linked list structures must be acyclic. This will give another invariant clause, which we may express as the requirement that, in any state *s*

> **[A30]** *injective* ([*first . right***] (*s*))

where *injective* (*r*), for a relation *r* (including the case of a function) indicates that *r* never pairs two different source elements with the same target element; this can be defined as $r \circ r^{-1} \subseteq Id$ where *Id* is the identity relation. [A30] states that a *right* sequence may not include the same *LINKABLE* [*G*] cell twice, although two of its cells may of course have the same *G* content.

We must also preclude tail sharing: no two lists may share *LINKABLE* [*G*] cells (although they may again share cell values). The invariant clause is

> **[A31]** *injective* ([first . right*] (· s ·))

This is almost the same as [A30], using the reflexive transitive closure of *right* rather than sequence closure. Because this yields a relation, not a function, we need the image operator (·....·) [13] rather than function application.

The correctness rule [S19] requires every exported routine of the class to maintain [A30] and [A31].

9 Proving Correctness of List Removal

Let's apply the theory to prove the procedure *remove_front* introduced earlier.

> It is in general meaningless to talk of "proving software": you prove the correctness of a software element not in the absolute but with respect to a certain specification. Our classes and their routines, however, are equipped with contracts, so "proving a routine" simply means proving that it satisfies its specification as expressed by the contract.

The postcondition, labeled *head_chopped_off* in section 3, is *model* = **old** *model.tail*. [S18] tells us that the property to prove is then

> $\overline{remove\_front}$ ■ *model* = *model . tail*

From [S10], $\overline{remove\_front}$ is **function** *a* | $\overline{body}$ where *body* denotes the body of the procedure and we can ignore *a* since the procedure has no argument. Its body is the single instruction *first := first.right* whose semantics is an example of case [S7], giving

> $\overline{remove\_front}$ = [*first := first . right*]

So we have to prove

> [*first := first. right*] ■ *model* = *model . tail*

that is to say, the property [T29] as proved in the preceding section.

Preservation of the acyclicity invariant [A30] follows from the property that if *f*** contains no cycle neither does its tail. Preservation of the no-tail-sharing invariant [A31] follows from the property that replacing a sequence by its tail cannot introduce tail sharing. (These properties can be made more formal and proved in the style of the properties in section 7.)

10 Proving Correctness of List Reversal

We now turn to a more sophisticated algorithm, list reversal (given in section 3). As originally noted, the result to be proved (apart from termination, and preservation of the class invariants) is that the body preserves the loop invariant, which read

> [I32] *spliced*: **old** *model* = *first. right*** □ *mirror* + *next. right***

We have to prove that

> $\overline{spliced} \overset{*}{\Rightarrow} \overline{Body}$ ∎ $\overline{spliced}$

where *Body* is the body of the loop:

> [*previous, first, next*] := [*first, next, next. right*]   -- *Shift*
> *first. put_right* (*previous*)   -- *Reattach*

Let us compute $\overline{Body}$ ∎ $\overline{spliced}$. From the instruction sequencing rule [S8] it is $\overline{[Shift \blacksquare Reattach]}$ ∎ $\overline{spliced}$ where *Shift* and *Reattach* are the two instructions.
    Associativity applies so we first compute $\overline{Reattach}$ ∎ $\overline{spliced}$. From [S12], $\overline{Reattach}$ is $\overline{first\ put\_right\ (previous)}$. Procedure *put_right* (*x*), in class *LINKABLE*, performs the assignment *right* := *x*, so its semantics $\overline{put\_right}$ is, from the assignment rule [S6] and the procedure [S10]

> $\overline{put\_right}$ = **function** *a* | $\overline{right := a}$

Combining this with the qualified call rule [S12] gives:

> $\overline{Reattach}$ = $\overline{first}$ ∎ $\overline{[right := previous]}$

Applying this to $\overline{spliced}$ and retaining the **old** expression as per [S18] yields

> $\overline{Reattach}$ ∎ $\overline{spliced}$ =
>   [**old** *model* = [*first* ∎ $\overline{[right := previous]}$] ∎
>   [*first . right*** □ *mirror* + *next. right***]]

Distributing over + and applying [T25]:

$\overline{Reattach}$ ■ spliced =
  [**old** model = [<first> + previous . right**] □ mirror +
              next . right**]

What we are computing is $\overline{Shift}$. $\overline{Reattach}$ ■ spliced, so we must compose $\overline{Shift}$ with the right-hand side. From the multiple assignment axiom [S7]:

$\overline{Shift}$ = [previous, first, next := first, next, next . right]

so that, applying the property [A4] of multiple assignment to all operands:

$\overline{Body}$ ■ spliced =
  [**old** model = [<next> + first . right**] □ mirror +
              next . right . right**]

so that from the property [T26] of mirror we may write $\overline{Body}$ ■ spliced as

[I33]   **old** model = [first . right**] □ mirror +
              <next> + next . right . right**]

That this is an immediate consequence of the loop invariant spliced is clear from the picture that illustrated the invariant

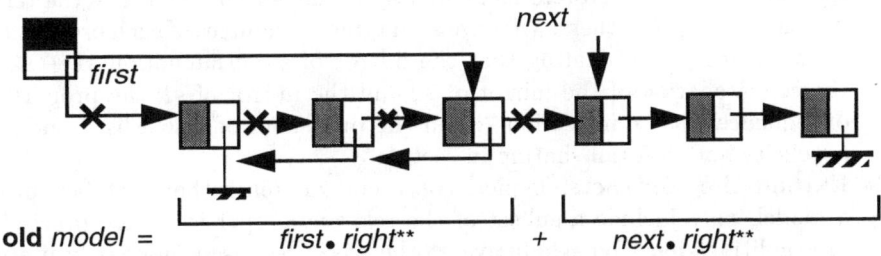

Fig. 13. List reversing: intermediate state

and is proved by using [T22] to simplify the second line of [I33], giving

[I34]   **old** model = [first . right**] □ mirror +
              next . right**

which is the original invariant spliced [I32]. So we have proved that $\overline{spliced}$ implies $\overline{Body}$ ■ spliced.

To prove termination we may use a similar technique to compute $\overline{Body}$ ▪ [next.right**.count], the value of the loop variant (the length of the sequence next.right**) after an execution of the loop body, and find that it is one less than the initial value.

Preservation of the class invariants follows from the property that replacing the *model* by its reversed form, as expressed by the postcondition, cannot introduce any cycle or tail sharing.

The proof of procedure *put_front* or other routines that create object present no particular difficulty but needs the associated modeling of object creation and management discussed in [13].

11 Conclusion and Plan of Work

The approach described here appears to provide a workable basis for a systematic effort at proving the classes of a contracted library such as EiffelBase, covering the fundamental structures that application developers use daily.

The Process

The example of class *LINKED_LIST* suggests a standard approach for proving library classes.

P1● **Devise a model.** Choose a mathematical structure that will support expressing the properties of the instances of the class.

P2● **Build a static theory.** In this step one must explore the properties of the model in a fixed state, independently of any execution (hence the term "static"), and prove them. We have seen typical examples of such properties: for sequences, [T26] stating that the mirror of a concatenation $s1 + s2$ is the concatenation of the mirror of $s2$ and the mirror of $s1$; the properties of sequence closure in section 7; and the properties of linked lists, such as acyclicity and non-tail sharing in section 8.

P3● **Extend the contracts.** Typical contracts, written without the benefit of a model, only include a subset of the relevant properties. More precisely, preconditions must be exhaustive – otherwise the class is not safely usable – but postconditions and class invariants often miss important information that are hard to express without a model, for example, in an insertion operation, that all previous elements are still there. Loop invariants and variants are often omitted. All these must be filled in.

P4● **Translate the class to mathematical form.** The denotational semantics of section 6 is the basis here. This step should be performed by an automated tool relying on a parser of the source language.

P5● **Perform the proofs.** Although this paper has used a manual approach, the intent is to perform proofs mechanically; this explains the need for the previous step, since a proof tool will need to manipulate formulae expressed in an appropriate notation. The mechanically-checked proof effort may still, of course, require substantial manual support.

In line with the rest of the present discussion, this description covers proofs of individual classes. The framework described in [14], taking advantage of inheritance, involves both an effective (concrete) class such as *LINKED_LIST* and its deferred (abstract) ancestors, such as *LIST* describing general lists independent of an implementation. In this case there may be both an abstract model and a concrete one, requiring two extra steps:

P6• **Prove that the abstract assertions imply the model assertions** in the deferred class.

P7• **Prove the consistency of the concrete model against the abstract model** in the effective class.

Contrary to appearances this actually simplifies the process, since step P6, in the case of multiple descendants describing specific implementations of an abstract structure, moves up to the common ancestor part of the work that would have to be done anew for each descendant. See [14] for details.

Even for a single class, the process is unlikely to be strictly sequential. The proof step P5 may in particular encounter obstacles that require refining the model (step P1) or proving new properties of it (step P2).

One may also need to go back to the class texts. It is well known that the prospect of picking an ordinary piece of software and proving its correctness is an illusion: the software must have been written with correctness proofs in mind. We are starting from a better situation than usual since our target is the EiffelBase library, equipped with extensive contracts that are part of the design and documentation, not an afterthought, and indeed the idea of possible proofs has been there from the beginning. But we still expect that the proof process will require – aside from the correction of any actual bugs that it might uncover – simplifications and other changes to EiffelBase as it exists today.

Other Object-Oriented Mechanisms

The present discussion has not accounted for classes, genericity, inheritance, the resulting type system, and dynamic binding. To add these mechanisms, the envisioned strategy is: introduce the notion of class, with room for generic parameterization, into the model; include support for expressing the inheritance relation between classes; and add a function *generator* that, for any object, gives the corresponding type (class plus actual generic parameters if any). The generator is set on object creation and does not change thereafter. One of the basic type rules is that for each attribute function f there is a type T such that

$$\textbf{domain}\,(f) \subseteq \textit{instances}\,(\cdot\,\{T\}\,\cdot)$$

where *instances* is the inverse of *generator*. Note subset operator rather than equality, to account for possibly void references; for expanded attributes, which can't be void, it's an equality. The other significant change to the model of the present paper is that in the interpretation $\bar{x}.\bar{f}(a)$ of a feature call $\bar{f}$ is obtained no longer directly from f but as *dynamic* $(f, \textit{generator}\,(x))$ where the function *dynamic*, accounting for dynamic binding, yields the version of a certain feature for a certain type.

Future Work

Aside from the extension of the model to cover the whole of object-oriented programming, the tasks lying ahead are clear: apply the above process to a growing set of classes covering the fundamental data structures and algorithms of computing

science. This involves building models, developing the associated theories, completing the contracts of the corresponding classes, attempting the proofs, and refining the library in the process.

Acknowledgments. An early presentation of the results reported here benefited from important comments by Robert Stärk and Armin Biere, as well as Bernd Schoeller who also provided useful feedback on an early draft of this article. Emil Sekerinski's criticism led to the correction of a significant error. The article benefited from a detailed reading and important suggestions (not all yet taken into account at this stage of the work) from Peter Müller, who also pointed out some existing work that should be referenced, and Robert Switzer. Finally, a presentation at an IFIP WG2.3 meeting was the occasion of invaluable criticism from the working group members.

References

[1] Martín Abadi and Luca Cardelli: *A Theory of Objects*, Monographs in Computer Science, Springer-Verlag, 1996.
[2] Jean-Raymond Abrial, *The B Book*, Cambridge University Press, 1995.
[3] Ralph Back, X. Fan and Viorel Preoteasa: *Reasoning about Pointers in Refinement Calculus*, Technical Report, Turku Centre for Computer Science, Turku (Finland), 22 August 2002.
[4] Richard Bornat: *Proving Pointer Programs in Hoare Logic*, in *Mathematics of Program Construction*, Springer-Verlag, 2000, pages 102–106.
[5] ClearSy [name of company, no author listed]: Web documents on Atelier B, www.atelierb.societe.com, last consulted December 2002.
[6] C.A.R. Hoare: *Proof of Correctness of Data Representations*, in Acta Informatica 1 (1972), pp. 271–281. Also in C.A.R. Hoare and C. B. Jones (ed.): *Essays in Computing Science*, Prentice Hall International, Hemel Hempstead (U.K.), 1989, pages 103–115.
[7] C. A. R. Hoare. *Procedures and parameters: An axiomatic approach*. In E. Engeler, editor, *Symposium on Semantics of Algorithmic Languages*, volume 188 of Lecture Notes in Mathematics, pages 102–116. Springer-Verlag, 1971.
[8] C.A.R. Hoare and He Jifeng: *A Trace Model for Pointers*, in *ECOOP '99 – Object-Oriented Programming*, Proceedings of 13th European Conference on Object-Oriented Programming, Lisbon, June 1999, ed. Rachid Guerraoui, Lecture Notes in Computer Science 1628, Springer-Verlag, pages 1–17.

[9] Bertrand Meyer: *Introduction to the Theory of Programming Languages*, Prentice Hall, 1990.
[10] Bertrand Meyer: *Object-Oriented Software Construction*, *2nd edition*, Prentice Hall, 1997.
[11] Bertrand Meyer, Christine Mingins and Heinz Schmidt: P*roviding Trusted Components to the Industry*, in *Computer* (IEEE), vol. 31, no. 5, May 1998, pages 104–105.
[12] Bertrand Meyer et al.: Trusted Components papers at se.inf.ethz.ch, last consulted December 2002.
[13] Bertrand Meyer: *Proving Pointer Program Properties*, series of columns to appear in *Journal of Object Technology*, draft version available at www.inf.ethz.ch/~meyer/ ongoing/references/, last consulted January 2003.
[14] Bertrand Meyer: *A Framework for Proving Contract-Equipped Classes*, to appear in *Abstract State Machines 2003 – Advances in Theory and Applications*, Proc. 10th International Workshop, Taormina, Italy, March 3–7, 2003, eds. Egon Boerger, Angelo Gargantini, Elvinia Riccobene, Springer-Verlag 2003. Prepublication copy at www.inf.ethz.ch/~meyer/publications/, last consulted January 2003.
[15] Bernhard Möller: *Calculating with Pointer Structures*, in *Algorithmic Languages and Calculi*, Proceedings of IFIP TC2/WG2.1 Working Conference, Le Bischenberg (France), February 1997, Chapman and Hall, 1997, pages 24–48.
[16] Joseph M. Morris, *A general axiom of assignment*; *Assignment and linked data structures*; *A proof of the Schorr-Waite algorithm*. In *Theoretical Foundations of Programming Methodology*, Proceedings of the 1981 Marktoberdorf Summer School, eds. Manfred Broy and Gunther Schmidt, Reidel 1982, pages 25–51.
[17] John C. Reynolds: *Separation Logic: A Logic for Shared mutable Data Structures*, in Proceedings of 17th Annual IEEE Symposium on Logic in Computer Science, Copenhagen, July 22–25 2002.
[18] Norihisha Suzuki, *Analysis of Pointer "Rotation"*, in *Communications of the ACM*, vol. 25, no. 5, May 1982, pages 330–335.

Automatically Generating Information from a Z Specification to Support the Classification Tree Method

Robert M. Hierons[1], Mark Harman[1], and Harbhajan Singh[2]

[1] Department of Information Systems and Computing, Brunel University, Uxbridge, Middlesex, UB8 3PH, UK
[2] DaimlerChrysler AG, Research Information and Communication Software Technology Research Lab (RIC/SM), Alt-Moabit 96a, D-10559 Berlin, Germany

Abstract. The Classification Tree Method provides a flexible basis for systematic testing. Traditionally the generation of a classification tree has been entirely manual. This paper introduces a new approach that extracts predicates from the Z specification of an operation and builds a Classification Tree from these predicates. It thus shows how the generation of a Classification Tree may be semi-automated on the basis of a Z specification. The paper also defines the notion of the test context of a predicate that determines when the value of this predicate is relevant. The test context is used to reduce the number of tests produced from the Classification Tree.

Keywords: Classification tree method, test automation, formal methods, Z notation.

1 Introduction

Formal Methods and Software Testing are two important approaches that aim to improve software quality. While these approaches were seen as rivals, they are now widely seen as complementary [6,13]. Importantly the presence of a formal specification allows the automatic or semi-automatic generation of information that may assist testing. The presence of a formal specification may help reduce the cost of testing while making testing more systematic.

The Classification Tree Method [2,3,7,17] involves choosing a set of *classification aspects*, each of which represents factors that the tester believes to be important. The tester then chooses a set of ranges of values, called *classes*, for each classification aspect. The set of classes corresponding to a classification aspect represent a partition of the values the classification aspect may take. Typically, all values within a class are considered, by the tester, to be equivalent. The classification aspects and classes are visually represented as a tree. Abstract test cases are produced from this classification tree, each abstract test case being defined by a set of classes. An abstract test case thus represents a constraint on the test input and equivalently a set of test cases. Concrete test cases are produced from each abstract test case. By allowing the tester to choose ways in which the classes are combined, the Classification Tree Method allows the tester to apply their expertise and domain knowledge. A further advantage of the Classification Tree Method is that it is supported by a tool [7]. The Classification Tree Method and previous work on testing from a Z specification will be briefly reviewed in Section 2.

A number of authors have considered the problem of automating test generation on the basis of a specification written in a model based notation such as Z or VDM [1,4,5,8,9,15,18]. One of the earliest, and most important, approaches to test automation is the *DNF method* [5]. Here the specification is rewritten to Disjunctive Normal Form and a partition of the input domain is formed from the preconditions of the disjuncts. Test cases are drawn from each subdomain of the partition.

While the DNF approach has many advantages, it may lead to a combinatorial explosion. Where the application of the DNF approach is impractical, an alternative is to produce a classification tree from the specification and combine classes from this tree to form abstract test cases [17]. While the use of all combinations of classes might reproduce the combinatorial explosion found in the DNF approach, the tester may choose to use only some of the combinations. This paper extends the work of [17] to show how information, that supports the application of the Classification Tree Method, may be automatically derived from a Z specification.

This paper makes the following contributions. First, Section 3 shows how classification aspects and classes may be automatically generated from the Z specification of an operation in order to assist the production of the classification tree. The analysis described in Section 3 is semantic in nature and typically will be expensive to apply. However, Section 4 introduces an efficient but approximate syntactic analysis. Section 5 shows how the test effort may be reduced by choosing appropriate abstract test cases. Specifically, information contained in the specification is used to automatically limit the combinations of classes used in testing. Finally, in Section 6 conclusions are drawn.

2 Preliminaries

Throughout this paper S will denote the body of a schema that specifies the operation under test. In order to simplify the exposition it will be assumed that S is in the form of a sequence of quantifiers followed by a quantifier free predicate S^* such that: S^* contains no logical operators other than $\vee$, $\wedge$ and $\neg$; and, in S^*, $\neg$ is only applied to atomic predicates. This form is called *Prenex Normal Form (PNF)*. Any predicate can be rewritten to PNF using standard rules. Note that the transformation to PNF may be preceded by the application of transformation steps. For example, $x \in \{y \in \mathbb{Z} \mid y > 0\}$ might be rewritten to $x > 0$.

2.1 Testing from a Z Specification

This section will briefly describe the DNF approach [5] to generating tests from a Z or VDM specification of an operation.

The example in Figure 1 will be used as a running example throughout the paper. Here Q represents the rational numbers. This specification specifies a system that determines the cost of a rail ticket. The price depends upon the following factors: the start and destination of the journey; whether it is being booked more than a week in advance; whether the journey time is peak or off-peak; whether the customer has a railcard; and, if the person has a railcard, whether it is a student railcard or a pensioner's railcard. To simplify the specification it will be assumed that only the dates are considered when determining how far in advance the ticket is being booked. It will also be assumed that there are functions, $price\_peak$ and $price\_off\_p$, that give the basic cost of tickets during the peak and off-peak periods respectively. Railcards provide a discount as long as the journey is off-peak. The discount provided by booking more than a week in advance depends on whether the journey is peak or off-peak (10% if peak, 40% if off-peak).

Within this specification, RAILCARD denotes the types of railcard (STUDENT, OAP, and NONE), STATIONS denotes the set of stations, DATE denotes the set of dates and PERIOD denotes the travel period (peak and off-peak).

Price

$r? : RAILCARD$
$start?, end? : STATIONS$
$current\_date?, outward\_date? : DATE$
$travel\_period? : PERIOD$
$price! : Q$

$outward\_date? \geq current\_date?$
$(travel\_period? = peak \wedge$
$(outward\_date? - current\_date? > 7$
$\wedge price! = 0.9 * price\_peak(start?, end?)$
$\vee outward\_date? - current\_date? \leq 7$
$\wedge price! = price\_peak(start?, end?))$
$) \vee$
$(travel\_period? = off\_peak \wedge \exists p1, p2 : Q \bullet$
$(r? = NONE \wedge p1 = 1 \vee r? = STUDENT \wedge$
$p1 = 0.9 \vee r? = OAP \wedge p1 = 0.7) \wedge$
$(outward\_date? - current\_date? > 7 \wedge p2 = 0.6 \vee$
$outward\_date? - current\_date? \leq 7 \wedge p2 = 1) \wedge$
$price! = p1 * p2 * price\_off\_p(start?, end?))$

Fig. 1. The specification of *Price*

It is easy to confirm that *Price* may be rewritten to PNF by simply moving the quantifiers to the front.

The DNF approach considers the specification of an operation and generates a partition $P = \{D_1, \ldots, D_n\}$ of the input domain of that operation. The partition generated has the property that, according to the specification, all values in a subdomain should be treated in the same manner. Note that the input domain for an operation is formed from both the input received from the environment and the internal state space. Tests are produced from each subdomain.

Given a specification S of an operation op, the DNF approach initially involves rewriting S to DNF. Suppose this produces disjuncts $C_1, \ldots, C_m$. Then the precondition $pre(C_i)$ of each C_i is found. This produces m predicates that, between them, partition the input domain. Initially, the $pre(C_i)$ may not themselves partition the input domain: the $pre(C_i)$ need not define disjoint sets. However, the partition may be formed from the $pre(C_i)$ [5,9].

Consider, for example, $Price$. Rewriting the body of this to disjunctive normal form gives nine disjuncts, including the following:

$$outward\_date? \geq current\_date? \wedge travel\_period? = peak \wedge$$
$$outward\_date? - current\_date? > 7$$
$$\wedge price! = 0.9 * price\_peak(start?, end?))$$

and

$$outward\_date? \geq current\_date? \wedge travel\_period? = off\_peak \wedge$$
$$\exists p1, p2 : Q \bullet r? = STUDENT \wedge p1 = 0.9 \wedge$$
$$outward\_date? - current\_date? \leq 7 \wedge p2 = 1$$
$$\wedge price! = p1 * p2 * price\_off\_p(start?, end?)$$

The above lead to the following conditions of subdomains of the partition:

$$outward\_date? \geq current\_date? \wedge$$
$$travel\_period? = peak \wedge$$
$$outward\_date? - current\_date? > 7$$

and

$$outward\_date? \geq current\_date? \wedge$$
$$travel\_period? = off\_peak \wedge$$
$$r? = STUDENT \wedge outward\_date? - current\_date? \leq 7$$

It has been noted [9] that it is not always necessary to rewrite the specification of an operation all the way to DNF. For example, suppose the specification of an operation is $(x? > 0 \vee y? > 0) \wedge r! = "ok"$. Here there is only one specified behaviour $(r! = "ok")$ with one precondition $(x? > 0 \vee y? > 0)$. The DNF approach will split this, making it appear that there are two separate behaviours with separate preconditions. Thus, the DNF approach produces more subdomains than required and, as a consequence, may suggest more tests than necessary. This may reduce the set of problems for which the approach is practical. Another example of a case where the DNF approach splits the behaviour too far, is a specification of the form $x? > 0 \wedge (r! = "ok" \vee r! = "positive")$. The DNF approach will again produce two disjuncts but here the two have the same precondition.

An alternative approach, which tackles some of the problems described above, is based on estimating the role of predicates [9]. For example, in $x? > 0 \wedge (r! = "ok" \vee r! = "positive")$ it is clear that the two predicates $r! = "ok"$ and $r! = "positive"$ are not involved in defining any partition produced since they only refer to output. Thus, it is not necessary to rewrite the predicate $x? > 0 \wedge (r! = "ok" \vee r! = "positive")$.

While the approach of Ref. [9] overcomes the problems described above, it may still suffer from a combinatorial explosion. The approach outlined in this paper avoids the combinatorial explosion by not actually generating the partition. Instead, it identifies the predicates responsible for defining the partition and uses these to produce a classification tree. If all combinations of classes are chosen then the combinatorial explosion returns. However, using the approach introduced here, the tester may choose the combinations used in a way that avoids this.

2.2 The Classification Tree Method

The Classification Tree Method provides a flexible basis for test generation. The tester identifies a number of aspects, called *classification aspects*. Each aspect represents a property to be considered in testing. For example, for *Price*, the tester might identify the aspect: the period during which the journey will occur.

For each aspect a number of *classes*, which represent different values or sets of values for the aspect, are defined. For example, for the period in which the journey will occur, there might be two classes: peak and off-peak. If the number of days, between the booking and the date on which the outward journey is made, forms a classification aspect there might be two classes: the interval is greater than 7 days; and the interval is at most 7 days.

Typically, a class will represent some range of values for the classification aspect that are deemed to be treated in an equivalent manner. The classes must be disjoint and should be complete with respect to the classification aspect: the union of the classes should give the complete range of values. Where appropriate, classes might be included to represent values that are likely to find certain types of fault. For example, where there is a boundary between two ranges of interest, a class might represent values around this boundary. The addition of such classes allows the tester to specify the use of special values of interest (such as 0).

The tester defines an *abstract test case* by choosing a set of leaves from the classification tree. This set contains at most one class for each classification aspect. Each abstract test case is graphically represented by a horizontal line in which the classes defining the abstract test case are identified. Thus an abstract test case is effectively a set of constraints on the input and the internal state before the test. Given an abstract test case, the tester will subsequently find concrete values that satisfy these constraints. An abstract test case thus represents a set of concrete test cases, any one of which suffices. Where the classes are formally defined, an automated or semi-automated process might construct concrete test cases from abstract test cases.

As well as defining classification aspects and classes, the tester is able to include a precondition on the operation. This precondition forms part of the set of properties defining each abstract test case. Further, it is possible to add constraints that relate the classes. For example, it is possible to say that if one class c_1 has been chosen then some other class c_2, from a different classification aspect, must not be chosen.

The classification tree might be formed as a flat tree, by placing each classification aspect as a child of the root and, for each classification aspect, having each of its classes as a leaf of this node. Often, however, the tester places some structure on the classification tree. It is possible to place a classification aspect C below a class c. This means that the classification aspect C is only relevant where the class c has been chosen. Similarly, it means that if some class from C is chosen then the class c is also chosen.

Consider the classification tree in Figure 2. This classification tree is for the operation Price specified in Figure 1. The figure shows two abstract test cases. In the first, the travel period is off-peak, the person has a student railcard and is purchasing the ticket no more than a week in advance of the journey. In this classification tree the classification aspect *Railcard* being below the class *Yes* for *Off Peak* indicates that the classification aspect *Railcard* is only relevant when the travel period is *Off Peak*.

By allowing a range of classification aspects and classes to be chosen, the Classification Tree Method allows the tester to apply expert knowledge in both producing the classification tree and choosing abstract test cases. This allows the tester to concentrate effort on the parts of the system that are most likely to contain faults or are particularly critical. This is important where the number of classification aspects and classes does not allow the use of all combinations of classes.

Note that many systems will have an internal state and multiple operations. In such cases, once abstract test cases have been formed for each operation, it may be necessary to determine how to sequence these abstract test cases. This sequencing may be based on a finite state model of the system generated on the basis of the partitions [5,8,9,11]. For information regarding the automatic

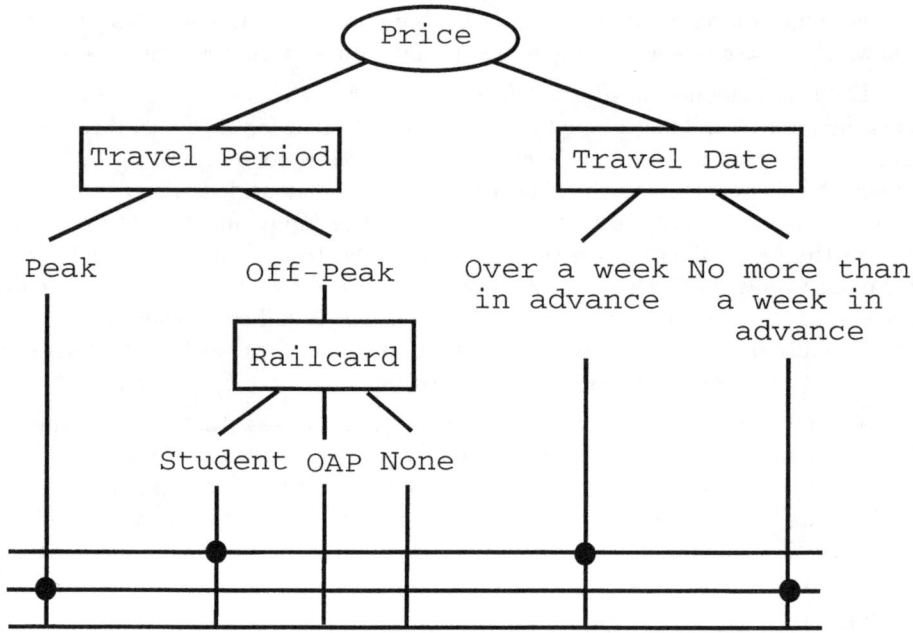

Fig. 2. A Classification Tree for Price

generation of test sequences from finite state models see, for example [10,12,14,16].

3 Generating the Classification Tree

This section describes an approach to automatically generating elements of the classification tree based on the Z specification of an operation. Much of the analysis described is semantic in nature and is therefore unlikely to scale up to large examples. However, the material in this section motivates the syntactic approximation, introduced in Section 4, which allows the classification tree to be automatically developed in a more efficient way.

3.1 Generating Information from the Signature

The Z specification of an operation has a number of input variables and starting state variables to which the classification aspects should refer. Syntactic conventions allow these variables to be identified automatically. As described in Ref. [17], for each such variable, it is possible to generate a set of classes based on its type and expert knowledge.

Suppose an input variable or starting state variable x has an enumerated type T that contains only a few possible values. A class might be chosen for each of these values. Using this approach, if T is the *booleans* then x will have two classes: *True* and *False*.

Clearly this approach cannot be applied for infinite types and is of little value with a type that is finite but large. For such types, a number of standard partitions can be provided to the tester. Consider, for example, the type of natural numbers for which one commonly used partition is $\{\{0\}, \{1\}, \{2, \ldots\}\}$. Thus, given a variable x that represents a natural number, the tester can be offered a classification aspect with three classes defined by: $x = 0$, $x = 1$ and $x > 1$.

Given the specification S of an operation, it is possible to automatically identify the input and starting state variables from S and to provide a set of possible classifications for each of these. The tester might choose from this set of possibilities, basing their decision for a variable x on their knowledge of the role of x and the ways in which it is used. Section 4 describes how this information might be combined with information derived from the predicates.

3.2 Basing Information on the Predicates

This section shows how a classification tree may be based on the body of S. The analysis in this section will assume that the predicates in S are uniquely identified and thus, when considering a predicate p from S, it may be assumed that p occurs only once in S. Recall that it is assumed that S is in PNF.

The precondition of the operation may be found in the normal manner. This forms a condition for the classification tree and thus forms a condition for every abstract test case.

The problem now is to determine which predicates contribute to the precondition of some behaviour in S. Since these predicates are involved in determining which behaviour is applied, they will form the classification aspects of the classification tree. In order to determine which predicates do this, it is sufficient to rewrite S to DNF and consider the individual disjuncts, since each disjunct may be seen to form a specified behaviour. Thus, the following process may be applied in order to determine whether a predicate p of S contributes to the precondition of some behaviour:

1. Rewrite S to DNF, forming $c_1, \ldots, c_n$.
2. p contributes to the precondition of some behaviour if and only if there exists some $1 \leq i \leq n$ such that c_i has a different precondition when p is removed.

The predicates identified by the above process are those that define the partitioning of the DNF approach. However, in order to apply this approach it is necessary to define what it means to remove p from S. This is defined in Figure 3, in which $remove(p, c)$ denotes c with p removed.

Essentially, the function *remove* only alters the (single) occurrence of either p or $\neg p$ and replaces this by *true*. Note that this definition relies on S being in PNF: for some disjunct c, if c contains p or $\neg p$ there is no possibility of a term containing this being negated in c.

$$remove(p, q) = q \text{ (atomic predicate } q \neq p)$$
$$remove(p, \neg q) = \neg q \text{ (atomic predicate } q \neq p)$$
$$remove(p, p) = true$$
$$remove(p, \neg p) = true$$
$$remove(p, P \wedge Q) = remove(p, P) \wedge remove(p, Q)$$
$$remove(p, P \vee Q) = remove(p, P) \vee remove(p, Q)$$

Fig. 3. The function *remove*

The classification tree may be constructed from the predicates that contribute to the precondition of a behaviour: these each have two classes, *True* and *False*.

Consider now the following, formed by rewriting the example to DNF and let this be denoted c.

$$outward\_date? \geq current\_date? \wedge$$
$$travel\_period? = peak \wedge$$
$$outward\_date? - current\_date? > 7$$
$$\wedge price! = 0.9 * price\_peak(start?, end?)$$

$remove(travel\_period? = peak, c)$ and c have different preconditions and thus the predicate $travel\_period? = peak$ contributes to the precondition of a behaviour. In contrast, c and $remove(price! = 0.9 * price\_peak(start?, end?), c)$ have the same preconditions and thus $price! = 0.9 * price\_peak(start?, end?)$ does not contribute to the precondition of this behaviour.

The above process is likely to be highly inefficient: it combines the costs associated with rewriting to DNF, determining preconditions, and determining whether two predicates are equivalent. In fact, since the procedure involves determining whether c_i and $remove(p, c_i)$ have equivalent preconditions, the above procedure is not, in general, computable. We will now introduce a syntactic approximation that avoids these problems.

4 A Syntactic Approach to Generating Information from Predicates

This section describes how classification aspects and classes may be derived automatically using a syntactic analysis of the predicates of a Z specification S of an operation. This process of deriving the classification aspects and classes is based on classifying the predicates on the basis of the variables they mention and the structure of S.

In the analysis described in this section it will be assumed that the predicates in the specification are uniquely identified. Thus, if two copies of a predicate are contained in S then we can distinguish between these copies.

Section 4.1 introduces a way of partitioning the predicates of S into input and output predicates. The input predicates will be used, both in forming and using the classification tree. Essentially, the input predicates are the predicates that define the partition formed by the DNF approach.

Section 4.2 shows how the input predicates are further classified as either partitioning predicates or defining predicates. The partitioning predicates will form classification aspects, each classification aspect having two classes: *True* and *False*.

4.1 Input and Output Predicates

Consider the Z specification given in Figure 1. It is possible to identify predicates that are involved in determining whether an input satisfies the precondition of the operation and which behaviour is applied when it does. These predicates are:

1. $outward\_date? \geq current\_date?$
2. $travel\_period? = peak$
3. $travel\_period? = off\_peak$
4. $outward\_date? - current\_date > 7$
5. $outward\_date? - current\_date \leq 7$
6. $r? = NONE$
7. $r? = STUDENT$
8. $r? = OAP$

By noting that this list contains some pairs of predicates, such that one is the negation of the other, this list may be further reduced to:

1. $outward\_date? \geq current\_date?$
2. $travel\_period? = peak$
3. $outward\_date? - current\_date? > 7$
4. $r? = NONE$
5. $r? = STUDENT$
6. $r? = OAP$

The problem now is to find a syntactic approach that will identify such predicates.

The predicates given above are responsible for defining the preconditions of the behaviours in the specification. Given this role, they mention only input variables (this specification has no state variables). For this reason they will be called input predicates. This can be extended to the case where a term mentions state variables, by defining a predicate to be an *input predicate* if each variable it mentions is either an input variable or a starting state variable [9].

Some predicates, such as $price! = price\_peak(start?, end?)$, are involved in defining an input/output behaviour. A predicate that is not an input predicate is an *output predicate* [9].

The process of classifying the predicates into sets of input and output predicates relies on one assumption: that no output predicate contributes to the precondition of any behaviour. This assumption might contribute to part of a definition of testability for Z specifications. Note that for a specification to fail to satisfy this it must describe a precondition in terms of output and final state values: something that is often possible, but which is likely to make the specification relatively difficult to understand. For example, if part of the precondition for an operation requires the state variable x to be non-negative, and the operation does not change the value of x, then this may be expressed by stating that the final value of x is non-negative ($x' = x \land x' \geq 0$). Where output predicates contribute to preconditions of behaviours, the impact on the approach outlined in this paper is simply that it may fail to identify some of the relevant predicates. However, the information returned should still be of value to the tester; it is sound but incomplete.

The classification of predicates into input and output predicates assumes the absence of locally quantified variables. However, even where there are locally quantified variables, the classification can be used to assist in the production of a classification tree: relevant predicates that do not contain locally quantified variables will be identified. This may be extended to predicates that mention locally quantified variables, by classifying the locally quantified variables as either input locally quantified variables or output locally quantified variables. This classification may be achieved by noting the predicates that mention each locally quantified variable and the variables mentioned in these predicates. For example, in *Price*, the locally quantified variables appear in predicates that mention output variables. Thus, the locally quantified variables in *Price* are all output locally quantified variables. The problem of classifying predicates containing locally quantified variables has been considered elsewhere [9] and will not be described further here for reasons of space.

The input predicates will now be further analysed.

4.2 Classifying Input Predicates

An input predicate may perform one of two roles: it might form part of the precondition of the operation as a whole or it might be involved in determining which of the behaviours is applied. For example, in *Price*, the input predicate *outward_date?* $\geq$ *current_date?* forms part of the precondition of the operation as a whole, while the input predicate *travel_period?* = *peak* is involved in determining which input/output relation is applied. An input predicate that forms part of the precondition of the whole operation will be called a *defining predicate*. The other input predicates, which determine which of the behaviours is applied, will be called *partitioning predicates*.

The partitioning predicates define the partition and thus are the predicates that will be used to form the classification tree. The defining predicates will contribute to a precondition on the operation and thus to every abstract test case. The problem now is to automatically determine which input predicates are defining predicates and which input predicates are partitioning predicates.

Recall that S is in PNF and that S^* denotes S with the quantifiers removed. In the following analysis it will be assumed that each input predicate appears only once in S^*. If an input predicate p does appear more than once, then copies of p may be treated as separate predicates.

Suppose $S^* = p \wedge Q$ for some input predicate p. Clearly, all specified behaviour must satisfy p and this suggests that p is a defining predicate. Suppose now that $S^* = (P_1 \vee P_2) \wedge P_3$ for predicates P_1, P_2, and P_3. The disjunction suggests that there are at least two possible behaviours with their own preconditions: $P_1 \wedge P_3$ and $P_2 \wedge P_3$ may be seen as separate behaviours. From this observation, it is possible to conclude that the input predicates from P_1 and P_2 are partitioning predicates and not defining predicates.

The above observation provides an initial way of classifying input predicates: an input predicate, p, is a defining predicate if the whole operation can be rewritten as $p \wedge P$ for some predicate P and otherwise it is a partitioning predicate. However, there is an exception: if the schema is of the form $(P_1 \vee P_2) \wedge P_3$ and P_1 and P_2 contain input predicates only then $P_1 \vee P_2$ forms part of the precondition for the whole operation and thus $P_1 \vee P_2$ is a (non-atomic) defining predicate. Thus, if P is a non-atomic predicate that contains only input predicate then P is a defining predicate in $P \wedge Q$. To see this consider the predicate $(x? \geq 0 \vee y? \geq 0) \wedge z! = x?$. This has precondition $x? \geq 0 \vee y? \geq 0$ and only one behaviour: the output $z!$ is equal to $x?$. To consider $x? \geq 0$ and $y? \geq 0$ as partitioning predicates would incorrectly suggest that there were two separate behaviours that need testing. Of course, the tester might still choose to make $x? \geq 0$ and $y? \geq 0$ form separate classification aspects.

From the above observations it is clear that the defining predicates need not be atomic. Let *out* denote a function that takes a predicate T and returns the (atomic) output predicates contained in T and *in* denote a function that takes a predicate T and returns the (atomic) input predicates contained in T. Further, let *atomic* denote a function that takes a predicate T and returns the set of atomic predicates contained in T and let $\overline{atomic}$ denote a function that takes a set $\overline{P}$ of predicates and returns the set of atomic predicates contained in the predicates in $\overline{P}$. The recursive function *def*, that returns the sets of defining predicates, is defined by the rules in Figure 4; these will now be explained. The function *part*, that returns the partitioning predicates, will be defined in terms of *def*.

The first two rules provide base cases and simply require that *def* applied to a constant returns no defining predicates. The third and fourth rules are also base cases, stating that $def(p)$ returns p if p is an atomic input predicate or the negation of an atomic input predicate. Essentially, p is a defining predicate in p if and only if p is an input predicate and $\neg p$ is a defining predicate in $\neg p$ if and only if p is an input predicate.

The fifth rule considers a predicate that is a conjunction of two predicates P and Q. Observe here that if P can be rewritten to the form $p \wedge P'$ then $P \wedge Q$ can be rewritten to the form $p \wedge R'$ (here $R' = P' \wedge Q$). Thus, if a predicate p is a defining predicate for either P or Q then it is a defining predicate for

$P \wedge Q$. Further, if $P \wedge Q$ can be rewritten to the form $p \wedge R'$ then either P can be rewritten to the form $p \wedge P'$ or Q can be rewritten to the form $p \wedge Q'$. Thus a predicate p is a defining predicate for $P \wedge Q$ if and only if it is either a defining predicate for P or it is a defining predicate for Q.

The final rule deals with predicates of the form $P \vee Q$ and essentially encapsulates two cases. If either P or Q contain one or more output predicates then P and Q represent separate sets of behaviours with their own preconditions. In this case, $P \vee Q$ will have no defining predicates. The second case is that $P \vee Q$ is, itself, a defining predicate if it contains only input predicates.

$$\begin{aligned}
def(true) &= \varnothing \\
def(false) &= \varnothing \\
def(p) &= \text{if } out(p) = \varnothing \text{ then } \{p\} \\
&\quad \text{else } \varnothing \ (p \text{ is an atomic predicate}) \\
def(\neg p) &= \text{if } out(p) = \varnothing \text{ then } \{\neg p\} \\
&\quad \text{else } \varnothing \ (p \text{ is an atomic predicate}) \\
def(P \wedge Q) &= def(P) \cup def(Q) \\
def(P \vee Q) &= \text{if } out(P \vee Q) = \varnothing \text{ then } \{P \vee Q\} \\
&\quad \text{else } \varnothing
\end{aligned}$$

Fig. 4. A recursive definition of *def*

The set of defining predicates of S is $def(S^*)$. Since each input predicate appears only once and a predicate cannot be both a partitioning predicate and part of a defining predicate, we have that:

$part(S) = in(S) \setminus \overline{atomic}(def(S^*))$.

Each partitioning predicate will form a classification aspect with two classes: *True* and *False*.

It is possible to combine the classification aspects based on the predicates with those based on data type information to form a classification tree. The data type information should be compared with the defining predicates. For example, suppose that the following partition of Q is chosen for an input variable $a?$.

$\{\{x : Q \mid x < 0\}, \{0\}, \{x : Q \mid x > 0\}\}$

If there is a defining predicate $a? \geq 0$ then this reduces to:

$\{\{0\}, \{x : Q \mid x > 0\}\}$

4.3 Classifying the Predicates of the Example

Consider the application of *def* to *Price*. Applying the rule for conjunction gives the following term:

$$\begin{aligned}
def(Price) = &\, def(outward\_date? \geq current\_date?) \cup \\
&\, def((travel\_period? = peak \land \\
&\, (outward\_date? - current\_date? > 7 \\
&\, \land price! = 0.9 * price\_peak(start?, end?) \\
&\, \lor outward\_date? - current\_date? \leq 7 \\
&\, \land price! = price\_peak(start?, end?)) \\
&\,) \lor \\
&\, (travel\_period? = off\_peak \land \exists p1, p2 : Q \bullet \\
&\, (r? = NONE \land p1 = 1 \lor r? = STUDENT \\
&\, \land p1 = 0.9 \lor r? = OAP \land p1 = 0.7) \land \\
&\, (outward\_date? - current\_date? > 7 \\
&\, \land p2 = 0.6 \lor \\
&\, outward\_date? - current\_date? \leq 7 \\
&\, \land p2 = 1) \land \\
&\, price! = p1 * p2 * price\_off\_p(start?, end?)))
\end{aligned}$$

Applying the rule for disjunction and the rules for atomic predicates, this reduces to:

$$def(Price) = \{outward\_date? \geq current\_date?\}.$$

Thus *Price* has one defining predicate only: $outward\_date? \geq current\_date?$ and each test case is given the precondition $outward\_date? \geq current\_date?$. All other input predicates are partitioning predicates.

The following are thus the partitioning predicates of *Price*:

1. $travel\_period? = peak$
2. $travel\_period? = off\_peak$
3. $outward\_date? - current\_date? > 7$
4. $outward\_date? - current\_date? \leq 7$
5. $r? = NONE$
6. $r? = STUDENT$
7. $r? = OAP$

As the corresponding leaves of the classification tree have two associated values, *True* and *False*, this set may be reduced to the following:

1. $travel\_period? = peak$
2. $outward\_date? - current\_date? > 7$
3. $r? = NONE$
4. $r? = STUDENT$
5. $r? = OAP$

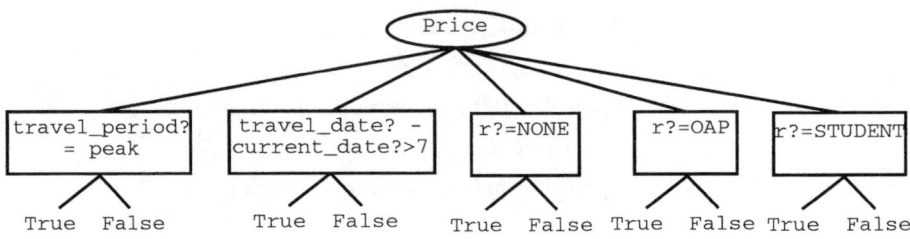

Fig. 5. Classification tree based on predicates only

The classification tree produced by this process is shown in Figure 5. The classification tree is flat: it has five nodes below the root, each leaf being capable of taking on one of the values *True* and *False*. Further, there are dependencies between these nodes. Specifically, if any of the three nodes that refer to $r?$ takes on the value *True* then the others must be *False*. It is thus desirable to add some structure to this classification tree. The tester might provide this structure. The automatic identification of situations in which the structure may be improved is a problem for future work. Note that while the example does not include state variables, the inclusion of these does not affect the overall procedure.

Given the classification tree, the tester may choose any combination of leaves. For example, they might choose an abstract test case defined by the classes: $travel\_period? = peak$ being *True*, $travel\_date? - current\_date? > 7$ being *True*, and $r? = NONE$ being *True*. This places the constraint $travel\_period? = peak \land travel\_date? - current\_date? > 7 \land r? = NONE$ on the input. The tester then has to find concrete input values that satisfy this constraint.

5 Test Size Reduction

This section will show how analysis based on the structure of S may be used to avoid certain combinations of classes. This may reduce the test effort by identifying abstract test cases that make little sense.

Suppose that the partitioning predicates p_1 and p_2 are conjoined in S, p_1 and p_2 appear only once in S and p_1 and p_2 have been chosen as classification aspects. Suppose further that, for an abstract test case being developed, the class *False* has been chosen for p_1. Since p_2 is conjoined with p_1, the value of p_2 is irrelevant. If the tester does not realise this, there are at least two potential consequences:

1. The tester chooses abstract test cases, with p_1 being *False*, that differ only in the value of p_2, believing these to test different behaviours.
2. In order to explore the impact of the value of p_2, the tester chooses abstract test cases that differ only in the value of p_2. However, in these abstract test cases, p_1 is *False*.

From the first case it is clear that there may be pairs of abstract test cases that test the same behaviour: the test contains unintended redundancy. This may reduce the efficiency of testing. From the second case it is clear that there may be a pair of abstract test cases, intended to test the impact of p_2, that cannot achieve this. This may reduce the effectiveness of testing. This section will consider an approach to automatically devising constraints in order to avoid the problems described above.

Ideally a constraint for p in S should give the conditions under which the value of p may affect the selection of a behaviour from S. This is when there is some disjunct c_i, formed by rewriting S to DNF, whose precondition differs from that of the predicate produced by replacing p in c_i with $\neg p$. Determining this condition is likely to be expensive. A further disadvantage is that the information returned by the above process might appear to bear little relationship to the predicates in the classification tree. Where this is the case, it does not help the tester to choose sensible combinations of classes.

A syntactic approximation, called the test context, will be introduced. The analysis will be computationally cheap to perform and the result of the analysis will be expressed in terms of the classes of the classification tree. The analysis will produce a necessary condition for the value of a predicate to be relevant. While the condition need not be sufficient, it is capable of warning the tester to avoid certain combinations of classes. Thus, the use of the test context should make testing more efficient and effective.

As before, it will be assumed that each partitioning predicate appears only once in S; where a partitioning predicate appears more than once the test context will be constructed for each separate occurrence and the disjunction of these taken.

Observe that the value of p is relevant if and only if, were S^* to be rewritten to DNF, one of the disjuncts containing either p or $\neg p$ contains no other term that takes on the value *false*. Thus the test context of p in S may be formed in the following way:

1. Rewrite S^* to DNF to form T_1.
2. Delete all disjuncts from T_1, that do not mention p, to form T_2.
3. Delete the references to p in T_2 to form T_3.
4. Delete the output predicates from T_3 to form T_4.
5. Return T_4 as the test context.

Although the above algorithm determines the test context of p in S, the first step may lead to a combinatorial explosion. Instead, a recursive definition will be given. Given S, let S' denote S with the output predicates removed and any quantifiers removed. Given partitioning predicate p from S, the test context of p in S will be denoted $tc(p, S')$. The function tc, which will be defined below, is more efficient than the above algorithm since it avoids the combinatorial explosion. tc has a precondition: when applied to (p, S'), the predicate p must appear exactly once in S'.

The test context is defined by the rules in Figure 6. Here, the first two rules form the base case: the value of p is always relevant to the values of both p and $\neg p$. The third rule considers the test context of p in $S' = P \wedge Q$. Suppose p appears in P (and thus does not appear in Q). The value of p appears in some disjunct, formed by rewriting S' to DNF, whose other predicates are all $true$, if and only if two conditions are satisfied:

1. P, when rewritten to DNF, has some disjunct that contains p and whose other predicates are $true$; and
2. Q, when rewritten to DNF, contains some disjunct whose predicates are all $true$.

The first of these conditions is equivalent to $tc(p, P)$ being $true$; the second is equivalent to Q being $true$.

The final rule deals with the case where $S' = P \vee Q$. Suppose that p is contained in P. Thus, p is in a disjunct, formed by rewriting S' to DNF, in which all other predicates are $true$, if and only if p is in a disjunct, formed by rewriting P to DNF, in which all other predicates are $true$. Thus, if p is contained in P then $tc(p, S') = tc(p, P)$ and otherwise $tc(p, S') = tc(p, Q)$.

$$tc(p, p) = true$$
$$tc(p, \neg p) = true$$
$$tc(p, P \wedge Q) = \text{if } p \in atomic(P) \text{ then } tc(p, P) \wedge Q$$
$$\text{else } tc(p, Q) \wedge P$$
$$tc(p, P \vee Q) = \text{if } p \in atomic(P) \text{ then } tc(p, P)$$
$$\text{else } tc(p, Q)$$

Fig. 6. The test context

Consider now the application of the test context to the predicate $r? = OAP$ in *Price*. This is:

$$tc(r? = OAP, outward\_date? \geq current\_date? \wedge$$
$$(travel\_period? = peak \wedge$$
$$(outward\_date? - current\_date? > 7$$

$$\lor\ outward\_date? - current\_date? \leq 7)) \lor$$
$$(travel\_period? = off\_peak \land$$
$$(r? = NONE \lor r? = STUDENT \lor r? = OAP) \land$$
$$(outward\_date? - current\_date? > 7 \lor$$
$$outward\_date? - current\_date? \leq 7)))$$

Applying the rule for conjunction, this becomes:

$$outward\_date? \geq current\_date? \land$$
$$tc(r? = OAP, travel\_period? = peak \land$$
$$(outward\_date? - current\_date? > 7$$
$$\lor\ outward\_date? - current\_date? \leq 7) \lor$$
$$(travel\_period? = off\_peak \land$$
$$(r? = NONE \lor r? = STUDENT \lor r? = OAP) \land$$
$$(outward\_date? - current\_date? > 7 \lor$$
$$outward\_date? - current\_date? \leq 7)))$$

Applying the rule for disjunction, reduces this to:

$$outward\_date? \geq current\_date? \land$$
$$tc(r? = OAP, travel\_period? = off\_peak \land$$
$$(r? = NONE \lor r? = STUDENT \lor r? = OAP) \land$$
$$(outward\_date? - current\_date? > 7 \lor$$
$$outward\_date? - current\_date? \leq 7))$$

Two more applications of the rule for conjunction reduces this to:

$$outward\_date? \geq current\_date? \land$$
$$travel\_period? = off\_peak \land$$
$$(outward\_date? - current\_date? > 7 \lor$$
$$outward\_date? - current\_date? \leq 7) \land$$
$$tc(r? = OAP, r? = NONE \lor r? = STUDENT \lor r? = OAP)$$

Applying the rule for disjunction, followed by the rule that states $tc(p, p) = true$, gives:

$$outward\_date? \geq current\_date? \land$$
$$travel\_period? = off\_peak \land$$
$$(outward\_date? - current\_date? > 7 \lor$$
$$outward\_date? - current\_date? \leq 7)$$

This reduces to:

$outward\_date? \geq current\_date? \wedge travel\_period? = off\_peak$

The first of these predicates is a defining predicate. Thus, if a class for the classification aspect $r? = OAP$ is chosen then the class *True* for the classification aspect $travel\_period? = off\_peak$ should also be chosen. This tells the tester that it is not necessary to have any abstract test cases that have the class *True* for $r? = OAP$ and the class *False* for $travel\_period? = off\_peak$.

6 Conclusions

This paper has introduced an approach that supports the Classification Tree Method. This approach partially automates the generation of a classification tree from a Z specification, providing a mechanism to avoid the combinatorial explosion inherent in previous approaches. The tester may further augment the tree constructed in order to exploit expert knowledge.

The approach described here uses two sources of information: the signature of a schema and the predicates contained within it. For each type of an input or state variable it is possible to devise a number of standard partitions. Thus, for example, with the integers one partition is: integers less than zero, zero, and integers greater than zero.

An algorithm has been given to identify predicates in the specification that are involved in either describing the precondition of the operation (defining predicates) or in determining which behaviour is applied (partitioning predicates). The defining predicates provide a precondition for each test case while the partitioning predicates are used to form nodes of the classification tree.

The paper has also defined the test context of a predicate. Given a partitioning predicate p in specification S, the test context of p in S identifies other choices that must be made in order for the value of p to be relevant. This allows the tester to avoid certain abstract test cases that make little sense, increasing test efficiency and effectiveness.

References

1. N. Amla and P.Ammann. Using Z specifications in category partition testing. In *COMPASS '92, Seventh Annual Conference on Computer Assurance*, pages 15–18, Gaithersburg, MD, USA, 1992.
2. T. Y. Chen and P. L. Poon. Construction of classification trees via the classification-hierarchy table. *Information and Software Technology*, 39:889–896, 1997.
3. T. Y. Chen and P. L. Poon. On the effectiveness of classification trees for test case construction. *Information and Software Technology*, 40:765–775, 1998.
4. J. Derrick and E. Boiten. Testing refinements of state-based formal specifications. *Journal of Software Testing, Verification, and Reliability*, 9:27–50, 1999.

5. J. Dick and A. Faivre. Automating the generation and sequencing of test cases from model-based specifications. In *FME '93, First International Symposium on Formal Methods in Europe*, pages 268–284, Odense, Denmark, 19–23 April 1993. Springer-Verlag, Lecture Notes in Computer Science 670.
6. M. C. Gaudel. Testing can be formal too. In *TAPSOFT'95*, pages 82–96. Springer-Verlag, March 1995.
7. M. Grochtmann and K. Grimm. Classification trees for partition testing. *Journal of Software Testing, Verification and Reliability*, 3:63–82, 1993.
8. P. A. V. Hall and R. M. Hierons. Formal Methods and Testing. Technical Report 91/16, Computing Department, The Open University, August 1991.
9. R. M. Hierons. Testing from a Z specification. *Journal of Software Testing, Verification and Reliability*, 7:19–33, 1997.
10. R. M. Hierons and M. Harman. Testing comformance to a quasi-non-determinstic stream X-machine. *Formal Aspects of Computing*, 12:423–442, 2000.
11. R. M. Hierons, S. Sadeghipour, and H. Singh. Testing a system specified using statecharts and Z. *Information and Software Technology*, 43:137–149, 2001.
12. R. M. Hierons and H. Ural. Reduced length checking sequences. *IEEE Transactions on Computers*, 51:1111–1117, 2002.
13. C. A. R. Hoare. How did software get so reliable without proof? In *Proceedings of Formal Methods Europe, 96 (Lecture Notes in Computer Science 1051)*, pages 1–17. Springer-Verlag, 1996.
14. M. Holcombe and F. Ipate. *Correct Systems: Building a Business Process Solution*. Springer-Verlag, 1998.
15. G. Laycock. Formal specification and testing: A case study. *Journal of Software Testing, Verification and Reliability*, 2:7–23, 1992.
16. D. Lee and M. Yannakakis. Principles and methods of testing finite-state machines. *Proceedings of the IEEE*, 84:1089–1123, 1996.
17. H. Singh, M. Conrad, and S. Sadeghipour. Test case design based on Z and the classification-tree method. In *First IEEE Conference on Formal Engineering Methods*, pages 81–90, Hiroshima, Japan, November 1997. IEEE Computer Society.
18. P. Stocks and D. Carrington. A Framework for Specification-Based Testing. *IEEE Transactions on Software Engineering*, 2:777–793, 1996.

Refinement Preserves *PLTL* Properties

Christophe Darlot, Jacques Julliand, and Olga Kouchnarenko

Laboratoire d'Informatique de l'Université de Franche-Comté, FRE CNRS 2661
16, route de Gray, 25030 Besançon Cedex
Ph:(33) 3 81 66 64 52, Fax:(33) 3 81 66 64 50
{darlot,julliand,kouchna}@lifc.univ-fcomte.fr,
http://lifc.univ-fcomte.fr

Abstract. We are interested in verifying dynamic properties of reactive systems. The reactive systems are specified by B event systems in a refinement development. We use labelled transition systems to express the semantics of these event systems on which we define a refinement relation. The main advantage is that the user does not need to express a variant and a loop invariant to obtain automatic proofs of dynamic properties, at least for finite state event systems. Another advantage is that the model-checking is done on an abstraction with few states and the property is preserved in the following refinements of the system.
The originality of this work concerns the proof that this refinement relation preserves the properties expressed with propositional linear temporal logic.

Keywords: Presevation of *PLTL* properties, B event systems, Refinement development.

1 Introduction

The introduction of dynamic properties is necessary for the design and the verification of event systems [12,2,11]. In our approach, the specification of a B event systems enriched with Propositional Linear Temporal Logic [12] (*PLTL*) formulae. Finite or infinite transition systems give the semantics of B event systems. In the finite case, we can algorithmically verify *PLTL* properties on these systems. We are mainly interested in the *preservation* of these dynamic properties through refinement.

As a way of comparison, our approach for addressing the introduction of dynamic constraints in B is quite different from the propositions of J.-R. Abrial and L. Mussat in [2]: In B, the verification of *dynamic invariants* and of the liveness modalities *leads to* and *until* uses proof techniques which requires the user to give explicitly *variants* and *loop invariants*. Moreover, the user has to express a *variant* to prove that the refinement introduces no live-lock. Our technique frees the user from these variants and loop invariants since the temporal properties are verified by model-checking and the refinement is verified algorithmically.

Since we introduce new details in the refinement, the abstract system is usually small in number of states while the refinements are likely to be very large, so that model-checking can not be easily performed.

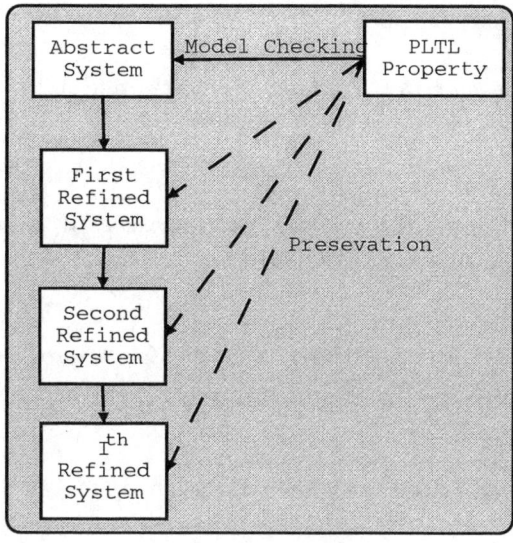

Fig. 1. Specification and verification approach

Finite state systems provide a nice framework for the verification of B event systems. Anyway, robust systems design requires the designer to restrict the number of states to something finite (it would be for example inconceivable for a flight control computer to ask the pilot for more disk space in the middle of an astable flight !). So, in this paper, we deal with the specification and the verification of finite state systems. This allows us to verify fully automatically any $PLTL$ property, i.e. safety, liveness and fairness properties. The main idea of this paper is that our refinement relation is compatible with $PLTL$ properties, so that any property verified at a given level of the refinement design is preserved in the following refinements. This also means that we have temporal properties verified "for free" in the refined levels of the specification provided that the refinement relation verification succeeds. This approach is illustrated in Fig. 1.

The paper is organized as follows. Section 2 gives some definitions and shows how to express B event systems semantics by transition systems. Then we define our refinement relation in Section 3. In Section 4, we show how temporal properties are preserved through refinement. Finally, we give some ideas about future works in Section 5.

2 B Event Systems and Labelled Transitions Systems

In the next section, we introduce the notations and definitions of transitions systems and B event systems and then show how to express the semantics of the last using the first in order to be able to verify temporal properties by model-checking.

2.1 Preliminaries

In the following, $s, s_0, s_1, s_2, \ldots$ designate states and V is a set of variables $\{x_1, \ldots, x_n\}$ of type $Dom(x_i)$, which is a finite set.

Definition 1 (Atomic Propositions). *We call $AP_V \stackrel{def}{=} \{ap, ap_0, ap_1, ap_2, \ldots\}$ the set of atomic propositions over the set of variables V where ap is a formula $x_i = d_j$, with $x_i \in V$ and $d_j \in Dom(x_i)$.*

Definition 2 (State Proposition). *The set of state propositions over the set of variables V, written $SP_V \stackrel{def}{=} \{sp, sp_1, sp_2, \ldots\}$, is defined by the following grammar:*

$$sp ::= ap \mid sp \vee sp \mid \neg sp, \text{ where } ap \in AP_V$$

Definition 3 (Labelled Transition Systems (LTS)). *A transition system TS labelled over a set of variables V ranging on finite domains is defined by the quintuple $TS = (Q, Q_0, L, T, l)$ where:*

- *Q is a set of states;*
- *Q_0 is a set of initial states ($Q_0 \subseteq Q$);*
- *$L \stackrel{def}{=} \{a, a_1, \ldots\}$ is a set of transitions' labels that we call actions;*
- *$T \in \mathbb{P}(Q \times L \times Q)$ is the transition relation;*
- *$l : Q \to SP_V$ is an injective mapping such that for a state s, $l(s)$ is a conjunction $\bigwedge_{i=1}^{n} (x_i = d_j)$ expressing the value of each variable where $d_j \in Dom(x_i)$.*

For convenience, we note $s_1 \stackrel{a}{\to} s_2$ the transition (s_1, a, s_2), and we say transition system for short.

Definition 4 (sp holds on s). *Let $TS = (Q, Q_0, L, T, l)$ be a transition system over V. A state $s \in Q$ satisfies a state proposition $sp \in SP_V$, written $s \models sp$, iff $l(s) \Rightarrow sp$.*

We now give a few definitions about paths of transition systems:

Definition 5 (Path of a LTS). *Let $\sigma = s_0, s_1, \ldots$ be a sequence of states in $TS = (Q, Q_0, L, T, l)$. σ is a path of TS iff $\forall i.(i \geq 0 \Rightarrow \exists a.(a \in L \wedge (s_i \stackrel{a}{\to} s_{i+1} \in T)))$.*

We note $\sigma(i)$ to designate the state s_i of the path σ and $\Sigma(TS)$ for the set of paths of TS.

2.2 From B Event Systems ...

Definition 6 (B Event System). *A B event system is a quintuple $SE = (E, V, I, Init, D)$ where:*

- *E is a finite set of event labels;*
- *V is a finite set of variables;*
- *I is a state proposition which defines the event system invariant ($I \in SP_V$);*
- *$Init$ is a substitution which defines the initial states of the system, and*
- *D is a set of events $e \hat{=} S$ for each $e \in E$ where S is a generalized substitution.*

We restrict the generalized substitutions to the following grammar:

$$S' ::= \text{SELECT } p \text{ THEN } S \text{ END}$$
$$| \text{ANY } z \text{ WHERE } p \text{ THEN } S \text{ END}$$
$$| \text{CHOICE } S \text{ OR } S \text{ END}$$
$$| S \parallel S$$
$$| v := exp$$

where p is a state proposition, v is a variable from V, z is a n-tuple of variables which are not in V, and exp is standard expression of the B-language as defined in [1].

2.3 ... to Labelled Transitions Systems

In order to build the transition system from an event system, we mainly use the method introduced in [8]. We firstly need to give the definitions of the weakest preconditions and the conjugate weakest preconditions.

Definition 7 (Weakest Precondition). *Let S be a generalized substitution and sp a state proposition, $[S]sp$ is the weakest precondition for S to establish sp.*

This means that given a state s_1 satisfying $[S]sp$ and an event $e \hat{=} S$ which allows us to go from s_1 to a state s_2, then s_2 satisfies sp. Notice that the generalized substitution calculus is described in [1].

Definition 8 (Conjugate Weakest Precondition). *Let S be a generalized substitution and p a state proposition, then $< S > sp \stackrel{def}{=} \neg[S]\neg sp$ defines the conjugate weakest precondition for S to possibly establish sp.*

This definition can be read as follows. "It is not true that S establishes $\neg sp$", which can also be understood as "If an execution of S exists, at least one of them leads to a state where sp holds".

Definition 9 (Event Systems Semantics). *The definition of a transition system $TS = (Q, Q_0, L, T, l)$ over V expresses the semantics of a B event system $SE = (E, V, I, Init, D)$ to these rules:*

- Q is the set of states satisfying the invariant I, i.e. $Q = \{s \mid l(s) \Rightarrow I\}$;
- the transitions are labelled by the names of the events, i.e. $L = E$;
- the set of initial states Q_0 is such that $Q_0 = \{s \in Q \mid <Init> l(s)\}$;
- for each pair of states $s_1, s_2 \in Q$ and each event (labelled by a) of SE that can be activated in the state s_1 and can lead to the state s_2, we add to T the transition $s_1 \stackrel{a}{\rightarrow} s_2$; formally,

$$T = \{s_1 \stackrel{a}{\rightarrow} s_2 \mid (a \stackrel{\wedge}{=} S) \in D \wedge l(s_1) \Rightarrow <S> l(s_2)\}.$$

Considering the first item in the above definition, notice that either the transitions system is built from a proven event system – in this case we do not need to verify the invariant, or the invariant is checked on the fly while constructing the transition system.

3 Refinement of Labelled Transition Systems

3.1 Refinement and Transitions Systems

We want to express and to verify the refinement algorithmically, i.e. as a relation between transition systems. For this, we define in this section the refinement as a kind of τ-simulation. This part mostly sums up the work presented in [6] for finite state systems, and in [4] for parametric state ones.

Let $TS_1 = (Q_1, Q_{0_1}, L_1, T_1, l_1)$ and $TS_2 = (Q_2, Q_{0_2}, L_2, T_2, l_2)$ be two transitions systems with respective sets of variables V_1 and V_2. They give the semantics of two B event systems modelling a system on two successive levels of refinement.

We first define a binary relation $\mu \subseteq Q_2 \times Q_1$ which allows us to express the gluing invariant between the states of TS_1 and TS_2.

Definition 10 (Relation μ). Let $I_{1,2}$ be the gluing invariant of the systems TS_1 and TS_2. The state $s_2 \in Q_2$ is glued to the state $s_1 \in Q_1$ by $I_{1,2}$, written $s_2 \mu s_1$, iff $(l_2(s_2) \wedge I_{1,2}) \Rightarrow l_1(s_1)$.

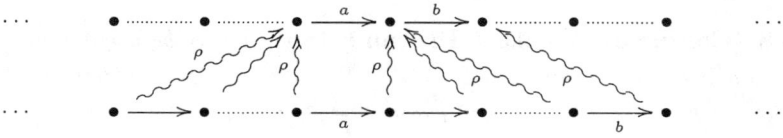

Fig. 2. Path refinement

We now define the refinement as a τ-simulation. For this, we restrict the relation μ to a relation ρ having the following properties:

1. In order to describe the refinement, we keep the transitions of TS_2 whom labels are in L_1 (those labelled by the "old" events) and we consider the new transitions introduced during the refinement process (those whom label is in $L_2 \setminus L_1$) as being non-observable; they are called τ-transitions. Each portion of path containing τ-transitions must end by a transition labelled from L_1. Then, the refinement relation is either a strict relation or a stuttering relation (see Fig. 2).
2. The new events should not take the control forever. So, we forbid the paths containing an infinity of successive τ-transitions in order to avoid the live-locks.
3. Moreover, the new events should not introduce dead-locks.

Notice that these features are those given informally for the refinement of B event systems. They are common to other formalisms such as action systems refinement [9] or LTL refinement [10].

Now we gave an informal description of the refinement properties, here is its formal definition:

Definition 11 (Relation ρ). Let $TS_1 = (Q_1, Q_{0_1}, L_1, T_1, l_1)$ and $TS_2 = (Q_2, Q_{0_2}, L_2, T_2, l_2)$ be two transition systems. Let $a \in L_1$. We define the relation $\rho \subseteq Q_2 \times Q_1$ as

1. the greatest binary relation included in μ, and
2. satisfying the following conditions:
   a) **Strict transition refinement:** (see Fig. 3)
      $(s_2 \rho s_1 \wedge s_2 \xrightarrow{a} s'_2 \in T_2) \Rightarrow \exists s'_1.(s_1 \xrightarrow{a} s'_1 \in T_1 \wedge s'_2 \rho s'_1)$
   b) **Stuttering transitions refinement:** (see Fig. 5)
      $(s_2 \rho s_1 \wedge s_2 \xrightarrow{\tau} s'_2 \in T_2) \Rightarrow s'_2 \rho s_1$
   c) **Non-introduction of deadlocks:** (see Fig. 4)
      $(s_2 \rho s_1 \wedge s_2 \not\rightarrow_2) \Rightarrow (s_1 \not\rightarrow_1)$ [1]
   d) **Non τ-divergence:**
      $\forall \sigma_2, k.(\sigma_2 \in \Sigma(TS_2) \wedge k \geq 0 \Rightarrow \exists a, k'.(a \in L_1 \wedge k' \geq k \wedge \sigma_2(k'-1) \xrightarrow{a} \sigma_2(k') \in T_2))$
   e) **External non-determinism preservation:** (see Fig. 6)
      $(s_1 \xrightarrow{a} s'_1 \wedge s_2 \rho s_1) \Rightarrow \exists s'_2, s''_2, s''_1.(s'_2 \rho s_1 \wedge s'_2 \xrightarrow{a}_2 s''_2 \in T_2 \wedge s_1 \xrightarrow{a} s''_1 \in T_1 \wedge s''_2 \rho s''_1)$

Definition 12 (Refinement of Transition Systems). A transition system $TS_1 = (Q_1, Q_{0_1}, L_1, T_1, l_1)$ is refined by a transition system $TS_2 = (Q_2, Q_{0_2}, L_2, T_2, l_2)$, written $TS_1 \sqsubseteq_\rho TS_2$), iff

$$\forall s_2.(s_2 \in Q_{0_2} \Rightarrow \exists s_1.(s_1 \in Q_{0_1} \wedge s_2 \rho s_1))$$

Definition 13 (Refinement of Paths). Let TS_1 and TS_2 be to transition systems such that $TS_1 \sqsubseteq TS_2$. Let σ_1 and σ_2 be some respective paths of $\Sigma(TS_1)$ and $\Sigma(TS_2)$. σ_1 is refined by σ_2, written $\sigma_1 \sqsubseteq \sigma_2$, iff

$$\forall i.(\sigma_2(i) \in Q_2 \Rightarrow \exists j.(\sigma_1(j) \in Q_1 \wedge \sigma_2(i) \rho \; \sigma_1(j)))$$

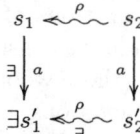
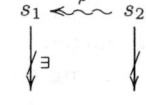

Fig. 3. Strict transition refinement

Fig. 4. Non-introduction of deadlocks

Fig. 5. Stuttering transition refinement

Fig. 6. External non-determinism preservation

Last, we give an important property of this relation stating the existence of an abstract path for any refined path.

Lemma 1 (Existence of an Abstract Path). *Let $TS_1 = (Q_1, Q_{0_1}, L_1, T_1, l_1)$ and $TS_2 = (Q_2, Q_{0_2}, L_2, T_2, l_2)$ be two transition systems such that $TS_1 \sqsubseteq_\rho TS_2$. Then,*

$$\forall s_2.(s_2 \in Q_2 \Rightarrow \exists s_1.(s_1 \in Q_1 \wedge s_2 \rho \ s_1)).$$

Sketch of proof : (by construction) Suppose that s_2 can be reached by a path σ_2 such that $\sigma_2(0) \in Q_{0_2}$ and $\sigma_2(k) = s_2$. By Clause 2d in Definition 11, σ_2 contains a finite number of τ-transitions. σ_2 can then be written $\sigma_2(0) \xrightarrow{\tau} \ldots \xrightarrow{a_1} \ldots \xrightarrow{\tau} \ldots \xrightarrow{a_n} \xrightarrow{\tau} \ldots \sigma_2(k)$.

Moreover, it is easy to see that it exists a state $s_{1_0} \in Q_{1_0}$ such that $(\sigma_2, 0)\rho s_{1_0}$. We can then construct a path σ_1 issued from $s_{1_0} = \sigma_1(0)$ such that the states of σ_1 are linked by transitions labelled by $a_1 \ldots a_n$. That way, we reach a state $\sigma_1(j)$ and from the clauses 2a and 2b of Definition 11, we know that $\sigma_2(k)\rho\sigma_1(j)$. □

In the case of finite systems, this relation ρ can be computed fully algorithmically. This computation is detailed in [6] ; informally, it is performed by a joint enumeration of the abstract and the refined systems. This frees the user from expressing a global *variant* for the specification. We can extend this method in order to handle parameterized (infinite) systems that refines finite systems. Notice that no model-checking is done on the infinite systems for which we only consider the preserved properties defined in the next section. Some early results were published in [4].

---

[1] we note $s \not\rightarrow_i$ when $\forall s', s''.(s' \xrightarrow{a} s'') \in T_i \Rightarrow s \neq s'$.

4 Preservation of *PLTL* Properties

In this section, we define the temporal logic we use and then, show how temporal properties are preserved through the refinement process.

4.1 Propositional Linear Temporal Logic (*PLTL*)

To express the dynamic properties, we use Propositional Linear Temporal Logic (*PLTL*) defined in [12]. On one hand, *PLTL* is more expressive than the dynamic invariants and *B* modalities without `While` list. On the other hand, *PLTL* can be verified by model-checking in a fully automatic way whereas interactive proof is often required when proving modalities.

Definition 14 (*PLTL*). *Given temporal formulae ϕ, ϕ_1, ϕ_2 and a path σ, we define ϕ to be valid at $j \geq 0$ on a path $\sigma = s_0, s_1, \ldots, s_j, \ldots$, written $\sigma(j) \models \phi$, as follows:*

$\sigma(j) \models sp$ iff $s_j \models sp$ and $sp \in SP_V$
$\sigma(j) \models \neg \phi$ iff it is not true that $\sigma(j) \models \phi$
$\sigma(j) \models \phi_1 \vee \phi_2$ iff $\sigma(j) \models \phi_1$ or $\sigma(j) \models \phi_2$
$\sigma(j) \models \bigcirc \phi$ iff $\sigma(j+1) \models \phi$
$\sigma(j) \models \phi_1 \mathcal{U} \phi_2$
    iff $\exists k.(k \geq j \wedge \sigma(k) \models \phi_2 \wedge \forall i.(j \leq i < k \Rightarrow \sigma(i) \models \phi_1))$

We also define $\sigma \models \phi$ by $\sigma(0) \models \phi$ and we say that "ϕ holds on σ".

Here, two temporal operators, Next ($\bigcirc$) and Until ($\mathcal{U}$) are defined. We also use the following notations: $\Diamond \phi$ (eventually ϕ) defined as $true\ \mathcal{U} \phi$, $\Box \phi$ (always ϕ) defined as $\neg \Diamond \neg \phi$, and $\phi_1 \Rightarrow \phi_2$ defined as $\neg \phi_1 \vee \phi_2$.

We extend the previous definition to transition systems:

Definition 15 (Validity of a *PLTL* Property on a Transition System). *We define a temporal property ϕ to be valid[2] for a transition system as follows:*

$$TS \models \phi \text{ iff } \forall \sigma.(\sigma \in \Sigma(TS) \Rightarrow \sigma \models \phi)$$

4.2 Preservation

In many formalisms using refinement design such as *LTL* [10] or *TLA* [11], properties are preserved through the refinement process. We show in this section that *PLTL* properties are also preserved in our refinement approach.

The set of variables is not the same in both abstract and refined specifications. In order to be able to reason with the abstract variables of an abstract system at a refined level, we have to give a new validity definition.

---
[2] we also say that "ϕ holds on TS"

Definition 16 (Validity of a State Proposition through the Gluing Invariant). Let a transition system TS_1 be refined by a transition system TS_2. Let $I_{1,2}$ be their gluing invariant. Let $s_2 \in Q_2$ and let sp_1 be a state proposition expressed with the variables of TS_1, we say that s_2 satisfies p_1 through the gluing invariant (written $(s_2, I_{1,2}) \models_c p_1$) iff $l_2(s_2) \wedge I_{1,2} \Rightarrow p_1$.

Now we can formally define what is a $PLTL$ property preserved through refinement.

Definition 17 (Semantics of Preserved $PLTL$ Formulae). Let TS_1 and $TS_2 = (Q_2, Q_{0_2}, L_2, T_2, l_2)$ be two transitions system such that $TS_1 \sqsubseteq_\rho TS_2$, and let $I_{1,2}$ be their gluing invariant. Let σ_2 be a path of $\Sigma(TS_2)$. Let ϕ and ψ be two temporal properties of TS_1. σ_2 satisfies ϕ by preservation, written $(\sigma_2(j), I_{1,2}) \models_p \phi$, iff:

- $(\sigma_2(j), I_{1,2}) \models_p sp$, iff $(\sigma_2(j), I_{1,2}) \models_c sp$ and $sp \in SP_{V_1}$,
- $(\sigma_2(j), I_{1,2}) \models_p \neg \phi$, iff it is not true that $(\sigma_2(j), I_{1,2}) \models_p \phi$,
- $(\sigma_2(j), I_{1,2}) \models_p \phi \vee \psi$ iff $(\sigma_2(j), I_{1,2}) \models_p \phi$ or $(\sigma_2(j), I_{1,2}) \models_p \psi$,
- $(\sigma_2(j), I_{1,2}) \models_p \bigcirc \phi$ iff $\exists j'.(j < j' \wedge (\sigma_2(j'), I_{1,2}) \models_p \phi)$,
- $(\sigma_2(j), I_{1,2}) \models_p \phi \mathcal{U} \psi$, iff $\exists j'.(j \leq j' \wedge (\sigma(j') I_{1,2}) \models_p \psi \wedge \forall j''.(j \leq j'' < j' \Rightarrow (\sigma_2(j'), I_{1,2}) \models_p \phi)$.

We define $(TS_2, I_{1,2}) \models_p \phi$ by $\forall \sigma_2.(\sigma_2 \in \Sigma(TS_2) \Rightarrow (\sigma_2(0), I_{1,2}) \models_p \phi)$.

We want to emphasize that the properties containing the *Next* operator are preserved in a specific way. Intuitively, in order to know their preserved form, it suffices to replace each *Next* operator by a *Strict Eventually*[3]. In other words, a property ϕ that happenes "in the next state" ($\bigcirc \phi$) of the abstract system level will happen eventually (but at least at the next step) in the next refinements because of the interwoven transitions introduced by the refinement.

Now, we prove that $PLTL$ properties are preserved according to the previous definition by the refinement relation ρ defined in Section 3.

Theorem 1 (Preservation of a $PLTL$ Property on a Path). Let ϕ be a formula of $PLTL$, TS_1 and TS_2 two transitions systems such that $TS_1 \sqsubseteq_\rho TS_2$ with $I_{1,2}$ as gluing invariant, and σ_1 and σ_2 respectively belong to $\Sigma(TS_1)$ and $\Sigma(TS_2)$, then

$$\forall j, k.(j \geq 0 \wedge k \geq 0 \wedge \sigma_2(k) \rho\, \sigma_1(j) \wedge (\sigma_1(j) \models \phi) \Rightarrow (\sigma_2(k), I_{1,2}) \models_p \phi).$$

Sketch of proof:

Let σ_2 de TS_2 be a path a $\Sigma(TS_2)$ and refining a path σ_1 of TS_1 (Lemma 1 ensures that this path exits). Besides, $a, a', \ldots, a^{(n)}$ label the transitions of TS_1 $(a, a'', \ldots, a^{(n)} \in L_1)$ and τ labels each transition introduced during refinement $(\tau \in L_2 \setminus L_1)$.

---

[3] *Strict Eventually* $\phi \stackrel{def}{=} \bigcirc \Diamond \phi$

Refinement Preserves PLTL Properties

The proof is performed by structural induction on the following syntax of temporal properties:

$$\phi ::= sp \mid \bigcirc\phi \mid \phi\mathcal{U}\phi \mid \phi \vee \phi \mid \neg\phi$$

Note that this grammar covers all *PLTL* properties.

1. Let us prove that a state proposition sp is preserved by refinement.
   Let be $\sigma_1(j)$ such that $\sigma_2(k)\rho\sigma_1(j)$, so $\sigma_2(k)\mu\sigma_1(j)$. By definition of the μ relation, we have got $l_2(\sigma_2(k)) \wedge I_{1,2} \Rightarrow l_1(\sigma_1(j))$. Besides, $l_1(\sigma_1(j)) \Rightarrow sp$ since $\sigma_1(j) \models sp$ (by definition of the semantics of *PLTL*).
   We can infer that $l_2(\sigma_2(k)) \wedge I_{12} \Rightarrow sp$ by transitivity of the implication. So, $(\sigma_2(k), I_{1,2}) \models_c sp$ (see definition 16), and $(\sigma_2(k), I_{1,2}) \models_p sp$ (see definition 17).

2. Let us prove that $\bigcirc\phi$ is preserved by refinement, with the recurrence hypothesis that ϕ is preserved.
   We know that $\sigma_1(j) \models \bigcirc\phi$, so $\sigma_1(j+1) \models \phi$. Besides, $\sigma_2(k)\rho\sigma_1(j)$.

   a) First case : $\sigma_2(k) \xrightarrow{a} \sigma_2(k+1) \in T_2$

   $\sigma_1 \cdots\cdots \sigma_1(j) \xrightarrow{a} \sigma_1(j+1) \cdots\cdots$

   $\ \rho\uparrow\quad\quad\quad\quad \rho\uparrow$

   $\sigma_2 \cdots\cdots \sigma_2(k) \xrightarrow{a} \sigma_2(k+1) \cdots\cdots$

   According to the Clause 2a of the ρ relation definition, $\sigma_1(j) \xrightarrow{a} \sigma_1(j+1) \in T_1$ and $\sigma_2(k+1)\rho\sigma_1(j+1)$. By recurrence hypothesis, $(\sigma_2(k+1), I_{1,2}) \models_p \phi$, so $(\sigma_2(k), I_{1,2}) \models_p \bigcirc\phi$ according to definition 17.

   b) Second case : $\sigma_2(k) \xrightarrow{\tau} \sigma_2(k+1) \in T_2$

   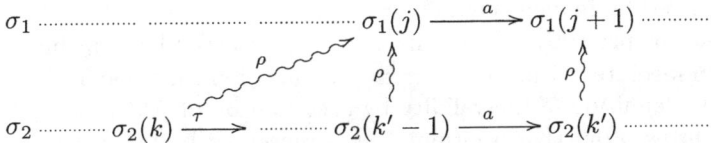

   According to Clause 2d of Definition 11, the transitions labelled by τ cannot take the control forever, and according to Clause 2c, the refinement does not introduce deadlocks. So, $\exists a, k'.(a \in L_1 \wedge k' > k \wedge \sigma_2(k) \xrightarrow{\tau} \sigma_2(k+1) \xrightarrow{\tau} \ldots \xrightarrow{\tau} \sigma_2(k'-1) \xrightarrow{a} \sigma_2(k'))$. According to Clause 2b of Definition 11, $\sigma_2(k'-1)\rho(\sigma_1,j)$.
   As $\sigma_2(k'-1)\rho\sigma_1(j)$ and $\sigma_2(k'-1) \xrightarrow{a} \sigma_2(k') \in T_2$, according to Clause 2a of Definition 11, $\sigma_1(j) \xrightarrow{a} \sigma_1(j+1) \in T_1 \wedge \sigma_2(k')\rho\sigma_1(j+1)$. however, $\sigma_1(j+1) \models \phi$ and as $\sigma_2(k')\rho\sigma_1(j+1)$, by recurrence hypothesis, $(\sigma_2(k'), I_{1,2}) \models_p \phi$, which implies $(\sigma_2(k), I_{1,2}) \models_p \phi$.

   As a conclusion of the last two points, we can deduce that $(\sigma_2(k), I_{1,2}) \models_p \bigcirc\phi$ so the formulae $\bigcirc\phi$ are preserved by refinement (assuming ϕ is preserved by refinement).

3. Let us prove that $\phi \mathcal{U} \psi$ is preserved by refinement with the recurrence hypothesis that ϕ and ψ are preserved.

By hypothesis, we know that $\sigma(j) \models \phi \mathcal{U} \psi$, so, by definition of $\mathcal{U}$,

$$\exists j''.(j \leq j'' < |\sigma| \wedge \sigma_1(j'') \models \psi \tag{1}$$
$$\wedge \forall j'.(j \leq j' < j'' \Rightarrow \sigma_1(j') \models \phi)) \tag{2}$$

where the $\mathcal{U}$ operator is defined on one hand by a *eventuality* (1) and on the other hand by a *maintenance* (2).

Let be $\sigma_2' = \sigma_2(k) \to \ldots \xrightarrow{a^{(n)}} \sigma_2(k'')$. σ_2' refined a finite portion of σ_1' and the states of the paths σ_1' and σ_2' are related by ρ as seen on the following figure (according to Lemma 1):

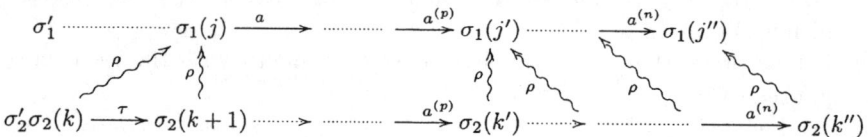

If we interpret the $\mathcal{U}$ operator definition, we can deduce that it exists a sequence of transitions labelled by $a, a', \ldots, a^{(n)} \in L_1$ de σ_1 such that we have in σ_1 the following finite path part: $\sigma_1' = \sigma_1(j) \xrightarrow{a} \ldots \xrightarrow{a^{(n)}} \sigma_1(j'')$.

a) *(Eventuality)* $\sigma_1' \sqsubseteq_\rho \sigma_2'$ so $\sigma_2(k'') \rho \sigma_1(j'')$. Besides, $\sigma_1(j'') \models \psi$. By recurrence hypothesis, we know that ψ is preserved, so $(\sigma_2(k''), I_{1,2}) \models_p \psi$.

b) *(Maintenance)* $\sigma_1' \sqsubseteq_\rho \sigma_2'$ so $\sigma_2(k') \rho \sigma_1(j')$ for any k' and j' such that $k \leq k' < k'' \wedge j \leq j' < j''$. Besides, $\sigma_1(j') \models \phi$. By recurrence hypothesis, we know that ϕ is preserved so $(\sigma_2(k'), I_{1,2}) \models_p \phi$.

As a conclusion of the last two points, we can deduce that $(\sigma_2(k), I_{1,2}) \models_p \phi \mathcal{U} \psi$ so the formulae $\phi \mathcal{U} \psi$ are preserved by refinement (if ϕ and ψ are preserved by refinement).

4. Let us prove that a formula $\phi \vee \psi$ is preserved by refinement.

Immediate, with the recurrence assumption that ϕ and ψ are preserved and by definition of the validity by preservation of $\phi \vee \psi$ (see definition 17).

5. Let us prove that a formula $\neg \phi$ is preserved by refinement.

Immediate, with the recurrence assumption that ϕ is preserved and by definition of the validity by preservation of $\neg \phi$ (see definition 17).

□

Theorem 2 (Preservation of *PLTL* Properties). *Let ϕ be a PLTL formula, TS_1 and TS_2 be two transition systems. If $TS_1 \models \phi$ and $TS_1 \sqsubseteq_\rho TS_2$, $I_{1,2}$ being the gluing invariant, then $(TS_2, I_{1,2}) \models_p \phi$.*

Proof: Immediate. If $TS_1 \sqsubseteq_\rho TS_2$, then $\forall \sigma_2.((\sigma_2, 0) \in Q_{0_2} \Rightarrow \exists \sigma_1.((\sigma_1, 0) \in Q_{0_1} \wedge (\sigma_2, 0) \rho (\sigma_1, 0)))$. Moreover, if $TS_1 \models \phi$, then $\forall \sigma_1.((\sigma_1, 0) \in Q_{0_1} \Rightarrow (\sigma_1, 0) \models \phi)$. We then can use Theorem 1.

□

5 Conclusion

In this paper, we propose a technique for verification by abstraction and refinement based on a specific notion of refinement relation. This relation is defined in the style of Milner-Park simulation relation between concrete and abstract finite transition systems.

However, it is well-known that the algorithmic verification quickly meets its limits when applied to huge systems. So, we have to face the problem of combinatory explosion during refinement since the details introduced in this process tend to drastically increase the number of states of the systems. It is also the case while verifying temporal properties by model-checking. Preservation partially avoids this problem by expressing properties on a system abstract enough, and then, refining this system. In [7], we give conditions of refinement of a whole system from the refinement of its components to avoid a combinatory explosion problem during the refinement verification.

We propose to free the user from expressing variants and loop invariants. In our opinion, these artifacts of proof should not be a constraint imposed to the user for specification and verification. Expressing dynamic properties with the $PLTL$ logics allows us to verify them using fully automatic model-checking tools. Moreover, the refinement relation between transition systems can also be verified by a non-interactive computation. This way, $PLTL$ temporal properties expressed and established for an abstract system, are also established for the refined levels, provided that the refinement relation verification succeeds.

We are also working on extending this work to particular infinite systems with parametric counters, in the case where the abstract systems are finite and the refined systems are infinite ones. The interest of refining a finite system into an infinite system can be the verification of a whole class of finite systems expressed by one parameterized (infinite) system. The reader can find an example of such a refinement in [4].

To conclude, this work on property preservation is used as a hypothesis for running work on reformulation [3,5] of properties through refinement. In this framework, preserved properties are "enriched" with the refinement details, and then, are verified with a technique combining proof and model-checking. This method allows the validation of properties weaker than the preserved ones, and captured by reformulation patterns.

References

1. J.-R. Abrial. *The B Book*. Cambridge University Press - ISBN 0521-496195, 1996.
2. J.-R. Abrial and L. Mussat. Introducing dynamic constraints in B. In *Second Conference on the B method*, volume 1393 of *LNCS*, pages 83–128, 1998.
3. F. Bellegarde, C. Darlot, J. Julliand, and O. Kouchnarenko. Reformulate dynamic properties during B refinement and forget variants and loop invariants. In *Proc. First Int. Conf. ZB'2000, York, GB, volume 1878 of Lecture Notes in Computer Science*, pages 230–249. Springer-Verlag, September 2000.

4. F. Bellegarde, C. Darlot, J. Julliand, and O. Kouchnarenko. How to verify LTL properties on infinite refined systems by proof and model-checking cooperation. In *AVIS'01*, March 2001.
5. F. Bellegarde, C. Darlot, J. Julliand, and O. Kouchnarenko. Reformulation: a way to combine dynamic properties and B refinement. In J.N. Oliveira and P. Zave, editors, *FME'01*, volume 2021 of *LNCS*, pages 2–19, Berlin, Allemagne, March 2001. Springer-Verlag.
6. F. Bellegarde, J. Julliand, and O. Kouchnarenko. Ready-simulation is not ready to express a modular refinement relation. In *FASE'2000*, volume 1783 of *LNCS*, pages 266–283, April 2000.
7. F. Bellegarde, J. Julliand, and O. Kouchnarenko. Synchronized parallel composition of event systems in B. In D. Bert, J. P. Bowen, M. C. Henson, and K. Robinson, editors, *ZB 2002 : Formal specification an development in Z and B*, volume 2272 of LNCS, pages 436–457. Springer-Verlag, 2002.
8. D. Bert and F. Cave. Construction of finite labelled transition systems from B abstract systems. In *Proc. of the 2nd Int. Conf. on Integrated Formal Methods (IFM 2000)*, volume 1945 of *LNCS*, pages 235–254, Dagstuhl, Germany, novembre 2000. Springer-Verlag.
9. M.J. Butler. Stepwise refinement of communicating systems. *Science of Computer Programming*, 1996.
10. Y. Kesten, Z. Manna, and A. Pnueli. Temporal verification of simulation and refinement. In J.W. de Bakker, W.-P. de Roever, and G. Rozenberg, editors, *A Decade of Concurrency*, volume 803 of *LNCS*, pages 273–346. Springer-Verlag, 1994.
11. L. Lamport. A temporal logic of actions. *ACM Transactions On Programming Languages And Systems, TOPLAS*, 16(3):872–923, May 1994.
12. Z. Manna and A. Pnueli. *The Temporal Logic of Reactive and Concurrent Systems: Specification*. Springer-Verlag, 1992.

Proving Event Ordering Properties for Information Systems*

Marc Frappier[1,**] and Régine Laleau[2]

[1] Département de mathématiques et d'informatique, Université de Sherbrooke
Sherbrooke, Québec, Canada J1K 2R1, +1 819 821-8000x2096,
Marc.Frappier@dmi.usherb.ca

[2] Laboratoire CEDRIC, Institut d'Informatique d'Entreprise
Conservatoire National des Arts et Métiers
18 allée Jean Rostand, 91025 Évry Cedex France, +33 1 69 36 73 47,
laleau@iie.cnam.fr

Abstract. This paper presents an approach to prove event ordering properties for B specifications of information systems. The properties are expressed using the EB^3 notation, where input event ordering properties are defined using a process algebra similar to CSP and output events are specified by recursive functions on the input traces associated to the process expression. By proving that the EB^3 specification is refined by the B specification, using the B theory of refinement, we ensure that both specifications accept and refuse exactly the same event traces. The proof relies on an extended labeled transition system, generated using the operational semantics of the process algebra, in order to deal with unbounded systems. The gluing invariant is generated from the EB^3 recursive functions.

Keywords. EB^3, B, process algebra, trace-based specifications, refinement.

1 Introduction

Organisations are increasingly developing external access to their information systems (IS) through the internet. This may put data integrity at risk if IS are not completely robust. External users may play with the IS in unexpected ways, or have malicious objectives, something which is usually less expected from internal users. Hence, the pressure to develop highly reliable IS is increasing, which may open a new application domain for formal methods.

The most widely used paradigm for specifying information systems is state transition. A state transition specification (STS) consists of a state space, defined

---

* This paper is dedicated to the memory of Philippe Facon, our friend and colleague, who contributed to this work. The research described in this paper was supported in part by the Natural Sciences and Engineering Research Council of Canada (NSERC).
** Part of this research was conducted while Marc Frappier was visiting the Institut d'Informatique d'Entreprise, Conservatoire National des Arts et Métiers, Évry, France.

by state variables, and operations describing transitions by modifications of the state variables. Upon reception of an external event, an operation is called to compute the new state and to produce an output if necessary. There exist several notations for describing state transition specifications (e.g., extended state machines, UML with OCL, model-based notations like B, Z, VDM). In this paper, we use the B notation and we assume that B machines are written in the style defined in [10]. In this style, the structure of the B machines is derived from a class diagram defining the entities of the IS. A set of state variables define the entities and their attributes.

One difficulty with STS of information systems is the *validation of event ordering properties*. Because this ordering is expressed through conditions on state variables, it is not easily checked by human inspection. State variables constitute an encoding of the event history, and the human inspector must have a very good understanding of the state transformations in order to validate these properties. For instance, to check that a given sequence of external events $e_1, \cdots, e_n$ is possible, one may check that the sequential execution of operations $op_{e_1}, \cdots, op_{e_n}$ is possible, which means proving that the execution of $init; op_{e_i}; \ldots; op_{e_i}$ establishes the precondition of $op_{e_{i+1}}$ for $1 \leq i < n$.

This paper presents an approach to prove event ordering properties for B specifications of information systems. The properties are expressed using the EB^3 notation [7,8]. In EB^3, the specification of inputs is decoupled from the specification of outputs. Input event ordering properties are defined using a process algebra similar to CSP [9]; output events are specified by recursive functions on the input traces associated to the process expression.

The main idea is to prove that the EB^3 specification is refined by the B STS. This proof is achieved by first translating the EB^3 specification into an equivalent B specification, and then proving refinement by the B STS. The gluing invariant, which relates the state of the EB^3 process expression to the state of the STS, is provided by the recursive functions of the EB^3 specification. The proof involves an analysis of the labeled transition system (LTS) associated to an EB^3 process expression. In order to handle unbounded LTS, we introduce the notion of an extended LTS (ELTS).

This paper is structured as follows. Sect. 2 briefly introduces the EB^3 notation on a trivial example. Then, Sect. 3 illustrates the proof for this trivial example. In Sect. 4, a proof is presented for an unbounded IS specification using an ELTS. Sect. 5 provides a comparison with related work and concludes with some remarks on future work.

2 The EB^3 Notation

An EB^3 specification consists of a process expression E and an input-output relation R. The traces accepted by E, denoted by $\mathcal{T}(E)$, are called the *valid input traces*. The relation R is defined on $\mathcal{T}(E) \times O$ using the predicate calculus, where O is the set of output events.

The operational behavior of an EB³ specification may be explained as follows. Let $E \xrightarrow{\sigma} E'$ denote that E can execute the event σ and transform into E' and let t denote the system trace.

```
t := [];
forever do
    receive input event σ;
    if ∃ E' : E ─σ→ E' then
        E := E';
        t := t ← σ;
        send output event o such that (t, o) ∈ R;
    else
        send error message;
```

The process algebra used in EB³ is inspired from regular expressions, CSP, CCS, and Lotos [3, 9, 12]. The main differences between EB³ and these process algebras are: i) EB³ allows one to use a single state variable, the system trace, in predicates of guard statements; the system trace denotes the *valid* events accepted so far; ii) EB³ uses a single operator, concatenation (as in regular expressions), instead of prefixing and sequential composition, which makes specifications easier to read and write. Moreover, input events constitute elementary process expressions (as in regular expressions). Operators for composing process expressions are . (concatenation), | (choice), $\Longrightarrow$ (guard), * (Kleene closure), $\|$ (parallel composition of CSP), and $\|\|$ (interleave). Operators | and $\|\|$ can be quantified. For example, $\|\|x : 1..n : E(x)$ denotes $E(1) \|\| \cdots \|\| E(n)$. The EB³ process algebra has an operational semantics defined by transition rules, in the CCS style [12].

As a simple example, consider the following requirement:

"The system must accept A, followed by an arbitrary number of B, and then accept C; output ok is produced for each input received." (1)

This requirement is represented by the following EB³ specification.

$$E \triangleq A . B^* . C$$

$$R \triangleq \mathcal{T}(E) \times \{\mathsf{ok}\}$$

Note that, according to the operational semantics of EB³, an error message is sent when an input cannot be accepted by the process expression. Fig.1 illustrates this EB³ specification by providing an equivalent state-transition diagram (STD) and a sample execution sequence. As usual, a transition with input σ and output o is denoted by $q \xrightarrow{\sigma/o} q'$. An input σ is of the form $a(v_1, \ldots, v_n)$, where a is the input label and $v_1, \ldots, v_n$ are parameters. When there is no parameter, we simply write a, for the sake of brevity.

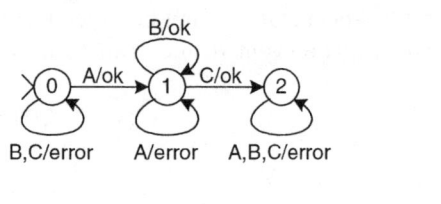

Order No.	Input	Output
1	B	error
2	A	ok
3	B	ok
4	A	error
5	C	ok

(a)   (b)

Fig. 1. (a) The STD of the EB³ specification; (b) A sample execution sequence

3 Proving Event Ordering Properties for B: A Small Example

To illustrate and discuss the issue of proving event ordering properties for a B specification, let us first provide a B specification which satisfies the same requirement as the one used in the previous section. This machine is simply a B transcription of the STD in Fig. 1(a).

MACHINE *BasicExample*

VARIABLES s

INVARIANT $s \in \{0, 1, 2\}$ (2)

INITIALISATION $s := 0$

OPERATIONS
$x \longleftarrow \mathbf{A} \triangleq$ IF $s = 0$ THEN $s := 1 \parallel x := $ ok ELSE $x := $ error END;

$x \longleftarrow \mathbf{B} \triangleq$ IF $s = 1$ THEN $s := 1 \parallel x := $ ok ELSE $x := $ error END;

$x \longleftarrow \mathbf{C} \triangleq$ IF $s = 1$ THEN $s := 2 \parallel x := $ ok ELSE $x := $ error END
END

The EB³ specification and the B specification express exactly the same behavior. However, ordering properties are more explicit in the EB³ specification. The STD is also a nice way of representing ordering properties. Unfortunately, STDs fail to easily represent the *complete* behavior of information systems: STDs are good at describing the behavior of one object (e.g., a book), but it is impossible to represent the behavior of a set of objects; extended STDs must be used (e.g., statecharts), but then the use of state variables makes the event ordering properties as difficult to view as in a B specification. Process algebras do not suffer from this problem: representing a set of objects simply requires the use of a quantification on the expression representing the single object. An example of EB³ IS specification will illustrate this fact in the next section.

Note that the IF-THEN-ELSE structure used for the operations is mandatory. When an input event is received out of order, the system must notify the user about it, and preserve the current value of the system state. This style differs from the traditional one in B where PRE-THEN are usually used, and from the event-driven style where SELECT-THEN [2,4,5] are used.

Several strategies are possible to prove that the B specification satisfies the event ordering properties of the EB^3 specification. A general solution is to show that the B specification refines, in the B sense, the EB^3 specification. Recall that, in B, a machine M is refined by a machine M' (denoted $M \sqsubseteq M'$) iff their operation's signatures are the same and the operations of M' preserve the *observable behaviour* of the operations of M [1]. The preservation of observable behavior for operations can be defined as follows. Let s be an arbitrary sequence of operation calls starting from the initialisation of the machine. If machine M can successfully execute s, then M' must also be able to successfully execute it. Moreover, let x be an output produced by an operation call in s. If a call in M' delivers output x, then output x must be allowed by machine M.

Consequently, if we provide a B semantics for EB^3 specification, which is easy to do, we can use refinement to show that a sequence of events (both input and outputs) in the EB^3 specification is preserved by the B specification. The B machine corresponding to an EB^3 specification is structured as follows.

1. The machine has only one state variable, t, which contains the current value of the valid system trace. The invariant states that variable t is always valid, that is, $t \in \mathcal{T}(E)$.
2. The initial state of the machine is the empty trace.
3. The machine contains one operation for each input event of the EB^3 specification. All the operations have the same structure: the IF condition checks that the system trace appended (using sequence operator $\leftarrow$) with the input event corresponding to the operation call constitutes a valid trace; the THEN part appends the input event to the system trace and produces any output allowed by the EB^3 specification. The ELSE part deals with error processing. We will discuss the choice of the IF substitution at the end of the section.

Here is the machine.

MACHINE *EB3Translation*

SEES ...   /* machines defining set of EB^3 events, E, $\mathcal{T}$, ... */

VARIABLES t

INVARIANT $t \in \mathcal{T}(E)$ (3)

INITIALISATION t := []

OPERATIONS

$x \longleftarrow \mathbf{A} \triangleq$ IF $t \leftarrow A \in \mathcal{T}(E)$ THEN $t := t \leftarrow A \parallel x := \text{ok}$
ELSE $x := \text{error}$ END;

$x \longleftarrow \mathbf{B} \triangleq$ IF $t \leftarrow B \in \mathcal{T}(E)$ THEN $t := t \leftarrow B \parallel x := \text{ok}$
ELSE $x := \text{error}$ END;

$x \longleftarrow \mathbf{C} \triangleq$ IF $t \leftarrow C \in \mathcal{T}(E)$ THEN $t := t \leftarrow C \parallel x := \text{ok}$
ELSE $x := \text{error}$ END
END;

3.1 The Refinement Proof

To prove refinement, one must find a gluing invariant which relates the concrete state to the abstract state. For the simple EB^3 example, the following formula is a possible gluing invariant which is added as a conjunct to the invariant of machine *BasicExample*.

$$\begin{array}{l}(s = 0 \Leftrightarrow t = []) \land \\ (s = 1 \Leftrightarrow last(t) \in \{A, B\}) \land \\ (s = 2 \Leftrightarrow last(t) = C)\end{array} \qquad (4)$$

A refinement proof in B contains two parts. First, one must show that the initialisation establishes the invariant. Second, one must show that each operation of the concrete machine preserves the behavior of the abstract machine. Let us first discharge the initialisation proof. In the sequel, we use equation numbers in formulas (e.g., $(2) \land (4)$) for the sake of concision.

$$[s := 0][t := []]((2) \land (4))$$
$\Leftrightarrow$ ⟨ apply both substitutions to (2) and (4) ⟩
$$\begin{array}{l}0 \in \{0, 1, 2\} \land \\ (0 = 0 \Leftrightarrow [] = []) \land \\ (0 = 1 \Leftrightarrow last([]) \in \{A, B\}) \land \\ (0 = 2 \Leftrightarrow last([]) = C)\end{array}$$
$\Leftrightarrow$
true □

The proof for an operation has the following form. Under the hypotheses

$$(2) \land (3) \land (4)$$

prove

$$\begin{array}{l}[[x := x'](\text{ IF } c_c \text{ THEN } U_c \parallel x := \text{ok ELSE } x := \text{error END })] \\ \quad [\text{ IF } c_a \text{ THEN } U_a \parallel x := \text{ok ELSE } x := \text{error END }] \\ \quad ((2) \land (4) \land x = x')\end{array}$$

The $_c$ subscripts and the $_a$ subscripts denote parts of the concrete machine and abstract machine, respectively. Applying the substitutions, we obtain four cases.

1. $c_a \wedge c_c \Rightarrow [U_a][U_c]((2) \wedge (4)) \wedge \text{ok} = \text{ok}$
2. $\neg c_a \wedge \neg c_c \Rightarrow \text{error} = \text{error}$
3. $c_a \wedge \neg c_c \Rightarrow [U_a]((2) \wedge (4)) \wedge \text{ok} = \text{error}$
4. $\neg c_a \wedge c_c \Rightarrow [U_c]((2) \wedge (4)) \wedge \text{error} = \text{ok}$

The proof of case 1 is very simple. For operation **A**, it amounts to proving the following statement, which is easily discharged.

$1 \in \{0, 1, 2\} \wedge$
$(1 = 0 \Leftrightarrow \text{t} \leftarrow A = []) \wedge$
$(1 = 1 \Leftrightarrow last(\text{t} \leftarrow A) \in \{A, B\}) \wedge$
$(1 = 2 \Leftrightarrow last(\text{t} \leftarrow A) = C) \wedge$
$\text{ok} = \text{ok}$

The proof of case 2 is trivial. The most interesting proofs are for cases 3 and 4. Because the right-hand side of each $\Rightarrow$ is false, due to the conjunct $\text{ok} = \text{error}$, these two statements are equivalent to $c_a \Leftrightarrow c_c$. Here is the proof of this equivalence.

$(c_a \wedge \neg c_c \Rightarrow [U_a]((2) \wedge (4)) \wedge \text{ok} = \text{error})$
$\wedge$
$(\neg c_a \wedge c_c \Rightarrow [U_c]((2) \wedge (4)) \wedge \text{error} = \text{ok})$
$\Leftrightarrow \qquad \langle (p \Rightarrow \textbf{false}) \Leftrightarrow \neg p \rangle$
$\neg(c_a \wedge \neg c_c) \wedge \neg(\neg c_a \wedge c_c)$
$\Leftrightarrow$
$c_a \Leftrightarrow c_c \qquad\qquad\qquad\qquad\qquad\qquad\qquad\qquad\qquad\qquad\qquad\qquad\square$

Hence, the refinement proof requires to show that the abstract condition and the concrete condition of the IF statements are equivalent. In other words, it requires to show that the B specification and the EB^3 specification accept the same events (i.e., output x is ok), and refuse the same events (i.e., output x is error). This illustrates that the refinement proof captures all the important aspects of event ordering properties. If we had used the traditional, so-called "generous" style, based on PRE-THEN, instead of the "defensive" style, based on IF-THEN-ELSE, then this part of the proof would not be required, and the proof of the ordering properties would not be complete. In that case, the B specification of the IS could accept event sequences that the EB^3 specification refuses, which is not desirable. For instance, consider the following abstract operation.

$x \longleftarrow \textbf{A} \triangleq \text{PRE } \text{t} \leftarrow A \in \mathcal{T}(E) \text{ THEN } \text{t} := \text{t} \leftarrow A \parallel x := \text{ok END};$

It is refined by the following concrete operation.

$x \longleftarrow \textbf{A} \triangleq \text{PRE } s = 0 \vee \textbf{s} = \textbf{1} \text{ THEN } s := 1 \parallel x := \text{ok END};$

There is refinement, because the concrete operation has a "weaker" precondition than the abstract operation. This operation allows an arbitrary number of A followed by an arbitrary number of A or B to be executed. Hence, this behavior does not satisfy the requirements. Fig. 2(a) illustrates the STD of the EB^3

Fig. 2. (a) The STD of a PRE-THEN abstract machine; (b) The STD of a concrete refining machine

abstract machine when PRE-THEN are used instead of IF-THEN-ELSE, while Fig. 2(b) illustrates a concrete machine which refines it using also PRE-THEN. The STD of Fig. 2(b) is not a refinement of the STD in Fig. 1(a).

The proof of $c_a \Leftrightarrow c_c$ is the most interesting part. It involves a case analysis on the labeled transition system (LTS) associated to the process expression E. The LTS corresponds to the transitions that E can execute, which are derived from the operational semantics associated to the EB^3 process algebra. These transitions are the following.

$$A \, . \, B^* \, . \, C \xrightarrow{A} B^* \, . \, C$$
$$B^* \, . \, C \xrightarrow{B} B^* \, . \, C$$
$$B^* \, . \, C \xrightarrow{C} \square$$

Process expression $\square$ denotes a process that has successfully completed its execution. These transitions are graphically represented in Fig. 3. For the sake of concision, process expressions are denoted by q_0, q_1, q_2.

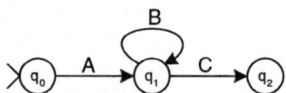

Fig. 3. The LTS of the EB^3 process expression $E \triangleq A \, . \, B^* \, . \, C$

The proof of $c_a \Leftrightarrow c_c$ for operation **A** is conducted as follows.

$\quad c_a$
$\Leftrightarrow$
$\quad\quad t \leftarrow A \in \mathcal{T}(E)$
$\Leftrightarrow \quad\quad\quad \langle \text{ definition of } \mathcal{T}(E) \rangle$
$\quad\quad \exists \, E', E'' : E \overset{t}{\leadsto} E' \wedge E' \xrightarrow{A} E''$

This last statement can be understood as follows. Relation $\leadsto$ is the extension of relation $\rightarrow$ to traces; $E \overset{t}{\leadsto} E'$ denotes that E can accept t and transform into E'; E' can then accept event A (i.e., $E' \xrightarrow{A} E''$). In other words, E' is reachable from the initial state and it can execute A. The only state in Fig. 3 that satisfies this statement is q_0. The only trace leading to q_0 is $t = []$. Hence, this last statement is equivalent to $t = []$. Resuming the proof, we obtain the following.

$$\begin{array}{ll} \Leftrightarrow & \\ & t = [] \\ \Leftrightarrow & \qquad \langle \text{ hypothesis (4) } \rangle \\ & s = 0 \\ \Leftrightarrow & \\ & c_c \end{array}$$

$\square$

This concludes the proof of refinement for operation **A**. The proofs of operations **B** and **C** are of the same style.

In summary, we have shown in this section how to prove that a B specification M satisfies event ordering properties expressed by an EB^3 specification P. This proof is conducted by first translating P into an equivalent B specification M_P; this translation can be automated, since it requires no creativity. The properties are verified by proving that $M_P \sqsubseteq M$. This proof ensures that M accepts the same traces as P. The proof involves a case analysis that covers the state space of the LTS associated to an EB^3 process expression. In general, the state space of the LTS of an IS is unbounded, but finite. The next section will show how to handle this case.

4 Proving Ordering Properties for Unbounded IS

An IS is usually made of entities interacting together. For instance, a library system is made of two entity types, books and members. A member entity can borrow books, reserve them, and so on. For the sake of illustration, consider the following EB^3 process expression of a book entity type.

$$E \triangleq |||y : V : A(y, \_) \, . \, B(y)^* \, . \, C(y)$$

This process expression is very similar to the one of Sect. 3, except that i) a quantified interleave is used to denote that book entities evolve concurrently; V is a finite set denoting the possible values for book ids; ii) events now have input parameters; the reader may assume that the event $A(y, n)$ denotes the creation of a book y of title n, event $B(y)$ denotes that book y is lent, and event $C(y)$ denotes that the book y is deleted. The wildcard '_' can be used in input events; it denotes that any value of the parameter type is accepted. The signature of events is part of an EB^3 specification; it has been omitted here for the sake of concision.

For now, we do not consider the specification of members, since it is not necessary to illustrate the principles used for reasoning about large state spaces. The state space of this LTS is unbounded since V is finite but unbounded.

The input-output relation R of this EB^3 specification is based on recursive functions defined on the system trace t. There is one function for each entity type and one for each attribute. For the sake of illustration, we provide only two, f_{books}, which returns the set of books created, and f_{active}, a Boolean function which returns true when a book has not been deleted yet. These functions are defined using a CAML-like syntax. Their types are $f_{books} \in \mathcal{T}(E) \to \mathbb{P}(V)$ and $f_{active} \in \mathcal{T}(E) \times V \to BOOL$.

$$f_{books}(t) \triangleq$$
$$\text{match } t \text{ with}$$
$$[\,] \qquad\qquad : \{\}$$
$$t' \leftarrow A(y,\_) : \{y\} \cup f_{books}(t')$$
$$t' \leftarrow \_ \qquad : f_{books}(t')$$

$$f_{active}(t, y) \triangleq$$
$$\text{match } t \text{ with}$$
$$[\,] \qquad\qquad : \bot$$
$$t' \leftarrow A(y,\_) : \textbf{true}$$
$$t' \leftarrow C(y) \quad : \textbf{false}$$
$$t' \leftarrow \_ \qquad : f_{active}(t')$$

The B translation of this EB³ specification is almost the same as the one of Sect. 3, except that operations have input parameters. Here is the translation of operation **A**.

$$x \longleftarrow \mathbf{A}(y, n) \triangleq$$
$$\text{PRE } y \in V \,\wedge\, n \in TITLE \text{ THEN}$$
$$\quad \text{IF } \text{t} \leftarrow (A, y, n) \in \mathcal{T}(E) \text{ THEN } \text{t} := \text{t} \leftarrow (A, y, n) \,||\, x := \text{ok}$$
$$\quad \text{ELSE } x := \text{error END}$$
$$\text{END};$$

The B specification of this small library information system is somewhat different from the one used in Sect. 3. It has two state variables: s is now a subset of the set of possible books V and it contains the books created so far; $active$ is a total function from s which indicates if a book has been deleted. The operations must properly update these two variables in order to provide exactly the same behavior as the EB³ specification. A precondition must be added to each operation in order to type the input parameters. Note that no other constraint can be specified in this precondition, because operations must always terminate, whatever the values of their input parameters are.

MACHINE *BasicExampleExtended*

SETS $V, TITLE$

VARIABLES $s, active$

INVARIANT $s \subseteq V \,\wedge\, active \in s \to BOOL$ \hfill (5)

INITIALISATION $s := \{\} \,||\, active := \{\}$

OPERATIONS
$x \longleftarrow \mathbf{A}(y, n) \triangleq \text{PRE } y \in V \,\wedge\, n \in TITLE \text{ THEN}$
$\quad \text{IF } y \notin s \text{ THEN } s := s \cup \{y\} \,||\, active(y) := \textbf{true} \,||\, x := \text{ok}$
$\quad \text{ELSE } x := \text{error END END};$

$x \longleftarrow \mathbf{B}(y) \triangleq \text{PRE } y \in V \text{ THEN}$
    IF $y \in s \land active(y)$ THEN $x := $ ok ELSE $x := $ error END END;

$x \longleftarrow \mathbf{C}(y) \triangleq \text{PRE } y \in V \text{ THEN}$
    IF $y \in s \land active(y)$ THEN $active(y) := $ **false** $\parallel$ $x := $ ok
    ELSE $x := $ error END END;
END

Note that machine *BasicExampleExtended* is significantly more complex to understand, when compared to *BasicExample* of Sect. 3. On the other hand, the process expression of the EB^3 specification has not changed much from the basic example to the extended example. This illustrates the ease with which ordering constraints can be expressed in EB^3.

4.1 The Refinement Proof

The first step is to find a gluing invariant. This gluing invariant is derived directly from the recursive functions of the EB^3 specification. Typically, the state variables of a B IS specification denote the attributes of entities. These same attributes are defined in EB^3 by recursive functions on the system trace. There are two kinds of attributes: key and non-key. For instance, state variable s is a key attribute, and state variable *active* is a non-key attribute; s corresponds to function f_{books}, and *active* corresponds to f_{active}. The gluing invariant for a key attribute k, with corresponding EB^3 function f_k, has the following simple form: $k = f_k(\mathbf{t})$. The gluing invariant for a non-key attribute a, with corresponding EB^3 function f_a, has the following form: $a = \lambda z \cdot (z \in dom(a) \mid f_a(\mathbf{t}, z))$. When a is a total function from k, we may simply use k instead of $dom(a)$. Thus, for the example at hand, the gluing invariant is the following.

$$s = f_{books}(\mathbf{t}) \quad \land \quad active = \lambda z \cdot (z \in s \mid f_{active}(\mathbf{t}, z)) \tag{6}$$

The proof of the initialisation is quite straightforward. We concentrate on the gluing invariant only.

$\qquad [s := \{\} \parallel active := \{\}][\mathbf{t} := [\,]\,](6)$
$\Leftrightarrow \qquad \langle$ apply both substitutions to (6) $\rangle$
$\qquad \{\} = f_{books}([\,]) \quad \land \quad \{\} = \lambda y \cdot (y \in \{\} \mid f_{active}([\,], y))$
$\Leftrightarrow$
    true   □

The proof for operations is illustrated with operation **A**. Recall from Sect. 3.1 that there are two cases to handle.

1. $c_a \land c_c \Rightarrow [U_a][U_c]((5) \land (6))$
2. $c_a \Leftrightarrow c_c$

Proof of case 1. Again we concentrate on the proof of the gluing invariant, i.e., $[U_a][U_c](6)$, which is the most interesting part. The proof consists of simply applying the definition of the recursive functions of the EB^3 specification, and to use the gluing invariant (6) which is an hypothesis of this proof. Assume $c_a \wedge c_c$.

$$[U_a][U_c](6)$$
$\Leftrightarrow$
$$s \cup \{y\} = f_{books}(\mathbf{t} \leftarrow (A, y, n)) \wedge \quad (7)$$
$$active \cup \{y \mapsto \mathbf{true}\} = \lambda z \cdot (z \in s \cup \{y\} \mid f_{active}(\mathbf{t} \leftarrow (A, z, n), y)) \quad (8)$$

We now split the proof in two parts: (7) and (8). For (7), we have:

$$f_{books}(\mathbf{t} \leftarrow (A, y, n))$$
$= \qquad \langle \text{ def. of } f_{books} \rangle$
$$f_{books}(\mathbf{t}) \cup \{y\}$$
$= \qquad \langle\ (6)\ \rangle$
$$s \cup \{y\}$$

For (8), we have:

$$\lambda z \cdot (z \in s \cup \{y\} \mid f_{active}(\mathbf{t} \leftarrow (A, y, n), z))$$
$= \qquad \langle \text{ split in two functions } \rangle$
$$\lambda z \cdot (z \in s \wedge z \neq y \mid f_{active}(\mathbf{t} \leftarrow (A, y, n), z))$$
$$\cup$$
$$\{y \mapsto f_{active}(\mathbf{t} \leftarrow (A, y, n), y)\}$$
$= \qquad \langle \text{ def. of } f_{active}, \text{ hypothesis } c_c \equiv y \notin s \rangle$
$$\lambda z \cdot (z \in s \mid f_{active}(\mathbf{t}, z)) \cup \{y \mapsto \mathbf{true}\}$$
$= \qquad \langle\ (6)\ \rangle$
$$active \cup \{y \mapsto \mathbf{true}\} \qquad \square$$

This concludes the proof of case 1.

Proof of case 2. This proof is more interesting. As in the basic example of Sect. 3.1, we need to explore the LTS of the EB^3 process expression. However, this LTS is unbounded. To reason about the transitions, we introduce the notion of an *extended* LTS (ELTS). An ELTS contains two types of states: simple and extended. Simple states are like LTS states. Extended states contains sub-states, and a sub-state can be either simple or extended. For instance, the quantified interleave of E is translated into an extended state q_3 which contains a map $m \in V \rightarrow Q$, where Q is the set of states of the ELTS. Map m defines the sub-states of q_3. The ELTS of E is graphically represented by Fig. 4. The dotted arrow indicates that the codomain of m is restricted to the states inside the dotted rectangle. This rectangle contains the LTS of $A(y, \_) \cdot B(y)^* \cdot C(y)$. The formal definition of the transition relation for state (q_3, m) is the following.

$$\exists v, q', \sigma' \cdot m(v) \xrightarrow{\sigma'} q' \wedge \sigma = [y := v]\sigma' \Rightarrow (q_3, m) \xrightarrow{\sigma} (q_3, m \triangleleft \{v \mapsto q'\})$$

This formula states that there is a transition from (q_3, m) to (q_3, m') on σ when there exists a sub-state of q_3 (denoted by $m(v)$) which can execute a transition. The initial state of this ELTS is $(q_3, V \times \{q_0\})$.

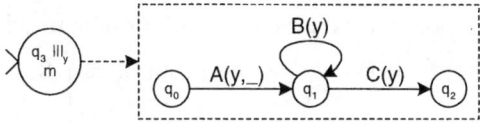

Fig. 4. The ELTS of the EB^3 process expression $|||y : V : A(y,\_) . B(y)^* . C(y)$

The first step in the proof of case 2 is to develop each condition in terms of t.

c_a	c_c
$\Leftrightarrow$	$\Leftrightarrow$
$\exists E', E'' :$	$y \notin s$
$E \stackrel{t}{\leadsto} E' \wedge E' \xrightarrow{(A,y,n)} E''$	$\Leftrightarrow$
	$y \notin f_{books}(t)$

We can prove that these last two statements are equivalent using a case analysis on the occurrence of an element (A, y, n') in t.

Case 2.1 Assume that, for all n', (A, y, n') does not occur in t. We can prove by induction on the structure of t that $y \notin f_{books}(t)$ holds. For $t = []$, it trivially holds; for the induction step, it also follows very easily, due to the recursive definition of f_{books}. The proof of $\exists E', E'' : E \stackrel{t}{\leadsto} E' \wedge E' \xrightarrow{(A,y,n)} E''$ requires an analysis of the ELTS. First, observe that the initial sub-state $m(y) = q_0$ can only execute $(A, y, \_)$. Since (A, y, n') does not occur in t, the state of the ELTS after accepting t satisfies the property $m(y) = q_0$. Therefore $E' \xrightarrow{(A,y,n)} E''$, hence the statement $\exists E', E'' : E \stackrel{t}{\leadsto} E' \wedge E' \xrightarrow{(A,y,n)} E''$ holds, and we have $c_a \Leftrightarrow c_c$.

Case 2.2 Assume that there exists n' such that (A, y, n') occurs in t. We can decompose t into sub-traces t', t'' such that $t = t' \frown [(A, y, n')] \frown t''$ and t'' does not contain an event of the form $(A, y, \_)$. Then, we can prove by induction on the structure of t'' that $f_{books}(t' \frown [(A, y, n')] \frown t'') = f_{books}(t' \frown [(A, y, n')])$. Therefore

$$f_{books}(t)$$
$$= f_{books}(t' \frown [(A, y, n')] \frown t'')$$
$$\langle \text{ by induction on } t'' \rangle$$
$$= f_{books}(t' \frown [(A, y, n')])$$
$$= \{y\} \cup f_{books}(t')$$

Hence, $y \notin f_{books}(t)$ is false. We must then prove that $\exists E', E'' : E \stackrel{t}{\leadsto} E' \wedge E' \xrightarrow{(A,y,n)} E''$ is also false. This is done by analysis of the structure of the ELTS. Recall that (A, y, n') occurs in t. The only sub-state of q_3 which can execute (A, y, n') is $m(y) = q_0$. Hence, after accepting t, the state E' satisfies $m(y) \in \{q_1, q_2\}$. Neither q_1 nor q_2 can execute (A, y, n). Therefore, the transition

$E' \xrightarrow{(A,y,n)} E''$ is impossible. Therefore, the statement $\exists E', E'' : E \stackrel{\mathsf{t}}{\leadsto} E' \wedge E' \xrightarrow{(A,y,n)} E''$ is false. This concludes the proof of case 2. □

4.2 Summary and Discussion the Refinement Proof Structure

The refinement proof of an unbounded EB^3 specification P by a machine M is conducted as follows.

- Translate P into a B machine M_P.
- Generate the gluing invariant from the recursive functions in P.
- Generate the ELTS of P.
- Prove the refinement of M_P by M.

Steps 1 to 3 can be automated; they do not require human intervention. The generation of the ELTS can be done for all operators except process call. Tail recursive calls can be translated; non tail-recursive calls would require the use of stacks in the ELTS, which make their analysis more complex. Fortunately, IS specification rarely require non tail-recursive calls. Most of the time, the Kleene closure is used for iteration (see [8] for classical patterns of EB^3 specifications which are derived from entity-relationship diagram patterns). When tail recursion is insufficient, another solution is to define a recursive function on the system trace and to use it in guard statements of the EB^3 specification.

The creative part is in step 4, mainly in the proof obligation $c_a \Leftrightarrow c_c$, where the essence of event ordering resides. The main idea used in the proof is to find a case analysis condition $\phi(\mathsf{t})$ such that $\phi(\mathsf{t}) \Rightarrow c_a \wedge c_c$ and $\neg\phi(\mathsf{t}) \Rightarrow \neg c_a \wedge \neg c_c$. $\phi(\mathsf{t})$ characterises the state reached after accepting t. We can then reason about the transitions executable from this state in the ELTS.

5 Conclusion

Specification errors are often found by stating the same thing twice, in different ways, and proving their consistency. The orthogonality in specification style between EB^3 and B allows that. Our approach probably applies to other model-based language like Z and to other application domains.

The work of Butler on CSP2B [5] is probably the closest to ours. CSP2B allows one to write a B specification which includes CSP expressions to define ordering constraints. The CSP part is translated by the CSP2B tool into a machine with one operation per event and a LTS encoded in state variables. Operations are written using the event-driven style of B; hence operations use SELECT instead of IF-THEN-ELSE. CSP2B is limited to a single level interleave quantification. Roughly speaking, a CSP2B specification is at the same level of abstraction as an EB^3 specification, except that entity attributes in EB^3 are defined by recursive functions on the system trace. The refinement of a CSP2B specification corresponds to the refinement of our EB^3 specification into a B specification. However, the associated proof obligations are not the same due to the use of SELECT statements in CSP2B. SELECT statements can be refined by strengthening the condition, which is not desirable in the context of information system specification. The gluing invariant in CSP2B is manually derived and it relates the state of the LTS to more concrete state variables, whereas our gluing invariant is based on the system trace and generated automatically from attribute definitions in EB^3. Our ELTS can be seen as a generalisation of CSP2B's LTS. It allows multiple level of quantifications and arbitrary parallel compositions.

The structure of the B specifications used in our work are inspired from the method presented in [10], which translates UML models into B. There are other proposals for the translation of UML models or statecharts into B [13–15].

Fischer, Derrick and Smith [6, 16] have studied the integration of CSP and Object Z. Their semantics is based on failure-divergence, as in CSP. They study proof of properties using the sat relation of CSP and refinement using an abstraction relation (i.e., a gluing invariant).

As future work, we wish to investigate how our approach could be supported by the standard case tools supporting B (i.e., Atelier B and the B-Tool). It will require an encoding of the ELTS in the B theory. We also wish to define heuristics to generate the condition and the THEN part of the operations in the B machine from the EB^3 specification.

References

1. Abrial, J.-R.: *The B-Book*. Cambridge University Press, Cambridge, UK, 1996.
2. Abrial, J.-R., Mussat, L.: Introducing Dynamic Constraints in B. In *Second International B Conference*, D. Bert, ed., LNCS 1393, Springer-Verlag, 83–128, April 1998.
3. Bolognesi, T. and Brinksma, E.: Introduction to the ISO Specification Language LOTOS. *Computer Networks and ISDN Systems*, 14(1):25–59, 1987.
4. Butler, M. J., Waldén, M.: Distributed System Development in B. In First B Conference, H. Habrias, ed., November 1996.
5. Butler, M.: csp2B: A Practical Approach to Combining CSP and B. *Formal Aspects of Computing*, 12(4):182–198, 2000.
6. Fischer, C.: CSP-OZ: A combination of Object-Z and CSP. In *Formal Methods for Open Object-Based Distributed Systems (FMOODS'97)*, volume 2, 423–438, Chapman & Hall, 1997.
7. Frappier, M., St-Denis, R.: Combining JSD and Cleanroom for Object-Oriented Scenario Specification. In *Object-Oriented Behavioral Specifications*, H. Kilov, B. Rumpe, I. Simmonds, eds., Kluwer Academic Publishers, 1999.
8. Frappier, M., St-Denis, R.: Specifying Information Systems through Structured Input-Output Traces, Technical Report, Département de mathématiques et d'informatique, Université de Sherbrooke, Sherbrooke (Québec), Canada J1K 2R1, 2002.
9. Hoare, C. A. R.: *Communicating Sequential Processes*. Prentice Hall, Englewood Cliffs, 1985.
10. Laleau, R. Mammar, A.: An Overview of a Method and its Support Tool for Generating B Specifications from UML Notations. In *ASE: 15th IEEE Conference on*

Automated Software Engineering, Grenoble, France, IEEE Computer Society Press, September 2000.
11. Meyer, E., Souquières, J.: A Systematic approach to Transform OMT Diagrams to a B specification. In *Formal Methods (FM'99)*, J.M. Wing, J. Woodcook, J. Davies, eds., LNCS 1708 vol. 1, Springer-Verlag, 875–895, September 1999.
12. Milner, R.: *Communication and Concurrency*. Prentice Hall, Englewood Cliffs, 1989.
13. Sekerinski, E., Zurob, R.: Translating Statecharts to B, In *3rd International Conference on Integrated Formal Methods (IFM'02)*, M. Butler, L. Petre, K. Sere, eds, LNCS 2335, Springer-Verlag, 128-144, Turku, Finland, May 2002.
14. Butler, M., and Snook, C.: Verifying Dynamic Properties of UML Models by Translation to the B Language and Toolkit. In *UML 2000 Workshop, Dynamic Behaviour in UML Models: Semantic Questions*. York, UK, 2-6 October, 2000.
15. Snook, C., Walden, M.: Use of U2B for Specifying B Action Systems. In *International workshop on Refinement of Critical Systems: Methods, Tools and Experience (RCS'02)*, Grenoble, France, January 2002.
16. Smith, G., Derrick, J.: Specification, Refinement and Verification of Concurrent SystemsAn Integration of Object-Z and CSP. *Formal Methods in System Design*, 18:249-284, 2001.

ZML: XML Support for Standard Z

Mark Utting[1], Ian Toyn[2], Jing Sun[4], Andrew Martin[3], Jin Song Dong[4], Nicholas Daley[1], and David Currie[5]

[1] The University of Waikato, Hamilton, NZ
{marku,ntd1}@cs.waikato.ac.nz
[2] The University of York
ian@cs.york.ac.uk
[3] Oxford University
Andrew.Martin@comlab.ox.ac.uk
[4] The National University of Singapore
{sunjing,dongjs}@comp.nus.edu.sg
[5] IBM UK Labs, Hursley Park, Winchester, Hants, UK
david_currie@uk.ibm.com

Abstract. This paper proposes an XML format for standard Z. We describe several earlier XML proposals for Z, the problems and issues that arose, and the rationales behind our new proposal. The new proposal is based upon a comparison of various existing Z annotated syntaxes, to ensure that the mark-up will be widely usable. This XML format is expected to become a central feature of the CZT (Community Z Tools) initiative.

1 Why an XML format for Z?

The publication during 2002 of the ISO Z Standard [3] represents a significant milestone for the development and interoperability of Z tools. It has established what notation should be exchanged, but not necessarily how. Technology has advanced during the development of the standard, so it now seems most natural for tools to interact using an XML mark-up [9].

This paper describes such a mark-up, intended to be a development of the Standard's work, as a contribution to the Community Z Tools[1] (CZT) initiative. CZT has been proposed in response to the observation that many interesting Z tools have been developed, but few have built large user communities, and many have found it necessary to invest disproportionately large amounts of effort in the relatively mundane activities of parser and pretty-printer development. The initiative aims to define interfaces and interchange facilities (and later, code libraries) which Z tool developers can draw on in an open-source spirit, with the aim both of promoting interoperability and of relieving those wishing to develop novel tools for visualisation, animation, refinement, proof, and so on, from the need to invest effort in the user interface code.

XML is a development, like HTML, from the SGML [4]. Early drafts of the Z Standard included an SGML mark-up, but it was found hard to maintain. XML now

---

[1] See http://web.comlab.ox.ac.uk/oucl/work/andrew.martin/CZT.

enjoys a much wider take-up than SGML, having quickly become a new standard for structured information interchange between tools.

Without such a mark-up, Standard Z allows specifications to be exchanged using Unicode (UCS[1,2]). However, this representation is suitable only for interchanging raw (unparsed) Z specifications, without annotation. Tools (and sometimes authors) benefit from being able to annotate terms with type information, anticipated usage and refinement targets, free-form comments, and so on. A particular presentation (on paper, on screen, or within program data structures) may make use of some of these annotations and discard others. An XML format facilitates the inclusion of such annotations, with as little or as much structure as is appropriate. In the longer term, when this use of XML reaches greater maturity, we would expect the format described here to become part of the ISO Z Standard.

1.1 Requirements of a Z Interchange Mark-Up

We have three requirements for an XML mark-up for Z.

Annotations. The already mentioned annotations should be accommodated in the interchange mark-up wherever tools wish to put them. The forms of individual annotations should not be constrained. There should be some pre-defined annotations for types and for source-file locations (so that error messages can refer to the source of an error), but it should also be possible for tools to define additional annotations. Tools that do not understand such annotations should simply ignore them.

Injectivity. The concrete syntax of Z provides different ways of writing the same things. For example, a boxed schema paragraph may be written in an equivalent definitional form, without the box. After a specification has been transferred between tools, the user wants to be reassured as much as possible (by avoiding unexpected changes of presentation) that their specification document has not been changed. Consequently, the interchange mark-up for Z should capture sufficient information from the concrete representation to be able to resurrect the same concrete phrases (though not necessarily the same layout). In other words, we want the conversion of a textual Z specification into XML format to be one-to-one (injective), so that the concrete representation before and after interchange, ignoring annotations, remains recognisably the same. For the schema paragraph example, this means keeping a note of whether or not the boxed representation is used. In this paper, we avoid using the traditional term *abstract syntax* because of this avoidance of loss of information from the concrete form.

Commonality. Conversely, for reasons of simplicity and demonstrable soundness, tools should need to deal with as few cases as possible. This implies that we should merge equivalent concrete constructs whenever possible (the Z standard has a large number of transformation rules that do exactly this). For example, a tool might offer to display the signature of a schema paragraph regardless of whether or not it is boxed. This is easier if a common *annotated syntax* is used for both of the concrete representations of the schema paragraph. Interchange will be eased if the mark-up is based on an annotated syntax that identifies similar commonalities to those exploited by tools. In this paper, we use two approaches to merging constructs while preserving injectivity:

1. using a common XML tag for two similar constructs, but adding attributes to distinguish between the constructs;
2. using distinct XML tags and adding a common type hierarchy above them to reflect their commonality.

The second approach has an additional advantage: the type hierarchy of commonality is similar to a typical inheritance hierarchy in object-oriented programs, which makes it easier to map between the XML structure and Java or C++ classes. This is useful, because one of the CZT aims is to develop a Java library for building Z tools.

The annotated syntaxes used within existing tools have already addressed these issues of annotations, injectivity and commonalities. The annotated syntax used within Standard Z addresses some of these issues. An interchange mark-up for Z will be easier for a tool to use if the mark-up is similar to the tool's own annotated syntax, but there is considerable variation between existing tools.

This paper compares some existing annotated syntaxes and describes an XML mark-up based on their common features or best features. We aim to define a mark-up that will be usable not only by proposed CZT developments but also by developments of existing tools. Hence, we are interested to receive feedback from other tool builders.

1.2 Specifying the XML Structure: DTD or XML Schema?

There are many different ways in which Z specifications could be expressed in XML. To specify exactly which structures of XML we propose to use, and the well-formedness conditions on those structures, we need to specify a particular subset of XML. Such a specification is typically written in either of two languages: as a *Document Type Definition* (DTD), or as an *XML Schema*. The provision of such a specification allows a *validating parser* to perform more accurate well-formedness checking, and is useful to toolbuilders for defining what tools should be able to interchange.

The DTD notation is older and simpler than the XML Schema notation, and more human-readable, but the XML Schema language allows better specification of the data types of elements than the DTD language. XML Schema has many built-in datatypes such as string, integer, boolean, float, date, time and so on, and provides mechanisms to constrain the allowable content of an element or attribute, such as setting a valid range of values or defining a regular expression to which the content must conform. New types can be defined from scratch or by constraining or extending an existing type. This allows hierarchies of complex types to be constructed. Furthermore, XML Schemas are themselves written in XML. This makes the document descriptions more verbose, but also far more extensible than they were in the original DTD syntax. Declarations can have richer and more complex internal structures than declarations in DTDs. Thus XML Schemas can be stored along with other XML documents in XML-oriented data stores, referenced, and even styled, using tools like XLink, XPointer, and XSLT[2]. For our purposes, we prefer to use XML schema notation, to obtain a tighter specification of the structure, and to take advantage of XML tools, such as XSLT.

---

[2] See www.w3.org.

2 Previous Work

There were earlier attempts to define XML mark-ups for Z [16,13] but these did not support the interchange of annotations such as the types of expressions, and were based on an earlier version of Z, described by Spivey [12]. For example, Z/EVES [11] supports an XML mark-up for communication between tools, based on Spivey Z.

Before ZB2002, Toyn wrote a DTD for Standard Z, influenced by the abstract syntaxes of CADiZ and Zeta. This DTD has heavily influenced our proposal in this paper.

For example, here is the top-level element declaration from that DTD:

```
<!ELEMENT Z:Spec; (((Z:Sect;*), Z:SpecAnns;?) | Z:PCDATA)>
```

This defines a Z specification to be either a sequence of sections followed by an optional *specification annotations* element, or a PCDATA alternative, which is another element that is defined to contain just #PCDATA (*parsed character data*). Every element in the DTD includes a Z:PCDATA alternative, so that if one part of a specification contains an error, the whole specification can still be passed between tools. For example, a fully-parsed specification might be passed to an editor, and after editing is complete, the editor might pass it back with unchanged portions still in parsed form, but the edited portions in Z:PCDATA form.

During 2002, David Currie validated the DTD, and Utting and Daley manually derived a Java class hierarchy from it [5]. During this process, we identified several difficulties with the DTD structure:

1. The presence of an 'unparsed' alternative for *every* element allowed extremely fine-grained portions of the specification to be left unparsed, but dramatically complicated the Java class hierarchy. Basically, every element E of the DTD had to be translated into *three* Java classes: an abstract class E and two concrete subclasses, EParsed and EUnparsed, where EParsed contained fields that matched the parsed structure and EUnparsed contained just an unparsed string. The real disadvantage of this was that every piece of Java code that accessed an E object had to immediately check whether it was parsed or unparsed. This issue was not specific to Java, but would affect processing in every language.

   To solve this problem, our new proposal in this paper limits the *granularity* of the unparsed portions so that an entire paragraph (for example, one schema) is the smallest unparsed portion allowable. This simplifies processing, because it means that only the top-level of processing needs to consider unparsed portions and once we see a parsed paragraph, we know that everything inside it will also be parsed.

2. Each element in the DTD has its own kind of annotation, as illustrated in the example above (SpecAnns). Each kind of annotation is given a default definition in the DTD (expression annotations contain just a type, schema annotations contain a signature etc.), but can be overridden by providing an extended DTD that adds extra fields. However, because each kind of expression has its own kind of annotation, it is necessary to override all 23 kinds of expressions to add a new annotation to expressions (or 7 kinds for predicates, 5 kinds for paragraphs, etc.).

   To solve this problem, and make it easier to add new kinds of annotations, we have changed to a more loosely-typed view of annotations that is similar to the annotations

in Zeta. Each Z construct can contain a list of arbitrary annotations. This means that a tool could attach an annotation to an inappropriate construct (such as putting a type annotation on a predicate), but such annotations do no harm and can simply be ignored. On the other hand, there are many kinds of annotations (such as hyperlinks, source-code positions and comments), that we want to be able to attach to arbitrary constructs, and this is easier with these loosely-typed annotations.
3. In an object-oriented class hierarchy, it is possible to organise the hierarchy to reflect commonality, so that common fields and methods can be inherited. This is more flexible than the DTD structure, which does not have any kind of inheritance. This resulted in more differences between the DTD structure and our ideal Java class hierarchy than we would have liked.

Our new proposal solves this problem by using XML Schema to specify the structure of the Z mark-up. XML Schema offers a rich set of (single) inheritance features between types, as well as a *substitution group* facility which is similar to subtyping in object-oriented languages.

Also in 2002, at the National University of Singapore, Dong and Sun developed a new version of their XML Schema, based more closely on the annotated syntax structure of the Z standard. This did not support unparsed alternatives or annotations, and made less use of commonalities than Toyn's DTD, but it included extensions for supporting Object-Z and TCOZ (Timed Communicating Object Z) [10]. They demonstrated that it is possible to use the XSLT transformation language to transform the XML form of Z into elegant HTML with proper boxes and mathematical symbols.[3] The generated HTML includes cross-references, and buttons for expanding schema expressions and folding them again. The impressive feature is that this transformation system actually runs in your own browser, using standard technologies (XML, XSLT and Unicode).

This shows the promise of our XML proposal—it allows one to download a parsed and type-checked Z specification in an XML format that is ideal for importing into tools, yet still view it and explore it (following cross references etc.) with a standard web browser.

Furthermore, Dong and Sun have defined an XSLT stylesheet for automatically transforming the Object-Z/TCOZ models in XML into UML class diagrams [14]. The XSLT encodes the projection rules from the formal notations into their corresponding UML counterparts. Recently this work has been extended to support the auto-generation of UML statechart diagrams from Object-Z/TCOZ specifications via Java XML parser [6]. Both implementations take the customized XML format as a standard input and performs XML transformation into XMI (XML Metadata Interchange) format for visualization. In addition, an XML-based type checker was built for the static type checking of Z/Object-Z/TCOZ specifications in XML format.

3 Influences on Our Design

The structure of our proposed XML mark-up is based on Toyn's DTD, which was designed by comparing and merging the best features of three annotated syntaxes used

---

[3] See http://nt-appn.comp.nus.edu.sg/fm/zml for a demonstration of this system. It requires an appropriate Unicode font on your computer, such as Microsoft Arial Unicode.

by the Z standard, CADiZ and Zeta. This section briefly describes each of these systems and how they differ from our goals.

3.1 Standard Z

Standard Z's annotated syntax provides the basis for its definition of the type system and semantics of Z. These are the only functions defined on its annotated syntax. In particular, the standard has no need to resurrect concrete syntax. It has annotations for types of expressions, signatures of paragraphs, and section-type environments of sections. Commonalities are identified by *syntactic transformation rules*, which define the translation of concrete syntax to equivalent annotated syntax. Some of these rules are quoted below.

XML mark-up differs from Standard Z's annotated syntax because of the need to resurrect concrete syntax and the need to support a greater variety of functions and annotations.

3.2 CADiZ

CADiZ's annotated syntax supports typechecking, prettyprinting (i.e. resurrection of concrete syntax), interactive browsing (i.e. tracking of references to declarations and inspection of types, signatures and environments), and logical inference (i.e. transformation to equivalent notation, as in the course of proofs). Z notation is also used as patterns in tactics for automated reasoning.

In CADiZ's annotated syntax, the representation of declarations plays many roles. As well as representing the name and expression of a declaration, it records the declared variable's type, allowing signatures to be represented as lists of declarations, and it records which expressions refer to it. An inclusion declaration brings new copies of a declaration into scope, so that uses of the included declaration are not confused with uses of the original declaration. Expressions record the declarations to which they refer—this supports interactive browsing. They also support logical inference rules, correctly handling variable capture side-conditions: the inference rules maintain bindings of references to declarations, and the prettyprinter does renaming wherever variable capture would otherwise seem to occur. The representation of declarations causes CADiZ's annotated syntax to be not a tree structure but a more general graph, which would be inconvenient for a textual interchange mark-up such as XML (but more on this later).

CADiZ[15] can be said to support Standard Z—the deviations are very minor. (It does have some extensions to Standard Z, but we will ignore those.) CADiZ's annotated syntax is not fixed, and has changed frequently in the past (and may change in the future to be closer to this proposal).

3.3 Zeta

Zeta's annotated syntax supports typechecking, prettyprinting (i.e. resurrection of concrete syntax), and animation (i.e. automatic reduction of expressions). Those are the functions of the core edition of Zeta.

XML mark-up differs from Zeta's annotated syntax wherever Zeta[8] deviates from Standard Z.

3.4 Standard Terminology

The main syntactic rules (Specification, Section, Paragraph, Predicate and Expression) are present in all annotated syntaxes for Z, though not with the same names. In some tools, this renaming reflects the widening of syntactic rules to include non-Z phrases. The following table summarises these names, and suggests names to be used for the elements in XML. The Z: prefix is just a namespace prefix, and can be omitted in XML documents whose default namespace is our XML Schema. We use a postfix ∗ symbol to indicate possible repetition of a construct (zero or more times) and + to indicate one or more repetitions.

Standard Z	CADiZ	Zeta	XML
Specification	doc*	UnitAbsy*	Z:Spec
Section	doc	UnitAbsy.Section	Z:Sect
Paragraph	def	Item	Z:Para
Predicate	pred	Predicate	Z:Pred
Expression	term	Expr	Z:Expr

4 Our XML Schema Proposal

In this section, we go through each major construct of the Z notation, briefly comparing the Z standard, CADiZ and Zeta, and describing our proposed XML structure. The XML Schema was developed and validated using the XML-Spy tool[4], and the diagrams were also partly generated with XML-Spy. The diagrams use two connectors: the three-dots connector defines a *sequence* of the elements on its right, while the three-way switch connector defines a *choice* between the elements on its right. Dashed lines indicate optional components–this is usually obvious from the repetition counts, like $0 \ldots \infty$, below the optional constructs.

4.1 Specifications and Sections

Standard Z specifications are either anonymous or sectioned. The standard syntactically transforms anonymous specifications to sectioned specifications, as follows (Z standard, clause 12.2.1.1).

$D_1 \ldots D_n \implies$ *Math toolkit* ZED section *Specification* parents *standard_toolkit* END $D_1 \ldots D_n$

The name *Specification* can be anything distinct (CADiZ uses the name of the file that the specification came from). To allow the concrete syntax to be resurrected precisely, it is necessary to know whether a section was originally anonymous—we do this by associating a Boolean attribute Anon with each section.

So, a specification can be represented as just a sequence of sections, and both CADiZ and Zeta use that representation. The following table lists the components of a Z section.

---

[4] See www.xmlspy.com

Standard Z	CADiZ	Zeta	XML
Section	doc	UnitAbsy.Section	Z:Sect
NAME	word	Name	Z:Word
seq NAME	parent*	Name*	Z:Word*
seq Paragraph	def*	Item*	Z:Para*
SectTypeEnv			Z:Anns/Z:SectTypeEnvAnn

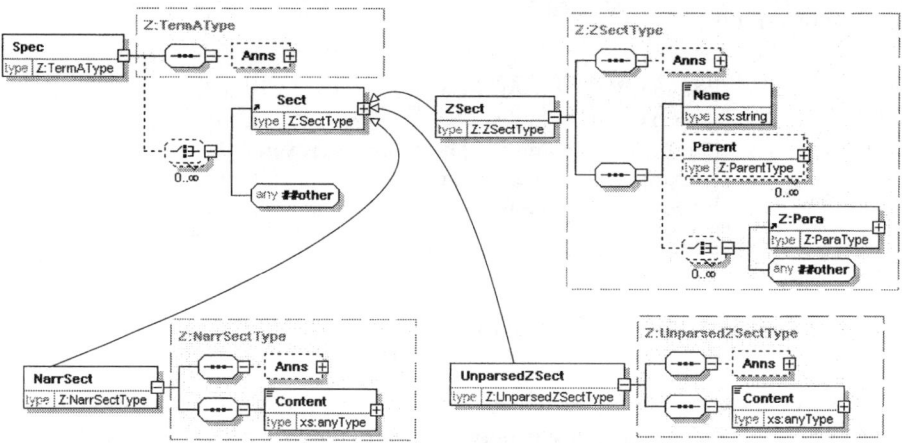

Fig. 1. XML structure for an entire Specification. The arrows pointing towards Sect indicate that ZSect, UnparsedZSect and NarrSect are in the Sect substitution group, so each Sect element can be replaced by any one of them.

Fig. 1 shows a diagrammatic presentation of the corresponding XML structure, omitting some details such as attributes. It shows that a specification is a sequence of zero or more constructs, where each construct is either a parsed section (ZSect), an unparsed section (UnparsedZSect), a narrative portion (NarrSect) or some other kind of arbitrary (non Z-related) XML element (the any ##other). Each parsed ZSect section must be a sequence of an optional set of annotations, then a name, then zero or more parents, then zero or more paragraphs (or other XML elements). The top-level Spec element also has three optional attributes (not shown) to record its *Creator* and the *Date* and *Time* of the last modification. Note that inside an Anns tag, *any* XML elements are allowed—our XML proposal pre-defines several annotations, but other tools are free to define more. We have set *processing* = *lax* within the Anns element, which means that Z tools and other validation tools should simply ignore any annotations they do not understand.

Within a ZSect, the list of parent names need not include *prelude*, as that is implicitly a parent of all sections. If there are no parents, the ZSect element does not record whether or not the keyword parents occurred in the concrete representation. This doesn't matter sufficiently to deserve the declaration of an attribute.

Support for Z Extensions. There have been numerous extensions of Z in the past, and this will probably continue. Furthermore, within a Z specification, we want to allow complementary kinds of specification, such as CSP specifications, UML diagrams, or new kinds of paragraphs defined by some extension of Z like Object-Z or TCOZ. Fig. 1 shows that, within specifications and sections, our XML mark-up allows arbitrary elements from *other* namespaces to be interspersed with Z constructs. This means that the XML tags that belong to the standard Z namespace will be checked and processed by Z tools, while text and unknown tags (from other namespaces) will be ignored. In other words, the formal Z constructs (sections and paragraphs) are viewed as being part of a larger narrative, which may contain other kinds of top-level mark-up. This is a more permissive, egalitarian style of mark-up than allowing only standard Z constructs to appear at the top level.

4.2 Paragraphs

Toyn's DTD defined Z:Para to be a *choice* between six kinds of paragraph. XML Schema gives us several different ways of doing this, and we have decided to use a newish XML Schema feature, *Substitution Groups*, rather than choice groups, because substitution groups are similar to an object-oriented subtyping structure (where a subtype object can replace a supertype object), and can support inheritance of attributes and elements.

Substitution groups make it easy to extend the structure. For example, a Z extension can add a new kind of paragraph simply by defining a new element with substitutionGroup="Para". It is also easy to add new features to one of the subtypes, like AxPara, by declaring a new element whose type extends or restricts the type of AxPara and says substitutionGroup="AxPara" (the substitution relationship is transitive).

Here is the XML Schema definition for Para. It is declared to be abstract so that XML files *must* contain a more specific kind of paragraph, wherever a Para element is expected.

```
<xs:element name="Para" type="ParaType" abstract="true"/>
```

The following subsections go through each kind of paragraph, describing their structure.

Given Types Paragraph. The following table lists the components of a given types paragraph.

Standard Z	CADiZ	Zeta	XML
Given types Paragraph	givdef	Item.AxiomaticDef*	Z:GivenPara
seq NAME	dec*	Expr.GivenType	Z:DeclName*
Signature			Z:Anns/Z:TypeEnvAnn

In CADiZ, all declarations (given types, generic parameters, variables) share the same dec representation. This has the advantage of providing a basis for tracking all references to each declaration.

In Zeta, a given types paragraph is represented as an Item.AxiomaticDefs sequence, in which each Item.AxiomaticDef's expression is an Expr.GivenType containing the name of a given type. This is an instance of a more general approach: Zeta represents each Z global definition as an Item.AxiomaticDef, using additional kinds of expressions beyond those of Standard Z to make this possible. Concretely, a given types paragraph (or a single given type) is not an expression, and so Zeta's representation seems a bit forced.

In XML, a given types paragraph is marked-up using the Z:GivenPara element, whose type is shown in Fig. 2. To save space, we do not show the annotation elements (Anns) in this and future diagrams, because they appear on virtually all constructs.

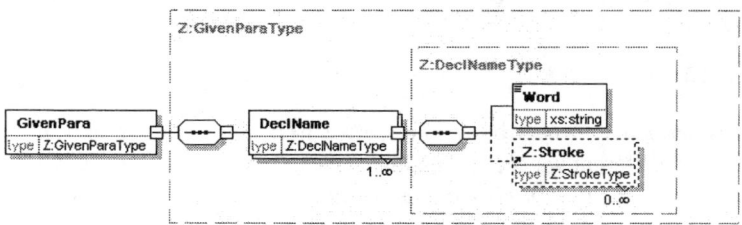

Fig. 2. XML structure for Given Type paragraphs

Axiomatic Description Paragraph. The following table lists the components of an axiomatic description paragraph.

Standard Z	CADiZ	Zeta	XML
(Generic) axdef Paragraph	axidef	Item.AxiomaticDef	Z:AxPara
seq NAME	dec*	NameDecl*	Z:DeclName*
Expression	sch	Expr.Text	Z:SchText
Signature			Z:Anns/Z:TypeEnvAnn

In CADiZ and Zeta, non-generic axiomatic description paragraphs are represented as generic ones with an empty list of generic parameters. Standard Z differs, as it was thought that the semantics of generics would be easier to understand if the semantics of non-generics were defined separately first.

The declarations and predicate parts of an axiomatic description paragraph are represented differently in the different annotated syntaxes. Standard Z transforms them to an expression. CADiZ retains the schema text, represented by a distinct rule in the annotated syntax. Zeta views the schema text as an expression. We believe that some annotations can usefully be placed on schema texts, and that any single expression appearing where a schema text is expected is best represented as an inclusion in a schema text, so that there is somewhere to record those annotations.

Fig. 3 shows our XML structure for the AxPara element, as well as for schema text and declarations. Note the three 'subtypes' of Decl. These are all declared as belonging to the Decl substitution group so that they can appear wherever a Decl is required.

The following definitions from the Z standard (syntactic transformations 12.2.3.1—12.2.3.4) show how to represent (generic) schema definition paragraphs and (generic) horizontal definition paragraphs as (generic) axiomatic description paragraphs. The *SCH, END* etc. are box tokens, which abstract away from the exact appearances of paragraph outlines.

$$\text{SCH } i \ t \text{ END} \implies \text{AX } [i == t] \text{ END}$$

$$\text{GENSCH } i \ [i_1, ..., i_n] \ t \text{ END} \implies \text{GENAX } [i_1, ..., i_n] \ [i == t] \text{ END}$$

$$\text{ZED } i == e \text{ END} \implies \text{AX } [i == e] \text{ END}$$

$$\text{ZED } i \ [i_1, ..., i_n] == e \text{ END} \implies \text{GENAX } [i_1, ..., i_n] \ [i == e] \text{ END}$$

Generic operator definition paragraphs have their operator names syntactically transformed to ordinary names (syntactic transformations 12.2.9.1—12.2.9.4) and hence they become generic horizontal definition paragraphs that can be represented as generic axiomatic description paragraphs.

To support resurrection of the original concrete representation, we add an attribute Box with values: OmitBox, AxBox (the default), or SchBox. A further Boolean attribute called Mixfix, distinguishes whether mixfix syntax is used in the definition of a generic operator e.g. $\_ \leftrightarrow \_[X, Y] == \mathbb{P}(X \times Y)$.

Free Types Paragraph. The following tables list the components of a free types paragraph.

Standard Z	CADiZ	Zeta	XML
Free types Paragraph	datdef	Item.AxiomaticDef*	Z:FreePara
seq Freetype	fret+	Expr.FreeType	Z:FreeType+
Signature			Z:Anns/Z:TypeEnvAnn

In Zeta, the representation of free types paragraphs is similar to that of other global definitions (see the earlier discussion in the Given Types section).

Standard Z	CADiZ	Zeta	XML
Freetype	fret	Expr.FreeType	Z:FreeType
NAME	dec	NameDecl	Z:DeclName
seq Branch	bra+	Branch+	Z:Branch+

The representation of a branch is very different in different tools, and so cannot readily be tabulated.

Standard Z	XML
Branch	Z:Branch
NAME	Z:DeclName
Expression	Z:Expr?

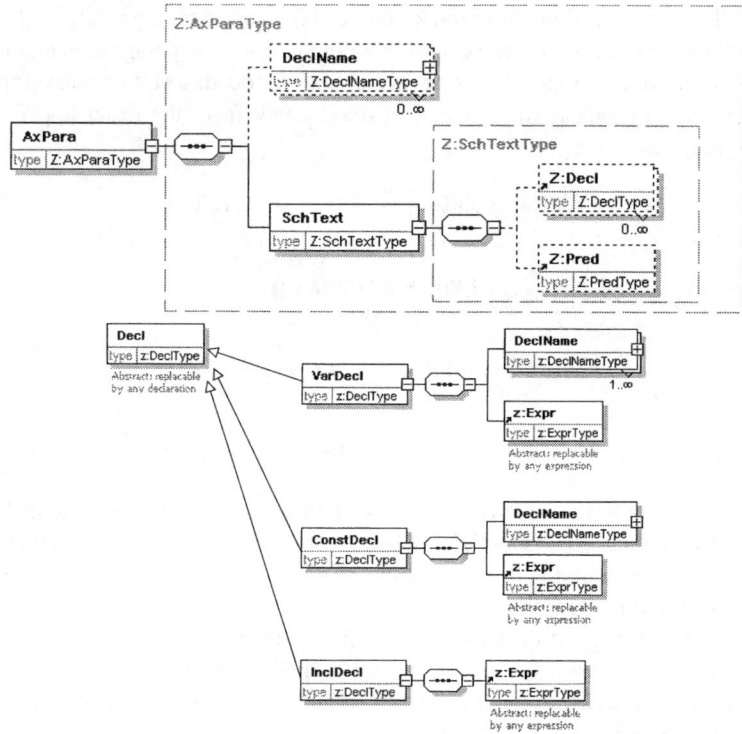

Fig. 3. XML structure for Axiomatic Definition paragraphs, Schema Text and Declarations. The arrows pointing towards Decl indicate that VarDecl, ConstDecl and InclDecl are in the Decl substitution group, so each Decl element can be replaced by any one of them.

In CADiZ, a Branch's name and optional expression are both represented by a single dec value, allowing references to the name to be tracked.

In Zeta, a Branch is either a Constant or a Function. A Constant has just a NameDecl, whereas a Function has both a NameDecl and an Expr.

In XML, a free types paragraph is marked-up using the Z:FreePara element, whose type is shown in Fig. 4.

Conjecture Paragraph. Standard Z conjectures have a single consequent predicate and zero or more generic parameters.

Zeta does not support conjecture paragraphs.

In CADiZ, conjectures are represented as particular cases of a more general syntax for sequents. Sequents allow for zero-or-more generic parameters, zero-or-more levels of nested DeclParts, zero-or-more antecedent predicates, zero-or-more consequent predicates, and a name for the sequent. This more general syntax assists humans doing proofs interactively, but adds nothing semantically: any sequent can be rearranged into an equivalent single-consequent form that conforms to the Z standard (ignoring the se-

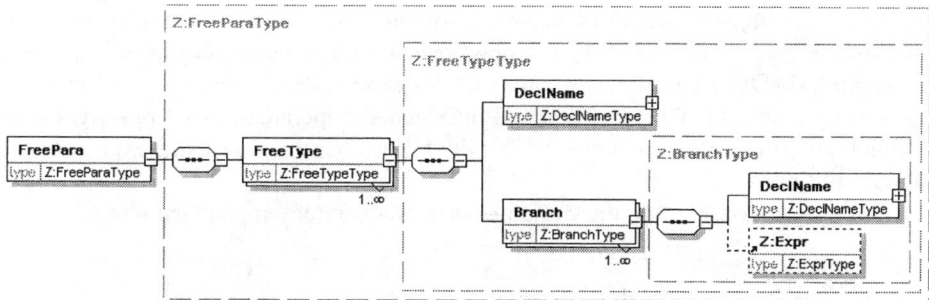

Fig. 4. XML structure for Free Type paragraphs

quent's name, which can be thought of as an annotation). Other reasoning tools for Z may use different representations for sequents. So it seems inappropriate to define an XML mark-up for anything more complicated than a Standard Z (generic) conjecture.

The following table lists the components of a conjecture paragraph.

Standard Z	XML
(Generic) conjecture Paragraph	Z:ConjPara
seq NAME	Z:DeclName*
Predicate	Z:Pred
Signature	Z:Anns/Z:TypeEnvAnn

In XML, a conjecture paragraph is marked-up using the Z:ConjPara element (Fig. 5). This representation suffices for both generic and non-generic conjecture paragraphs: the sequence of generic parameters is empty in the non-generic case.

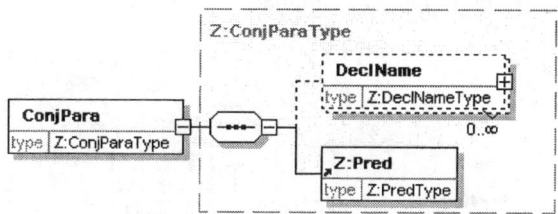

Fig. 5. XML structure for Conjecture paragraphs

Operator Template Paragraph. Standard Z has operator template paragraphs in its concrete syntax but not in its annotated syntax, because they affect how the specification is parsed but have no further meaning themselves. To be able to interchange them and resurrect their concrete syntax, and the concrete syntax of the operators they define, the XML mark-up must provide a representation of them.

Operator templates are one of the innovations of Standard Z and were subject to some late changes, so tools are unlikely to support operator templates exactly as in Standard Z (excepting CADiZ). The concrete syntax allows explicit declaration of precedence and associativity only for infix function and infix generic operators. Other operators have implicit precedences and associativities, which it is convenient to make explicit in the annotated syntax.

The following table lists the components of an operator template paragraph.

Standard Z	CADiZ	Zeta	XML
Operator template Paragraph	fixdef	Fixity	Z:OptempPara
Category	cat	isGeneric	Z:Cat (Attr)
Prec	nat	prio	Z:Prec (Attr)
Assoc	boole	?	Z:Assoc (Attr)
Template	(nat,word)+	Component*	See Fig. 6

In CADiZ, a Template is represented as a list of pairs. While this enforces alternation of operators and operands, it may unfortunately appear to add an unwanted operand at the beginning and/or an unwanted operator at the end, for which distinguishable values are needed to avoid confusion.

In Zeta, a Template is represented as a list of Components. Each Component is either a Keyword, Operand or OperandList. Zeta appears to parse declarations of associativity, but it does not appear to keep a representation of associativity in its annotated syntax. Its annotated syntax also appears not to distinguish relation and function categories.

In XML, an operator template paragraph is marked-up using the Z:OptempPara element (Fig. 6). In addition, each Z:OptempPara has three attributes:

Cat (category) which can equal Relation, Function or Generic.
Assoc which can be Left or Right.
Prec (precedence) which is a natural number.

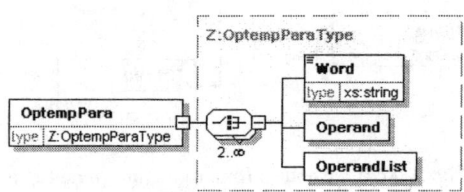

Fig. 6. XML structure for Operator Template paragraphs

Narrative Paragraph. To allow natural language narrative to appear between Z paragraphs, we define a NarrPara element, containing annotations and a Contents element which contains arbitrary unicode and markup. This is similar to NarrSect in Fig. 1.

Unparsed Paragraph. Our final kind of paragraph does not appear in Zeta or the Z standard, because their annotated syntax representations are used only *after* an entire specification has been successfully parsed. However, since our XML format may be our source representation, we need to be able to represent erroneous (unparsable) specifications as well. Similar to the ErrorDef paragraph in CADiZ, we use a special paragraph called UnparsedPara, whose structure is the same as UnparsedZSect (see Fig.1). If a tool attempts to parse an UnparsedPara, it may return a parse error, or one or more paragraphs (which will replace the UnparsedPara). Similarly, at the top level of a specification, an UnparsedZSect may become one or more sections if it can be parsed.

4.3 Predicates and Expressions

We shall not go into details about the structure of predicates and expressions etc., but will discuss some specific features and give a few short XML examples to give the flavour of our approach.

As for paragraphs, declarations and strokes, we define Expr and Pred to be abstract elements, and use substitution groups to allow specific concrete kinds of expressions and predicates to be used in their place. To capture the commonalities between various kinds of expressions, we define a hierarchy of XML types (Fig. 7). We expect that this same hierarchy can be used in Z tools that are written in object-oriented languages. Then the various concrete predicate and expression elements are defined as members of these types, as the following examples illustrate (grp stands for substitutionGroup):

```
<element name="OrPred"        type="Z:Pred2Type"     grp="Z:Pred"/>
<element name="ImpliesPred"   type="Z:Pred2Type"     grp="Z:Pred"/>
<element name="ForallPred"    type="Z:QntPredType"   grp="Z:Pred"/>
<element name="ExistsPred"    type="Z:QntPredType"   grp="Z:Pred"/>
<element name="FalsePred"     type="Z:FactType"      grp="Z:Pred"/>
<element name="TruePred"      type="Z:FactType"      grp="Z:Pred"/>

<element name="LambdaExpr"    type="Z:Qnt1ExprType"  grp="Z:Expr"/>
<element name="MuExpr"        type="Z:QntExprType"   grp="Z:Expr"/>
<element name="LetExpr"       type="Z:Qnt1ExprType"  grp="Z:Expr"/>
<element name="SetCompExpr"   type="Z:QntExprType"   grp="Z:Expr"/>
```

Some expressions and predicates have special features to enable the concrete syntax to be resurrected. Z has several conjunction operators ($\wedge$, ; , newline and the implicit conjunctions within $a < b < c$), which are all represented by the AndPred element (of type Pred2Type) with an attribute to record which kind of conjunction it came from. The RefExpr, ApplExpr and MemPred elements have a Boolean attribute called Mixfix to record whether the application uses mixfix notation or not.

The Challenge of Nested Identical Names. In Z it is quite common to have several levels of declarations nested inside one another. If two levels declare the same name X, then expressions inside the inner's scope cannot normally refer to the outer X. However, there are situations like the following example, where the instantiation of generic operators during type checking must introduce references to the outer X (the $\#\{a\}$ becomes

```
TermType                          supertype of all Z constructs
    StrokeType                    supertype of the 4 kinds of name decorations
    AnnType                       supertype of all annotations
    TermAType                     supertype of all annotatable constructs
        Spec
        SectType                  supertype of all section types
            ZSectType
            UnparsedZSectType
            NarrSectType
        ParaType                  supertype of all paragraph types
            GivenParaType
            AxParaType
            FreeParaType
            ConjParaType
            OptempParaType
            UnparsedParaType
        DeclType                  supertype of all declarations
            VarDecl
            ConstDecl
            InclDecl
        PredType
            Pred2Type             supertype of all binary predicates
            QntPredType           supertype of all quantifier predicates
            FactPredType          supertype of the true/false predicates
        ExprType
            Expr1Type             supertype of all unary expressions
            Expr2Type             supertype of all binary expressions
                LogExprType       supertype of all binary schema operators
            QntExprType           supertype of all quantifier exprs
                Qnt1ExprType      supertype of quantifier exprs with compulsory body
                    ExistsExprType supertype of existential schema exprs
            Expr0NType            supertype of exprs with 0 or more subexprs
                Expr2NType        supertype of exprs with 2 or more subexprs
        TypeType                  supertype of all Z base types used in annotations
        ParentType
        FreeTypeType
        BranchType
        SchTextType
        NameType
```

Fig. 7. The hierarchy of XML complex types in ZML.

$\#[X]\{a\}$). This creates a problem, because naively introducing X at this point causes it to bind to the inner X rather than the outer X.

$[X]$

$$\frac{a : X}{\exists X : \mathbb{N} \bullet \#\{a\} = X}$$

None of the previous DTD or XML Schema proposals solve this problem. The traditional solution is to rename the bound X. But to allow exact resurrection of concrete syntax we do *not* want to rename bound variables. The Z standard solves this problem by creating suit-decorated synonyms of type names (e.g., $X\heartsuit$) and making implicit instantiations refer to those synonyms. We want a more general solution than this, so that tools can perform a variety of transformations, then produce correct XML using the original names, even though the scopes of those names may have changed.

CADiZ solves this problem by using references to link each name to a corresponding declaration. We do the same thing in XML, by using the ID and IDREF cross-reference features of XML to allow a variable reference to point to a specific variable declaration (which may not be the nearest nested name). Declarations of names may have an ID-valued attribute called Id, while references to names may have an IDREF-valued attribute called Decl which links to a declaration. Since soundness relies on following these references correctly, every Z tool must be capable of following them, and pretty printers must display the output unambiguously (either by renaming one of the bound variables, or by making the generic instantiations implicit again to hide the problem reference).

The full mark-up of the above example is shown in Appendix A. The XML for the declaration of the global name X is:

`<GivenPara><DeclName Id="X.3"><Word>X</Word></DeclName></GivenPara>`

while an expression that references this X can be marked up as:

`<RefExpr><RefName Decl="X.3"><Word>X</Word></RefName></RefExpr>`

5 Conclusions

We have defined an XML mark-up format for standard Z, based on combining the best features from the standard and several existing tools. The XML Schema has been validated, and several small examples have been validated against the schema. We are now seeking feedback and comments on the design, particularly on the following issues:

1. Two alternative approaches to annotations: the approach taken here is for each term to have an optional Anns slot that can contain arbitrary XML (which is not validated or checked in any way). An alternative approach would be to put new kinds of annotations into separate documents (with their own XML Schema) and use IDREF links to link each annotation to the appropriate Z term (which would have an ID attribute).
2. Two alternative approaches to narrative and non-standard portions of Z specification documents. Should narrative paragraphs and non-Z XML mark-up be viewed as subordinate to the Z, or should it be mixed in with the Z constructs on an equal basis (as in this paper)? The former approach allows stricter XML validation of the document, because every top-level paragraph is of a known type and can be checked (except that Narrative paragraphs would be allowed arbitrary contents). The latter approach (which we have taken) makes it easy to add new kinds of paragraphs (e.g., for Z extensions), even without extending the XML Schema, but means that standard Z tools will quietly ignore all unknown kinds of paragraphs.
3. Unparsed fragments. Is it really useful to be able to have some paragraphs or sections unparsed? Would an even finer granularity be useful (Expr and Pred etc.)? Or should we disallow unparsed portions and insist that this XML mark-up be used only for syntactically correct specifications?
4. Mathematical Symbols. We expect that the special symbols used in Z will normally be represented in XML documents using their binary Unicode representation (e.g., UTF8). However, this means that the documents are not ASCII-based and are only

human-readable if you have a full Unicode font. Would it be useful to define symbolic names for all the Z symbols (this can be done using DTD entities, or XML Schema elements with fixed contents) so that the Z specifications can be pure ASCII? Or will this be irrelevant once full Unicode fonts and Unicode editors become widely available?

Combining the best features from the Z standard and several existing tools has been worthwhile, as can be seen by considering the main influences on the XML structure. The Specification representation is influenced mainly by the form of XML. The Section representation is influenced mainly by Zeta. The Paragraph representation is influenced mainly by Standard Z, with the commonality between generics and non-generics taken from both CADiZ and Zeta, and the template representation in operator templates taken from Zeta. The Predicate representation is influenced mainly by CADiZ and Zeta, which use remarkably similar representations. The Expression representation falls between those of CADiZ and Zeta. The representations of schema text and names are influenced mainly by Zeta.

Next we plan to derive a set of open-source Java classes from this XML schema, preferably by using either JAXB[5] or XSLT to transform the schema into Java source. These Java classes will support the visitor design pattern [7], so that functionality such as type checkers, transformation tools, simplifiers and pretty printers can easily be written as add-on packages. This will dramatically reduce the usual initial barriers of creating new Z tools (parsing, type-checking etc.) and make it easier for student projects and other researchers to experiment with building new Z tools.

Another important step is for existing Z tools to support this XML format, by adding import and export functions that read and write it. CADiZ already exports an XML format that is close to this one.

References

1. ISO/IEC 10646-1. *Information Technology – Universal Multiple-Octet Coded Character Set (UCS) – Part 1: Architecture and Basic Multilingual Plane*. 2000.
2. ISO/IEC 10646-2. *Information Technology – Universal Multiple-Octet Coded Character Set (UCS) – Part 2: Supplementary Planes*. 2001.
3. ISO/IEC 13568. *Information Technology – Z Formal Specification Notation – Syntax, Type System and Semantics*. 2002. First Edition 2002-07-01.
4. ISO 8879-1986. *Information Processing – Text and Office Systems – Standard Generalized Mark-up Language (SGML)*. ISO, 1986.
5. Nicholas Daley. Abstract syntax tree for Z. 591 Project Report, The Department of Computer Science, Waikato University, Hamilton, New Zealand, October 2002. Available from marku@cs.waikato.ac.nz.
6. Jin Song Dong, Yuan Fang Li, Jing Sun, Jun Sun, and Hai Wang. XML-based static type checking and dynamic visualization for TCOZ. In *4th International Conference on Formal Engineering Methods*, pages 311–322. Springer-Verlag, October 2002.
7. Erich Gamma, Richard Helm, Ralph Johnson, and John Vlissides. *Design Patterns: Elements of Reusable Object-Oriented Software*. Addison Wesley, USA, 1995.

---

[5] See http://java.sun.com/xml/jaxb.

8. W. Grieskamp. ZETA. http://uebb.cs.tu-berlin.de/zeta, 2000.
9. E.R. Harold and W.S. Means. *XML in a Nutshell*. O'Reilly, 2001.
10. B. Mahony and J. S. Dong. Timed Communicating Object Z. *IEEE Transactions on Software Engineering*, 26(2), February 2000.
11. M. Saaltink. The Z/EVES system. In J. Bowen, M. Hinchey, and D. Till, editors, *Proc. 10th Int. Conf. on the Z Formal Method (ZUM)*, volume 1212 of *Lecture Notes in Computer Science*, pages 72–88, Reading, UK, April 1997. Springer-Verlag, Berlin.
12. J. Michael Spivey. *The Z Notation: A Reference Manual*. International Series in Computer Science. Prentice-Hall International (UK) Ltd, second edition, 1992.
13. J. Sun, J.S. Dong, J. Liu, and H. Wang. An XML Schema for Z family. http://nt-appn.comp.nus.edu.sg/fm/zml/zml.xsd, 2001.
14. Jing Sun, Jin Song Dong, Jing Liu, and Hai Wang. A Formal Object Approach to the Design of ZML. *Annals of Software Engineering*, 13(1-4):329–356, June 2002.
15. I. Toyn. CADiZ. http://www-users.cs.york.ac.uk/~ian/cadiz/, 2001.
16. J. Wordsworth. An XML DTD for Z, October 1999.

A XML Mark-Up of Example from Sect. 4.3

```
<NarrPara>
  <Content>First we declare X to be a given set.</Content>
</NarrPara>
<GivenPara>
  <DeclName Id="X.3"> <Word>X</Word> </DeclName>
</GivenPara>

<NarrPara>
  <Content>This axiomatic definition declares a:X, with the
  constraint: (∃ X:ℕ @ #{a} = X)</Content>
<NarrPara>
<AxPara>
  <SchText>
    <VarDecl>
      <DeclName> <Word>a</Word> </DeclName>
      <RefExpr><RefName><Word>X</Word></RefName></RefExpr>
    </VarDecl>

    <ExistsPred>
      <SchText>
        <VarDecl>
          <DeclName> <Word>X</Word> </DeclName>
          <RefExpr><RefName><Word>ℕ</Word></RefName></RefExpr>
        </VarDecl>
      </SchText>
      <MemPred>
        <TupleExpr>
          <ApplExpr>
            <RefExpr>
              <RefName><Word>#</Word></RefName>
              <RefExpr>
```

```
              <RefName Decl="X.3"> <Word>X</Word>
              </RefName>
            </RefExpr>
          </RefExpr>
          <SetExpr>
            <RefExpr><RefName><Word>a</Word></RefName></RefExpr>
          </SetExpr>
        </ApplExpr>
        <NumExpr Value="1"/>
      </TupleExpr>
      <RefExpr><RefName><Word>=</Word></RefName></RefExpr>
    </MemPred>
  </ExistsPred>
 </SchText>
</AxPara>
```

Formal Derivation of Spanning Trees Algorithms

Jean-Raymond Abrial[1], Dominique Cansell[2], and Dominique Méry[3]*

[1] Consultant
Marseille, France
jr@abrial.org
[2] LORIA,Université Henri Poincaré Nancy 1
Dominique.Mery@loria.fr
[3] LORIA,INRIA Lorraine
Dominique.Cansell@loria.fr
BP 239
Vandœuvre-lès-Nancy Cédex,France

Abstract. Graphs algorithms and graph-theoretical problems provide a challenging battle field for the incremental development of proved models. The B event-based approach implements the incremental and proved development of abstract models which are translated into algorithms; we focus our methodology on the minimum spanning tree problem and on Prim's algorithm. The correctness of the resulting solution is based on properties over trees and we show how the greedy strategy is efficient in this case. We compare properties proven mechanically to the properties found in a classical algorithms textbook.

1 Introduction

Overview. Developing distributed algorithms can be improved by the use of refinement techniques. A refinement technique allows one to gradually develop a distributed algorithm step by step, or to tackle complex problem like the PCI Transaction Ordering Problem [7] or the IEEE 1394 Tree Identification Protocol [3]. The B event-based method provides a framework for deriving abstract systems modeling distributed algorithmic solutions like the Minimum Spanning Tree algorithms, MST algorithms for short. This paper analyses the proof-based development of MST algorithms and Prim's algorithm in particular [20] is produced in fine: this is an illustration of the effectiveness of refinement for such algorithms.

Proof-based Development. Proof-based development methods integrate formal proof techniques in the development of software systems. The main idea is to start with a very abstract model of the system under development. We then gradually add details to this first model by building a sequence of more concrete ones. The relationship between two successive models in this sequence is that of *refinement* [6,5,9]. It is controlled by means of a number of *proofs obligations*,

---

* Supported in part by PRST Intelligence Logicielle/QSL/DIXIT project and by PRST Intelligence Logicielle/QSL/ADHOC project

which guarantee the correctness of the development. Such proof obligations are proved by automatic (and interactive) proof procedures supported by a proof engine. The essence of the refinement relationship is that it preserves already proved *system properties* including safety properties and termination properties. The invariant of an abstract model plays a central role for deriving safety properties and our methodology focuses on the incremental discovery of the invariant; the goal is to obtain a formal statement of properties through the final invariant of the last refined abstract model. When developing formal models for the IEEE 1394 protocol, we use the Atelier B environment [10] for generating and proving proof obligations.

Refining Formal Models. Formal models, as described in this paper, contain *events* which preserve some invariant properties; they also include aspects related to the termination. Such models are thus very close to action systems introduced by R.J. Back [6] and to UNITY programs [9]. The refinement of formal models plays a central role in these frameworks and is a key concept for developing algorithmic systems. When one refines a formal model, the corresponding more concrete model may have new variables and new events, it may also strengthen the *guards* of more abstract events. As already mentioned, some proof obligations are generated in order to prove that a refinement is correct. Notice that, if some proof obligations remain unproved, it means that, either the formal model is not correctly refined, or that an interactive proving session is required. The prover allows us to get a complete proof of the development.

Organization of the paper. Section 2 introduces the MST problem and known MST algorithms; the different steps of Prim's algorithm and the correctness are informally explained. Section 3 recalls the proof-based development methodology. Section 4 describes the formal development of a first spanning tree algorithm; the problem is formally stated in the B event-based framework and the resulting model is called the generic model. Section 5 uses the previous development by adding effective cost functions to edges and Prim's algorithm is then obtained with the complete proof. Section 6 details properties over trees proved to ensure that the resulting algorithm returns the minimum spanning tree. Section 7 compares our approach to related approaches. Section 8 concludes our paper.

2 The Minimum Spanning Tree Problem

The Minimum Spanning Tree Problem, MST problem for short, is the problem of finding a minimum spanning tree with respect to a connected graph. The literature contains several algorithmic solutions like Prim's algorithm [20] or Kruskal's algorithm [16]. Both algorithms implement the greedy method. Typically, we assume that a cost function is related to every edge and the problem is to infer a globally minimum spanning tree, which covers the initial graph. The cost function returns integer values. The MST problem is strongly related to practical problems like the optimisation of circuitry and the greedy strategy advocates making the choice that is the best one at the moment; It does not always guarantee the optimality but certain greedy strategies yield a MST.

Prim's algorithm is easy to explain but it underlies mathematical properties related to the graph theory and especially the general theory of trees. We consider two kinds of solutions; a first one is called *generic algorithm* because it does not use a cost function. This first *generic* solution allows us to develop a second solution: the MST one.

Let us summarize how Prim's algorithm works. The state of the algorithm while executing contains two sets of nodes of the current graphs. A first set of nodes, equipped with a restriction of the relation over the global set of nodes, defines the current spanning tree starting from a special node called the root of the spanning tree. A second set of nodes is the complement of the first set. The acyclicity of the spanning tree must be preserved, while adding a new edge in the current spanning tree and the basic computation step consists of taking an edge between a node in the current spanning tree and a node which is in the other set. The choice leads to maintaining the acyclicity of the current spanning tree with the new node, since both sets of nodes are disjoint. The process is repeated as long as the set of remaining and unchosen nodes is empty. The final computed tree is a spanning tree computed by the generic algorithm. Now, if one adds the cost function, one gets Prim's algorithm by modifying the choice of the new node and edge to add to the current spanning tree. In fact, the minimum edge is chosen and the final spanning tree is then the minimum spanning tree. However, the addition of the cost function is a refinement of the generic solution.

The generic MST algorithm without cost function is sketched as follows:

- Precondition: *A undirected connected graph, g, over a set of nodes ND and a node r*
- Initial Step *tr_nodes (the current set of nodes) contains only r and is included into ND and tr (the current set of edges) is empty*
- Computation Step *If $ND - tr\_nodes$ is not empty, then choose a node x in tr_nodes and a node y in $ND - tr\_nodes$ such that the link (x, y) is in g with the minimum cost and add it to tr; then add y to tr_nodes and (x, y) to tr*
- Termination Step *If $ND - tr\_nodes$ is empty $(ND = tr\_nodes)$, then tr is a minimum spanning tree on ND*
- Postcondition *(ND, tr) is a minimum spanning tree*

The termination of the algorithm is ensured by decreasing the set $ND - tr\_nodes$. The genericity of the solution leads us to the refinement by introducing the cost function in the computation step. We have a clear simple abstract view of the problem and of the solution. We can, in fact, state the problem in the B event-based framework. It remains to prove the optimality of the resulting spanning tree and that will be derived using tools and models. Before starting the modeling, we recall the B-event-based modeling technique.

3 Proof-Based Development

3.1 Event-Based Modeling

Our event-driven approach [2,4] is based on the B notation [5]. It extends the methodological scope of basic concepts such as set-theoretical notations and generalized substitutions in order to take into account the idea of *formal models*. Roughly speaking, a formal model is characterized by a (finite) list x of *state variables* possibly modified by a (finite) list of *events*; an invariant $I(x)$ states some properties that must always be satisfied by the variables x and *maintained* by the activation of the events. Abstract models are close to guarded commands of Dijkstra [12], action systems of Back [6] and to UNITY programs [9]. In what follows, we briefly recall definitions and principles of formal models and explain how they can be managed by Atelier B [10].

Definition 1. *Generalized Substitution. Generalized substitutions are borrowed from the B notation. They provide a way to express the transformations of the values of the state variables of a formal model. In its simple form, $x := E(x)$, a generalized substitution looks like an assignment statement. In this construct, x denotes a vector build on the set of state variables of the model, and $E(x)$ a vector of expressions of the same size as the vector x. The interpretation we shall give here to this statement is not however that of an assignment statement. We interpret it as a logical simultaneous substitution of each variable of the vector x by the corresponding expression of the vector $E(x)$. There exists a more general form of generalized substitution. It is denoted by the construct $x : P(x_0, x)$. This is to be read: "x is modified in such a way that the predicate $P(x_0, x)$ holds", where x denotes the* new value *of the vector, whereas x_0 denotes its* old value. *It is clearly non-deterministic in general. This general form could be considered as a* normal *form, since the simplest form $x := E(x)$ is equivalent to the more general form $x : (x = E(x_0))$.*

Definition 2. *Events and Before-After Predicates. An event is essentially made of two parts: a guard, which is a predicate built on the state variables, and an action, which is a generalized substitution. An event can take one of the forms shown in the table below. In these constructs, evt is an identifier: this is the event name. The first event is not guarded: it is thus always enabled. The guard of the other events, which states the necessary condition for these events to occur, is represented by $G(x)$ in the second case, and by $\exists t \cdot G(t, x)$ in the third one. The latter defines a non-deterministic event where t represents a vector of distinct local variables. The, so-called, before-after predicate $BA(x, x')$ associated with each event shape, describes the event as a logical predicate expressing the relationship linking the values of the state variables just before (x) and just after (x') the event "execution".*

Event	Before-after Predicate $BA(x, x')$
$evt \;\widehat{=}\; \text{BEGIN}\; x : P(x_0, x)\; \text{END}$	$P(x, x')$
$evt \;\widehat{=}\; \text{SELECT}\; G(x)\; \text{THEN}\; x : Q(x_0, x)\; \text{END}$	$G(x) \wedge Q(x, x')$
$evt \;\widehat{=}\; \text{ANY}\; t\; \text{WHERE}\; G(t, x)\; \text{THEN}\; x : R(x_0, x, t)\; \text{END}$	$\exists t \cdot (G(t, x) \wedge R(x, x', t))$

Proof obligations are produced from events in order to state that the invariant condition $I(x)$ is preserved. We next give the general rule to be proved. It follows immediately from the very definition of the before-after predicate, $BA(x, x')$ of each event:

$$I(x) \wedge BA(x, x') \;\Rightarrow\; I(x')$$

Notice that it follows from the two guarded forms of the events that this obligation is trivially discharged when the guard of the event is false. When it is the case, the event is said to be "disabled".

3.2 Model Refinement

The refinement of a formal model allows us to enrich a model in a *step by step* approach. Refinement provides a way to construct stronger invariants and also to add details in a model. It is also used to transform an abstract model in a more concrete version by modifying the state description. This is essentially done by extending the list of state variables (possibly suppressing some of them), by refining each abstract event into a corresponding concrete version, and by adding new events. The abstract state variables, x, and the concrete ones, y, are linked together by means of a, so-called, *gluing invariant* $J(x, y)$. A number of proof obligations ensure that (1) each abstract event is correctly refined by its corresponding concrete version, (2) each new event refines *skip*, (3) no new event take control for ever, and (4) relative deadlock-freeness is preserved.

Definition 3. *Refinement. We suppose that an abstract model AM with variables x and invariant $I(x)$ is refined by a concrete model CM with variables y and gluing invariant $J(x, y)$. If $BAA(x, x')$ and $BAC(y, y')$ are respectively the abstract and concrete before-after predicates of the same event, we have to prove the following statement:*

$$I(x) \wedge J(x, y) \wedge BAC(y, y') \;\Rightarrow\; \exists x' \cdot (BAA(x, x') \wedge J(x', y'))$$

This says that under the abstract invariant $I(x)$ and the concrete one $J(x, y)$, a concrete step $BAC(y, y')$ can be simulated ($\exists x'$) by an abstract one $BAA(x, x')$ in such a way that the gluing invariant $J(x', y')$ is preserved. A new event with before-after predicate $BA(y, y')$ must refine skip ($x' = x$). This leads to the following statement to prove:

$$I(x) \land J(x,y) \land BA(y,y') \Rightarrow J(x,y')$$

Moreover, we must prove that a variant $V(y)$ is decreased by each new event (this is to guarantee that an abstract step may occur). We have thus to prove the following for each new event with before-after predicate $BA(y,y')$:

$$I(x) \land J(x,y) \land BA(y,y') \Rightarrow V(y') < V(y)$$

Finally, we must prove that the concrete model does not introduce more deadlocks than the abstract one. This is formalized by means of the following proof obligation:

$$I(x) \land J(x,y) \land \mathsf{grds}(AM) \Rightarrow \mathsf{grds}(CM)$$

where $\mathsf{grds}(AM)$ stands for the disjunction of the guards of the events of the abstract model, and $\mathsf{grds}(CM)$ stands for the disjunction of the guards of the events of the concrete one. The MST problem can now be stated in the B-event based framework.

4 Development of a Spanning Tree Algorithm

4.1 Formal Specification of the Spanning Tree Problem

First we define elements of the current graph namely g over the set of nodes namely ND. The graph is assumed to be undirected, which is modeled by the symmetry of the relation of the graph. Node r is the root of the resulting tree and we obtain the following B definitions:

$$\begin{array}{l} g \subseteq ND \times ND \;\land \\ g = g^{-1} \;\land \\ r \in ND \end{array}$$

The termination of the algorithm is clearly related to properties of the current graph; the existence of the spanning tree is based on the connectivity of the graph. The modelling of a tree uses the acyclicity of the graph. A tree is defined by a root r, a node: $r \in ND$, and a parent function t (each node has an unique parent node, but the root): $t \in ND - \{r\} \longrightarrow ND$. A tree is an acyclic graph. A cycle c in a finite graph t built on a set ND, is a subset of ND whose elements are members of the inverse image of c under t, formally $c \subseteq t^{-1}[c]$. To fulfill the requirement of acyclicity, the only set c that enjoys this property is necessarily the empty set. We formalize it by the left predicate that follows, which can be proved to be *equivalent* to the one on the right, which can be used as an induction rule:

$$
\forall c \cdot (\; c \subseteq ND \;\land\; c \subseteq t^{-1}[c] \;\Rightarrow\; c = \emptyset\;) \quad\Leftrightarrow\quad \forall q \cdot (\; q \subseteq ND \;\land\; r \in q \;\land\; t^{-1}[q] \subseteq q \;\Rightarrow\; ND = q\;)
$$

We prove the equivalence using Atelier B. We can now define a spanning tree (rooted by r and with the parent function t) of a graph g as one whose parent function is included in g, formally:

$$
\text{spanning}\,(t, g) \;\widehat{=}\; \begin{pmatrix} t \in ND - \{r\} \longrightarrow ND \;\land\\ \forall q \cdot (\, q \subseteq ND \;\land\; r \in q \;\land\; t^{-1}[q] \subseteq q \;\Rightarrow\; ND = q\,) \;\land\\ t \subseteq g \end{pmatrix}
$$

Now we can define the set tree (g) of all spanning trees (with root r) of the graph g, formally:

$$
\text{tree}\,(g) \;=\; \{t\,|\,\text{spanning}\,(t, g)\}
$$

We define the property of *being a connected graph* by connected(g):

$$
\text{connected}\,(g) \;\widehat{=}\; \begin{pmatrix} g \in ND \leftrightarrow ND \;\land\\ \forall S \cdot (\, S \subseteq ND \;\land\; r \in S \;\land\; g[S] \subseteq S \;\Rightarrow\; ND = S\,) \end{pmatrix}
$$

The graph g and the node r are two global constants of our problem and must satisfy properties stated above. Moreover, we assert that there is at least one solution to our problem. The optimality of the solution will be analyzed later, while introducing the cost function. Now, we build the first model which computes the solution in one shot. The event span corresponds to producing a spanning tree among the non-empty set of possible spanning trees for g. The variable st contains the resulting spanning tree.

$$
\begin{array}{l}
\text{span} \;\widehat{=}\\
\quad \text{BEGIN}\\
\quad\quad st :\in \text{tree}(g)\\
\quad \text{END}
\end{array}
$$

The invariant is very simple and only a type invariant.

$$
st \in ND \leftrightarrow ND
$$

The initialization establishes this invariant.

The current model is in fact the specification of the simple spanning tree problem; we have not yet mentioned the cost function. The next step is to refine the current model into a simple spanning tree algorithm.

4.2 Development of a Simple Spanning Tree Algorithm

The second model introduces a new event which gradually computes the spanning tree by constructing the spanning tree in a progressive way. The new event adds a new edge to the current tree tr which partly spans g. The chosen edge is such that the first component of the pair is in tr_nodes and the second one is in $remaining\_nodes$. These two new variables partition the set of nodes and we obtain the following new properties to add to the invariant of the current model.

$$
\begin{array}{l}
tr\_nodes \subseteq ND \quad \wedge \\
remaining\_nodes \subseteq ND \quad \wedge \\
tr\_nodes \cup remaining\_nodes = ND \quad \wedge \\
tr\_nodes \cap remaining\_nodes = \emptyset
\end{array}
$$

A new event, progress, simulates the computation step of the current solution by choosing a pair maintaining the updated invariant.

```
progress ≙
  SELECT
    remaining_nodes ≠ ∅
  THEN
    ANY x, y WHERE
      x, y ∈ g  ∧  x, y ∈ tr_nodes × remaining_nodes
    THEN
      tr := tr ∪ {y ↦ x} ||
      tr_nodes := tr_nodes ∪ {y} ||
      remaining_nodes := remaining_nodes − {y}
    END
  END
```

The event span is simply refined by modifying the guard of the previous instance of the event in the abstract model. The event is triggered when the set of remaining nodes is empty: the variable st contains a spanning tree for the graph g.

$$\begin{array}{l} \text{span} \;\widehat{=}\\ \quad \text{SELECT}\\ \qquad remaining\_nodes = \emptyset\\ \quad \text{THEN}\\ \qquad st := tr\\ \quad \text{END} \end{array}$$

The invariant of the new model states the properties of the two new variables and relates them to previous ones.

$$\begin{array}{l} tr\_nodes \subseteq ND \;\wedge\\ remaining\_nodes \subseteq ND \;\wedge\\ tr\_nodes \cup remaining\_nodes = ND \;\wedge\\ tr\_nodes \cap remaining\_nodes = \emptyset \;\wedge\\ tr \in tr\_nodes - \{r\} \longrightarrow tr\_nodes \;\wedge\\ \forall q \cdot (\, q \subseteq tr\_nodes \;\wedge\; r \in q \;\wedge\; tr^{-1}[q] \subseteq q \;\Rightarrow\; tr\_nodes = q\,) \end{array}$$

The following initialization establishes the invariant:

$$\begin{array}{l} tr := \emptyset \;||\\ tr\_nodes := \{r\} \;||\\ remaining\_nodes := ND - \{r\} \end{array}$$

The expression of the absence of deadlock is simply stated as follows:

$$\begin{array}{l} remaining\_nodes = \emptyset \;\vee\\ remaining\_nodes \neq \emptyset \;\wedge\; \exists (x,y) * \left(\begin{array}{l} x,y \in g \;\wedge\\ x,y \in tr\_nodes \times remaining\_nodes \end{array}\right) \end{array}$$

We have obtained a simple iterative solution for the simple MST problem; the solution follows the sketch of the algorithm given in the section describing the so called generic algorithm in the book of Cormen et al. [11]. We can derive the following algorithm from the current model:

```
ALGORITHM generic_MST
  tr := ∅;
  tr_nodes = {r};
  WHILE remaining_nodes ≠ ∅ DO
    LET x, y WHERE
      x, y ∈ g  ∧  x, y ∈ tr_nodes × remaining_nodes
    THEN
      tr := tr ∪ {y ↦ x};
      tr_nodes := tr_nodes ∪ {y};
      remaining_nodes := remaining_nodes − {y}
    END
  END_WHILE
  st := tr
```

The next step refines the current model into a model where the cost function is effectively used.

4.3 A Proof View of the Spanning Tree Algorithm

The previous model computes a spanning tree, when the graph is connected. This algorithm looks like a proof of existence of a spanning tree; the following lemma allows us to prove that the set of spanning trees is not empty and hence a minimum spanning tree exists:

Lemma 1 *(Existence of a spanning tree)*
  connected $(g) \Rightarrow$ tree $(g) \neq \emptyset$

However, the previous lemma requires to construct a tree from the hypothesis related to the connectivity of the graph. Hence, we must prove a first inductive theorem on finite sets, which will include the existence of a tree. We suppose that the set ND is finite and there exists a function from ND to $1..n$, where n is the cardinality of ND.

Lemma 2 *(An inductive theorem on finite sets)*

$$
\begin{array}{l}
\forall P \cdot (\\
\quad P \subseteq \mathbb{P}(ND) \;\wedge \\
\quad \emptyset \in P \;\wedge \\
\quad \forall A \cdot (A \in P \wedge A \neq ND \;\Rightarrow\; \exists a \cdot (a \in ND - A \;\wedge\; A \cup \{a\} \in P)) \\
\Rightarrow \\
\quad ND \in P)
\end{array}
$$

We can use the previous lemma with the following set:

$$\{A | A \subseteq ND \land \exists f \cdot \begin{pmatrix} f \in A - \{r\} \longrightarrow A \land \\ f \subseteq g \land \\ \forall S \cdot \begin{pmatrix} S \subseteq ND \land r \in S \land f^{-1}[S] \subseteq S \\ \Rightarrow \\ A \subseteq S \end{pmatrix} \end{pmatrix} \}$$

to prove that the set of spanning trees of g is not empty.

5 Development of Prim's Algorithm

The cost function is defined on the set of edges and is extended over the global set of possible pairs of nodes.

$$cost : g \longrightarrow \mathbb{Z} \land$$
$$\forall (x,y) \cdot (x, y \in g \Rightarrow cost(x \mapsto y) = cost(y \mapsto x)) \land$$
$$Cost : \mathbb{P}(g) \longrightarrow \mathbb{Z} \land$$
$$Cost(\{\}) = 0 \land$$
$$\forall (s, x, y) \cdot \begin{pmatrix} s \in \mathbb{P}(g) \land x, y \in g - s \\ \Rightarrow \\ Cost(s \cup \{x \mapsto y\}) = Cost(s) + cost(x \mapsto y) \end{pmatrix}$$

We have proved that tree(g) is not empty, since the graph g is connected; the $mst\_set(g)$ containing every minimum spanning tree of the graph g is defined as follows:

$$mst\_set(g) = \{mst | mst \in \text{tree}(g) \land \forall tr \cdot (tr \in \text{tree}(g) \Rightarrow Cost(mst) \leq Cost(tr))\}$$

The set $mst\_set(g)$ is clearly not empty. The first ¡¡one shot¿¿ model is refined into the new model which contains only one event span. We strengthen the definition of the choice of the resulting tree by strengthening the condition over the set and by choosing a candidate in the set of possible MST trees.

$$\text{span} \; \widehat{=}$$
$$\text{BEGIN}$$
$$st :\in mst\_set(g)$$
$$\text{END}$$

The second model gradually computes the spanning tree by adding a new edge to the current ¡¡under construction¿¿ tree tr spanning a part of g. The tree tr is defined over the set of already treated nodes, called tr_nodes. The event progress is modified to handle the minimality criterion: the guard is modified to integrate the choice of the minimum edge among the remaining possible ones.

```
progress ≙
  SELECT
    remaining_nodes ≠ ∅
  THEN
    ANY x, y WHERE
      x, y ∈ g  ∧  x, y ∈ tr_nodes × remaining_nodes  ∧
      ∀(a, b) · (a ∈ tr_nodes ∧
                 b ∈ remaining_nodes ∧
                 a, b ∈ g
                 ⇒
                 cost(y ↦ x) ≤ cost(b ↦ a))
    THEN
      tr := tr ∪ {y ↦ x} ||
      tr_nodes := tr_nodes ∪ {y} ||
      remaining_nodes := remaining_nodes − {y}
    END
END
```

The event span remains unchanged:

```
span ≙
  SELECT
    remaining_nodes = ∅
  THEN
    st := tr
  END
```

The invariant includes the invariant of the refined model of the generic refinement and we add that the current spanning tree tr is a part of a minimum spanning tree of the graph g:

$$\exists T \cdot (T \in mst\_set(g) \ \land \ tr \subseteq T)$$

The invariant implies that after completion, when the event span occurs, the current spanning tree tr is finally a minimal one. Since $\text{tree}(g)$ is not empty, then $mst\_set(g)$ is not empty and a tree can be chosen in this non-empty set to prove that a MST exists (this MST contains ∅). So the invariant holds for the initialization, using the lemma 1. The difficult task is to prove that the event progress maintains the invariant. We can take the minimum spanning tree given by the invariant, if $y \mapsto x$ is in this tree. Or else we must provide another minimum tree which includes the current one and the new edge $y \mapsto x$.

In fact, textbooks provide algorithms implementing the greedy strategy and we refer our explanations to the book of Cormen et al. [11]. The authors prove a theorem page 501 numbered 24.1 to assert that the choice of the two edges is done following a given requirement, namely a safe edge (a safe edge is a edge allowing the progress of the algorithm). We recall the theorem:

Theorem 1. *(24.1, p 501from [11]) Let g be a connected, undirected graph on ND (set of nodes) with a real-valued weight function cost defined on g (edges). Let tr be a subset of g that is included in some minimum spanning tree for g, let $(tr\_nodes, ND - tr\_nodes)$ be any cut of g that respects tr_nodes, and let (x, y) be a light edge crossing $(tr\_nodes, ND - tr\_nodes)$. Then edge (x, y) is safe for tr_nodes.*

Let us explain notions of cut, crosses and light edge. A cut $(tr\_nodes, ND - tr\_nodes))$ of an undirected graph g is a partition of ND. An edge (x, y) crosses the cut $(tr\_nodes, ND - tr\_nodes)$ if one of its endpoints is in tr_nodes and the other is in $ND - tr\_nodes$. An edge is a light edge crossing a cut if its weight is the minimum of any edge crossing the cut. A light edge is not unique.

Proof: *Let T be a minimum spanning tree that includes tr, and assume that T does not contain the light edge (x, y), since if it does, we are done. We shall construct another minimum spanning tree T' that includes $tr \cup \{(x, y)\}$ by using a cut-and-paste technique, thereby showing that (x, y) is a safe edge for tr. The edge (x, y) forms a cycle with the edges on the path p from x to y in T. Since x and y are on opposite sides of the cut $(tr\_nodes, ND - tr\_nodes)$, there is at least one edge in T on the path p that also crosses the cut. Let (a, b) be any such edge. The edge (a, b) is not in tr, because the cut respects tr. Since (a,b) is on the unique path from x to y in T, removing (a,b) breaks T into two components. Adding (x, y) reconnects them to form a new spanning tree $T' = T - \{(a,b)\} \cup \{(x,y)\}$. We next show that T' is a minimum spanning tree. Since (x, y) is a light edge crossing $(tr\_nodes, ND - tr\_nodes)$ and (a, b) also crosses this cut, $cost(x, y) \leq cost(a, b)$. Therefore,*

$$Cost(T') = Cost(T) - cost(a, b) + cost(x, y)$$
$$\leq Cost(T)$$

But T is a minimum spanning tree, so that $Cost(T) \leq Cost(T')$; thus, T' must be a minimum spanning tree also. It remains to show that (x, y) is actually a safe edge for tr. We have $tr \subseteq T'$, since $tr \subseteq T$ and $(a, b) \notin tr$; thus, $tr \cup \{(x, y)\} \subseteq T'$. Consequently, since T' is a minimum spanning tree, (x, y) is safe for tr. □

We have to prove the property above that has been in fact adapted into the B proof engine. However, it is not a simple exercise of translation but a complete formulation of graph-theoretical aspects; moreover, the proof has been completely mechanized, as we will show in the next section. Let us compare the theorem and our formulation. The pair $(tr\_nodes, ND - tr\_nodes)$ is a cut in the left part of the implication; the restriction of the tree f to the set of nodes tr_nodes is a tree rooted by r; (x, y) crosses the cut. Those assumptions imply that there exists a spanning tree sp rooted by r that is minimum on tr_nodes and such that there exists a light cut (a, b) preserving the minimality property.

We must give a formal description of this theorem. We introduce a predicate atree($root, nodes, tree$) stating that a structure $tree$ is a tree on the set $nodes$ and whose root is $root$:

$$\begin{array}{l}\mathsf{atree}(root, nodes, tree) \;\widehat{=}\; \\ \left(\begin{array}{l} root \in nodes \;\wedge\; \\ tree \in nodes - \{root\} \longrightarrow nodes \;\wedge\; \\ \forall q \cdot (\, q \subseteq nodes \;\wedge\; root \in q \;\wedge\; tree^{-1}[q] \subseteq q \;\Rightarrow\; nodes = q\,) \end{array}\right) \end{array}$$

Hence, we must add the following property which is proved separately.

$$\begin{array}{l} \forall (T, tr\_nodes, x, y) \cdot (\\ \quad tr\_nodes \subseteq ND \;\wedge\; \\ \quad y \in ND \;\wedge\; \\ \quad \mathsf{atree}(r, ND, T) \\ \quad r \in tr\_nodes \;\wedge\; \\ \quad x \in tr\_nodes \;\wedge\; \\ \quad (y \notin tr\_nodes) \;\wedge\; \\ \quad \mathsf{atree}(r, tr\_nodes, (tr\_nodes - \{r\} \triangleleft T \triangleright tr\_nodes)) \;\wedge\; \\ \quad \forall S \cdot (S \subseteq ND \;\wedge\; y \in S \;\wedge\; T[S] \subseteq S \Rightarrow S \cap tr\_nodes \neq \emptyset) \\ \Rightarrow \\ \quad \exists (a, b, T') \cdot (\\ \quad\quad a, b \in T \;\wedge\; a \notin tr\_nodes \;\wedge\; b \in tr\_nodes \;\wedge\; \\ \quad\quad \mathsf{atree}(r, ND, T') \;\wedge\; \\ \quad\quad T' \subseteq (T \;\cup\; T^{-1} - \{b \mapsto a, a \mapsto b\}) \cup \{y \mapsto x\} \;\wedge\; \\ \quad\quad Cost(T') = Cost(T) - cost(b \mapsto a) + cost(y \mapsto x) \;\wedge\; \\ \quad\quad y \mapsto x \in T' \;\wedge\; \\ \quad\quad (tr\_nodes - \{r\} \triangleleft T \triangleright tr\_nodes) \subseteq T')) \end{array}$$

The property is the key result for ensuring the optimality of the greedy strategy in this process. In the next section, we detail the proof of our theorem.

6 On the Theory of Trees

As we have mentioned previously, trees play a central role in the justification of the algorithm; the optimality of the greedy strategy is mainly based on the proof of the theorem used by Cormen et al. [11]. We should now detail the theory of trees and intermediate lemmas required for deriving the theorem. Both the development of the tree identification protocol IEEE 1394 [3] and the development of recursive functions [8] require proofs related to the closure of relations; we apply the same technique for the closure of a function defining a tree.

Let (T, r) be a tree defined by a tree function T and a root r; they satisfy the following axioms atree(r, ND, T).

The closure cl of T^{-1} is the smallest relation containing $\mathsf{id}(ND)$ and stable by application of T^{-1}, that is:

$$
\begin{aligned}
&cl \in ND \leftrightarrow ND \ \wedge \\
&\mathsf{id}(ND) \subseteq cl \ \wedge \\
&(cl; T^{-1}) \subseteq cl \ \wedge \\
&\forall r \cdot (\\
&\qquad r \in ND \leftrightarrow ND \ \wedge \\
&\qquad \mathsf{id}(ND) \subseteq r \ \wedge \\
&\qquad (r; T^{-1}) \subseteq r \ \wedge \\
&\quad \Rightarrow \\
&\qquad cl \subseteq r \\
&)
\end{aligned}
$$

Useful properties on the closure can be derived from those definitions; for instance, the closure is a fix-point; the root r is connected to every node of the connected component; the closure is transitive, etc. We summarize those properties using our notations:

$$
\begin{aligned}
&cl = \mathsf{id}(ND) \cup (cl; T^{-1}); \\
&r \times ND \subseteq cl; \\
&(T^{-1}; cl) \subseteq cl; \\
&(cl; cl) \subseteq cl; \\
&T \cap cl = \emptyset; \\
&cl \cap cl^{-1} \subseteq \mathsf{id}(ND);
\end{aligned}
$$

Figure 1 contains a tree with the edge $b \mapsto a$ and without the edge $y \mapsto x$. The construction of a new tree which contains the edge $y \mapsto x$ but not the edge $b \mapsto a$ is done according to the following points (see the result in Figure 3):

1. remove the edge $b \mapsto a$
2. reverse all edges between y to b (dashed arrows)
3. add the edge $y \mapsto x$

The resulting object seems to be a tree rooted by r. On Figure 2 we observe that the both parts are subtrees rooted by r or b. We should prove these two facts.

Lemma 3 *(Concatenation of two separate trees)*

Let $T_1, r_1, N_1, T_2, r_2, N_2, x$ be such that: $\begin{cases} \mathsf{atree}(r_1, N_1, T_1) \\ \mathsf{atree}(r_2, N_2, T_2 \\ N_1 \cap N_2 = \emptyset \\ N_1 \cup N_2 = ND \\ x \in N_1 \end{cases}$

Then $\mathsf{atree}(r_1, ND, T_1 \cup T_2 \cup \{r_2 \mapsto x\})$.

Proof Sketch: The proof is made up of several steps. A first step proves that the concatenation is a total function over the set $N_1 \cup N_2$. A second one leads to a more technical task and we should prove the inductive property over trees using a splitting of the inductive variable S ($S \cap N_1$ and $S \cap N_2$). □

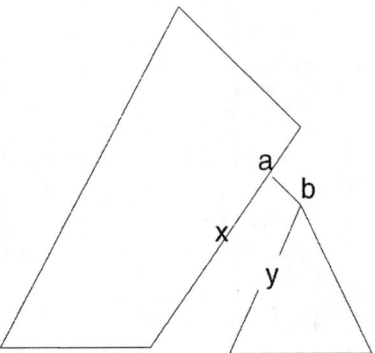

Fig. 1. A spanning tree containing b, a

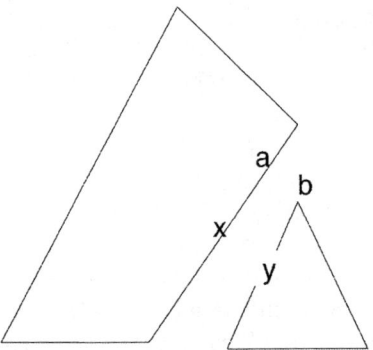

Fig. 2. Two trees

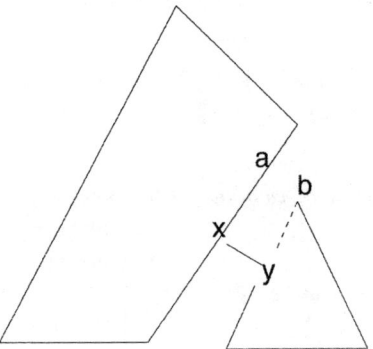

Fig. 3. A spanning tree containing y, x

Lemma 4 *(Subtree property)*
  Let (T, r) be a tree on ND (atree(r, ND, T)) and b a node in ND.

Then $\text{atree}(b, cl[\{b\}], (cl[\{b\}] - \{b\} \triangleleft T))$

Proof Sketch: The main difficulty is related to the inductive part. We must prove that, if $S \subseteq cl[\{b\}]$, $b \in S$ and $(cl[\{b\}] - \{b\} \triangleleft T)^{-1}[S] \subseteq S$, then $cl[\{b\}] \subseteq S$. We use the inductive property on T with the set $S \cup ND - cl[\{b\}]$. □

Lemma 5 *(Complement of a subtree)*
    Let (T, r) be a tree on ND and b a node in ND.
    Then $\text{atree}(r, ND - cl[\{b\}], (cl[\{b\}] \not\triangleleft T))$.

Proof Sketch: We should prove that, if $S \subseteq ND - cl[\{b\}]$, $b \in S$ and $(cl[\{b\}] \not\triangleleft - T)^{-1}[S] \subseteq S$, then $ND - cl[\{b\}] \subseteq S$. A hint is to use the inductive property on T with the set $S \cup cl[\{b\}]$. □

Now, we must characterize the subtree, where we have reversed the edge between y to the root b. Let $subtree(T, b)$ be the subtree of T with b as root (it's $cl[\{b\}] - \{b\} \triangleleft T$). This following function seems to be a good choice:

$$(cl^{-1}[\{y\}] \not\triangleleft subtree(T, b)) \cup (cl^{-1}[\{y\}] \triangleleft subtree(T, b))^{-1}$$

$(cl^{-1}[\{y\}] \triangleleft subtree(T, b))^{-1}$ is exactly all reverse edges. $cl^{-1}[\{y\}]$ is the set of all parents of y.

Lemma 6 *(Reverse from y to b produces a tree)*
    Let b, y such that: $\begin{cases} b \in ND \\ y \in cl[\{b\}] \end{cases}$
    Then $\text{atree}(y, cl[\{b\}], (cl^{-1}[\{y\}] \triangleleft -subtree(T, b)) \cup (cl^{-1}[\{y\}] \triangleleft subtree(T, b))^{-1})$

Proof Sketch: In this case we must use an induction on the tree $cl[\{b\}]$ and sometimes use an second induction with the inductive property in hypothesis.□

Lemma 7 *(Existence of a spanning tree)*
    Let a, b, x, y such that $\begin{cases} b, a \in T \\ y \in cl[\{b\}] \\ x : ND - cl[\{b\}] \end{cases}$
    Then there exists a tree T' such that:
    $\begin{cases} T' \subseteq (T \cup T^{-1} - \{a \mapsto b, b \mapsto a\}) \cup \{y \mapsto x\} \\ \text{atree}(r, ND, T') \\ Cost(T') = Cost(T) - cost(b \mapsto a) + cost(y \mapsto x) \\ y \mapsto x \in T' \\ cl[\{b\}] \not\triangleleft T \subseteq T' \end{cases}$

Proof Sketch: T' is obtained by concatenation of . the two trees identified in the two previous lemmas. Both trees are linked by the edge $y \mapsto x$. □

Finally, we have to prove the existence of an edge $b \mapsto a$ which is safe in the sense of the greedy strategy.

Lemma 8 *(Existence of $b \mapsto a$)*

Let tr_nodes, y such that: $\begin{cases} tr\_nodes \subseteq ND \\ y \in ND - tr\_nodes \\ r \in tr\_nodes \\ \forall S \cdot \begin{pmatrix} S \subseteq ND \land y \in S \land T[S] \subseteq S \\ \Rightarrow \\ S \cap tr\_nodes \neq \emptyset \end{pmatrix} \end{cases}$

Then there exists a and b such that: $\begin{cases} a \in tr\_nodes \\ b \mapsto a \in T \\ b \notin tr\_nodes \\ b \in cl^{-1}[\{y\}] \end{cases}$.

The property of the existence of a minimum spanning tree can now be derived using lemmas and the proof of the property is then completely mechanized.

7 Related Works

The refinement is a concept introduced by Back in his seminal paper [6] and it is developed from the wp semantics defined by E. Dijkstra [12]. Those seminal works inspire notations or methods for developing programs and systems (Morgan[19], Abrial [1,5], Gribomont [14] ...). Temporal aspects are integrated into notations for extending the expressivity of the modeling language (UNITY [9], TLA/TLA$^+$ [17,18]). Clearly, our contribution is based on the B event-based method, which is a proposal for an integrated mechanization of the refinement process and a methodology for developing (reactive, distributed, sequential) systems; the B event-based approach proposes a complete environment supporting the methodological approach. However, as it was pointed out by previous readers, our works require comparisons with development of MST-like systems using a formal framework.

First at all, Cormen et al. [11] present a collection of algorithms which are justified in a pseudo-mathematical language, leaving details of formalization to the reader; we obtain a complete verified version of the algorithm. The paper of Stroetman [21] addresses a similar kind of case study, the *constrained minimal spanning tree* problem, using the ASM [15] notation. Proofs are clearly done in a very classical way using the ASM mathematical framework and no reference to the use of a proof tool is given. Moreover, our case study is related to Prim's algorithm and we used an incremental process, namely the refinement. Although Stroetman mentions a refinement, it is not systematically used for constructing the final solutions. Fraer [13] has developed the Kruskal algorithm using the ¡¡classical¿¿ B method. In fact, the main difference is our use of the B event-based approach for developing events systems. Even if Fraer has proved a part of proof obligations, it is clear that some proof obligations might be found false in the remaining unproved proof obligations. We recall that the goal of the refinement is to produce systems which are completely proved with respect to the target properties. Finally, we can reuse a part of our development for obtaining the Kruskal algorithm.

Our paper illustrates a systematic approach for developing event systems combining the refinement and the proof process supported by a tool; formalizations of concepts like graphs and trees are designed using the proof tool and are checked by the proof tool; they can be reused in other case studies.

8 Conclusion

The development of Prim's algorithm leads us to state and to prove properties over trees. The inductive definition of trees helps in deriving intermediate lemmas asserting that the growing tree converges to the MST, according to the greedy strategy. The resulting algorithm is completely proved and we can partially reuse current developed models to obtain Dijkstra's algorithm or Kruskal's one. The greedy strategy is not always efficient and the optimality of the resulting algorithm is proved by the theorem 24.1. The gain is clear, since we have a mechanized and verified proof of Prim's algorithm. The mechanized proof looks like the proof given in the book of Cormen et al.; we think that it is a proof readable by specialists of graph theory. Moreover, sketches of proofs are directly derived from the mechanized proofs; in fact, the tool provides a way to discover these sketches. We can plan the re-writing of a book like Cormen et al including algorithms, complete developments of each algorithm, proofs of developed algorithms and the possibility to replay the developments to explain how each algorithm is really working. Future work will study other techniques related to algorithmics for graph theory, since only one chapter in the book of Cormen et al. is treated!

References

1. J.-R. Abrial. A formal approach to large software constructions. In J. L. A van de Snepscheut, editor, *Mathematics for Program Construction*, pages 1–20. Springer-Verlag, june 1989. LNCS 375.
2. J.-R. Abrial. Extending B without changing it (for developing distributed systems). In H. Habrias, editor, *1st Conference on the B method*, pages 169–190, November 1996.
3. J.-R. Abrial, D. Cansell, and D. Méry. A mechanically proved and incremental development of the IEEE 1394 Tree Identify Protocol . *Formal Aspects of Computing*, ??(??), 2002. accepted for publication.
4. J.-R. Abrial and L. Mussat. Introducing dynamic constraints in B. In D. Bert, editor, *B'98 :Recent Advances in the Development and Use of the B Method*, volume 1393 of *Lecture Notes in Computer Science*. Springer-Verlag, 1998.
5. J.R. Abrial. *The B Book – Assigning Programs to Meanings*. Cambridge University Press, 1996. ISBN 0-521-49619-5.
6. R. J. R. Back. On correct refinement of programs. *Journal of Computer and System Sciences*, 23(1):49–68, 1979.
7. Dominique Cansell, Ganesh Gopalakrishnan, Mike Jones, Dominique Méry, and Airy Weinzoepflen. Incremental proof of the producer/consumer property for the pci protocol. In D. Bert, editor, *ZB 2002*, Lecture Notes in Computer Science. Springer-Verlag, January 2002.

8. Dominique Cansell and Dominique Méry. Développement de fonctions définies récursivement en b. Technical report, LORIA, 2002.
9. K. M. Chandy and J. Misra. *Parallel Program Design A Foundation*. Addison-Wesley Publishing Company, 1988. ISBN 0-201-05866-9.
10. ClearSy, Aix-en-Provence (F). *Atelier B*, 2002. Version 3.6.
11. Thomas H. Cormen, Charles E. Leiserson, Ronald L. Rivest, and Cliff Stein. *Introduction to Algorithms*. MIT Press and McGraw-Hill, 2001.
12. E. W. Dijkstra. *A Discipline of Programming*. Prentice-Hall, 1976.
13. R. Fraer. Formal Development in B of a Minimum Spanning Tree Algorithm. In H. Habrias, editor, 1st *Conference on the B method*, pages 169–190, November 1996.
14. E. Pascal Gribomont. Concurrency without toil : a systematic method for parallel program design. *Science of Computer Programming*, 21:1–56, 1993.
15. Y. Gurevitch. *Specification and Validation Methods*, chapter "Evolving Algebras 1993: Lipari Guide", pages 9–36. Oxford University Press, 1995. Ed. E. Börger.
16. J. B. Kruskal. On the shortest spanning subtree and the traveling salesman problem. *Proc. Am. Math. Soc.*, 7:48–50, 1956.
17. L. Lamport. A temporal logic of actions. *Transactions On Programming Languages and Systems*, 16(3):872–923, May 1994.
18. Leslie Lamport. *Specifying Systems: The TLA+ Language and Tools for Hardware and Software Engineers*. Addison-Wesley, 2002.
19. C. Morgan. *Programming from Specifications*. Prentice Hall International Series in Computer Science. Prentice Hall, 1990.
20. R. C. Prim. Shortest connection and some generalizations. *Bell Syst. Tech. J.*, 36, 1957.
21. K. Stroetmann. The constrained shortest path problem: A case study in using ASMs. *J. of Universal Computer Science*, 3(4):304–319, 1997.

Using B Refinement to Analyse Compensating Business Processes

Carla Ferreira and Michael Butler

Department of Electronics and Computer Science,
University of Southampton,
Highfield, Southampton SO17IBJ, United Kingdom
{cf,mjb}@ecs.soton.ac.uk

Abstract. This paper explores the refinement of compensating business processes, which are modelled in a heterogeneous notation that combines StAC and B. In our refinement approach, the StAC behavioural and compensation information are explicitly embedded in a B machine. As the resulting machine is standard B one can use the B notion of refinement to prove the refinement of business processes. We also show how the *Atelier-B* prover can help in constructing the gluing invariant.

1 Introduction

StAC (**St**ructured **A**ctivity **C**ompensation) [8] is a formal business process modelling language. The distinctive feature of the language is the concept of compensation, which can be defined as the action taken to correct any errors or when there is a change of plan. The motivation for developing StAC came from a collaboration with IBM concerning the extension of existing notions of compensation for business transactions within the BPBeans enterprise technology [9].

A model of a business process is specified as a set of StAC processes plus a B machine [2]. The StAC processes describe the execution order of the operations and the compensation information, while the B machine describes the state of the system and its basic operations. A model involving compensation does not always give a clear view of the overall properties of the system. Consequently, we need to provide a way of verifying that such a model (involving compensation) satisfies certain properties. We propose to use refinement as a way of verifying StAC specifications, by representing the property as a more abstract system and show that it is refined by the model with compensation.

In this paper we explore a refinement approach where both specification parts – StAC and B – are refined simultaneously. The refinement strategy presented here follows the csp2b approach [5] and combines the StAC processes and the B machine into a new B machine that deals explicitly with compensation and operation ordering. The fact that the resulting machine is standard

B allows the use of the B notion of system refinement to validate refinement between StAC specifications. The contribution of this paper is:

- demonstration of refinement in context of heterogeneous specifications, and
- showing how the *Atelier-B* prover can help in the construction of the gluing invariant.

Also, to simplify the construction of invariant of our case study (the *e-bookstore*) we started by constructing the invariant for a single client and then generalised it to any number of number clients. This strategy made the determination of the invariant simpler, as *Atelier-B* suggested most of the invariant clauses.

The next section describes briefly the StAC language. Section 3 describes our strategy to system refinement. Section 4 presents the abstract and concrete specifications of the *e-bookstore*. In Section 5 we apply our refinement approach to a single client, and Section 6 shows how to extend the results of a single client to a bookstore with any number of clients.

2   StAC Language

The StAC language allows sequential and parallel composition of processes, and the usual process combinators. It also has specific combinators to deal with compensation. Most of the language operators are presented in Table 2. A complete description of StAC, including a formal semantics, can be found in [8,10].

Table 1. StAC Syntax

Process ::=	A	(activity label)
	$null$	(null)
	$b \rightarrow P$	(condition)
	$rec(N)$	(recursion)
	$P;Q$	(sequence)
	$P \parallel Q$	(parallel)
	$\parallel x \in X. P_x$	(generalised parallel)
	$P [] Q$	(choice)
	$[]_{x \in X}. P_x$	(generalised choice)
	$P \div_i Q$	(compensation pair)
	$\boxtimes_i$	(reverse)
	$\boxed{\checkmark}_i$	(accept)
	$J \triangleright i$	(merge)

Each activity label A (in StAC) has an associated activity $\xrightarrow{A}$ (in B) representing an atomic change in the state. The sequential construct is a binary operator that composes two processes, P and Q. In the process $P;Q$, P is executed first. When P completes, Q is executed. There are two forms of concurrent construct, the binary form, $P \parallel Q$, which composes two process in parallel, and the generalized form, $\|\ x{\in}X.P_x$, which models concurrent invocation of multiple instances of a process. The choice $P \,[]\, Q$ selects whichever of P or Q is enabled. Generalised choice extends choice over a set of processes.

A compensation pair $P \div_i Q$ is a grouping of two tasks, where P is the primary task, and Q is the compensation task. When a compensation pair is executed, it only executes the primary task. Once the primary task has completed, the compensation task is remembered on compensation task i[1]. We have to differentiate the compensation tasks as a process may have several simultaneous compensation tasks associated with it. A process decides which task to attach compensation activities to, and individual tasks can be accepted or reversed. The instruction that performs compensation on task i is the reversal operator, $\boxtimes_i$. For example, consider the following process, where A and B are activities:

$$(A \div_i B); \boxtimes_i$$

This process will perform activity A and remember the compensation B on task i. The reversal instruction will then cause compensation activity B to be executed. A sequence of compensation pairs is compensated in reverse order, so the process:

$$(A1 \div_i B1); (A2 \div_i B2); (A3 \div_i B3); \boxtimes_i$$

executes $A1$, $A2$ and $A3$ sequentially and then, because of the reversal on task i, executes $B3$, $B2$, $B1$ sequentially. The acceptance operator, $\boxdot_i$, indicates that currently remembered compensations of task i should be forgotten as they will no longer be required. For example the process:

$$(A1 \div_i B1); \boxdot_i; (A2 \div_i B2); \boxtimes_i$$

performs $A1$ followed by $A2$ and then performs the compensation $B2$. Compensation $B1$ is not performed as it will have been removed by the accept instruction before the reversal. Until now we have only used a single compensation task, but the next example illustrates the use of several compensation tasks:

$$(A1 \div_i B1); (A2 \div_j B2); \boxtimes_i; (A3 \div_j B3); \boxtimes_j$$

This process will invoke $A1$, $A2$ and then the reversal causes compensation $B1$ to be invoked. Compensation $B2$ will not be invoked at this stage as it is on compensation task j and only compensation task i is invoked by the first reversal operator. After the first compensation, activity $A3$ is performed. Reversal is then invoked on compensation task j which causes $B3$ followed by $B2$ to be executed.

An important operator in StAC is the merge operator. The expression $J \triangleright i$, where J is set of indices, merges all compensation tasks belonging to J

---

[1] Informally we can say that the compensation information is maintained as a function that for each task index returns the associated compensation process.

into the compensation task i. When merging compensation tasks, those tasks are merged in parallel. For example the process

$$(A1 \div_i B1); (A2 \div_j B2); (A3 \div_k B3); \{i,j\} \triangleright k$$

initially it executes $A1$, $A2$, and $A3$ and then merges compensation tasks i and j into compensation task k. Joining compensation tasks i and j results in the parallel process $B1 \parallel B2$, which will be put in front of the compensation task k, giving $(B1 \parallel B2); B3$ as the resulting compensation for task k.

2.1 Example: E-bookstore

The *e-bookstore* is a typical example of an e-business. In this example each client defines a limited budget and has an e-basket where the selected books are kept. Every time the client selects a book, the budget is checked to see if it was exceeded, in this case the book is returned to the e-shelf. When the client finishes shopping s/he can either pay or abandon the bookstore, in the later case all selected books have to be returned to the shelf.

The e-bookstore is defined as an infinite set of parallel *Client* processes, over the set $CLIENT$ of all possible on-line clients:

$$Bookstore = \parallel c \in CLIENT \ . \ Client(c)$$

The first activity in process *Client* is **Arrive**. The next process is *ChooseBooks*, followed by a choice between paying the books in the basket or abandon the bookstore without buying any books. If the client chooses to quit, the reversal is invoked causing the return of all books in the client's basket to the shelf. Notice that each client has an independent compensation task c, so the reversal $\boxtimes_c$ will only return the books of client c. If the client decides to pay for his/her order, **Pay** will process the client's card. If the card is rejected, the reversal instruction will be invoked. **Exit** represents the packaging of all books in the client's basket.

$$\begin{aligned}
Client(c) = \ &\textbf{Arrive}(c); \\
&ChooseBooks(c); \\
&(\textbf{Quit}(c); \boxtimes_c \\
&[\!] \\
&\textbf{Pay}(c); (\neg \textbf{accepted}(c) \rightarrow \boxtimes_c)); \\
&\textbf{Exit}(c)
\end{aligned}$$

To select books the client iterates over the selection of individual books until **Checkout** is invoked:

$$ChooseBooks(c) = \textbf{Checkout}(c) \ [\!] \ (ChooseBook(c); \ ChooseBooks(c))$$

In *ChooseBook* a new compensation process is created for each book selected. The new compensation $c1$ is only related to the selected book. Within *ChooseBook* there is a compensation pair, **AddBook** compensated by **ReturnBook**, and the compensation process is only executed if adding that book to the basket exceeds the budget. In this case executing the compensation

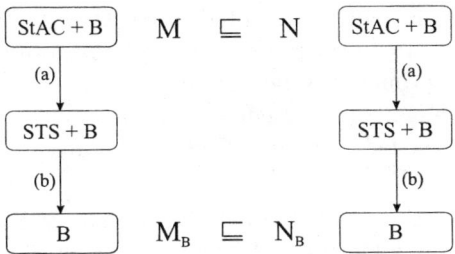

Fig. 1. StAC refinement

task implies returning the book that has just been added to the basket, rather than all books in the basket. If the budget is not exceeded, the compensation is preserved by the merge constructor.

$$ChooseBook(c) = [\!] \, b \in BOOK \, . \, (\mathbf{AddBook}(c,b) \div_{c1} \mathbf{ReturnBook}(c,b));$$
$$(\mathbf{overBudget}(c) \;\rightarrow\; \boxtimes_{c1}); \; c1 \triangleright c$$

3 StAC Refinement

The strategy we have defined for refinement of StAC specifications is described in Fig. 1, and it is based on the csp2b [5] approach. The first step (a) extracts a State Transition Diagram (STS) from a set of StAC processes. The STS describes the execution order of the activities. In the second step (b) the information of the STS is explicitly included in the original B specification. The resulting M_B and N_B specifications are standard B machines that deal explicitly with compensation and operation ordering. With this approach, to prove that N is a refinement of M, it is necessary to build both M_B and N_B machines and prove within the B method that N_B is a refinement of M_B. Because the resulting B machines are standard B we have used *Atelier-B* to generate the proof obligations and its prover to assist in proving those obligations.

In this paper we apply the approach of Fig. 1 to the e-bookstore example, and explain by example the embedding of StAC into B (for a detailed description see [10]).

4 Case Study

The e-bookstore example will be used to show how refinement can be use to verify system properties, and to study the applicability of the proposed refinement strategy. We will start by defining a more abstract specification of the e-bookstore that provides a simplified functionality of the system without using compensation. This specification captures the basic properties that must be preserved by the system. Some of the e-bookstore properties are: a client cannot exceed his/her predefined budget; books are transferred from the shelf to the basket; transactions can be accepted or rejected; if rejected, books are returned to the shelf. Notice that the concrete e-bookstore (Section 2.1) does not always preserve this property. When adding a book to the basket, the system only verifies if the budget was exceeded after the book is already in the basket. If the budget was exceeded, compensation will be invoked restoring the system consistency.

The abstract e-bookstore will be called *Bookstore0*, while the concrete specification will be renamed *Bookstore1*. Ultimately we want to prove that

$$Bookstore0 \sqsubseteq Bookstore1$$

by using the event-B [1] notion of system refinement. In event-B the concrete system may introduce extra operations that refine *skip*.

4.1 Abstract Model

The abstract e-bookstore is defined as an infinite set of parallel *Client0* processes:

$$Bookstore0 = \|_{c \in CLIENT} . Client0(c)$$

Process *Client0* is a sequential process, which starts with activity **Arrive** that initialises the client information. The next activity is **Checkout**, which represents a client choosing simultaneously all the books s/he wants to buy. Activity **Checkout** is followed by a choice between paying for the books or abandoning the bookstore without buying any books. The **Pay** activity verifies whether the card of the client is accepted and if the card is rejected the books in the basket will be returned. In the **Quit** activity the client's basket and its content will be returned to the shelves. The last process **Exit** represents the packaging of the all books in the client's basket.

$$Client0(c) = \mathbf{Arrive}(c)\,;\, \mathbf{Checkout}(c)\,;\, (\mathbf{Pay}(c) \,[\!]\, \mathbf{Quit}(c))\,;\, \mathbf{Exit}(c)$$

The state of the *Bookstore0* machine has two sets: $CLIENT$ that represents all clients that can be on-line simultaneously; and $BOOK$ that represents all books available in the bookstore. Variables *basket*, *budget*, and *accepted* are partial functions that return for each client, respectively, the selected books, the allowed spending money, and the card status. These functions have the same domain, which represents the set of clients accessing on-line the bookstore. The variable *shelf* returns for each book its availability, and *price* contains the price of each book. The first clause in the invariant states that if a client is on-line, then s/he must have a basket, a budget, and a card status. The second clause states that every on-line client must keep his/her basket within the predefined budget.

MACHINE $Bookstore0$
SETS $CLIENT, BOOK$
VARIABLES $basket, budget, accepted, shelf, price$
DEFINITIONS
  $overBudget(c) == \sum b \,.\, (b \in basket(c) \mid price(b)) \geq budget(c)$
  $inBudget(s, c) == \sum b \,.\, (b \in s \mid price(b)) \geq budget(c)$
INVARIANT
  $basket \in CLIENT \pfun \mathcal{F}(BOOK) \wedge$
  $budget \in CLIENT \pfun \mathbb{N}_1 \wedge$
  $accepted \in CLIENT \pfun \mathbf{BOOL} \wedge$
  $shelf \in BOOK \rightarrow \mathbb{N} \wedge$
  $price \in BOOK \rightarrow \mathbb{N}_1 \wedge$
  $dom(basket) = dom(budget) = dom(accepted) \wedge$
  $\forall c \in CLIENT \,.\, c \in dom(basket) \Rightarrow \neg overBudget(c)$

Next, we will describe in detail most of the *Bookstore0* operations. If client c is not already on-line, **Arrive** will initialise the new client's information.

$\mathbf{Arrive}(c : CLIENT)^2 \;\hat{=}\;$
  SELECT $c \notin dom(basket)$ **THEN**
    ANY a **WHERE** $a \in \mathbb{N}_1$ **THEN**
      $basket := basket \cup \{c \mapsto \emptyset\} \;\|$
      $budget := budget \cup \{c \mapsto a\} \;\|$
      $accepted := accepted \cup \{c \mapsto \text{FALSE}\}$
    END
  END

Checkout is enabled for clients that are already on-line, and it chooses nondeterministically a set of books that are within the client's budget and in stock, and puts them in the basket. This operation gives a very simplified view of choosing books in a bookstore, usually a client would want to choose the books him/herself.

$\mathbf{Checkout}(c : CLIENT) \;\hat{=}\;$
  SELECT $c \in dom(basket)$ **THEN**
    ANY $books$ **WHERE** $books \subseteq BOOK \wedge inStock(books) \wedge inBudget(books, c)$
    THEN
      $basket(c) := books \;\|$
      $shelf := shelf \mathbin{\lhd\mkern-14mu-} \lambda(book) \,.\, (book \in books \mid shelf(book) - 1)$
    END
  END

Operation **Pay** describes the payment of the books at a very abstract level. **Pay** performs two actions, verifying the client's card and returning the books in the basket to the shelves, if the card is rejected.

---
[2] The notation $A(x : X) \,\hat{=}\, S$ is an abbreviation for $A(x) \,\hat{=}\, \mathbf{PRE}\, x : X\, \mathbf{THEN}\, S\, \mathbf{END}$.

$\mathbf{Pay}(c : CLIENT) \;\hat{=}$
  $\mathbf{SELECT}\; c \in dom(basket)\; \mathbf{THEN}$
    $\mathbf{CHOICE}$
      $accepted(c) := \mathrm{TRUE}$
    $\mathbf{OR}$
      $accepted(c) := \mathrm{FALSE}\;\|$
      $basket(c) := \emptyset\;\|$
      $shelf := shelf \lhd \lambda(book).(book \in basket(c)\;|\;shelf(book)+1)$
    $\mathbf{END}$
  $\mathbf{END}$

Quit represents the client leaving the bookstore without buying any books, so it just returns the books in the client's basket to the shelf. The last operation **Exit** does not alter any state variable it just assigns the basket to an output variable.

4.2 Concrete Model

The StAC specification of the concrete e-bookstore was already presented in Section 2.1, so we will continue by describing the *Bookstore*1 machine. The main difference between the abstract and concrete specifications is that in the later books are added one at the time, and compensation is used to return books. The state of *Bookstore*1 is similar to the abstract state (each abstract variable v will be replaced by a concrete variable $v1$), so we will only describe the concrete activities that are not identical to their abstract representations. **AddBook** is enabled if c is a on-line client, b is not in the client's basket and it is available. If all conditions are met, b is added to the basket of client c. The operation **ReturnBook** has similar enabling conditions, but instead it removes a book from the client's basket.

$\mathbf{AddBook}(c : CLIENT, b : BOOK) \;\hat{=}$
  $\mathbf{SELECT}\; c \in dom(basket1) \wedge b \notin basket1(c) \wedge shelf1(b) > 0\; \mathbf{THEN}$
    $basket1(c) := basket1(c) \cup \{b\}\;\|$
    $shelf1(b) := shelf1(b) - 1$
  $\mathbf{END}$

Checkout is used in process *ChooseBooks* to exit its recursive definition, so it does not need to perform any explicit action. Operation **Quit** is similar to operation **Checkout**. **Quit** is used to determine which action the client wants to perform, quit the bookstore or pay the books.

$\mathbf{Checkout}(c : CLIENT) \;\hat{=}\; \mathbf{SELECT}\; c \in dom(basket1)\; \mathbf{THEN}\; skip\; \mathbf{END}$

Both *accepted1* and *overBudget* are used as guards of conditional processes, so they are specified in B as boolean expressions (process guards do not change the machine state). Operation **Pay** sets the variable *accepted1*, which is used to trigger the execution of the compensation process when the card is rejected.

$\mathbf{Pay}(c : CLIENT) \;\hat{=}$
  $\mathbf{SELECT}\; c \in dom(basket1)\; \mathbf{THEN}$
    $\mathbf{CHOICE}\; accepted1(c) := \mathrm{TRUE}\; \mathbf{OR}\; accepted1(c) := \mathrm{FALSE}\; \mathbf{END}$
  $\mathbf{END}$

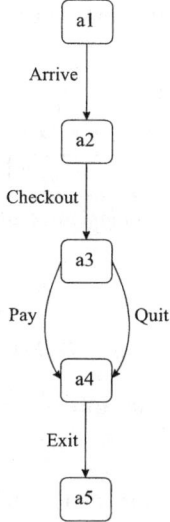

Fig. 2. STS for *Client0*

Operation **Pay** is described as a choice between attributing the value TRUE or FALSE to *accepted1*, depending on the card being accepted or rejected.

5 Dealing with Single Clients

Both abstract and concrete e-bookstore are generalised parallel processes, executing concurrently all clients accessing on-line the bookstore. Therefore, to simplify the determination of the gluing invariant, we decided to deal first with a single client and later extend the invariant for any number of concurrent clients.

5.1 Constructing the $Client0_B$ Machine

To prove that *Client1* refines *Client0* we will follow the steps described in Fig. 1. Fig. 2 shows the STS extracted from process *Client0*. A client must first execute operation **Arrive**, followed by **Checkout**. Next, there are two alternative transitions labelled **Pay** and **Quit**. These transitions are the STS representation for the choice between the activities **Pay** and **Quit**. Last, a client has to execute operation **Exit**.

Next, we need to extend the *Client0* machine to deal the behavioural information of its STS. The extended machine $Client0_B$ has two additional components: a set $STATE$ that contains the states of the STS; and a variable *state* that will keep track of the machine current state.

MACHINE $Client0_B$
SETS
  $BOOK$;
  $\boxed{STATE = \{\, a1,\, a2,\, a3,\, a4,\, a5 \,\}}$
VARIABLES $basket,\ budget,\ accepted,\ shelf,\ price,\ \boxed{state}$
INVARIANT
  $\ldots \wedge$
  $\boxed{state \in STATE}\ \wedge$
  $budget \geq \Sigma(book).(book \in basket \mid price(book))$

The last clause in the invariant guarantees the initial requirement of the client buying within the budget.

Because process *Client0* does not deal with compensation, we only have to extend each operation with a SELECT statement that assures the operation will be executed in the order defined by the STS of Fig. 2. In **Checkout** the SELECT statement enables the operation when the system is on state $a2$. The remaining operations are extended in a similar way.

Checkout $\hat{=}$
  $\boxed{\textbf{SELECT}\ state = a2\ \textbf{THEN}\ state := a3\ \textbf{END}}\ \|$
  ANY $books$ **WHERE** $books \subseteq BOOK \wedge inStock(books) \wedge \neg overBudget(books)$
  THEN
    $basket := books\ \|$
    $shelf := shelf \triangleleft \lambda(book).(book \in books \mid shelf(book) - 1)$
  END

5.2 Constructing the $Client1_B$ Machine

The STS extracted from the process *Client1* is presented in Fig. 3. This STS deals with compensation operators, like compensation pair, merge, and reversal. The operators merge and compensation pair are represented by a single transition labelled with the operator name, as for example the transition from $c2$ to $c3$ labelled **AddBook**$(b) \div_i$ **ReturnBook**(b) (we have changed the compensation task identifier $c1$ and c to $i1$ and i to avoid confusion with the STS concrete states).

The reversal has a more complex representation, because it has to invoke sequentially the activities in the compensation. In the general form, $\boxtimes_j$ is represented by the following STS:

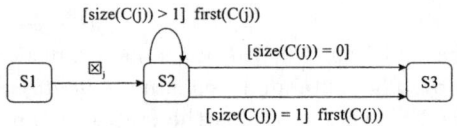

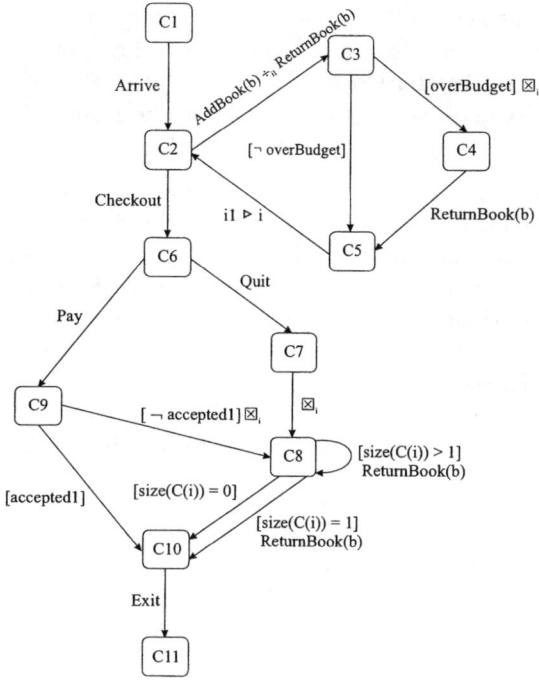

Fig. 3. STS for *Client1*

where $C \in INDEX \to seq(ACTIVITY)$ is the compensation function that for each task index returns a sequence of compensation activities. The occurrence of $\boxtimes_j$ causes the state to evolve from $S1$ to $S2$. In state $S2$ only one of the three transitions will be enabled, depending on the number of compensation activities on task j. If compensation task j is empty, the STS will evolve to $S3$ without performing any action. If the compensation task j has a single compensation activity, that activity will be executed and the STS will evolve to $S3$. Otherwise, the compensation activities will be executed sequentially until a single activity remains. A more systematic approach to the construction of STS from StAC processes is presented in [10].

In the STS of Fig. 3 we can simplify the transitions that occur after the reversal (starting from $c4$ and $c8$). Those transitions can invoke directly the operation **ReturnBook**, because it is the only operation name in both compensation tasks:

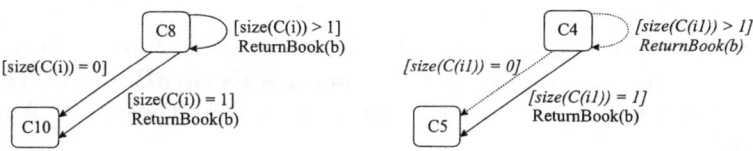

The transitions that occur after state $c4$ can be simplified even further, because we know that the sequence that represents task $i1$ has exactly one element, and that this element is **ReturnBook**. Therefore state $c4$ has a single transition that causes the last book added to the basket to be returned to the shelves. So, all guards and dotted transitions can be ignored.

Now that we have the STS for the *Client1* process, the next step is to embed it into the *Client1* machine. Two new sets and variables where added to the state of *Client1* machine. $STATE1$ has the states used in the STS and $INDEX$ has the compensation task indices used in the e-bookstore processes. Given that **ReturnBook** is the only compensation operation in the system we only need to "store" in compensation function C the value of the argument of **ReturnBook**. When the primary activity of the compensation pair **AddBook**$(b) \div_{i1}$ **ReturnBook**(b) occurs, its necessary to keep the value of b stored so that if a reversal occurs **ReturnBook** will be invoked with the correct argument.

REFINEMENT $Client1_B$
REFINES $Client0_B$
SETS
$STATE1 = \{\, c1,\ c2,\ \cdots,\ c10,\ c11\,\};$
$INDEX = \{\, i,\ i1\,\}$
VARIABLES $basket1,\ budget1,\ accepted1,\ shelf1,\ price1,\ \boxed{state1, C}$
INVARIANT
$\cdots \wedge$
$state1 \in STATE1 \wedge$
$C \in INDEX \rightarrow seq(BOOK)$

The concrete operation **Checkout** is used to exit the recursive process of adding single books to the basket, and it becomes enabled in state $c2$ and its execution causes the state to evolve to $c6$.

Checkout $\,\hat{=}\,$
SELECT $state1 = c2$ **THEN** $state1 := c6$ **END**

The operation **Quit** also does not perform any action besides changing the machine state.

The extensions to operation **AddBook** are more complex because **AddBook** is the primary task of **AddBook**$(b) \div_{i1}$ **ReturnBook**(b). Therefore, the parameter b has to be added to compensation task $i1$ whenever **AddBook** is executed.

AddBook$(b : BOOK) \cong$

| **SELECT** $state1 = c2$ **THEN** |
| $state1 := c3$ ∥ |
| $C(i1) := b \leftarrow C(i1)$ |
| **END** |

∥
SELECT $b \notin basket1 \land shelf1(b) > 0$ **THEN**
$\quad basket1 := basket1 \cup \{b\}$ ∥
$\quad shelf1(b) := shelf1(b) - 1$
END

Operation **ReturnBook** is a compensation action, so it will be invoked after the occurrence of the reversal in states $c4$ and $c8$. In state $c4$ the operation is called after the reversal of task $i1$ and it will enabled if the parameter b is equal to the book on top of $C(i1)^3$. In state $c8$ the operation **ReturnBook** is successively invoked until the compensation task i is empty.

ReturnBook$(b : BOOK) \cong$

| **SELECT** $state1 = c4 \land size(C(i1)) = 1 \land first(C(i1)) = b$ **THEN** |
| $C(i1) := tail(C(i1))$ ∥ |
| $state1 := c5$ |
| **WHERE** $state1 = c8 \land size(C(i)) \geq 1 \land first(C(i)) = b$ **THEN** |
| $C(i) := tail(C(i))$ ∥ |
| **IF** $size(C(i)) = 1$ **THEN** $state1 := c10$ **END** |
| **END** |

∥
SELECT $b \in basket1$ **THEN**
$\quad basket1 := basket1 - \{b\}$ ∥
$\quad shelf1(b) := shelf1(b) + 1$
END

The **Reverse**, **Merge** and **Null** are new operations to be added to $Client1_B$ machine. The **Reverse** may be invoked in three different states, $c3$, $c7$, and $c9$. In each of one this states, and if the its other conditions hold, the reversal will cause the state to evolve.

Reverse$(index : INDEX) \cong$
$\quad$**SELECT** $state1 = c3 \land index = i1 \land overBudget(basket1)$ **THEN** $state1 := c4$
$\quad$**WHEN** $state1 = c7 \land index = i$ **THEN** $state1 := c8$
$\quad$**WHEN** $state1 = c9 \land index = i \land \neg accepted1$ **THEN** $state1 := c8$
$\quad$**END**

The **Merge** is enabled on state $c5$, and if applied with the expected task indices. **Merge** will put compensation task $i1$ on top of task i and clear task $i1$.

$\quad$**Merge**$(index1 : INDEX, index2 : INDEX) \cong$
$\quad\quad$**SELECT** $index1 = i1 \land index2 = i \land state1 = c5$
$\quad\quad$**THEN**
$\quad\quad\quad C := \{index2 \mapsto C(index1)^\frown C(index2), index1 \mapsto []\}$ ∥
$\quad\quad\quad state1 := c2$
$\quad\quad$**END**

---

[3] $C(i1)$ does not need to be a sequence as it contains at most one element.

The **Null** operator is used when the STS has unlabelled guarded transitions. The STS for *Client1* has two empty transitions. In state $c3$ the empty transition occurs when the book added to basket keeps the basket within the budget, no action has to be done and the client may continue choosing books. In state $c9$ the client has decided to pay for the books and his/her card was accepted, again no further action needs to be done and the state evolves to $c10$.

Null $\hat{=}$
   SELECT $state1 = c3 \land \neg overBudget(basket1)$ **THEN** $state1 := c5$
   WHEN $state1 = c9 \land accepted1$ **THEN** $state1 := c10$
   END

5.3 Devising an Abstraction Invariant

We need to devise an invariant I that relates the variables of the abstract system to those of the refined system:

Abstract	basket	budget	accepted	shelf	price	state	
Concrete	basket1	budget1	accepted1	shelf1	price1	state1	C

Atelier-B was used to generate the proofs obligations and to help construct most of the invariant clauses in a incremental way. We will explain next how we used *Atelier-B* to help us deducing the invariant.

When applying the *Atelier-B* automatic prover to a refinement there are two possible outcomes, all proofs are proved (the specification is proven correct) or there are some proof obligations left unproved. When the automatic prover fails to prove an obligation, the user has to examine each failed proof obligation and determine the reason for that failure:

1. The proof obligation is to complex too be done automatically.
2. The proof obligation is impossible to prove with the present invariant clauses.
3. The proof obligation is false, so the refinement claim is invalid.

In the first case, the user has to assist the automatic prover in its demonstration, by using a set of interactive commands provided by *Atelier-B*. In the second case, the invariant is too weak as its clauses are not sufficient to prove all proof obligations. This can be solved by strengthen the invariant with new clauses. With some specifications, the clauses to be added can be extracted almost directly from unproved obligations. This is what we called earlier "*Atelier-B* helping to construct the invariant" which is done by strengthening the invariant with the failed proof obligations. In the last case, either the specification or the refinement (or both) have to change.

Initially we just added the clause C_1 to the invariant, stating that the concrete variables *price1*, *budget1* and *accepted1* are equal to the correspondent abstract variables[4]. This incremental approach of building the invariant is based on [7].

    C_1 $price1 = price \land budget1 = budget \land accepted1 = accepted$

---
[4] This is generated automatically by *Atelier-B* if abstract and concrete variables have the same name.

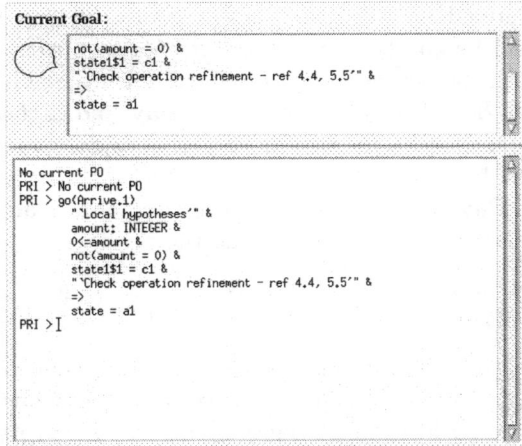

Fig. 4. *Atelier-B* interactive prover

After using the automatic prover on $Client1_B$ with the clause C_1 several proof obligations where left unproved. Fig. 4 shows *Atelier-B* interactive prover applied to one of those unproved obligations, where the user is asked to help the automatic prover discharging the proof obligation *Arrive1*. This proof obligation corresponds directly to $C_{2.1}$. The other unproved obligations corresponded to the remaining clauses of C_2. The clauses C_2 relate the abstract variable *state* to the concrete variable *state1*. Those clauses could be deduced directly from analysing both the abstract and concrete STS. For example, in any of the states $\{c2, c3, c4, c5\}$ the transition *Arrive* has occurred and the only external operation that may occur next is **Checkout**, which are the incoming and outgoing transitions of $a2$.

$C_{2.1}$ $\quad state1 = c1 \quad \Rightarrow \quad state = a1$
$C_{2.2}$ $\quad state1 \in \{c2, c3, c4, c5\} \quad \Rightarrow \quad state = a2$
$C_{2.3}$ $\quad state1 = c6 \quad \Rightarrow \quad state = a3$
$C_{2.4}$ $\quad state1 \in \{c7, c8, c9, c10\} \quad \Rightarrow \quad state = a4$
$C_{2.5}$ $\quad state1 = c11 \quad \Rightarrow \quad state = a5$

The invariant C_3 describes in which states both abstract and concrete baskets have the same books. Clause $C_{3.1}$ was not suggested directly by *Atelier-B*, but it was introduced in the process of interactively proving the proof obligation for **Checkout**. $C_{3.1}$ shows that after **Checkout** both systems baskets are equal, because in the concrete system the client has finished choosing individually each book of *basket1* and in the abstract system a set of books was placed in *basket*. Also in the final state both baskets must have the same books. Clause $C_{3.2}$ was constructed by *Atelier-B* and it shows that if the client's card was accepted, both baskets must have the same books.

$C_{3.1}$ $\quad state1 \in \{c6, c10\} \quad \Rightarrow \quad basket1 = basket$
$C_{3.2}$ $\quad state1 = c9 \wedge accepted1 = TRUE \quad \Rightarrow \quad basket1 = basket$

Clause $C_{4.1}$ was added in order to preserve clause $C_{3.1}$ and it says that the abstract basket will be empty after the occurrence of **Quit**, while the concrete basket still has all the books chosen by the client. The clause $C_{4.2}$ was constructed directly by *Atelier-B* and it states that after **Pay** and if the client's card was not accepted the abstract basket will be empty, because operation **Pay** removes the books from the basket at the same times the card is rejected. The concrete system operation **Pay** just verifies the card maintaining all the books in the basket, as they will be removed by invoking the reversal.

$$C_{4.1} \quad state1 \in \{c7, c8\} \Rightarrow basket = \emptyset$$
$$C_{4.2} \quad state1 = c9 \wedge accepted1 = FALSE \Rightarrow basket = \emptyset$$

The clauses C_5 relates the compensation tasks to the concrete basket. Clauses $C_{5.1}$ and $C_{5.2}$ say that each book on the basket must be in one of the compensation tasks but not in both. The last clause is necessary to prove the two previous clauses.

$$C_{5.1} \quad ran(C(i1)) \cup ran(C(i)) = basket1$$
$$C_{5.2} \quad ran(C(i1)) \cap ran(C(i)) = \emptyset$$
$$C_{5.3} \quad state1 \in \{c2, c6, c7, c8, c9\} \Rightarrow C(i1) = [\,]$$

Although in the abstract system the value of the books in the basket is always within the budget, in the concrete system after the operation **AddBook** the basket may exceed the budget, and as a result the last book added to basket must be returned. The fact that there are states in the concrete machine where the budget is exceeded does not breach the abstract invariant, because this only happens with internal operations that are not visible to the abstract machine. Clause $C_{6.1}$ asserts that before adding a new book to the basket (state $c2$) and after returning the last book added if the budget was exceeded (state $c5$), the basket is within the budget. Clauses $C_{6.2}$ and $C_{6.3}$ where constructed directly by *Atelier-B* after we added clause $C_{6.1}$. This two clauses show that if the budget was exceeded after the occurrence of **AddBook**, this was caused by adding the last book to the basket.

$$C_{6.1} \quad state1 \in \{c2, c5\} \Rightarrow inBudget(basket1)$$
$$C_{6.2} \quad state1 = c3 \wedge overBudget(basket1) \Rightarrow$$
$$\qquad\qquad inBudget(basket1 - \{first(C(i1))\}$$
$$C_{6.3} \quad state1 = c4 \Rightarrow inBudget(basket1 - \{first(C(i1))\})$$

The last clause of the invariant (C_7) says that each book in the abstract and concrete system are either in basket or in the shelf, although the abstract and concrete values may not agree. For example, a book might be in the shelf in the abstract system and in the basket in the concrete system.

$$C_7 \quad \forall book \,.\, book \in BOOK \Rightarrow shelf(book) + inBasket(book, basket) =$$
$$\qquad\qquad shelf1(book) + inBasket(book, basket1)$$

5.4 Proving the Refinement

We have proved using *Atelier-B* that the clause $C_1 \wedge C_2 \wedge \cdots \wedge C_7$ is a gluing invariant for the refinement of $Client0_B$ by $Client1_B$. The total number of proof obligations adds up to 202, of those 171 where automatically proved by the prover of *Atelier-B*. From the remaining 31 proofs, 13 of those where fairly easy to prove by interaction with the prover. For the remaining 18 unproved obligations it was necessary to define a user rule file to assist the automatic prover. The user rules are necessary when the prover rule database does not have rules to deal with a specific type of proof. Most of our rules where concerned with sequences or lambda expressions, for which the rule database had a very limited set of rules. Even with the user rules 4 proofs where difficult and time consuming.

Proving the refinement for a single client was very useful, because it allowed us to develop a gluing invariant in a incremental way. The *Atelier-B* prover constructed most of the invariant clauses and by attempting to prove proof obligations for weak gluing invariants we have constructed some invariant clauses needed to prove other proof obligations.

6 Dealing with Multiple Clients

In this section we show how to generalise the gluing invariant for a single client to deal with any number of concurrent clients.

6.1 Alterations on Both B Machines

In the machine and refinement the variables associated to the client where extended to partial functions, where the domain of those functions describe the clients currently on-line.

MACHINE $Bookstore0_B$ **SETS** $\quad CLIENT$ $\quad BOOK$ $\quad STATE = \{\,a1, a2, a3, a4, a5\,\}$ ... **INVARIANT** $\quad basket \in CLIENT \nrightarrow \mathcal{F}(BOOK) \wedge$ $\quad budget \in CLIENT \nrightarrow \mathbb{N}_1 \wedge$ $\quad accepted \in CLIENT \nrightarrow \textbf{BOOL} \wedge$ $\quad state \in CLIENT \nrightarrow STATE \wedge$ $\quad shelf \in BOOK \rightarrow \mathbb{N} \wedge$ $\quad price \in BOOK \rightarrow \mathbb{N}_1$	**REFINEMENT** $Bookstore1_B$ **REFINES** $Bookstore0_B$ **SETS** $\quad STATE1 = \{\,c1, c2, \cdots, c10, c11\,\}$ $\quad INDEX = \{\,i, i1\,\}$ ... **INVARIANT** $\quad basket1 \in CLIENT \nrightarrow \mathcal{F}(BOOK) \wedge$ $\quad budget1 \in CLIENT \nrightarrow \mathbb{N}_1 \wedge$ $\quad accepted1 \in CLIENT \nrightarrow \textbf{BOOL} \wedge$ $\quad state1 \in CLIENT \nrightarrow STATE1 \wedge$ $\quad C \in CLIENT \nrightarrow (INDEX \rightarrow seq(BOOK)) \wedge$ $\quad shelf1 \in BOOK \rightarrow \mathbb{N} \wedge$ $\quad price1 \in BOOK \rightarrow \mathbb{N}_1$

Each operation of the abstract and concrete system will have an extra parameter, the client that is invoking the operation.

6.2 Alterations on the Abstraction Invariant

The gluing invariant I_B for the bookstore refinement will be similar to the client invariant I_C. Although the invariant I_B needs an extra clause asserting that the domains of the variables related to the bookstore clients are the same. The last conjunction of the clause B_0 states that the set of clients on-line in the abstract and concrete system must be the same.

$$B_0 \quad dom(basket1) = dom(budget1) = dom(accepted1) = dom(state1)$$
$$= dom(thread1) \wedge dom(basket1) = dom(basket)$$

As we said I_B is similar to I_C and, with the exception of B_0, all the clauses of I_B where obtained by generalising each I_C clause for a set of clients. The gluing invariant I_B is defined as the following conjunction:

$$I_B = B_0 \wedge C_1 \wedge B_2 \wedge \cdots \wedge B_7$$

The clause C_1 stays unaltered, generalising it over a set of clients does not alter the original clause. We will describe in more detail the clauses $B_{4.1}$ and B_7.

Clause $B_{4.1}$ universally quantify clause $C_{4.1}$ over the set of on-line clients. A client is on-line if it is defined for the any of the client's partial functions. In $B_{4.1}$ we used function $state1$.

$$B_{4.1} \quad \forall\, client\,.\ client \in dom(state1) \wedge$$
$$state1(client) \in \{c7, c8\} \;\Rightarrow\; basket(client) = \emptyset$$

Clause B_7 states the same property of clause C_7, that a book can either in the shelf or in the basket, although in the former clause one has to consider that a book might be in baskets of several clients.

$$B_7 \quad \forall\, book\,.\ book \in BOOK \;\Rightarrow\; shelf(book) + booksSold(book, basket) =$$
$$shelf1(book) + booksSold(book, basket1)$$

6.3 Proving the Refinement

The fact that almost every clause of the invariant has a universal quantification increased considerably the complexity of the proof obligations. The total number of proofs amounts to 250 and only 93 where automatically proved by the *Atelier-B* prover. From the remaining 157 proofs, 100 of those where time consuming but not difficult because we replicated the strategies used in the refinement of the single client system. Of the other 57 proofs, 45 where fairly difficult, and the last 12 proof obligations where extensive and difficult to prove. Nevertheless, all were proved.

7 Conclusions

In this paper we have showed how refinement can be used to analyse business processes with compensation. A model involving compensation may not give a clear view of the overall properties of the system. Moreover, as we have seen in the e-bookstore example, such a model may temporarily falsify those properties, and then use the compensation information to restore the system consistency.

We have explored an approach to the refinement of StAC specifications, where both StAC processes and B machine are refined simultaneously. This approach combines the both parts of a business process specification into a B machine that deals explicitly with compensation tasks and the ordering of operations. We have used *Atelier-B* to help constructing the refinement invariant, and also to prove the necessary proof obligations.

Our initial experience of applying our refinement approach to the bookstore example was that it is a difficult process. That view changed when we tried to prove the refinement of a single client, as most of the invariant clauses where constructed by the *Atelier-B* prover and it was possible to check informally if the proof obligations where provable or not. We can conclude that the difficulty level of applying the StAC refinement strategy depends significantly on the system under study. The difficulty level was reasonable for the single client system, but too high for the bookstore system. The complexity in proving the invariant for the bookstore refinement was the result of the universal quantification on the invariant clauses. Those clauses where necessary because the bookstore was defined as a generalised parallel process. Considering that for the case study presented here, the invariant for the refinement of a single process was easily extended to a set of concurrent processes, possibly this tactic could be used for other systems defined as generalised parallel processes.

Although the approach we used in employing *Atelier-B* to construct the refinement invariant was fairly systematic, some reasoning is needed to deduce new obligations required by the invariant. It has to be investigated whether this approach could be automated, as found, for example, the automatic invariant generation provided by STeP [4].

An alternative to refinement would be to develop a model checker for StAC processes. A model checker would allow the verification of several types of properties, as for example invariants and assertions. Within this line of work, the paper [3] describes the use of both SPIN and STeP to verify StAC processes.

References

1. J.-R. Abrial and L. Mussat. Introducing dynamic constraints in B. In *Recent Advances in the Development and Use of the B Method (B'98)*, volume 1393. Springer-Verlag, 1998.
2. J.R. Abrial. *The B-Book: Assigning Programs to Meanings*. Cambridge University Press, 1996.
3. J. Augusto and M. Butler. Some observations about using SPIN and STeP to verify StAC specifications. Technical report, Department of Electronics and Computer Science, University of Southampton, October 2002.
4. N. Bjorner, A. Browne, and Z. Manna. Automatic generation of invariants and intermediate assertions. *Theoretical Computer Science*, 173(1):49–87, 1997.

5. M. Butler. csp2B: A practical approach to combining CSP and B. *Formal Aspects of Computing*, 12:182–198, 2000.
6. M. Butler. On the use of data refinement in the development of secure communications systems. *Formal Aspects of Computing*, To appear, 2002.
7. M. Butler. A system-based approach to the formal development of embedded controllers for a railway. *Design Automation for Embedded Systems*, 6(4):355–366, 2002.
8. M. Butler and C. Ferreira. A process compensation language. In *Integrated Formal Methods(IFM'2000)*, volume 1945 of *LNCS*, pages 61 – 76. Springer-Verlag, 2000.
9. M. Chessell, D. Vines, C. Griffin, M. Butler, C. Ferreira, and P. Henderson. Extending the concept of transaction compensation. *IBM Systems Journal*, 41(4):743–758, 2002.
10. C. Ferreira. *Precise Modelling of Business Processes with Compensation*. PhD thesis, Department of Electronics and Computer Science, University of Southampton, 2002.

A Formal Specification in B of a Medical Decision Support System

Christine Poerschke, David E. Lightfoot, and John L. Nealon

Department of Computing, Oxford Brookes University, Oxford, OX33 1HX, UK
{cpoerschke, delightfoot, jlnealon}@brookes.ac.uk

Abstract. We have used the B notation to formally specify an existing medical decision support system. The system runs on a palmtop computer and helps patients with insulin-dependent diabetes decide on a dose of insulin to inject. Using extracts we both qualitatively and quantitatively describe the formal specification and compare it with the existing C/C++ implementation of the system. We also report our experience of the specification process, the benefits derived from and the challenges presented by it. We conclude that the use of an abstract machine notation such as B for the formal specification and documentation of a knowledge-based medical decision support system is both feasible and viable.

This paper is divided into five sections. Section 1 briefly describes the actual application that was specified as well as the context in which it is used. Given this background, Section 2 looks at the motivations behind and the aims of this project. Section 3 concerns the actual specification, whilst Section 4 considers the process of producing the specification. The final section summarises and concludes the paper.

1 Background

Diabetes is a disease currently affecting some two percent of the population with the number of people with diabetes forecast to double worldwide by 2010 to 221 million [1]. Diabetes mellitus is characterised by a partial or complete inability to control blood glucose levels due to a lack of the hormone insulin and/or insulin resistance. In the long-term, people with diabetes are two to four times more likely to suffer from cardiovascular diseases and complications such as blindness, renal failure and nerve damage. However, recent large scale studies such as the American Diabetes Control and Complications Trial (DCCT) [2] and the United Kingdom Prospective Diabetes Study (UKPDS) [3] have demonstrated that good glycaemic (blood glucose) control can significantly reduce the risk of long-term complications in both Type-1 (early onset) and Type-2 (late onset) diabetes respectively. These findings have changed both medical and public attitudes towards diabetes management; with good glycaemic control no longer being seen as merely desirable but as essential outcomes. However, in practice, achieving and maintaining good control is difficult due to a number of factors and it has been suggested that information technology can play a useful part in the process.

The Department of Computing at Oxford Brookes University and the Diabetes Trials Unit at Oxford University have jointly developed a handheld decision support system for use by patients with insulin-dependent diabetes [4] [5]. The latest version of the system is based on a Handspring Visor device running the Palm OS operating system. It was evaluated in a clinical study with 8 patients who during a 7-week period used the device as part of their everyday life. Although all patients had no or moderate computer experience, they enjoyed using the device and found it easy to operate, reliable and not time consuming. Following this successful proof of concept study we are currently preparing for a larger clinical trial to assess the system's potential to improve glycaemic control and its use in routine clinical practice.

2 Motivation

In this work we have formally specified the main parts of the Insulin Advisor system introduced above. This specification work was independent of the actual system development work but was motivated by and considered worthwhile for the following reasons.

2.1 Safety-Critical Nature of the Application

The Insulin Advisor provides decision support by suggesting, to the user i.e. the patient, a dose of insulin to inject. The algorithms used to derive this dose are based on published clinical guidelines and require patient-specific information entered by the patient's physician as well as current and past information entered by the patient. Upon request, the system can provide a short explanation of its dose advice. The patient may or may not follow the system's advice and hence always enters the dose they actually decided to inject themselves with.

Although it is ultimately the patient who decides upon each dose, one might consider this type of system to be safety-critical, particularly in view of the system's use in normal everyday life and the potential consequences of way too low or way too high insulin doses being taken. Too little insulin leads to hyperglycaemia (unacceptably high blood glucose levels), which in the long-term leads to the serious complications described above. On the other hand, too much insulin causes hypoglycaemia (unacceptably low blood glucose levels) symptoms of which include sweating and increasing mental confusion leading to coma. Of course, people with diabetes are trained to recognise the symptoms and counteract the effects of hypoglycaemia, but they are not always able to do so.

We are hence dealing with a safety-critical system with multiple, related and possibly missing inputs which are processed according to complex clinical guidelines, all system characteristics which make a formal specification of what the system does valuable.

2.2 Complexity of the Knowledge Embedded in the System

Clearly, the knowledge embedded in the Insulin Advisor system i.e. the rules and concepts it uses to generate advice are not trivial. Another aim of this research was to explore the possibility of using a formal specification in B as a form of knowledge representation and documentation.

Items of information and the relationships between them. Items of information preset by the patient's physician or entered by the patient form a crucial part of the overall decision support system. Whilst the type and meaning of each individual item is fairly easily documented in natural language and encoded in a program, the relationships that exist between individual items of information are not. Examples of this are the timestamps of glucose and meal events and the *is_preprandial_to* relationship between glucose and meal events. However, given the availability of a formal notation such as B with user defined types, sets, functions, relations and quantifiers, the expression and thus explicit documentation of such relationships becomes much more practical. The formal specification of the *is_preprandial_to* relation can be found in Fig. 3.

Safety-related properties. Relationships between items of information include safety-related properties like for example the fact that a dose change made by the system must result in a dose that does not exceed the relevant minimum and maximum limits set by the patient's physician.

Knowledge documentation. It was hoped that the project would produce a complete and unambiguous formal specification of the system, a form of documentation that is concise, authoritative and implementation-independent. It was also thought that the process of developing the specification might potentially uncover ambiguities and/or inconsistencies within the existing documentation and implementations.

2.3 Feasibility and Viability of a Formal Specification

Finally, using our existing system as a case study, the project hoped to explore the feasibility and viability of producing a formal specification of a future or an existing medical computer system. A literature search for publications describing the use of formal methods, in particular the Z notation and the B method, in the context of medical computer systems, identified the following work in this area.

In 1987 Todd [6] presents a model-based diagnostic program, in 1995 Todd and Ledger [7] describe a computer-based flowcharting system for clinical protocols, and in 1999 Todd and Andrews [8] present a formal specification of an electrocardiogram compressor. In 1996 Kasurinen and Sere [9] describe a medical computer system used to train the reaction abilities of patients with severe brain damage. In the same year, the work of Groenboom et al [10] concerns the formal specification of knowledge in anaesthesiology and the development of a support system for anesthesists. Finally, between 1990 and 1997 Jacky and colleagues [11] [12] [13] [14] [15] describe the development of a control system for a clinical cyclotron for radiation therapy. With the exception of [10] all the above projects made use of the Z notation.

Prior to the start of this project the authors have had some experience of using both the Z notation and the B method. Given its local availability and the B-Toolkit's support for writing and checking of specifications as well as its proof obligation generation and machine-assisted proof facilities, the B method was chosen for this project. No other specification notations or tools were investigated or considered.

3 The Specification

3.1 The InsulinAdvisor Machine

The overall final specification is composed of fifteen machines as shown in Fig. 1.

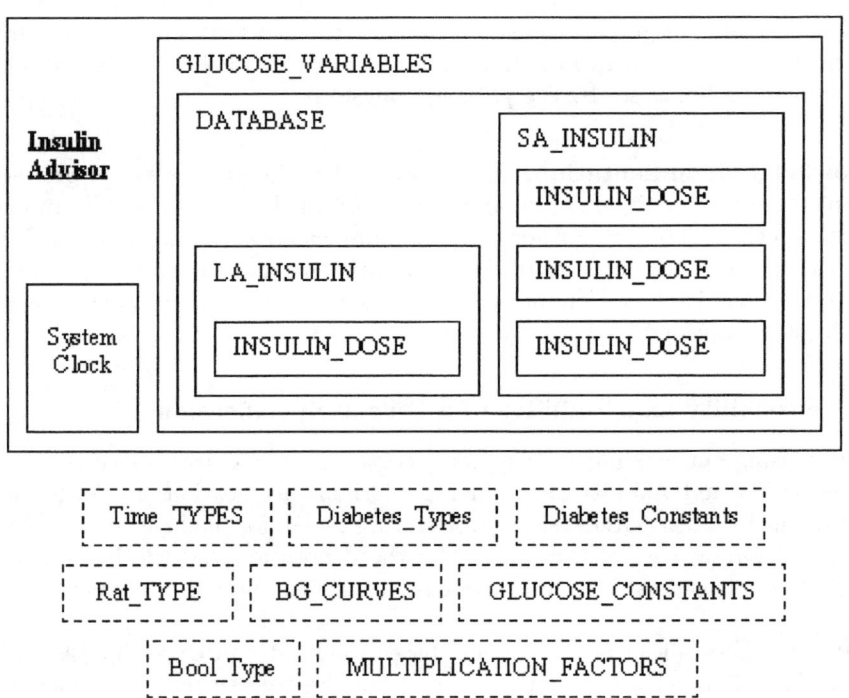

Fig. 1. The specification's machines: solid line = INCLUDES, dashed line = SEES

The seven operations of the top level machine (InsulinAdvisor.mch) mirror the data entry items of the actual Insulin Advisor's user interface.

EnterGlucoseEvent (current_BG) $\triangleq$
PRE current_BG $\in$ **GLUCOSE_READING**

Having pricked one of their fingers and used the drop of blood and their glucose meter to measure the capillary blood glucose concentration, patients use the calculator-style glucose entry screen of the Insulin Advisor to record this glucose reading. The above operation models this data entry screen.

EnterMealEvent (MealTime, MealSize) $\triangleq$
PRE MealTime $\in$ **MEAL_TIME** $\wedge$ MealSize $\in$ **MEAL_SIZE**

EnterExerciseEvent (ExerciseLevel) $\triangleq$
PRE ExerciseLevel $\in$ **EXERCISE_LEVEL** $\wedge$ MealEvents $\neq \emptyset$

EnterHealthEvent (HealthStatus) $\triangleq$
PRE HealthStatus $\in$ **HEALTH_STATUS**

Lifestyle-related factors such as the meal type and size, the anticipated amount of exercise after the meal and the current state of health are entered as descriptive quantities selected from a list. As denoted by the *MealEvents* $\neq \emptyset$ precondition an exercise event can only be entered after at least one meal event has been entered. This is so because an exercise event is in fact an amount of exercise planned for after a meal and clearly one cannot make plans for after something that doesn't exist.

UsualDose, SuggestedDose $\leftarrow$ **CalculateAdvisedDose (InsulinType)**
$\triangleq$
PRE InsulinType $\in$ **INSULIN_TYPE** $\wedge$ recent_meal_available(now)

A patient can request insulin dose advice by selecting, on the insulin screen, an insulin from a list. The *recent_meal_available(now)* precondition states that insulin advice can only be requested and provided if a meal event has recently been entered.

EnterInsulinEvent (TakenDose) $\triangleq$
PRE TakenDose $\in$ **DOSE**
$\wedge$
advice_still_valid_at(most_recent(AdviceEvents), now)
$\wedge$
not(new_info_available=TRUE)

Having taken notice of the system's advice and decided upon the dose of insulin to inject, patients record the dose of insulin that they actually took on the insulin screen. The *advice_still_valid_at(most_recent(AdviceEvents), now)* precondition states that the insulin screen can only be used whilst the most recent dose advice provided by the system is still valid i.e. it's not yet too old. The *not(new_info_available = TRUE)* precondition states that as soon as new information is entered, any previous advice becomes out of date since it does not consider the new piece of information.

EnterHypoEvent (SeverityGrade, HoursAgo) $\triangleq$
PRE SeverityGrade $\in$ **HYPO_SEVERITY** $\wedge$
 HoursAgo $\in \mathbb{N} \wedge$ HoursAgo $\in$ **0..99**

When recording a hypoglycaemic episode (hypo), patients, by selecting from a list, grade its severity as 'transient' (Grade 1), 'interfered with normal life' (Grade 2) or 'required third party assistance' (Grade 3). Due to their debilitating symptoms hypos are usually entered after they occurred and again using a calculator-style screen patients enter how many hours ago they experienced the hypo. The precondition *HoursAgo* $\in$ *0..99* indicates how the user interface should constrain the value of this data item.

3.2 The Diabetes_Types Machine

As an example, Fig. 2 shows the full Diabetes_Types machine.

3.3 The DATABASE Machine

The DATABASE machine (i) stores all the items of information entered by the patient and (ii) models and maintains certain relationships between those items. Each of the operations in the InsulinAdvisor machine, amongst other things, references a corresponding operation in the DATABASE machine. The extract in Fig. 3 illustrates the principles.

When the *EnterGlucoseEvent* operation references the *AddGlucoseEvent* operation it provides the glucose reading entered by the patient and the current system time as parameters. *AddGlucoseEvent* then adds a new member to the *GlucoseEvents* set and updates the *datetime, glucose_value* and *is_preprandial_to* relationships so as to maintain the invariant properties. Where certain similar but complex expressions are used repeatedly, predicates such as *correct_meal_to_glucose_distance(m, g)* are defined. *upto_from_to(d, f, t)* in turn is a predicate defined in the Time_TYPES machine and in it *d, f* and *t* of the user-defined types DURATION and TIME.

Overall, the DATABASE machine contains 28 variables. Of these 7 variables (e.g. *GlucoseEvents*) model the events themselves, 12 (e.g. *glucose_value*) model events' attributes, 8 (e.g. *is_preprandial_to*) model relationships between different types of events and 1, namely *new_event*, is strictly modelling-independent. Including type-determining invariants such as *GlucoseEvents* $\in \mathbb{P}(EVENT)$, the

```
MACHINE  Diabetes_Types

SEES  Rat_TYPE  /* Provides a type RAT for rational numbers. */

SETS
      GLUCOSE_READING;

      GLUCOSE_LEVEL = { VERY_LOW, LOW, IN_RANGE,
                       HIGH, VERY_HIGH};

      MEAL_TIME = {BREAKFAST, LUNCH, DINNER, BEDTIME, SNACK};

      MEAL_SIZE = { NOTHING_MEAL, LIGHT_MEAL,
                    NORMAL_MEAL, LARGE_MEAL};

      EXERCISE_LEVEL = { NONE_EXERCISE, MINIMAL_EXERCISE,
                         NORMAL_EXERCISE, HEAVY_EXERCISE};

      HEALTH_STATUS = { WELL_HEALTH, UNWELL_HEALTH,
                        VERYSICK_HEALTH};

      INSULIN_TYPE = {SHORT_ACTING, LONG_ACTING};

      HYPO_SEVERITY = {GRADE_1, GRADE_2, GRADE_3}

PROPERTIES  GLUCOSE_READING = RAT − NEGATIVE

END
```

Fig. 2. Diabetes_Types machine (without annotations)

DATABASE machine contains 44 AND-ed predicates over its variables, 9 of which include universal and/or existential quantifiers. However, having said all that, the DATABASE machine is by far the most complex machine in this specification. Related metrics which also compare this specification and an implementation of the system can be found in Section 3.6 of this paper.

3.4 Modelling Patient-Specific Settings

With the exception of the insulin doses themselves and a glucose-related target value, all patient-specific settings are determined by and must only be changed by the patient's physician and are hence, within this specification, modelled as constants. An example of a patient-specific constant is the *GlucoseLevel* ∈ $GLUCOSE\_READING \rightarrow GLUCOSE\_LEVEL$ abstraction function defined in the GLUCOSE_CONSTANTS machine.

MACHINE DATABASE

SETS EVENT

PROPERTIES EVENT = ℕ

DEFINITIONS

correct_meal_to_glucose_distance(m, g) $\triangleq$ upto_from_to(
kMaxDuration_Meal_to_GlucoseEntry, datetime(m), datetime(g))
;
AllEvents $\triangleq$ GlucoseEvents ∪ MealEvents ∪ ExerciseEvents ∪
HealthEvents ∪ InsulinEvents ∪ HypoEvents ∪ AdviceEvents

INVARIANT

GlucoseEvents ∈ ℙ(EVENT)
∧
datetime ∈ AllEvents → TIME
∧
glucose_value ∈ GlucoseEvents → GLUCOSE_READING
∧
is_preprandial_to ∈ GlucoseEvents ↔ MealEvents
∧
is_preprandial_to = { glucose, meal | glucose, meal ∈ GlucoseEvents × MealEvents
   ∧
   (correct_glucose_to_meal_distance(glucose, meal)
   ∨
   correct_meal_to_glucose_distance(meal, glucose)) }
∧
new_event ∈ EVENT ∧ new_event ∉ AllEvents

OPERATIONS

AddGlucoseEvent (value, timestamp) $\triangleq$
PRE value ∈ GLUCOSE_READING ∧ timestamp ∈ TIME
THEN
   GlucoseEvents := GlucoseEvents ∪ {new_event} ∥ new_event := new_event + 1
   ∥
   datetime := datetime ∪ {new_event ↦ timestamp}
   ∥
   glucose_value := glucose_value ∪ {new_event ↦ value}
   ∥
   is_preprandial_to := is_preprandial_to ∪ {new_event} × { meal |
   meal ∈ MealEvents ∧ correct_meal_to_glucose_distance(meal, new_event) }
END

Fig. 3. Extract from the DATABASE machine

3.5 Insulin Doses, Insulin Dose Advice, and Safety Parameters

It is the INSULIN_DOSE machine with its ten parameters, that models the characteristics of a generic insulin dose. As shown in Fig. 1, the LA_INSULIN and SA_INSULIN machines instantiate copies of this machine and thus model the concrete LONG_ACTING and SHORT_ACTING insulin components of an insulin regimen. A typical such regimen consists of three doses of short-acting insulin taken before each main meal (breakfast, lunch, dinner) and doses of long-acting insulin taken at bedtime and possibly also at breakfast time. Unlike other systems, the Insulin Advisor does not require patients to eat and take insulin at fixed predetermined times, something that increases patients' quality of life as well as the system's complexity.

Dose-by-dose insulin advice is generated and recorded by the DATABASE's *Add_SHORTACTING_AdviceEvent* and *Add_LONGACTING_AdviceEvent* operations which amongst others make use of the MULTIPLICATION_FACTORS and INSULIN_DOSE machines. Between them the GLUCOSE_CONSTANTS, GLUCOSE_VARIABLES, BG_CURVES and INSULIN_DOSE machines model the patient's blood glucose control and thus assess and optimise the effectiveness of each insulin dose. For safety reasons, permanent dose changes as opposed to one-off dose adjustments are constrained by four of the INSULIN_DOSE machine's ten parameters: absolute minimum and maximum dose limits and relative limits that proportionate to the current insulin dose constrain the magnitude of any one dose change. The extract given in Fig. 4 illustrates this.

3.6 Specification and Implementation Size and Complexity

This section provides some metrics which we believe help quantify the size and complexity of this formal specification and the previously existing C/C++ implementation of the system.

The figures in Table 2 describe the previously existing C/C++ implementation for the Palm OS handheld platform. This implementation included a few features not modelled in this specification (see Section 4) and accordingly adjusted the implementation is approximately 10400 lines of annotated code long. The previous non-C/C++ [4] as well as the latest C/C++ [5] version of the system were largely specified using natural language. Work on both systems formed part of two successive PhD projects and it is thus difficult to provide meaningful person-time estimates of the effort required for their specification and development.

During the Insulin Advisor pilot study [5] each patient entered about 145 events per week. However, these included a small number of notebook entries, information of interest to the patient's physician but not used by the Insulin Advisor itself and hence not modelled in this specification. Furthermore, the existing implementation used a different way of recording advice events. The correspondingly adjusted number of events generated by a patient i.e. the size of the *AllEvents* set in the DATABASE machine (Fig. 3) would be about 170 events per week.

Table 1. Metrics describing the formal specification in B

Machine name	Pages[a] with annotations	Pages[a] without annotations[b]	Parameters, Constants, Variables	Constraints, Properties, Invariants	Operations	Definitions	Proof obligations total[c]	Proof obligations non-trivial[d]	Proof obligations undischarged[e]
BG_CURVES	3	2	5	14	0	0	1	1	1
Bool_TYPE	1	1	0	0	0	0	N/A	N/A	N/A
DATABASE	16	11	28	45	8	10	5558	2485	2485[f]
Diabetes_Constants	2	1	7	14	0	0	4	4	0
Diabetes_Types	2	1	0	1	0	0	1	1	1
GLUCOSE_CONSTANTS	2	2	12	29	0	0	16	16	13
GLUCOSE_VARIABLES	9	7	5	6	2	3	962	186	117
INSULIN_DOSE	14	9	22	34	6	9	201	76	66[g]
InsulinAdvisor	6	5	1	1	7	2	1015	780	776
LA_INSULIN	2	2	11	22	0	6	23	13	0
MULTIPLICATION_FACTOR	4	2	5	18	0	0	22	22	22
Rat_TYPE	4	3	16	23	0	49	1	1	1
SA_INSULIN	4	3	11	22	4	5	75	53	33
SystemClock	1	1	1	1	1	0	2	1	0
Time_TYPES	3	1	6	9	0	15	3	3	3

[a] Pages of A4 required to display the document produced by the B-Toolkit's DocumentMarkUp facility and LaTex.
[b] Annotations are natural language summaries of the meaning of individual parts of a machine. If appropriate, annotations are also used to justify particular specification details (e.g. use of a partial vs. total function).
[c] The proof obligations (POs) generated by the POGenerator Setting 'generate all obligations' was selected.
[d] The POs generated when the POGenerator Setting 'generate non-trivial obligations' and a 'Max Generated Hypotheses' (MGH) value of 300 was selected.
[e] The (non-trivial) POs that the AutoProver could not discharge without user theory and with a MGH value of normally 300.
[f] Even with the B platform capacity increased to 134,217,726 (the maximum possible value for our installation) and an MGH value of 1 the AutoProver could not complete any proofs.
[g] Due to the B platform capacity limits, the proofs for this machine could only be run with a MGH value of 79.

> **MACHINE** INSULIN_DOSE (MIN_Dose, USUAL_Dose0, MAX_Dose, percentage_decrease, percentage_increase, ...)
>
> **INVARIANT**
> USUAL_Dose ∈ DOSE ∧
> MIN_Dose ≤ USUAL_Dose ∧ USUAL_Dose ≤ MAX_Dose
> ∧
> MaxDecrement ∈ DOSE ∧ MaxDecrement = MaxDecrementDef(
> USUAL_Dose, percentage_decrease, MIN_Dose)
> ∧
> MaxIncrement ∈ DOSE ∧ MaxIncrement = MaxIncrementDef(
> USUAL_Dose, percentage_increase, MAX_Dose)
> ∧
> Updated_Dose ∈ RAT → DOSE
> ∧
> ∀ rr . (rr ∈ RAT
> ⇒
> (MIN_Dose ≤ Updated_Dose(rr) ∧ Updated_Dose(rr) ≤ MAX_Dose))
> ∧
> ∀ rr . (rr ∈ RAT
> ⇒
> (Updated_Dose(rr) < USUAL_Dose
> ⇒
> USUAL_Dose − Updated_Dose(rr) ≤ MaxDecrement)
> ∧
> (Updated_Dose(rr) > USUAL_Dose
> ⇒
> Updated_Dose(rr) − USUAL_Dose ≤ MaxIncrement))

Fig. 4. Extract from the INSULIN_DOSE machine

Table 2. Metrics describing the existing C/C++ implementation

Number of header files: 39	1500 lines of annotated code
Number of source files: 30	11300 lines of annotated code
Number of routines: 257	

4 The Specification Process

As mentioned previously, this project concerned the formal specification of an existing as opposed to a 'future' computer system. Besides the existing C/C++ implementation work and the B specification development were both carried out by one and the same person. It is in this context that the experiences reported below should be viewed.

Given the size and complexity of the system it was clear that the overall specification would be a **combination of several smaller machines**. However, the number of and the relationships between the different machines varied throughout the specification process i.e. could not be determined up front but only emerged gradually. Two main factors that contributed to this were: (i) our lack of experience in the development of multiple-machine, realistic-size specifications combined with little guidance on larger specifications' structure from standard textbooks on B, and (ii) the restrictions imposed via the machine INCLUDES mechanism (e.g. one machine cannot be explicitly included by several other machines) compounded perhaps also by certain implementation-biased preconceptions (see below) as to what information should be stored in what machine.

B's lack of a type for **non-natural numbers** posed something of a challenge. The solution adopted was to model rational numbers (positive and negative fractions) with a user-defined type RAT. Arithmetic operations such as addition, subtraction, multiplication, etc. were modeled as constant function e.g. $ADD \in RAT \times RAT \rightarrow RAT$.

Benefits and drawbacks derived from the implementation experience.
No doubt the in-depth knowledge and understanding of the system gained during its implementation considerably facilitated the formal specification process. However, on occasions it also caused prejudice and resulted in implementation-biased 'specification code' only later to be recognised as such and thus replaced or changed. Described below are 'patterns found' or 'lessons learnt' during the process. With the benefit of hindsight, one could conjecture that some of the 'mistakes' described might not have been made by more experienced B users and that hence other less experienced users of B might find our learning experience of interest.

Variables versus constants. Not every program variable need necessarily be represented as a machine variable. An implementation must initially read patient-specific settings from a file and then store them as variables. However, such settings might in fact be constants, i.e. variables that will and must never be changed by the system. Dose limits for example must only be changed by a doctor (outside the system's scope) and are hence for specification purposes constant. Unlike most implementations, the specification can explicitly represent these settings as constants. It was also found that this explicit distinction between patient-specific constants and variables helped identify intuitive boundaries along which the specification could be divided into smaller machine (e.g. GLUCOSE_CONSTANTS and GLUCOSE_VARIABLES).

Few complex versus several simple data structures. In an actual implementation the use of a particular complex data structure (e.g. a three-dimensional array) can in various ways be the best possible way of working with the data concerned. However, in a specification the use of the very same structure can cause confusion by disguising similarities between items of information in it and/or by suggesting similarities that don't actually exist. In some situations the use of several simple data structures may hence be less 'efficient' but more readable.

Operations, constants, variables, definitions. The specification equivalent of a function or procedure in the system implementation is not necessarily an operation. In fact, it was found that in this specification the only operations needed were those that changed a machine's state, everything else could be expressed with constants, variables, definitions. Constants that combined and were thus defined in terms of several other constants proved particularly useful.

Identification of ambiguous, inconsistent or missing rules within the knowledge base. No major problems were discovered, but the specification process helped identify a few minor inconsistencies in the implementation (as opposed the design) of the algorithms. The (i) addition of a new rule in one particular situation, (ii) amendment of an existing rule and (iii) clarification of the meaning of one particular timestamp and following that the introduction of two additional timestamps removed those inconsistencies.

Specification scope. The actual Insulin Advisor system's features include a number of information display screens and various helpful 'intelligent' message screens. Although these are important components of the overall system, they have virtually no complex knowledge 'behind them' and were hence not included in the formal specification.

Suitability of abstract machine notation for knowledge documentation. Overall, B was found to be suitable for the documentation of our particular knowledge-based system, a system which uses rules and algorithms but which does not have a traditional rule base plus inference engine type of structure. In this context the parallel substitution operator || or rather the absence of a sequential substitution operator ; was initially a bit awkward but eventually helped focus attention on what the system does as opposed to how and in what order it might do it. The division of the specification into logical components i.e. machines helped cope with the system's complexity. However, the system's complexity and the specification's conciseness and density presented us with the challenge of making the specification document accessible to different types of readers. To this purpose, we have prefixed the specification with (i) suggested 'reading routes' through the document and (ii) an annotated mini specification i.e. an adapted extract from the real specification that explains the notation and specification constructs most commonly used.

Specification : implementation size ratio. As detailed in Section 3.6, the overall specification is about 73 pages long, roughly a third of which consisted of annotations. The previously existing C/C++ implementation for the Palm OS platform is about 10,400 lines of annotated code. This gives a ratio of about 7 to 8 pages of annotated specification per 1000 lines of annotated code. The above page count does not include the 10 or so pages preface with the suggested reading routes and notation overview. In comparison, for the formal description in Z of a control program for a radiation therapy machine Jacky et al [15] report figures of about 1200 and 6000 lines of noncomment, nonblank Z description and code respectively. However, in this context it must be noted, that their control program's development made use of the Z specification work, whilst our code already existed before the B specification work commenced.

Generation and discharging of proof obligations. This was not a key part of the project. The proof obligations (POs) were both numerous and complex and their generation and attempted discharging required us to increase the B platform's capacity from initially 1,500,000 to 134,217,726, the maximum possible value for our installation of the B toolkit. The proportion of POs discharged by auto-proof varied between machines (Table 1) and was about 55 % (4366 out of 7884) overall. We believe that the high level of abstraction achieved through the use of quantifiers, set comprehension and complex relations explains this perhaps rather low proof rate. Furthermore, the discharging of certain POs related to rational numbers would clearly require user theory; the experimental addition for example of four straightforward formulae related to GLUCOSE_READINGs and RATional numbers resulted in the discharging of 12 of the remaining 13 POs of the GLUCOSE_CONSTANTS machine.

Refinement and implementation of the specification. A re-implementation of our system via the B method's specification-refinement-implementation route would, given this formal specification, be theoretically possible. However, we believe the process of developing successive refinements and the discharging of related proof obligations would, in practice, be too onerous. Besides, a handheld platform such as Palm OS imposes certain program size, memory requirements and execution speed related constraints. In this context it is unclear (i) if and how any C/C++ code generated by the B toolkit could be deployed on the Palm OS or any other handheld platform, and (ii) if and how specification-refinement-implementation developed applications of this kind would differ from 'traditionally' developed applications, in terms of program size, memory requirements, execution speed and so on.

Related to these questions (and faced with even more extreme programming constraints) is work at Gemplus concerning the use of formal methods for smart cards. Lanet and Lartigue [16] have shown in 1998 that under some conditions some CASE tools can, with an acceptable overhead, generate code for smart cards. However, specifically concerning B, Requet and Bossu [17] reported in 2000 that code generated from a B specification does not (yet) meet the constraints of smart cards and they hence present optimisation techniques that when included in a code generator will make specification to machine code conversion more efficient.

Future re-implementation of the system. We believe that, supplemented by a specification of the user interface, our formal specification could form the basis for a 'traditional' new implementation of the system, for either a handheld or a desktop platform. Comparison of the formal specification and the existing implementation shows that there are considerable differences in terms of the number, structure and scope of the variables used and the number and order-of-use of the various operations i.e. procedures. Although any re-implementation informed by this specification document would in turn exhibit characteristics different from the specification, we consider it likely that any such re-implementation would nevertheless differ considerably from the existing implementation.

5 Summary and Conclusion

We have formally specified an existing medical decision support system and thus shown that such an undertaking is both feasible and viable.

In particular:

- A formal abstract machine notation such as B can be used to produce an unambiguous, authoritative, implementation-independent and concise system specification and documentation.
- The process of developing such a formal specification, in the absence of implementation-related distractions, helps focus attention on what the system does and this may help identify problems within existing documentation and/or implementations.
- For our particular system the formal discharging of all proof obligations was prohibitive. However, the formal and explicit documentation of certain safety-related properties is in itself valuable and may facilitate testing and non-formal reasoning about the holding and maintenance of those properties.
- An implementation of our system via the B method's specification-refinement-implementation route would appear to be theoretically possible but practically impractical. However, we believe that supplemented by a specification of the user interface, our formal specification could form the basis for a 'traditional' new implementation of the system, an implementation which in many of its details would probably vary considerably from the existing implementations.

Acknowledgements. Thanks to Peter Ells for over and over again increasing the B platform's capacity, Kim Yong Chun and Dang Van Hung whose spatial data types [18] inspired our time and rational number data types, and Silvina Gallo and three anonymous reviewers for their comments and suggestions.

References

1. Amos AF, McCarty DJ, Zimmet P (1997) The rising global burden of diabetes and its complications: estimates and projections to the year 2010. *Diabetic Medicine*, 14 Suppl 5, S1–85.

2. National Institute of Diabetes and Digestive and Kidney Diseases. *American Diabetes Control and Complications Trial.* Retrieved on 22 October 2002 from: http://www.niddk.nih.gov/health/diabetes/pubs/dcct1/dcct.htm.
3. Diabetes Trials Unit, Oxford University. *United Kingdom Prospective Diabetes Study.* Retrieved on 22 October 2002 from: http://www.dtu.ox.ac.uk/ukpds/index.html.
4. Holman RR, Smale AD, Pemberton E, Riefflin A, Nealon JL (1996) Randomized controlled pilot trial of a hand-held patient-oriented, insulin regimen optimizer. *Medical Informatics (London),* 21, 317–326.
5. Gallo S, Poerschke C, Barrow BA, Blackwell L, Nealon JL, Holman RR (2002) Handheld insulin dose advisor. *Diabetes,* 51 Suppl 2, A1933.
6. Todd BS (1987) A model-based diagnostic program. *Software Engineering Journal,* 2, 54–63.
7. Todd BS, Ledger WL (1995) A computer-based flowcharting system for clinical protocols. *Medical Informatics (London),* 20, 177–198.
8. Todd BS, Andrews DC (1999) The formal specification of an electrocardiogram compressor. *Medical Informatics and the Internet in Medicine,* 24, 11–32.
9. Kasurinen V, Sere K (1996) Integrating Action Systems and Z in a Medical System Specification. *FME '96: Industrial Benefit and Advances in Formal Methods* (Lecture Notes in Computer Science 1051), 105–119.
10. Groenboom R, Saaman E, Rotterdam E, de Lavalette G (1996) Formalizing Anaesthesia: a Case Study in Formal Specification. *FME '96: Industrial Benefit and Advances in Formal Methods* (Lecture Notes in Computer Science 1051), 120–139.
11. Jacky J (1990) Formal specification for a clinical cyclotron control system. *ACM SIGSOFT Software Engineering Notes* (Conference Proceedings on Formal Methods in Software Development), 15, 45–54.
12. Jacky J (1993) Specifying a Safety-Critical Control System in Z. *FME '93: Industrial-Strength Formal Methods* (Lecture Notes in Computer Science 670), 388–402.
13. Jacky J (1995) Specifying a Safety-Critical Control-System in Z. *IEEE Transactions on Software Engineering,* 21, 99–106.
14. Jacky J, Unger J (1995) From Z to Code: A Graphical User Interface for a Radiation Therapy Machine, *ZUM '95: The Z Formal Specification Notation* (Lecture Notes in Computer Science 967), 315–333.
15. Jacky J, Unger J, Patrick M, Reid D, Risler R (1997) Experience with Z Developing a Control Program for a Radiation Therapy Machine, *ZUM '97: The Z Formal Specification Notation* (Lecture Notes in Computer Science 1212), 317–328.
16. Lanet JL, Lartigue P (1998) The Use of Formal Methods for Smart Cards, a Comparison between B and SDL to Model the T=1 Protocol. *Proceedings of International Workshop on Comparing Systems Specification Techniques.*
17. Requet A, Bossu G (2000) Embedding Formally Proved Code in a Smart Card: Converting B to C. *Proceedings of ICFEM '00,* 15–24.
18. Chun KY, Hung DV (2002) Specification and Verification of Spatial Data Types with B-Toolkit. *Proceedings of COMPSAC '02,* 711–716.

Extending B with Control Flow Breaks

Lilian Burdy and Antoine Requet

Gemplus Research Lab
La Vigie
Avenue du Jujubier - ZI Athelia IV
13705 La Ciotat CEDEX - France
{lilian.burdy,antoine.requet}@gemplus.com

Abstract. This paper describes extensions of the B language concerning control flow breaks in implementations and specification of operations with exceptional behaviors. It does not claim to define those extensions in a pure formal and complete way. It is rather a presentation of what could be done and how it could be done. A syntax is proposed and proof obligations are defined using a weakest precondition calculus extended to deal with abrupt termination. Examples emphasizing the advantages of these extensions are also given.

1 Introduction

The B method [1], as a specification method, notably with its new event based features, begins to be very well known and used, in academic and research world but also in industry. Nevertheless one can obviously remark that B, as a development method, does not seem to follow the same successful story. Except for the railway transport industry, which is the historical user domain, it is really difficult to find industrials that are ready to use it to develop their software from specification to code. We do not claim that extending B with control flow breaks is the way to change this situation, but we consider it as a little step that can bring B to be more attractive as a development method.

If we focus on the developer point of view, concerning the difficulty to adopt B, we can often remark that some reservations are expressed. Those reservations usually concern the B language itself and not the methodology. Some of them could be rubbed out if B could be presented as a real development language on which correctness proof can be done. But, for the moment, developers do not find in B all the classical language features they are used to appreciate. In this way, introducing return, break, continue and exceptions is a way to bring B0 closer to other development languages such as Ada, Java, CAML, C or C++ and to make it more attractive.

On the other hand, introducing exceptions and moreover allowing to specify exceptional behaviors can improve development clarity. This feature really provides a new way to specify operations, by clearly distinguishing normal behaviors from exceptional ones.

The remainder of this paper is organized as follows. Section 2 describes a possible syntax that allows to talk more formally and to give examples of the introduced features. Section 3 describes more in details the motivations to introduce control flow breaks in B. The semantics, consisting on a new proof obligations calculus, is described in Section 4. Section 5 gives some examples and Section 6 concludes.

2 Syntax

Before arguing on their usefulness, the syntax of the new features is introduced. We do not claim that it is the best one, but we need to define one in order to define its semantics and to give examples. The syntax is presented distinguishing two parts, the first one concerns the specification language and the second one the implementation language (B0). Associating to the syntax, some syntactical rules are given. Most of them are obvious and all can be checked statically.

2.1 Specifying Exceptional Behaviors

Exceptional behaviors can be specified in machines and refinements. Exceptions are declared in machines in a specific **EXCEPTIONS** clause, this clause behaves the same as the **SETS** clause, that is, all declared exceptions seen from a machine, should have different names. In operations body, a new clause is introduced. The body of an operation should follow the rules described in the definition 1.

Definition 1. *An operation's body syntax in machine or refinement*

$Operation\_body ::=$ PRE *Predicate* THEN *Substitution* END
       | BEGIN *Substitution* END
       | PRE *Predicate*
        THEN *Substitution*
        EXCEPTION *Exceptional_behavior* END
       | BEGIN *Substitution*
        EXCEPTION *Exceptional_behavior* END

$Exceptional\_behavior ::=$ exception WHEN *Predicate* THEN *Substitution*
           | *Exceptional_behavior* ALSO *Exceptional_behavior*

An operation can describe different exceptional behaviors but thrown exceptions should be distinct. Moreover all thrown exceptions in an operation should be declared in a visible **EXCEPTIONS** clause. There is no way to catch or to throw exceptions in machine, since this corresponds to implementation and not to specification matter. This implies that operations defining exceptional behavior in included or seen machines cannot be called from other machines.

2.2 Abrupt Termination

The B0 implementation language is extended (see definition 2) to allow abrupt termination with a RETURN. One can also define labelled blocks and allow to abruptly exit them with a BREAK. BREAK and CONTINUE can also be used in labelled loops. Considering exceptions, they can be raised and caught in implementations.

Definition 2. *Substitution syntax extension in implementation*

Extended_Substitution ::= *Substitution*
  | BREAK [*label*]
  | CONTINUE [*label*]
  | LABEL *label* THEN *Extended_Substitution* END
  | RETURN
  | RAISE *exception*
  | BEGIN *Extended_Substitution*
    CATCH *Catch_clause* END

Catch_clause ::= *exception* THEN *Extended_Substitution*
  | *Catch_clause* WHEN *Catch_clause*

A BREAK corresponds to a jump to the end of the corresponding labelled block or loop. A CONTINUE corresponds to a return to the beginning of the loop on the test condition. BREAK and CONTINUE with label should be used in a block where this label is defined. Labels should be distinct within a method and are local to methods. Raised and caught exceptions should be declared in a visible EXCEPTIONS clause. Catched exceptions in a CATCH clause should be distinct.

3 Technical Vision

After having introduced the syntax with some syntactic rules, we describe in this section the reasons that have guided us to propose those extensions of the B language. Those reasons are multiple, nevertheless, one can focus on two points. The first one, coming from our experience in formalizing and developing with B convinces us that those extension could be useful. The second one, coming from our experience in proving Java application correctness convinces us that it was possible to generate proof obligations considering this kind of substitution.

3.1 It Could Be Useful

From our experience developing with B : mainly the Java byte-code verifier [3, 4], other smart card applications [7] and also Meteor for one of the authors, we consider that those features are a way to ease the use of B. Those features exist in classical languages : CAML, Ada, Java and C++. They are usually good ways to reduce code size. Moreover, using exceptions usually provides more readable and maintainable code. Other control flow breaks have not this advantage as break usage for instance often gives less readable code. Nevertheless, as implementation correction is proved, there is not any reason to reduce B0 capabilities. On the other hand, we consider that specifying exceptional behaviors can also be useful. To emphasize this point, we have rewritten the first example of the B Book concerning seat reservation. Figure 1 shows the specification of this example using exceptional behaviors. The main part of the specification is described as the normal behavior: the free seats are decreased from the booked number. And, in the appropriate clause, the exceptional behavior condition and action are also described: when the number of free seats is too small, the free seats number remains unchanged. Moreover, the operation does not need to return a parameter anymore. In the implementation, the test is done in a classical way

```
MACHINE
    booking
EXCEPTIONS
    book_failed
ABSTRACT_VARIABLES
    seat
INVARIANT
    seat ∈ N
OPERATIONS
    book(nbr) ≜
    PRE
        nbr ∈ NAT
    THEN
        seat := seat - nbr
    EXCEPTION
        book_failed
            WHEN nbr > seat
            THEN skip
    END
END
```

```
IMPLEMENTATION
    booking_i
REFINES
    booking
OPERATIONS
    book(nbr) ≜
    IF nbr ≤ seat
    THEN
        seat := seat - nbr
    ELSE
        RAISE book_failed
    END
END
```

Fig. 1. Specifying and implementing with exception

and the exception is raised when it fails. Clearly identifying normal behaviors from exceptional ones can really be another way to obtain clearer and easier to read specifications.

3.2 It Is Possible

Working on Java applet correctness [2] have brought us to develop a tool that applies a weakest precondition calculus to Java statements. This calculus [5,6]

has been firstly used in the LOOP tool [8]. In fact, the classical Hoare logic
is extended to deal with control flow breaks. Regarding this, it is possible to
generate automatically proof obligations for the Java language which contains
exceptions, returns, breaks and continue.

From this point of view, we have considered that it was possible to use
this same calculus within the B method. Since B uses the classical Hoare logic
to generate proof obligations, we have used the extended one to apply it to
extended B substitutions. The next section describes the calculus applied to this
previously defined syntax.

4 Semantics

After defining some notations, this section describes the extended weakest precondition calculus applied to the classical B substitutions and the newly introduced one. In the last part, proof obligations are defined dealing with this new calculus. The semantics is given in term of proof obligations and not by giving new definitions for trm and prd, since we consider that it is the more simpler to understand. For instance, $trm(S)$ and $prd_x(S)$ are in effect no more predicates since S can have different termination.

4.1 Notations

Given the set of formulas $\mathcal{F}$, the set of labels $\mathcal{L}$ and the set of exceptions $\mathcal{E}$:

- φ^{norm}, with $\varphi^{norm} \in \mathcal{F}$ corresponds to a formula that must hold in case of normal termination.
- φ^{ret}, with $\varphi^{ret} \in \mathcal{F}$ represents a formula that must hold in case of abrupt termination on RETURN.
- φ^{brk} and φ^{cont}, where $\varphi^{brk} \in \mathcal{L} \nrightarrow \mathcal{F}$ and $\varphi^{cont} \in \mathcal{L} \nrightarrow \mathcal{F}$ are partial functions mapping labels to formulas that must hold after abrupt termination, respectively on BREAK and CONTINUE.
- φ^{ex}, with $\varphi^{ex} \in \mathcal{E} \nrightarrow \mathcal{F}$ corresponds to a partial function mapping exceptions to formulas. It represents the formula that must hold when the corresponding exception occurs.

We assume the existence of a special label $\bar{l}$, the unnamed label, that is different from all the declared labels in the program. This special label is used for handling non-labelled BREAK and CONTINUE statements. In the following, φ^{brk}_{label} and φ^{cont}_{label} will be used as shortcuts to $\varphi^{brk}(label)$ and $\varphi^{cont}(label)$. In a similar way, φ^{ex}_e will correspond to $\varphi^{ex}(e)$ if $e \in dom(\varphi^{ex})$ and $false$ otherwise.

Using those definitions, $[S]^i(\varphi^{norm}, \varphi^{ret}, \varphi^{brk}, \varphi^{cont}, \varphi^{ex})$, where S is an extended substitution, corresponds to the necessary precondition that must hold to ensure that:

- φ^{norm} holds after S if S terminates normally;
- φ^{ret} holds after S if it terminates abruptly on a RETURN;

- for all label l defined in the context, φ_l^{brk} holds after S if it terminates abruptly on a BREAK l.
- for all label l defined in the context, φ_l^{cont} holds after S if it terminates abruptly on a CONTINUE l.
- for all exception e defined in the context, φ_e^{ex} holds after S if it terminates abruptly on a RAISE e.

In the following, we will use $X = (\varphi^{norm}, \varphi^{ret}, \varphi^{brk}, \varphi^{cont}, \varphi^{ex})$ in order to ease the notation.

4.2 Weakest Precondition Calculus

This section presents the extended weakest precondition calculus that is used to generate proof obligations. In order to handle exceptions and control flow breaks, we have to differentiate the cases where the program terminates normally from the cases where it terminates abruptly. We define the $[]^i$ operator (where i means implementation as opposed to machine) on extended generalized substitutions.

Definition for classical substitutions. Definition 3 defines $[]^i$ for the classical substitutions. Those definitions are close to the classical ones. The definition for the sequencing operator is a bit different: it can be explained by the fact that the result of $[S_2]^i X$ is relevant only if S_1 terminates normally. Otherwise, as S_2 will never be executed, S_1 should establish the formulas concerning the abrupt terminations.

Definition 3. *Definition of $[]^i$ for the classical substitutions*

$[x := E]^i X \Leftrightarrow [x := E]\varphi^{norm}$

$[P \Longrightarrow S]^i X \Leftrightarrow P \Rightarrow [S]^i X$

$[S_1 \| S_2]^i X \Leftrightarrow [S_1]^i X \wedge [S_2]^i X$

$[@x.S]^i X \Leftrightarrow \forall x.([S]^i X)$

$[S_1; S_2]^i X \Leftrightarrow [S_1]^i([S_2]^i X, \varphi^{ret}, \varphi^{brk}, \varphi^{cont}, \varphi^{ex})$

Definition for operation calls. We consider the operation as defined on Figure 2. When calling such an operation, the cases where the operation terminates normally must be distinguished from the cases where the operation raises an exception. This is handled by the definition of $[]^i$ for operation call given in definition 4.

Definition 4. *Definition of $[]^i$ for operation calls*

$[c_1, \ldots, c_n \leftarrow op(p_1, \ldots, p_m)]^i X \Leftrightarrow$

$\begin{bmatrix} arg_1, & p_1, \\ \ldots, & := & \ldots, \\ arg_m & & p_m \end{bmatrix} \begin{pmatrix} P \wedge \\ (P \wedge \bigwedge_{1 \leq i \leq p} (\neg W_i) \Rightarrow [[r_1, \ldots, r_n := c_1, \ldots, c_n]S]\varphi^{norm}) \wedge \\ \bigwedge_{1 \leq i \leq p} (P \wedge W_i \Rightarrow [[r_1, \ldots, r_n := c_1, \ldots, c_n]T_i]\varphi_{e_i}^{ex}) \end{pmatrix}$

$r_1, \ldots, r_n \leftarrow \text{op}(arg_1, \ldots, arg_m) \triangleq$
PRE
$\quad P$
THEN
$\quad S$
EXCEPTION
$\quad e_1$ WHEN W_1 THEN T_1
$\quad \ldots$
ALSO e_p WHEN W_p THEN T_p
END

Fig. 2. Operation specification

Note that the classical definition for $[]$ is used within the definition of operation calls, since the substitutions allowed for specification do not allow abrupt termination or raising exceptions. Note, also, that when the called operation does not declare exceptional behaviors, the definition remains valid (with p equals 0). Moreover, since the guards associated to exceptions can overlapped, each exception case leads to an independant proof obligation.

Definition for loops. The definition for loops is updated to handle abrupt termination from the loop as shown on definition 5.

Definition 5. *Definition of $[]^i$ for loops*
[WHILE P DO S INVARIANT I VARIANT V END$]^i X$

$$\Leftrightarrow \begin{cases} I \wedge \\ \forall x.(I \wedge P \Rightarrow [S]^i \begin{pmatrix} I, \\ \varphi^{ret}, \\ \varphi^{brk} \triangleleft \{\bar{l} \mapsto \varphi^{norm}\}, \\ \varphi^{cont} \triangleleft \{\bar{l} \mapsto I\}, \\ \varphi^{ex} \end{pmatrix}) \wedge \\ \forall x.(I \Rightarrow V \in \mathbb{N}) \wedge \\ \forall x.(I \wedge P \Rightarrow [n := V][S]^i \begin{pmatrix} V < n, \\ \mathcal{L} \times \{true\}, \\ \mathcal{L} \times \{true\}, \\ V < n, \\ \mathcal{E} \times \{true\} \end{pmatrix}) \wedge \\ \forall x.(I \wedge \neg P \Rightarrow \varphi^{norm}) \end{cases}$$

The invariance property of the loop ensures that a terminating iteration of the loop, as well as an abrupt termination on a CONTINUE statement will establish the loop invariant. The same applies for the variant property, that must be ensured both by the normal termination and the continuing abrupt termination.

In the case of an abrupt termination of the iteration leaving the loop (that is, an operation return, an exception or a BREAK statement), proving the loop invariant is not required, but the formula corresponding to the normal behavior has to. Moreover, the variant property does not need to be proved.

Accordingly, the finalization part of the loop only requires proving the φ^{norm} formula, since it is reached only in the case of a normal termination of the loop.

Finally, the typing of the variant is left unchanged.

Definition for new substitutions. The definition of $[]^i$ for the new substitutions is quite straightforward. In the case of label declaration, the definition is given in definition 6. This corresponds to adding the label to the set of known labels, and ensuring that the current φ^{norm} holds when the block is exited abruptly.

Definition 6. *Definition of $[]^i$ for labels*

$$\left[\begin{array}{l} \text{LABEL } l \\ \text{THEN } S \\ \text{END} \end{array}\right]^i X \Leftrightarrow [S]^i \begin{pmatrix} \varphi^{norm}, \\ \varphi^{ret}, \\ \varphi^{brk} \triangleleft \{l \mapsto \varphi^{norm}\}, \\ \varphi^{cont}, \\ \varphi^{ex} \end{pmatrix}$$

Labeled loops. Labels enclosing a loop are treated as special cases since the execution of the loop can be resumed using the CONTINUE *label* keyword. The definition of $[]^i$ for those loops is given in definition 7. This definition is very close to the one used for classical loops (Definition 5), except that it uses both the unnamed label $\bar{l}$ and the defined label l.

Definition 7. *Definition of $[]^i$ for labeled loops*

[LABEL l THEN WHILE P DO S INVARIANT I VARIANT V END END$]^i X$

$$\Leftrightarrow \begin{cases} I \wedge \\ \forall x.(I \wedge P \Rightarrow [S]^i \begin{pmatrix} I, \\ \varphi^{ret}, \\ \varphi^{brk} \triangleleft \{l \mapsto \varphi^{norm}, \bar{l} \mapsto \varphi^{norm}\}, \\ \varphi^{cont} \triangleleft \{l \mapsto I, \bar{l} \mapsto I\}, \\ \varphi^{ex} \end{pmatrix}) \wedge \\ \forall x.(I \Rightarrow V \in \mathbb{N}) \wedge \\ \forall x.(I \wedge P \Rightarrow [n := V][S]^i \begin{pmatrix} V < n, \\ \mathcal{L} \times \{true\}, \\ \mathcal{L} \times \{true\}, \\ V < n, \\ \mathcal{E} \times \{true\} \end{pmatrix}) \wedge \\ \forall x.(I \wedge \neg P \Rightarrow \varphi^{norm}) \end{cases}$$

The case definition for control-flow breaks is given by the definition 8. It simply selects the relevant formula to prove. The definition for the BEGIN CATCH END substitution corresponds to the precondition of S with the exception handlers added to φ^{ex}.

Definition 8. *Definition of $[]^i$ for control-flow breaks*

$[\text{ CONTINUE label }]^i X \Leftrightarrow \varphi_{label}^{cont}$

$[\text{ BREAK label }]^i X \quad \Leftrightarrow \varphi_{label}^{brk}$

$[\text{ RETURN }]^i X \quad \Leftrightarrow \varphi^{ret}$

$[\text{ RAISE } e]^i X \quad \Leftrightarrow \varphi_e^{ex}$

$$\begin{bmatrix} \text{BEGIN } S \\ \text{CATCH } e_1 \text{ THEN } C_1 \\ \ldots \\ \text{WHEN } e_n \text{ THEN } C_n \\ \text{END} \end{bmatrix}^i X \Leftrightarrow [S]^i \begin{pmatrix} \varphi^{norm}, \\ \varphi^{ret}, \\ \varphi^{brk}, \\ \varphi^{cont}, \\ \varphi^{ex} \triangleleft \bigcup_{1 \leq i \leq n} \{e_i \mapsto [C_i]^i X\} \end{pmatrix}$$

4.3 Proof Obligations

We have defined in the previous section the new operator $[]^i$. We are now defining the new proof obligations calculus in machines, refinements and implementations.

Machine proof obligations. As substitutions with control flow breaks are only usable in implementation, one can keep the classical B operator $[]$ to generate machine proof obligations. We only have to extend it with the new introduced machine substitution that corresponds to an exceptional behavior description (see definition 9).

Definition 9. *Extending $[]$ definition*

$$\begin{bmatrix} \text{BEGIN} \\ \quad S \\ \text{EXCEPTION} \\ \quad e_1 \text{ WHEN } W_1 \text{ THEN } T_1 \\ \quad \ldots \\ \text{ALSO} \\ \quad e_n \text{ WHEN } W_n \text{ THEN } T_n \\ \text{END} \end{bmatrix} P \Leftrightarrow \begin{cases} \bigwedge_{1 \leq i \leq n} (W_i \Rightarrow [T_i]P) \wedge \\ \bigwedge_{1 \leq i \leq n} (\neg W_i) \Rightarrow [S]P \end{cases}$$

This definition looks like the definition for a SELECT clause where the normal substitution S corresponds to the ELSE branch and each exception description to a WHEN branch. So, a way of understanding it is that if an exception condition W_i is valid, then the corresponding exceptional behavior will occur, otherwise if no exception condition is valid, then the normal behavior will occur. Moreover, one can notice that exceptional conditions do not have to be distinct and obviously should not cover all the cases. For the other substitutions, the proof obligations calculus remains unchanged.

Refinement Proof Obligations. To generate proof obligations for refinement, one has to take into account exceptional behaviours. Exceptional behaviours can be refined but an operation that declares exceptions can only be refined by an operation that declares the same exceptions or fewer exceptions. This means that one can suppress exceptional behaviours during the refinement but not create new ones.

$$\begin{array}{l} \text{BEGIN} \\ \quad S' \\ \text{EXCEPTION} \\ \quad e_1 \text{ WHEN } W'_1 \text{ THEN } T'_1 \\ \quad \ldots \\ \quad \text{ALSO } e_p \text{ WHEN } W'_p \text{ THEN } T'_p \\ \text{END} \end{array}$$

Fig. 3. Operation specification

Definition 10. *Exceptional behaviour refinement proof obligations*

When an operation with body as described figure 3 refines an operation in a machine or a refinement that declares exceptional behaviours (see a description figure 2), the proof obligation is

$$\begin{cases} \bigwedge_{1 \leq i \leq p} W'_i \Rightarrow W_i \\ \bigwedge_{1 \leq i \leq p} (\neg W_i) \wedge \bigwedge_{1 \leq i \leq p} (\neg W'_i) \Rightarrow [S']\neg[S]\neg I \\ \bigwedge_{1 \leq i \leq p} (W_i \wedge W'_i \Rightarrow [T'_i]\neg[T_i]\neg I) \end{cases}$$

Note that the exceptions that are not refined can be considered as refined with $false$ as guard. Note also that the guards can get stronger during the refinement.

Implementation Proof Obligations. To generate refinement proof obligations for implementations, one has to take into account control flow breaks. This means that the classical refinement proof obligation ($[T]\neg[S]\neg I$ when T refines S under invariant I) is no longer valid, since the $[]^i$ operator should be used. The definitions 11 and 12 define refinement proof obligations depending on the refined substitution.

Definition 11. *Normal behaviour implementation proof obligations.*
When an operation with body T in an implementation refines an operation with body S that does not declare exceptional behaviours, the proof obligation is

$$[T]^i \begin{pmatrix} \neg[S]\neg I, \\ \neg[S]\neg I, \\ \emptyset, \\ \emptyset, \\ \emptyset \end{pmatrix}$$

If the refined substitution does not declare an exceptional behaviour, then the implementation has to ensure that it can only terminates normally or on a RETURN. In those two cases, one has to ensure classical refinement correctness; all other cases are initialized with the empty set corresponding to the fact that no formula has to be proved. It will lead to false if such abrupt termination occurs.

Definition 12. *Exceptional behaviour implementation proof obligations*

When an operation with body T in an implementation refines an operation that declares exceptional behaviours (see a description figure 2), the proof obligation is

$$[T]^i \begin{pmatrix} \bigwedge_{1 \leq i \leq p} (\neg W_i) \wedge \neg[S]\neg I, \\ \bigwedge_{1 \leq i \leq p} (\neg W_i) \wedge \neg[S]\neg I, \\ \emptyset, \\ \emptyset, \\ \bigcup_{1 \leq i \leq p} \{e_i \mapsto W_i \wedge \neg[S_i]\neg I\} \end{pmatrix}$$

If the refined substitution declares exceptional behaviours, the implementation should respect them. This means, that if it terminates normally or abruptly on a RETURN, one should prove that no exceptional behaviour condition is valid and that the refinement is correct in the classical sense. One also has to prove that if the refinement terminates abruptly on an exception, then the condition of this exception is valid and the refinement refines correctly the exceptional behaviour corresponding to this exception. Moreover, abrupt termination on BREAK or CONTINUE is still not valid for a method.

Proof obligations calculus becomes quite more complex than it was previously. But our experience generating proof obligations for Java has shown that after the calculation, generated proof obligations remain with the same complexity.

5 Examples

This section provides little examples that highlight the advantages of having control flow break substitutions.

5.1 Loop Termination

The example given figure 4 describes two implementations of a loop. This loop implements the search of an element a in the range of an integer array t with domain 0..10. On the left side, a classical B operation is shown, the right side shows an implementation with a return inside the body of the loop. One can

$$
\begin{array}{l}
\text{res} \leftarrow \text{search(a)} \triangleq \\
\text{BEGIN} \\
\quad \text{res} := \text{FALSE;} \\
\quad \text{i} := 0; \\
\quad \text{WHILE i} \leq 10 \land \\
\quad\quad \text{res} = \text{FALSE DO} \\
\quad\quad \text{IF t(i)} = a \\
\quad\quad \text{THEN} \\
\quad\quad\quad \text{res} := \text{TRUE} \\
\quad\quad \text{END;} \\
\quad\quad \text{i} := \text{i} + 1 \\
\quad \text{INVARIANT} \\
\quad\quad \text{i} \in 0..11 \land \\
\quad\quad \text{res} = \text{bool(a} \in \text{t[0..i-1]}) \\
\quad \text{VARIANT} \\
\quad\quad 11 - \text{i} \\
\quad \text{END} \\
\text{END}
\end{array}
\qquad
\begin{array}{l}
\text{res} \leftarrow \text{search(a)} \triangleq \\
\text{BEGIN} \\
\quad \text{i} = 0; \\
\quad \text{WHILE i} \leq 10 \text{ DO} \\
\quad\quad \text{IF t(i)} = a \\
\quad\quad \text{THEN} \\
\quad\quad\quad \text{res} := \text{TRUE;} \\
\quad\quad\quad \text{RETURN} \\
\quad\quad \text{END;} \\
\quad\quad \text{i} := \text{i} + 1 \\
\quad \text{INVARIANT} \\
\quad\quad \text{i} \in 0..11 \land \\
\quad\quad a \notin \text{t[0..i-1]} \\
\quad \text{VARIANT} \\
\quad\quad 11 - \text{i} \\
\quad \text{END;} \\
\quad \text{res} := \text{FALSE} \\
\text{END}
\end{array}
$$

Fig. 4. Loop termination

consider two improvements when using abrupt exiting from a loop:

- the loop stop condition can be simplified, one does not need to test if the value has been found anymore. This allows to reduce code size and execution time.
- the invariant is simplified too, since we can consider that if we are in the loop, it is only if the searched for value has not been found. While the classical invariant should deal with the two cases : already found or not, the new invariant only deals with the second one.

One can consider that those advantages are not so important but in big development, it can really save code size, execution time and development time.

5.2 Exceptional Behaviors

The examples (figures 5 and 6) show the advantages to have the possibly of specifying a method with exceptional behaviors. The first example shows the

specification of a read operation on a partial function. On the left side, the
classical specification is given, the right side describes the specification with
an exceptional behavior. The second specification can be understood as: the
operation returns the value of the function for this index and exceptionally if
the index does not belong to the function domain, an exception will be raised
and the returned value is not relevant.

The figure 6 describes the use of the previous read method. The implemented
specification is given on top and two implementations are given. The left one
has to test the validity parameter before using the returned value. The right one
implements the test in normal way and in the catch part treats the exceptional
behavior by returning false. Even in this simple example where two values are
read sequentially, it is clear that the code with exception is more readable than
the classical code. If one takes an example with more calls to the read function, the classical B code would be even harder to follow whereas the code with
exception would not lose its readability.

Moreover, in such cases, tests are performed twice: once by the read function,
in order to initialize the result value, and a second one by the caller of the read
operation, in order to check wether the read operation succeeded. When using
exception treatment, in the normal case, that can be considered as the usual
one, the test has only to be performed in the read function.

It is really obvious to demonstrate that programming with exception provides
clearer code. The new point on which we argue here is that specifying with
exceptional behaviors allows also to obtain clearer specifications.

6 Conclusion

In this paper, an extension of the B language corresponding to the control-flow
breaks in implementation and the specification of operations with exceptional
behavior is presented. It shows that those extensions could be useful for writing
implementations, but also for differentiating the normal behavior from the exceptional one in specifications. It can also be a way to obtain more efficient code
when translating B0, even if the introduced features do not exist in all targeted
language.

Moreover, a surprising result is that those extensions also allow writing simpler loop invariants and can ease the proof process. This was unexpected, since
control-flow breaks require more complicated handling.

Introducing those features has the side effect that B0 is not a subset of
the languages supported by the converter anymore. More exactly, C does not
have exception, and Ada has more restricted control flow breaks. For those languages, it could be easily possible to handle those features in the converter: for
example, converting control flow breaks into Ada could use exceptions, and the
setjmp/longjmp feature of C could be used to handle exceptions. However, this
complexifies the converter, so if this complexity increase is an issue, it could also
be possible to add additional B0 checks depending on the target language used.

is_valid, value ⟵ read(i) ≜
PRE
    $i \in INT$
THEN
    IF $i \in dom(t)$
    THEN
        is_valid := TRUE ∥
        value := t(i)
    ELSE
        is_valid := FALSE ∥
        value :∈ INT
    END
END

value ⟵ read(i) ≜
PRE
    $i \in INT$
THEN
    value := t(i)
EXCEPTION
    outofdomain
    WHEN
        $i \notin dom(t)$
    THEN
        value :∈ INT
END

Fig. 5. Exceptional behaviors

res ⟵ test(i,j) ≜
PRE
    $i \in INT \wedge$
    $j \in INT$
THEN
    res := bool($i \in dom(t) \wedge$
                $j \in dom(t) \wedge$
                t(i) = t(j))
END

res ⟵ test(i,j) ≜
BEGIN
    res, l1 ⟵ read(i);
    IF res = TRUE
    THEN
        res, l2 ⟵ read(j);
        IF res = TRUE
        THEN
            res := bool(l1 = l2)
        END
    END
END

res ⟵ test(i,j) ≜
BEGIN
    l1 ⟵ read(i);
    l2 ⟵ read(j);
    res := bool(l1 = l2)
CATCH
    outofdomain
    THEN
        res := FALSE
END

Fig. 6. Catching exceptions

So B0 using control flow breaks could not be converted to Ada and B0 with exceptions could not be converted to C.

Finally, although the new event B can reduce the need to directly specify exceptional behavior at the start, we consider that exceptional behavior and control-flow breaks are a complementary feature, that would prove useful for providing the link between event B and the classical B required for implementation.

References

1. Jean-Raymond Abrial. *The B Book, Assigning Programs to Meanings.* Cambridge University Press, 1996.
2. Lilian Burdy and Antoine Requet. Jack : Java Applet Correctness Kit. In *GDC 2002, Singapore*, November 2002.
3. Ludovic Casset. Development of an Embedded Verifier for Java Card Byte Code using Formal Methods. In Lars-Henrik Eriksson and Peter Alexander Lindsay, editors, *Formal Methods – Getting IT Right*, volume 2391 of *Lecture Notes in Computer Science*, pages 290–309. Springer-Verlag, July 22–24 2002.
4. Ludovic Casset, Lilian Burdy, and Antoine Requet. Formal Development of an Embedded Verifier for Java Card Byte Code. In *DSN 2002, International Conference on Dependable Systems & Networks*, pages 51–56, Washington, D.C., USA, June 2002.
5. Marieke Huisman. *Java Program Verification in Higher-Order Logic with PVS and Isabelle.* PhD thesis, University of Nijmegen, The Netherlands, 2001.
6. Marieke Huisman and Bart Jacobs. Java Program Verification via a Hoare Logic with Abrupt Termination. In T. Maibaum, editor, *Fundamental Approaches to Software Engineering (FASE)*, volume 1783, pages 284–303. Springer-Verlag, 2000.
7. Pierre Lartigue and Denis Sabatier. The use of the B formal method for the design and the validation of the transaction mechanism for smart card applications. In *Formal Methods in System Design, Special Issue on FM'99*, November 1999.
8. Joachim van den Berg and Bart Jacobs. The LOOP Compiler for Java and JML. *Lecture Notes in Computer Science*, 2031:299–312, 2001.

Towards Dynamic Population Management of Abstract Machines in the B Method*

Nazareno Aguirre[1]**, Juan Bicarregui[2], Theo Dimitrakos[2], and Tom Maibaum[1]

[1] Department of Computer Science, King's College London,
Strand, London WC2R 2LS, United Kingdom, {aguirre, tom}@dcs.kcl.ac.uk
[2] Rutherford Appleton Laboratory, Chilton, Didcot,
OXON, OX11 0QX, United Kingdom {J.C.Bicarregui, T.Dimitrakos}@rl.ac.uk

Abstract. We study some restrictions associated with the mechanisms for structuring and modularising specifications in the B abstract machine notation. We propose an extension of the language that allows one to specify machines whose constituent modules (other abstract machines) may change dynamically, i.e., at run time. In this way, we increase the expressiveness of B by adding support for a common activity of the current systems design practice.

The extensions were made without having to make considerable changes in the semantics of standard B. We provide some examples to show the increased expressive power, and argue that our proposed extensions respect the methodological principles of the B method.

Keywords: Structuring mechanisms, modularisation, object orientation, dynamic reconfiguration.

1 Introduction

Formal methods support precise and rigorous specifications of those aspects of a computer system capable of being expressed in a formal language. One of the main advantages of formal methods is that, in addition to aiding in the elimination of ambiguities in specification, they allow for analysis and verification of system properties prior to implementation. Since defining what a system should do and understanding the implications of these decisions are amongst the most troublesome problems in software engineering, the use of formal methods has major benefits.

However, formal methods are hard and expensive to use, and they may require a strong background in formal reasoning in order to perform the analysis

---

* This work was partially supported by the Engineering and Physical Sciences Research Council of the U.K., through projects: *The Integration of Two Industrially Relevant Formal Methods (VDM+B)*, Grants GR/L68445 and GR/L68452, and *Objects, Associations and Subsystems: A Hierarchical Approach to Encapsulation*, Grants GR/M72630 and GR/N00814.
** Contact author. Phone number: +44 (0)207 848 1166. Fax: +44 (0)207 848 2851. Nazareno Aguirre is currently on leave from Departamento de Computación, FCEFQyN, Universidad Nacional de Río Cuarto, Río Cuarto, Córdoba, Argentina.

and verification tasks. In the formal specification process, and even more so in the formal analysis process, appropriate tool support is then a necessity. In order to be able to provide tool support, it is generally required that the semantics underlying formal languages have to be simple. Simpler semantics usually leads to having restricted expressive power. So, a balance has to be found in order to achieve what is considered important for the take-up of a formal method (and its successful use in the development of systems), namely, simple but sufficiently expressive semantics, tool support, structure and relevance to the current systems engineering practice, etc.

Model based formal methods such as B [1], VDM [14] and Z [15] are among the few formal methods currently in use by industry and supported by commercial tools. They have been used in a variety of industrial case studies for the specification and verification of mission critical systems, in application domains varying from the rail industry to smart cards. Using such formal methods in the development of an information system is about: eliminating all ambiguity beginning right from the interpretation of the need, constructing a specification which is both coherent and conformant with the need (the model), and elaborating the software system which realises the specification, in successive stages. The coherence of the model and the conformity of the final program in relation to this model are guaranteed by mathematical proofs.

The languages referred to above are considerably less expressive than many object-oriented formalisms, but also considerably simpler, better structured, and in some cases with important tool support and proof assistance [9][4][12], due to their simpler semantics. One of these languages, the B language, has an associated method, described in [1], and commercial tool support [9][4]. A useful feature present in object-oriented languages is the possibility of dynamically creating or deleting modules or components (objects in the object-oriented terminology). In fact, dynamic object management has now become a common task in systems design practice. The B language and its associated method lack this useful feature of object-oriented languages: having it in the specification language of the B method would be equivalent to being able to dynamically create or delete abstract machines. The work in [16] and the different object-oriented variants of model-oriented specification languages provide evidence of the need for this feature.

In this paper, we make a first attempt to provide an extension of the B language and its semantics, in order to support dynamic management of abstract machine populations. In recognition of the fact that maintaining compatibility with the existing tool support for the B method is very important, we concentrate on "extending" (conservatively) the current language and semantics, rather than "changing" it. In effect, we ensure that:

1. one can possibly reduce the semantics associated with the proposed extension of the B specification language to the standard semantics of the B method,
2. the proposed extension does not affect the semantics of the core specification language of B.

The resulting language is in some aspects clearly more expressive than standard B, without being in the realm of object-oriented languages. We therefore increase the expressiveness of B by building into the language support for common activities of the current systems design practice, while avoiding the introduction of the complexity that is often associated with the semantics of fully-fledged object-oriented languages, including the object-oriented variants of the above-mentioned model oriented formal methods.

2 Adding Dynamism to B

In B, the declaration of an abstract machine corresponds to the declaration of a kind of "template" of a component. An abstract machine is not a component itself, since it might prescribe the way many different components work. The creation of a number of different specification components corresponding to a single abstract machine declaration can be achieved by means of renaming and inclusion, using some of the structuring mechanisms available, of the renamed machines in some "super" machine M, in a way similar to what is called *cloning* in some object-oriented languages. However, the machines included in a super machine M are *fixed*: clearly, during the run time of M, neither the modular structure of M, in terms of the submachines it is built out of, nor the number of included machines can change. So, abstract machines cannot be considered as *objects* in an object-oriented sense, but instead they are closer to standard *modules* of traditional imperative programming languages. The advantages of the concept of *object* over that of *primitive module* are well-known; many of them could be considered differences between traditional imperative and object-oriented languages.

We extend the notation of abstract machines to allow for dynamic management of abstract machine populations. The notation of single, basic abstract machines is preserved. The changes are in the way we build bigger machines in terms of more primitive ones, i.e., in the structuring notation. In this paper, we restrict ourselves to studying a particular type of INCLUDES, the one characterised by the EXTENDS clause. For the sake of simplicity, we also ignore for the moment the issues related to the use of parameterised machines, and explain the concepts for machines without parameters, although it will be clear how the same concepts apply to parameterised machines straightforwardly.

3 Population Management: The Standard B Approach

To motivate our work, let us introduce an example that shows how a specification might be structured in B. This example is shown in Figure 1, and consists of an extension of a variant of the primitive machine *Scalar*, found in pages 320 and 321 of [1]. Machine *Scalar* consists only of an integer variable, and operations to update and return the value of the variable.

A structured machine built on top of *Scalar* is proposed in [1] as well, as machine *TwoScalars*. We show the definition of *TwoScalars* in Figure 2. As seen

```
MACHINE
    Scalar
VARIABLES
    var
INVARIANT
    var ∈ INT
INITIALIZATION
    x :∈ INT
OPERATIONS
    chg(v)  ≙  PRE  v ∈ INT  THEN  var := v  END
    v ⟵ val  ≙  BEGIN  v := var  END
END
```

Fig. 1. Abstract machine *Scalar*.

there, multiple copies of *Scalar* are "imported" in *TwoScalars*, by means of copy and renaming of (some of) the language elements of the original *Scalar* machine definition [1]. An extra operation *swap* is declared in this machine, calling in parallel the *chg* operations of machines *xx* and *yy*.

```
MACHINE
    TwoScalars
EXTENDS
    xx.Scalar, yy.Scalar
OPERATIONS
    swap  ≙  BEGIN  xx.chg(yy.var)  ||  yy.chg(xx.var)  END
END
```

Fig. 2. Abstract machine *TwoScalars*.

Now, suppose we decided we need a generalisation of this previous machine, one in which the number of scalars varies over time by creating or deleting dynamically new scalars, and where the *swap* operation might be applied to any two machines. The standard way of dealing with this problem in B, as shown in several examples of Chapter 8 in [1] and also in [13], is by defining a new machine, which includes both the operations of *Scalar*, relativised to names for the "instances", and the population management operations. Machine *SeveralScalars*, described in Figure 3, is defined using this approach. For this new machine, machine definition *Scalar* had to be discarded, and all the operations corresponding to it had to be adapted and included in *SeveralScalars*. A set, *scalars*, is used to denote the names of the active scalar instances. Operations *chg* and *val*, originally defined in *Scalar*, had to be rewritten in this machine specification, now relativised to the corresponding instances (see the extra parameter in each of these operations). Variable *var* was also incorporated to *SeveralScalars*, now representing the values of the original *var* for each of the active instances of scalar.

The initialisation substitution of *Scalar* became an assignment (in fact, part of a parallel assignment) in *add_sc*, the operation that adds a new scalar in this machine.

MACHINE
　SeveralScalars
SETS
　SCALARSET
VARIABLES
　var, scalars
INVARIANT
　$(var \in scalars \rightarrow \mathsf{INT}) \wedge (scalars \subseteq SCALARSET)$
INITIALIZATION
　$var, scalars := \emptyset, \emptyset$
OPERATIONS
　$chg(v,p)\ \ \hat{=}$
　　PRE　$v \in \mathsf{INT} \wedge p \in scalars$
　　THEN　$var := (\mathsf{dom}(var) - \{p\}) \triangleleft var) \cup \{(p,v)\}$
　　END

　$v \longleftarrow val(p)\ \ \hat{=}\ \ $PRE　$p \in scalars$　THEN　$v := var(p)$　END

　$swap(p,q)\ \ \hat{=}$
　　PRE　$p \in scalars \wedge q \in scalars$
　　THEN　$var := var <+ \{(p, var(q)), (q, var(p))\}$
　　END

　$add\_sc(p)\ \ \hat{=}$
　　PRE　$p \in (SCALARSET - scalars)$
　　THEN　$(scalars := scalars \cup \{p\})$　$||$
　　(ANY v WHERE $v \in \mathsf{INT}$ THEN $var := var \cup \{(p,v)\}$ END)
　　END

　$rem\_sc(p)\ \ \hat{=}$
　　PRE　$p \in scalars$
　　THEN　$scalars := scalars - \{p\}$　$||$
　　　$var := (\mathsf{dom}(var) - \{p\}) \triangleleft var$
　　END
END

Fig. 3. Abstract machine *SeveralScalars*.

This is a standard approach to the management of multiple instances of certain objects. It is, certainly, a problem, since the whole specification of a scalar had to be rewritten. Imagine a case in which the machine whose population we need to manage, say M, is not as simple as our *Scalar* machine, and instead consists of a complex structure in terms of "submachines"; if we want to specify a machine that manages the population of M, then the whole specification of M must be rewritten. Therefore, specifications cannot be modularised into natural conceptual entities, proofs cannot be "localised" to relevant specification parts, etc.

4 A Notation for Dynamic Creation of Machines

We suggest that it is possible to provide B with a richer notation, that allows us to dynamically manage the population of abstract machines, partly overcoming the problems mentioned in the previous section. The general form of our notation is not difficult to understand. The AGGREGATES M_1 clause in a machine M indicates that multiple machines of type M_1 are available in M, in the same style as for EXTENDS, i.e., *promoting* all operations of the included machine. Included machines are declared to belong to an *instance set*, whose name is $M_1 Set$ (in our case *ScalarSet*). Instance sets are used to characterise live instances of machine types.

A machine equivalent to the *SeveralScalars* machine in Figure 3 is written in our proposed extended notation as follows:

```
MACHINE
    SeveralScalars'
AGGREGATES
    Scalar
OPERATIONS
    swap(p, q)  ≙
        PRE    p ∈ ScalarSet ∧ q ∈ ScalarSet
        THEN   p.chg(q.var) ||| q.chg(p.var)
        END
END
```

In contrast to machine *SeveralScalars*, machine *SeveralScalars'* is indeed defined in terms of the primitive machine *Scalar*. It does not include the declaration of a set of instances (*scalars* in machine *SeveralScalars*), since it is declared *implicitly*, by the AGGREGATES clause. Two operations, called *add_Scalar* and *del_Scalar*, are automatically generated and implicitly included by the AGGREGATES clause. These operations are meant to manipulate the population of instances of scalar. For our example, they are defined in the following way:

```
add_Scalar(p)  ≙
    PRE    p ∈ (NAME − ScalarSet)
    THEN   ScalarSet := ScalarSet ∪ {p}   ||   p.init
    END

del_Scalar(p)  ≙
    PRE    p ∈ scalars
    THEN   ScalarSet := ScalarSet − {p}   ||
           var := (dom(var) − {p}) ◁ var
    END
```

The set NAME is assumed to be predefined in some way in B (see the section regarding the semantics of the extension). It denotes the set of all names of machines (more than one machine type might be aggregated by a particular machine). It is assumed that the graph corresponding to the AGGREGATES dependency between machines is *acyclic*; in other words, no recursive (either direct or indirect) aggregation is allowed. The notation $p.chg(x)$ is in fact just a convenient more readable way (borrowed from object orientation) of writing $chg(x, p)$, i.e., p is simply an extra argument of chg.

The substitution *init* used in the definition of operation *add_Scalar* is not explicitly declared in the aggregated machine as an operation, but corresponds to the substitution defined in the INITIALIZATION clause, now relativised to an instance. For example, for the case of scalars, the initialisation was:

$$var :\in \mathsf{INT}$$

Then, $p.init$ is defined as:

$$\mathsf{ANY}\ v\ \mathsf{WHERE}\ v \in \mathsf{INT}\ \mathsf{THEN}\ var := var \cup \{(p,v)\}\ \mathsf{END}$$

This expression is rather complicated, because we need to maintain the nondeterminism in the original substitution. We can use the syntax sugaring defined in pages 266 and 267 of [1] to express the above substitution in the following more readable form:

$$var(p) :\in \mathsf{INT}$$

To better understand the meaning of $p.init$, consider a simpler initialisation assignment, such as:

$$var := 0$$

Then, $p.init$ would be simply defined as:

$$var := var \cup \{(p, 0)\}$$

In case any of the automatically generated operations of the aggregating abstract machine should not be exported, a wrapper machine promoting the interface operations could be declared, as is usual in the B method.

Note that a new combination of substitutions, that we call *interleaving parallel composition* (denoted by the triple bar), is used in the above machine. We describe below the semantics of this operator in detail, and our need for it.

5 Providing Semantics to the Extension

A straightforward way to provide semantics to the proposed syntax extension to B would be to simply indicate that specifications like *SeveralScalars'* are syntax sugaring for an equivalent *flat* specification, like *SeveralScalars*. We could in this way take advantage of the already well-defined semantics and consistency checking of standard B for the syntax extension.

However, we wish to treat AGGREGATES as a proper structuring mechanism. Certainly, the above straightforward way of giving semantics to the extension does not treat AGGREGATES as a proper structuring mechanism. For instance, it would be necessary to flatten the specification in order to perform the consistency checking of a specification structured using AGGREGATES, and therefore there would not be, as for the other structuring mechanisms, a way of checking consistency of the structured machine in terms of the consistency of the simpler composing submachines.

On the contrary, the way we provide semantics for the AGGREGATES clause relies on the generation of a *population manager* for each aggregated machine. Given a basic (or flat) machine M, we construct a machine $M\,Manager$, in such a way that its internal consistency is guaranteed, provided that M is internally consistent. We define the clause AGGREGATES M to mean simply EXTENDS $M\,Manager$.

The generation of the population manager is described below.

5.1 Generating Population Managers

Let M be a generic basic abstract machine, of the form:

$$
\begin{array}{l}
\text{MACHINE} \\
\quad M \\
\text{SETS} \\
\quad s \\
\text{CONSTANTS} \\
\quad c \\
\text{PROPERTIES} \\
\quad PROP(s,c) \\
\text{VARIABLES} \\
\quad v \\
\text{INVARIANT} \\
\quad I(s,c,v) \\
\text{INITIALIZATION} \\
\quad INIT(v) = P_{INIT}(v) \mid @x' \cdot (Q_{INIT}(x',v) \Longrightarrow v := x') \\
\text{OPERATIONS} \\
\quad r \longleftarrow op(\overline{p}) \;\;\widehat{=}\;\; P(\overline{p},v) \mid @\overline{x}' \cdot (Q(\overline{x}',\overline{p},v) \Longrightarrow v,r := \overline{x}') \\
\quad \vdots \\
\text{END}
\end{array}
$$

Note that we have written the substitutions corresponding to the initialisation and the operations in the most general form (according to Theorem 6.1.1 in page 284 of [1], all substitutions are reducible to this *normal form*). Also, for the sake of simplicity, we have considered a generic machine without parameters, although it will be clear that our techniques can be straightforwardly extended to cope with parameterised machines.

Let us assume that M is internally consistent, i.e., it satisfies its proof obligations, and that $\overline{T}$ are the types assigned to its variables v [1]. The population manager $MManager$ for the abstract machine specification M has the following form:

MACHINE
    $MManager$
SETS
    s
CONSTANTS
    c
PROPERTIES
    $PROP(s,c)$
VARIABLES
    $MSet, v$
INVARIANT
    $(\forall n \cdot n \in MSet \Rightarrow I(s,c,v(n))) \wedge (MSet \subseteq \mathsf{NAME}) \wedge (v \in MSet \to \overline{T})$
INITIALIZATION
    $MSet, v := \emptyset, \overline{\emptyset}$
OPERATIONS
    $add\_M(n) \;\; \widehat{=}$
    PRE $n \in (\mathsf{NAME} - MSet)$
    THEN $MSet := MSet \cup \{n\} \quad || \quad INIT(v(n))$
    END
    $del\_M(n) \;\; \widehat{=}$
    PRE $n \in MSet$
    THEN $MSet := MSet - \{n\} \quad || \quad v := (\mathsf{dom}(v) - \{n\}) \triangleleft v$
    END
    $r \longleftarrow op(\overline{p}, n) \;\; \widehat{=}$
    $P(\overline{p}, v(n)) \wedge (n \in MSet) \mid @x' \cdot (Q(x', \overline{p}, v(n)) \Longrightarrow v(n), r := x')$
    $\vdots$
END

We can describe then the construction of the population manager of M as follows:

- The sets, constants and properties defined in M are included without any change in $MManager$,
- An extra variable $MSet$, representing the set of live instances of M, is declared,
- all variables defined in M are included as variables of $MManager$, relativised to names of live instances, i.e., each variable V of type T becomes a mapping from $MSet$ to T,
- the invariant M is relativised to names of instances, and incorporated as a conjunct of the invariant of $MManager$,

---

[1] Recall that in the B method, it is a requeriment for the invariant to imply that all variables are assigned, directly or indirectly, a corresponding type.

- all operations defined in M are included as operations of $MManager$, adding an extra parameter of type $MSet$, which indicates in which instance the operation should be executed,
- population management operations add_M and del_M, which are automatically generated from the definition of M, are defined.

To clarify the generation of population managers, consider the machine in Figure 4. It is the result of the generation of a population manager for machine $Scalar$, given in Figure 1.

MACHINE
    $ScalarManager$
VARIABLES
    $var, ScalarSet$
INVARIANT
    $(\forall n \cdot n \in ScalarSet \Rightarrow var(n) \in \mathsf{INT}) \wedge (ScalarSet \subseteq \mathsf{NAME}) \wedge$
    $(var \in ScalarSet \rightarrow \mathsf{INT})$
INITIALIZATION
    $ScalarSet, var := \emptyset, \emptyset$
OPERATIONS
    $add\_Scalar(n) \;\; \widehat{=}$
    PRE $\;\; n \in (\mathsf{NAME} - ScalarSet)$
    THEN $\;\; (ScalarSet := ScalarSet \cup \{n\}) \;\; || \;\; var(n) :\in \mathsf{INT}$
    END

    $del\_Scalar(n) \;\; \widehat{=}$
    PRE $\;\; n \in ScalarSet$
    THEN $\;\; ScalarSet := ScalarSet - \{n\} \;\; ||$
    $var := (\mathsf{dom}(var) - \{n\}) \triangleleft var$
    END
    $chg(v, n) \;\; \widehat{=}$
    PRE $\;\; v \in \mathsf{INT} \wedge n \in ScalarSet$
    THEN $\;\; var(n) := v$
    END

    $v \longleftarrow val(n) \;\; \widehat{=} \;\;$ PRE $\;\; n \in ScalarSet \;\;$ THEN $\;\; v := var(n) \;\;$ END

END

Fig. 4. Abstract machine $ScalarManager$.

There are just a few very basic differences between the meaning of machine $SeveralScalars'$ (as an extension of $ScalarManager$) and the meaning of machine $SeveralScalars$; we use a general sort, called NAME, as the domain of names for machine instances (recall that in the flat specification $SeveralScalars$, a special local set named $SCALARSET$ is used). It is easy to extend the core of B with a definition of a set NAME, and a sufficiently large number of constants of this sort; in fact, it is even not necessary to incorporate this to B's core, but instead a stateless abstract machine containing the definition might be declared, and implicitly used in all other machine declarations.

5.2 Consistency of Generated Population Managers

As we mentioned before, if the abstract machine M is internally consistent, i.e., it satisfies its proof obligations, then we guarantee that the generated $MManager$ is also internally consistent, by construction. We justify this claim here.

Let us consider then the generic abstract machine specification M described above. Adapting the style used in [10] to the more general form of substitutions, we express the proof obligations corresponding to M as follows:

IC1 $\exists s_0, c_0 : PROP(s_0, c_0)$
IC2 $PROP \Rightarrow \exists v_0 : I(v_0)$
IC3 $PROP \Rightarrow [INIT]I(v)$
IC4 $(PROP \wedge I(v) \wedge P(\bar{p}, v) \wedge Q(x', \bar{p}, v)) \Rightarrow [v, r := x']I(v)$

The proof obligations for machine $MManager$ would then be:

M-IC1 $\exists s_0, c_0 : PROP(s_0, c_0)$
M-IC2 $PROP \Rightarrow \exists v_0', MSet_0 : I_{Man}(v_0', MSet_0)$
M-IC3 $PROP \Rightarrow [MSet, v := \emptyset, \overline{\emptyset}]I_{Man}(v, MSet)$
M-IC4a $(PROP \wedge I_{Man}(v, MSet) \wedge (n \in (\mathsf{NAME} - MSet)) \Rightarrow$
$[INIT(v(n)) \parallel MSet := MSet \cup \{n\}]I_{Man}(v, MSet)$
M-IC4b $(PROP \wedge I_{Man}(v, MSet) \wedge (n \in MSet) \Rightarrow$
$[MSet := MSet - \{n\} \parallel v := (\text{dom}(v) - \{n\}) \triangleleft v]I_{Man}(v, MSet)$
M-IC4c $(PROP \wedge I_{Man}(v, MSet) \wedge P(\bar{p}, v(n)) \wedge (n \in MSet) \wedge Q(x', \bar{p}, v(n))) \Rightarrow$
$[v(n), r := x']I_{Man}(v, MSet)$

where $I_{Man}(X, Y)$ represents the invariant of $MManager$ for X and Y, i.e., the formula:

$$(\forall n \cdot n \in Y \Rightarrow I(X(n))) \wedge (Y \subseteq \mathsf{NAME}) \wedge (X \in Y \to T)$$

Let us assume that the proof obligations of machine M have already been *discharged*. We prove that this implies the satisfaction of each of the proof obligations of $MManager$:

M-IC1: Trivial, due to the validity of IC1.
M-IC2: Let us consider $MSet_0 = \emptyset$ and $v_0' = \overline{\emptyset}$. We have to prove that $I(v_0', MSet_0)$ is satisfied:
  - $\forall n \cdot n \in \emptyset \Rightarrow I(v_0(n))$: Trivially true (the antecedent of the implication is false).
  - $\emptyset \subseteq \mathsf{NAME}$: Trivially true, since NAME is defined to be a set.
  - $\overline{\emptyset} \in \emptyset \to \overline{T}$: Trivially true, since $(\emptyset \to \overline{T}) = \overline{\{\emptyset\}}$.
M-IC3: valid (see proof for M-IC2).

M-IC4a: This proof obligation indicates that operation add_M preserves the invariant. So, under the hypothesis:

$PROP \wedge$
$(\forall n \cdot n \in MSet \Rightarrow I(s,c,v(n))) \wedge (MSet \subseteq \mathsf{NAME}) \wedge (v \in MSet \rightarrow \overline{T}) \wedge$
$(n \in (\mathsf{NAME} - MSet))$

we have to prove that the invariant is re-established after the assignment:

$$INIT(v(n)) \parallel MSet := MSet \cup \{n\}$$

Let us assume $P_{INIT}(v(n))$ (the precondition of $INIT$), and let x' be an arbitrary expression such that $Q_{INIT}(x', v(n))$. We prove that each of the conjuncts of the invariant is preserved:

- $\forall n_0 \cdot n_0 \in MSet \cup \{n\} \Rightarrow I(s,c,(v <+\{n \mapsto x'\})(n_0))$: If n_0 is distinct from n, then this holds due to the hypothesis. It remains to be proved then that this also holds when $n_0 = n$, i.e., that $I(s,c,x')$ holds. we know this is true, because the initialisation of M preserves I (IC3).
- $MSet \cup \{n\} \subseteq \mathsf{NAME}$: Trivially true, due to the hypothesis $MSet \subseteq \mathsf{NAME}$ and $n \in (\mathsf{NAME} - MSet)$.
- $(v <+\{n \mapsto x'\}) \in (MSet \cup \{n\}) \rightarrow \overline{T}$: Holds trivially, due to our hypothesis

$$v \in MSet \rightarrow \overline{T}$$

and x' being of type $\overline{T}$ (enforced because $INIT$ is well-formed).

M-IC4b: This proof obligation indicates that operation del_M preserves the invariant. So, under the hypothesis:

$PROP \wedge$
$(\forall n \cdot n \in MSet \Rightarrow I(s,c,v(n))) \wedge (MSet \subseteq \mathsf{NAME}) \wedge (v \in MSet \rightarrow \overline{T}) \wedge$
$(n \in MSet)$

we have to prove that the invariant is re-established after the assignment

$$MSet := MSet - \{n\} \quad \parallel \quad v := (\mathsf{dom}(v) - \{n\}) \triangleleft v$$

i.e., that the following holds:

$(\forall n_0 \cdot n_0 \in MSet - \{n\} \Rightarrow I(s,c,((\mathsf{dom}(v) - \{n\}) \triangleleft v)(n_0))) \wedge$
$(MSet - \{n\} \subseteq \mathsf{NAME}) \wedge$
$((\mathsf{dom}(v) - \{n\}) \triangleleft v) \in (MSet - \{n\}) \rightarrow \overline{T}$

The first conjunct reduces to

$$\forall n_0 \cdot n_0 \in MSet - \{n\} \Rightarrow I(s,c,v(n_0))$$

because n_0 is distinct from n. Due to our hypothesis, the above holds. The second and third conjuncts follow immediately from the hypothesis.

M-IC4c: This proof obligation indicates that the operations that were originally defined in M preserve the invariant when adapted and incorporated into the manager of M. So, under the hypothesis:

$$(PROP \land I_{Man}(v, MSet) \land P(\overline{p}, v(n)) \land (n \in MSet) \land Q(x', \overline{p}, v(n)))$$

the invariant is re-established, i.e., that $I_{Man}(x', MSet)$ holds. The second conjunct of the invariant is trivially preserved, since the substitution does not write on $MSet$. The first conjunct of the invariant is also preserved, since according to IC4, an assignment based on relation Q preserves I under hypothesis P. The third conjunct of the hypothesis is trivially preserved, according to the definition of assignments of the form $f(x) := E$ (page 267 of [1]).

5.3 Proof Obligations for AGGREGATES

Using the extension described above, we would be provided with a more suitable notation for dynamic population management of components in B. To check for consistency of a machine M_1 aggregating an internally consistent machine M, we just need to check the proof obligations corresponding to EXTENDS $MManager$, according to the semantics described above for the proposed extension. In this way, we are treating AGGREGATES as a proper structuring mechanism, and not just as a short-hand for an unstructured flat specification; in other words, we do not need to flatten specifications involving AGGREGATES in order to check for consistency.

6 Using Aggregated Machines: Interleaving Parallel Composition

In the abstract machine *TwoScalars* that we described in Figure 2, an operation *swap* was defined. This operation simultaneously *called* two other operations, namely $xx.chg$ and $yy.chg$. This is allowed because these two operations belong to different extended machines. If two (or more) operations belong to the same abstract machine, then they cannot be called in parallel. Several researchers noticed this restriction, and proposed different extensions to B and languages with similar characteristics, incorporating write frames, modifying the semantics of parallel composition, etc [6][5][11]. A common restriction on the parallel composition of statements, which is reasonable, is that composed statements should not write on the same variables.

In the case of our machine *SeveralScalars'*, which aggregates *Scalar*, we would like to be able to call in parallel operations $p.chg(q.var)$ and $q.chg(p.var)$, which, at least when p and q are different, naturally *seem* to belong to different machines. However, because of the way we provide meaning to the AGGREGATES clause, even when p are q are different, they will be writing on the same variable, namely the mapping var. Therefore, according to the definitions of parallel composition we know of, we cannot define an operation similar to the *swap* operation in *SeveralScalars* when, instead of redefining scalar in a flat specification, we aggregate scalars.

Due to this problem, we are forced to introduce an extra operator for combining substitutions, in order to be able to use combinations of operations of aggregated machines. The operation we provide is different from the extensions or alternatives to parallel substitution we are aware of. For all substitutions S and T, and formula P, we define the *interleaving parallel composition* of S and T as follows:
$$[S \,|||\, T]P \;\hat{=}\; ([S][T]P) \land ([T][S]P)$$

In the presence of a sequencing operator (not present in the set of operations at the specification stage in the B method), $S \,|||\, T$ can be described as $(S;T)[](T;S)$. There are good reasons for the absence of sequencing at the specification stage in B; methodologically, it forces the specifier to describe behaviour in an abstract way, without allowing one to enforce a particular order in the substitutions that define an operation. We believe our interleaving parallel composition respects this philosophy, since the order in which the substitutions are applied in unknown. In fact, the interesting case is when $[S][T] = [T][S]$, which, intuitively, leads to a definition of non-interference between S and T [7][2]. Note that the definition of *swap* in *SeveralScalars'* is a case of a use of $|||$ with non-interfering substitutions: $(p.chg(q.var); q.chg(p.var))$ and $(q.chg(p.var); p.chg(q.var))$ both give the same result, i.e., they are non-interferent.

There are no side conditions for the well-formedness of $(S\,|||\,T)$. In particular, as we wanted, two substitutions S and T can be combined using $|||$ even when they write on the same variables.

It is important to say that it is not our aim to provide an alternative to parallel composition. As we indicated before, we need to introduce this extra substitution operator to be able to express in a natural way operations defined in terms of other operations in aggregated machines. In fact, substitutions of the form
$$x := y \,\|\, y := x$$
for instance, are not equivalently defined using $|||$ instead. Note that
$$x := y \,|||\, y := x$$
does not swap the values of x and y, but instead lets variables x and y with the same value (either the original value of x or the original value of y).

An interesting special case of the use of interleaving parallel composition is the one in which the composing substitutions write on the same mapping variable, as, for instance, in the following substitution:
$$f(x) := E_1 \,|||\, f(y) := E_2.$$

---

[2] Our definition of interleaving parallel composition is related but not equivalent to the interleaving semantics of parallel composition: in our interleaving parallel composition, non-interference of the composed statements is not a requirement for the well-formedness of the composite statement.

Here, if x and y are distinct elements of the domain of f, the substitution changes the image of x by E_1 and the image of y by E_2. This clearly is not possible if we use $||$ instead of $|||$, since both composing substitutions write on the same variable (the mapping f).

The reader might argue that an equivalent substitution can be expressed, without the use of parallel composition (for our case, $f := f \mathbin{<\!\!+} \{(x, E_1), (y, E_2)\}$ would be an equivalent substitution without the use of parallel composition). However, this is just an alternative when defining substitutions in a flat specification. On the other hand, when the composing substitutions correspond to operations defined in "submachines", this alternative is no longer possible. So, for instance, we cannot define the *swap* operation using this approach in a machine extending *ScalarManager*.

We need to justify that the introduction of this new combination of substitutions does not affect the standard semantics of B. The following Theorem complements the result of Theorem 6.1.1 in page 284 of [1]. It proves that substitutions built using interleaving parallel composition reduce to the normal form, thus indicating that our extension is within B's standard semantics.

Theorem 1. *Let S and T be two substitutions which reduce to the normal form defined in 284 of [1]. Then, the substitution*

$$S \mathbin{|||} T$$

also reduces to the normal form.

Proof. Let S and T be two substitutions, which reduce to the normal form. If we prove that both $S;T$ and $T;S$ reduce to normal form, then $S|||T$ will also reduce to normal form, due to Theorem 6.1.1, since nondeterministic choice of reducible substitutions reduces to normal form.

Since S and T are reducible to normal form, they can be expressed respectively as follows:

$$P_S \mid @x' \cdot (Q_S \Longrightarrow x := x')$$
$$P_T \mid @x'' \cdot (Q_T \Longrightarrow x := x'')$$

We prove that $S;T$ also reduces to normal form. The proof for $T;S$ is similar. We refer to the basic properties of ";", given in pages 375 and 376 of [1], as "BP ;". We also refer to the laws of substitutions given in pages 284 and 285 of [1].

$(P_S \mid @x' \cdot (Q_S \Longrightarrow x := x')) ; (P_T \mid @x'' \cdot (Q_T \Longrightarrow x := x'')) = \{\text{BP ; (2)}\}$
$P_S \mid (@x' \cdot (Q_S \Longrightarrow x := x')) ; (P_T \mid @x'' \cdot (Q_T \Longrightarrow x := x'')) = \{\text{BP ; (8)}\}$
$P_S \mid ([@x' \cdot (Q_S \Longrightarrow x := x')]P_T \mid$
$\qquad @x' \cdot (Q_S \Longrightarrow x := x') ; @x'' \cdot (Q_T \Longrightarrow x := x'')) = \{\text{Law 3}\}$
$P_S \wedge ([@x' \cdot (Q_S \Longrightarrow x := x')]P_T) \mid (@x' \cdot (Q_S \Longrightarrow x := x') ; @x'' \cdot (Q_T \Longrightarrow x := x''))$

We now go on reducing $(@x' \cdot (Q_S \Longrightarrow x := x')\,;\, @x'' \cdot (Q_T \Longrightarrow x := x''))$.

$(@x' \cdot (Q_S \Longrightarrow x := x')\,;\, @x'' \cdot (Q_T \Longrightarrow x := x'')) = \{\text{BP ; (11)}\}$
$@x'' \cdot (@x' \cdot (Q_S \Longrightarrow x := x')\,;\, (Q_T \Longrightarrow x := x'')) = \{\text{BP ; (5)}\}$
$@x'' \cdot @x' \cdot ((Q_S \Longrightarrow x := x')\,;\, (Q_T \Longrightarrow x := x'')) = \{\text{BP ; (3)}\}$
$@x'' \cdot @x' \cdot Q_S \Longrightarrow ((x := x')\,;\, (Q_T \Longrightarrow x := x'')) = \{\text{BP ; (9)}\}$
$@x'' \cdot @x' \cdot Q_S \Longrightarrow ([x := x']Q_T \Longrightarrow x := x'; x := x'') = \{\text{Law 6}\}$
$@x'' \cdot @x' \cdot (Q_S \wedge [x := x']Q_T) \Longrightarrow (x := x'; x := x'') = \{\text{Def. ;}\}$
$@x'' \cdot @x' \cdot (Q_S \wedge [x := x']Q_T) \Longrightarrow x := [x := x']x''$

So, as we wanted to prove, $S;T$ reduces to normal form, which implies (together with $T;S$ reducing to normal form) that $S|||T$ also reduces to normal form.

6.1 Relating Parallel Composition and Interleaving Parallel Composition

It is interesting to compare the use of parallel substitution and interleaving parallel substitution. In [11], S. Dunne compares

$$(skip \,||\, x := x + 1) \text{ and } (x := x \,||\, x := x + 1),$$

illustrating that $skip$ and $x := x$ are not *absolutely* equivalent. Surprisingly, substitutions

$$(skip \,|||\, x := x + 1) \text{ and } (x := x \,|||\, x := x + 1)$$

are well-formed, and indeed equivalent, since both reduce to $x := x + 1$. In fact, they are also equivalent to $(skip \,||\, x := x + 1)$.

To finish our introduction to the interleaving parallel composition, we state a Proposition, which gives a sufficient condition for the equivalence between $||$ and $|||$.

Proposition 1. *Let S and T be two substitutions, of the form:*

$$P_S \mid @x' \cdot (Q_S \Longrightarrow x := x')$$
$$P_T \mid @x'' \cdot (Q_T \Longrightarrow y := x'')$$

respectively. If $x \cap y = \emptyset$, $x\backslash P_T, Q_T$ and $y\backslash P_S, Q_S$, then

$$(S||T) = (S|||T)$$

7 Conclusions

We have argued for the benefits of extending the notation of the B language to support dynamic management of abstract machine populations. We proposed a preliminary notation, in which we generalise the EXTENDS clause (by defining a new clause AGGREGATES) to support dynamic creation and deletion of machines. The semantics of standard B is preserved by the extension, and just very simple machinery had to be built on top of B's core.

The mechanisms via which we can extend the B language have been used in [8], in the context of object-oriented modelling languages, and in [2][3], in the context of axiomatic specifications of reconfigurable architectures. Other concepts introduced in this previous work, such as the use of associations and inheritance, remain to be studied in the context of model-oriented specifications.

Among our priorities for future research in this direction are:

- to generalise the concept of *aggregate* to support associations between dynamic sets of instance machines;
- to study similar concepts to *aggregate* supporting specification structuring within the IMPLEMENTATION construct of the B method;
- to study the generalisation of the REFINEMENT construct to accomodate refinement between aggregates of dynamically managed instances;
- to provide a mechanism that allows instances and associations to be composed into a *subsystem* instance.

All the above are necessary for acheiving a general theory of dynamic management of component populations within specifications in the B language. A similar approach should also be possible for a larger group of similar model-oriented specifications such as Z and the module version of VDM.

An interesting new combination of substitutions, the interleaving parallel composition, emerged as a consequence of the use of machine aggregations. We plan to explore in more detail the implications of introducing this new operation in the B method.

Acknowledgements. We would like to thank the anonymous referees for their useful comments and suggestions.

References

1. J.-R. Abrial, *The B-Book, Assigning Programs to Meanings*, Cambridge University Press, 1996.
2. N. Aguirre and T. Maibaum, *A Temporal Logic Approach to the Specification of Reconfigurable Component-Based Systems*, in Proceedings of the 17th International Conference Automated Software Engineering ASE 2002, IEEE Press, 2002.
3. N. Aguirre and T. Maibaum, *A Logical Basis for the Specification of Reconfigurable Component-Based Systems*, to appear in Proceedings of Fundamental Aspects of Software Engineering FASE 2003, Poland, LNCS, Springer, 2003.
4. *The B-Toolkit User Manual*, B-Core (UK) Limited, 1996.
5. R.-J. Back and M. Butler, *Fusion and Simultaneous Execution in the Refinement Calculus*, Acta Informatica 35, vol 11, 1998.
6. D. Bert, M.-L. Potet and Y. Rouzaud, *A Study on Components and Assembly in B*, in Proceedings of the First B Conference, IRIN, Nantes, 1996.

7. J.C. Bicarregui, *Do Not Read This*, in Proceedings of FME 2002: Formal Methods – Getting IT Right, Denmark, LNCS 2391, Springer, 2002.
8. J. Bicarregui, K. Lano and T. Maibaum, *Towards a Compositional Interpretation of Object Diagrams*, in Proceedings of IFIP TC 2 working conference on Algorithmic Languages and Calculi, Bird and Meertens (eds), Chapman and Hall, 1997.
9. Digilog, *Atelier B - Générateur d'Obligation de Preuve, Spécifications*, Technical Report, RATP SNCF INRETS, 1994.
10. T. Dimitrakos, J. Bicarregui, B. Matthews and T. Maibaum, *Compositional Structuring in the B-Method: A Logical Viewpoint of the Static Context*, in Proceedings of the International Conference of B and Z Users ZB2000, York, United Kingdom, LNCS, Springer-Verlag, 2000.
11. S. Dunne, *A Theory of Generalised Substitutions*, in Proceedings of the International Conference of B and Z Users ZB2002, Grenoble, France, LNCS, Springer-Verlag, 2002.
12. R.Elmstrøm, P.G.Larsen, P.B.Lassen, *The IFAD VDM-SL Toolbox: A Practical Approach to Formal Specifications*, ACM Sigplan Notices, 1994.
13. K. Lano, *The B Language and Method, A Guide to Practical Formal Development*, Fundamental Approaches to Computing and Information Technology, Springer, 1996.
14. C. Jones, *Systematic Software Development Using VDM*, 2nd edition, Prentice Hall International, 1990.
15. M. Spivey, *The Z Notation: A Reference Manual*, 2nd edition, Prentice Hall International, 1992.
16. H. Treharne, *Supplementing a UML Development Process with B*, in Proceedings of FME 2002: Formal Methods – Getting IT Right, Denmark, LNCS 2391, Springer, 2002.

Author Index

Abrial, Jean-Raymond 168, 457
Aguirre, Nazareno 528
Amálio, Nuno 339

Bicarregui, Juan 528
Blazy, Sandrine 40
Bramble, Marchia 58
Burdy, Lilian 513
Butler, Michael 477

Cansell, Dominique 457
Currie, David 437

Daley, Nicholas 437
Darlot, Christophe 408
Derrick, John 127, 300
Deutsch, Moshe 103, 148
Dimitrakos, Theo 528
Dong, Jin Song 437
Dunne, Steve 178

Ferreira, Carla 477
Frappier, Marc 421

Gervais, Frédéric 40

Hallerstede, Stefan 101
Harman, Mark 388
Henson, Martin C. 103, 148
Hierons, Robert M. 388
Hoang, Thai Son 216, 240

Jackson, Daniel 1
Jin, Zhendong 240
Julien, David 79
Julliand, Jacques 408

Kouchnarenko, Olga 408

Laleau, Régine 40, 421
Lightfoot, David E. 497

Maibaum, Tom 528
Martin, Andrew 437
McIver, Annabelle 216, 240
Méry, Dominique 457
Meyer, Bertrand 359
Morgan, Carroll 216, 240

Nealon, John L. 497

Peschanski, Frédéric 79
Poerschke, Christine 497
Polack, Fiona 2, 20, 339
Pouzancre, Guilhem 98

Reeves, Steve 103
Requet, Antoine 513
Robinson, Ken 240

Schneider, Steve 58
Singh, Harbhajan 388
Smith, Graeme 260, 280
Stepney, Susan 2, 20
Stoddart, Bill 197
Sun, Jing 437

Toyn, Ian 2, 20, 437
Treharne, Helen 58

Utting, Mark 319, 437

Wang, Shaochun 319
Wehrheim, Heike 127
Winter, Kirsten 260, 280

Zeyda, Frank 197

Lecture Notes in Computer Science

For information about Vols. 1–2579

please contact your bookseller or Springer-Verlag

Vol. 2580: H. Erdogmus, T. Weng (Eds.), COTS-Based Software Systems. Proceedings, 2003. XVIII, 261 pages. 2003.

Vol. 2581: J.S. Sichman, F. Bousquet, P. Davidsson (Eds.), Multi-Agent-Based Simulation II. Proceedings, 2002. X, 195 pages. 2003. (Subseries LNAI).

Vol. 2582: L. Bertossi, G.O.H. Katona, K.-D. Schewe, B. Thalheim (Eds.), Semantics in Databases. Proceedings, 2001. IX, 229 pages. 2003.

Vol. 2583: S. Matwin, C. Sammut (Eds.), Inductive Logic Programming. Proceedings, 2002. X, 351 pages. 2003. (Subseries LNAI).

Vol. 2584: A. Schiper, A.A. Shvartsman, H. Weatherspoon, B.Y. Zhao (Eds.), Future Directions in Distributed Computing. X, 219 pages. 2003.

Vol. 2585: F. Giunchiglia, J. Odell, G. Weiß (Eds.), Agent-Oriented Software Engineering III. Proceedings, 2002. X, 229 pages. 2003.

Vol. 2586: M. Klusch, S. Bergamaschi, P. Edwards, P. Petta (Eds.), Intelligent Information Agents. VI, 275 pages. 2003. (Subseries LNAI).

Vol. 2587: P.J. Lee, C.H. Lim (Eds.), Information Security and Cryptology – ICISC 2002. Proceedings, 2002. XI, 536 pages. 2003.

Vol. 2588: A. Gelbukh (Ed.), Computational Linguistics and Intelligent Text Processing. Proceedings, 2003. XV, 648 pages. 2003.

Vol. 2589: E. Börger, A. Gargantini, E. Riccobene (Eds.), Abstract State Machines 2003. Proceedings, 2003. XI, 427 pages. 2003.

Vol. 2590: S. Bressan, A.B. Chaudhri, M.L. Lee, J.X. Yu, Z. Lacroix (Eds.), Efficiency and Effectiveness of XML Tools and Techniques and Data Integration over the Web. Proceedings, 2002. X, 259 pages. 2003.

Vol. 2591: M. Aksit, M. Mezini, R. Unland (Eds.), Objects, Components, Architectures, Services, and Applications for a Networked World. Proceedings, 2002. XI, 431 pages. 2003.

Vol. 2592: R. Kowalczyk, J.P. Müller, H. Tianfield, R. Unland (Eds.), Agent Technologies, Infrastructures, Tools, and Applications for E-Services. Proceedings, 2002. XVII, 371 pages. 2003. (Subseries LNAI).

Vol. 2593: A.B. Chaudhri, M. Jeckle, E. Rahm, R. Unland (Eds.), Web, Web-Services, and Database Systems. Proceedings, 2002. XI, 311 pages. 2003.

Vol. 2594: A. Asperti, B. Buchberger, J.H. Davenport (Eds.), Mathematical Knowledge Management. Proceedings, 2003. X, 225 pages. 2003.

Vol. 2595: K. Nyberg, H. Heys (Eds.), Selected Areas in Cryptography. Proceedings, 2002. XI, 405 pages. 2003.

Vol. 2596: A. Coen-Porisini, A. van der Hoek (Eds.), Software Engineering and Middleware. Proceedings, 2002. XII, 239 pages. 2003.

Vol. 2597: G. Păun, G. Rozenberg, A. Salomaa, C. Zandron (Eds.), Membrane Computing. Proceedings, 2002. VIII, 423 pages. 2003.

Vol. 2598: R. Klein, H.-W. Six, L. Wegner (Eds.), Computer Science in Perspective. X, 357 pages. 2003.

Vol. 2599: E. Sherratt (Ed.), Telecommunications and beyond: The Broader Applicability of SDL and MSC. Proceedings, 2002. X, 253 pages. 2003.

Vol. 2600: S. Mendelson, A.J. Smola, Advanced Lectures on Machine Learning. Proceedings, 2002. IX, 259 pages. 2003. (Subseries LNAI).

Vol. 2601: M. Ajmone Marsan, G. Corazza, M. Listanti, A. Roveri (Eds.) Quality of Service in Multiservice IP Networks. Proceedings, 2003. XV, 759 pages. 2003.

Vol. 2602: C. Priami (Ed.), Computational Methods in Systems Biology. Proceedings, 2003. IX, 214 pages. 2003.

Vol. 2603: A. Garcia, C. Lucena, F. Zambonelli, A. Omicini, J. Castro (Eds.), Software Engineering for Large-Scale Multi-Agent Systems. XIV, 285 pages. 2003.

Vol. 2604: N. Guelfi, E. Astesiano, G. Reggio (Eds.), Scientific Engineering for Distributed Java Applications. Proceedings, 2002. X, 205 pages. 2003.

Vol. 2606: A.M. Tyrrell, P.C. Haddow, J. Torresen (Eds.), Evolvable Systems: From Biology to Hardware. Proceedings, 2003. XIV, 468 pages. 2003.

Vol. 2607: H. Alt, M. Habib (Eds.), STACS 2003. Proceedings, 2003. XVII, 700 pages. 2003.

Vol. 2609: M. Okada, B. Pierce, A. Scedrov, H. Tokuda, A. Yonezawa (Eds.), Software Security – Theories and Systems. Proceedings, 2002. XI, 471 pages. 2003.

Vol. 2610: C. Ryan, T. Soule, M. Keijzer, E. Tsang, R. Poli, E. Costa (Eds.), Genetic Programming. Proceedings, 2003. XII, 486 pages. 2003.

Vol. 2611: S. Cagnoni, J.J. Romero Cardalda, D.W. Corne, J. Gottlieb, A. Guillot, E. Hart, C.G. Johnson, E. Marchiori, J.-A. Meyer, M. Middendorf, G.R. Raidl (Eds.), Applications of Evolutionary Computing. Proceedings, 2003. XXI, 708 pages. 2003.

Vol. 2612: M. Joye (Ed.), Topics in Cryptology – CT-RSA 2003. Proceedings, 2003. XI, 417 pages. 2003.

Vol. 2613: F.A.P. Petitcolas, H.J. Kim (Eds.), Digital Watermarking. Proceedings, 2002. XI, 265 pages. 2003.

Vol. 2614: R. Laddaga, P. Robertson, H. Shrobe (Eds.), Self-Adaptive Software: Applications. Proceedings, 2001. VIII, 291 pages. 2003.

Vol. 2615: N. Carbonell, C. Stephanidis (Eds.), Universal Access. Proceedings, 2002. XIV, 534 pages. 2003.

Vol. 2616: T. Asano, R. Klette, C. Ronse (Eds.), Geometry, Morphology, and Computational Imaging. Proceedings, 2002. X, 437 pages. 2003.

Vol. 2617: H.A. Reijers (Eds.), Design and Control of Workflow Processes. Proceedings, 2002. XV, 624 pages. 2003.

Vol. 2618: P. Degano (Ed.), Programming Languages and Systems. Proceedings, 2003. XV, 415 pages. 2003.

Vol. 2619: H. Garavel, J. Hatcliff (Eds.), Tools and Algorithms for the Construction and Analysis of Systems. Proceedings, 2003. XVI, 604 pages. 2003.

Vol. 2620: A.D. Gordon (Ed.), Foundations of Software Science and Computation Structures. Proceedings, 2003. XII, 441 pages. 2003.

Vol. 2621: M. Pezzè (Ed.), Fundamental Approaches to Software Engineering. Proceedings, 2003. XIV, 403 pages. 2003.

Vol. 2622: G. Hedin (Ed.), Compiler Construction. Proceedings, 2003. XII, 335 pages. 2003.

Vol. 2623: O. Maler, A. Pnueli (Eds.), Hybrid Systems: Computation and Control. Proceedings, 2003. XII, 558 pages. 2003.

Vol. 2625: U. Meyer, P. Sanders, J. Sibeyn (Eds.), Algorithms for Memory Hierarchies. Proceedings, 2003. XVIII, 428 pages. 2003.

Vol. 2626: J.L. Crowley, J.H. Piater, M. Vincze, L. Paletta (Eds.), Computer Vision Systems. Proceedings, 2003. XIII, 546 pages. 2003.

Vol. 2627: B. O'Sullivan (Ed.), Recent Advances in Constraints. Proceedings, 2002. X, 201 pages. 2003. (Subseries LNAI).

Vol. 2628: T. Fahringer, B. Scholz, Advanced Symbolic Analysis for Compilers. XII, 129 pages. 2003.

Vol. 2631: R. Falcone, S. Barber, L. Korba, M. Singh (Eds.), Trust, Reputation, and Security: Theories and Practice. Proceedings, 2002. X, 235 pages. 2003. (Subseries LNAI).

Vol. 2632: C.M. Fonseca, P.J. Fleming, E. Zitzler, K. Deb, L. Thiele (Eds.), Evolutionary Multi-Criterion Optimization. Proceedings, 2003. XV, 812 pages. 2003.

Vol. 2633: F. Sebastiani (Ed.), Advances in Information Retrieval. Proceedings, 2003. XIII, 546 pages. 2003.

Vol. 2634: F. Zhao, L. Guibas (Eds.), Information Processing in Sensor Networks. Proceedings, 2003. XII, 692 pages. 2003.

Vol. 2636: E. Alonso, D, Kudenko, D. Kazakov (Eds.), Adaptive Agents and Multi-Agent Systems. XIV, 323 pages. 2003. (Subseries LNAI).

Vol. 2637: K.-Y. Whang, J. Jeon, K. Shim, J. Srivastava (Eds.), Advances in Knowledge Discovery and Data Mining. Proceedings, 2003. XVIII, 610 pages. 2003. (Subseries LNAI).

Vol. 2638: J. Jeuring, S. Peyton Jones (Eds.), Advanced Functional Programming. Proceedings, 2002. VII, 213 pages. 2003.

Vol. 2639: G. Wang, Q. Liu, Y. Yao, A. Skowron (Eds.), Rough Sets, Fuzzy Sets, Data Mining, and Granular Computing. Proceedings, 2003. XVII, 741 pages. 2003. (Subseries LNAI).

Vol. 2641: P.J. Nürnberg (Ed.), Metainformatics. Proceedings, 2002. VIII, 187 pages. 2003.

Vol. 2642: X. Zhou, Y. Zhang, M.E. Orlowska (Eds.), Web Technologies and Applications. Proceedings, 2003. XIII, 608 pages. 2003.

Vol. 2643: M. Fossorier, T. Høholdt, A. Poli (Eds.), Applied Algebra, Algebraic Algorithms and Error-Correcting Codes. Proceedings, 2003. X, 256 pages. 2003.

Vol. 2644: D. Hogrefe, A. Wiles (Eds.), Testing of Communicating Systems. Proceedings, 2003. XII, 311 pages. 2003.

Vol. 2645: M.A. Wimmer (Ed.), Knowledge Management in Electronic Government. Proceedings, 2003. XI, 320 pages. 2003. (Subseries LNAI).

Vol. 2646: H. Geuvers, F, Wiedijk (Eds.), Types for Proofs and Programs. Proceedings, 2002. VIII, 331 pages. 2003.

Vol. 2647: K.Jansen, M. Margraf, M. Mastrolli, J.D.P. Rolim (Eds.), Experimental and Efficient Algorithms. Proceedings, 2003. VIII, 267 pages. 2003.

Vol. 2648: T. Ball, S.K. Rajamani (Eds.), Model Checking Software. Proceedings, 2003. VIII, 241 pages. 2003.

Vol. 2649: B. Westfechtel, A. van der Hoek (Eds.), Software Configuration Management. Proceedings, 2003. VIII, 241 pages. 2003.

Vol. 2651: D. Bert, J.P. Bowen, S. King, M, Waldén (Eds.), ZB 2003: Formal Specification and Development in Z and B. Proceedings, 2003. XIII, 547 pages. 2003.

Vol. 2653: R. Petreschi, Giuseppe Persiano, R. Silvestri (Eds.), Algorithms and Complexity. Proceedings, 2003. XI, 289 pages. 2003.

Vol. 2656: E. Biham (Ed.), Advances in Cryptology – EUROCRPYT 2003. Proceedings, 2003. XIV, 649 pages. 2003.

Vol. 2663: E. Menasalvas, J. Segovia, P.S. Szczepaniak (Eds.), Advances in Web Intelligence. Proceedings, 2003. XII, 350 pages. 2003. (Subseries LNAI).

Vol. 2665: H. Chen, R. Miranda, D.D. Zeng, C. Demchak, J. Schroeder, T. Madhusudan (Eds.), Intelligence and Security Informatics. Proceedings, 2003. XIV, 392 pages. 2003.

Vol. 2667: V. Kumar, M.L. Gavrilova, C.J.K. Tan, P. L'Ecuyer (Eds.), Computational Science and Its Applications – ICCSA 2003. Proceedings, Part I. 2003. XXXIV, 1060 pages. 2003.

Vol. 2668: V. Kumar, M.L. Gavrilova, C.J.K. Tan, P. L'Ecuyer (Eds.), Computational Science and Its Applications – ICCSA 2003. Proceedings, Part II. 2003. XXXIV, 942 pages. 2003.

Vol. 2669: V. Kumar, M.L. Gavrilova, C.J.K. Tan, P. L'Ecuyer (Eds.), Computational Science and Its Applications – ICCSA 2003. Proceedings, Part III. 2003. XXXIV, 948 pages. 2003.

Vol. 2670: R. Peña, T. Arts (Eds.), Implementation of Functional Languages. Proceedings, 2002. X, 249 pages. 2003.

Vol. 2675: M. Marchesi, G. Succi (Eds.), Extreme Programming and Agile Processes in Software Engineering. Proceedings, 2003. XV, 464 pages. 2003.

Vol. 2692: P. Nixon, S. Terzis (Eds.), Trust Management. Proceedings, 2003. X, 349 pages. 2003.

Vol. 2707: K. Jeffay, I. Stoica, K. Wehrle (Eds.), Quality of Service – IWQoS 2003. Proceedings, 2003. XI, 517 pages. 2003.